HOMER

ILIAD

BOOK XXIII

EDITED BY

ADRIAN KELLY

Tutorial Fellow in Ancient Greek Languages and Literature,
Balliol College
Professor of Ancient Greek Literature,
University of Oxford

CAMBRIDGE
UNIVERSITY PRESS

Shaftesbury Road, Cambridge CB2 8EA, United Kingdom

One Liberty Plaza, 20th Floor, New York, NY 10006, USA

477 Williamstown Road, Port Melbourne, VIC 3207, Australia

314–321, 3rd Floor, Plot 3, Splendor Forum, Jasola District Centre,
New Delhi – 110025, India

Cambridge University Press is part of Cambridge University Press & Assessment,
a department of the University of Cambridge.

We share the University's mission to contribute to society through the pursuit of
education, learning and research at the highest international levels of excellence.

www.cambridge.org
Information on this title: www.cambridge.org/9781107150157

DOI: 10.1017/9781316576793

When citing this work, please include a reference to the
DOI 10.1017/9781316576793

First published 2026

A catalogue record for this publication is available from the British Library

A Cataloging-in-Publication data record for this book is available from the Library of Congress

ISBN 978-1-107-15015-7 Hardback
ISBN 978-1-316-60451-9 Paperback

CONTENTS

ACKNOWLEDGEMENTS

This book has been long and interrupted in the making, and its list of creditors is extensive. First of all, to the editors of the series, Richard Hunter and Oliver Thomas (and their predecessors Pat Easterling and Neil Hopkinson, who dealt with first drafts and initial proposals), huge thanks is due for both their patience and careful reading of the many drafts I have sent their way. They have saved me from error and embarrassment on countless occasions. Similarly patient have been my colleagues at Balliol, Alexander Bown, Matthew Robinson, and Rosalind Thomas, alongside the list of those I have been lucky enough to call colleagues there, including Joe Barber, Bob Cowan, Sarah Cullinan-Herring, Andrea Doda, Lucy Jackson, Edward Jones, Nicolas Liney, Tom McConnell, Jessica Moss, Liz Potter, and Stefan Sienkiewicz. Hugely enduring have been the Balliol undergraduates, who received my rantings (not only) on *Iliad* Book 23 with tolerance, good humour, and no little scepticism; and beyond the immediate Classics school in college, I am particularly indebted to Penny Bulloch, James Forder, Simon Skinner, and Nicky Trott. For their advice and relentless improvement of my work, in general but especially in reading and commenting on sections of the MS, I owe enormous thanks to Bill Allan, Angus Bowie, Felix Budelmann, Patrick Finglass, Andre Lardinois, Irene Lemos, Henry Spelman, Jenny Strauss Clay, and Laura Swift. Moreover, no work of scholarship done in Oxford can be conducted without the wonderful staff of the Lower Reading Room in the Bodleian Library and of the Art, Architecture, and Ancient World Library. And finally, to return to the beginning of this catalogue, I thank Michael Sharp, Katie Idle, Liz Davey, and the whole of the superb team at Cambridge University Press, Jane Burkowski for her superb copyediting, and John Jacobs and Mary Morton for their magnificent proofing. They have all saved me from many errors.

To my family, especially my wife, I owe a great deal more. This book is dedicated to the youngest member of the clan, Endy, in the hope that it justifies my standing as the 'Classics nerd' of the household.

FIGURES

TABLES

ABBREVIATIONS

Abbreviations follow, with some modifications, those of *The Oxford Classical Dictionary* (4th ed., Oxford) and *L'Année philologique*.

Andronikos   Andronikos, M. (1968), *Totenkult: Archaeologia Homerica W*, Göttingen.

B   Bernabé, A. (1987), *Poetarum Epicorum Graecorum testimonia et fragmenta: Pars I*, Leipzig.

BA   Talbert, R. J. A. (ed.) (2000), *The Barrington Atlas of the Greek and Roman World*, Princeton.

BDAG   Montanari, F., with Goh, M. and Schroeder, C. (eds) (2015), *The Brill Dictionary of Ancient Greek*, Leiden.

CEG   Hansen, P. A. (ed.) (1983–9), *Carmina epigraphica Graeca*, Berlin.

C–G   Chantraine, P. and Goube, H. (1972), *Homère Iliade: Chant XXIII. Édition, introduction et commentaire*, Paris.

C–M   Cavanagh, W. and Mee, C. (1998), *A Private Place: Death in Prehistoric Greece*, Jonsered.

DELG   Chantraine, P. (1986), *Dictionnaire étymologique de la langue grec*, 2 vols, Paris.

EDG   Beekes, R. (2009), *Etymological Dictionary of Greek*, 2 vols, Leiden.

Edwards   Edwards, M. W. (1991), *The Iliad: a Commentary. Volume V: Books 17–20*, Cambridge.

Erbse   Erbse, H. (1969–88), *Scholia Graeca in Homeri Iliadem (scholia vetera)*, 6 vols, Berlin.

GD   Buck, C. D. (1955), *The Greek Dialects*, Chicago.

GH I   Chantraine, P. (1951), *Grammaire homérique I: Phonetique et morphologie*, Paris (revised and corrected by M. Casevitz, 2013).

GH II   Chantraine, P. (1953), *Grammaire homérique II: Syntaxe*, Paris (revised and corrected by M. Casevitz, 2015).

GHS   Wachter, R. (2009), 'Grammatik der homerischen Sprache', in J. Latacz, *Homers Ilias Gesamtkommentar: Prolegomena*, 3rd ed., Munich and Leipzig: 61–108.

GM   West, M. L. (1982), *Greek Metre*, Oxford.

Hainsworth   Hainsworth, J. B. (1993), *The Iliad: a Commentary. Volume III: Books 9–12*, Cambridge.

HG   Monro, D. B. (1891), *A Grammar of the Homeric Dialect*, 2nd ed., Oxford.

HW	Leumann, M. (1950), *Homerische Wörter*, Basel.
Janko	Janko, R. (1992), *The Iliad: a Commentary. Volume IV: Books 13–16*, Cambridge.
KG	Kühner, R. and Gerth, B. (1898–1904), *Ausführliche Grammatik der griechischen Sprache*, 3rd ed., 2 vols, Hannover and Leipzig.
Kirk I, II	Kirk, G. S. (1985), *The Iliad: a Commentary. Volume I: Books 1–4*, Cambridge; (1990), *The Iliad: a Commentary. Volume II: Books 5–8*, Cambridge.
Laser	Laser, S. (1987), *Sport und Spiel: Archaeologia Homerica T*, Göttingen.
Leaf	Leaf, W. (1900–2), *Homer: The Iliad*, 2 vols, London.
LfrgE	Snell, B. et al. (eds) (1955–2011), *Lexicon des frühgriechischen Epos*, Göttingen.
LH	Ebeling, H. (1885), *Lexicon Homericum*, 2 vols, Stuttgart.
LIMC	*Lexikon Iconographicum Mythologiae Classicae* (1981–1999, 2009), Zurich.
LSJ	Liddell, H. R., Scott, R., and Jones, H. S. (1940), *A Greek–English Lexicon*, 9th ed. (with revised Supplement 1996), Oxford.
M–W	Merkelbach, R. and West, M. L. (1967), *Fragmenta Hesiodea*, Oxford.
OACG	Sommerstein, A. et al. (2011), *The Oath in Archaic and Classical Greece*, database hosted by the University of Nottingham: www.nottingham.ac.uk/greatdatabase/brzoaths/public_html/index.php.
PMGF	Davies, M. (1991), *Poetarum Melicorum Graecorum Fragmenta*, Oxford.
Richardson	Richardson, N. J. (1993), *The Iliad: a Commentary. Volume VI: Books 21–4*, Cambridge.
Vendryès	Vendryès, J. (1945), *Traité d'accentuation grecque*, Paris.
West	West, M. L. (1998–2000), *Homeri Ilias*, 2 vols, Munich and Leipzig.
WHS	Risch, E. (1974), *Wortbildung der homerischen Sprache*, 2nd ed., Berlin.

INTRODUCTION

1 BOOK 23 IN THE *ILIAD*

> If one had lived only in order to read the twenty-third book of the *Iliad*, one could not then complain about one's existence.
>
> Friedrich Schiller (von Wolzogen 1885: 335)

> What this part of the poem lacks is grandeur, and therefore an essentially Homeric character.
>
> Antoine Croiset (Croiset et Croiset 1896–8: I.158)

> ... the most diverse prizes are won by the most varied heroes in the most varied of ways.
>
> Johann Wolfgang von Goethe (Lehrs 1882: 428)

One scholar, two poets, encapsulating nicely the somewhat disjointed and polarised manner in which Book 23 has been received in the modern world.[1] Certainly this portion of the *Iliad*, which tells of Patroclos' Funeral and then his Funeral Games, has not always been treated as kindly as Goethe and Schiller would have had it; roundly condemned by the Analysts, even today its authenticity is sometimes doubted in whole or in part, or felt not to have the same kind of dramatic or emotional intensity as the rest of the poem.[2] Thankfully, fashion seems to have realised that 'the poet's art, above all, must hold our attention',[3] and so scholars have turned instead to analysing the narrative techniques[4] and reflective character of Book 23, and the meaningful way it fills the gap between the death of Hector in Book 22 and the ransom of his corpse in Book 24. Yet the structure of the poem suggests that it is much more than an interlude between what we have come to feel are the emotional high points of the *Iliad*, and so it is there that we should begin.

---

[1] For its extensive ancient reception, see Intro. § 2.2.

[2] For example, Wilamowitz 1916: 69–70 traces Books 22 and 23 to a separate poem about Achilleus; Malten 1923–4: 302–4 separates the poet of the funeral from that of the games; von der Mühll 1952: 350–1 ascribes the whole book to his 'second *Iliad* poem'; Van Thiel 1982: 550–77 attributes the funeral to the 'early *Iliad*' and the games to the 'late *Iliad*', but only the chariot race, the wrestling, and the spear throwing (the other contests are additions by the 'Redaktor'); West 2011: 399, 411, considers the games the poet's own expansion of his story, an 'afterthought' (255–7n.).

[3] C–G 7 (7–8 on the funeral, 12–15 on the games).

[4] Excellent recent studies in Scott 1997; Minchin 2001a: 43–53; Grethlein and Huitink 2017; Scodel 2021; von Alvensleben 2022: 99–118; Ready 2023: 100–10.

The events of Book 23 may be easily and meaningfully accommodated within the overall shape of the *Iliad*, a brief consideration of which is essential to appreciating the thematic significance of this book's events for the work as whole.[5] Scholars generally conceive of the poem's macrostructure in two ways. The first sets ring-composition as its basic structural principle, and seeks to match the events of corresponding books:[6] the action of Book 1 is mirrored and reversed by that in Book 24, and Book 23 most closely corresponds to the action of Book 2, and so on. In this case, the main character (Agamemnon/Achilleus) is visited by a dream which motivates a gathering of the community directed by that character (mustering of army/funeral) before a large-scale catalogue plays out the ramifications of that gathering (the Catalogue of Ships/Funeral Games).[7] The parallels draw out the transfer of authority and narrative focus from the army's overlord to Achilleus[8] and the emotional intensification of the situation in Book 23, where the cavalcade of those about to participate in the battle in Book 2 has been whittled down and their deaths manifest in the figure of Patroclos' corpse (and Hector's). It also allows a matching 'curtain call' (to use Taplin's phrase) to the great cast list in the Catalogue; revealingly, this can only be partial, because there are no Trojans here except those subject to Greek domination[9] – the sacrificed youths (21–3, 175–7nn.), the dead Hector (20–3, 24–6n., 179–83, 184–91nn.), the victorious chariot team of Diomedes taken from Aineias (344–8n.), and the memories preserved in the stories behind some of the prizes offered during the contests (560–2n., 741–9, 798–800nn.).

However far into the structure of the *Iliad* one wishes to follow the implications of this model (and most scholars would accept at least the parallels between Books 1–3 and 22–4), one might criticise it for relying

---

[5] There are many individual approaches to, and studies of, the poem's architecture; for useful overviews, see Kirk I.44–7; Richardson 1–14; Schein 1997; Latacz 2009; and nn. 6 and 15 below.

[6] See e.g. Bethe 1914–27: I.61–2; Myres 1932; Whitman 1958: 257–60; Reinhardt 1961: 63–8; Baltes 1987; Gordesiani 1987: 26–67, esp. 37, 53–5; Lohmann 1970: 169–73; Stanley 1993: 241–4; Richardson 4–6; Heiden 2000 (~ 2008: 67–84) combines the two approaches; Létoublon 2023. For another way of thinking about Homeric structure, see the démonstration of Reichel 1994: 329–40 that relatively few books explicitly look forward to Book 23 (and only from Book 18 onwards), but it looks back much further into the poem (starting with the taking of Aineias' horses in Book 5).

[7] We might also see the diversions of the Myrmidons (2.773–9) – discus, spear throwing, archery, and the stillness of the chariots – as a foreshadowing of the later athletic contests: see generally Schein 1997: 346; Scott 1997: 214; Richardson 7–8.

[8] The point is repeatedly made on a smaller scale as well. See 35–58, 35–7, 38, 49–51, 54, 110[b], 154–5, 158–60, 233–5, 448–99, 490–1, 809–10, 892–4, 895–7, 884–97nn.

[9] Another parallel to the Catalogue, where the Greeks (2.484–760) massively outnumber the Trojans (815–77).

on the authenticity of the book divisions,[10] a matter on which there is unlikely to be consensus anytime soon. A slightly modified form of such a structure (Fig. 1), which obviates this issue, revolves around four central days of battle surrounded by narrative sections setting up and then 'resolving' (whatever that may mean) the theme announced in the *Iliad*'s very first line, the anger of Achilleus.[11]

A¹ 'Construction' of Achilleus' anger (1.1–611)

    B¹ Battle: first day (2.1–7.380)

        C¹ Battle: second day (8.1–9.713 *or* –10.579)

        C² Battle: third day (11.1–18.617)

    B² Battle: fourth day (19.1–23.108)

A² 'Resolution' of Achilleus' anger (23.109–24.804)

1. The structure of the *Iliad*

Within this scheme, the actions of the first and fourth days (B¹ and B²) mirror one another not only in position but also in detail and outline, like those of the second and third (C¹ and C²), as the following schemes make clear:

The first (B¹) and fourth (B²) days of battle

1. Daylight preparation
   - B¹: Assemblies and Catalogues (2.1–877)
   - B²: Assembly and Arming Scene (Achilleus) (19.351–20.3)
2. Delayed joining (narration) of battle
   - B¹: Duel between Menelaos and Paris, and its consequences (3.15–4.445)
   - B²: Preparation for the theomachia (20.4–75)
3. Single Greek figure drives the narrative
   - B¹: Diomedes

---

[10] The terms of the debate are usefully set out in Jensen et al. 1999; see also Heiden 1996 and 1998.

[11] This section repeats material from Kelly 2007b: 382–7; 2012: 41–3; and 2017. In Figure 1, no view is necessary, or taken, on the authenticity of the *Doloneia*.

- B²: Achilleus
4. Single Greek figure personally aided by Athene
   - B¹: against Aineias and Pandaros (5.114–318)
   - B²: against Hector (22.187–375)
5. Single Greek figure fights deities
   - B¹: Aphrodite / Apollo (5.318–67, 432–48 / 793–867)
   - B²: Scamandros (21.211–384)
6. Single Greek figure almost fights Apollo protecting a Trojan
   - B¹: Diomedes v. Aineias (5.432–70)
   - B²: Achilleus v. Agenor (21.544–22.20)
7. Deities fight one another
   - B¹: Athene/Ares (5.793–867); and almost Athene/Apollo (7.17–43)
   - B²: Theomachia (21.385–520)
8. Duel with Hector closes the day of battle
   - B¹: Aias v. Hector (7.44–322)
   - B²: Achilleus v. Hector (22.21–515)
9. Day concluded by funeral scenes (Greek and Trojan dead/Patroclos)
   - B¹: Gathering and burning of corpses (7.381–432)
   - B¹: Construction of the wall (7.433–82)
   - B²: Patroclos' Funeral (23.109–257)
   - B²: Funeral Games (23.257–897)

The second (C¹) and third (C²) days of battle
1. Zeus on Mt Ida isolated from other Gods
   - C¹: 8.41–52
   - C²: 11.78–83, 181–4
2. Initial Greek success followed by Trojan gains
3. Teucros and Telamonian Aias fight as a pair until Hector counterattacks
   - C¹: against Hector (8.266–334); Teucros wounded by Hector (322–34), who attacks (335f.)
   - C²: against (a) Sarpedon (12.370–436), and Hector attacks (437f.)
   - C²: against (b) Hector (15.442–83); Teucros' bowstring broken by Zeus (15.463–5), and Hector attacks (484f.)
4. Diomedes faces down Hector, and is prevented from following up
   - C¹: Thunderbolts from Zeus (8.117–29/130ff.)
   - C²: Wounded by Paris (11.349–68/369ff.)
5. Hera joins forces with another deity unsuccessfully to counteract Trojan success
   - C¹: with Athene (8.350–96)
   - C²: with Hypnos (and Poseidon) (14.153–361)
6. Zeus openly threatens recalcitrant pair
   - C¹: Athene and Hera – threats delivered by Iris (8.461–84)

- C²: Hera – delivered by Zeus himself (15.13–78); Poseidon – by Iris (15.157–219)
7. Hector worsted by major Greek hero in battle
   - C¹: Diomedes (8.116–29)
   - C²: Diomedes (11.310–60) and Telamonian Aias (14.402–32)
8. Paris wounds important Greek with a bow
   - C¹: Nestor('s horse) (8.81–2)
   - C²: Diomedes (11.369–78), Makhaon (11.505–7), and Eurypylos (11.581–4)
9. Day ends with Trojans on plain, in assembly led by Hector
   - C¹: Hector is the only speaker (8.493–541)
   - C²: Poulydamas speaks first and suggests retreat, Hector contradicts (18.284–313)

According to this view, the overall structure of the poem pairs and contrasts the fighting and achievements of Diomedes on the first day of battle with those of Achilleus on the fourth,[12] while the narrative of the second day prepares for the massively increased importance and scale of the third; it introduces its major actions and general plight, plunges the Greeks into the desperate situation in Books 17–18 which requires Achilleus' return, and motivates that return as revenge for Patroclos. Book 23 straddles the boundary between the sections labelled as B² and A² above, and thus represents a structural hinge in moving from the course of combat and Achilleus' successful revenge to the question of resolution and closure.

In this way, Book 23 reinforces the links between the first and fourth days, for much of its narrative mirrors and hugely expands the closing events of the first day of battle in Book 7, i.e. a funeral after a major duel in which Hector comes off second:[13] where Hector was rescued with some difficulty from Aias in Book 7, he is now a corpse at Achilleus' hands in the Greek camp; where the dead after the first day are unnamed and numerous, Book 23 focuses on an individual and the hugely increased scale of his funeral process.[14] The importance of this last day of fighting is made even more clear, as is the greater influence and significance of Achilleus – and Patroclos – within the story.

---

[12] This dynamic will be played out in the Funeral Games as well, as Diomedes usurps the position of the 'second best after Achilleus' (288–9, 290–2nn.) in two events in particular, the chariot race (against Eumelos) and the fight in armour (against Aias *meizōn*).
[13] For the typical structures involved, see Intro. § 2.1.
[14] See, e.g., Bethe 1914–27: I.61–2; Heiden 2000: 37, 48–9 (~ 2008: 79–80); also n. 6 above.

The book is thus doubly anchored within the *Iliad*'s multiply articulated macrostructure; it alerts the audience to both the opening and closing of that first day of fighting, as well as the poet's attempt to locate Achilleus within the narrative and political structures of the Greek camp. Where his physical absence posed a problem which helped to cause the events of Books 2–7 (and beyond), for the majority of Book 23 after the funeral he will be an 'absent presence' somewhat above the action, pointedly not competing whilst exercising individualised and general control over those who do. These links back into the poem combine to reinforce the transfer of narrative prominence and political power from Agamemnon to Achilleus, the personalisation of death in the form of Patroclos' corpse, and the final result of the battle threatened in Book 2 – and indeed the whole story initiated by that new phase in the fighting.

The second major macrostructural conception of the *Iliad* is that of the 'move' or 'group', in which sets of books mirror one another across the course of the poem. Often complementary to the ring-compositional model, and sometimes related to performative as well as thematic criteria, this perspective generally suggests a tripartition of the *Iliad*, of the sort e.g. Books 1–9, 10/11–18, and 19–24.[15] The resonances thereby suggested for Book 23 are largely the same as those outlined above, since Patroclos' Funeral and Games are located within the closing phase of any of the groupings which scholars have made along the lines of this model. This supports the dynamic with the (similarly located) close of the first day of fighting in Book 7, and adds the battle over Patroclos' corpse in Book 17. If Patroclos exists in epos[16] principally to die (65, 89–90nn.), the structure of the poem neatly and constantly enshrines this role.

Amidst all these maps and tables, one might also reflect on the absence of the Trojans as living characters from the narrative in Book 23: whatever their role in the rest of the poem, they are as far from the forefront as they

---

[15] See e.g. Wade-Gery 1952: 15–16 (Books 1–9, 10–18.353, 18.354–24; Schadewaldt 1975: 23–4 (cf. 39–74); Taplin 1992: 11–31, 200–2 (Books 1–9, 11–18.353, 18.354–24); Stanley 1993, Schein 1997, and Louden 2006 (Books 1–7, 8–17, and 18–24); Heiden 2000 (~ 2008: 67–84) (Books 1–8, 9–15, 16–24). Some scholars argue for a four-part model: see Kirk I.44–7; Thornton 1984: 46–63. For even more segmentation, see Nicolai 1973: 141–58 (esp. 156), whose model reflects an alternation of success and failure realised in six stages over five conflicts (roughly Books 1, 2–7, 8–17, 18–23, 24), where Book 23 closes the fourth conflict, between Hector and Achilleus, and looks back not only to Book 7 but also to Book 17 (the fight over Patroclos' corpse).

[16] Derived from ἔπος, this term denotes all epic poetry in dactylic hexameter (for which, see § 3.2), including Homer, Hesiod, the *Homeric Hymns*, and the fragments of the Epic Cycle. The comparable term 'melos' (from μέλος 'song') is used for all lyric poetry, and the recitative mode of elegiac: see Kelly 2022: 35–6.

could be here, as we turn from the city at the opening of the book and are confronted with events in the Greek camp. Yet this fact, and the almost subcutaneous presence of dead and dominated Trojans in Book 23,[17] keys us into a third informative structural framework for Patroclos' Funeral and Games, one which this time looks forward rather than back. What is to be done with Hector's corpse, and, indeed, how is the poem to finish? The presence of his body in the Greek camp, especially when contrasted with the sumptuousness of Patroclos' funeral rituals, is a problem which sits unresolved at the back of the narrative, and poses questions about resolution which will only be answered in Book 24.

Thus, the events of this book play an important role in the 'decreasing doublet' comprising the poem's end by serving as the major element to the minor in Hector's funeral.[18] In this strategy, the process by which Patroclos is returned to the Greek camp, which begins with the battle over his corpse in Book 17 and is interrupted by the revenge taken upon his killer in Books 18–22, sets up a broad parallel for the return of Hector's corpse, which begins with a divine assembly at the start of Book 24, a heroic journey by Priam often likened to a *katabasis* or 'journey down' (i.e. to Hades), his meeting with Achilleus, and the return of his son's corpse to Troy for burial. The link between these two event sequences is broad, once more, but obvious, and not only in their ending point.[19]

The structural or compositional purpose of the parallel is to draw the poem to a close, discouraging the audience from expecting continuation, and to allow the thematic contrasts between the poem's two final funeral sequences to become clear. It also, simultaneously, looks forward to the future of the story beyond the end of the poem, with the imminent death of Achilleus and the destruction of Troy prominently figured into the narrative at several points (for more details see Intro. § 2). But in the *Iliad* itself, while Patroclos' funeral is huge and hugely celebrated over the course of the whole book, Hector's is a little over a hundred verses long – smaller,

---

[17] See above, p. 2.   [18] Kelly 2007b: 382–4.
[19] Among the many other links between them, consider also the unique and memorable three verses pairing their demise (16.855–7 = 22.361–3: ὣς ἄρα μιν εἰπόντα τέλος θανάτοιο κάλυψεν, | ψυχὴ δ' ἐκ ῥεθέων πταμένη Ἄϊδόσδε βεβήκει | ὃν πότμον γοόωσα, λιποῦσ' ἀνδροτῆτα καὶ ἥβην), the divine protection afforded to each corpse (19.38–9 ~ 23.185–7), and the fact that both are lamented well before the actual funeral, Patroclos at several points during his extended *prothesis* (see Intro. § 2.1 for the term) after the return of his body to the camp (18.22–77, 314–55), and Hector in his absence as the Trojans look with horror on the scene below them on the plain (22.405–515). This underlines not only their causal connection in the narrative, but also the differences in their situations and the pressing need for resolution – Hector has to be returned to Troy; see generally Segal 1971: 48–56; Di Benedetto 1998: 289–301.

more intimate, devoted instead to the wider community and its now very
endangered status, with the mourners women from his own family, figures
who represent the generations of those about to suffer Troy's sack, and not
'spear-won' slaves with little choice about their presence in the Greek camp
as they mourn for Patroclos but in reality for themselves (19.301–2). The
communal activity is a meal in Priam's house, not an enormous sporting
festival; in the *Iliad*'s vision, the Trojans have neither the desire nor, practi-
cally, the space to exercise their competitive drives. Furthermore, the sun-
dering of political ties between Agamemnon and Achilleus which opened
the poem requires another demonstration in the Greek camp, after the
somewhat awkward Assembly of Book 19, that the usual dynamics holding the army together have been re-established. This is not to isolate tones
of disturbance and death to Troy, of course; consider only the plight of
Briseis (19.282–300) and the other enslaved women among the Greeks
(and more generally the similarities between the precarious position of the
women on either side), or what the families of the Greek soldiers endure in
their absence and/or from their failure to return home at all. Yet there is an
emotional as well as scalar intensification evident in the pairing, one which
acknowledges in Hector's fate the other side to all the splendour enshrined
in the funeral of Patroclos and the games commemorating his death.

An important shared feature for both of these sequences is that Achilleus
stands at the centre of a nexus 'of death that unites all three (characters)
together',[20] the driving force and host in the first funeral and the obstacle
who ends up becoming a host and thus the enabler of the second funeral.
In each he exercises ultimate power over the success of the narrative and the
continuation of the story, and the poet's focus is determinedly held on him as
he comes to terms with his responsibilities and duties. How well he performs
these roles, and what if anything he has learned from his experiences in the
poem, remains an open question. The emotional focus on him throughout
Patroclos' Funeral[21] is continued in the contests that follow, and he certainly
shows little sign of coming to terms with his friend's death at the start of Book
24, so perhaps we might think less of rupture or development in his previous
character and more of continuity. Indeed, this commentary argues that his
conduct of the Funeral Games is intended to strike an audience as problematic or questionable,[22] especially in his interventions (257[b]–897, 490–1,
534–41, 618–23, 700–39, 733–4, 798–825, 809–10, 884–97nn.), and this
problematisation will continue into the poem's last book (and beyond); as

[20] Di Benedetto 1998: 293. See 12, 17–34, 17–18, 99–101[a], 105–7, 222–5nn.
[21] See recently Austin 2021: 96–104; Lesser 2022: 214–41.
[22] See, e.g., Stanley 1993: 224–32; Sauge 1994; Postlethwaite 1995; Allan and
Cairns 2011: 136; Kelly 2017; Stocking 2023: 111–66.

we shall see in § 2 of this Introduction, it is also to be found in his conduct of the funeral itself, where scholars have found the process disturbing in several regards. All this is a function of Achilleus' exceptional character, and its ability to bend the norms of epos around itself, but the vast majority of critics see him acting positively in both sections of Book 23 (and beyond), someone who has learned to accept his place in the world, to respond to the needs of others, and who can now behave in a community-oriented manner to soothe crises as they arise, a powerful contrast to his earlier anger and withdrawal.[23]

That we can even ponder these sorts of questions is largely, of course, because of the positioning of Book 23 and the structural maps presented earlier, since they almost demand that we see the Funeral, and especially the Games, as a 'mirror-story' or *mise-en-abyme* for the whole of the *Iliad*,[24] a chance for the poet to represent in a different setting the issues which have driven the narrative. This is represented by a series of culminating themes in Book 23, such as the deployment of the repeated idioms χάλκεα μαρμαίροντα 'gleaming bronze' (26–7n.), ταφὼν δ' ἀνόρουσεν 'and astonished he leapt up' (101b–2n.), and θεσπιδαὲς πῦρ 'god-kindled fire' (214–16n.), and the tree-felling (118–21an.), and parent–child similemes (222–5n.). It is also an opportunity, more broadly, to reflect on the success or otherwise of the characters in dealing with the drives and imperatives of Homeric society.[25] After all, the competitors in these 'most hotly contested of competitions'[26] are βασιλῆες keenly and ever aware of the need to protect their standing,[27] both before their own people and their peers; conflict is for that reason never far from the surface.[28] As a place where power is (re-)performed in front of the λαός, whose reactions and views are considered important enough to be a repeated element in the event sequence (257b–897n.), the

[23] See, e.g., Willcock 1973; Schadewaldt 1975: 69–71; Dunkle 1981 and 1987; Macleod 1982: 30–1; Clay 1983: 176–80; Taplin 1992: 251–60; Richardson 165–6; Hammer 1997 and 2002; Scott 1997; Kitchell 1998; Minchin 2001a: 48–72, esp. 61–2; Wilson 2002: 124–5; Ulf 2004; Clay 2007; Scodel 2008: 153–7; Kyle 2015: 53–69; Lovatt 2019: 413–22; von Alvensleben 2022: 99–118. It is a daunting list.

[24] See respectively Ulf 2004 and Bierl 2019 for the terms, though their conception of Achilleus is very different from mine.

[25] Many scholars have situated this dynamic within a historical frame, reading the book as evidence for the growth of the polis and the development of political discourse between elite and non-elite in the Archaic period: see esp. Hammer 1997: 13–22; Brown 2003; Seaford 2004: 159–90; Grethlein 2007b; Elmer 2013: 187–203, 204–24; Bierl 2019: 56–7.

[26] Van Wees 1992: 89–100, at 91; see also Thalmann 1988: 143–53 on the risks attendant in the Scherian games.

[27] For the contested status of Epeios, see 664–6n.

[28] This need not even be limited just to the moment of competition, dangerous though that may be, as in the deadly reaction of the Thebans to being bested by the somewhat provocative Tydeus (4.385–95).

contests especially permit us to observe the position and roles of the other Greek chieftains, and the efficacy of the entire basileutic system. The whole episode, thus, harks back to the opening quarrel and basic problem of the poem, and Homer hereby encourages his audiences to ponder the kind of resolution possible in the heroic world of epos.

2 FUNERALS AND FUNERAL GAMES

2.1 FUNERAL

... a veritable meditation on death
(C–G 7)

Patroclos' funeral rites are conducted over three separate days (1–61, 109–225, 226–57), with the episode of the shade's visitation interposed during the night (62–108) between the first and second, and matched on a smaller scale by Achilleus making libations all night long before the third (217–25). Homeric funerals typically extend over multiple days (Table 1),[29] beginning with a period of varying length for the gathering of wood, construction of the pyre, tending of the corpse, and formal lamentations; the first day of the ritual proper is concerned with the burning of the body, and the second with the gathering of the ashes, burial, and construction of the tomb mound, and a social activity to affirm the community's continuation.[30] The enormously greater scale of this funeral is seen at every stage: not only a series of preview rituals on the first day (4–34n.), but more lamentations over a longer period (beginning with Achilleus' initial *cri de coeur* in Book 18), the largest description of tendance of the corpse and wood gathering (110–28), the longest and most complex burning (161–225) and burial/mound construction (226–57), and by far the largest and most thoroughly narrativised communal activity (257–24.3). On the other hand, one each of the obsequies for both Hector and Achilleus is extended over many days (24.777–84 wood

---

[29] Adapted from Kelly 2017: 89.

[30] See Garland 1982 (= 1984); Schnapp-Gourbeillon 1982; Edwards 1986; Seaford 1994: 159–90. Of the other two Homeric burials given some detail, Sarpedon's is foreshadowed in general terms by Hera (16.453–7) but then amplified by Zeus (16.667–75: 671–3 ~ 454–5, 674–5 = 456–7), who instructs Apollo to clean the body and anoint it with ambrosia and clothe it, before sending it with Sleep and Death to Lycia for burial (carried out at 679–83); while the hurried burial for Elpenor (*Od.* 12.8–16) is more compressed, with all the narrated events (procession, wood gathering, mourning, and tomb construction) apparently happening on the same day.

Table 1 The funeral sequence in Homer

Elements	7.416–41 (Greeks and Trojans)	18.22–24.3 (Patroclos)	24.719–804 (Hector)	Od. 24.43–92 (Achilleus)
(1) tendance of the corpse	7.424–6	18.231–8	24.719–20	24.43–5
(2) lamentation	7.427 (*)	18.22–77 18.314–55 19.282–338 23.12–23	22.405–36/460–515 24.720–76	24.45–64 (17 days)
(3) gathering of wood	7.416–17/418–20	23.110–28	24.777–84 (9 days)	–
1st day				
(4) burning the corpse(s)	7.429/430–2	23.161–225	24.786–7	24.65–70
2nd day				
(5) gathering of ashes, burial, mound construction	7.435–6	23.226–57	24.789–801	24.71–84
(6) communal activity	7.436–41 (wall)	23.257–24.3 (games)	24.802–4 (meal)	24.85–92 (games)

gathering, *Od.* 24.45–64 lamentation), while Patroclos is relatively swiftly committed to the pyre.

Moreover, though Patroclos' funeral is obviously and thoroughly paired with Hector's in the closure of the poem (Intro. § 1), there are also several specific links with the narrative of Achilleus' burial in the *Odyssey* beyond those visible in Table 1:[31] the cutting of hair (23.135–6, *Od.* 24.45–6), armed procession around the corpse (23.128–34, *Od.* 24.68–70), sacrifice of sheep and cattle (23.166–7, *Od.* 24.65–6), and the use of oil and honey as offerings on the fire (23.170–1, *Od.* 24.67–8). These parallels may be significant for the Neoanalytical contention that Patroclos 'does not, in heroic terms, rate the honors paid to him',[32] according to which we should think instead of the poet drawing on or alluding to another poem on Achilleus' own burial.[33] That Book 23 of the *Iliad* looks forward to future events in the story is undoubtedly true (see 13–14, 708–9, 726–8, 798–825, 895–7nn.), as is the idea that Achilleus' impending doom is summoned at several points (see 69–92, 91–2, 136–7, 140–4, 144–5nn.), but 'there is no need to hypothesize an external source'[34] in order to make sense of this dynamic; one suspects that, if we had more examples of narrated funerals from early epos, all of these features would recur.

In the archaeological and historical record, all of the elements in Patroclos' funeral (with exception of the human sacrifice)[35] are attested in the practices of the Iron Age (for details, see 45–7, 83–4[a], 91–2, 127–39, 166–7[a], 171–2, 175–7, 245–8, 250–4nn.).[36] The process seems to have remained remarkably stable in its basic outline from the Bronze Age onwards, beginning with the washing, laying out, and mourning over the corpse (*prothesis*), the procession to the place of internment/cremation (*ekphora*), and finally the cremation and/or interment of the remains.

---

[31] Garland 1982: 72 (= 1984: 12).   [32] Willcock 1997: 188 n. 28.
[33] See esp. Pestalozzi 1945: 22–33, esp. 30–3; Kakridis 1949: 83–95; Edwards 145–6; Burgess 2009: 56–71. The same argument is made with regard to the games (see § 2.2 below).
[34] Willcock 1997: 188.   [35] Though see n. 49 below.
[36] Andronikos 37–128, 129–35; Crielaard 2016. For treatments of Greek funeral customs from the Bronze Age to the Classical period and beyond, see Schnaufer 1970; Kurtz and Boardman 1971: 142–61, 186–7; Ahlberg-Cornell 1971; Vermeule 1979: esp. 2–3, 63 on stability; Garland 1985: 21–37; Morris 1987; Cavanagh and Mee 1998; Lemos 2002: 151–90; Gallou 2005; Galanakis 2020. The Homeric focus on cremation suggests generally a post-Mycenaean vision, but cremation and inhumation are found together in the early Geometric period and jostle for supremacy thereafter, and it is difficult to assign a universal rule or distribution – which makes the unanimity of Homer's practice all the more noticeable. The inhumation without burning of Aias (*Little Iliad* fr. 3 B) is at least a partial exception, and may be a Mycenaean relic (Holt 1992).

This tripartition is not inconsistent with the typical sequence, especially as it is realised in Book 23 – a very extended and interrupted *prothesis* takes place in the initial, variable period (18.22–23.61), while *ekphora* and cremation occur together on the first day, and the interment on the second day – but does not map easily onto it: the *prothesis* actually begins in Book 18 with the recovery, cleaning, and initial lamentations over Patroclos (18.22–137, 314–55, 19.282–338), and is woven together with several actions between the third and fourth days of battle (Intro. § 1); the whole process is held in abeyance from the last third of Book 19 to the end of Book 22 as Achilleus takes his revenge on Hector, before starting once more here in Book 23.[37]

Yet the individuality of Patroclos' funeral is not just a question of scale. Several features are unusual either in the typical narrative frame or when compared to historical practice. Achilleus himself, firstly, blurs the distinction between *prothesis* and *ekphora* when he orders a procession around the corpse whilst it is still laid out (4–34n.), an action which previews the actual procession on the next day (13–14n.) and allows the poet to turn straight to the games after the funeral. Other, more noticeably anomalous elements include the laying of hair on the body (135–6n.), the famous sacrifice of the twelve Trojan captives (175–7n.), the apparent preparation of animals for a post-sacrificial meal which never occurs (4–34, 166–7[a]nn.), the use of animal fat to cover Patroclos' body before the burning (166–76n.), and both the range and type of victims. Much of this crosses ritual lines between cremation and sacrifice, for the animals (and humans) are as much a part of the cremation as Patroclos himself, and the human and divine dividends of the sacrifice are not clearly demarcated. We might ascribe all this to the fact that some of these details are reminiscent of hero cult, though its presence in Homer is disputed,[38] or that this is a 'chthonian' ritual, where the animal is burned whole and there is no accompanying meal,[39] though the validity of the chthonian/Olympian dichotomy has been increasingly

---

[37] This has an important ramification, as the request of Patroclos' shade for immediate burial (23.69–92) has good justification within the text (despite Thetis' tendance for the corpse's integrity 19.38–9) as an almost metatextual nod to the length of the funeral process, and the practical issues thereby raised. Differently, West 1997a: 343 thinks this a sign that Homer derived the whole scene from *Gilgamesh* (69–108n.), where the funeral is delayed until a worm drops from Enkidu's nose: 'the horrid realism of the older story has been refined away by the Greek poet. He has banished the appalling worm, but not forgotten it.'

[38] See 151n., and esp. Clay 2025.

[39] For example, Naiden 2013: 169–70 n. 196 lists it as such without further comment, while Vermeule 1974: 99–100 does not include it amongst her examples of sacrificial offerings. The omission of the meal seems pointed not only in itself, but also when compared with the meal in Priam's house to close Hector's funeral (24.801–3).

questioned,[40] and the relationship between Homeric sacrificial practices and those reconstructed from later periods is not a simple one.[41] In line with our view of Achilleus' behaviour during the Funeral Games (Intro. § 1), Schnapp-Gourbeillon considers these features a sign that 'the funeral of Patroclus is to be entirely set under the symbol of excess, of immoderation ... this ritual is therefore both misappropriation and transgression',[42] while for Hitch they express the hero's isolation and special, quasi-divine, status within the epic world.[43] Certainly Achilleus repurposes other ritual processes in this scene (140–4n.), but, whatever the conclusion, we can agree that the particularity of this funeral is deliberate, the epic imagining of such an event on the largest, most lavish possible scale, all reflecting once more on the exceptional character driving it. In seeking to understand him, we have to recognise that quality and the way it forces itself into the narrative and on all its participants, displacing ritual actions and states as he comes to terms with his own fate.[44] Consequently, we should not look to bind his shaping of the funeral too closely to any one historical place or practice, any more than we should tie Homer's language with any one historical region or period of Greek.

That does not mean archaeology has nothing to offer. This portion of the *Iliad* has long been linked with a tenth-century BCE site at Lefkandi in Euboia that was brought to the world's notice in the early 1980s, when several features – remains of a huge building over the site, a large tumulus, burial of a cremated warrior in an imported cauldron, horse sacrifice, and the presence of costly, international, grave goods – immediately invited comparisons and understandable speculation about its relationship with

[40] Indeed, even the applicability of the term 'chthonian' requires examination in a Homeric context (see next n.), since none of the conditions listed as typical of such sacrifices by Scullion 1994: 76 are fulfilled here except the holocaust (*contra* Hitch 2009: 103), while Naiden 2020: 368 suggests that Odysseus' promise and fulfilment of sacrifice to Teiresias and the shades (*Od.* 10.521–5 = 11.29–33) are the two 'other' examples of Homeric holocausts (so also Vermeule 1974: 99–100), but πυρήν τ' ἐμπλησέμεν ἐσθλῶν (*Od.* 10.523 = 11.31) does not mean that the whole animal was to be placed in the fire. For the wider debate, see e.g. Schlesier 1992; Scullion 1994; Hägg and Alroth 2005; Deacy 2015; Sekita 2022.

[41] See Kirk 1981: 62–70; Hitch 2009: 18–39; Naiden 2013: 15–32.

[42] Schnapp-Gourbeillon 1982: 82–3 (= 2017: 86); cf. similarly Kitts 2011: 234–6 (and 2007: 28–33) with regard to the earlier sacrifice, which is unusual in focusing on the animals' 'suffering' and the blood (23.30–4), though neither ὀρέχθεον nor μηκάδες can really bear the weight required (see 30–3, 34nn.).

[43] Hitch 2009: 194–6; cf. Kitts 2007: 33–41 for a different view, focusing on the notion of *poinē*. On Homeric sacrifice as narrative, see Arend 1933: 64–78; Vermeule 1974: 95–100; Foley 1999: 171–82.

[44] For examples of his ability to disrupt the narrative conventions of Homer's world, see Kelly 2007a: 67 n. 3.

Homer's major burials, especially that of Patroclos.[45] Some scholars maintain that the site is relatively isolated in the material record,[46] and Euboia must generally have been an influential location in the history of early Greek epos as we have it;[47] both factors might seem to hint tantalisingly at a link between Homeric poetry and an actual, historical site. However, all of these features are increasingly evidenced in the contexts of the so-called 'warrior burials' across the Mediterranean world in the tenth to eighth centuries BCE, at sites stretching from Crete to Italy, and therefore they probably represent a wider phenomenon.[48] So the line from Lefkandi to the Homeric poems in the eighth or seventh century is unlikely to be a simple or direct one,[49] however we choose to explain the still very striking similarities in this case. Certainly one cannot just claim that epic poetry 'produced' the burial, any more than Lefkandi or sites like it 'produced' the funerary practices in Homer; it is better to see them as concurrent, interlocked, and developing strands in Iron Age discourse about honouring the elite dead.

Scholars have also looked for parallels or sources further afield, to Ancient Near Eastern death processes, particularly in the 'sallis wastais' rituals of Hittite royal burials of the thirteenth century BCE, where funeral sacrifices, lamentation, cremation by night, and careful tendance of the remains are all shared with the *Iliad*.[50] Other Homeric features, such as the placing of the bones in an urn, the construction of the mound, and the athletic games, are absent; and in the Hittite ritual there are various magic operations, and the remains are placed on a chair or a stool, none of which are paralleled in Book 23. Thus, whilst the comparison may bolster the idea that cremation came to the Greek world from Anatolia at the end of the Bronze Age, 'the differences are perhaps more significant than the similarities ... Homer is doing something different'.[51] Some of the features in the funeral of Book 23, of course, may have originated in

---

[45] Popham et al. 1982; Antonaccio 1995a, 2002; Lemos 2002: 140–6.

[46] Morris 1999.

[47] West 1988: 166–9 (= 2011–13: I.61–7); Cassio 1998; Debiasi 2004. Indeed, the Ionic of the epic language is that of West Ionic spoken in Euboia, not the East Ionic of Asia Minor: see Intro. § 3.1.

[48] Antonaccio 2002; Vlachou 2012: 368–70; Crielaard 2016.

[49] Cf., *contra*, e.g. Powell 1991: 185; 1993a; 1993b. This must also apply to the late eighth-century burial at Eleutherna, which Stampolidis 1995 has closely linked with Patroclos' funeral, especially because of the decapitated figure at the edge of the pyre.

[50] Cf. Gurney 1990: 137–40; Puhvel 1991: 18–19; West 1997a: 398–9.

[51] Rutherford 2008: 230.

Hittite contexts and passed from there into the Greek epic tradition,[52] but the line to our *Iliad* is once again somewhat indirect.

2.2 FUNERAL GAMES

The second major section of Book 23, athletic contests in a funeral context, 'were a regular part of Greek life and had a continuing effect on several aspects of Greek society ... well into the Hellenistic period'.[53] The origins of such a practice, however, are more obscure: a Mycenaean background has been particularly explored, especially on a famous thirteenth-century *larnax* from Tanagra in Boiotia which contains panels with several apparently athletic images surrounding a central funeral procession,[54] while archaeologists have tentatively interpreted an area in front of a royal tomb in Late Bronze Age Thebes as a racecourse which could have held funeral contests.[55] Scholars have once more sought parallels and/or sources in the other civilisations of the ancient Mediterranean and Near East,[56] but none of this evidence is sufficiently close to the Homeric 'Totenagon' to suggest that the narrative of Book 23 is drawing on, or particularly influenced by, non-Greek sources or practices.[57]

Wherever it came from, the idea of funeral games was sufficiently familiar and widespread by the time of the *Iliad* as to be thoroughly embedded within that world: aside from a memorable simile image which helps to prepare for Book 23 (22.162–4: see 431–3n.), the concept is considered by Achilleus (23.274–5) and Agamemnon as a habitual occurrence (*Od.* 24.87–9), and Homer mentions other games in honour of Achilleus (*Od.* 24.85–92), Oidipous (23.677–80), and Amarynceus (23.629–43), while Hesiod claims to have competed successfully in singing at the funeral games of an Amphidamas (*WD* 654–9: see 87–8n.). Beyond this generic background, some scholars have looked especially to Achilleus' games as the model for Patroclos' contests, within the wider Neoanalytical argument that the *Iliad* depends on or alludes to the *Aithiopis* (or a similar

---

[52] See, e.g., Finkelberg 2005 for a similar argument about royal inheritance patterns in early Greek myth. For the still popular theory that the Achilleus–Patroclos storyline owes something to the notion of a ritual substitute for the Hittite king (Nagy 1990a and often; Clarke 2019: 244–9), see now Rutherford 2020 (and 89–90n.).

[53] Roller 1981a: 1; see esp. Malten 1923–4: 307–17; Roller 1977, 1981a, 1981b; Nielsen 2018: 15–21.

[54] Decker 1982–3, 2012; Mouratidis 1990; Gallou 2005; *contra* Roller 1977: 113–18; Benzi 1999.

[55] Gallou 2005: 125–8.

[56] Puhvel 1988; Decker 2004: esp. 18–21; Decker 2012; Kyle 2015: 22–52.

[57] Carter 1988; Kyle 2015: 24–6, 45–6.

poem) composed at some point in the Archaic period. Though neither the *Odyssey* (24.71–92, esp. 85ff.) nor the direct evidence for the *Aithiopis* (arg. 22–4 Bernabé) gives much detail, pseudo-Apollodoros (second century CE) relates that 'Eumelos won in the chariot race, Diomedes in the running race, Aias in the discus, and Teucros in the archery', with a final 'victory prize for the best man' (τῶι ἀρίστωι νικητήριον) being Achilleus' divinely made armour, which lay at the heart of the quarrel between Odysseus and Aias *meizōn* and would lead to the latter's suicide (*Epit.* 5.5).[58] There is a pattern of Homeric losers becoming or being already victors in the *Aithiopis* (though not in Diomedes' case) but no mention of boxing, wrestling, or the fight in armour. The absence of a parallel for the latter event, whose presence in Book 23 has often troubled scholars (798–825n.), is perhaps unsurprising, but that of the first two events is more noticeable, given their ubiquity in other games. The events reported by pseudo-Apollodoros proceed roughly in the same order, but this seems to have been more or less the standard pattern in early epos (257[b]–897n.). Doubtless a story (or stories) of Achilleus' funeral games was known to Homer, for he seems to allude to that event on several occasions,[59] but his dependence on or allusion to any single version of the story remains uncertain (see § 2.1 above).

Though it may surprise Homerists, another story of funeral games, this time for the Thessalian Pelias and involving the Argonauts, was a much *more* popular doublet to our event in the Archaic imaginary. These contests were reflected in several no longer extant artefacts, such as the Chest of Cypselos and the throne of Apollo at Amyclai (both as described by Pausanias), in many depictions of the events on vases, and known in a literary form from a lost work 'The Games for Pelias' by the sixth-century lyric poet Stesichoros.[60] A lost epic version has been hypothesised, and in fact one would be surprised if there was just one, but there is no strong evidence for that story's particular influence on Patroclos' Games.[61]

Funerals for powerful people continued to be a prominent location for contests well into the Hellenistic period, long after the main festival

---

[58] West 2013: 156–9; Currie 2016: 242, with further references.

[59] Willcock 1997: 188–9; Burgess 2009: 41–2, 63, 92, 94–6. See 708–9n. for hints at Aias *meizōn*'s future.

[60] Roller 1981b: 109–12; Davies and Finglass 2014: 212–21.

[61] Davies and Finglass 2014: 217–18 raise two points in favour, the similar ordering of events on the Chest of Cypselos and the presence of Eumelos, whose father Admetos competed in Pelias' Games. Neither point is compelling, as they recognise: the similarity in order could point to influence in either direction (though they do not note that it is traditional anyway: see 257[b]–897, 262–652nn.), and Eumelos' team was famous (344–8n.).

games were established.[62] Indeed, the Pindaric scholia claim that all athletic contests were originally established 'for the dead' (*Hyp. Isthm.* Drachmann iii.192), and the four major Panhellenic Games celebrated foundational heroic deaths (Pelops and Oinomaos at Olympia, Python at Delphi, Melicertes at the Isthmia, Opheltes-Archemoros at Nemea).[63] The prestige of epic poetry doubtless helped to fuel the process, whatever the precise historical relationships between established and occasional contests (as indeed with the burial at Lefkandi), and it allowed for a fruitful interpretive dynamic between the athlete's toils and the achievements of the commemorated hero.[64] Yearly athletic contests were established in honour of the war dead, city founders, and civic heroes later in the Classical period and beyond, with well-known cases including Miltiades (Herodotos 6.38) and Brasidas (Thucydides 5.11),[65] so for centuries Homer's games enjoyed a continuing resonance with an audience able to connect them with recognisable contemporary practices.

Athletic competition beyond these contexts was a defining element of Greek culture at all periods of antiquity;[66] examples in early epos include the events on Scheria (*Od.* 8.104–30), in Thebes where Tydeus showed his quality (*Il.* 4.389–90), the diversions of the Myrmidons (*Il.* 2.773–5), the suitors' continual amusements on Ithaca (*Od.* 4.625–7 = 17.167–9; cf. *Od.* 4.659), the despatch of a chariot team to Elis to race (*Il.* 11.698–702), the 'prize-winning horses' which Agamemnon offers to Achilleus (*Il.* 9.123–4 = 265–6), and the reference to 'the kinds of prizes set for men' in the (dis)simile describing the race for Hector's life (*Il.* 22.158–61). Athletics provides several Iliadic similes (15.358–9, 16.589–92, 23.431–3, 23.517–23, 23.528–9), while Hesiod refers to games as a typical context for Hecate's favour and assistance, where victory is a source of joy to the

---

[62] Roller 1981a; Nielsen 2018: 17–22.

[63] Homer makes no explicit reference to these festivals, though some have argued that the reference to sending a chariot team to Elis (11.698–702) is an allusion to Olympia (Strabo, *Geographica* 8.3.30): see Roller 1981b: 113–15; Scanlon 2004.

[64] Bohringer 1979 (~ de Polignac 2014); Miller 2004b: 160–5; Nagy 2021.

[65] See further Roller 1981a; Proietti 2014; Nagy 2021: 296.

[66] For the early period, see Perry 2014; Younger 2021. The bibliography on ancient athletics is huge, and there are good recent companions (Christesen and Kyle 2014, Futrell and Scanlon 2021) and general overviews (esp. Kyle 2015, Miller 2004b). Researchers cannot go past the exhaustive collection of sources in the series *Quellendokumentation zur Gymnastik und Agonistik im Altertum* under the general editorship of Ingomar Weiler (Weiler et al. 1991–2002), while more readily digestible collections can be found in Sweet 1987, Miller 2004a, Stocking and Stephens 2021, and the main journals devoted to ancient sport are *Nikephoros* and *Stadion*.

contestant and 'glory to his parents' (*Th.* 435–8).[67] Achievement at these contests is always presented positively, as when the young Phaeacian Laodamas claims that 'there is no greater glory for a man | than whatever he achieves on foot and with his hands' (*Od.* 8.147–8), but one may suspect hyperbole in that setting, given what then occurs.

As an elite activity, athletics were deeply implicated in the political discourse of the ancient world, and constantly therefore the subject of both affirmation and interrogation.[68] If extant epos generally tends towards valorisation (though cf. 664–75, 664–6nn. on Epeios and his status), critique begins early in other poetic forms: Xenophanes prioritises the social order which his wisdom may bring over the glory available to an athlete (fr. 2.1–12 W²), while Tyrtaios prefers a steadfast warrior to any other kind of achievement (fr. 12.1–14 W²), in the first visible signs of a more critical tradition which would find considerable purchase in the ancient world; a speaker in Euripides' *Autolycos*, for instance, could claim that 'of all the countless ills in Greece | nothing is worse than the race of athletes' (fr. 282.1–2 Kannicht).[69] Nonetheless, the enduring importance of athletics is clear not only in the many visual and literary depictions of individual events in the ancient world (see event notes in the commentary for details), or in the briefly flourishing genre of *epinikion* (literally a song 'for the victory') devoted specifically to commemorating achievements of this sort, but even in the vibrant contribution of sport to the paroemographical tradition:[70] down to its daily metaphors and clichés, Greek culture was thoroughly enfolded in athletic arms.[71]

It is no surprise then, that Archaic visual discourse reflects this cultural prominence with some regularity from the eighth and seventh centuries onwards,[72] but Patroclos' Games are explicitly identified (with inscriptions) amongst these images for the first time only in the early sixth century, when Pelias' Games also become prominent in the record.[73] The

---

[67] Nielsen 2018: 16–17.

[68] See Golden 1998, Bertolín-Cebrián 2002, Papakonstantinou 2019: 24–61, and Valavanis 2021 for recent overviews and much further bibliography.

[69] See further Müller 1995; Visa-Ondarçuhu 1999: 213–46; Papakonstantinou 2014; Stewart 2014.

[70] García Romero 2001: 97–131.

[71] For two recent, excellent studies on the pervasiveness of athletics in ancient Greece, see Nielsen 2014 and 2024; of earlier works, Golden 1998 is a classic treatment.

[72] See Laser, and the evidence collected in Weiler et al. 1991–2002.

[73] Kossatz-Deissman 1981; Roller 1981b; Kavvadias 2010. The funeral, by contrast, does not seem to have attracted the early artists; when it is represented from the late Classical period onwards, the most popular theme is the sacrifice of the Trojans (*LIMC* s. Achilleus 487–90a).

François Vase and Sophilos *dinos* from Pharsalos (*LIMC* s. Achilleus 491, 493) definitely depict the chariot race, as the labelled characters make clear, in the former case with some striking and significant differences from the *Iliad* (262–652n.). A proto-Corinthian *aryballos* from the last third of the seventh century (*LIMC* 494) depicting a chariot race but without labels is sometimes linked with our episode, as is an early sixth-century band cup (*LIMC* 492), also unlabelled, which reflects Homer's order in placing images of boxing, wrestling, and running from left to right (but this order is traditional: 257[b]–897n.).[74] There are a few even more tentative or controversial identifications,[75] but this is not much of a return, and the short-lived early prominence is centred on the north-eastern Peloponnesos and may be connected with the growing importance of the Panhellenic Games.[76] It reflects the underwhelming impact of the Homeric poems on early Greek art more generally,[77] while later representations are few and far between (though see below).[78]

[74] Kotsonas 2019: 613 notes that the first two running figures (closest to the tripod representing victory) are bearded, but the third is not, which would map well onto the relative ages of Homer's cast and the outcome.

[75] I know of three possible cases, all with unlabelled figures: (1) horses and a group of spectators on a fragment from another *dinos* attributed to Sophilos (Tuna-Nörling 2002: 10, pl. 4; Brownlee 1988: 82–4); (2) a chariot race on a mid-sixth-century amphora from Tarquinia by the Castellani Painter, with an overturned chariot (*LIMC* s. Amazones 12; Shapiro 1994: 34, 37); (3) a synoptic depiction of the end of the *Iliad*, including the runners in the race from Patroclos' Games (740–97n.) on a seventh-century cup from Kommos on Crete (Kommos C2396; Heraklion Archaeological Museum Π25787; Kotsonas 2019). Brownlee 1988: 82–4 discusses (1) and (2) but did not know (3), all of which might reflect the *Iliad* or its story, though final certainty is impossible. Finally, Nagy 2012: 53–6 also suggests that 'we see the hero Achilles himself in the act of participating in the chariot race held in honor of Patroclus' (56) on a late sixth-century *hydria* in Münster (*LIMC* s. Achilleus 596). This vase depicts on the right a (fragmentary) female figure, a four-horse chariot team in the middle, and (directly over them but smaller) an armed figure running to the left, emerging from a tomb and labelled 'shade' (ΦΣΥΧΕ), with a lion on the ground beneath the team. No charioteer is visible, and to the left of the team is a poorly preserved figure running to the right, also in armour (presumably Achilleus). From this, Nagy 2009 ~ 2005: 315 suggests 'the version of the *Iliad* that was performed in that era (late 6th cent. BCE) must have featured the same apobatic moment'; he refers to the *apobatēs* race, an Athenian institution in which the fully armed passenger periodically runs next to the vehicle and its separate driver (Reed 1990). This is very speculative, and there is no other trace of this version of the Funeral Games. Indeed, most scholars link this *hydria* instead with a series of synoptic depictions of the scene where Hector's corpse is brought to the camp (*LIMC* 585–600): see Stähler 1967; Kossatz-Deissmann 1981: 134–6.

[76] Roller 1981b.   [77] Cf. Snodgrass 1998 against e.g. Friis Johansen 1967.

[78] Kossatz-Deissmann 1981: 121–2.

The literary reception of Patroclos' Games is, on the other hand, weighty, since it became *de rigueur* for an epic poem to have such an episode, and Book 23 remained a prime target for invocation, imitation, and competition (details and citations are provided with the headline notes for each event in the commentary).[79] Those following in Homer's footsteps spanned the whole of antiquity, from the epic and lyric poets of the Archaic period all the way to Lucian of Samosata and Nonnos of Panopolis;[80] even Apollonios' decision to omit from the *Argonautica* a discrete and full-scale episode of this sort was a deliberate choice not to deepen that particular wheel-rut.[81] This later prominence was heralded well before any specific recreation appeared, since 'Patroclos' contests' is evidenced as a title for a depiction of the chariot race on the Sophilos *dinos*, and the phrase ἐπὶ Πατρόκλωι ἆθλα proved a ready shorthand, taking its place among the other titles for segments of the Homeric poems (such as the Catalogue of Ships, the Battle at the Ships, and the *Doloneia*) which Aelian cited as evidence for ancient episodic performance of the *Iliad* and *Odyssey* (*VH* 13.14.5).[82]

Aside from the many direct recreations of the episode and its individual events in authors as generically and temporally diverse as Sophocles (262–652n.), Apollonios, and Theocritos (653–99n.) – to name just a few – different kinds of reception and supplementation were possible, but they all attest to the lasting influence and impact of Patroclos' Games. Phainias, for instance, apparently saw an inscription on a tripod in Delphi in the fourth century BCE claiming to be that originally won by Diomedes in Homer's chariot race (Athenaios 6.21.9 = Phainias, fr. 11.29–33 Wehrli);[83] intriguingly, the inscription also sought to fill out the *Iliad*'s silence on that item's provenance by sourcing it to the Trojan Helicaon, son of Antenor (see 264–5ᵃn.)! This tendency towards supplementing Homeric narrative can also be seen much later, in the fourth century CE,

---

[79] See the notes to 262–652 (chariot race), 653–99 (boxing), 700–39 (wrestling), 740–97 (running), 798–825 (fight in armour), 826–49 (iron throwing), 850–83 (archery), 884–97 (spear throwing).

[80] For surveys, see Willis 1941; Frangoulidis 1999: 4–5; Nicholson 2014; Lovatt 2019.

[81] Visa-Ondarçuhu 2015; Forte 2017: 85–95.

[82] Burkert 2012 uses this evidence as a parallel for a similar 'Ransom of Hector' title, once more found in Aelian and on a Corinthian vase of the early sixth century, to argue for precise knowledge of our *Iliad* at that date.

[83] For other inscriptions on votives sourced in funerary contests, see Roller 1981a: 2–4. In keeping with the general absence of writing from Homer's world, this is not part of his discourse.

in Libanios' decription of a painting 'around the edges', as it were, of
the running race (see 740–97n.), focusing on details which are not mentioned, but equally not precluded, by Homer. Indirect in a different way,
the first-century BCE Lindian Chronicle links Meriones and Teucros in
their dedications at the local temple to Athene. Though the votives do not
come from the archery contest in Homer, their positioning as the last two
dedicatees from the Trojan War is surely a nod to the competition in Book
23 (see 850–83n.). Beyond his pictorial interest, Libanios seems to have
been particularly struck by the Funeral Games, since he cites them several
times in his *Progymnasmata* to prove the moral worth of both Diomedes
and Achilleus (*Encomium* 1.15–16, 3.20; *Invective* 1.21),[84] while Synesios in
the fifth century CE shrewdly noted that the actual outcomes in Patroclos'
contests frequently go against expectations (see 257^b–897n.), illustrating
his contention that the poet was 'the first of the Greeks to realise that
human beings are the plaything of god' (*Egyptian Tale* 2.2.11 Hose et al.
2012). To close with parody, Lucian reran the whole episode selectively
in the 'Thanatousia' or Festival of the Dead (*Ver. hist.* 2.22), where the
original cast and some interlopers went at it a second time on the Isle
of the Blest: Achilleus and Theseus were the umpires, Odysseus lost the
wrestling to Caranos, Epeios tied with Areios the Egyptian in the boxing,
there was no pancration, 'but as for the footrace, no longer do I recall
who won'.[85]

Yet here too we need caution: Hyginus in the first century BCE/CE lists
fifteen famous games down to those of Vergil (the first four in his list are
missing), and omits reference to most of those known or referred to in
Archaic Greek epos, while his record of Patroclos' Games is fourteenth
on his list and at variance with Homer in every detail given – Aias is the
victor in the wrestling and Menelaos (!) in spear throwing, the sacrifice of
the Trojan youths occurs after the events, and the prizes are all different
(*Fabulae* § 273). It is not contended here that these variations suggest a
widely divergent tradition for the Homeric episode at the turn of the era
(see Intro. § 4), simply that reception – even of such a prominent figure
as the poet of the *Iliad* – was never a straightforward process in antiquity,[86]
and we must reckon with the possibility of a large number of early comparanda now entirely lost to us.

---

[84] See now Decloquemont 2023.
[85] To the author's chagrin, Hesiod defeated Homer in the poetic contest,
'though in truth (Homer) was much better': see Mal-Maeder 1992. I have never
had more faith in Lucian.
[86] See, most recently, Hunter 2018; Manolea 2022.

3 LANGUAGE, METRE, AND STYLE

3.1 LANGUAGE

3.1.1 Dialect

Homer's language was famously termed by Meister a *Kunstsprache* or 'art(istic) language', a form of Greek never actually spoken in one time or place, combining elements from several different dialects at several different stages of their existence, passed down and developed by many generations of singers. The chief principle for this agglutination – found also in the language of Hesiod, the *Homeric Hymns*, and what little we have left of the Epic Cycle – is that of compositional utility, and it works through a constant process of retaining, adopting, discarding, and even creating features according to the opportunities and flexibility they afford to the orally composing poet.[87] The two main dialects in the language of epos are Aeolic and Ionic, with the latter dominant throughout (to the point that the dialect is often said to be 'Epic-Ionic' *vel sim.*).[88]

a. Ionic[89]

- Proto-Greek ᾱ > η (unlike Attic, this holds even after ε, ι, and ρ): γενεή, μελίη, etc.; cf. πυρῆς (22: A. πυρᾶς), κλισίην (38: A. κλισίαν), etc.
- ν mobile (like A.): ὦρσεν (14), στήθεσσιν (18), δόμοισιν (19), etc.

---

[87] This commentary adopts no position over the Homeric Question(s) on the identity or whereabouts of the poet, nor indeed on whether or not writing was necessary for the conception and fixation of the *Iliad*. The above statement merely reflects the fact that the language used was developed for a framework of oral (re)composition in performance; we have the poems as written texts, of course, and in some sense we have to respect that fact, but we should not downplay our uncertainties as to how that text came into being: see further Intro. § 4.

[88] For discussions of the epic dialect, see Palmer 1962, Hainsworth 1988, Janko 8–19, Horrocks 1997, West 1997; Willi 2011. In the lists below, we use the sigla AI. for Attic-Ionic, A. for Attic, WG for West Greek (the term for Doric and 'North-West Greek' dialects north of the Gulf of Corinth, and many of the Greek communities in Italy), and PG for Proto-Greek (the reconstructed hypothetical ancestor of all known Greek dialects). This latter dialect is often the first experienced by most students coming to Ancient Greek, and many Ionic features are shared with Attic, as will be seen.

[89] The particular type of Ionic in the epic language is that of Central (Cyclades) and Western (Euboia) Ionic, not Eastern (Asia Minor, Anatolia): that is clear in the treatment of the sound *$k^w o$- in words like που (East Ionic κου), ὅπου (ὅκου), πω (κω), πῶς, πως (κῶς, κως), ὅπως (ὅκως), ποῖος (κοῖος), ὁποῖος (ὁκοῖος), πότε, ποτε (κότε, κοτε), ὁπότε (ὁκότε), πόσος (κόσος), ὁπόσος (ὁκόσος). For a recent discussion of the features of all varieties of Ionic and their complex interactions, see del Barrio 2014. Another East Ionic feature lacking from our texts is psilosis, or loss of aspiration, which is not found either in Homer (generally), West and Central Ionic, or Attic, but is found in Aeolic.

- athematic infinitives in -ναι (like A.; cf. Aeol. -μεν, -μεναι): εἶναι (343, 595), ἐπιδοῦναι (559), δοῦναι (593).
- potential particle ἄν (like A.; cf. Aeol. κε): 275, 339.
- conditional particle εἰ (like A.; cf. Aeol. αἰ): 155, 274, 344, 383, etc.
- 1st/2nd person pronouns ἡμεῖς/ὑμεῖς etc. (like A.; cf. Aeol. ἄμμες/ὔμμες etc.): ὑμῖν (445), ὑμεῖς (458, 495, etc.).
- demonstrative pronoun (~ article) οἵ, αἵ (like A.; cf. Aeol. τοί, ταί).
- general lack of contraction (unlike A.): νόος (484, 590, 604: A. νοῦς, which Hom. uses at *Od.* 10.240), ἔρρεε (34, 688: A. ἔρρει, which Hom. uses at 17.86), ποδώκεες (376: A. ποδώκεις), ἀολλέες (674: A. ἀολλεῖς), προσέειπε (722: A. προσεῖπε), νεφέων (874: A. νεφῶν), φρονέων (545: A. φρονῶν), etc.
- -σσ- (unlike A. -ττ-): πρήσσοντε (501: A. πράττω), κασσιτέρωι (503, 561: A. καττίτερος), κρείσσων (578: A. κρείττων), etc.
- 'quantitative metathesis' (i.e. change of length, like A.: PG/Myc. ᾱο > I. ηο > AI. εω): Τυδεῖδεω (405: < *Τυδεῖδηο < Τυδεῖδᾱο 5.281, 8.254).
- 1st person plural active ending in -μεν (like A.; cf. Aeolic -μες): κλαίωμεν (9), δορπήσομεν (11), etc.
- compensatory lengthening of vowels after a consonant loss (like A.; Aeol. usually 'geminates' or doubles the consonant): I. κούρη < κόρϝᾱ (A. κόρη, Aeol. κόρα), I. ξεῖνος < ξένϝος (Aeol. ξέννος; A. ξένος).
- temporal adverbs τότε, πότε, ὅτε (like A.; cf. WG τόκα, πόκα, ὄκα): τότε (374, 497, etc.), ὅτε (38, 87, 117, etc.).
- adverb/preposition πρός (like A.; Aeol. προτί, ποτί): 68, 171, 235, 868, etc.

b. Aeolic[90]

- extension/retention of -σσ-: ἐτέλεσσα (i.e. ἐτέλεσ-σα 149, 543, 559; AI. ἐτέλεσα), but also ὄμοσσεν (42 < ὄμνυμι), κοτέσσατο (383 < κοτέομαι), ἀγασσάμενοι (639 < ἄγαμαι) etc.; μέσσον (685, 704, 701; AI. μέσον).
- infinitives in -μεν, -μεναι: θέμεναι (45), ἀξέμεναι (50), τιθήμεναι (83), ἀξέμεν (111), δαπτέμεν (183), ἐλθέμεν (197), διδασκέμεν (308), ἔμμεναι (791), etc.
- dative plural for consonant stems (i.e. 3rd decl.) in -εσσι. Originally from s-stem nouns like ἔτεσ-σι or στήθεσ-σι (18), the ending is then applied to other stems (ἄνδρ-εσσι, κηρύκ-εσσι 39, Μυρμιδόν-εσσιν 60, κύν-εσσιν 183, etc.), and then back into s-stems (λεχέ-εσσι 25).[91]

---

[90] Wathelet 1970; Haug 2002: 70–106; for a recent survey, see Hodot 2014.
[91] This is an important illustration of how compositional utility drives the way in which Homer's language developed.

- patronymics in -ιος: Τελαμώνιος (708, 722, etc.).
- potential particle κε (AI. ἄν): 82, 244, 247, 322, 346, 382, etc.
- conditional particle αἰ (AI. εἰ): 82, 413, 543.
- thematic inflection of contract verbs: φορῆναι (2.107, etc. < φορέω) for φορεῖν.
- 3rd person plural endings in -εν (AI. -ησαν): ἄγερθεν (287: AI. ἠγέρθησαν), πλῆσθεν (397: AI. ἐπλήσθησαν).
- 1st/2nd person pronouns ἄμμες/ὔμμες etc. (AI. ἡμεῖς/ὑμεῖς etc.): ἄμμι (160: AI. ἡμῖν), ὔμμι (787: AI. ὑμῖν).
- perfect participles with present endings: κεκλήγοντες (AI. κεκληγότες).
- apocope of prepositions/preverbs: πὰρ λεχέεσσι (25), κὰδ δ᾽ ἷζον (28), παρπεπιθόντες (37), etc.
- demonstrative pronoun (~ article) τοί, ταί. (AI. οἵ, αἵ): ταί (119, 121), τοί (202, 212, 241, etc.).
- * masc. a-stem (1st decl.) genitive singular in -αο: Πολυποίταο (848: AI. Πολυποίτου).
- * o-stem (2nd decl.) genitive singular in -οιο: δειλοῖο (65: AI. δειλοῦ), ποταμοῖο (73: AI. ποταμοῦ), etc.
- adverb/preposition προτί, ποτί (AI. πρός): 64 (see n.), 510, 869.
- labialisation of *kʷ-: πίσυρες ('four' 171: AI. τέσσαρες).
- asseverative particle μάν (A. μήν, I. μέν): 441.

The asterisked items may not be specifically or only Aeolic features, as they are shared with the language of **Mycenaean** as preserved in the Linear B tablets.[92] To the features of this older group we add the instrumental case ending -φι, the genitive plural of 1st decl. nouns in -ᾱων (cf. ἀράων 199), the prefix ἐρι- (ἐρίηρες 6, ἐρίβωλον 215, ἐριμύκων 775), and many deeply embedded items of Homeric vocabulary, such as ἄναξ, δέπας, ἔγχος, κόρυς, τεύχω, φάσγανον, etc. Scholars debate the significance of the Mycenaean inheritance (does it show unbroken continuity from the Bronze Age? or distantly remembered and preserved forms?), but they cannot deny its presence.

c. Attic

The final major group of linguistic features in the *Kunstsprache* is Attic, though there are times when it is hard to separate a specifically Attic feature from Ionic, especially for such an early period, because our

---

[92] See Ruijgh 1995, 2011 (expansive); Thompson 2024.

external evidence for the dialects is so poor.[93] Nonetheless, here are some features in epos which scholars generally associate with it:[94]

- οὖν (I. ὦν): 813.
- ἐνταῦθα, ἐντεῦθεν, ἐνταυθοῖ (East I. ἐνθαῦτα, ἐνθεῦτεν).[95]
- χίλια (I. χείλια); μείζων (I. μέζων); κρείσσων (I. κρέσσων): 578.
- μήν (I. μέν; Aeol. μάν: 441): 410.
- δέχομαι (I. δέκομαι): 647.
- aspiration more generally (like West and Central I.; cf. psilosis in East I.): ἀφῆκεν (432: East I. ἀπῆκεν), ἀφίσταται (517: East I. ἀπίσταται), etc.
- -ντο 3rd pl. athematic secondary ending: μαχέοιντο (1.344: I. μαχεοίατο, the usual optative ending in Homer); ἐπεκείντο (Od. 6.19; I. ἐπεκείατο).
- assorted cases of α for I. η: ἀγξηράνηι (21.347: I. ἀγξηρήνηι), μισγαγκείαν (4.453: I. μισγαγκείην), Ἀνεμώρειαν (2.521: I. *Ἀνεμωρείην).

As is evident, this last type of influence – when we can be certain that we are not dealing with a feature shared by Attic and West Ionic, or an independent innovation – is very apparent in our text but does not penetrate deep into the language, i.e. into the formula systems; clearly there was some influence on the paradosis, but it may not have been at the level of performance or bardic recreation.[96]

How these dialects relate to one another, and what they tell us about the prehistory of Greek epos, is very controversial. The presence of Attic features, for example, though most scholars now would grant many fewer cases than were originally proposed by Wackernagel, suggests that Athens did play a role in the fixation/recording of the text (Intro. § 4). Whether that amounts to a thoroughgoing 'recension' of the sort proposed for the sixth-century tyrant Peisistratos is unclear. When it comes to the wider picture about the relationship between Aeolic and Ionic features, one model suggests an 'Aeolic phase', a largely direct line from the Mycenaean world through the Aeolic-speaking areas at the end of the Bronze Age, spreading later into Ionian areas and becoming thoroughly 'Ionicised', as it were, before being written down (possibly) in a West Ionic area such as Euboia. This demands a single stream of transmission for epos from the Bronze Age into the Iron Age, and the

---

[93] Wackernagel 1916: 1–159 (expansive); GH I § 7; Shipp 1972: 10–15; Ruijgh 1995: 49–50; West 2001a: 31–2; Cassio 2002: 116–17; Reece 2005: 80–6. Scholars are increasingly inclined to view these forms as less categorically Attic (see e.g. Willi 2011: 460 on κεῖντο as an analogically created form rather than a dialect borrowing).

[94] See also the nn. in the commentary on ἆσσον (8), κλισιῶν (112), Ἑωσφόρος (226), τέσσαρα (268), ἐφομαρτεῖτον (414), περιδώμεθον (485).

[95] Ruijgh 1995: 49–50 notes that the aspiration here would have been a feature of Euboian (West) Ionic, and so need not be a sign of Attic influence (cf. also δέχομαι, and aspiration more generally in the above list).

[96] See esp. Reece 2005, and Intro. § 4.

concomitant belief that all memory of hexameter poetry died out entirely in other parts of Greece, only to be spread back to them later on. One of the best arguments in its favour is the predominance of Aeolic forms over old Ionic forms in a sequence like the genitive singular of a-stem masculine nouns: -āo > *-ηo > -εω. The first and last inflections are attested in Homer (e.g. Ἀτρεΐδαο and Ἀτρεΐδεω); we might expect a process of thorough Ionicisation to replace the Aeolic (and older) -āo with its Ionic equivalent -ηo, but we do not find that form. This model would help to explain, *inter al.*, the dominance of Achilleus, a Thessalian Aeolic figure, in all surviving material to do with the Trojan War.

Another model demands a more 'diffusionist' process, where independently evolved and developing traditions in Ionic- and Aeolic-speaking areas were constantly interacting and regenerating the language. One of its best arguments is the presence of older Ionic forms in the following sequence, the genitive singular forms of the word for 'ship': *νᾱ(ϝ)ός > νηός (1.476, etc.) > νεός (15.423 etc.). The first form is never attested in Homer, but the two stages of Ionic are (the second where quantitative metathesis has not completed the lengthening of the final vowel to νεώς, by analogy with other forms ending in -ος). If the phase theory were correct, the argument goes, the Homeric text would have retained the spelling with long α (as it does with -āo above). This model would help to account for several shared features between East Ionic and Aeolic, such as psilosis, or even the creation of the -μεναι infinitive ending (only in Lesbian Aeolic) as a combination of Aeolic -μεν and Ionic -ναι; there is also some evidence for Aeolic hexameters in Sappho (frr. 106, 142–3 V), but they are hardly probative of a long-standing or separate epichoric tradition.[97] Neither side holds the field; the debate continues.[98]

3.1.2 Grammar

The heterogeneity of Homer's dialect(s), and the flexibility it gives to the poet, is reflected also in his morphology. I merely aim to set out here the range of basic forms most particularly characteristic of his language, especially (but not only) where they differ from Attic.[99] Peculiarities and

---

[97] Kelly 2021: 56–7.

[98] See e.g. Horrocks 1997: 200, 212–17; Haug 2002: 145–64; Jones 2012.

[99] Aside from the very handy individual guides to Homeric grammar in other volumes from this series (esp. the superb treatment in Bowie 2013: 29–54 and Bowie 2019: 43–67, to which every reader of this commentary is directed enthusiastically), the standard work remains Chantraine's *Grammaire homérique* (2 vols, 2nd ed., Paris 1951–3; now updated by Michel Casevitz, and referenced in this book as *GH*); more recent is Wachter's 'Grammatik der homerischen Sprache' (*GHS*) in the Prolegomena volume to the Basel commentary (3rd ed., Berlin and New York

features of Homer's syntax are reserved for § 3.3 'Style' below, and the commentary itself.

a. Pronouns

i. Personal

1st person sing. ἐγώ(ν)[100] nom., με/ἐμέ[101] acc., ἐμεῖο/ἐμέο*/ἐμεῦ/μευ[102]/ ἐμέθεν gen., μοι/ἐμοί dat.
2nd person sing. σύ/τύνη nom., σε/σέ acc., σεῖο/σέο/σεο/σεῦ/σευ/ σέθεν/τέοιο* gen., σοί/σοι/τοι[103]/τεῖν* dat.
3rd person sing. – nom.,[104] ἑ/ἕ/ἑέ (refl.)*/μιν acc., εἷο/ἕο/ἑο/εὗ/εὑ/ ἕθεν/ἔθεν gen., οἷ/οἱ/ἑοῖ dat.

1st person dual νώ, νῶϊ nom. acc., νῶϊν gen. dat.
2nd person dual σφώ, σφῶϊ nom. acc., σφῶϊν gen. dat.
3rd person dual σφωε nom. acc., σφωϊν gen. dat.

1st person pl.[105] ἡμεῖς/ἄμμες nom., ἡμέας/ἄμμε acc., ἡμέων/ἡμείων gen., ἡμῖν/ἡμίν/ἄμμι dat.

2nd person pl. ὑμεῖς/ὕμμες nom., ὑμέας/ὕμμε acc., ὑμέων/ὑμείων gen., ὑμῖν/ὑμίν/ὕμμι dat.

3rd person pl. – nom., σφέας/σφεας (not refl.)/σφας*/σφε acc., σφείων/ σφῶν/σφεων (not refl.) gen., σφίσι/σφισι (not refl.)/σφι (not refl.) dat.

2009, now translated into English). See also Willi 2011, and still useful are Palmer 1962, and D. B. Monro's venerable *Grammar of the Homeric Dialect* (Oxford 1891). In the lists below, an asterisk marks a form rarely found in the MSS.

[100] For the so-called 'epenthetic' ν, see 243–4n.

[101] The variation in accentuation for these and other pronominal forms listed below (σέ/σε, σέο/σεο, σεῦ/σευ, σοί/σοι, ἕ/ἑ, ἕο/ἑο, εὗ/εὑ) is generally held to depend on whether or not the pronoun is considered to be emphatic (in which case it is accented; if unemphatic, it is considered 'enclitic', so its accent leans on the previous word), but the MSS show considerable variation; see e.g. 126 (φράσσατο Πατρόκλωι μέγα ἤριον ἠδέ οἱ αὐτῶι), where ἠδε οἷ is a plausible minority reading, given the constant focus on Achilleus and his future (and some rules in antiquity would have it accented anyway because it is reflexive).

[102] On forms in -ευ, see 69–70n.

[103] On this form, see 19–20n.

[104] There is no separate nominative form for this pronoun; Homer uses a demonstrative instead.

[105] There is some, albeit controversial, trace of initial accent in the acc., gen., and dat. of these forms, which has been considered a mark of emphasis (Vendryes 97) or not (Probert 2003: 150–1), while *GHS* § 96 n. 37 judges it 'doubtful from the point of view of linguistic history'.

ii. Demonstrative

	masc.	fem.	neut.
gen. sing.	τοῖο, τοῦ	τῆς	τοῖο, τοῦ
nom./acc. dual	τώ	τώ	τώ
gen./dat. dual	τοῖϊν	τοῖϊν	τοῖϊν
nom. pl.	οἵ, τοί	αἵ, ταί	τά
dat. pl.	τοῖσι, τοῖς	τῆισι, τῆις	τοῖσι, τοῖς

iii. τις Interrogative/Indefinite

gen. sing.	AI. τίνος/τινος is not found; instead, Hom. uses τεῦ/ τευ, τέο/τεο.
dat. sing. masc.	AI. indef. τινι, and also τεωι.
gen. pl.	AI. τίνων is not found; instead, Hom. uses τέων.

The corresponding 'compound' pronoun ὅς τις (ὅστις), ἥ τις, ὅ τι 'whoever, whatever' has a number of notable forms: aside from the expected forms in the nom. and acc. (ὅς τις, ὅν τινα, ἥ τις, ἥν τινα, οἵ τινες, οὕς τινας, αἵ τινες ἅς τινας, and ἅσσα = A. ἅττα), we also find a series of 'shorter' forms from a nom. masc. sing. ὅτις (494) where the first element is invariable (as often in Attic poetry), giving masc. acc. sing. ὅτινα, gen. sing. ὅττεο, ὅττευ, or ὅτευ, dat. sing. ὅτεωι, masc. acc. pl. ὅτινας, gen. pl. ὅτεων, dat. pl. ὁτέοισι, and neut. nom. and acc. sing. ὅττι (71, 403, 414, 670).

b. Adjectives

i. Possessive

> 1st person sing. ἐμός -ή -όν
> 2nd person sing. σός -ή -όν, τεός -ή -όν
> 3rd person sing. ὅς ἥ ὅν, ἑός -ή -όν

> 1st person dual νωΐτερος -η -ον* 'belonging to us two'
> 2nd person dual σφωΐτερος -η -ον 'belonging to you two'

> 1st person pl. ἡμέτερος -η -ον, ἁμός -ή -όν
> 2nd person pl. ὑμέτερος -η -ον, ὑμός -ή -όν[106]
> 3rd person pl. σφός -ή -όν, σφέτερος -η -ον

---

[106] This form is also used in the sing. (i.e. = σός, as in later Greek) at 5.489, 13.815 (where on both occasions the speaker is addressing one person). Both ὑμός and ἁμός have been classed as Doric, or explained as derived from the Aeolic first- and second-person plural pronominal stems (ἁμμ-, ὑμμ-).

c. Nouns

i. a-Stems (1st Declension)

- masc. nom. sing. in -ᾰ (originally vocatives): ἱππότᾰ (89: see n.).
- masc. gen. sing. in -ᾱο and -εω (A. -ου): Ἀΐδαο (19: A. Ἅιδου); Τυδεΐδεω (405: Τυδειδοῦ), etc. by quantitative metathesis (i.e. -ᾱο > *-ηο > -εω).
- masc. nom. acc. dual in -α: Ἀτρεΐδα (1.16, etc.).
- fem. dat. pl. in -ῃσι(ν) -ῃς (rarely -αις); cf. A. -αις): ξυνοχῇσιν (330: A. συνοχαῖς), πνοιῇς (367: A. πνοαῖς), ἐμῇς (675: A. ἐμαῖς), etc. Homeric forms with -αις are rare and often suspect, though they may be ancient and/or the result of Attic influence.[107]
- fem. gen. pl. in -ᾱων and -εων (lacking older Ionic *-ηων) and even 'Attic' -ων: ἀράων (199: A. ἀρῶν); κλισιῶν (112).

ii. o-Stems (2nd Declension)

- gen. sing. in -οιο: δειλοῖο (65: AI. δειλοῦ), ποταμοῖο (73: AI. ποταμοῦ), etc.
- dat. pl. in -οισι and -οις (A. always -οις): ἑτάροισι (5: A. ἑταίροις), etc.[108]

iii. Athematic[109] Stems (3rd Declension)

General

- extension of s-stem dative plurals in -εσσι to other stems: κηρύκ-εσσι (39), Μυρμιδόν-εσσιν (60), κύν-εσσιν (183; cf. κυ-σί 11.365 etc.), νή-εσσι (248, 829; cf. also νέ-εσσι 3.46 etc., and more regularly νηυ-σί, etc.), χείρεσσι (554; cf. χέρσιν 1.14, etc.), σταχύ-εσσιν (598), πόδ-εσσιν (622, 636, 696, 764; cf. πόσ(σ)ι 2.44 etc.), λιμέν-εσσι (845; cf. λίμεσι 12.284, etc.), κτεάτ-εσσιν (829).[110]

iv. s-Stems

Neuter nouns in -ος such as γένος, ἔπος, κέρδος, σάκος, στῆθος, τεύχεα, etc.

- uncontracted vowels revealing original -σ-, as ἔπεος gen. sing. (< *ἔπεσ-ος: A. ἔπους), ἔπεϊ dat. sing. (< ἔπεσ-ι), ἔπεα nom. acc. pl.

---

[107] See GH I § 85.

[108] 'Long' dative plurals are originally old locative formations, with the shorter forms either elided versions of -οισι, influenced by Attic (which used -οις), or old instrumentals (GH I § 81).

[109] This term, as with the verbs below, denotes the fact that nouns in this pattern add the case ending straight onto the noun stem (βασιλῆ-α).

[110] The ending is also grafted back onto the s-stems as well: ἐπέ-εσσι (363, 489, 492), λεχέ-εσσι (25).

(< *ἔπεσ-α: A. ἔπη), ἐπέων gen. pl. (< *ἐπέσ-ων: A. ἐπῶν), ἔπε(σ)-σι and ἐπέ-εσσι dat. pl. (< ἔπεσ-σι: A. ἔπεσι): στήθεος gen. sing. (761, 763: A. στήθους), τεύχεα nom. acc. pl. (15, 800, 803, 809: A. τεύχη), κέρδεα acc. pl. (709: A. κέρδη), σάκεος (820: A. σάκους), etc.

v. i-Stems

Masc. and fem. nouns such as πόλις, μάντις, δύναμις, πόσις, νέμεσις, μῆτις with the -ι- of the stem retained through most forms.

- dat. sing. sometimes -ι but more usually -εϊ/-ει: μάντι and μάντεϊ, μήτι (315, 316, 318), πόσεϊ and πόσει, νέμεσσι.
- nom. pl. usually in -ιες (A. -εις).
- acc. pl. can be -ῑς (ἀκοίτις*, πόλῑς minority reading at 2.648), -ιας, -εις.[111]
- dat. pl. adds -εσσι to stem (πολίεσσι).
- the declension of πόλις is thus:
  (i) a complete range of -ι- forms: πόλις nom. sing., πόλιν acc., πόλιος gen. (A. πόλεως[112]), πόλιες* nom. pl. (A. πόλεις), πόλιας* acc. pl. (A. πόλεις), πολίων gen. pl. (A. πόλεων), πολίεσσι dat. pl. (A. πόλεσι);
  (ii) forms with -η-/-ε-: πόληος πόλεος* gen., πόληϊ* πόλεϊ/πόλει dat., πόληες nom. pl., πόλεις πόληας* πόλεας* acc. pl., πολέεσσι dat. pl.

vi. u-Stems

A few nouns like πέλεκυς, ἄστυ, and many adjectives like βραδύς, ἡδύς, etc., show some -υ- forms, but forms in -ε- as well.

- they are generally similar to the i-stem nouns (-εος gen. sing., -εϊ dat. sing., -εες, -εις nom. pl., -εας -εις acc. pl., -εων gen. pl., -σι, -εσσι dat. pl.).
- πολύς has some original -υ- forms (πολύς nom. masc. sing., πολύν acc. masc. sing.), some -ε- forms (πολέος gen. sing., πολέες, πολεῖς* nom. pl., πολέας acc. pl., πολέσι, πολέσσι dat. pl.), and many borrowed from the 1st and 2nd declensions as well (πολλός nom. masc. sing., πολλή fem. nom. sing., πολλόν nom. neut. sing., etc.).
- the word for 'son' (stem υἱ-) has (i) a partial athematic declension, (ii) some -ε- forms, and (iii) a thematic declension as well (and a dat. pl. υἱάσι borrowed from πατράσι[113]):

---

[111] Sometimes viewed as an Atticisim (Intro. § 3.1).

[112] This is actually a majority reading at 11.168.

[113] Though πατράσι is not actually attested in Homer, this -ασι is part of the pattern we see with words for father, mother, daughter, and man (below, viii), within which the form ἀνδράσι is extremely common.

(i) υἷα acc. sing., υἷος gen. sing., υἷϊ dat. sing., υἷε nom. acc. dual, υἷες nom. pl., υἷας acc. pl.

(ii) υἱέα* acc. sing., υἱέος gen sing., υἱεῖ and υἱέϊ dat. sing., υἱεῖς and υἱέες nom. pl., υἱέας acc. pl.

(iii) υἱός nom. sing., υἱόν acc sing., υἱοῦ gen. sing., etc.

On the other hand, a series of nouns like νέκυς, σῦς, ἰχθύς, and δρῦς retain -υ- throughout.

- νέκυς nom. sing., νέκυν acc. sing., νέκυος gen. sing., νέκυϊ dat. sing., νέκυες nom. pl., νέκυας and νέκῦς acc. pl., νεκύων gen. pl., νέκυσσι and νεκύεσσι dat pl.

vii. Diphthong Stems (-ευ-, -ηυ-)

Nouns like βασιλεύς, νηῦς, βοῦς, and names like Πηλεύς, Ἀχιλλεύς, Ὀδυσσεύς, and Ζεύς, with an original -ηϝ- in the stem.

- βασιλεύς retains -η: βασιλῆα, βασιλῆος, βασιλῆϊ/βασιλῆϊ, βασιλῆες, βασιλῆας, βασιλήων, βασιλεῦσι.
- νηῦς varies between -η-/-ε-: νηῦς, νῆα/νέα*, νηός/νέος, νῆϊ, νῆες/νέες, νῆας/ νέας, νηῶν/νεῶν, νηυσί/νήεσσι/νέεσσι.
- βοῦς (stem βοϝ-) shows an ancient form in acc. sing. (βοῦν; βῶν Σ 7.238), but otherwise builds on βο- (βοός., no dat. sing., βόες, βόας/ βοῦς, βοῶν, βουσί. and βόεσσι).
- Ἀχιλλεύς retains -η (except Ἀχιλλεῖ at 23.792: see n.), and also shortens -λλ- to -λ- (Ἀχιλεύς, Ἀχιλῆα, Ἀχιλῆος, Ἀχιλῆϊ).
- Ὀδυσσεύς shows more variation, with -η- retention (Ὀδυσσῆα, Ὀδυσσῆος, Ὀδυσσῆϊ), shortening to -ε (Ὀδυσσέα, Ὀδυσσέος*), and some shortening of -σσ- to -σ- (Ὀδυσεύς, Ὀδυσῆα, Ὀδυσῆος, Ὀδυσῆϊ).
- 'Zeus' has a regular and original declension in Ζεύς, Ζῆν, Διός, Διΐ (< *dy-, *di-), but an accusative Δία was 'back-formed' from the genitive, and Ζῆνα (whence Ζηνός, Ζηνί) created to regularise the declension in line with other athematic accusatives in -α (see 43–4n.).

viii. Stems in λ, μ, ν, ρ

Most nouns of this sort are quite regular (ποιμήν, λιμήν, etc.), but four show tremendous flexibility (πατήρ, μήτηρ, θυγάτηρ, and ἀνήρ). These originally exhibited variation in their stem length (-ηρ- in the nom., -ερ- in the voc. sing., acc. sing., nom. pl., and possibly acc. pl., and simply -ρ- in the gen. sing., possibly acc. pl., gen. pl., and dat. pl.). Bardic need and Greek's capacity for analogical extension gave rise to a more varied system, thus:

πατήρ	μήτηρ	θυγάτηρ	ἀνήρ
πατέρα	μητέρα	θυγατέρα, θύγατρα	ἀνέρα, ἄνδρα
πατέρος*, πατρός	μητέρος, μητρός	θυγατέρος, θυγατρός	ἀνέρος, ἀνδρός
πατέρι, πατρί	μητέρι, μητρί	θυγατέρι, θυγατρί	ἀνέρι, ἀνδρί
–	–	θυγατέρες, θύγατρες	ἀνέρες, ἄνδρες
πατέρας*	μητέρας*	θυγατέρας*, θύγατρας	ἀνέρας, ἄνδρας
πατέρων, πατρῶν*	–	θυγατρῶν	ἀνδρῶν
–	–	θυγατέρεσσι*	ἀνδράσι, ἄνδρεσσι

ix. Case Endings and Suffixes

Epos is particularly rich in suffixes to express certain adverbial relationships.

- accusatival: -δε 'towards' (also -σε, -ζε): κλισίηνδε (58, 275, 662), Ἄϊδόσδε (137: see n.), οἶκόνδε (229: see n., 856), πεδίονδε (189), χαμᾶζε (508), ἑτέρωσε (231: see n., 697).
- genitival: -θεν 'from', very frequently in adverbs (ἐγγύθεν, etc.), and sometimes used as an equivalent to a genitive: οὐρανόθεν (189), σέθεν (312 = σεῦ, etc.), κλισίηθεν (564), οἴκοθεν (592).
- locatival: -θι 'at': also frequently in adverbs (ὅθι 'where', αὖθι 'there'): αὐτόθι (147).
- -φι is a Mycenaean instrumental plural ending used in epos as a general datival and genitival suffix; the resulting words can also be modified by prepositions/preverbs: ὄχεσφι (7), ὑπ' ὄχεσφιν (130), βίηφιν (315), ἐκ θεόφιν (347), δακρυόφι (397), σὺν ὄχεσφιν (518), παρ' αὐτόφι (640: GHI § 104f.; Ruijgh 2011: 274–7).

d. Verbs

i. Endings

There are two sets of endings for the Greek verb[114] – primary and secondary. The primary endings are used for the present, future, perfect, and future perfect tenses of the indicative, and for all tenses of the subjunctive mood.

---

[114] There are also two patterns of conjugation, the 'thematic' (-ω) and 'athematic' (-μι); in the former case, a vowel is used to join the tense stem to the ending (λύ-ο-μεν, λύ-ε-τε), and in the second the ending is joined straight onto that stem (τίθε-μεν, τίθε-τε).

The secondary endings are used for everything else, the imperfect, aorist, and pluperfect tenses of the indicative, and all tenses of the optative mood.

Active	*Primary*	*Secondary*
sing.	-ω/-μι, -ς/-θα, -ι/-σι (< -τι)	-ν, -ς/-σθα
dual	-τον, -τον	-τον, -την
pl.	-μεν, -τε, -σιν	-μεν, -τε, -ν/-σαν

- athematic 1st and 3rd sing. forms (-μι, -σι) are used for thematic subjunctive forms as well (ἴδωμι 18.63 but ἴδω 24.555; ἄγησι 6.37 but ἄγηι 7.335): παρεκπροφύγηισιν (314).[115]
- athematic 2nd sing. -θα (οἶσθα) is treated as though the ending was -σθα, and used as an alternative to 2nd sing. -ς (esp. in thematic subjunctives): παρεξελάσηισθα (344: = παρεξελάσηις), ἐθέλησθα = ἐθέλης, εἴπηισθα = εἴπηις, διδοῖσθα = διδοῖς, etc.
- 2nd sing. ἐσ-σί from εἰμί 'I am' preserves the old -σι ending, later simplified to -ς.
- 3rd pl. athematic endings generally show the lengthened stem vowel: see τιθεῖσι, διδοῦσι, ἱεῖσιν, ἱστᾶσι (A. τιθέασι, διδόασι, ἵασι), but cf. ἔασι and εἰσί (311: see n.), and ἴασι < εἰμι.
- 3rd pl. -ν (Aeolic) is a very common alternative for -σαν (AI): βάν/ἔβαν (352) versus ἔβησαν· ἄγερθεν (287: A. ἠγέρθησαν).

Medio-passive[116]	*Primary*	*Secondary*
sing.	-μαι, -σαι, -ται	-μην, -σο, -το
dual	-σθον, -σθον	-σθον, -σθην
pl.	-με(σ)θα, -σθε, -νται/-αται	-με(σ)θα, -σθε, -ντο/-ατο

- 2nd sing. -σαι loses -σ- between vowels, which gives -εαι and then -ηι by contraction: ἐπιτέλλεαι (95: < *ἐπιτέλλεσαι), ἱππάζεαι (426: < *ἱππάζεσαι), etc. Athematic verbs often show this *sigma* in the present tense of the indicative (δύνασαι, δαίνυσαι but also δαινύηι, ἧσαι, κεῖσαι), as do some verbs in the perfect (e.g. μέμνησαι 648,[117] δεδάκρυσαι 16.7).

---

[115] West I.xxxi does not print *ι* adscript for this form, on the basis of one word on Nestor's cup from Pithecoussai (*CEG* 454) and the greater antiquity of -ησι, but the very common -ηι form encouraged reanalysis of Archaic -ησι as -η(ι)-σι, and *ι* is both well attested in the MSS and integral to the wider subjunctive morphology (e.g. -ηισθα: Peters 1998).

[116] The passive voice actually developed from the middle, with which it shares many forms (or, rather, never developed alternative forms): it has its own forms for the future and aorist indicatives (both with -θη-), though the former is never found in Homer.

[117] See 648–9n.

- 2nd sing. -σο also loses post-vocalic *sigma* in this way, resulting either in -ευ < -εο < *-εσο (ἔπλευ < ἔπλεο < *ἔπλεσο), or -ω < -αο < *-ασο (ἐλύσαο < *ἐλύσασο, ἐκτήσω < *ἐκτήσαο < *ἐκτήσασο *Od.* 24.193) by contraction; cf., however, athematic imperf. κεῖσο (*Od.* 24.40) and imperatives ἵστασο (3×) κάθησο (2×), ἧσο (6×).
- 3rd pl. -αται/-ατο are the forms which athematic and consonant stem verbs show instead of -νται/-ντο, with the ν effectively becoming an α in order to avoid a run of unpronounceable consonants, though epos (and Ionic) deploys them even with some verbs whose stem ends in a vowel. We see them in the imperfect (κείατο), perfect (ἐρηρέδαται 284, 329), and pluperfect indicative (εἵατ᾽ 128: see n.), and in all tenses of the optative (where the -ι- in e.g. φλεγεθοίατο 197 is treated almost as a consonant). Homer sometimes uses -ντ- and -ατ- interchangeably with the same verb: μαχοίατο but μαχέοιντο (1.544), κεῖντο (2×) but κείατο (2×).

ii. Reduplication

In Attic Greek we are accustomed to seeing this in the perfect tenses (λε-λυ-) and the present (and perfect) system of the athematic verbs: τι-θη-, δι-δω-, τε-θη-, δε-δω-, etc.), as well as in presents of the sort μίμνω, but epos enjoys a wide range of such reduplications – not differing from later Greek in type, so much as in extent.[118]

- in the aorist (κέ-κλοντο 371 < κέλομαι, ἀμπε-παλών < πάλλω, πε-πιθ- < πείθω) and future (κε-χολώσομαι < χολόω: 543–4n.; κε-κλήσηι < καλέω) by repeating the initial consonant + ε.
- particularly productive, especially in the present tense, by repeating the initial consonant + ι (aor. βι-βάς < βαίνω, cf. βάς; κι-κλήσκω < καλέω; cf. μί-μνω, γί-γνομαι, etc.).
- in 'expressive' presents (μαρ-μαίροντα 27: see n., παμ-φανόωντος 509) where the verb root is repeated.

iii. Augment

Rare in Mycenaean, the augment has been explained as a general marker of past time (whether originally as a separate particle or not), a marker of immediacy, and a reduplicating syllable.[119] However we explain it, the

---

[118] The debate on the semantic difference between ι-reduplicated and simplex forms is unresolved, though some general shift towards reduplication expressing 'perfective' meaning (i.e. looking to the result or end-state of the action) seems to be gaining ground (see, e.g., 465–8n.): see Giannakis 1997; Willi 2018.

[119] The first view is more or less general, the second Bakker 2001 (= 2005: 114–35), the third Willi 2018: 357–416.

reader needs to be aware of its variable appearance in the Homeric text; indeed, Aristarchos considered its absence characteristic of the poet and a sign of Archaic usage, and so favoured it wherever possible.[120]

- It can be either 'syllabic', adding another syllable (ε) to the start of a verb which begins with a consonant, or 'temporal', lengthening the vowel/diphthong which begins the verb (α > η, ε > η, ῐ > ῑ, ο > ω, ῠ > ῡ, αι > ηι, αυ > ηυ, ει > ηι, ευ > ηυ, οι > ωι).
- for the compositional freedom this gives, ἱκέσθην (215) with no augment allows the poet to place the dual form at the end of the verse where the first syllable must be light, and ἱκέσθην with augment (14.283) at the start of the second foot where that syllable must be heavy.[121]

iv. 'Tmesis' of Compound Verbs

The term tmesis (lit. 'cutting') describes the separation of a preposition from its verb, which is especially common in Homer: κὰδ δ' ἷζον (28), ἐπὶ δ' ὅρκον ὄμοσσεν (42), ἐπὶ ἔργα τράπωνται (53), πρὸς μῦθον ἔειπεν (68), etc. Though epos definitely knows compound verbs (ἀποσκίδνασθαι 4, μετηύδα 5, ὑπέστην 20, ἀφωπλίζοντο 26, ἐφοπλίσσαντες 55, κακκείοντες 58), from a diachronic perspective the 'preposition' was originally a floating preverb, which later gravitated towards verbs to form compounds (hence in this commentary we call them preverbs/prepositions, or adverbs). The phenomenon in Homer can thus be viewed either as a very old inheritance (already largely disappeared from Mycenaean) which is retained because of its extraordinary compositional usefulness or, for the same reason, a deliberate stylistic choice to separate the preposition from its natural home.[122]

v. Subjunctive

- 'short vowel' subjunctives: alongside the usual -ω-/-η- formations (λύωμεν, λύητε, etc.), epos uses a short thematic vowel (the original way for athematic verbs to form the subjunctive): δορπήσομεν (11), θείομεν

---

[120] See Intro. § 4.
[121] For these terms, and Homer's metre, see Intro. § 4.
[122] See Horrocks 1997: 201–2; Bortone 2010: 131–40; Haug 2012; McConnell 2025: 128–52.

(244, 486 = θέωμεν *Od.* 24.485; cf. θείω, θήηις, θήηι), δοάσσεται (339), παραθήσομεν (810: see n.).

• athematic -σθα ending (see above) very common in thematic subjunctives: παρεξελάσηισθα (344: = παρεξελάσηις), ἐθέλησθα = ἐθέλης, εἴπησθα = εἴπης, etc.

vi. Imperative

• athematic 2nd sing. imperative ending -θι is much more common than in Attic: στῆθι (97), ἄνωχθι (158), ὄμνυθι (585), κλῦθι (770).

vii. Infinitive

• athematic present and aorist in -ναι (AI.): εἶναι (343, 595, 669), δοῦναι (593).
• athematic (all tenses) in -μεν (Aeol.) and -μεναι (Lesb. Aeolic): θέμεναι (45), τιθήμεναι (247), παραδύμεναι (416), ἔμ(μ)μεναι (459, 479), δόμεναι (551); also extended to thematic verbs (Aeol.): ἀξέμεναι (50: see 49–51n.), δαπτέμεν (183), πεπληγέμεν (660).
• thematic present and future in -ειν (AI.): ἀποδειροτομήσειν (22), ῥέξειν (146), ἱερεύσειν (147), θείειν (310), ἐλαύνειν (434), ἄγειν (512, 613), φέρειν (513), etc.
• thematic future and aorist in -έειν: κερέειν (146: see n.), ἰδέειν (463; cf. ἰδεῖν 4×), σχεθέειν (466), ἐκπεσέειν (467), πεσέειν (595).

viii. εἰμί 'I am'

As a showcase of the Homeric verb's varied morphology, εἰμί has the following forms:

• pres. indic. εἰμί, εἶς/ἐσσί, ἐστί, εἰμέν, ἐστέ, εἰσί/ἔᾱσι.
• pres. infin. εἶναι, ἔμεν, ἔμμεν, ἔμεναι, ἔμμεναι.
• pres. opt. εἴην, εἴης/ἔοις, εἴη/ἔοι, 2nd pl. εἶτε, 3rd pl. εἶεν.
• pres. subj. ἔω, 3rd sing. ἦισι/ἔηισι/ἔηι, 3rd pl. ὦσι/ἔωσι.
• fut. indic. 1st sing. ἔσομαι/ἔσσομαι, 2nd sing. ἔσεαι/ἔσσεαι/ἔσηι, 3rd sing. ἔσται/ἔσεται/ἔσσεται/ἐσσεῖται, 1st pl. ἐσόμεθα/ἐσσόμεθα, 2nd pl. ἔσεσθε/ἔσσεσθε, 3rd pl. ἔσονται/ἔσσονται.
• imperf. indic. 1st sing. ἦα/ἔα/ἔον/ἔσκον, 2nd sing. ἦσθα/ἔησθα, 3rd sing. ἦν/ἦεν/ἔην/ἤην/ἔσκε, 1st pl. ἦμεν, 2nd pl. ἦτε, 3rd pl. ἦσαν/ἔσαν.

What this brief survey should reveal, above all, is the extraordinary creative and poetic potential of epos, giving its practitioners the options of

retaining, extending, and developing the linguistic and artistic resources
of the Greek language.[123]

3.2 METRE

Ancient Greek verse is 'quantitative', which means that its rhythms, patterns,
and structures depend upon the arrangement of syllables which take
different amounts of time to pronounce.[124] Any syllable may be 'heavy' or
'light', though common usage prefers 'long' and 'short' respectively.[125]

(i)   A syllable is heavy when it contains a long vowel (η, ω, and sometimes
      α, ι, υ) or diphthong (αι, αυ, ει, ευ, ηυ, οι, ου, υι);[126] or

(ii) when it contains a vowel of any length followed by two consonants,
      including the so-called digraphs ζ, ξ, ψ, which count as two letters.

(iii) A syllable is light when it contains a short vowel (ε, ο, and sometimes
      α, ι, υ) followed by a single consonant.

(iv) A heavy syllable with a long vowel or a diphthong may be rendered
      light if the long vowel or diphthong meets another vowel (usually,
      but not always, at the start of the next word). This is termed 'epic
      correption': see e.g. ἠδέ οἱ αὐτῶι (126), χρυσέου ἐκ (219), etc.

(v)   A heavy syllable with a short vowel followed by two consonants may be
      rendered light when the consonant cluster is made up of a 'plosive' (π,
      τ, κ; φ, θ, χ; β, δ, γ) and a 'liquid' or 'nasal' (λ, μ, ν, ρ). This is known as
      'Attic correption', since it is common in Athenian poetry but less so in
      Homer: see ὡς ἐτράφην (84), πτερόεντᾰ προσηύδα (557, 601, 625), etc.

(vi) A heavy syllable may be formed by two vowels or a vowel and a
      diphthong run together to form one syllable (termed 'synizesis',

---

[123] This is not an exhaustive list of the forms created in the Homeric language.
For 'metrical lengthening' of words, see § 3.2 'Metre' below, and for the common phenomenon of 'diectasis', where new forms are created by dragging out
contracted vowel sounds so as to fit the word into new parts of the line, see nn.
to 105–7 (on γοόωσα < γοῶσα < γοάουσα), 140–4 (on τηλεθόωσαν < τηλεθῶσαν
< τηλεθάουσαν), 146–8 (on κερέειν < κερά-εϊν), 226–8 (on φόως < φῶς < φάος), 319–21 (on
πλανόωνται < πλανῶνται < πλανάονται), 509 (on παμφανόωντος < παμφανῶντος
< παμφανάοντος), 629 (on ἡβώοιμι: < ἡβῶιμι < ἡβά-οιμι), 643–5 (on ἀντιοώντων
< ἀντιῶντων < ἀντια-όντων), 785–8 (μειδιόων < μειδιῶν < μειδιάων) and *GH* I §§ 31–4.

[124] The best basic treatment in English is West 1982, with slightly greater detail
for Homer in West 1997b; cf. also Raven 1962: 21–6, 43–5. For an excellent survey
of analyses of Homeric metre (especially colometry) in the twentieth century, see
Janse 2020: 3–13. Every volume on Homer in the Cambridge Greek and Latin
Classics series has its own section on metre.

[125] Since long and short are also commonly used to describe vowel length within
a syllable, the potential for confusion is great; a syllable, as we shall see, may have a
long or short vowel and not for that reason alone be either heavy or light.

[126] These sounds need not be inevitably run together, in which case the second
vowel is printed with a diaeresis (¨): see e.g. Πηλεΐδης at 17, scanned –∪∪– (17–18n.).

'synecphonesis', and sometimes 'crasis'[127]), usually in the same word. This is especially common with -εω < -αο (gen. sing. of a-stem nouns: Τυδεΐδεω 405, Ἀτρεΐδεω 434) and -εων (gen. pl. of a-stem nouns): see πελέκεας (114, 851, 856, 882), Βορέηι (195), Ἐωσφόρος (226), σφεας (235), χρυσέηι (243), χρεώ (308), χρεώμενος (834).

(vii) Some light syllables are treated as heavy simply for compositional convenience, in a phenomenon known as 'metrical or epic lengthening'.[128] This is usually confined to the first position within the 'foot' (see below for this term), but may be of several types, caused by several factors, and is often revealed orthographically:

(a) otherwise unmetrical polysyllables lengthen a vowel to fit into the line: ἠνεμόεσσαν (64), γεινόμενον (79), τιθήμεναι (83), εἰλήλουθας (94), ἀνέρας (111), κυάνεον (188), ἀθανάτοις (207; cf. 277, 788), δῖογενής (294), θείειν (310), πουλυβοτείρηι (368), Ἀπόλλωνι (872); cf. other words like οὐλόμενος, οὔνομα, οὔρεος (οὔρεϊ etc., oblique cases < ὄρος), and Οὔλυμπος;

(b) some words beginning with λ, μ, ν, ρ, and σ can treat their initial consonant as though it was doubled ('gemination'), thus rendering heavy a preceding light open syllable: e.g. δὲ μεγάλα (119) is scanned as though δὲ *μμεγάλα; ἀπὸ νύσσης as though ἀπὸ *ννύσσης (758). Papyri and some medieval MSS can write out the two consonants in these cases (118–21[a]n.). Sometimes this doubling has linguistic justification, i.e. the word did at some point in the history of Greek before Homer begin with a lost letter or two, and sometimes it does not;[129] similarly,

(c) some other examples of lengthening are explained by the loss of such letters in a following word or in the same word: ὑπείρ (226: see 226–8n.), γοῦνα for γόνϝα (444), ὑποδδείσαντες for ὑποδϝείσαντες (417);

(d) some light syllables are simply treated as heavy, whether that is reflected in the spelling (like εἰν for ἐν) or not, as where a light syllable opens the line in the so-called 'acephalous' or headless verses (e.g. | ἐπεὶ δή 3, | Βορέηι 193)[130] or is placed in the first position of the foot somewhere else in the line (e.g. εὐρυπυλὲς Ἄϊδος δῶ | 74).

---

[127] This is, actually, a separate thing, where the meeting vowels are joined graphically as well as prosodically: see e.g. ἐπήν (76) = ἐπεί + ἄν, οὔνεκα (385, 640) = οὗ ἕνεκα (GH I § 35).

[128] Wyatt 1969.

[129] GH I §§ 69–72. It is particularly common with the forms of *(σ)λαμβάνω (465–8n. on ἔλλαβε).

[130] See also 3.357, 5.539, 5.827, Od. 9.109, 10.141. See Wyatt 1969: 201–32, who emends or otherwise explains away these examples.

Finally, we have already encountered two things which may happen when vowels collide: epic correption (iv) and synizesis (vi). But two other things may happen:

(viii) Elision, when a word-final vowel is simply lopped off the end of its word, and this is represented in the text by an apostrophe: ἄρ᾽ ἐσκίδναντο (3), δ᾽ οὐκ (4), ὑπ᾽ ὄχεσφι (7), κ᾽ ὀλοοῖο (10), ἔφαθ᾽, οἳ (12), etc. The vowels so affected are commonly short α, ε, and ο (as in the above examples), sometimes ι (Ἕκτορ[ι] 64, θίν[ι] 693); some middle endings in -αι can be elided, as can -οι in the datives of the personal pronouns μοι and σοι (μ[οι] … ἐπιπλήξειν 579–80n.).[131]

(ix) Hiatus or 'yawning', where the two meeting vowels bear their face value without any effect. This is frequently, though not always,[132] due to the loss of a letter or a historic change in the form of the word of the sort we have already observed just above: e.g. ἠδέ οἱ αὐτῶι (126), where οἱ/οἷ < ϝοῖ (earlier *sw-) continues to show the effect of the lost *digamma* in not forcing the elision of ἠδέ (similarly ἄρα οἱ 765; δέ οἱ 139, 149, 303, 304, 387, 390, 392, 396, 397, 500, 562, 674, 677, 683; κε οἱ 540; ὅτι οἱ 545, 556, 577; ῥά οἱ 384; τέ οἱ 337), while it fails to bring about correption in δή οἱ (537), δώσω οἱ (560), εἴ οἱ 832; καί οἱ (564), μή οἱ (297), and 'makes position' (i.e. renders a light syllable heavy by closing it) for γάρ sometimes (298, 530, 834), sometimes not (865). For more examples, especially frequent with the *digamma*, see ἐσκίδναντο ἑήν (3), γε ἄνακτα (35), γε ἄνακτι (173), ὑπερθύμοιο ἄνακτος (302), γε ἑκάστου (374), οὗ ἑτάροιο (748), etc., and look out for common words like ἄναξ, ἄστυ, ἑ (3rd person pronoun), ἔλπομαι, ἔπος and εἰπεῖν, ἔργον, ἰδεῖν, οἶκος, and οἶνος.[133] This does not mean that the poet pronounced the ϝ (or any other lost letter[s]) in these cases, for there are plenty of occasions before these words where *digamma* is not observed (see e.g. ἄκουσέν ἄναξ 161, μέν ἄναξ 288, ἠπείλησέν ἄνακτι 863, ἀπίθησέν ἄναξ 895, etc., where the observance of *digamma* would render the previous syllable heavy, but has not). Instead, he had just learned that hiatus is permitted before these words because he had inherited many expressions where it was.

* * *

---

[131] *GH* I § 36.
[132] For a particularly noticeable example, see μέγα ἠρίον (126); the noun has no certain etymology, and the hiatus leads *EDG* s.v. to reconstruct a forebear *ϝηρίον.
[133] See the full list at *GH* I §§ 54–8.

Armed with this rather supple attitude towards prosody, Homer's metre is arranged around the dactylic rhythm (so called because it apparently reflects the finger, δάκτυλος, in having one long and two short sections), comprising one heavy syllable followed by two light syllables (denoted – ◡ ◡). The two light syllables can be replaced by one heavy syllable (in 'contraction' or 'resolution'), rendering what is termed a 'spondee' (– – ; for the derivation of this term, see 218–21n.). The standard verse contains six of these units (or, more accurately, five units and one shortened or 'catalectic' unit), whence it gets its name 'hexameter' or 'six measure':

$$- \underset{\smile\smile}{} \mid - \underset{\smile\smile}{} \mid - \underset{\smile\smile}{} \mid - \underset{\smile\smile}{} \mid - \underset{\smile\smile}{} \mid - \times$$

Contraction/resolution is permitted in any of the first five units, but more commonly occurs in the first half of the verse (1st and 2nd foot, c. 40 per cent; 3rd, c. 15 per cent; 4th, c. 30 per cent; 5th, c. 5 per cent).[134] The last syllable of the line is frequently marked × as being of indeterminate weight (or 'anceps' in the handbooks), but the pause in delivery after the end of each verse renders the final position always effectively heavy.[135] Each of the dactyls comprises a portion or 'foot' in the verse, a metaphor we also find in describing the two portions of the foot, as the first is termed 'arsis' ('lifting' i.e. the foot) and the second 'thesis' ('placing' the foot). In some handbooks, these two portions are called 'princeps' and 'biceps'.

Each verse is also punctuated by pauses or breaks, both within the feet or the units of which they are comprised ('caesurae') and at the end of those units ('diaereses'). The most common of these pauses, identified by the ancients themselves, occurs in the middle of the verse, in the 3rd foot after the first heavy syllable ('penthemimeral' caesura, also known as 'masculine')[136] or the first light syllable (caesura 'at the third trochee',[137] also known as the 'feminine'), or – much more rarely – after the first heavy syllable in the 4th foot ('hepthemimeral' caesura). Almost every verse in Homer has one of these pauses, with those in the 3rd foot being the most common (and showing a slight preference for the 'third trochee' caesura

---

[134] There are only six verses in Homer with complete resolution/contraction (2.544, 11.130, 23.221, *Od.* 15.334, 21.15, 22.175), though editors try to emend them in some other way (see 218–21n.).

[135] Daitz 1991.

[136] The penthemimeral caesura, or the penthemimerus, occurs after 'five half-portions' (i.e. two-and-a-half feet); the hepthemimeral after 'seven half-portions' (three-and-a-half feet).

[137] The 'trochee' is the name given to the rhythm unit – ◡.

over the penthemimeral).[138] There is also a very common pause at the
end of the 4th foot, sometimes called the 'bucolic' diaeresis because it is
typical of later bucolic poetry. If we try to represent these pauses on the
above scheme (with forward slashes), we get:

$$- \smile\smile \mid - \smile\smile \mid - / \smile / \smile \mid - / \smile\smile \mid / - \smile\smile \mid - \times$$

Sometimes these breaks fall between elided words, but they are never
placed before δέ, μέν, γάρ, κεν, ἄν or after καί, ἀλλά, or after monosyllabic
prepositions (εἰς, ἐκ, ἐν, πρός, πρό, σύν).[139] The other side of the coin,
where breaks are avoided, are called 'bridges': the most important of
these for Homeric poetry is Hermann's Bridge, an observation that word
break rarely falls between the two light syllables of the fourth foot (about
once every 550 verses): in Book 23, see ἐπήν με πυρὸς λελάχητε | (76), νέον
περ ἐόντ' ἐφίλησαν | (306), ἔγωγε νεώτερός εἰμι | (587), τίς τε γυναικὸς
ἐϋζώνοιο | (760).[140]

But what do these breaks tell us about the relationship between sentence and verse structure, or between the rhythmic and semantic content
of the verse? The modern starting point for addressing these questions
was Hermann Fränkel's breakthrough division of the Callimachean and
Homeric hexameter into 'cola' (from κῶλον 'limb'). He proceeded from
the understanding that sense pauses and caesurae were the same thing,
and that they tended to cluster around three points in the line (which he
named A, B, and C) resulting in four cola as follows (! marks a delayed
caesura of that sort):[141]

$$- {}^{A1} \smile {}^{A2} \smile {}^{A3} \mid - {}^{A4} \smile {}^{A!} \smile \mid - {}^{B1} \smile {}^{B2} \smile \mid - {}^{C1} \smile \smile {}^{C2} \mid - {}^{C!} \smile {}^{C!} \smile \mid - \times$$

The great benefit of this system, and its many subsequent modifications
by other scholars, is that it tries to come to grips with what the poets of
early Greek epos thought they were doing, and this kind of approach
undoubtedly captures better the essence of Homeric composition – the
(re)use and (re)combination of rhythmically shaped phrases (what are
now called by some scholars 'intonation units' or 'discourse units').
Fränkel's theory was not without difficulty, including a certain arbitrari-
ness in working out which of the pauses to use, and it has been adopted

[138] West 1982: 36 and 1997b: 222–3.
[139] They may be found rarely between disyllabic prepositions and their nouns,
occasionally before other enclitics like ποτέ or between demonstratives and their
nouns.
[140] Schein 2016: 93–116 claims to find semantic effects here (75–6n.).
[141] Fränkel 1926 (revised and expanded in Fränkel 1960).

or rejected in equal measure. In fact, there is no real consensus at the moment on how we should reconcile colometry and versification, nor even on whether sense pauses should, or always do, correspond to rhythmic pauses (see below, § 3.3 'Style' for exemplification). This commentary, therefore, does not adopt an exclusivising attitude to the question, and counsels the reader to remain open to the metrical and syntactic variety possible in Homeric composition and versification.[142] In keeping with the lack of agreement about colometry, there are a huge number of notation systems for the hexameter currently available, but for ease of reference this commentary adopts that of Janse (2003):

$$^1 - \underset{1a}{\smile} \underset{1b}{\smile} \underset{1c}{\smile} \Big|^2 - \underset{2a}{\smile} \underset{2b}{\smile} \underset{2c}{\smile} \Big|^3 - \underset{3a}{\smile} \underset{3b}{\smile} \underset{3c}{\smile} \Big|^4 - \underset{4a}{\smile} \underset{4b}{\smile} \underset{4c}{\smile} \Big|^5 - \underset{5a}{\smile} \underset{5b}{\smile} \underset{5c}{\smile} \Big|^6 - \underset{6a}{\smile} \underset{6c}{\times}$$

The scheme combines the traditional 'feet' numbers with the variety of caesura positions, 'a' falling after the first element in the foot, 'b' after the trochee, and 'c' at the end of the foot. Of the major pauses identified in standard handbooks and mentioned earlier, the penthemimerus is 3a, the 'trochaic' caesura is 3b, the hephthemimerus is 4a, the bucolic diaeresis is 4c.

Finally, what of the semantic effect, the meaning of metre? It is a rule of thumb in Homer that metre by itself is not meaningful, in the sense that a heavily dactylic or spondaic rhythm in a line is intended, without reference to the meaning of the words themselves, to have some kind of effect on the listener. Scholars have found some examples where combined effects seems plausible,[143] and, in one of the few all-spondaic lines in Homer in our book (ψυχὴν κικλήσκων Πατροκλῆος δειλοῖο 23.221: see 218–21n.), the heavy rhythm rather fits the sad action denoted by the words.[144] But 'it is more prudent to think of the sound and metre as being well adapted or well suited to the sense; they cannot normally convey the meaning of the line independently of the listener's understanding'.[145] One general effect, however, is the pleasing, almost ritualistic repetition of the verse pattern,

[142] The most recent and exciting studies of Homer's colometry by Mark Janse and Rutger Allan, building on several earlier studies by Egbert Bakker, offer us a path towards a much better understanding of the structural, rhythmic, and semantic units at the poet's disposal. See e.g. Janse 2020 (esp. 3–13 for a review of the modern history of this question); Allan 2023a, 2023b.

[143] See, e.g., *Od.* 11.593–8, where the mixed rhythms of Sisyphos pushing the boulder up the hill (593–7) are contrasted with the purely dactylic rhythm of the boulder falling down once more (598).

[144] See also 503–4n. for another example.

[145] Rutherford 2019: 55.

one line after the other, with regular pauses and an engagingly variable rhythm that constantly helps to propel the poetry forward.

3.3 STYLE

Style is an evanescent concept, and its separation from the study of Homer's language, syntax, and metre is always going to be somewhat artificial, since they work together to produce the world of early Greek epos, and can hardly be imagined as isolated entities.[146] Homer's style cannot exist without the unique sounds and morphology of his language, nor the way in which those units combine to form larger units on every level of composition, from the colon to the verse to the entire scene, from the famous noun–epithet expressions all the way to the widespread narrative patterns that structure the whole epic. Yet there are things which the student of epos can appreciate as they approach reading Homer, even if they are not trying to approximate the circumstance, knowledge, and familiarity of an original audience listening to an orally recomposing bard. Perhaps the best way to illuminate Homer's style, rather than simply listing concepts to look out for, is to take the first sixteen verses of Book 23 and see how they are constructed and how they convey meaning, in terms of language, metre, verse structure, colon structure, formularity, rhetorical techniques, and their traditional references.[147]

ὣς οἳ μὲν στενάχοντο³ᵇ| **κατὰ πτόλιν**· αὐτὰρ Ἀχαιοί,|

ἐπεὶ δὴ **νῆάς τε**³ᵇ| **καὶ Ἑλλήσποντον** ἵκοντο, |

οἳ μὲν ἄρ' ἐσκίδναντο³ᵇ| ἑὴν ἐπὶ νῆα ἕκαστος, |

Μυρμιδόνας δ' οὐκ εἴα³ᵇ| ἀποσκίδνασθαι Ἀχιλλεύς, |

ἀλλ' ὅ γε οἷς **ἑτάροισι**³ᵇ| **φιλοπτολέμοισι** μετηύδα· | 5

'Μυρμιδόνες ταχύπωλοι,³ᵇ| **ἐμοὶ ἐρίηρες ἑταῖροι**, |

μὴ δή πω ὑπ' ὄχεσφι³ᵇ| λυώμεθα **μώνυχας ἵππους**, |

ἀλλ' αὐτοῖς **ἵπποισι**³ᵇ| **καὶ ἅρμασιν** ἆσσον ἰόντες |

Πάτροκλον κλαίωμεν·³ᵇ| **ὃ γὰρ γέρας ἐστὶ θανόντων**. |

---

[146] Again, the corresponding sections of several volumes in this series can be consulted with enormous profit, including Macleod 1982: 35–53; Graziosi and Haubold 2010: 13–24; De Jong 2012: 18–28; Bowie 2019: 52–67; Rutherford 2019: 34–50; Bakker 2025: 53–9.

[147] Formulae are boldened, medial caesurae are denoted by superscript numbers before a vertical stroke |, and end-stopped verses (see below) by a vertical stroke |.

αὐτὰρ ἐπεί κ' ὀλοοῖο³ᵇ| τεταρπώμεσθα γόοιο, | 10

ἵππους λυσάμενοι³ᵃ| δορπήσομεν ἐνθάδε πάντες.' |

ὡς ἔφαθ', οἱ δ' ᾤμωξαν³ᵇ| ἀολλέες, ἦρχε δ' Ἀχιλλεύς. |

οἳ δὲ τρὶς περὶ νεκρὸν³ᵇ| ἐΰτριχας ἤλασαν ἵππους |

μυρόμενοι· μετὰ δέ σφι³ᵇ| Θέτις γόου ἵμερον ὦρσεν. |

δεύοντο ψάμαθοι,³ᵃ| δεύοντο δὲ τεύχεα φωτῶν | 15

δάκρυσι· τοῖον γὰρ³ᵃ| πόθεον μήστωρα φόβοιο. |

Casting our minds back to matters of dialect and morphology, we see several examples of the kinds of layering encountered above in Homer's language: thematic gen. sing. in both οιο (ὀλοοῖο ... γόοιο, φόβοιο) and -ου (γόου), augment observed (ἐσκίδναντο, εἷα, μετηύδα, ἔφαθ', ᾤμωξαν, ἦρχε, ἤλασαν, ὦρσεν) and unobserved (στενάχοντο, ἵκοντο, δεύοντο, πόθεον), 1st pl. ending in -μεθα (λυώμεθα) and -μεσθα (τεταρπώμεσθα), dative plurals of consonant stem nouns in -σι (ἄρμασι) and -φι (ὄχεσφι), long and short dative plurals for thematic nouns (οἷς ἑτάροισι, αὐτοῖς ἵπποισι), long- and short-vowel subjunctives for thematic verbs (κλαίωμεν, τεταρπώμεσθα, δορπήσομεν), uncontracted vowels (ἀολλέες, τεύχεα, πόθεον) where Attic would contract (ἀολλεῖς, τεύχη, ἐπόθουν), diachronically distinct stems (ἑτάροισι, ἑταῖροι), and Aeolic features (κε) sprinkled among the prevalent Ionic (aspiration, words like νηᾶς, Ἑλλήσποντον, νῆα, etc.), together with older, consciously Archaic forms (-φι). The variety in this language helps to create its own, almost timeless, poetic world.

Among the notable metrical or prosodic features is the 'acephalous' verse 2, with heavy ἐπεὶ δή at the start of the verse; epic correption in καὶ Ἑλλήσποντον (2), ἀποσκίδνασθαῖ Ἀχιλλεύς (4), ταχύπωλοῖ, ἐμοὶ (6), καῖ ἄρμασιν (8), γόοῦ ἵμερον (14); the effect of a lost consonant to obviate hiatus in νῆα ἕκαστος (3 < *σϝ-), ἀλλ' ὅ γε οἷς (5 < *σϝ-), and such an effect without apparent etymological justification in ἐμοὶ ἐρίηρες (6);[148] on the other hand, hiatus without correption in | μὴ δή πω ὑπ' ὄχεσφι (7). Again, the poet uses the full range of his resources, and the several licences afforded him, to help create his verse. The special rules which allow the same sound to be both heavy and light in different places within the same few lines, or which permit and deny hiatus to the same sounds, bespeak a world which operates on its own terms.

---

[148] Similar hiatus before this word at 8.332 = 13.421 (τὸν μὲν ἔπειθ' ὑποδύντε δύω ἐρίηρες ἑταῖροι), but elision at 16.363 (ἀλλὰ καὶ ὡς ἀνέμιμνε, σάω δ' ἐρίηρας ἑταίρους) and epenthetic ν at 4.266 (Ἀτρεΐδη μάλα μέν τοι ἐγὼν ἐρίηρος ἑταῖρος); cf. esp. *Od.* 19.271 (ἀτὰρ ἐρίηρας ἑταίρους).

But metre is not simply a matter of prosody. Note, firstly, how often the end of the verse coincides with a semantic pause of various degrees (sometimes given the term **end-stopping**, and marked with | after the end of the verse); this is a general characteristic of Homeric versification.[149] In fact, only verses 1 and 8 end with what has been termed **harsh/necessary/violent run-over** (also called 'enjambement'), i.e. situations where there is no semantic pause in the flow of the sentence at the verse-end because the main verb of the clause is yet to appear: though other verses close with sentences still incomplete (verse 2 has not yet hit the main clause initiated at 4c in verse 1 with αὐτάρ, but it is at least its own complete syntactical unit within the boundaries of the line; verse 6 similarly is a self-contained vocative expression extending, honorifically, over the whole line), only these two verses lack any such sense of closure. This is noticeable, since the mismatch between expecting a pause and not receiving it directs our attention towards the actions so denoted.[150] In the second case, falling within a speech, it corresponds to the most important issue from Achilleus' perspective – the need to mourn his dead comrade (Πάτροκλον κλαίωμεν). The first case falls in the poet's narrative, and helps to foreground the further fissure in that group as expressed in verse 3, where οἳ μέν looks forward to the narrowing of focus to one *laos* and its leader (Μυρμιδόνας δέ ... Ἀχιλλεύς 4) within the Greeks as a whole, and the alternation between his people and him dominates verses 4 and 5 so as to introduce his speech. The delay allows the poet to get the army back to the camp and split from the conglomerate group into its other constituent units on the one hand (ἕκαστος 3) and the Myrmidons on the other (4); this location is where he will stay for the duration of the funeral and is obviously a significant change of scene.

There is another kind of run-over here, termed variously elsewhere **soft/unnecessary/progressive**, where the thought from a previous verse is continued with a word grammatically unnecessary to that previous verse, in the sense that the clause or thought is already complete, however much we might desire continuation or supplementation: μυρόμενοι (14) is an example, where the qualifying participle agrees with the subject of the previous verse οἳ δέ (13); so too is δάκρυσι (16), for the previous verse does

---

[149] Over 75 per cent of all Homeric verses, according to Higbie 1990: 66. See also Kirk I: 30–7. There are different ways of categorising run-over/enjambement, but the two basic categories adopted here are sufficiently widespread to capture the phenomenon.

[150] Bakker 1990, adopted, e.g., by Graziosi and Haubold 2010: 12–13, criticised by Friedrich 2000. It is not the only way the poet directs our attention to significant moments, but it is one of those strategies.

not strictly require that detail in order for it to be understood (though it is natural to expect some such fulfilment or further qualification). In both cases the continuation is significant because the run-over element retains the audience's attention *on that element* as the basis for continuation: note that μυρόμενοι is then followed by clauses in which the sorrowing Myrmidons are the agents of several acts of grief, whilst δάκρυσι resumes the emphasis on that collective sorrow which is then qualified by explanatory γάρ.

But run-over is not the only way of joining verses together. Most of the rest of the lines are new beginnings, as it were, with connective particles like μέν (1, 3), δέ (4, 12), ἀλλά (5, 8), αὐτάρ (10), etc. showing the start of a new thought or action. Coupled with the high frequency of end-stopping, this reveals the basically 'paratactic' or 'adding' style of epos, in which chains of clauses are joined on a co-ordinate level. This is not to say we do not find 'hypotaxis' in Homer, or clauses on different syntactical levels (i.e. main clause followed by a causal/conditional/temporal etc. clause), simply that the relentlessly onwards march of the narrative brings us back to co-ordination as frequently and as quickly as possible.[151]

Turning our attention to the 'inner metric', every verse has a median caesura at 3a or 3b. However, formular construction (marked in bold above) might suggest that some colon boundaries should be differently placed, if they are also to serve as sense boundaries or intonation units. Some formular units do fit well with those boundaries, such as e.g. 3bκατὰ πτόλιν4c (1), 3bἐμοὶ ἐρίηρες ἑταῖροι (6), 3bὃ γὰρ γέρας ἐστὶ θανόντων (9), 3bἐΰτριχας [verb] ἵππους (13), 4aμήστωρα φόβοιο (16).[152] Others straddle that median boundary, such as 2aνῆάς τε3b| καὶ Ἑλλήσποντον ἵκοντο (2), [noun] + 3bφιλοπτολέμοισι5b (5), 2aἵπποισι καὶ ἅρμασιν4c (8), 2aὀλοοῖο3b| τεταρπώμεσθα γόοιο (10), [verb]3b + ἀολλέες, ἦρχε δέ [noun] (12), while the very common ὣς ἔφαθ' (12) is clearly intended to close a speech and introduce a reaction as quickly as possible at 1c. Note how common it is for these expressions to have variable units within them across those boundaries, such as the dative noun qualified by φιλοπτολέμοισι, or the verb before ἀολλέες; the break was clearly important for compositional reasons, but may not have marked a pause in sense, much less delivery, within the verse. So, although a formal caesura in the middle of the line can be observed, it was just as important to a poet composing colon by colon to

---

[151] See esp. Bakker 1997: 35–85.
[152] There might be a case for considering οἳ μὲν ἄρ' ἐσκίδναντο ἑὴν ἐπὶ νῆα ἕκαστος (3) a whole-verse formula, but it only occurs here and 19.277; so also τεύχεα φωτῶν (15, 16.566).

be able to fit units of several shapes into several different positions within the verse as well.

Mention of formulae leads into the most easily recognisable element of Homeric verse – its formular nature, and its reliance on repetition of every sort, on every level of composition. Before tackling the thorny question of meaning, the cumulative effect of the famous noun–epithet expressions in the passage should be noted: Achilleus does not just address his comrades, but his comrades 'at home in war', he calls them not 'Myrmidons' but 'Myrmidons swift-foaled', they are 'my deeply honoured companions', lamentation is 'destructive', the horses are 'single-hoofed' and 'fair-tressed',[153] their lost companion is not just 'Patroclos', but (poignantly) a 'deviser of rout'. In this way of describing a world, the listener is constantly lured away from the onward flow of the narrative by punctual indications of context, different ways of looking at people and objects within the epic world. This colouring, suppletive quality has to be appreciated, for 'mean or humdrum objects and persons and animals do not trail | such clouds of verbal glory behind them'.[154]

The wider semantics of formulae, idioms, and repeated expressions of any sort in Homer is a contentious area, but the approach taken in this commentary is that each of them has a resonance arising from their use elsewhere in Greek epic, their 'traditional referentiality',[155] and that this meaning is observable in our text and relatable to other features in the narrative pointing the same way: for instance, the formula ὃ γὰρ γέρας ἐστὶ θανόντων (9) is used, as its denotation might suggest, to qualify actions concerned with funeral processes, here in Book 23 the ritual procession around Patroclos' corpse but elsewhere the process represented by the construction of a mound and a *stele* (16.457 = 675), the washing, laying out, and mourning of each suitor's corpse which his family could not perform (*Od.* 24.190), and the similarly contrafactual configuration of Penelope's inability to mourn her husband uttered by the aged Laertes

----

[153] And only in this book: see 13–14n.

[154] Macleod 1982: 38–9. Related are the similes for which Homer is justly famous, and of which there are many examples in Book 23: see nn. to 99–101ᵃ (100), 222–5, 364ᵇ–7 (366), 431–3, 517–23, 597ᵇ–600, 692–4, 712–13, 760–3, 782–3 (783), 844–7. However they reflect on the surrounding narrative, they are pictures which demand the auditor/reader to stop, if only briefly, and consider the action, object, or character so qualified from a different angle.

[155] See Foley 1991, 1999, etc.; Kelly 2007a. It is much the same kind of thing as the concept of 'resonance' set out in Graziosi and Haubold 2005, and the 'immanence' somewhat briefly sketched in Turkeltaub 2020. It has become a widespread method in Homeric scholarship; for a recent extension of the theory to the language of Sappho, see Nelson 2024; for critique, see Danek 2002; Currie 2016: 4–9; and (much more hostile) Rutherford 2019: 40.

before his son relents and reveals himself (*Od.* 24.296). In each case the γέρας is envisaged as being performed by the blood relatives of the deceased, but here in Book 23 by Achilleus and the rest of the Myrmidons: the usual usage, its traditional reference, bestows a quasi-familial dynamic on the relationship between the two men, and is the first of many signs in this portion of the *Iliad* that their bond is a singular one.

Of course, whether one accepts this way of reading the poem or not, even the identification of formulae is a contentious area, since the terms 'formular' and 'formulaic' still have somewhat negative connotations in the context of poetic creation. Perhaps we should do better if we think of the *Kunstsprache* as a living language characterised on every level by repetition: repeated elements of a variety of types, whatever term we use for them, may be subject to greater or lesser levels of fixity within the verse on a continuum of regularity, rather than being defined exclusively, and reductively, as either a 'formula' or 'not a formula'.[156] Moreover, these elements do not need to be interpreted solely by reference to a tradition, excluding all possibility of direct individual reference or recall between examples.[157] There is no doubt, for instance, that the hospitality scenes which structure the *Odyssey* are to be understood both as individual scenes manipulating a traditional sequence, and as mirroring or interacting with one another and developing patterns and movements across the whole poem.[158] In this way of viewing the traditional resources of Homeric language, it is a question of seeing how they combine within the text. Even then, as John Foley always sought to stress, this is not some totally new way of reading the poetry; it is, instead, an attempt to restore its idiomatic nature, the conventional understanding which the original audience(s) brought to the experience of this kind of narrative.

Nonetheless, if epos is characterised by repetition, it is also important to recognise that epos is *not only* characterised by repetition: a commentary concerned only with tracing the presence and impact of formularity cannot reveal everything of the poet's art. The usual range of rhetorical and 'literary' strategies are available to any artist trained in this tradition: even in our passage above, the asyndeton opening verse 15, for instance, when

---

[156] See recently, e.g., Rodda 2021; Bozzone 2024.

[157] Rutherford 2019: 40 points out that Kelly 2007a: 68 and 73 does not comment on the repetition of 8.452 at 18.310 but instead places them within a generic framework of the assembly scene. His point is well taken, and the repetition itself would fit very well with the structural map of the poem in § 1 of this Introduction as another direct parallel between the actions of the second and third battle days. In this commentary, these sorts of parallels in Book 23 are noted and their possible allusive value recognised.

[158] See especially the brilliant study of Reece 1993.

coupled with the anaphora of its verb δεύοντο at the median caesura (a different kind of repetition), emphasises the extent of the crying in terms of its most physical effect on its surroundings. This point is underlined by the multiplicity expressed in having neuter plural τεύχεα with a plural verb, and leads naturally into the soft run-over word δάκρυσι (16). Not a traditional formula, idiom, or resonance anywhere in sight, but plenty of interlacing and mutually reinforcing poetic effects and deliberation. Or note the way the same 'group > individual' progression is applied in verses 3–4 around a μέν/δέ contrast, so as to achieve the splintering of the army and turn the focus on the Myrmidons, with the repetition of the verb ἐσκίδναντο/ἀποσκίδνασθαι on either side of the 3b caesura. Where every man in the rest of the army 'scatters' to his own ship, seemingly without order, structure, or commanders, Achilleus stops his own λαός 'scattering', so as to begin the funeral process. Again, no traditional units, but careful narrative progress through mirroring and contrast.

But the diachronically and synchronically sourced elements can, indeed they must, reinforce one another: for example, the hard run-over of Πάτροκλον κλαίωμεν (9) and its attendant emotional stress is perfectly explained, or complemented, by the quasi-familial reference/resonance of ὃ γὰρ γέρας ἐστὶ θανόντων. Sometimes a deliberately jarring effect is achieved: the formula μήστωρα φόβοιο (16) is usually applied to a victorious or aggressive opponent; that it should be used here of the Myrmidons' sense of loss, and juxtaposed with a verb like πόθεον, bestows a sense of hostility to that desire as a measure of their grief and pain, and encourages the audience to reflect on that fact once more, and from another angle.

4 TEXT AND TRANSMISSION

When we consider how well attested, how varied, and how lacking in desperate corruption of sense is the Homeric text, it may sound strange to say that the textual criticism of the *Iliad* and *Odyssey* is a difficult task. These are, after all, not obscure texts. They lie at the very centre of the ancient Greek literary tradition, and scholars working on other authors would love to have the Homerist's range of evidence – hundreds of partial and whole MSS, including a singular wealth of papyri, long and short quotations in other ancient authors, centuries of scholarly commentary preserved in voluminous scholia. This abundance brings with it, however, some particularly thorny questions, or perhaps it throws the old questions into even starker relief. The original where, when, and how of the poem's composition and recording is unknown, as is the relationship between composition and recording; the primary means of transmission is also contested; moreover, the role, practices, and effects of the Alexandrian scholars in the third and second centuries BCE are all matters of controversy.

Nonetheless, the following outline would probably not cause too much disagreement:[159] our medieval MSS reflect a largely stabilised text which, at least in terms of its famous *numerus versuum* ('number of verses') and intralinear readings, was established during the Alexandrian period, or perhaps more accurately was one of the effects of that period. Whether Zenodotos of Ephesos, Aristophanes of Byzantion, and Aristarchos of Samothrace produced their own texts in Alexandria or chose texts that they particularly favoured as the basis for their work, it seems clear that their combined efforts helped to bring the now standard, 'vulgate' text to the fore.[160] There were other versions known to them, and hence to us mainly from the Homeric scholia – the so-called 'city texts', the 'κατ' ἄνδρα' texts apparently associated with individual scholars – but the level of variation we find in them, and in the early quotations of Homer and the earliest Ptolemaic papyri, begins to tail off in later papyri as the vulgate seems to emerge in the middle of the second century BCE.

So the Alexandrian period is a bottleneck; beforehand, the text is quite a bit 'flabbier':[161] we find differences in phrasing and numbers of verses (usually additions rather than subtractions), but no changes in substance or storyline, even within individual sections and scenes. The Homeric text is able, then, to 'move' in fairly circumscribed ways; control like this might be attributed to professionalised guilds of performers like the 'Children of Homer',[162] or a proliferation of authoritative written texts from which performers – and indeed scribes – felt themselves able to diverge depending on their performance setting (expanding abbreviated typical scenes, for instance); a moment of such proliferation or standardisation seems to be reflected in the (also controversial) later story of the 'Peisistratean recension', according to which the sixth-century tyrant of Athens gathered the work of Homer and issued in some way an authoritative version and/or a performance rule for it.[163]

Trying to bridge the gap between the later Classical period and the origins of the poems in the eighth to sixth centuries BCE is beyond the

---

[159] For narratives of the transmission, with references to its voluminous earlier scholarship, see esp. S. West 1988: 33–48; Janko 20–38; Haslam 1997; Nardelli 2001a; West 2001a: 1–157; Cassio 2002; Reece 2005; Graziosi 2007; Pontani 2024.

[160] For their work, see Nickau 1977 (Zenodotos); Janko 22–8; West 2001a: 33–45 (Zenodotos), 61–4 (Aristarchos); Montanari 2002; Rengakos 2002; Schironi 2018 (Aristarchos); Montana 2020; Le Feuvre 2022 (Zenodotos).

[161] Haslam 1997: 68.

[162] See Graziosi 2002: 21–40, 201–17, esp. 208ff; West 2011: 15–17.

[163] See S. West 1988: 36–40; Janko 29–32; Jensen 2011; also n. 168 below.

scope of this section, and involves us in the great unanswerables of
the Homeric Question(s), but the first acknowledged, direct quotation
of Homer occurs in the early fifth century with Simonides (frr. 19–20 W²,
quoting *Il.* 6.146), though scholars have argued for allusions especially to
the *Iliad* well before then.[164] It was once accepted that Homer emerged
triumphantly into the wider Greek consciousness as soon as he composed his poems in the eighth or seventh century BCE, but evidence for
that awareness only becomes available in the sixth century BCE, shortly
before Simonides.[165] It is probably fair to say that a majority of scholars
would until recently have agreed that the text was written down early,
we know not when and where and how, and then transmitted largely by
written means, with some scope for performance variations, down to the
Alexandrian period.[166] The big question here is how to conceptualise the
differences we find especially in the earlier part of the paradosis mentioned above – are they changes to a fixed text or evidence of many different, concurrent texts?[167]

In any attempt at an answer, much depends on the predicates of the
method used to deal with the evidence. The traditional concept is one
of an original text, to which additions, alterations, and interpolations of
various sorts are made by scribes or performers over the long and somewhat uncontrolled process of transmission; textual critical methods are
employed to remove these later, secondary phenomena, and reveal the
original text. But, according to a school of scholarship associated with
Gregory Nagy and his students, this is entirely wrong: we should not think
of an original or fixed text of Homer, because that was only achieved
shortly before the Alexandrian period.[168] Prior to that date, in decreasing

---

[164] See Kelly 2015 for Homer's early reception in lyric poetry; also Nelson 2023.

[165] West 1999: 377 (= 2011–13 I.429): 'from the last third of the 6th century,
Homer springs into life. Author after author names him and comments on his
achievements. The epics are no longer treated as free-standing records of the past,
but as the artistic creations of an individual, to be praised or criticized.' This does
not translate into a date for the poems' composition, of course; it is simply an
awareness of their existence.

[166] Perhaps the two most influential models are: (i) the orally dictating poet
first championed by Lord 1953, restated by Janko 1998, and now advanced from
a comparative perspective in Ready 2019: 101–81 (though he opts for a sixth-century date); and (ii) the poet who writes (West 2001a, etc.).

[167] See now the superb discussion of Pontani 2024.

[168] The idea that textual fixation is not coterminous with the act of creation,
or not even necessarily to be linked with a master poet, is of course not new; the
Peisistratean recension is the earliest attested of such theories and, in the form
of the 'Panathenaic bottleneck', helps to contribute an important stage in Nagy's
model. For some of his many statements of the theory, see Nagy 1980, 1995,
1996a, 1996b, etc., now conveniently summarised in Nagy 2020, with further

levels or stages of (re)creative freedom, transmission was largely a matter
of recomposition by bards/rhapsodes/performers – hence the amount
of variation found in a range of early sources we just mentioned. While
the adherents of this school would probably agree that the transmission
from the Alexandrian period onwards is relatively stable and conducted
through written means, before that date much is now very controversial.

This perspective has found a great deal of purchase, but it has also
been pointed out that the level of variation in the paradosis is not great
enough,[169] nor consistently responsive enough to what we can reconstruct
of bardic practice, to match the image required by this evolutionary/
multiform/crystallisation model (all three terms have been used, but
this edition will just use multiform).[170] All of the textual *cruces* encountered in Book 23 are more readily explicable as just that, 'variants' of an
established version, rather than 'alternants' proving a multiform, i.e. the
sorts of changes which a traditionally trained and attuned bard would
produce.[171] Of course, it always possible that one's methods and assumptions could misidentify the latter as the former; equally, scribes *and* readers can learn the traditional language to the point that they alter a text in
ways that look authentic;[172] performers can make changes to an otherwise
fixed text in the course of a performance which can make their way into

references. The model is centrally enshrined in the Homer Multitext project at
Harvard University (www.homermultitext.org; critiqued in both digital and scholarly terms by Magnani 2018; cf. Dué 2023 for the most recent delineation of its
aims and methods), has been applied to *Iliad* Book 10 (Dué and Ebbot 2010), and
serves as the ideological underpinning for the *Cambridge Guide to Homer* (Pache
2020: see the pertinent critique of Scully 2020), showing how far it has triumphed
even since the excellent (and critical) review of Reece 2005.

[169] A point made well by Finkelberg 2000, and still unanswered. See Jensen
2011: 214–24 for more detail on the level and type of variation expected, and
attested, in other epic traditions.

[170] For the same conclusion by the recent editors of *Iliad* Book 6 for this series,
see Graziosi and Haubold 2015: 5–6. The most recent volume in the series, on
Odyssey Book 9, is silent on this issue (Bakker 2025: 68–71).

[171] For this original differentiation between these terms, see Kelly 2007a: 378–
409. The distinction suggested there was one in which the variant reading shows
signs of traditional referentiality, i.e. the kinds of understanding about the meaning of the reading in question which would not generally be available to a scribe
making a slip, but it need not be limited to it. There are other kinds of cases
imaginable, as with the formula πολυπίδακος Ἴδης (117n.), where πολυπιδάκου is
also widely attested in the MSS, since the thematism of athematic words is an established feature in the *Kunstsprache*, and so possibly reflective of bardic practice.
What the presence of such cases might tell us, we deal with at the end of this
section.

[172] See now the stimulating notion of the scribe as performer in Ready 2019:
185–234.

written copies; and the process of textualisation itself, however it happened, may have been drawn out and multiple in its stages. For all these reasons, the criteria we use to evaluate these differences should be both stringent and themselves of several types.

All too often, however, the argumentation of the multiform school sets a very low bar: any difference, no matter where it is reported or how great its support, can be an authentic part of the text, as long as one can show often no more than a minimal reflection of Homeric, or more generally epic, Greek.[173] Other explanations for the fact of difference are too quickly discarded, if at all considered, as driven by the wrong stance on the status of the text at this period. But difference is not only to be explained as the result of oral recomposition in performance. As with every other literary figure from the Greek and Roman world, we need to remember that performers do not always stick religiously to their scripts, people make mistakes when they write and misremember when they quote, and ancient authors recomposed their authoritative texts for their own ends.[174]

As an example of the stakes involved, one can look to the several *zētēmata* found in Aischines' extensive quotation (*Against Timarchos* § 149) from Patroclos' speech to Achilleus at the beginning of Book 23 (69–92; the quoted section is 77–91). A brief treatment of all his differences from the 'vulgate' is reserved for the Appendix, but let us look at his reading of οὐ γὰρ ἔτι at 77 instead of the usual οὐ μὲν γάρ. Taking an explicitly multiform stance, Casey Dué points out that either phrase is perfectly Homeric, and so her job is largely done; the potential authenticity of the variant is all that needs to be proven.[175] Yet, assuming that the text from which Aischines quotes was not confined to 23.77–91, we should note that the same phrase οὐ γὰρ ἔτι appears two lines before the quoted passage at 75, and so proximate a repetition of this expression is unparalleled in Homer.[176] Of course, we do not have Aischines' text of 75, and it may be different from the one we read (for what it is worth, there are no significant variants recorded in the paradosis), but this looks like a case where ordinary textual criticism gives a ready answer: the orator himself, in the

---

[173] See, e.g., Bird 2010, with critique in Kelly 2014 and Magnani 2018: 95–7; cf. also Sansom 2021: 139. It would be too harsh to term them 'sophistic' (Nardelli 2001b: iii.4), but a tendency to justify too easily the differences in the earliest papyri is typical of the approach, following the arguments of di Luzio 1969 to a similar end. Cantilena 2012: 89–95 persuasively (to my mind) refutes this approach to the evidence of the papyri.

[174] See, e.g., Labarbe 1949 on Plato's extensive quotations of Homer.

[175] Dué 2001a: 40–1 = 2019: 74–5.

[176] For the agonistic, capping uses of the expression by Achilleus (23.619) and Nestor (23.627), see 618–20n.

process of excerpting and quoting from a longer passage, has been led by a very nearby example of a very common expression to include it where it does not belong. That the greater explicit stress on the future afforded by οὐ γὰρ ἔτι was on his mind here was even directly foreshadowed in the paraphrase of this part of the passage earlier in his speech (λέγει ὅτι οὐκέτι περὶ τῶν μεγίστων, κτλ. § 147). Aischines' οὐ γὰρ ἔτι is, thus, either a simple mistake or a deliberate alteration to help him make his point.[177] By not considering other explanations for the phenomenon of difference, one can find the multiform simply because one is looking for it.

On the other hand, textual critics who favour the notion of an *Iliad* fixed just the once, early in the Archaic period, and then transmitted by largely written means can also be at least as circular in their thinking, for their methods are all designed to reveal an original, fixed text; it should be no surprise when those methods triumphantly unveil the expected object. They depend on – sometimes unspoken – predicates about just what Homer's text was and when it was established: if one thinks that Homer was an eighth- or seventh-century figure, then the text one establishes will look like that; similarly, if one thinks that the Homeric poems were first written down in Athens under Peisistratos, then the Atticisms in the text (see Intro. § 3, and below) are only to be expected (and are in fact good evidence for the whole event).[178] This is not a new development in Homeric scholarship, since 'Aristarchus was correcting the text in order to make it as *his own Homer* would have written it'.[179]

Inexplicitness is not, however, a criticism which can be fairly levelled at Martin West, whose Teubner texts of both poems have set the standard for the reporting of the Homeric tradition, because he was perfectly open about what kind of text he was trying to reconstruct and how he went about doing it.[180] His predicates led him, for example, to normalise features to their earliest possible form, as e.g. with the participles of ἰδεῖν, where he frequently goes against the majority of MSS in printing ἔργα

---

[177] It is also one which was found 'in some of the city texts' (Σ A 23.77), though the proximity of the same figure in 75 accounts for that, similarly, as an error. For more discussion, and especially of Aischines' reputation for altering the substance of his text in order to make his rhetorical point all the better, see the Appendix.

[178] Bolling 1950 even printed this specifically Athenian text (*Ilias Atheniensium*).

[179] Schironi 2018: 495.

[180] This was clear from the early signposting in West 1998, the introductions to his editions (1998–2000, 2017a), and their companion volumes (2001a, 2011, 2017b), which served to set out in detail his suppositions and methods. He was also amusingly forthright in replies to his several critics (West 2001b). I agree with very few of his conclusions or editorial decisions, but one of the greatest merits of his scholarship was that West always presented clearly and fully all the information one needed entirely to disagree with his own analysis of it.

ἰδυῖαν rather than ἔργ᾽ εἰδυῖαν, because the former reading respects the *digamma*, the *digamma* is an older feature and extremely common with other forms of this verb, and so ἔργα ἰδυῖαν is more Homeric. Yet the MSS show that epos was also able to neglect *digamma* before this verb for compositional utility – which is above all the operative principle of the poetic *Kunstsprache* – and so one should not simply restore the linguistically oldest attested or possible form wherever one can: ἰδυῖαν is not necessarily more authentic than εἰδυῖαν. It is quite possible, in fact, to imagine a circumstance in which oral poets will use one form in one place, another in another, without bothering to standardise their usage[181] – and this is actually what our MSS offer us on a whole series of questions, such as the temporal augment in otherwise already heavy syllables:[182] in some places the augment is the more attested reading, in others it is not, and there does not seem to be any principle behind the distribution.[183] Aristarchus tried to remove both syllabic and temporal augments or favoured reading forms without them, on the basis that this was the more Ionic form,[184] but our MS tradition suggests that whenever and however the text was fixed, a certain variability was already inherent.[185]

So how do we explain this, and how do we avoid the charge of methodological circularity when addressing the evidence? The short answer to the latter question is that we cannot, at least not entirely. Our knowledge of Homeric transmission does not allow us to be certain of much in the earliest period so as to base our methods on absolutely irrefutable assumptions. Some things, however, we can know: there are 'Atticisms' in the text, though perhaps not as many as Wackernagel thought,[186] and they cannot all be evidence of post-compositional interpolation: many can be removed or emended away but, once you have one irreducible case, the justification for removing the rest becomes much weaker. Many, such as the spellings of μείζων and κρείσσων (which I print at 578) for Archaic

---

[181] Graziosi and Haubold 2015: 11.

[182] For 'heavy' and 'light' syllables, as opposed to 'long' and 'short' vowels within syllables, see Intro. § 3.2.

[183] *GH* I §§ 230–4, esp. 231–2; West I.xxvii.

[184] Schironi 2018: 616–19.

[185] For the complex linguistic arguments over this feature in Homer, see Intro. § 3.1.2.d.iii. A respect for the variability in our MSS guides my attitudes towards other matters, like the augment and psilosis; we cannot assume that the poets would have adopted a linguistically uniform response when composing in an artistic language which valorised its distance from the norms of everyday speech. The MSS do not give that picture, and it should not be imposed upon them.

[186] See Intro. § 3.1. For examples in Book 23, see nn. to 8–9 (ἆσσον), 111–12 (κλισιῶν), 226–8 (Ἑωσφόρος), 267–8 (τέσσαρα), 413–14 (ἐφομαρτεῖτον), 485–7 (περιδώμεθον).

MEZON or ΚΡΕΣΣΟΝ, look like superficial changes of orthography, and it is salutary to remember that Attic forms are not found embedded into the formula systems, but our MSS show us that messiness is the norm. Moreover, scholars are increasingly reluctant to categorise many of these features as borrowings rather than independent formations. So, however they got there, whatever title we should use for them, and whatever it tells us about composition and transmission, these forms are part of our Homeric text, and the *Kunstsprache* it represents, and they should be printed.

The editor must, therefore, respect the state of affairs in the medieval MS tradition. That does not mean failing to criticise or emend when their evidence can be judged in need of it, or respecting only a select group of MSS and disregarding all other evidence (as does Helmut van Thiel, for instance).[187] But it does mean acknowledging two facts: (i) this vulgate 'compares well with what we know of the overall textual *facies* of Homer in antiquity',[188] yet (ii) a not entirely consistent picture emerges from the paradosis about the date, time, place, and process of composition. Thus, we cannot just approach the evidence with a method which assumes only the presence of an early fixed text (like West et al.), nor can we just replace this method with one that assumes only the absence of an early fixed text (like Nagy et al.). Instead, any difference within the paradosis needs to be evaluated to see if it could be an 'alternant', which involves not just establishing that the reading is possible, but showing that it respects the poem's usual practices, idioms, and rhetoric. At the same time, we need to be certain that it could not just be a 'variant' produced in the usual manner for every other ancient author, a result of error, misremembering, or even deliberate recreation. The two possibilities, in other words, need to be left open, balanced in each case, and combined.

So, for example, at 23.767 this edition prints ἱεμένωι referring to Odysseus, rather than the ἱέμενοι found in the bT scholia, some papyri, and some medieval MSS, because it is both much better attested and fits with the other examples of this traditional 'striving for victory' idiom in referring to the competitors (369^b–71^{a}n.). It also contributes a powerful chiasmus placing Odysseus at its centre as the referent of two connected dative participles, another in a series of such signs of the crowd's (and the poet's) favour for him and his coming success. Rhetoric, traditionality, MS evidence, all point in favour of the dative singular over the nominative plural. A more multiformly inclined scholar could argue that ἱέμενοι is a possible alternant, but the evidence of this poem suggests that its application

---

[187] Van Thiel 1991, 1996.   [188] Pontani 2024: 234.

to someone other than the competitors is not the kind of thing a traditionally trained bard, on the evidence we have about this point, would produce. When one combines an oral traditional perspective with more established practices of textual criticism, one can use a method which does not simply prove its assumptions in a closed hermeneutic circle, but looks to survey all the possibilities and deploy all the critical tools available without prejudging the issue.

As foreshadowed earlier, there is only one example in Book 23 (and this includes Aischines' quotation of 23.77–91 discussed in the Appendix) where alternation seems to be a better explanation than variation, and that is the case of πολυπίδακος/πολυπιδάκου at 117 (see n.).[189] There are plenty more cases where one could theoretically argue for alternation as at least as possible an explanation as variation, and one might even, for the sake of argument, extend this to cover all the differences in Book 23 (see below for the list). The final question would remain the same: what kind of creature is a multiform *Iliad*? The difference between the readings is minor, and the kinds of difference on display hew so closely to the vulgate that any possible evolutionary process has finished long before the time these MSS were established; the evidence of Aischines suggests that this was already true in the fourth century BCE. My conclusion from this limited body of evidence is that the process by which we have the Homeric poems is more likely to be a big bang moment, or a closely linked series of such moments, at a relatively early stage in the history of the text at some point between the eighth and sixth centuries BCE. Variation and even some alternation was possible during that period, but all the later available evidence seems to stems back to that more or less single line of transmission, through the Alexandrian and Roman periods, into the medieval world, and so down to us.

* * *

This text is not based on a separate collation. Working from an XML version of the Allen–Monro OCT,[190] I have used West's Teubner and its apparatus as my first point of reference, and then examined differences from Thomas Allen's *editio maior* (Oxford 1931) and Helmut van Thiel's *Iliad* (2nd ed., Hildesheim 2010). With regard to general editorial practice, I always print *v* mobile at the end of the verse, as this seems to have been a consistent phenomenon in the early Ptolematic papyri and may

---

[189] See Pontani 2024: 251, on the Cretan *Odyssey* as 'one passage in Homer where textual variants may hint to a radical alternative', but Beck 2020 has effectively demolished the scholiastic basis for that theory.

[190] With many thanks to Tom McConnell for providing it.

reflect early bardic practice (S. West 1967: 17 and n. 22; West I.xxv–xxvi); Πηλεῖδης (and other patronymics) is always so printed rather than trisyllabic Πηλείδης (17–18n.); 3rd person singular subjunctives end in -ηισι rather than -ηισι (313–14n.); the digraph -ευ- for -εο- (or other remedies) is retained, as these forms are not confined to the fourth century (69–70n.); I make no attempt to impose uniformity on augmented versus unaugmented forms of the verb, or on psilotic versus aspirated forms (17–18, 530–1, 536–8nn.); on the same basis I follow Allen and extend West's favour for accented forms of the demonstrative pronoun (ὄ, ἥ, etc.) even to those cases where it closely approaches the function of the definite article (149, 276, 387, 392, 500, 877).

Punctuation is designed for modern readability, and the apparatus criticus is kept to a minimum. The most significant differences in MS readings are recorded there; almost all of them receive some attention in the commentary and/or have been dealt with above (full diplomatic details can be consulted in the Teubner apparatus). I do not comment e.g. on repeat examples of the principles enumerated above, but they are included as separate items in the apparatus for the reader's convenience.

Some individual papyri are encountered several times in the commentary. They are referred to as follows, using West's sigla:

Π 9   Bibl. Brit. Add. MS 17210 (sixth century CE)
Π 12 P. Grenf. 2.4 + P. Hibeh 1.22 + P. Heid. 1262–6 (third century BCE)
Π 13 P. Bibl. Brit. Inv. 128 (P. Lit. Lond. 27) (first century BCE)
Π 453 P.S.I. 1275 (second century CE)

ΟΜΗΡΟΥ ΙΛΙΑΔΟΣ ΡΑΨΩΙΔΙΑ Ψ

ΟΜΗΡΟΥ ΙΛΙΑΔΟΣ ΡΑΨΩΙΔΙΑ Ψ

ὣς οἳ μὲν στενάχοντο κατὰ πτόλιν· αὐτὰρ Ἀχαιοί,
ἐπεὶ δὴ νῆάς τε καὶ Ἑλλήσποντον ἵκοντο,
οἳ μὲν ἄρ' ἐσκίδναντο ἑὴν ἐπὶ νῆα ἕκαστος,
Μυρμιδόνας δ' οὐκ εἴα ἀποσκίδνασθαι Ἀχιλλεύς,
ἀλλ' ὅ γε οἷς ἑτάροισι φιλοπτολέμοισι μετηύδα·   5
Μυρμιδόνες ταχύπωλοι, ἐμοὶ ἐρίηρες ἑταῖροι,
μὴ δή πω ὑπ' ὄχεσφι λυώμεθα μώνυχας ἵππους,
ἀλλ' αὐτοῖς ἵπποισι καὶ ἅρμασιν ἆσσον ἰόντες
Πάτροκλον κλαίωμεν· ὃ γὰρ γέρας ἐστὶ θανόντων.
αὐτὰρ ἐπεί κ' ὀλοοῖο τεταρπώμεσθα γόοιο,   10
ἵππους λυσάμενοι δορπήσομεν ἐνθάδε πάντες.'
ὣς ἔφαθ', οἳ δ' ᾤμωξαν ἀολλέες, ἦρχε δ' Ἀχιλλεύς.
οἳ δὲ τρὶς περὶ νεκρὸν ἐΰτριχας ἤλασαν ἵππους
μυρόμενοι· μετὰ δέ σφι Θέτις γόου ἵμερον ὦρσεν.
δεύοντο ψάμαθοι, δεύοντο δὲ τεύχεα φωτῶν   15
δάκρυσι· τοῖον γὰρ πόθεον μήστωρα φόβοιο.
τοῖσι δὲ Πηλεΐδης ἁδινοῦ ἐξῆρχε γόοιο,
χεῖρας ἐπ' ἀνδροφόνους θέμενος στήθεσσιν ἑταίρου·
'χαῖρέ μοι, ὦ Πάτροκλε, καὶ εἰν Ἀΐδαο δόμοισιν·
πάντα γὰρ ἤδη τοι τελέω τὰ πάροιθεν ὑπέστην,   20
Ἕκτορα δεῦρ' ἐρύσας δώσειν κυσὶν ὠμὰ δάσασθαι,
δώδεκα δὲ προπάροιθε πυρῆς ἀποδειροτομήσειν
Τρώων ἀγλαὰ τέκνα, σέθεν κταμένοιο χολωθείς.'
ἦ ῥα, καὶ Ἕκτορα δῖον ἀεικέα μήδετο ἔργα,
πρηνέα πὰρ λεχέεσσι Μενοιτιάδαο τανύσσας   25
ἐν κονίῃς· οἳ δ' ἔντε' ἀφωπλίζοντο ἕκαστος
χάλκεα μαρμαίροντα, λύον δ' ὑψηχέας ἵππους,
κὰδ δ' ἷζον παρὰ νηΐ ποδώκεος Αἰακίδαο
μυρίοι· αὐτὰρ ὃ τοῖσι τάφον μενοεικέα δαίνυ.
πολλοὶ μὲν βόες ἀργοὶ ὀρέχθεον ἀμφὶ σιδήρωι   30
σφαζόμενοι, πολλοὶ δ' ὄϊες καὶ μηκάδες αἶγες·
πολλοὶ δ' ἀργιόδοντες ὕες θαλέθοντες ἀλοιφῆι
εὑόμενοι τανύοντο διὰ φλογὸς Ἡφαίστοιο·

8 ἆσσον: ἄσσον   17 ἁδινοῦ: ἀδινοῦ   26 ἀφωπλίζοντο: ἀφοπλίζοντο

πάντηι δ' ἀμφὶ νέκυν κοτυλήρυτον ἔρρεεν αἷμα.
αὐτὰρ τόν γε ἄνακτα ποδώκεα Πηλεΐωνα   35
εἰς Ἀγαμέμνονα δῖον ἄγον βασιλῆες Ἀχαιῶν,
σπουδῆι παρπεπιθόντες ἑταίρου χωόμενον κῆρ.
οἳ δ' ὅτε δὴ κλισίην Ἀγαμέμνονος ἷξον ἰόντες,
αὐτίκα κηρύκεσσι λιγυφθόγγοισι κέλευσαν
ἀμφὶ πυρὶ στῆσαι τρίποδα μέγαν, εἰ πεπίθοιεν   40
Πηλεΐδην λούσασθαι ἄπο βρότον αἱματόεντα.
αὐτὰρ ὅ γ' ἠρνεῖτο στερεῶς, ἐπὶ δ' ὅρκον ὄμοσσεν·
'οὐ μὰ Ζῆν', ὅς τίς τε θεῶν ὕπατος καὶ ἄριστος,
οὐ θέμις ἐστὶ λοετρὰ καρήατος ἄσσον ἱκέσθαι,
πρίν γ' ἐνὶ Πάτροκλον θέμεναι πυρὶ σῆμά τε χεῦαι   45
κείρασθαί τε κόμην, ἐπεὶ οὔ μ' ἔτι δεύτερον ὧδε
ἵξετ' ἄχος κραδίην, ὄφρα ζωοῖσι μετείω.
ἀλλ' ἤτοι νῦν μὲν στυγερῆι πειθώμεθα δαιτί,
ἠῶθεν δ' ὄτρυνον, ἄναξ ἀνδρῶν Ἀγάμεμνον,
ὕλην τ' ἀξέμεναι παρά τε σχεῖν ὅσσ' ἐπιεικὲς   50
νεκρὸν ἔχοντα νέεσθαι ὑπὸ ζόφον ἠερόεντα,
ὄφρ' ἤτοι τοῦτον μὲν ἐπιφλέγηι ἀκάματον πῦρ
θᾶσσον ἀπ' ὀφθαλμῶν, λαοὶ δ' ἐπὶ ἔργα τράπωνται.'
ὣς ἔφαθ', οἳ δ' ἄρα τοῦ μάλα μὲν κλύον ἠδ' ἐπίθοντο.
ἐσσυμένως δ' ἄρα δόρπον ἐφοπλίσσαντες ἕκαστοι   55
δαίνυντ', οὐδέ τι θυμὸς ἐδεύετο δαιτὸς ἐΐσης.
αὐτὰρ ἐπεὶ πόσιος καὶ ἐδητύος ἐξ ἔρον ἔντο,
οἳ μὲν κακκείοντες ἔβαν κλισίηνδε ἕκαστος,
Πηλεΐδης δ' ἐπὶ θινὶ πολυφλοίσβοιο θαλάσσης
κεῖτο βαρὺ στενάχων πολέσιν μετὰ Μυρμιδόνεσσιν   60
ἐν καθαρῶι, ὅθι κύματ' ἐπ' ἠϊόνος κλύζεσκον·
εὖτε τὸν ὕπνος ἔμαρπτε, λύων μελεδήματα θυμοῦ,
νήδυμος ἀμφιχυθείς — μάλα γὰρ κάμε φαίδιμα γυῖα
Ἕκτορ' ἐπαΐσσων προτὶ Ἴλιον ἠνεμόεσσαν —
ἦλθε δ' ἐπὶ ψυχὴ Πατροκλῆος δειλοῖο,   65
πάντ' αὐτῶι μέγεθός τε καὶ ὄμματα κάλ' ἐϊκυῖα
καὶ φωνήν, καὶ τοῖα περὶ χροΐ εἵματα ἔστο.
στῆ δ' ἄρ' ὑπὲρ κεφαλῆς καί μιν πρὸς μῦθον ἔειπεν·

48 πειθώμεθα: τερπώμεθα **53** θᾶσσον: θάσσον **59** Πηλεΐδης: Πηλείδης **66** ἐϊκυῖα:
εἰκυῖα

εὕδεις, αὐτὰρ ἐμεῖο λελασμένος ἔπλευ, Ἀχιλλεῦ.
οὐ μέν μευ ζώοντος ἀκήδεις, ἀλλὰ θανόντος·   70
θάπτε με ὅττι τάχιστα, πύλας Ἀΐδαο περήσω·
τῆλέ με εἴργουσι ψυχαί, εἴδωλα καμόντων,
οὐδέ μέ πω μίσγεσθαι ὑπὲρ ποταμοῖο ἐῶσιν,
ἀλλ' αὔτως ἀλάλημαι ἀν' εὐρυπυλὲς Ἄϊδος δῶ.
καί μοι δὸς τὴν χεῖρ'· ὀλοφύρομαι, οὐ γὰρ ἔτ' αὖτις   75
νίσομαι ἐξ Ἀΐδαο, ἐπήν με πυρὸς λελάχητε.
οὐ μὲν γὰρ ζωοί γε φίλων ἀπάνευθεν ἑταίρων
βουλὰς ἑζόμενοι βουλεύσομεν, ἀλλ' ἐμὲ μὲν Κὴρ
ἀμφέχανε στυγερή, ἥ περ λάχε γεινόμενόν περ.
καὶ δὲ σοὶ αὐτῶι μοῖρα, θεοῖς ἐπιείκελ' Ἀχιλλεῦ,   80
τείχει ὕπο Τρώων εὐηγενέων ἀπολέσθαι.
ἄλλο δέ τοι ἐρέω καὶ ἐφήσομαι, αἴ κε πίθηαι·
μὴ ἐμὰ σῶν ἀπάνευθε τιθήμεναι ὀστέ', Ἀχιλλεῦ,
ἀλλ' ὁμοῦ, ὡς ἐτράφην περ ἐν ὑμετέροισι δόμοισιν,
εὖτέ με τυτθὸν ἐόντα Μενοίτιος ἐξ Ὀπόεντος   85
ἤγαγεν ὑμέτερόνδ' ἀνδροκτασίης ὕπο λυγρῆς,
ἤματι τῶι ὅτε παῖδα κατέκτανον Ἀμφιδάμαντος,
νήπιος, οὐκ ἐθέλων, ἀμφ' ἀστραγάλοισι χολωθείς·
ἔνθά με δεξάμενος ἐν δόμασιν ἱππότα Πηλεὺς
ἔτρεφέ τ' ἐνδυκέως καὶ σὸν θεράποντ' ὀνόμηνεν·   90
ὡς δὲ καὶ ὀστέα νῶϊν ὁμὴ σορὸς ἀμφικαλύπτοι
χρύσεος ἀμφιφορεύς, τόν τοι πόρε πότνια μήτηρ.
τὸν δ' ἀπαμειβόμενος προσέφη πόδας ὠκὺς Ἀχιλλεύς·
'τίπτέ μοι, ἠθείη κεφαλή, δεῦρ' εἰλήλουθας,
καί μοι ταῦτα ἕκαστ' ἐπιτέλλεαι; αὐτὰρ ἐγώ τοι   95
πάντα μάλ' ἐκτελέω καὶ πείσομαι, ὡς σὺ κελεύεις.
ἀλλά μοι ἆσσον στῆθι· μίνυνθά περ ἀμφιβαλόντε
ἀλλήλους ὀλοοῖο τεταρπώμεσθα γόοιο.'
ὡς ἄρα φωνήσας ὠρέξατο χερσὶ φίλῃσιν,
οὐδ' ἔλαβε· ψυχὴ δὲ κατὰ χθονὸς ἠΰτε καπνὸς   100
ὤιχετο τετριγυῖα. ταφὼν δ' ἀνόρουσεν Ἀχιλλεύς
χερσί τε συμπλατάγησεν, ἔπος δ' ὀλοφυδνὸν ἔειπεν·
'ὢ πόποι, ἦ ῥά τίς ἐστι καὶ εἰν Ἀΐδαο δόμοισιν,

---

78 Κήρ: κήρ 81 εὐηγενέων: εὐηφενέων 84 ἐτράφην: ἐτράφημεν, τράφομεν
91 ἀμφικαλύπτοι: ἀμφικαλύπτῃ 92 om., secl., dubit. nonnulli 97 ἆσσον:
ἄσσον ἀμφιβαλόντε: ἀμφιβαλόντες 103 τὶς: τι

ψυχὴ καὶ εἴδωλον, ἀτὰρ φρένες οὐκ ἔνι πάμπαν·
παννυχίη γάρ μοι Πατροκλῆος δειλοῖο 105
ψυχὴ ἐφεστήκει γοόωσά τε μυρομένη τε,
καί μοι ἕκαστ' ἐπέτελλεν, ἔϊκτο δὲ θέσκελον αὐτῶι.'
ὣς φάτο, τοῖσι δὲ πᾶσιν ὑφ' ἵμερον ὦρσε γόοιο·
μυρομένοισι δὲ τοῖσι φάνη ῥοδοδάκτυλος Ἠώς
ἀμφὶ νέκυν ἐλεεινόν. ἀτὰρ κρείων Ἀγαμέμνων 110
οὐρῆάς τ' ὤτρυνε καὶ ἀνέρας ἀξέμεν ὕλην
πάντοθεν ἐκ κλισιῶν· ἐπὶ δ' ἀνὴρ ἐσθλὸς ὀρώρει,
Μηριόνης, θεράπων ἀγαπήνορος Ἰδομενῆος.
οἳ δ' ἴσαν ὑλοτόμους πελέκεας ἐν χερσὶν ἔχοντες
σειράς τ' εὐπλέκτους· πρὸ δ' ἄρ' οὐρῆες κίον αὐτῶν, 115
πολλὰ δ' ἄναντα κάταντα πάραντά τε δόχμιά τ' ἦλθον.
ἀλλ' ὅτε δὴ κνημοὺς προσέβαν πολυπίδακος Ἴδης,
αὐτίκ' ἄρα δρῦς ὑψικόμους ταναήκεϊ χαλκῶι
τάμνον ἐπειγόμενοι· ταὶ δὲ μεγάλα κτυπέουσαι
πίπτον· τὰς μὲν ἔπειτα διαπλήσσοντες Ἀχαιοὶ 120
ἔκδεον ἡμιόνων· ταὶ δὲ χθόνα ποσσὶ δατεῦντο
ἐλδόμεναι πεδίοιο διὰ ῥωπήϊα πυκνά.
πάντες δ' ὑλοτόμοι φιτροὺς φέρον· ὣς γὰρ ἀνώγει
Μηριόνης θεράπων ἀγαπήνορος Ἰδομενῆος.
κὰδ δ' ἄρ' ἐπ' ἀκτῆς βάλλον ἐπὶ σχερῶι, ἔνθ' ἄρ' Ἀχιλλεὺς 125
φράσσατο Πατρόκλωι μέγα ἠρίον ἠδέ οἱ αὐτῶι.
αὐτὰρ ἐπεὶ πάντηι παρακάββαλον ἄσπετον ὕλην,
εἷατ' ἄρ' αὖθι μένοντες ἀολλέες. αὐτὰρ Ἀχιλλεὺς
αὐτίκα Μυρμιδόνεσσι φιλοπτολέμοισι κέλευσεν
χαλκὸν ζώννυσθαι ζεῦξαί θ' ὑπ' ὄχεσφιν ἕκαστον 130
ἵππους· οἳ δ' ὤρνυντο καὶ ἐν τεύχεσσιν ἔδυνον,
ἂν δ' ἔβαν ἐν δίφροισι παραιβάται ἡνίοχοί τε,
πρόσθε μὲν ἱππῆες, μετὰ δὲ νέφος εἵπετο πεζῶν,
μυρίοι· ἐν δὲ μέσοισι φέρον Πάτροκλον ἑταῖροι.
θριξὶ δὲ πάντα νέκυν καταείνυον, ἃς ἐπέβαλλον 135
κειρόμενοι· ὄπιθεν δὲ κάρη ἔχε δῖος Ἀχιλλεὺς
ἀχνύμενος· ἕταρον γὰρ ἀμύμονα πέμπ' Ἄϊδόσδε.
οἳ δ' ὅτε χῶρον ἵκανον, ὅθί σφισι πέφραδ' Ἀχιλλεύς,

111 ὤτρυνε: ὄτρυνε 112 κλισιῶν: κλισιάων 117 πολυπίδακος: πολυπιδάκου 120 πίπτον: πῖπτον 123 ὑλοτόμοι: ὤμοισιν 124 Μηριόνης: ὀτρηρός 125 ἐπὶ σχερῶι: ἐπισχερῶ 126 οἱ: οἵ 135 καταείνυον: καταείνυσαν

κάτθεσαν, αἶψα δέ οἱ μενοεικέα νήεον ὕλην.
ἔνθ᾽ αὖτ᾽ ἄλλ᾽ ἐνόησε ποδάρκης δῖος Ἀχιλλεύς· 140
στὰς ἀπάνευθε πυρῆς ξανθὴν ἀπεκείρατο χαίτην,
τήν ῥα Σπερχειῶι ποταμῶι τρέφε τηλεθόωσαν·
ὀχθήσας δ᾽ ἄρα εἶπεν ἰδὼν ἐπὶ οἴνοπα πόντον·
'Σπερχεῖ᾽, ἄλλως σοί γε πατὴρ ἠρήσατο Πηλεύς,
κεῖσέ με νοστήσαντα φίλην ἐς πατρίδα γαῖαν 145
σοί τε κόμην κερέειν ῥέξειν θ᾽ ἱερὴν ἑκατόμβην,
πεντήκοντα δ᾽ ἔνορχα παρ᾽ αὐτόθι μῆλ᾽ ἱερεύσειν
ἐς πηγάς, ὅθι τοι τέμενος βωμός τε θυήεις.
ὣς ἠρᾶθ᾽ ὃ γέρων, σὺ δέ οἱ νόον οὐκ ἐτέλεσσας.
νῦν δ᾽, ἐπεὶ οὐ νέομαί γε φίλην ἐς πατρίδα γαῖαν, 150
Πατρόκλωι ἥρωϊ κόμην ὀπάσαιμι φέρεσθαι.'
ὣς εἰπὼν ἐν χερσὶ κόμην ἑτάροιο φίλοιο
θῆκεν, τοῖσι δὲ πᾶσιν ὑφ᾽ ἵμερον ὦρσε γόοιο.
καί νύ κ᾽ ὀδυρομένοισιν ἔδυ φάος ἠελίοιο,
εἰ μὴ Ἀχιλλεὺς αἶψ᾽ Ἀγαμέμνονι εἶπε παραστάς· 155
'Ἀτρεΐδη, σοὶ γάρ τε μάλιστά γε λαὸς Ἀχαιῶν
πείσονται μύθοισι, γόοιο μὲν ἔστι καὶ ἆσαι,
νῦν δ᾽ ἀπὸ πυρκαϊῆς σκέδασον καὶ δεῖπνον ἄνωχθι
ὅπλεσθαι. τάδε δ᾽ ἀμφὶ πονησόμεθ᾽ οἷσι μάλιστα
κήδεός ἐστι νέκυς· παρὰ δ᾽ οἵ τ᾽ ἀγοὶ ἄμμι μενόντων.' 160
αὐτὰρ ἐπεὶ τό γ᾽ ἄκουσεν ἄναξ ἀνδρῶν Ἀγαμέμνων,
αὐτίκα λαὸν μὲν σκέδασεν κατὰ νῆας ἐΐσας,
κηδεμόνες δὲ παρ᾽ αὖθι μένον καὶ νήεον ὕλην,
ποίησαν δὲ πυρὴν ἑκατόμπεδον ἔνθα καὶ ἔνθα,
ἐν δὲ πυρῆι ὑπάτηι νεκρὸν θέσαν ἀχνύμενοι κῆρ. 165
πολλὰ δὲ ἴφια μῆλα καὶ εἰλίποδας ἕλικας βοῦς
πρόσθε πυρῆς ἔδερόν τε καὶ ἄμφεπον· ἐκ δ᾽ ἄρα πάντων
δημὸν ἑλὼν ἐκάλυψε νέκυν μεγάθυμος Ἀχιλλεὺς
ἐς πόδας ἐκ κεφαλῆς, περὶ δὲ δρατὰ σώματα νήει.
ἐν δ᾽ ἐτίθει μέλιτος καὶ ἀλείφατος ἀμφιφορῆας, 170
πρὸς λέχεα κλίνων· πίσυρας δ᾽ ἐριαύχενας ἵππους
ἐσσυμένως ἐνέβαλλε πυρῆι, μεγάλα στεναχίζων.
ἐννέα τῶι γε ἄνακτι τραπεζῆες κύνες ἦσαν,

---

155 Ἀγαμέμνονι: Ἀγαμέμνονα **157** μὲν ἔστι: μέν ἐστι **172** στεναχίζων: στοναχίζων

καὶ μὲν τῶν ἐνέβαλλε πυρῆι δύο δειροτομήσας,
δώδεκα δὲ Τρώων μεγαθύμων υἱέας ἐσθλοὺς   175
χαλκῶι δηϊόων· κακὰ δὲ φρεσὶ μήδετο ἔργα.
ἐν δὲ πυρὸς μένος ἧκε σιδήρεον, ὄφρα νέμοιτο.
ὤιμωξέν τ᾽ ἄρ᾽ ἔπειτα, φίλον δ᾽ ὀνόμηνεν ἑταῖρον·
᾽χαῖρέ μοι, ὦ Πάτροκλε, καὶ εἰν Ἀΐδαο δόμοισιν·
πάντα γὰρ ἤδη τοι τελέω τὰ πάροιθεν ὑπέστην.   180
δώδεκα μὲν Τρώων μεγαθύμων υἱέας ἐσθλοὺς
τοὺς ἅμα σοὶ πάντας πῦρ ἐσθίει· Ἕκτορα δ᾽ οὔ τι
δώσω Πριαμίδην πυρὶ δαπτέμεν, ἀλλὰ κύνεσσιν.᾽
ὣς φάτ᾽ ἀπειλήσας· τὸν δ᾽ οὐ κύνες ἀμφεπένοντο,
ἀλλὰ κύνας μὲν ἄλαλκε Διὸς θυγάτηρ Ἀφροδίτη   185
ἤματα καὶ νύκτας, ῥοδόεντι δὲ χρῖεν ἐλαίωι
ἀμβροσίωι, ἵνα μή μιν ἀποδρύφοι ἑλκυστάζων.
τῶι δ᾽ ἐπὶ κυάνεον νέφος ἤγαγε Φοῖβος Ἀπόλλων
οὐρανόθεν πεδίονδε, κάλυψε δὲ χῶρον ἅπαντα,
ὅσσον ἐπεῖχε νέκυς, μὴ πρὶν μένος ἠελίοιο   190
σκήλει᾽ ἀμφὶ περὶ χρόα ἴνεσιν ἠδὲ μέλεσσιν.
οὐδὲ πυρὴ Πατρόκλου ἐκαίετο τεθνηῶτος·
ἔνθ᾽ αὖτ᾽ ἀλλ᾽ ἐνόησε ποδάρκης δῖος Ἀχιλλεύς·
στὰς ἀπάνευθε πυρῆς δοιοῖς ἠρᾶτ᾽ ἀνέμοισιν,
Βορέηι καὶ Ζεφύρωι, καὶ ὑπίσχετο ἱερὰ καλά·   195
πολλὰ δὲ καὶ σπένδων χρυσέωι δέπαϊ λιτάνευεν
ἐλθέμεν, ὄφρα τάχιστα πυρὶ φλεγεθοίατο νεκροὶ
ὕλη τε σεύαιτο καήμεναι. ὠκέα δ᾽ Ἶρις
ἀράων ἀΐουσα μετάγγελος ἦλθ᾽ ἀνέμοισιν.
οἳ μὲν ἄρα Ζεφύροιο δυσαέος ἀθρόοι ἔνδον   200
εἰλαπίνην δαίνυντο· θέουσα δὲ Ἶρις ἐπέστη
βηλῶι ἔπι λιθέωι· τοὶ δ᾽ ὡς ἴδον ὀφθαλμοῖσιν,
πάντες ἀνήϊξαν κάλεόν τέ μιν εἰς ἓ ἕκαστος·
ἣ δ᾽ αὖθ᾽ ἕζεσθαι μὲν ἀνήνατο, εἶπε δὲ μῦθον·
᾽οὐχ ἕδος· εἶμι γὰρ αὖτις ἐπ᾽ Ὠκεανοῖο ῥέεθρα,   205
Αἰθιόπων ἐς γαῖαν, ὅθι ῥέζουσ᾽ ἑκατόμβας
ἀθανάτοις, ἵνα δὴ καὶ ἐγὼ μεταδαίσομαι ἱρῶν·
ἀλλ᾽ Ἀχιλεὺς Βορέην ἠδὲ Ζέφυρον κελαδεινὸν

---

180 τελέω τὰ πάροιθεν: τετελεσμένα ὥς περ **191** σκήλει᾽: σκήληι **195** Βορέηι:
Βορρῆι **197** νεκροί: νεκρόν **198** ὠκέα δ᾽ Ἶρις: ὦκα δὲ Ἶρις

ἐλθεῖν ἀρᾶται, καὶ ὑπίσχεται ἱερὰ καλά,
ὄφρα πυρὴν ὄρσητε καήμεναι, ἧι ἔνι κεῖται 210
Πάτροκλος, τὸν πάντες ἀναστενάχουσιν Ἀχαιοί.'
ἣ μὲν ἄρ' ὣς εἰποῦσ' ἀπεβήσετο, τοὶ δ' ὀρέοντο
ἠχῆι θεσπεσίηι, νέφεα κλονέοντε πάροιθεν.
αἶψα δὲ πόντον ἵκανον ἀήμεναι, ὧρτο δὲ κῦμα
πνοιῆι ὕπο λιγυρῆι· Τροίην δ' ἐρίβωλον ἵκέσθην, 215
ἐν δὲ πυρῆι πεσέτην· μέγα δ' ἴαχε θεσπιδαὲς πῦρ.
παννύχιοι δ' ἄρα τοί γε πυρῆς ἄμυδις φλόγ' ἔβαλλον,
φυσῶντες λιγέως· ὃ δὲ πάννυχος ὠκὺς Ἀχιλλεὺς
χρυσέου ἐκ κρητῆρος, ἔχων δέπας ἀμφικύπελλον,
οἶνον ἀφυσσόμενος χαμάδις χέε, δεῦε δὲ γαῖαν, 220
ψυχὴν κικλήσκων Πατροκλῆος δειλοῖο.
ὡς δὲ πατὴρ οὗ παιδὸς ὀδύρεται ὀστέα καίων
νυμφίου, ὅς τε θανὼν δειλοὺς ἀκάχησε τοκῆας,
ὣς Ἀχιλεὺς ἑτάροιο ὀδύρετο ὀστέα καίων,
ἑρπύζων παρὰ πυρκαϊήν, ἀδινὰ στεναχίζων. 225
ἦμος δ' Ἑωσφόρος εἶσι φόως ἐρέων ἐπὶ γαῖαν,
ὅν τε μέτα κροκόπεπλος ὑπεὶρ ἅλα κίδναται Ἠώς,
τῆμος πυρκαϊὴ ἐμαραίνετο, παύσατο δὲ φλόξ.
οἳ δ' ἄνεμοι πάλιν αὖτις ἔβαν οἶκόνδε νέεσθαι
Θρηΐκιον κατὰ πόντον· ὃ δ' ἔστενεν οἴδματι θυίων. 230
Πηλεΐδης δ' ἀπὸ πυρκαϊῆς ἑτέρωσε λιασθεὶς
κλίνθη κεκμηώς, ἐπὶ δὲ γλυκὺς ὕπνος ὄρουσεν·
οἳ δ' ἀμφ' Ἀτρεΐωνα ἀολλέες ἠγερέθοντο·
τῶν μιν ἐπερχομένων ὅμαδος καὶ δοῦπος ἔγειρεν,
ἕζετο δ' ὀρθωθεὶς καί σφεας πρὸς μῦθον ἔειπεν· 235
'Ἀτρεΐδη τε καὶ ἄλλοι ἀριστῆες Παναχαιῶν,
πρῶτον μὲν κατὰ πυρκαϊὴν σβέσατ' αἴθοπι οἴνωι
πᾶσαν, ὁπόσσον ἐπέσχε πυρὸς μένος· αὐτὰρ ἔπειτα
ὀστέα Πατρόκλοιο Μενοιτιάδαο λέγωμεν
εὖ διαγινώσκοντες· ἀριφραδέα δὲ τέτυκται· 240
ἐν μέσσηι γὰρ ἔκειτο πυρῆι, τοὶ δ' ἄλλοι ἄνευθεν
ἐσχατιῆι καίοντ' ἐπιμὶξ ἵπποι τε καὶ ἄνδρες.

219 ἔχων: ἑλών 220 ἀφυσσόμενος: ἀφυσσάμενος 225 ἀδινὰ στεναχίζων: ἀδινὰ στοναχίζων 226 Ἑωσφόρος: ἐωσφόρος 227 Ἠώς: ἠώς 230 θυίων: θύων 240 διαγινώσκοντες: διαγιγνώσκοντες   ἀριφραδέα δὲ τέτυκται: ἀριφραδέως γὰρ ἔκειτο

καὶ τὰ μὲν ἐν χρυσέηι φιάληι καὶ δίπλακι δημῶι
θείομεν, εἰς ὅ κεν αὐτὸς ἐγὼν Ἄϊδι κεύθωμαι.
τύμβον δ᾽ οὐ μάλα πολλὸν ἐγὼ πονέεσθαι ἄνωγα,   245
ἀλλ᾽ ἐπιεικέα τοῖον· ἔπειτα δὲ καὶ τὸν Ἀχαιοὶ
εὐρύν θ᾽ ὑψηλόν τε τιθήμεναι, οἵ κεν ἐμεῖο
δεύτεροι ἐν νήεσσι πολυκλήϊσι λίπησθε.᾽
ὣς ἔφαθ᾽, οἱ δ᾽ ἐπίθοντο ποδώκεϊ Πηλεΐωνι.
πρῶτον μὲν κατὰ πυρκαϊὴν σβέσαν αἴθοπι οἴνωι,   250
ὅσσον ἐπὶ φλὸξ ἦλθε, βαθεῖα δὲ κάππεσε τέφρη·
κλαίοντες δ᾽ ἑτάροιο ἐνηέος ὀστέα λευκὰ
ἄλλεγον ἐς χρυσέην φιάλην καὶ δίπλακα δημόν,
ἐν κλισίηισι δὲ θέντες ἑανῶι λιτὶ κάλυψαν·
τορνώσαντο δὲ σῆμα θεμείλιά τε προβάλοντο   255
ἀμφὶ πυρήν· εἶθαρ δὲ χυτὴν ἐπὶ γαῖαν ἔχευαν,
χεύαντες δὲ τὸ σῆμα πάλιν κίον. αὐτὰρ Ἀχιλλεὺς
αὐτοῦ λαὸν ἔρυκε καὶ ἵζανεν εὐρὺν ἀγῶνα,
νηῶν δ᾽ ἔκφερ᾽ ἄεθλα, λέβητάς τε τρίποδάς τε
ἵππους θ᾽ ἡμιόνους τε βοῶν τ᾽ ἴφθιμα κάρηνα   260
ἠδὲ γυναῖκας ἐϋζώνους πολιόν τε σίδηρον.
ἱππεῦσιν μὲν πρῶτα ποδώκεσιν ἀγλά᾽ ἄεθλα
θῆκε γυναῖκα ἄγεσθαι ἀμύμονα ἔργ᾽ εἰδυῖαν
καὶ τρίποδ᾽ ὠτώεντα δυωκαιεικοσίμετρον,
τῶι πρώτωι· ἀτὰρ αὖ τῶι δευτέρωι ἵππον ἔθηκεν   265
ἐξέτε᾽ ἀδμήτην, βρέφος ἡμίονον κυέουσαν·
αὐτὰρ τῶι τριτάτωι ἄπυρον κατέθηκε λέβητα
καλόν, τέσσαρα μέτρα κεχανδότα, λευκὸν ἔτ᾽ αὔτως·
τῶι δὲ τετάρτωι θῆκε δύω χρυσοῖο τάλαντα·
πέμπτωι δ᾽ ἀμφίθετον φιάλην ἀπύρωτον ἔθηκεν.   270
στῆ δ᾽ ὀρθὸς καὶ μῦθον ἐν Ἀργείοισιν ἔειπεν·
Ἀτρεΐδη τε καὶ ἄλλοι ἐϋκνήμιδες Ἀχαιοί,
ἱππῆας τάδ᾽ ἄεθλα δεδεγμένα κεῖτ᾽ ἐν ἀγῶνι.
εἰ μὲν νῦν ἐπὶ ἄλλωι ἀεθλεύοιμεν Ἀχαιοί,
ἦ τ᾽ ἂν ἐγὼ τὰ πρῶτα λαβὼν κλισίηνδε φεροίμην·   275
ἴστε γὰρ ὅσσον ἐμοὶ ἀρετῆι περιβάλλετον ἵπποι·
ἀθάνατοί τε γάρ εἰσι, Ποσειδάων δ᾽ ἔπορ᾽ αὐτοὺς

---

244 κεύθωμαι: κλεύθωμαι, κλεύσωμαι   **254** κλισίηισι δὲ θέντες: κλισίηι δ᾽ ἐνθέντες   **262**
ἱππεῦσιν: ἱπποῖσι   **263** ἔργ᾽ εἰδυῖαν: ἔργα ἰδυῖαν   **268** τέσσαρα: τέσσερα

πατρὶ ἐμῶι Πηλῆϊ, ὃ δ᾽ αὖτ᾽ ἐμοὶ ἐγγυάλιξεν.
ἀλλ᾽ ἤτοι μὲν ἐγὼ μενέω καὶ μώνυχες ἵπποι·
τοίου γὰρ σθένος ἐσθλὸν ἀπώλεσαν ἡνιόχοιο,   280
ἠπίου, ὅς σφωϊν μάλα πολλάκις ὑγρὸν ἔλαιον
χαιτάων κατέχευε, λοέσσας ὕδατι λευκῶι.
τὸν τώ γ᾽ ἑσταότες πενθείετον, οὔδεϊ δέ σφιν
χαῖται ἐρηρέδαται, τὼ δ᾽ ἕστατον ἀχνυμένω κῆρ.
ἄλλοι δὲ στέλλεσθε κατὰ στρατόν, ὅς τις Ἀχαιῶν   285
ἵπποισίν τε πέποιθε καὶ ἅρμασι κολλητοῖσιν.᾽
ὣς φάτο Πηλεΐδης, ταχέες δ᾽ ἱππῆες ἄγερθεν.
ὦρτο πολὺ πρῶτος μὲν ἄναξ ἀνδρῶν Εὔμηλος,
Ἀδμήτου φίλος υἱός, ὃς ἱπποσύνηι ἐκέκαστο·
τῶι δ᾽ ἐπὶ Τυδεΐδης ὦρτο κρατερὸς Διομήδης,   290
ἵππους δὲ Τρωιοὺς ὕπαγε ζυγόν, οὕς ποτ᾽ ἀπηύρα
Αἰνείαν, ἀτὰρ αὐτὸν ὑπεξεσάωσεν Ἀπόλλων·
τῶι δ᾽ ἄρ᾽ ἐπ᾽ Ἀτρεΐδης ὦρτο ξανθὸς Μενέλαος
διογενής, ὑπὸ δὲ ζυγὸν ἤγαγεν ὠκέας ἵππους,
Αἴθην τὴν Ἀγαμεμνονέην τὸν ἑόν τε Πόδαργον·   295
τὴν Ἀγαμέμνονι δῶκ᾽ Ἀγχισιάδης Ἐχέπωλος
δῶρ᾽, ἵνα μή οἱ ἕποιθ᾽ ὑπὸ Ἴλιον ἠνεμόεσσαν,
ἀλλ᾽ αὐτοῦ τέρποιτο μένων· μέγα γάρ οἱ ἔδωκεν
Ζεὺς ἄφενος, ναῖεν δ᾽ ὅ γ᾽ ἐν εὐρυχόρωι Σικυῶνι·
τὴν ὅ γ᾽ ὑπὸ ζυγὸν ἦγε, μέγα δρόμου ἰσχανόωσαν.   300
Ἀντίλοχος δὲ τέταρτος ἐΰτριχας ὡπλίσαθ᾽ ἵππους,
Νέστορος ἀγλαὸς υἱὸς ὑπερθύμοιο ἄνακτος,
τοῦ Νηληϊάδαο, Πυλοιγενέες δέ οἱ ἵπποι
ὠκύποδες φέρον ἅρμα· πατὴρ δέ οἱ ἄγχι παραστὰς
μυθεῖτ᾽ εἰς ἀγαθὰ φρονέων νοέοντι καὶ αὐτῶι·   305
᾽Αντίλοχ᾽, ἤτοι μέν σε νέον περ ἐόντ᾽ ἐφίλησαν
Ζεύς τε Ποσειδάων τε, καὶ ἱπποσύνας ἐδίδαξαν
παντοίας· τὼ καί σε διδασκέμεν οὔ τι μάλα χρεώ·
οἶσθα γὰρ εὖ περὶ τέρμαθ᾽ ἑλισσέμεν· ἀλλά τοι ἵπποι
βάρδιστοι θείειν· τῶ τ᾽ οἴω λοίγι᾽ ἔσεσθαι.   310
τῶν δ᾽ ἵπποι μὲν ἔασιν ἀφάρτεροι, οὐδὲ μὲν αὐτοὶ
πλείονα ἴσασιν σέθεν αὐτοῦ μητίσασθαι.

280 σθένος ἐσθλόν: κλέος ἐσθλόν   281 ὅς: ὃ   300 ἰσχανόωσαν: ἰχανόωσαν   301
ὡπλίσαθ᾽: ὁπλίσαθ᾽   303 Πυλοιγενέες: Πυληγενέες   307 ἐδίδαξαν: ἐδίδαξεν

ἀλλ᾽ ἄγε δὴ σύ, φίλος, μῆτιν ἐμβάλλεο θυμῶι
παντοίην, ἵνα μή σε παρεκπροφύγηισιν ἄεθλα.
μῆτι τοι δρυτόμος μέγ᾽ ἀμείνων ἠὲ βίηφιν,   315
μῆτι δ᾽ αὖτε κυβερνήτης ἐνὶ οἴνοπι πόντωι
νῆα θοὴν ἰθύνει ἐρεχθομένην ἀνέμοισιν,
μῆτι δ᾽ ἡνίοχος περιγίνεται ἡνιόχοιο.
ἀλλ᾽ ὃς μέν θ᾽ ἵπποισι καὶ ἅρμασιν οἷσι πεποιθὼς
ἀφραδέως ἐπὶ πολλὸν ἑλίσσεται ἔνθα καὶ ἔνθα,   320
ἵπποι δὲ πλανόωνται ἀνὰ δρόμον, οὐδὲ κατίσχει·
ὃς δέ κε κέρδεα εἰδῆι ἐλαύνων ἥσσονας ἵππους,
αἰεὶ τέρμ᾽ ὁρόων στρέφει ἐγγύθεν, οὐδέ ἑ λήθει
ὅππως τὸ πρῶτον τανύσηι βοέοισιν ἱμᾶσιν,
ἀλλ᾽ ἔχει ἀσφαλέως καὶ τὸν προύχοντα δοκεύει.   325
σῆμα δέ τοι ἐρέω μάλ᾽ ἀριφραδές, οὐδέ σε λήσει·
ἕστηκε ξύλον αὖον ὅσον τ᾽ ὄργυι᾽ ὑπὲρ αἴης,
ἢ δρυὸς ἢ πεύκης· τὸ μὲν οὐ καταπύθεται ὄμβρωι·
λᾶε δὲ τοῦ ἑκάτερθεν ἐρηρέδαται δύο λευκὼ
ἐν ξυνοχῆισιν ὁδοῦ, λεῖος δ᾽ ἱππόδρομος ἀμφίς·   330
ἤ τευ σῆμα βροτοῖο πάλαι κατατεθνηῶτος,
ἢ τό γε νύσσα τέτυκτο ἐπὶ προτέρων ἀνθρώπων·
καὶ νῦν τέρματ᾽ ἔθηκε ποδάρκης δῖος Ἀχιλλεύς.
τῶι σὺ μάλ᾽ ἐγχρίμψας ἐλάαν σχεδὸν ἅρμα καὶ ἵππους,
αὐτὸς δὲ κλινθῆναι ἐϋπλέκτωι ἐνὶ δίφρωι   335
ἦκ᾽ ἐπ᾽ ἀριστερὰ τοῖιν· ἀτὰρ τὸν δεξιὸν ἵππον
κένσαι ὁμοκλήσας, εἶξαί τέ οἱ ἡνία χερσίν,
ἐν νύσσηι δέ τοι ἵππος ἀριστερὸς ἐγχριμφθήτω,
ὡς ἄν τοι πλήμνη γε δοάσσεται ἄκρον ἱκέσθαι
κύκλου ποιητοῖο· λίθου δ᾽ ἀλέασθαι ἐπαυρεῖν,   340
μή πως ἵππους τε τρώσηις κατά θ᾽ ἅρματα ἄξηις·
χάρμα δὲ τοῖς ἄλλοισιν, ἐλεγχείη δὲ σοὶ αὐτῶι
ἔσσεται. ἀλλά, φίλος, φρονέων πεφυλαγμένος εἶναι.
εἰ γάρ κ᾽ ἐν νύσσηι γε παρεξελάσηισθα διώκων,
οὐκ ἔσθ᾽ ὅς κέ σ᾽ ἕληισι μετάλμενος οὐδὲ παρέλθοι, 345
οὐδ᾽ εἰ κεν μετόπισθεν Ἀρίονα δῖον ἐλαύνοι,
Ἀδρήστου ταχὺν ἵππον, ὃς ἐκ θεόφιν γένος ἦεν,
ἢ τοὺς Λαομέδοντος, οἳ ἐνθάδε γ᾽ ἔτραφεν ἐσθλοί.᾽

318 περιγίνεται: περιγίγνεται 319 ἀλλ᾽ ὅς: ἄλλος 337 ὁμοκλήσας: ὁμοκλήσας
345 παρέλθοι: παρέλθηι 348 γ᾽ ἔτραφεν: γ᾽ ἔτραφον, γ᾽ ἔτρεφεν, τέτραφεν

ὣς εἰπὼν Νέστωρ Νηλήϊος ἂψ ἐνὶ χώρηι
ἕζετ', ἐπεὶ ὧι παιδὶ ἑκάστου πείρατ' ἔειπεν.   350
Μηριόνης δ' ἄρα πέμπτος ἐΰτριχας ὡπλίσαθ' ἵππους.
ἂν δ' ἔβαν ἐς δίφρους, ἐν δὲ κλήρους ἐβάλοντο·
πάλλ' Ἀχιλεύς, ἐκ δὲ κλῆρος θόρε Νεστορίδαο
Ἀντιλόχου· μετὰ τὸν δ' ἔλαχε κρείων Εὔμηλος·
τῶι δ' ἄρ' ἐπ' Ἀτρεΐδης δουρικλειτὸς Μενέλαος·   355
τῶι δ' ἐπὶ Μηριόνης λάχ' ἐλαυνέμεν· ὕστατος αὖτε
Τυδεΐδης ὄχ' ἄριστος ἐὼν λάχ' ἐλαυνέμεν ἵππους.
στὰν δὲ μεταστοιχεί, σήμηνε δὲ τέρματ' Ἀχιλλεύς
τηλόθεν ἐν λείωι πεδίωι· παρὰ δὲ σκοπὸν εἶσεν
ἀντίθεον Φοίνικα, ὀπάονα πατρὸς ἑοῖο,   360
ὡς μεμνέωιτο δρόμου καὶ ἀληθείην ἀποείποι.
οἳ δ' ἄρα πάντες ἐφ' ἵπποιιν μάστιγας ἄειραν
πέπληγόν θ' ἱμᾶσιν ὁμόκλησάν τ' ἐπέεσσιν
ἐσσυμένως· οἳ δ' ὦκα διέπρησσον πεδίοιο
νόσφι νεῶν ταχέως· ὑπὸ δὲ στέρνοισι κονίη   365
ἵστατ' ἀειρομένη ὥς τε νέφος ἠὲ θύελλα,
χαῖται δ' ἐρρώοντο μετὰ πνοιῆις ἀνέμοιο.
ἅρματα δ' ἄλλοτε μὲν χθονὶ πίλνατο πουλυβοτείρηι,
ἄλλοτε δ' ἀΐξασκε μετήορα· τοὶ δ' ἐλατῆρες
ἕστασαν ἐν δίφροισι, πάτασσε δὲ θυμὸς ἑκάστου   370
νίκης ἱεμένων· κέκλοντο δὲ οἷσιν ἕκαστος
ἵπποις, οἳ δ' ἐπέτοντο κονίοντες πεδίοιο.
ἀλλ' ὅτε δὴ πύματον τέλεον δρόμον ὠκέες ἵπποι
ἂψ ἐφ' ἁλὸς πολιῆς, τότε δὴ ἀρετή γε ἑκάστου
φαίνετ', ἄφαρ δ' ἵπποισι τάθη δρόμος· ὦκα δ' ἔπειτα 375
αἳ Φηρητιάδαο ποδώκεες ἔκφερον ἵπποι,
τὰς δὲ μετ' ἐξέφερον Διομήδεος ἄρσενες ἵπποι,
Τρώϊοι, οὐδέ τι πολλὸν ἄνευθ' ἔσαν, ἀλλὰ μάλ' ἐγγύς·
αἰεὶ γὰρ δίφρου ἐπιβησομένοισιν ἐΐκτην,
πνοιῆι δ' Εὐμήλοιο μετάφρενον εὐρέε τ' ὤμω   380
θέρμετ'· ἐπ' αὐτῶι γὰρ κεφαλὰς καταθέντε πετέσθην.
καί νύ κεν ἢ παρέλασσ' ἢ ἀμφήριστον ἔθηκεν,
εἰ μὴ Τυδέος υἷι κοτέσσατο Φοῖβος Ἀπόλλων,

---

358 μεταστοιχεί: μεταστοιχί   **361** μεμνέωιτο: μεμνῆιτο   δρόμου: δρόμους   **362** ἄρα:
ἄμα   **363** ὁμόκλησαν: ὁμόκλησαν   **367** δ' ἐρρώοντο: δὲ ῥώοντο

ὅς ῥά οἱ ἐκ χειρῶν ἔβαλεν μάστιγα φαεινήν.
τοῖο δ᾽ ἀπ᾽ ὀφθαλμῶν χύτο δάκρυα χωομένοιο,   385
οὕνεκα τὰς μὲν ὅρα ἔτι καὶ πολὺ μᾶλλον ἰούσας,
οἳ δέ οἱ ἐβλάφθησαν ἄνευ κέντροιο θέοντες.
οὐδ᾽ ἄρ᾽ Ἀθηναίην ἐλεφηράμενος λάθ᾽ Ἀπόλλων
Τυδεΐδην, μάλα δ᾽ ὦκα μετέσσυτο ποιμένα λαῶν,
δῶκε δέ οἱ μάστιγα, μένος δ᾽ ἵπποισιν ἐνῆκεν·   390
ἡ δὲ μετ᾽ Ἀδμήτου υἱὸν κοτέουσα βεβήκει,
ἵππειον δέ οἱ ἧξε θεὰ ζυγόν, αἱ δέ οἱ ἵπποι
ἀμφὶς ὁδοῦ δραμέτην, ῥυμὸς δ᾽ ἐπὶ γαῖαν ἐλύσθη.
αὐτὸς δ᾽ ἐκ δίφροιο παρὰ τροχὸν ἐξεκυλίσθη,
ἀγκῶνάς τε περιδρύφθη στόμα τε ῥῖνάς τε,   395
θρυλίχθη δὲ μέτωπον ἐπ᾽ ὀφρύσι· τὼ δέ οἱ ὄσσε
δακρυόφι πλῆσθεν, θαλερὴ δέ οἱ ἔσχετο φωνή.
Τυδεΐδης δὲ παρατρέψας ἔχε μώνυχας ἵππους,
πολλὸν τῶν ἄλλων ἐξάλμενος· ἐν γὰρ Ἀθήνη
ἵπποις ἧκε μένος καὶ ἐπ᾽ αὐτῶι κῦδος ἔθηκεν.   400
τῶι δ᾽ ἄρ᾽ ἐπ᾽ Ἀτρεΐδης εἶχε ξανθὸς Μενέλαος.
Ἀντίλοχος δ᾽ ἵπποισιν ἐκέκλετο πατρὸς ἑοῖο·
᾽ἔμβητον καὶ σφῶϊ· τιταίνετον ὅττι τάχιστα.
ἤτοι μὲν κείνοισιν ἐριζέμεν οὔ τι κελεύω,
Τυδεΐδεω ἵπποισι δαΐφρονος, οἷσιν Ἀθήνη   405
νῦν ὤρεξε τάχος καὶ ἐπ᾽ αὐτῶι κῦδος ἔθηκεν·
ἵππους δ᾽ Ἀτρεΐδαο κιχάνετε, μηδὲ λίπησθον,
καρπαλίμως, μὴ σφῶϊν ἐλεγχείην καταχεύηι
Αἴθη θῆλυς ἐοῦσα. τίη λείπεσθε, φέριστοι;
ὧδε γὰρ ἐξερέω, καὶ μὴν τετελεσμένον ἔσται·   410
οὐ σφῶϊν κομιδὴ παρὰ Νέστορι ποιμένι λαῶν
ἔσσεται, αὐτίκα δ᾽ ὔμμε κατακτενεῖ ὀξέϊ χαλκῶι,
αἴ κ᾽ ἀποκηδήσαντε φερώμεθα χεῖρον ἄεθλον.
ἀλλ᾽ ἐφομαρτεῖτον καὶ σπεύδετον ὅττι τάχιστα·
ταῦτα δ᾽ ἐγὼν αὐτὸς τεχνήσομαι ἠδὲ νοήσω,   415
στεινωπῶι ἐν ὁδῶι παραδύμεναι, οὐδέ με λήσει.᾽
ὡς ἔφαθ᾽, οἳ δὲ ἄνακτος ὑποδδείσαντες ὁμοκλὴν

---

387 οἳ δέ οἱ: οἳ δ᾽ ἑοί   **400** ἔθηκεν: ἔδωκεν   **410** μήν: μάν, μέν   **414** ἐφομαρτεῖτον:
ἐφαμαρτεῖτον   **417** ὑποδδείσαντες: ὑποδείσαντες   ὁμοκλήν: ὀμοκλήν

μᾶλλον ἐπιδραμέτην ὀλίγον χρόνον· αἶψα δ' ἔπειτα
στεῖνος ὁδοῦ κοίλης ἴδεν Ἀντίλοχος μενεχάρμης.
ῥωχμὸς ἔην γαίης, ἧι χειμέριον ἀλὲν ὕδωρ   420
ἐξέρρηξεν ὁδοῖο, βάθυνε δὲ χῶρον ἅπαντα·
τῆι ῥ' εἶχεν Μενέλαος ἁματροχιὰς ἀλεείνων.
Ἀντίλοχος δὲ παρατρέψας ἔχε μώνυχας ἵππους
ἐκτὸς ὁδοῦ, ὀλίγον δὲ παρακλίνας ἐδίωκεν.
Ἀτρεΐδης δ' ἔδδεισε καὶ Ἀντιλόχωι ἐγεγώνει·   425
'Ἀντίλοχ', ἀφραδέως ἱππάζεαι· ἀλλ' ἄνεχ' ἵππους·
στεινωπὸς γὰρ ὁδός, τάχα δ' εὐρυτέρηι παρελάσσεις·
μή πως ἀμφοτέρους δηλήσεαι ἅρματι κύρσας.'
ὣς ἔφατ', Ἀντίλοχος δ' ἔτι καὶ πολὺ μᾶλλον ἔλαυνεν
κέντρωι ἐπισπέρχων, ὡς οὐκ ἀΐοντι ἐοικώς.   430
ὅσσα δὲ δίσκου οὖρα κατωμαδίοιο πέλονται,
ὅν τ' αἰζηὸς ἀφῆκεν ἀνὴρ πειρώμενος ἥβης,
τόσσον ἐπιδραμέτην· αἳ δ' ἠρώησαν ὀπίσσω
Ἀτρεΐδεω· αὐτὸς γὰρ ἑκὼν μεθέηκεν ἐλαύνειν,
μή πως συγκύρσειαν ὁδῶι ἔνι μώνυχες ἵπποι,   435
δίφρους τ' ἀνστρέψειαν ἐϋπλεκέας, κατὰ δ' αὐτοὶ
ἐν κονίηισι πέσοιεν ἐπειγόμενοι περὶ νίκης.
τὸν καὶ νεικείων προσέφη ξανθὸς Μενέλαος·
'Ἀντίλοχ', οὔ τις σεῖο βροτῶν ὀλοώτερος ἄλλος.
ἔρρ', ἐπεὶ οὔ σ' ἔτυμόν γε φάμεν πεπνῦσθαι Ἀχαιοί.   440
ἀλλ' οὐ μὰν οὐδ' ὣς ἄτερ ὅρκου οἴσηι ἄεθλον.'
ὣς εἰπὼν ἵπποισιν ἐκέκλετο φώνησέν τε·
'μή μοι ἐρύκεσθον μηδ' ἕστατον ἀχνυμένω κῆρ.
φθήσονται τούτοισι πόδες καὶ γοῦνα καμόντα
ἢ ὑμῖν· ἄμφω γὰρ ἀτέμβονται νεότητος.'   445
ὣς ἔφαθ', οἳ δὲ ἄνακτος ὑποδδείσαντες ὁμοκλὴν
μᾶλλον ἐπιδραμέτην, τάχα δέ σφισιν ἄγχι γένοντο.
Ἀργεῖοι δ' ἐν ἀγῶνι καθήμενοι εἰσορόωντο
ἵππους· τοὶ δ' ἐπέτοντο κονίοντες πεδίοιο.

418 ἐπιδραμέτην: ἐπεδραμέτην   420 ῥωχμός: ῥωγμός   424 παρακλίνας: παρακλινθείς,
παρεκκλίνας   427 εὐρυτέρηι παρελάσσεις: εὐρυτέρη παρελάσσαι, παρελάσσαις   433
ἐπιδραμέτην: ἐπεδραμέτην   441 ὥς: ὡς, ὡς οἴσηι: οἴσε'   446 ὑποδδείσαντες:
ὑποδείσαντες   ὁμοκλήν: ὁμοκλήν   447 ἐπιδραμέτην: ἐπεδραμέτην

πρῶτος δ' Ἰδομενεὺς Κρητῶν ἀγὸς ἐφράσαθ' ἵππους·   450
ἧστο γὰρ ἐκτὸς ἀγῶνος ὑπέρτατος ἐν περιωπῆι·
τοῖο δ' ἄνευθεν ἐόντος ὁμοκλητῆρος ἀκούσας
ἔγνω, φράσσατο δ' ἵππον ἀριπρεπέα προὔχοντα,
ὃς τὸ μὲν ἄλλο τόσον φοῖνιξ ἦν, ἐν δὲ μετώπωι
λευκὸν σῆμα τέτυκτο, περίτροχον ἠΰτε μήνη.   455
στῆ δ' ὀρθὸς καὶ μῦθον ἐν Ἀργείοισιν ἔειπεν·
'ὦ φίλοι, Ἀργείων ἡγήτορες ἠδὲ μέδοντες,
οἶος ἐγὼν ἵππους αὐγάζομαι, ἦε καὶ ὑμεῖς;
ἄλλοί μοι δοκέουσι παροίτεροι ἔμμεναι ἵπποι,
ἄλλος δ' ἡνίοχος ἰνδάλλεται· αἱ δέ που αὐτοῦ   460
ἔβλαβεν ἐν πεδίωι, αἱ κεῖσέ γε φέρτεραι ἦσαν·
ἤτοι γὰρ τὰς πρῶτα ἴδον περὶ τέρμα βαλούσας,
νῦν δ' οὔ πηι δύναμαι ἰδέειν, πάντηι δέ μοι ὄσσε
Τρωϊκὸν ἂμ πεδίον παπταίνετον εἰσορόωντι·
ἠὲ τὸν ἡνίοχον φύγον ἡνία, οὐδὲ δυνάσθη   465
εὖ σχεθέειν περὶ τέρμα, καὶ οὐκ ἐτύχησεν ἑλίξας·
ἔνθά μιν ἐκπεσέειν ὀΐω σύν θ' ἄρματα ἆξαι,
αἱ δ' ἐξηρώησαν, ἐπεὶ μένος ἔλλαβε θυμόν.
ἀλλὰ ἴδεσθε καὶ ὔμμες ἀνασταδόν· οὐ γὰρ ἔγωγε
εὖ διαγινώσκω· δοκέει δέ μοι ἔμμεναι ἀνὴρ   470
Αἰτωλὸς γενεήν, μετὰ δ' Ἀργείοισιν ἀνάσσει,
Τυδέος ἱπποδάμου υἱός, κρατερὸς Διομήδης.'
τὸν δ' αἰσχρῶς ἐνένιπεν Ὀϊλῆος ταχὺς Αἴας·
'Ἰδομενεῦ, τί πάρος λαβρεύεαι; αἱ δ' ἔτ' ἄνευθεν
ἵπποι ἀερσίποδες πολέος πεδίοιο δίενται.   475
οὔτε νεώτατός ἐσσι μετ' Ἀργείοισι τοσοῦτον,
οὔτέ τοι ὀξύτατον κεφαλῆς ἐκδέρκεται ὄσσε·
ἀλλ' αἰεὶ μύθοις λαβρεύεαι· οὐδέ τί σε χρὴ
λαβραγόρην ἔμεναι· πάρα γὰρ καὶ ἀμείνονες ἄλλοι.
ἵπποι δ' αὐταὶ ἔασι παροίτεραι, αἳ τὸ πάρος περ,   480
Εὐμήλου, ἐν δ' αὐτὸς ἔχων εὔληρα βέβηκεν.'
τὸν δὲ χολωσάμενος Κρητῶν ἀγὸς ἀντίον ηὔδα·
'Αἶαν, νεῖκος ἄριστε, κακοφραδές, ἄλλα τε πάντα
δεύεαι Ἀργείων, ὅτι τοι νόος ἐστὶν ἀπηνής.

---

452 ὁμοκλητῆρος: ὁμοκλητῆρος   **454** τόσον: δέμας   **455** σῆμα τέτυκτο: σῆμ' ἐτέτυκτο   **470** διαγινώσκω: διαγιγνώσκω   **471** ἀνάσσει: ἀνάσσειν   **472** ἱπποδάμου: ἱπποδάμοιο   **483** νεῖκος: νείκει

δεῦρό νυν, ἢ τρίποδος περιδώμεθον ἠὲ λέβητος,   485
ἵστορα δ' Ἀτρεΐδην Ἀγαμέμνονα θείομεν ἄμφω,
ὁππότεραι πρόσθ' ἵπποι, ἵνα γνώῃς ἀποτίνων.'
ὣς ἔφατ', ὤρνυτο δ' αὐτίκ' Ὀϊλῆος ταχὺς Αἴας
χωόμενος χαλεποῖσιν ἀμείψασθαι ἐπέεσσιν.
καί νύ κε δὴ προτέρω ἔτ' ἔρις γένετ' ἀμφοτέροισιν,   490
εἰ μὴ Ἀχιλλεὺς αὐτὸς ἀνίστατο καὶ φάτο μῦθον·
'μηκέτι νῦν χαλεποῖσιν ἀμείβεσθον ἐπέεσσιν,
Αἶαν Ἰδομενεῦ τε, κακοῖς, ἐπεὶ οὐδὲ ἔοικεν.
καὶ δ' ἄλλωι νεμεσᾶτον, ὅτις τοιαῦτά γε ῥέζοι.
ἀλλ' ὑμεῖς ἐν ἀγῶνι καθήμενοι εἰσοράασθε   495
ἵππους· οἱ δὲ τάχ' αὐτοὶ ἐπειγόμενοι περὶ νίκης
ἐνθάδ' ἐλεύσονται· τότε δὲ γνώσεσθε ἕκαστος
ἵππους Ἀργείων, οἳ δεύτεροι οἵ τε πάροιθεν.'
ὣς φάτο, Τυδεΐδης δὲ μάλα σχεδὸν ἦλθε διώκων,
μάστι δ' αἰὲν ἔλαυνε κατωμαδόν, οἱ δέ οἱ ἵπποι   500
ὑψόσ' ἀειρέσθην ῥίμφα πρήσσοντε κέλευθον.
αἰεὶ δ' ἡνίοχον κονίης ῥαθάμιγγες ἔβαλλον,
ἅρματα δὲ χρυσῶι πεπυκασμένα κασσιτέρωι τε
ἵπποις ὠκυπόδεσσιν ἐπέτρεχον· οὐδέ τι πολλὴ
γίνετ' ἐπισσώτρων ἁρματροχιὴ κατόπισθεν   505
ἐν λεπτῆι κονίηι· τὼ δὲ σπεύδοντε πετέσθην.
στῆ δὲ μέσωι ἐν ἀγῶνι, πολὺς δ' ἀνεκήκιεν ἱδρὼς
ἵππων ἔκ τε λόφων καὶ ἀπὸ στέρνοιο χαμᾶζε.
αὐτὸς δ' ἐκ δίφροιο χαμαὶ θόρε παμφανόωντος,
κλῖνε δ' ἄρα μάστιγα ποτὶ ζυγόν. οὐδὲ μάτησεν   510
ἴφθιμος Σθένελος, ἀλλ' ἐσσυμένως λάβ' ἄεθλον,
δῶκε δ' ἄγειν ἑτάροισιν ὑπερθύμοισι γυναῖκα
καὶ τρίποδ' ὠτώεντα φέρειν· ὃ δ' ἔλυεν ὑφ' ἵππους.
τῶι δ' ἄρ' ἐπ' Ἀντίλοχος Νηλήϊος ἤλασεν ἵππους,
κέρδεσιν, οὔ τι τάχεϊ γε, παραφθάμενος Μενέλαον·   515
ἀλλὰ καὶ ὣς Μενέλαος ἔχ' ἐγγύθεν ὠκέας ἵππους.
ὅσσον δὲ τροχοῦ ἵππος ἀφίσταται, ὅς ῥά τ' ἄνακτα
ἕλκῃσιν πεδίοιο τιταινόμενος σὺν ὄχεσφιν·

---

485 περιδώμεθον: περιδώμεθα   488 ὤρνυτο: ὄρνυτο   494 ῥέζοι: ῥέζῃ   505 γίνετ':
γίγνετ'   ἐπισσώτρων: ὀπισσώτρων   510 οὐδὲ μάτησεν: οὐδ' ἐμάτησεν   513 δ' ἔλυεν:
δὲ λῦεν   516 ὣς: ὡς, ὣς

τοῦ μέν τε ψαύουσιν ἐπισσώτρου τρίχες ἄκραι
οὐραῖαι, ὃ δέ τ' ἄγχι μάλα τρέχει, οὐδέ τι πολλὴ   520
χώρη μεσσηγύς, πολέος πεδίοιο θέοντος·
τόσσον δὴ Μενέλαος ἀμύμονος Ἀντιλόχοιο
λείπετ'· ἀτὰρ τὰ πρῶτα καὶ ἐς δίσκουρα λέλειπτο,
ἀλλά μιν αἶψα κίχανεν· ὀφέλλετο γὰρ μένος ἠΰ
ἵππου τῆς Ἀγαμεμνονέης, καλλίτριχος Αἴθης.   525
εἰ δέ κ' ἔτι προτέρω γένετο δρόμος ἀμφοτέροισιν,
τῶ κέν μιν παρέλασσ' οὐδ' ἀμφήριστον ἔθηκεν.
αὐτὰρ Μηριόνης, θεράπων ἐΰς Ἰδομενῆος,
λείπετ' ἀγακλῆος Μενελάου δουρὸς ἐρωήν·
βάρδιστοι μὲν γὰρ οἱ ἔσαν καλλίτριχες ἵπποι,   530
ἥκιστος δ' ἦν αὐτὸς ἐλαυνέμεν ἅρμ' ἐν ἀγῶνι.
υἱὸς δ' Ἀδμήτοιο πανύστατος ἤλυθεν ἄλλων,
ἕλκων ἅρματα καλά, ἐλαύνων πρόσσοθεν ἵππους.
τὸν δὲ ἰδὼν ὤικτειρε ποδάρκης δῖος Ἀχιλλεύς,
στὰς δ' ἄρ' ἐν Ἀργείοις ἔπεα πτερόεντ' ἀγόρευεν·   535
λοῖσθος ἀνὴρ ὤριστος ἐλαύνει μώνυχας ἵππους.
ἀλλ' ἄγε δή οἱ δῶμεν ἀέθλιον, ὡς ἐπιεικές,
δεύτερ'· ἀτὰρ τὰ πρῶτα φερέσθω Τυδέος υἱός.'
ὡς ἔφαθ', οἳ δ' ἄρα πάντες ἐπήινεον ὡς ἐκέλευεν.
καί νύ κέ οἱ πόρεν ἵππον, ἐπήινησαν γὰρ Ἀχαιοί,   540
εἰ μὴ ἄρ' Ἀντίλοχος μεγαθύμου Νέστορος υἱὸς
Πηλεΐδην Ἀχιλῆα δίκηι ἠμείψατ' ἀναστάς·
'ὦ Ἀχιλεῦ, μάλα τοι κεχολώσομαι, αἴ κε τελέσσηις
τοῦτο ἔπος· μέλλεις γὰρ ἀφαιρήσεσθαι ἄεθλον,
τὰ φρονέων, ὅτι οἱ βλάβεν ἅρματα καὶ ταχέ' ἵππω   545
αὐτός τ' ἐσθλὸς ἐών. ἀλλ' ὤφελεν ἀθανάτοισιν
εὔχεσθαι· τό κ' οὔ τι πανύστατος ἦλθε διώκων.
εἰ δέ μιν οἰκτείρεις καί τοι φίλον ἔπλετο θυμῶι,
ἔστι τοι ἐν κλισίηι χρυσὸς πολύς, ἔστι δὲ χαλκὸς
καὶ πρόβατ', εἰσὶ δέ τοι δμωιαὶ καὶ μώνυχες ἵπποι·   550
τῶν οἱ ἔπειτ' ἀνελὼν δόμεναι καὶ μεῖζον ἄεθλον,
ἠὲ καὶ αὐτίκα νῦν, ἵνα σ' αἰνήσωσιν Ἀχαιοί.
τὴν δ' ἐγὼ οὐ δώσω· περὶ δ' αὐτῆς πειρηθήτω

---

519 ἐπισσώτρου: ὀπισσώτρου   **526** δέ κ' ἔτι: δ' ἔτι καί   **531** ἥκιστος: ἥκιστος
533 πρόσσοθεν: ὠκέας, μώνυχας   **534** ὤικτειρε: ὤικτιρε   **536** ὤριστος: ὤριστος
548 οἰκτείρεις: οἰκτίρεις   φίλον: φίλος   **550** εἰσί: εἰσι

ἀνδρῶν ὅς κ' ἐθέλησιν ἐμοὶ χείρεσσι μάχεσθαι.'
ὣς φάτο, μείδησεν δὲ ποδάρκης δῖος Ἀχιλλεύς, 555
χαίρων Ἀντιλόχωι, ὅτι οἱ φίλος ἦεν ἑταῖρος,
καί μιν ἀμειβόμενος ἔπεα πτερόεντα προσηύδα·
'Ἀντίλοχ', εἰ μὲν δή με κελεύεις οἴκοθεν ἄλλο
Εὐμήλωι ἐπιδοῦναι, ἐγὼ δέ κε καὶ τὸ τελέσσω.
δώσω οἱ θώρηκα, τὸν Ἀστεροπαῖον ἀπηύρων, 560
χάλκεον, ὧι πέρι χεῦμα φαεινοῦ κασσιτέροιο
ἀμφιδεδίνηται· πολέος δέ οἱ ἄξιον ἔσται.'
ἦ ῥα, καὶ Αὐτομέδοντι φίλωι ἐκέλευσεν ἑταίρωι
οἰσέμεναι κλισίηθεν· ὃ δ' ὤιχετο καί οἱ ἔνεικεν.
[Εὐμήλωι δ' ἐν χερσὶ τίθει· ὃ δ' ἐδέξατο χαίρων.] 565
τοῖσι δὲ καὶ Μενέλαος ἀνίστατο θυμὸν ἀχεύων,
Ἀντιλόχωι ἄμοτον κεχολωμένος· ἐν δ' ἄρα κῆρυξ
χερσὶ σκῆπτρον ἔθηκε, σιωπῆσαί τ' ἐκέλευσεν
Ἀργείους. ὃ δ' ἔπειτα μετηύδα ἰσόθεος φώς·
'Ἀντίλοχε, πρόσθεν πεπνυμένε, ποῖον ἔρεξας; 570
ἤισχυνας μὲν ἐμὴν ἀρετήν, βλάψας δέ μοι ἵππους,
τοὺς σοὺς πρόσθε βαλών, οἵ τοι πολὺ χείρονες ἦσαν.
ἀλλ' ἄγετ', Ἀργείων ἡγήτορες ἠδὲ μέδοντες,
ἐς μέσον ἀμφοτέροισι δικάσσατε, μηδ' ἐπ' ἀρωγῆι,
μή ποτέ τις εἴπηισιν Ἀχαιῶν χαλκοχιτώνων· 575
'Ἀντίλοχον ψεύδεσσι βιησάμενος Μενέλαος
οἴχεται ἵππον ἄγων, ὅτι οἱ πολὺ χείρονες ἦσαν
ἵπποι, αὐτὸς δὲ κρείσσων ἀρετῆι τε βίηι τε.'
εἰ δ' ἄγ' ἐγὼν αὐτὸς δικάσω, καί μ' οὔ τινά φημι
ἄλλον ἐπιπλήξειν Δαναῶν· ἰθεῖα γὰρ ἔσται. 580
Ἀντίλοχ', εἰ δ' ἄγε δεῦρο, διοτρεφές, ἣ θέμις ἐστίν,
στὰς ἵππων προπάροιθε καὶ ἅρματος, αὐτὰρ ἱμάσθλην
χερσὶν ἔχε ῥαδινήν, ἧι περ τὸ πρόσθεν ἔλαυνες·
ἵππων ἁψάμενος γαιήοχον Ἐννοσίγαιον
ὄμνυθι μὴ μὲν ἑκὼν τὸ ἐμὸν δόλωι ἅρμα πεδῆσαι.' 585
τὸν δ' αὖτ' Ἀντίλοχος πεπνυμένος ἀντίον ηὔδα·
'ἄνσχεο νῦν· πολλὸν γὰρ ἔγωγε νεώτερός εἰμι
σεῖο, ἄναξ Μενέλαε, σὺ δὲ πρότερος καὶ ἀρείων.
οἶσθ' οἷαι νέου ἀνδρὸς ὑπερβασίαι τελέθουσιν·

565 secl. et nonnulli **568** χερσί: χειρί   τ' ἐκέλευσεν: τε κέλευσεν

κραιπνότερος μὲν γάρ τε νόος, λεπτὴ δέ τε μῆτις.   590
τῶ τοι ἐπιτλήτω κραδίη· ἵππον δέ τοι αὐτὸς
δώσω, τὴν ἀρόμην. εἰ καί νύ κεν οἴκοθεν ἄλλο
μεῖζον ἐπαιτήσειας, ἄφαρ κέ τοι αὐτίκα δοῦναι
βουλοίμην ἢ σοί γε, διοτρεφές, ἤματα πάντα
ἐκ θυμοῦ πεσέειν καὶ δαίμοσιν εἶναι ἀλιτρός.'   595
ἦ ῥα, καὶ ἵππον ἄγων μεγαθύμου Νέστορος υἱὸς
ἐν χείρεσσι τίθει Μενελάου. τοῖο δὲ θυμὸς
ἰάνθη, ὡς εἴ τε περὶ σταχύεσσιν ἐέρση
ληΐου ἀλδήσκοντος, ὅτε φρίσσουσιν ἄρουραι·
ὣς ἄρα σοί, Μενέλαε, μετὰ φρεσὶ θυμὸς ἰάνθη.   600
καί μιν φωνήσας ἔπεα πτερόεντα προσηύδα·
'Ἀντίλοχε, νῦν μέν τοι ἐγὼν ὑποείξομαι αὐτὸς
χωόμενος, ἐπεὶ οὔ τι παρήορος οὐδ' ἀεσίφρων
ἦσθα πάρος· νῦν αὖτε νόον νίκησε νεοίη.
δεύτερον αὖτ' ἀλέασθαι ἀμείνονας ἠπεροπεύειν.   605
οὐ γὰρ κέν με τάχ' ἄλλος ἀνὴρ παρέπεισεν Ἀχαιῶν·
ἀλλὰ σὺ γὰρ δὴ πόλλ' ἔπαθες καὶ πόλλ' ἐμόγησας,
σός τε πατὴρ ἀγαθὸς καὶ ἀδελφεός, εἵνεκ' ἐμεῖο·
τῶ τοι λισσομένωι ἐπιπείσομαι, ἠδὲ καὶ ἵππον
δώσω ἐμήν περ ἐοῦσαν, ἵνα γνώωσι καὶ οἵδε   610
ὡς ἐμὸς οὔ ποτε θυμὸς ὑπερφίαλος καὶ ἀπηνής.'
ἦ ῥα, καὶ Ἀντιλόχοιο Νοήμονι δῶκεν ἑταίρωι
ἵππον ἄγειν· ὃ δ' ἔπειτα λέβηθ' ἕλε παμφανόωντα.
Μηριόνης δ' ἀνάειρε δύω χρυσοῖο τάλαντα
τέτρατος, ὡς ἔλασεν. πέμπτον δ' ὑπελείπετ' ἄεθλον,   615
ἀμφίθετος φιάλη· τὴν Νέστορι δῶκεν Ἀχιλλεὺς
Ἀργείων ἀν' ἀγῶνα φέρων, καὶ εἶπε παραστάς·
'τῆ νῦν, καὶ σοὶ τοῦτο, γέρον, κειμήλιον ἔστω,
Πατρόκλοιο τάφου μνῆμ' ἔμμεναι· οὐ γὰρ ἔτ' αὐτὸν
ὄψει ἐν Ἀργείοισι. δίδωμι δέ τοι τόδ' ἄεθλον   620
αὔτως· οὐ γὰρ πύξ γε μαχήσεαι, οὐδὲ παλαίσεις,
οὐδέ τ' ἀκοντιστὺν ἐσδύσεαι, οὐδὲ πόδεσσιν
θεύσεαι· ἤδη γὰρ χαλεπὸν κατὰ γῆρας ἐπείγει.'
ὣς εἰπὼν ἐν χερσὶ τίθει· ὃ δ' ἐδέξατο χαίρων,
καί μιν φωνήσας ἔπεα πτερόεντα προσηύδα·   625

598 ἐέρση: ἐέρσηι   599 φρίσσουσιν: φρίσσωσιν   600 σοί: τοι   607 πόλλ' ἐμόγησας:
πολλὰ μόγησας   618 νῦν: νυν   620 ὄψει: ὄψε', ὄψηι   624 δ' ἐδέξατο: δὲ δέξατο

'ναὶ δὴ ταῦτά γε πάντα, τέκος, κατὰ μοῖραν ἔειπες·
οὐ γὰρ ἔτ' ἔμπεδα γυῖα, φίλος, πόδες, οὐδέ τι χεῖρες
ὤμων ἀμφοτέρωθεν ἐπαΐσσονται ἐλαφραί.
εἴθ' ὡς ἡβώοιμι βίη τέ μοι ἔμπεδος εἴη
ὡς ὁπότε κρείοντ' Ἀμαρυγκέα θάπτον Ἐπειοὶ   630
Βουπρασίωι, παῖδες δ' ἔθεσαν βασιλῆος ἄεθλα·
ἔνθ' οὔ τίς μοι ὁμοῖος ἀνὴρ γένετ', οὔτ' ἄρ' Ἐπειῶν
οὔτ' αὐτῶν Πυλίων οὔτ' Αἰτωλῶν μεγαθύμων.
πὺξ μὲν ἐνίκησα Κλυτομήδεα, Ἤνοπος υἱόν,
Ἀγκαῖον δὲ πάληι Πλευρώνιον, ὅς μοι ἀνέστη·   635
Ἴφικλον δὲ πόδεσσι παρέδραμον ἐσθλὸν ἐόντα,
δουρὶ δ' ὑπειρέβαλον Φυλῆά τε καὶ Πολύδωρον.
οἴοισίν μ' ἵπποισι παρήλασαν Ἀκτορίωνε,
πλήθει πρόσθε βαλόντες, ἀγασσάμενοι περὶ νίκης,
οὕνεκα δὴ τὰ μέγιστα παρ' αὐτόφι λείπετ' ἄεθλα.   640
οἳ δ' ἄρ' ἔσαν δίδυμοι· ὃ μὲν ἔμπεδον ἡνιόχευεν,
ἔμπεδον ἡνιόχευ', ὃ δ' ἄρα μάστιγι κέλευεν.
ὥς ποτ' ἔον· νῦν αὖτε νεώτεροι ἀντιοώντων
ἔργων τοιούτων. ἐμὲ δὲ χρὴ γήραϊ λυγρῶι
πείθεσθαι· τότε δ' αὖτε μετέπρεπον ἡρώεσσιν.   645
ἀλλ' ἴθι καὶ σὸν ἑταῖρον ἀέθλοισι κτερέιζε.
τοῦτο δ' ἐγὼ πρόφρων δέχομαι, χαίρει δέ μοι ἦτορ,
ὥς μευ ἀεὶ μέμνησαι ἐνηέος, οὐδέ σε λήθω
τιμῆς ἧς τέ μ' ἔοικε τετιμῆσθαι μετ' Ἀχαιοῖς.
σοὶ δὲ θεοὶ τῶνδ' ἀντὶ χάριν μενοεικέα δοῖεν.'   650
ὣς φάτο, Πηλεΐδης δὲ πολὺν καθ' ὅμιλον Ἀχαιῶν
ὤιχετ', ἐπεὶ πάντ' αἶνον ἐπέκλυε Νηλεΐδαο.
αὐτὰρ ὁ πυγμαχίης ἀλεγεινῆς θῆκεν ἄεθλα·
ἡμίονον ταλαεργὸν ἄγων κατέδησ' ἐν ἀγῶνι
ἑξέτε' ἀδμήτην, ἥ τ' ἀλγίστη δαμάσασθαι·   655
τῶι δ' ἄρα νικηθέντι τίθει δέπας ἀμφικύπελλον.
στῆ δ' ὀρθὸς καὶ μῦθον ἐν Ἀργείοισιν ἔειπεν·
'Ἀτρεΐδη τε καὶ ἄλλοι ἐυκνήμιδες Ἀχαιοί,
ἄνδρε δύω περὶ τῶνδε κελεύομεν, ὥ περ ἀρίστω,
πὺξ μάλ' ἀνασχομένω πεπληγέμεν· ὧι δέ κ' Ἀπόλλων   660

626 om. quaedam MSS, Σ   631 δ' ἔθεσαν: δὲ θέσαν   640 παρ' αὐτόφι: παρ' αὐτόθι
648 μέμνησαι: μέμνηαι

δώηι καμμονίην, γνώωσι δὲ πάντες Ἀχαιοί,
ἡμίονον ταλαεργὸν ἄγων κλισίηνδε νεέσθω·
αὐτὰρ ὃ νικηθεὶς δέπας οἴσεται ἀμφικύπελλον.'
ὣς ἔφατ', ὤρνυτο δ' αὐτίκ' ἀνὴρ ἠΰς τε μέγας τε
εἰδὼς πυγμαχίης, υἱὸς Πανοπῆος Ἐπειός,   665
ἅψατο δ' ἡμιόνου ταλαεργοῦ φώνησέν τε·
'ἆσσον ἴτω, ὅς τις δέπας οἴσεται ἀμφικύπελλον·
ἡμίονον δ' οὔ φημί τιν' ἀξέμεν ἄλλον Ἀχαιῶν
πυγμῆι νικήσαντ', ἐπεὶ εὔχομαι εἶναι ἄριστος.
ἦ οὐχ ἅλις, ὅττι μάχης ἐπιδεύομαι; οὐδ' ἄρα πως ἦν   670
ἐν πάντεσσ' ἔργοισι δαήμονα φῶτα γενέσθαι.
ὧδε γὰρ ἐξερέω, τὸ δὲ καὶ τετελεσμένον ἔσται·
ἀντικρὺ χρόα τε ῥήξω σύν τ' ὀστέ' ἀράξω.
κηδεμόνες δέ οἱ ἐνθάδ' ἀολλέες αὖθι μενόντων,
οἵ κέ μιν ἐξοίσουσιν ἐμῆις ὑπὸ χερσὶ δαμέντα.'   675
ὣς ἔφαθ', οἱ δ' ἄρα πάντες ἀκὴν ἐγένοντο σιωπῆι.
Εὐρύαλος δέ οἱ οἶος ἀνίστατο, ἰσόθεος φώς,
Μηκιστέος υἱὸς Ταλαϊονίδαο ἄνακτος,
ὅς ποτε Θήβασδ' ἦλθε δεδουπότος Οἰδιπόδαο
ἐς τάφον· ἔνθα δὲ πάντας ἐνίκα Καδμείωνας.   680
τὸν μὲν Τυδεΐδης δουρικλυτὸς ἀμφεπονεῖτο
θαρσύνων ἔπεσιν, μέγα δ' αὐτῶι βούλετο νίκην.
ζῶμα δέ οἱ πρῶτον παρακάββαλεν, αὐτὰρ ἔπειτα
δῶκεν ἱμάντας ἐϋτμήτους βοὸς ἀγραύλοιο.
τὼ δὲ ζωσαμένω βήτην ἐς μέσσον ἀγῶνα,   685
ἄντα δ' ἀνασχομένω χερσὶ στιβαρῆισιν ἅμ' ἄμφω
σύν ῥ' ἔπεσον, σὺν δέ σφι βαρεῖαι χεῖρες ἔμιχθεν.
δεινὸς δὲ χρόμαδος γενύων γένετ', ἔρρεε δ' ἱδρὼς
πάντοθεν ἐκ μελέων· ἐπὶ δ' ὤρνυτο δῖος Ἐπειός,
κόψε δὲ παπτήναντα παρήϊον· οὐδ' ἄρ' ἔτι δὴν   690
ἑστήκειν, αὐτοῦ γὰρ ὑπήριπε φαίδιμα γυῖα.
ὡς δ' ὅθ' ὑπὸ φρικὸς Βορέω ἀναπάλλεται ἰχθὺς
θίν' ἐν φυκιόεντι, μέλαν δέ ἑ κῦμ' ἐκάλυψεν,
ὣς πληγεὶς ἀνέπαλτ'· αὐτὰρ μεγάθυμος Ἐπειὸς
χερσὶ λαβὼν ὤρθωσε· φίλοι δ' ἀμφέσταν ἑταῖροι,   695

662 νεέσθω: φερέσθω 664 ὤρνυτο: ὄρνυτο 666 ἅψατο: ἥψατο 667 ἆσσον: ἆσσον 678 Μηκιστέος: Μηκιστῆος 683 παρακάββαλεν: περικάββαλεν 689 ὤρνυτο: ὄρνυτο 693 κῦμ' ἐκάλυψεν: κῦμα κάλυψεν

οἵ μιν ἄγον δι' ἀγῶνος ἐφελκομένοισι πόδεσσιν,
αἷμα παχὺ πτύοντα, κάρη βάλλονθ' ἑτέρωσε·
κὰδ δ' ἀλλοφρονέοντα μετὰ σφίσιν εἷσαν ἄγοντες,
αὐτοὶ δ' οἰχόμενοι κόμισαν δέπας ἀμφικύπελλον.
Πηλεΐδης δ' αἶψ' ἄλλα κατὰ τρίτα θῆκεν ἄεθλα,   700
δεικνύμενος Δαναοῖσι, παλαισμοσύνης ἀλεγεινῆς,
τῶι μὲν νικήσαντι μέγαν τρίποδ' ἐμπυριβήτην,
τὸν δὲ δυωδεκάβοιον ἐνὶ σφίσι τῖον Ἀχαιοί·
ἀνδρὶ δὲ νικηθέντι γυναῖκ' ἐς μέσσον ἔθηκεν,
πολλὰ δ' ἐπίστατο ἔργα, τίον δέ ἑ τεσσαράβοιον.   705
στῆ δ' ὀρθὸς καὶ μῦθον ἐν Ἀργείοισιν ἔειπεν·
'ὄρνυσθ', οἳ καὶ τούτου ἀέθλου πειρήσεσθον.'
ὣς ἔφατ', ὦρτο δ' ἔπειτα μέγας Τελαμώνιος Αἴας,
ἂν δ' Ὀδυσεὺς πολύμητις ἀνίστατο, κέρδεα εἰδώς.
ζωσαμένω δ' ἄρα τώ γε βάτην ἐς μέσσον ἀγῶνα,   710
ἀγκὰς δ' ἀλλήλων λαβέτην χερσὶ στιβαρῆισιν,
ὡς ὅτ' ἀμείβοντες τούς τε κλυτὸς ἤραρε Τέκτων
δώματος ὑψηλοῖο, βίας ἀνέμων ἀλεείνων.
τετρίγει δ' ἄρα νῶτα θρασειάων ἀπὸ χειρῶν
ἑλκόμενα στερεῶς· κατὰ δὲ νότιος ῥέεν ἱδρώς,   715
πυκναὶ δὲ σμώδιγγες ἀνὰ πλευράς τε καὶ ὤμους
αἵματι φοινικόεσσαι ἀνέδραμον· οἳ δὲ μάλ' αἰεὶ
νίκης ἱέσθην τρίποδος πέρι ποιητοῖο·
οὔτ' Ὀδυσεὺς δύνατο σφῆλαι οὔδει τε πελάσσαι,
οὔτ' Αἴας δύνατο, κρατερὴ δ' ἔχεν ἲς Ὀδυσῆος.   720
ἀλλ' ὅτε δή ῥ' ἀνίαζον ἐϋκνήμιδες Ἀχαιοί,
δὴ τότε μιν προσέειπε μέγας Τελαμώνιος Αἴας·
'διογενὲς Λαερτιάδη, πολυμήχαν' Ὀδυσσεῦ,
ἤ μ' ἀνάειρ', ἢ ἐγὼ σέ· τὰ δ' αὖ Διὶ πάντα μελήσει.'
ὣς εἰπὼν ἀνάειρε· δόλου δ' οὐ λήθετ' Ὀδυσσεύς·   725
κόψ' ὄπιθεν κώληπα τυχών, ὑπέλυσε δὲ γυῖα,
κὰδ δ' ἔβαλ' ἐξοπίσω· ἐπὶ δὲ στήθεσσιν Ὀδυσσεὺς
κάππεσε· λαοὶ δ' αὖ θηεῦντό τε θάμβησάν τε.
δεύτερος αὖτ' ἀνάειρε πολύτλας δῖος Ὀδυσσεύς,
κίνησεν δ' ἄρα τυτθὸν ἀπὸ χθονός, οὐδ' ἔτ' ἄειρεν,   730

---

701 παλαισμοσύνης: παλαιμοσύνης   **705** τεσσαράβοιον: τεσσεράβοιον   **712** Τέκτων:
τέκτων   **727** ἔβαλ': ἔπεσ'

ἐν δὲ γόνυ γνάμψεν· ἐπὶ δὲ χθονὶ κάππεσον ἄμφω
πλησίοι ἀλλήλοισι, μιάνθησαν δὲ κονίηι.
καί νύ κε τὸ τρίτον αὖτις ἀναΐξαντ' ἐπάλαιον,
εἰ μὴ Ἀχιλλεὺς αὐτὸς ἀνίστατο καὶ κατέρυκεν·
'μηκέτ' ἐρείδεσθον, μηδὲ τρίβεσθε κακοῖσιν· 735
νίκη δ' ἀμφοτέροισιν· ἀέθλια δ' ἶσ' ἀνελόντες
ἔρχεσθ', ὄφρα καὶ ἄλλοι ἀεθλεύωσιν Ἀχαιοί.'
ὣς ἔφαθ', οἳ δ' ἄρα τοῦ μάλα μὲν κλύον ἠδ' ἐπίθοντο,
καί ῥ' ἀπομορξαμένω κονίην δύσαντο χιτῶνας.
Πηλεΐδης δ' αἶψ' ἄλλα τίθει ταχυτῆτος ἄεθλα, 740
ἀργύρεον κρητῆρα τετυγμένον· ἓξ δ' ἄρα μέτρα
χάνδανεν, αὐτὰρ κάλλει ἐνίκα πᾶσαν ἐπ' αἶαν
πολλόν, ἐπεὶ Σιδόνες πολυδαίδαλοι εὖ ἤσκησαν,
Φοίνικες δ' ἄγον ἄνδρες ἐπ' ἠεροειδέα πόντον,
στῆσαν δ' ἐν λιμένεσσι, Θόαντι δὲ δῶρον ἔδωκαν· 745
υἱὸς δὲ Πριάμοιο Λυκάονος ὦνον ἔδωκεν
Πατρόκλωι ἥρωϊ Ἰησονίδης Εὔνηος.
καὶ τὸν Ἀχιλλεὺς θῆκεν ἄεθλιον οὗ ἑτάροιο,
ὅς τις ἐλαφρότατος ποσσὶ κραιπνοῖσι πέλοιτο·
δευτέρωι αὖ βοῦν θῆκε μέγαν καὶ πίονα δημῶι, 750
ἡμιτάλαντον δὲ χρυσοῦ λοισθήϊ' ἔθηκεν.
στῆ δ' ὀρθὸς καὶ μῦθον ἐν Ἀργείοισιν ἔειπεν·
'ὄρνυσθ', οἳ καὶ τούτου ἀέθλου πειρήσεσθε.'
ὣς ἔφατ', ὤρνυτο δ' αὐτίκ' Ὀϊλῆος ταχὺς Αἴας,
ἂν δ' Ὀδυσεὺς πολύμητις, ἔπειτα δὲ Νέστορος υἱός 755
Ἀντίλοχος· ὃ γὰρ αὖτε νέους ποσὶ πάντας ἐνίκα.
στὰν δὲ μεταστοιχεί· σήμηνε δὲ τέρματ' Ἀχιλλεύς.
τοῖσι δ' ἀπὸ νύσσης τέτατο δρόμος· ὦκα δ' ἔπειτα
ἔκφερ' Ὀϊλιάδης· ἐπὶ δ' ὤρνυτο δῖος Ὀδυσσεὺς
ἄγχι μάλ', ὡς ὅτε τίς τε γυναικὸς ἐϋζώνοιο 760
στήθεός ἐστι κανών, ὅν τ' εὖ μάλα χερσὶ τανύσσηι
πηνίον ἐξέλκουσα παρὲκ μίτον, ἀγχόθι δ' ἴσχει
στήθεος· ὣς Ὀδυσεὺς θέεν ἐγγύθεν, αὐτὰρ ὄπισθεν
ἴχνια τύπτε πόδεσσι πάρος κόνιν ἀμφιχυθῆναι·
κὰδ δ' ἄρα οἱ κεφαλῆς χέ' ἀΰτμένα δῖος Ὀδυσσεὺς 765

733 ἀναΐξαντ' ἐπάλαιον: ἀναΐξαντα πάλαιον 735 ἐρείδεσθον: ἐρίδεσθον, ἐρίζεσθον
754 ὤρνυτο: ὄρνυτο 757 μεταστοιχεί: μεταστοιχί 759 ὤρνυτο: ὄρνυτο 765 οἱ: ἐκ

αἰεὶ ῥίμφα θέων· ἴαχον δ᾽ ἐπὶ πάντες Ἀχαιοὶ
νίκης ἱεμένωι, μάλα δὲ σπεύδοντι κέλευον.
ἀλλ᾽ ὅτε δὴ πύματον τέλεον δρόμον, αὐτίκ᾽ Ὀδυσσεὺς
εὔχετ᾽ Ἀθηναίηι γλαυκώπιδι ὃν κατὰ θυμόν·
ʾκλῦθι, θεά, ἀγαθή μοι ἐπίρροθος ἐλθὲ ποδοῖιν.ʾ   770
ὣς ἔφατ᾽ εὐχόμενος· τοῦ δ᾽ ἔκλυε Παλλὰς Ἀθήνη,
γυῖα δ᾽ ἔθηκεν ἐλαφρά, πόδας καὶ χεῖρας ὕπερθεν.
ἀλλ᾽ ὅτε δὴ τάχ᾽ ἔμελλον ἐπαΐξεσθαι ἄεθλον,
ἔνθ᾽ Αἴας μὲν ὄλισθε θέων, βλάψεν γὰρ Ἀθήνη,
τῆι ῥα βοῶν κέχυτ᾽ ὄνθος ἀποκταμένων ἐριμύκων,   775
οὓς ἐπὶ Πατρόκλωι πέφνεν πόδας ὠκὺς Ἀχιλλεύς·
ἐν δ᾽ ὄνθου βοέου πλῆτο στόμα τε ῥῖνάς τε·
κρητῆρ᾽ αὖτ᾽ ἀνάειρε πολύτλας δῖος Ὀδυσσεύς,
ὡς ἦλθε φθάμενος· ὁ δὲ βοῦν ἕλε φαίδιμος Αἴας·
στῆ δὲ κέρας μετὰ χερσὶν ἔχων βοὸς ἀγραύλοιο,   780
ὄνθον ἀποπτύων, μετὰ δ᾽ Ἀργείοισιν ἔειπεν·
ʾὢ πόποι, ἦ μ᾽ ἔβλαψε θεὰ πόδας, ἣ τὸ πάρος περ
μήτηρ ὣς Ὀδυσῆϊ παρίσταται ἠδ᾽ ἐπαρήγει.ʾ
ὣς ἔφαθ᾽, οἱ δ᾽ ἄρα πάντες ἐπ᾽ αὐτῶι ἡδὺ γέλασσαν.
Ἀντίλοχος δ᾽ ἄρα δὴ λοισθήϊον ἔκφερ᾽ ἄεθλον   785
μειδιόων, καὶ μῦθον ἐν Ἀργείοισιν ἔειπεν·
ʾεἰδόσιν ὔμμ᾽ ἐρέω πᾶσιν, φίλοι, ὡς ἔτι καὶ νῦν
ἀθάνατοι τιμῶσι παλαιοτέρους ἀνθρώπους.
Αἴας μὲν γὰρ ἐμεῖ᾽ ὀλίγον προγενέστερός ἐστιν,
οὗτος δὲ προτέρης γενεῆς προτέρων τ᾽ ἀνθρώπων·   790
ὠμογέροντα δέ μίν φασ᾽ ἔμμεναι· ἀργαλέον δὲ
ποσσὶν ἐριδήσασθαι Ἀχαιοῖς, εἰ μὴ Ἀχιλλεῖ.ʾ
ὣς φάτο, κύδηνεν δὲ ποδώκεα Πηλεΐωνα.
τὸν δ᾽ Ἀχιλεὺς μύθοισιν ἀμειβόμενος προσέειπεν·
ʾἈντίλοχ᾽, οὐ μέν τοι μέλεος εἰρήσεται αἶνος,   795
ἀλλά τοι ἡμιτάλαντον ἐγὼ χρυσοῦ ἐπιθήσω.ʾ
ὣς εἰπὼν ἐν χερσὶ τίθει, ὁ δ᾽ ἐδέξατο χαίρων.
αὐτὰρ Πηλεΐδης κατὰ μὲν δολιχόσκιον ἔγχος
θῆκ᾽ ἐς ἀγῶνα φέρων, κατὰ δ᾽ ἀσπίδα καὶ τρυφάλειαν,
τεύχεα Σαρπήδοντος, ἅ μιν Πάτροκλος ἀπηύρα.   800

---

767 ἱεμένωι: ἱέμενοι   **773** ἐπαΐξεσθαι: ἐπαΐξασθαι   **792** ἐριδήσασθαι damn. West et
alii   **797** δ᾽ ἐδέξατο: δὲ δέξατο

στῆ δ᾽ ὀρθὸς καὶ μῦθον ἐν Ἀργείοισιν ἔειπεν·
'ἄνδρε δύω περὶ τῶνδε κελεύομεν, ὥ περ ἀρίστω,
τεύχεα ἑσσαμένω, ταμεσίχροα χαλκὸν ἑλόντε,
ἀλλήλων προπάροιθεν ὁμίλου πειρηθῆναι.
ὁππότερός κε φθῇσιν ὀρεξάμενος χρόα καλόν,   805
ψαύσῃ δ᾽ ἐνδίνων διά τ᾽ ἔντεα καὶ μέλαν αἷμα,
τῶι μὲν ἐγὼ δώσω τόδε φάσγανον ἀργυρόηλον,
καλὸν Θρηΐκιον, τὸ μὲν Ἀστεροπαῖον ἀπηύρων·
τεύχεα δ᾽ ἀμφότεροι ξυνήϊα ταῦτα φερέσθων,
καί σφιν δαῖτ᾽ ἀγαθὴν παραθήσομεν ἐν κλισίῃσιν.'   810
ὣς ἔφατ᾽, ὦρτο δ᾽ ἔπειτα μέγας Τελαμώνιος Αἴας,
ἂν δ᾽ ἄρα Τυδεΐδης ὦρτο κρατερὸς Διομήδης.
οἳ δ᾽ ἐπεὶ οὖν ἑκάτερθεν ὁμίλου θωρήχθησαν,
ἐς μέσον ἀμφοτέρων συνίτην μεμαῶτε μάχεσθαι,
δεινὸν δερκομένω· θάμβος δ᾽ ἔχε πάντας Ἀχαιούς.   815
ἀλλ᾽ ὅτε δὴ σχεδὸν ἦσαν ἐπ᾽ ἀλλήλοισιν ἰόντες,
τρὶς μὲν ἐπήϊξαν, τρὶς δὲ σχεδὸν ὡρμήθησαν.
ἔνθ᾽ Αἴας μὲν ἔπειτα κατ᾽ ἀσπίδα πάντοσ᾽ ἐΐσην
νύξ᾽, οὐδὲ χρό᾽ ἵκανεν· ἔρυτο γὰρ ἔνδοθι θώρηξ·
Τυδεΐδης δ᾽ ἄρ᾽ ἔπειτα ὑπὲρ σάκεος μεγάλοιο   820
αἰὲν ἐπ᾽ αὐχένι κῦρε φαεινοῦ δουρὸς ἀκωκῇι.
καὶ τότε δή ῥ᾽ Αἴαντι περιδδείσαντες Ἀχαιοὶ
παυσαμένους ἐκέλευσαν ἄεθλια ἶσ᾽ ἀνελέσθαι.
αὐτὰρ Τυδεΐδηι δῶκεν μέγα φάσγανον ἥρως
σὺν κολεῶι τε φέρων καὶ ἐϋτμήτωι τελαμῶνι.   825
αὐτὰρ Πηλεΐδης θῆκεν σόλον αὐτοχόωνον,
ὃν πρὶν μὲν ῥίπτασκε μέγα σθένος Ἠετίωνος·
ἀλλ᾽ ἤτοι τὸν ἔπεφνε ποδάρκης δῖος Ἀχιλλεύς,
τὸν δ᾽ ἄγετ᾽ ἐν νήεσσι σὺν ἄλλοισι κτεάτεσσιν.
στῆ δ᾽ ὀρθὸς καὶ μῦθον ἐν Ἀργείοισιν ἔειπεν·   830
'ὄρνυσθ᾽, οἳ καὶ τούτου ἀέθλου πειρήσεσθε.
εἴ οἱ καὶ μάλα πολλὸν ἀπόπροθι πίονες ἀγροί,
ἕξει μιν καὶ πέντε περιπλομένους ἐνιαυτοὺς
χρεώμενος· οὐ μὲν γάρ οἱ ἀτεμβόμενός γε σιδήρου
ποιμὴν οὐδ᾽ ἀροτὴρ εἶσ᾽ ἐς πόλιν, ἀλλὰ παρέξει.'   835

---

814 ἀμφοτέρων: ἀμφοτέρω **815** πάντας Ἀχαιούς: εἰσορόωντας **821** ἀκωκῇι:
ἀκωκήν **822** περιδδείσαντες: περιδείσαντες

ὣς ἔφατ', ὦρτο δ' ἔπειτα μενεπτόλεμος Πολυποίτης,
ἂν δὲ Λεοντῆος κρατερὸν μένος ἀντιθέοιο,
ἂν δ' Αἴας Τελαμωνιάδης καὶ δῖος Ἐπειός.
ἑξείης δ' ἵσταντο, σόλον δ' ἕλε δῖος Ἐπειός,
ἧκε δὲ δινήσας· γέλασαν δ' ἐπὶ πάντες Ἀχαιοί.   840
δεύτερος αὖτ' ἀφέηκε Λεοντεύς ὄζος Ἄρηος·
τὸ τρίτον αὖτ' ἔρριψε μέγας Τελαμώνιος Αἴας
χειρὸς ἄπο στιβαρῆς καὶ ὑπέρβαλε σήματα πάντων.
ἀλλ' ὅτε δὴ σόλον εἷλε μενεπτόλεμος Πολυποίτης,
ὅσσον τίς τ' ἔρριψε καλαύροπα βουκόλος ἀνήρ,   845
ἣ δέ θ' ἑλισσομένη πέτεται διὰ βοῦς ἀγελαίας,
τόσσον παντὸς ἀγῶνος ὑπέρβαλε· τοὶ δὲ βόησαν.
ἀνστάντες δ' ἕταροι Πολυποίταο κρατεροῖο
νῆας ἔπι γλαφυρὰς ἔφερον βασιλῆος ἄεθλον.
αὐτὰρ ὁ τοξευτῇσι τίθει ἰόεντα σίδηρον,   850
κὰδ δ' ἐτίθει δέκα μὲν πελέκεας, δέκα δ' ἡμιπέλεκκα·
ἱστὸν δ' ἔστησεν νηὸς κυανοπρῴροιο
τηλοῦ ἐπὶ ψαμάθοις, ἐκ δὲ τρήρωνα πέλειαν
λεπτῇι μηρίνθωι δῆσεν ποδός, ἧς ἄρ' ἀνώγει
τοξεύειν· 'ὃς μέν κε βάληι τρήρωνα πέλειαν,   855
πάντας ἀειράμενος πελέκεας οἶκόνδε φερέσθω·
ὃς δέ κε μηρίνθοιο τύχηι, ὄρνιθος ἁμαρτών,
ἥσσων γὰρ δὴ κεῖνος, ὁ δ' οἴσεται ἡμιπέλεκκα.'
ὣς ἔφατ', ὦρτο δ' ἔπειτα βίη Τεύκροιο ἄνακτος,
ἂν δ' ἄρα Μηριόνης, θεράπων ἐΰς Ἰδομενῆος.   860
κλήρους δ' ἐν κυνέηι χαλκήρεϊ πάλλον ἑλόντες,
Τεῦκρος δὲ πρῶτος κλήρωι λάχεν· αὐτίκα δ' ἰὸν
ἧκεν ἐπικρατέως, οὐδ' ἠπείλησεν ἄνακτι
ἀρνῶν πρωτογόνων ῥέξειν κλειτὴν ἑκατόμβην.
ὄρνιθος μὲν ἅμαρτε· μέγηρε γάρ οἱ τό γ' Ἀπόλλων·   865
αὐτὰρ ὁ μήρινθον βάλε πὰρ πόδα, τῆι δέδετ' ὄρνις·
ἀντικρὺ δ' ἀπὸ μήρινθον τάμε πικρὸς ὀϊστός.
ἡ μὲν ἔπειτ' ἤϊξε πρὸς οὐρανόν, ἡ δὲ παρείθη
μήρινθος ποτὶ γαῖαν· ἀτὰρ κελάδησαν Ἀχαιοί.
σπερχόμενος δ' ἄρα Μηριόνης ἐξείρυσε χειρὸς   870
τόξον· ἀτὰρ δὴ ὀϊστὸν ἔχεν πάλαι, ὡς ἴθυνεν.

846 δέ θ': δέ τ', δέ   854 ποδός: πόδα   856 οἴκόνδε: κλισίηνδε

αὐτίκα δ᾽ ἠπείλησεν ἑκηβόλωι Ἀπόλλωνι
ἀρνῶν πρωτογόνων ῥέξειν κλειτὴν ἑκατόμβην.
ὕψι δ᾽ ὑπαὶ νεφέων εἶδε τρήρωνα πέλειαν·
τῆι ῥ᾽ ὅ γε δινεύουσαν ὑπὸ πτέρυγος βάλε μέσσην, 875
ἀντικρὺ δὲ διῆλθε βέλος· τὸ μὲν ἂψ ἐπὶ γαίηι
πρόσθεν Μηριόναο πάγη ποδός· αὐτὰρ ἡ ὄρνις
ἱστῶι ἐφεζομένη νηὸς κυανοπρώιροιο
αὐχέν᾽ ἀπεκρέμασεν, σὺν δὲ πτερὰ πυκνὰ λίασθεν.
ὠκὺς δ᾽ ἐκ μελέων θυμὸς πτάτο, τῆλε δ᾽ ἀπ᾽ αὐτοῦ 880
κάππεσε· λαοὶ δ᾽ αὖ θηεῦντό τε θάμβησάν τε.
ἂν δ᾽ ἄρα Μηριόνης πελέκεας δέκα πάντας ἄειρεν,
Τεῦκρος δ᾽ ἡμιπέλεκκα φέρεν κοίλας ἐπὶ νῆας.
αὐτὰρ Πηλεΐδης κατὰ μὲν δολιχόσκιον ἔγχος,
κὰδ δὲ λέβητ᾽ ἄπυρον, βοὸς ἄξιον, ἀνθεμόεντα 885
θῆκ᾽ ἐς ἀγῶνα φέρων· καί ῥ᾽ ἥμονες ἄνδρες ἀνέσταν·
ἂν μὲν ἄρ᾽ Ἀτρεΐδης, εὐρὺ κρείων Ἀγαμέμνων,
ἂν δ᾽ ἄρα Μηριόνης, θεράπων ἐΰς Ἰδομενῆος.
τοῖσι δὲ καὶ μετέειπε ποδάρκης δῖος Ἀχιλλεύς·
"Ἀτρεΐδη, ἴδμεν γὰρ ὅσον προβέβηκας ἁπάντων 890
ἠδ᾽ ὅσσον δυνάμει τε καὶ ἥμασιν ἔπλευ ἄριστος·
ἀλλὰ σὺ μὲν τόδ᾽ ἄεθλον ἔχων κοίλας ἐπὶ νῆας
ἔρχευ, ἀτὰρ δόρυ Μηριόνηι ἥρωϊ πόρωμεν,
εἰ σύ γε σῶι θυμῶι ἐθέλοις· κέλομαι γὰρ ἔγωγε.᾽
ὣς ἔφατ᾽, οὐδ᾽ ἀπίθησεν ἄναξ ἀνδρῶν Ἀγαμέμνων· 895
δῶκε δὲ Μηριόνηι δόρυ χάλκεον· αὐτὰρ ὅ γ᾽ ἥρως
Ταλθυβίωι κήρυκι δίδου περικαλλὲς ἄεθλον.

---

874 ὑπαί: ὑπό   εἶδε: ἴδετο, ἴδε, ἴδε δέ   878 secl. West   879 λίασθεν: λιάσθη, λιάσθην,
λίασσεν   891 δυνάμει: δυνάμι   ἥμασιν: ῥήμασιν   894 ἐθέλοις: ἐθέλεις

COMMENTARY

1–257 THE FUNERAL OF PATROCLOS

1–61 First Day. After the death of Hector and the Trojan lamentations ending Book 22, the poet switches back to the Greeks and their return to camp, where his focus will remain until the council of the gods (24.23). Almost every change of scene from now until the end of the poem will involve ritual acts associated with funerals and lamentation (24.23, 83–6, 93–102, 120–5, etc.), so that the games and the *Iliad*'s closing cadences are informed on every side by death's processes. In terms of the funeral itself (Intro. § 2.1), the ritual actions conducted on this day preview the more fully described sequence on the second day (4–34n.), and allow the poet to connect the reclaiming of the corpse with the close of the poem's fourth day of battle (Intro. § 1) whilst amplifying the scale of the coming episode.

1–3 3 = 19.277, after the Greek assembly. Neither Hector's death nor the coming ritual will console Achilleus, since the 'scattered … each to his own' idiom introduces a differentiation or separation from a larger group after a combined activity, leaving the isolated figure unsatisfied (24.1–2, *Od.* 2.252, 258). **ὡς οἳ μέν … αὐτάρ** 'so they were … but': changing scene from Troy at the end of the previous book, this typical 'appositional summary' (De Jong 2001: xii) connects the lamentation in the city with the coming funeral in the camp, completing the movement observed by Andromache (22.464–5), and contributes to the parallelism in the poem's closure (Intro. § 1). Found at the start of books (9.1, *Od.* 6.1–2, 7.1–2) and elsewhere (16.124, 15.405, etc.), these devices cannot prove the originality or authenticity of the book division here (Hölscher 1939: 37–50, esp. 40–1; Richardson 1990: 110–19; Bitto 2019: 134–8: also Intro. § 1, n. 10). **πτόλιν:** an epic alternative for π- in πόλις, πόλεμος, etc. (5, 836–8nn.), πτ- is also found in Arcado-Cypriot, Thessalian, and Mycenaean (Ruijgh 1995: 265–6). πτόλιν is always used in this position after a preposition/preverb. **ἐπεὶ δή:** the first syllable of ἐπεί is only treated as heavy when this expression is moved to the verse-beginning from its usual position on the 1b colon boundary, resulting in an 'acephalous' or headless verse (*GH* I § 45; Wyatt 1969: 201–22, esp. 219–21). **νῆάς τε καὶ Ἑλλήσποντον** 'the ships and the Hellespont': metonymic hendiadys for the Greek camp when functioning as end point of disrupted or chaotic journeys (15.233, 17.432, 18.150); cf. 848–9n. The camp was constructed around the vessels at the Hellespontine shore ('the sea as far as

Sigeion': Σ bT), but no precise location is denoted (Trachsel 2007: 61–5). Continuing an ancient tradition of Homeric criticism (Ellis-Evans 2019: 19–29), some seek historical accuracy in Homer's geography, placing the camp west across the 'inner bay' from Troy revealed by deep-core drilling on the Karamenderes (Scamandros) plain, or in Beşik Bay to the south-west (Korfmann 1986; Luce 2003; Malfas 2008).   ἕκαστος: often in the singular after a plural subject + verb to emphasise individual partici-pation in the whole action (*GH* II § 18); the (frequent) hiatus before this word betrays original **sw-* (*GH* I § 55; also Intro. § 3.2.ix).

4–34 Previewing the formal funeral on the next day (109–225n.), Achilleus instructs the Myrmidons to drive around the bier before depart-ing to prepare dinner, an action which also distantly foreshadows the char-iot race around the σῆμα of some long-lost hero (331–3n.). The poet gives here a preliminary sequence of death ritual before its full array on the next day, with procession (13–14), formal lamentation (14–23), and the concluding sacrifice/meal (29–34). A meal is necessary anyway at the end of a day's fighting, but elsewhere occurs *after* the funeral (24.664–6, *Od.* 3.309–10); the lack of such an episode in the actual funeral is mirrored in the brief reporting of Achilleus' funeral (*Od.* 24.81–94) and reflects the poet's choice to narrativise the concluding community activity in the form of games (Edwards 1986: 87–8), but it may also imply something about Achilleus and that ritual (Intro. § 2.1; 166–76n.).

4 The Myrmidons were from Phthia in Thessaly and descended from an eponymous figure Myrmidon (Hes. fr. 10(a).99–101 M–W), but in another early tradition they were created by Zeus from ants (μύρμηκες) to ease the loneliness of Aiacos, Achilleus' grandfather, on Aigina (Hes. fr. 205.3–5 M–W; for the process bringing these originally Thessalian stories into the mythology of the island in the Saronic Gulf, see West 1985: 162–4 and n. 84).   εἴα 'he was (not) allowing': augmented 3rd sing. imperf. act. indic. of ἐάω (cf. unaugmented ἔα 5.517, 13.2, etc.), a form always negatived in Homer. The tense denotes the begin-ning and continuation of the Myrmidons' initial honouring of Patroclos, simultaneous with the departure of the Greeks to their ships (imperf. ἐσκίδναντο) and preparing for the start of Achilleus' speech (imperf. μετηύδα).

5–11 The instructions have an A–B–A structure, with the theme of unhar-nessing horses (λυώμεθα … ἵππους/ἵππους λυσάμενοι) surrounding the central, emphasised exhortation to grieve (8–10).

5 ἑτάροισι: epos retains the original stem ἑταρ- alongside the later form ἑταῖρος (6–7n.), though it is slightly less common and does not appear in the nominative singular (Pinsent 1983: 314; Hagen 2005).   **φιλοπτολέμοισι** 'war-loving': metre preserves -ττ- (1–3n.) in this adjective, since four successive light syllables could not fit into the verse. Homer applies the epithet to groups (mostly Trojans, Myrmidons, and Greeks) but not individuals (first in Hes. fr. 9.1 M–W).

6–7 ταχύπωλοι 'swift-horsed' or '-foaled' (*LfrgE* s.v., 336): otherwise used only of the Danaoi (Parry 1971: 101), the epithet introduces the horse-driving around Patroclos' tomb (7–9) and may allude to his role as charioteer (next n.).   **ἐμοὶ ἐρίηρες ἑταῖροι** 'my very faithful companions': Achilleus draws his group relationship as particularly close (only Odysseus in *Od.* so addresses his entire detachment), and suggests their surrogacy for Patroclos (cf. 16.269), 'the ἑταῖρος par excellence in the *Iliad*' (Pinsent 1983: 313; generally Haubold 2000: 126–37). The epithet's meaning in this formula is debated, but the prefix ἐρι- means 'very' or 'to a high degree', and the suffix has been linked with ἦρα 'service' (Willi 1999: 96–8; cf. Ruijgh 2011: 266–7).   **ὑπ' ὄχεσφι** 'from beneath the chariots': an easy extension of a usually locative phrase to express separation, referring to the place on the vehicle where the horses are attached (8.136, 13.23, 23.130; cf. 8.41; Delebecque 1951: 181). For the suffix -φι, see Intro. § 3.1.2.c.ix; ὄχεσφι = ὄχεσσι (not used in Homer).   **μώνυχας ἵππους** 'single-hoofed horses': the epithet in this formula is usually explained as *σμ-ῶνυξ 'one-horn' (*σμ- from *s(e) m- > e.g. εἷς, ὁμός) to differentiate the horse from cloven-hoofed animals (*EDG* 992). It is frequently deployed in vigorous contexts when the team is restrained or turned, perhaps to focus on the sound made by its contact with the ground (Delebecque 1951: 149–50), a connotation somewhat pathetic or anticlimactic in its frustration here (see 373–4n.).

8–9 Necessary run-over and delay of κλαίωμεν underlines Πάτροκλον, the speech's central theme.   **ἆσσον** 'closer': comparative adverb of ἄγχι, with gen. to denote 'motion to a point' and often postpositive. Wrongly condemned as an Atticism in favour of the minority's ἄσσον (printed by West), this form is not only an expected reflex of the root but well attested in the paradosis (*LfrgE* s. ἄγχι).   **Πάτροκλον:** short, o-declension of the hero's name, derived from the longer, consonant declension Πατροκλέης (< -κλέης; von Kamptz 1982: 131, 215). As Achilleus' retainer (θεράπων: 89–90n.) and closest friend (77–91n.), he is sometimes held to be an unusually gentle figure in the otherwise

hard-nosed world of Homeric masculinity (250–4n.). Patroclos' role
in his friend's narrative cannot be overstated, and his importance is
constantly underlined in this book (see generally von Scheliha 1943;
Sinos 1980; Lowenstam 1981; Mills 2000; Kanavou 2015: 55–62): also
65n.   ὃ γὰρ γέρας ἐστὶ θανόντων 'for this (lit. 'which') is the hon-
our-prize of the dead': the action is a traditional part of funeral ritual
(Myers 2019: 202), but these words suggest Achilleus' quasi-parental
role, since speakers invoke this consideration – referring to tomb construction (16.457 = 675, for Sarpedon) or funeral tendance (*Od.* 24.190,
296, for Achilleus) – only for their children or themselves (Garland 1982
= 1984). Derived from the same stem as γέρων and γῆρας, γέρας is either
a particular reward for military or political service or, as here, a long-
established right reflecting the honour of the receiver, whether that figure is dead, old (4.323, 9.422), or a god (4.49, 24.70; Van Wees 1992:
299–302; Scheid-Tissinier 1994: 196–7, 234–44, 251–3). The use of the
relative pronoun with what appears to be a superfluous γάρ is well established (*Od.* 24.190, 255, 286; cf. 6.59, 21.198, 22.201, etc.) and is sometimes seen as a trace of an older 'anaphoric' force of the relative (*GH* I
§ 129, Probert 2015: 393–8); whatever its origin, the persistence of the
syntax may also be encouraged by the demonstrative's frequent use as a
relative in epos (712–13n.).

10–11 ὀλοοῖο τεταρπώμεσθα γόοιο 'we are satisfied with (lit. 'from')
destructive lamentation': looking forward to the formal mourning at 17,
this formula (once with κρυεροῖο) strikingly makes lamentation almost
into a bodily need, like hunger and thirst (cf. 14 γόου ἵμερον; Latacz
1966: 184). τεταρπώμεσθα is 1st pl. redupl. aor. subj. mid. of τέρπω. The
ταρπ- forms of this verb generally mean 'sate oneself' rather than 'enjoy'
(Latacz 1966: 174–219, esp. 177–8). The γόος is 'formal lamentation
uttered by the next of kin' (Tsagalis 2004: 5) and normally concerns
the aretalogy and practical ramifications of the dead person's absence,
sometimes combined with a 'death wish' (Arnould 1990: 146–8; Tsagalis
2004: 27–51): see 17–34n.   **δορπήσομεν:** 1st pl. short vowel aor. subj.
(Intro. § 3.1.2.d.v; cf. 810). No explicit mention is made of Achilleus eating in either the funeral feast (29) or the following council scene (55–7),
after his early notable refusals to eat (19.206–14, 304–8) and subsequent
sustenance with ambrosia and nectar (19.340–54). He has resumed eating when Priam enters his tent (24.475–6), where he dines with his guest
almost immediately (621–8).

12 ὤιμωξαν ἀολλέες, ἦρχε δ': the link between group and led in this form
is elsewhere used of Trojan resistance and Hector's aggressive leadership

(13.136 = 15.306 = 17.262); this reallocation connects Hector and Achilleus, a familiar theme in this book, underlining the causal link between their fates (see Intro. § 1 with n. 19). Achilleus is reintroduced as chief mourner, picked up again by ἐξῆρχε (17–18n.). Underlining the event's importance is the fact that οἰμώζω (lit. 'I say οἴμοι'), denoting an immediate (usually male) reaction to grief, is everywhere else in Homer granted only to prominent characters (Spatafora 1997: 22–3; Arnould 1990: 150–5). ἀολλέες means 'all [collected] together', a masc. nom. pl. adj. derived from εἰλέω 'draw together', uncontracted (> -εῖς), as always with this word in archaic poetry and usually with other -ης -ες adjectives in Homer (GHI § 17; WHS 80–3).

13–14 This is the first we see of Patroclos' corpse since 19.211–12, where it was said to lie in Achilleus' tent; presumably it has been brought out and set on a bier for the procession to take place, but the poet is not bothered with such details. Though we are technically still at the stage of *prothesis* – i.e. the presentation, washing, and mourning over the corpse – this procession previews the funeral's actual *ekphora* (127–39n.: see Intro. § 2.1) and will also occur around Achilleus' own pyre (*Od.* 24.68–70; Andronikos 1968: 14–15). Adding run-over in 14 (and 16) keeps the narrative focused on Myrmidon grief.   τρίς 'thrice': the number three usually describes incomplete actions in Homer, showing a ritual insufficiency (1–3n.) that will be paralleled when Achilleus drags Hector's corpse thrice around the tomb (24.12–18; Germain 1954: 11–13; Kelly 2007a: 194–7); it is to be understood that here, too, Hector is dragged around Patroclos before being flung in the dust next to him (24–6n.; Mazon 1940: 255). For the associated 'triple attempt' motif in the wrestling and fight in armour events, see 733–4, 816–17nn.   ἐΰτριχας ἤλασαν ἵππους 'they drove their well-maned horses': the epithet only occurs in this book (301, 351), an example of 'phrase clustering' (Hainsworth 27–8) perhaps anticipating the thematic importance of the later hair offerings (135–6, 140–4nn.). Synonymous with the more common καλλίθριξ, it reflects their impressive appearance and expensive tending (Delebecque 1951: 151–2; Vivante 1982: 72–4).   γόου ἵμερον ὦρσεν: varies the usual formula ὑφ' ἵμερον ὦρσε γόοιο (108n.) to accommodate Thetis' unheralded and distant intervention (*pace* Kakridis 1949: 84, who thinks she is present here). The theme links with her participation in the last period of Greek mourning at the start of Book 18, and perhaps with extra-Homeric stories of Achilleus' death (Kelly 2012). For γόος, see 10–11n. ἵμερος is an immediate compulsion not to be refused, again making lamentation almost a bodily need (Weiss 1998: 47–56; Kloss 1994: 24–60 argues that ἵμερος/ἔρος = external/internal desire): cf. also 10n.

15–16 Grief is underlined by (the typically Achillean: Friedrich and Redfield 1978: 278–9) asyndeton and anaphora of δεύοντο, 3rd pl. imperf. indic. mediopass. of δεύω, whose plurality with neut. pl. τεύχεα stresses the subject's multiplicity (*GH* II §§ 23, 39). Patroclos' bloody death is here intimated, since garments may be drenched with tears (9.570, *Od.* 7.260), but nowhere else is the ground so affected, though the earth is typically wetted with blood in combat (218–21n.; cf. 9.570–1 δεύοντο δὲ δάκρυσι κόλποι): 34n. The focus is maintained by run-over δάκρυσι.   **πόθεον** 'they missed': Patroclos attracts ποθή, a 'desire for something not at hand' (Weiss 1998: 32), more than anyone else in the *Iliad* (17.439, 690, 19.321, 24.6: Austin 2021; Lesser 2022: 214–41).   **μήστωρα φόβοιο** 'planner of rout': μήστωρ is derived from μήδομαι 'I contrive/plan', and this expression is usually applied to a victorious/aggressive figure viewed from an opponent's perspective (5.272, 6.278, 8.108, 12.139, etc.). This example strikingly reconfigures that distance to the Myrmidons' sense of loss (Kelly 2007a: 152, 389–90).

17–34 The third of Achilleus' formal lamentations for Patroclos (18.314–55, 19.314–39), where an individual speech is set next to the supportive groaning of a larger group, in the first two cases the captive women (in the second (19.282–302) preceded by another formal lament from Briseis). These three speeches occur at progressively later stages of the funeral: washing and laying out the corpse (18.343–5), preparation of a meal in which Achilleus refuses to participate (19.303–13), and here his possible participation in the meal (11n.: also Intro. § 2.1, and Table 1). Such progression within repeated structures is a monumentalising device, but it also emphasises the structural and thematic importance of this funeral. Further linking the main characters (Intro. § 1 with n. 19), this lamentation also looks back to the initial Trojan grieving over Hector which closed the previous book (22.405–513), and forward to his funeral in the next.

17–18 = 18.316–17, Achilleus' first formal lament (19–23n.). The placing of hands on the dead companion's chest is also found in *Gilgamesh* SBV VIII.57–8 but, though unique in epos (where people usually touch the corpse's head, or beat their own chests), it is probably not derived from that poem (George 2003: I.54–7, Davies 2023; *contra* West 1997a: 340–3, Clarke 2019: 269–74). The chest attracts the hero's attention as the seat of several cognitive elements in the Homeric individual (*thymos, noos, phrenes*), and reflects Achilleus' confused distress at his friend's absence (Gazis 2018: 50–1): Intro. § 2.1; also 62–108, 99–101ᵃnn.   **Πηλεΐδης:** the most common of Achilleus' patronymics, the number and frequency of which lend him a particular traditional weight, evoking the history of his illustrious family and its (mis)deeds (Higbie 1995: 43–68, esp. 49–51; Willcock 2004: 56–7). Though it makes no metrical difference (ει could be either a heavy diphthong or two light syllables), εῖ is preferred here (and with similar names) as habitual in early *melos* and because Homer never places -ει- where a single heavy syllable is the only option (in the arsis of the foot); cf. 66–8n.   ἀδινοῦ ἐξῆρχε γόοιο 'he led off the repeated lamentation': underlining the uniqueness of the relationship with Patroclos, Achilleus is the only male predicated of this formula and the only subject unrelated by blood or marriage to the corpse (Derderian 2001: 52–7). Hiatus before ἐξ- does not entail epic correption, since -οῦ stands in the princeps position. ἀδινός denotes duration or repetition, both temporal and spatial, particularly in mourning or lamentation (Kaimio 1977: 49–52). I follow the majority of MSS in printing ἀδινοῦ instead of ἀδινοῦ (*GH* I § 76; Hackstein 2010: 402): cf. 530–1n. (ἥκιστος).   ἀνδροφόνους: of Achilleus' hands (= 18.317; 24.479), but more typically used of Hector in the role of 'the killed and not the killer' (Sacks 1987: 210, cf. 163–75); its usage underlines their connection (see Intro. § 1, n. 19 for others; Purves 2019: 164–5).

19–23 Achilleus recalls the original promise not to complete the funeral process until the two tasks were done (18.333–7; 23.22–3 = 18.336–7), which will be repeated at 179–83 after he slaughters the Trojan youths. For a γόος these are (thankfully) unusual themes, Achilleus typically outpacing the usual parameters of Homer's world.

19–20 = 179–80 (179–83n.).   χαῖρέ μοι 'have joy/feel goodwill towards me': though the imperative may be used as a greeting, here the pronoun is the source of Patroclos' satisfaction, as γάρ makes clear (cf. 10.462 χαῖρε, θεά, τοῖσδεσσι· σὲ γάρ ...; *Od.* 3.52; 13.59); the same is true at 179–80 below, where his imminent fulfilment of the promise is once more introduced by γάρ. This archaic syntax is the origin of the greeting formula, mostly visible in Homer in prayers but some other exchanges as well (Wachter 1998), and Achilleus is similarly exercised about his dead friend's attitude when ransoming Hector (24.591–5). Gazis 2018: 52–4 interprets it as a more formal greeting, viz. a sign of their distance.   καὶ εἰν Ἀΐδαο δόμοισιν 'even in the house of Hades': pathos is intensified because this formula is normally deployed by a fearful speaker speculating on the whereabouts of (a) missing person(s), but thrice in this book alone by Achilleus when speaking to or of Patroclos (103, 179; e.g. 22.52, *Od.* 4.834, etc.). εἰν is a metrically lengthened form of ἐν. Ἀΐδαο is a-stem gen. sing. of Ἀΐδης, the lord of the underworld, whose

name probably means 'unseen' or 'unknown' (*EDG* s.v.). Homer also uses
Ἀΐδεω (by quantitative metathesis < *-ηο in Ionic: Intro. § 3.1.2.c.i; see
71–4n. for another genitive form Ἀΐδος).   ἤδη τοι τελέω: τελέω either
pres. (as 2.286) or fut. indic., very suitable in the parallel passage below
(179–83n.). Achilleus' authority is extraordinary, as the 'fulfil as promised' idiom is deployed in the 1st person only elsewhere by Zeus (15.73–4;
cf. 13.375, *Od.* 10.483). τοι = σοί 'for you', the other dat. sing. of the 2nd
pers. pronoun in epos, and probably the origin of the asseverative particle
τοι 'surely' (*GH* I § 124).

21–3 22–3 = 18.336–7. On human sacrifice, see 175–7n. If not a standard figure (Germain 1954: 17–18; Hitch 2009: 990–100), the twelve victims may parallel the Thracians killed around Rhesus (10.487–8) or the
Trojans killed in the panic after Achilleus' shout (18.230–1).   κυσὶν
ὠμὰ δάσασθαι 'for the dogs to rend raw': a frightening threat, since these
formular mutilations are either themselves effected (*Od.* 22.476) or effective motivations to action (*Od.* 18.87), though Hector had tried much
the same with Patroclos (17.125), and the Trojan's corpse will remain
undefiled (184–91n.). The great taboo of animals rending corpses is
stressed in the proem (1.4–5) but only occurs once in the *Iliad* (21.203–4;
Kelly 2007a: 315–17; generally Segal 1971).   ἀποδειροτομήσειν 'to
cut away from (*or* at) the neck': reserved for Achilleus in the *Iliad*, this
chilling verb (even without the preposition/preverb) denotes specifically
decapitation (*Od.* 11.35, *Th.* 280) or just killing *tout court* (21.89), and is
used mostly for non-combat slaughter (Heubeck 1992: 277–8); it appears
also, as here, in unusual sacrifical settings (also 23.174, *Od.* 11.35, *HHerm.*
405).   ἀγλαὰ τέκνα: highly pathetic, since the formula figures the
youths as unmartial, resonating with themes of birth and home-life
(2.871–2, *Od.* 11.249, 285, 14.233, etc.); Thomas 2020: 179 interprets
the epithet as 'inducing pride and joy'. Run-over underlines their contrast with Hector, completing the emphatic pattern of foregrounding the
victims of Achilleus' anger.   σέθεν κταμένοιο χολωθείς 'made angry
by your death': as the poem's principal wrathful hero, Achilleus feels
χόλος (anger usually manifest in violence) for Patroclos more often than
any other character (Walsh 2005: 107–246, esp. 175–6; more generally
Clarke 1999: 92–7). Reactions in this form (χολωθείς is masc. nom. sing.
aor. pass. ppl. of χολόω) are usually consequent upon killing or serious
dishonour (cf. 87–8n.). σέθεν κταμένοιο is genitive of origin 'from'/'because of', showing one way in which the genitive absolute construction
developed (cf. 16.320; *GH* II § 472). Usually considered an Aeolic feature, σέθεν is 2nd pers. pronominal stem σε- + suffix -θεν 'from' used as an

equivalent to gen. σεῖο, σεῦ, in almost all the same constructions (cf. ἐμέθεν, ἔθεν, etc.: *GH* I § 110; Wathelet 1970: 287–8).

24–6 24 = 22.395, as Achilleus prepares to bind Hector to his chariot. Juxtaposition highlights the visual clash between δῖον 'shining'/'godlike' and ἀεικέα 'unseemly'.   ἦ 'he said': a 'petrified' 3rd sing. imperf. indic. (frequent and only Homeric form: also at 563, 596, and 612) which gave a 1st person ἦμί on the analogy of φημί (*EDG* s. ἦμί, 519).   **ἀεικέα μήδετο ἔργα** 'shaming deeds he planned': authoritative violence, a particular qualification (= 22.395ᵇ) of the verse-end formula only performed in epos by Achilleus and Zeus (2.38, 21.19, 23.176, etc.). ἀεικέα does not convey the poet's moral condemnation, i.e. that it was shameful for Achilleus to do this, but the idea that the treatment is shameful for Hector to suffer (as at 22.395; cf. Thersites receiving ἀεικέσσι πληγῇσιν at 2.264; Bassett 1933: 44–6; De Jong 2012: 162–3): see also 175–7n.   **πρηνέα ... τανύσσας | ἐν κονίῃς:** with the treatment repeated at 24.17–18 (τὸν δέ τ᾽ ἔασκεν | ἐν κόνι ἐκτανύσας προπρηνέα), Achilleus' vengeance is again unique, since he is the only character to inflict (as well as suffer 18.26) the otherwise passive 'stretch(ed) in the dust' theme (5× *Il.*: 13.393–4 = 16.486–7) and to cause (twice: 24.18) an enemy to be 'face down in the dust' outside combat (2.418, 4.544, 6.43; cf. *Scut.* 365; cf. Lather 2020: 280–2).   **πὰρ λεχέεσσι:** the preposition/preverb's last syllable has been lost (apocope) to avoid four consecutive light syllables, and the plural of λέχος is interchangeable with the singular (*GH* II § 39).   **Μενοιτιάδαο:** the patronymic bestows a sense of the traditional background, and may look forward to the migration story (84ᵇ–9on.). Menoitios was Patroclos' father and son of Actor, who was himself the son of Myrmidon (59–61n.), though another early tradition has Menoitios as Aiacos' son, along with Peleus, Telamon, and Phocos, which would make Patroclos and Achilleus cousins (Hes. fr. 212(a) M–W: see West 1985: 162–4 and n. 85).

26–7 (ἔντε᾽ ... |) **χάλκεα μαρμαίροντα** 'gleaming bronze': this formula helps to conclude the causal chain around the main characters (Intro. § 1 with n. 19), connecting the claiming of Sarpedon's armour (16.664, the prize for the fight in armour: 798–800n.) with the loss of Achilleus' original set (18.131) and its replacement (18.617 τεύχεα). There are several such culminating progressions or runs in Book 23 (Intro. § 1, p. 9). μαρμαίρω is an 'expressive' reduplication in the present tense, like παμφανόω, παπταίνω, δαιδάλλω, ὀλολύζω, etc. (*GH* I § 179).   **οἵ ... ἕκαστος** 'they ... each man': change in number captures the individuality, as well as the totality, of the Myrmidons' reaction: see 1–3n.   **ὑψηχέας**

ἵππους 'high-whinnying horses': preferred here to metrically equivalent ἐριαύχενας ἵππους because it resonates with the noise of lamentation and procession, and lacks that expression's connotation of failure (171–2n.). This formula helps to contrast the group's attitude towards the funeral's efficacy with their leader's view (1–3n.; *pace* Parry 1971: 113–14, 180). Kaimio 1977: 71–3 follows Σ A and some MSS in reading λύοντο δὲ μώνυχας ἵππους, probably produced to parallel the phrasing in Achilleus' speech (7) above.

28 Achilleus' ship is positioned on the far right of the Greek camp (8.222–6 = 11.5–9: Trachsel 2007: 52–65, esp. 55–7; Clay 2011: 41–51), and the Myrmidons' settlement here neatly enshrines his centrality to the coming narrative.   **κὰδ δ' ἷζον:** perhaps formulaic for a group returning from battle (21.560; cf. 9.87, 19.50). κὰδ = κατά with apocope and assimilation of -τ before δ'.   **ποδώκεος Αἰακίδαο** 'of the swift-foot (grand)son of Aiacos': reinforcing Achilleus' greater traditional status as a descendant of Zeus through his grandfather Aiacos (21.189–90; cf. Zunker 1988: 63–89), this formula uses a 'papponymic' in -ιδης (see Meyer 1907: 20; *WHS* 147–9), which in all grammatical cases is the second-least common of Achilleus' patronymics (Higbie 1995: 51–2, 58).

29–34 As with the main sacrifice later (166–76n.), this preview feast and sacrifice is linked with Phoinix's story of escape from his father's house (23.30–2 ~ 9.466–7; 33 = 9.468); this connects Achilleus' two most important advisors (84ᵇ–90n.) and equates Phoinix's symbolic death to his natal family with Patroclos' actual demise (Alden 2012: esp. 116, 122–3). No gods are referred to, no wine is mentioned, nor is there any narration of the consumption, de-emphasising the communal feast before the coming smaller-group meal (55–8; cf. *Od.* 9.469, 20.312–13, etc.) and continuing 'the gory tone of (the) grim treatment of Hector' (Hitch 2009: 55). Nonetheless, the event is important, since its victims encompass all sacrificial options (cattle, sheep, goats, and pigs: Van Straten 1995: 170–86; Ekroth 2002: 254–5) and there is to be no meal after the main sacrifice (Intro. § 2.1).

29 Whether or not he takes part in this meal (10–11n.), Achilleus' authority is underlined, since playing the host is one of the traditional functions of the Homeric *basileus*, especially in a funeral context (24.801–3, *Od.* 3.309–10; Andronikos 1968: 15–18).   **τάφον μενοεικέα δαίνυ** 'he gave the funeral feast': an acc. of the 'internal object', as e.g. εἰλαπίνην δαίνυντο (201). Connected with θάπτω, τάφος in Homer can refer to the entire process (23.619) or the associated meal (*Od.* 3.309; cf. γάμος 'wedding feast', *Od.* 4.3), but not the tomb itself (cf. *Scut.* 477). μενοεικής is conventionally used of food, and literally means 'suited/pleasing to the *menos*' ('life force', 'strength': Clarke 2004: 79–80) and so 'desirable' or 'suitable' (Blanc 2012: 64–82; also 138–9n.).

30–3 Building on μυρίοι (29), the triplication of πολλοί reinforces the ritual's scale and importance, and is found elsewhere in summary sacrifices (e.g. 9.466–8, *Od.* 9.45–6, 20.312–13; cf. Fehling 1969: 199–200).   ἀργοί 'white': elsewhere used of dogs in the sense 'swift', the adj. here refers to their bright colour or the gleam from their coats (*EDG* s. ἀργός); see 140–4, 188–91, 259–61, 454–5, 692–4nn. for other colour terms, the precise meaning of which often causes great difficulty in modern scholarship.   ὀρέχθεον 'were stretched out': linked with ὀρέγω (Le Feuvre 2011: 267–82), the origin and meaning of this Homeric hapax has been contentious, some ancient commentators suggesting a mimetic expression of groaning (cf. ῥοχθέω), others the notion of being struck or broken (cf. ἐρέχθω: see *DELG* s.v., 818).   σιδήρωι: while bronze is more usual for a cutting edge weapon in epos, iron is used metonymically in this sense (αὐτός ... ἐφέλκεται ἄνδρα σίδηρος, *Od.* 16.294 = 19.13), and found in a sword or dagger (18.34), arrowheads (4.123), and clubs (7.141, 143–4: see Sherratt 1990: 810–11; Létoublon 2018): also 259–61n.   μηκάδες αἶγες 'bleating she-goats': with its epithet derived from onomatopoeic μηκάομαι (*EDG* 942; Tichy 1983: 105, 158), this formula is more usually found where the group so denoted is being fostered (*Od.* 9.124, 244 = 341: cf. 11.383) and recalls the youthful Trojan victims (21–3n.).   ἀργιόδοντες ὕες θαλέθοντες ἀλοιφῆι 'pigs with gleaming teeth (i.e. 'tusks'), thriving with fat': the epithet is used mostly of domesticated animals and wild boar, once of dogs chasing a boar (11.292: Camerotto 2005: 122–3). The presence of pig-fat is a sign of good-quality meat (9.208, *Od.* 8.475–6). For the formation of θαλέθοντες, see φλεγέθω < φλέγω, τελέθω < τέλλω, etc. (*GH* I § 153).   διὰ φλογὸς Ἡφαίστοιο 'over the flame of Hephaistos': recalling the god's participation in the *Theomachy*, this idiom is linked with Achilleus' intimates (9.468, 17.88, *Od.* 24.71). These expressions tend to occur in contexts (food preparation, burning of the corpse) not usually linked with the god's essential powers (Graz 1965: 201–6).

34 The image draws upon the combat idiom '(with) blood flowed' (4.451, 8.65, 13.655, etc.; cf. *Od.* 11.36 below); blood is rarely mentioned in Homeric sacrifice (cf. 4.158) and very restricted in early sacrificial iconography (Ekroth 2005), so its mention here may suggest something wrong with the whole ritual (Kitts 2011: 234–6; Intro. § 2.1). The poet is forecasting the advent of Patroclos' shade (Vermeule 1974: 97), because blood is prominent in Odysseus' underworld ritual (*Od.* 11.36) where the ghosts drink it (10.537, 11.50, etc.), and in that scene's visual representations (Ekroth 2002: 254–7). Formed from ἀρύω 'I draw (water')' like εὐήρυτον (*HDem.* 106), the rare word κοτυλήρυτον 'that could be drawn off in a cup' (next in Nicander, *Ther.* 539; cf. Callim. fr. incert. auth. 773 Pfeiffer) may be an allusive metaphor (i.e. 'in quantities so great') or (perhaps less likely) an actual gathering and offering of blood to the corpse (cf. *Od.* 3.444 for a vessel to catch the fluid; Neal 2006: 264 n. 95; Andronikos 1968: 16–17): see also 43–4n.

35–58 The Greek leaders take Achilleus to Agamemnon. This small quasi-council scene removes him into Agamemnon's sphere of authority, just like Aias after his duel with Hector (7.311–44). As they both lead into funerals, the two episodes are deliberately connected, adding here to a general impression of Agamemnon's weakness: whilst other *boulai* allow several speakers (some openly critical: 9.96–113, 697–700, etc.), there is little sign of his command (as e.g. 7.321–2, 2.76-83, etc.). For the many other hints at this reversal between the two men in this book, see Intro. § 1, n. 8.

35–7 35–6 ~ 7.311–12, and the unique parallel phrasing here (23.36ᵃ = 7.312ᵃ) recalls the aftermath of the Aias–Hector duel.   ἄνακτα ποδώκεα Πηλεΐωνα | εἰς Ἀγαμέμνονα δῖον: in this succinct expression of reversed authority (cf. 1.7 Ἀτρεΐδης τε ἄναξ ἀνδρῶν καὶ δῖος Ἀχιλλεύς), Achilleus trumps Agamemnon in both formularity and genealogy: Agamemnon is rarely labelled δῖος and only in the accusative, and Achilleus is rarely termed ἄναξ (Yamagata 1997: esp. 7 n. 36, 9). On the other hand, ποδώκεα Πηλεΐωνα is common, and Πηλεΐωνα is Achilleus' third patronymic already in this book (17–18, 28nn.: Higbie 1995: 58).   σπουδῆι 'with difficulty': originally 'with effort', from σπεύδω 'I hurry, strive' (*EDG* 1381–2), but easily transferred here, as e.g. at 2.99, 5.893.   χωόμενον κῆρ 'angered in his heart': Achilleus' angry resentment continues, since characters so qualified are linked with revenge for losses or offences central to their identity (1.44, 9.555, *Od.* 12.376). κῆρ is (neut.) acc. of respect after χωόμενον, which is the object of παρπεπιθόντες, redupl. aor. ppl. of παραπείθω with apocope of παρά (24–6n.) to avoid a sequence of four light syllables.

38 οἳ δ' ὅτε δή: typical phrase for arrival (1.432, 3.15 = 5.14 = 630 = 850, etc.), but the poet avoids the formular οἳ δ' ὅτε δὴ κλισίηισιν ἐν Ἀτρεΐδαο γένοντο (7.313 = 9.669), possibly to deny Agamemnon the authority of a patronymic (which occurs the only other 2× οἵ δ' ὅτε δή denotes arrival at a tent: 10.566, 11.618). ἷξον ἰόντες 'they came in their going': εἶμι is particularly prone to subordinated redundancy of this and related sorts in Homer, as e.g. βάσκ' ἴθι and βῆ (δ') ἴμεν/ἰέναι (*GH* II § 441): see also 105–7, 229–30nn. ἷξον is a 3rd pl. indic. 'mixed aorist' of ἵκω (ἱκάνω, ἱκέσθαι), combining the sigmatic aorist stem and the thematic ending -ον (*GH* I § 199; Roth 1990: ch. 5): cf. ἀξέμεναι (49–51n.), -βήσετο (212–13n.), etc.

39–41 The bath is a central social ritual in the heroic world, and Achilleus' continued isolation is encapsulated in his refusal to bathe (Reece 1993: 33–4; Grethlein 2007a: esp. 31–8). Line 39 is one of Homer's not infrequent four-word verses, its syntactical integrity underlined by absence of particles/conjunctions (Bassett 1919: esp. 228), lending weight to the attempt to reintegrate Achilleus through bathing.   κηρύκεσσι λιγυφθόγγοισι κέλευσαν: this phrase is elsewhere restricted to calling assemblies (hence the epithet 'clear-voiced': Kaimio 1977: 42–7, 231–3), but heralds can function as retainers, and Talthybios and Eurybates (1.320–1) may well be imagined more or less permanently at Agamemnon's command (895–7n.). Often given speaking names reflecting their need to travel (Kanavou 2015: 141–2), κήρυκες play a particular role in ritual activities like sacrifice, libation, and washing (9.174 = *Od.* 1.146 etc.), a central part of their function already in Mycenaean Greek (Wéry 1967 = 1975; Karavites 1987; Pisano 2014: 51–66).   ἀμφὶ πυρὶ στῆσαι τρίποδα μέγαν 'place on the surrounding fire a great tripod': ἀμφί extends the local meaning of the dat. πυρί to convey the covering of the fire (*GH* II § 123) and the flames around the sides of the cauldron (*LfrgE* s.v. C I5d, 668). The formulaic action is always performed by the character's retainers/slaves, and we are drawn back to Achilleus' instructions to clean Patroclos' corpse (39ᵃ = 18.344ᵃ; 40 ~ 345), and the pathos of Andromache waiting for Hector's return (39ᵃ = 22.443ᵃ).   Πηλεΐδην: Achilleus' most common patronymic (17–18n.) is only rarely found in the accusative, reflecting the fact that he is, when the poet is stressing this aspect of his identity, the action's agent rather than its patient.   λούσασθαι ἄπο βρότον αἱματόεντα 'to wash off the bloody mess': Achilleus is close to his own death, as this formula usually denotes the blood of the corpse being washed (7.425 esp., 14.7, 18.345; cf. Burgess 2009: 72–92). The recessive accent on ἄπο emphasises the connection with λούσασθαι 'wash *off*', since the adverb is in 'anastrophe', following the word with which it is to be construed (Vendryès 240; Bortone 2010: 133–40).

42–53 Achilleus' refusal is powerful, in its oath and depiction of the meal, and his speech also sets out the action to occur on the next day. His command of the situation, if not of himself, is absolute. Oaths show great formal variation in Homer, but may include (i) an invitation/request to give an oath, (ii) invocation of usually divine witness(es), (iii) terms of the oath, whether a statement or a promise, (iv) confirmation and/or the verb of swearing, and (v) concluding transition (Arend 1933: 122–3; Callaway 1998: 159–62; Sommerstein 2014a). This example (*OACG* 420) has only (ii) 43, (iii) 43–7, and (iv) 42. Each is unusual (see nn.), in keeping with the speaker's character.

42 ἐπὶ δ' ὅρκον ὄμοσσεν 'and he swore a great oath on it': only Achilleus offers unbidden oaths in the *Il.* (1.233–46: Kozak 2014: 213–21, 217), and the poet uniquely transfers into his own voice, at the front of the sequence, the typical verb of swearing in the formula ἐπὶ [μέγαν] ὅρκον ὀμ[– ⌣], which is elsewhere found only in character speech, blurring the line between poet-narrator and character (von Alvensleben 2022: esp. 99–118): also 208–11, 250–4, 545–7, 658–63, 850–1, 855ᵇ–8, 884–97nn. for other examples of this strategy.

43–4 While Apollo (1.86–7) and Poseidon (584–5n.) are invoked in oaths, Zeus is the most common such figure (7.76, 7.411, 10.329, etc.). For groups of gods in invocations of this and other sorts, generally including Zeus, see 3.276–9, 15.36–9, 19.258–60, etc.   **οὐ μὰ Ζῆν'** 'no, by Zeus': only Achilleus uses this powerful negation to preface his oaths in the *Il.* (1.86; cf. 1.234; Sommerstein 2014b: 80–1). Ζῆν(α) is a 'normalisation' of original short accusative Ζῆν which epos preserves in the verse-end formula εὐρύοπα Ζῆν (Janko 1982: 62–3: Intro. § 3.1.2.c.vii).   **ὅς τίς τε θεῶν ὕπατος καὶ ἄριστος** 'who is always the gods' highest and best': Achilleus uniquely alters the oath-formula ἴστω νῦν Ζεὺς πρῶτα θεῶν ὕπατος καὶ ἄριστος to accommodate his denial at the verse-start. The modification explains the unusual combination of ὅς τις with ὅς τε, the normal expression in oaths (1.86 etc.; *GH* I § 130, II § 353; Ruijgh 1971: 447–8), which emphasises Zeus as the invoked deity and renews Achilleus' sense of their particular relationship (like 1.352–4, 9.607–8, 21.187–99). The latter tells against interpreting τις as expressing pious uncertainty over the way to address the god (Richardson 170).   **οὐ θέμις ἐστί** 'it is not right': Achilleus claims normative status for his refusal to wash, but such claims are frequently made when contentious or unparalleled (2.73, 9.33, etc.) and need not imply 'divine sanction' (Richardson 170; see Scodel 1999: 49–50). Achilleus will still determine his own path.   **λοετρὰ καρήατος ἆσσον ἱκέσθαι** 'that bathwater come near(er) my head': this unusual expression perhaps echoes phrases like μηδὲ ἐᾶν νεκύων ἀμενηνὰ κάρηνα | αἵματος ἆσσον ἴμεν (*Od.* 10.536–7 ~ 11.49–50, 11.88–9, 147–8), and once more suggests Achilleus' closeness to death (34n.). Elsewhere in Homer ἆσσον + verb of motion has an animate subject (667–9n.), and refusals to bathe are expressed differently (e.g. *HDem.* 50, Hes. *WD* 753). καρήατος is a unique genitive singular (next in Theocritos), formed by adding -ατος (from the usual contracted gen. κρατός) straight to the nom. κάρη; cf. dat. sing. (καρήατι) and acc. pl. (καρήατα). Other genitive forms include κρατός, κάρητος, and κράατος (*GH* I § 102; Nussbaum 1986: esp. 159–94; *WHS* 59). For the accent of ἆσσον, see 8–9n.

45–7 The order of events is reversed in *hysteron proteron* (lit. 'later earlier'), since the cutting of hair (46: see 135–6, 140–53) precedes the pyre burning and construction of the tomb (45: see 177, 255–7). Greater emphasis is thus laid on the first element, and Achilleus' preoccupation with memorialisation in the σῆμα (Bassett 1938: 120–8; Minchin 2001b = 2007: 102–16). The brief promise in 46 looks forward to more elaborate examples in 135–6 and 140–53. Death ritual in Homer is frequently accompanied by tearing (18.27, 22.77, 22.405–6, etc.) or cutting hair (23.135–6, 140–53, *Od.* 24.45–6, etc.; Andronikos 1968: 18–20). Both practices are reflected in the visual record from the late Bronze Age right into the Archaic period (Huber 2001: 59, 82, 84–5, 92–3, etc.). For hair as an offering to the dead, see 135–6, 140–4nn.   ἐνί ... θέμεναι 'place ... on': ἐνί is a metrically useful alternative for ἐν, with final -ι perhaps an old locative ending (*EDG* 419).   σῆμά τε χεῦαι: Achilleus later specifies a modest tomb for Patroclos (23.245–8) to be enlarged when he is dead (cf. *Od.* 24.80–4), though the pyre alone is 100 feet square (162–4n.). Standard for prominent epic characters (6.419, 7.86, 24.799, *Od.* 1.291, etc.), tombs were constructed by piling earth over the pyre's remains (255–7; cf. 7.435–41) to make a visible monument (7.86, *Od.* 24.80–4: Andronikos 1968: 32–4). Homer mentions several *tumuli* on the Trojan plain (2.793, 813–14, 24.349, etc.) and, though almost all of them were in fact settlement mounds, they were a conspicuous part of the local topography, with tourists from antiquity and beyond directed to the 'tombs' of major characters from Trojan myth (Rose 2014: 60–2 (and pl. 2); Rose and Körpe 2015: I.373–5, II.169–70; Chiai 2017: 219–43). Signs of a long inhabited past, they fill the landscape with the potential for memory, and suggest the tenuous Greek hold over, or connection with, the landscape (Taplin 1992: 94–6; Trachsel 2007: 62–4, 79–98; Clay 2011: 58–9, 118–19): cf. Nestor's uncertainty about the σῆμα in the chariot race (331–3n.).   ἵξετ' ἄχος κραδίην 'pain will come to my heart': the only necessary run-over in this speech underlines Achilleus' perturbation. Hesitant but assenting, he predicts with unique certainty the formula ἀλλὰ τόδ' αἰνὸν ἄχος κραδίην καὶ θυμὸν ἱκάνει, which elsewhere marks reluctant compliance despite prior distress (Kelly 2007a: 182–3). ζωοῖσι μετείω: reinforces Patroclos' importance to Achilleus' story, since this expression elsewhere accompanies an intention to persist in an action or opinion that always turns out as foreseen (22.387–8, *Od.* 10.52; cf. 14.487). In fact, Achilleus will die after avenging Antilochos by killing Memnon (*Aithiopis* arg. 12–14 B), to which this current assertion may be a competitive allusion (Burgess 2009: 79–81). μετείω is 1st sing. pres. subj. of μέτειμι 'I am among', with -ει- for -ε- for the sake of metre (cf. μετέω 22.388).

48 ἀλλ' ἤτοι νῦν μὲν στυγερῆι πειθώμεθα δαιτί 'well then, now let us start by yielding to the hateful meal': though he may already have broken his fast (10–11n.), Achilleus' reluctance to eat is clear; such 'let us yield' injunctions can introduce the night-time repast (8.502, 9.65, 12.241, *Od.* 12.291), but only here is a meal the object and qualified negatively (Kelly 2007a: 354–5). Failure to appreciate this singularity presumably explains the variant τερπώμεθα (Σ AT and Π 13). The particle combination ἀλλ' ἤτοι νῦν μέν is confined to these contexts (cf. 15.211): ἀλλά breaks off the last theme with clarification/qualification of the situation (ἤτοι), before νῦν μέν subordinates current necessities to (δέ) the morning's instructions (Ruijgh 1981: 278–9, Cuypers 2005: 63–5): see also 279n.

49–51 The instructions now move to the next day, with the gathering of wood and the preparation of items (50–1) to be placed on the pyre (166–76n.). ἠῶθεν 'from dawn': i.e. from that point onwards (for the formation, Intro. § 3.1.2.c.ix): tr. 'at dawn'. ἄναξ ἀνδρῶν Ἀγάμεμνον: Agamemnon's authority is undercut by this unique use of the 'short' vocative formula without the honorific Ἀτρεΐδη κύδιστε (cf. 19.146, 199): also 35–58n. This adaptation has produced a rare 'neglect' of initial *digamma* in ϝάναξ, so that the preceding -ον remains light (some editors wrongly emend it to -ε; Ruijgh 1957: 114). The linguistic origin of the term is disputed, but in the Mycenaean world it denoted a figure of higher rank and more centralised power than the locally influential βασιλεύς, a distinction blurred in Homer, where βασιλεύς has much greater formulaic purchase (Shear 2004; Carlier 2006; cf. Yamagata 1997). ἄναξ ἀνδρῶν is shared with several figures in epos (only once each: Parry 1971: 93–4, 147–8), but the expression is distinctive of Agamemnon's role (Whallon 1969: 2–5, 30; Yamagata 2012: 451). ἀξέμεναι 'that they bring': 'mixed aorist' act. infin. of ἄγω, created by adding -εμεναι to the sigmatic stem ἀξ-. The source for these mixed forms may have been the 'future' imp. ἄξετε, developed because ἄγε/ἄγετε are not used to mean 'bring' (*GH* I § 199; Roth 1990: ch. 2): also 38n. This infin. is elsewhere future (e.g. 23.668). **νεκρόν:**

though Homeric eschatology often distinguishes the corpse and the soul, the former remaining in the mortal world while the latter journeys to the underworld, the terms νέκυς/νεκρός are also used to denote those in Hades (e.g. *Od.* 11.93–4: Clarke 1999: 191–3).   ὑπὸ ζόφον ἠερόεντα: this formula refers to the underworld or the (north-)west in general (ζόφος) as the place where the sun disappears, as opposed to dawn in the east (cf. 12.239–40, *Od.* 13.240–1; Jouanna 2015: 27–8). ὑπό is either a preposition (tr. 'down to') or a preverb describing the direction of travel (tr. 'downwards': *Od.* 11.57, 155; cf. 21.56; *GH* II §§ 204, 213): see also 28, 296–300nn. The epithet ἠερόεντα 'misty' lit. means 'abounding with ἀήρ' (itself 'raised substance' < ἀείρω = 'fog', 'mist'), and only qualifies nouns associated with the underworld (Puhvel 1983: 224–6; Thomas 2020: 242 on *HHerm.* 172).

52–3 ἀκάματον πῦρ 'tireless fire': the epithet is derived from κάμνω with a privative prefix, and normally deployed of persistently violent or destructive fire, and so appropriate for Achilleus' sense of loss (5.4, 15.597–8, 731, etc.: Graz 1965: 88–104, esp. 101ff.).   **θᾶσσον:** comparative adverb of ταχύς, though often used without an explicit comparison, and means here only 'forthwith' (KG II.ii.305–6: 'recht schnell'). For the accent, see 8–9n. (ἄσσον).   **ἀπ' ὀφθαλμῶν** '(away) from our eyes': more usually deployed where a hindrance to sight is removed (5.127, 15.668, 20.341), the formula can also denote simple origin (23.385, *HHerm.* 45).   **λαοὶ δ' ἐπὶ ἔργα τράπωνται:** i.e. the resumption of life after the funeral (cf. 3.422) or an anticipation of the games to come. τράπωνται is 3rd pl. aor. mid. subj. of τρέπω.

54 ὣς ἔφαθ', οἳ δ' ἄρα τοῦ μάλα μὲν κλύον ἠδ' ἐπίθοντο: Achilleus' assumption of authority is complete (35–58n.), since this verse frequently marks the crucial suggestion in deliberative scenes, giving instructions for the night (7.379, 9.79). τοῦ is gen. masc. sing. of the demonstrative pronoun, genitive after κλύον 'they listened/hearkened to'. ἠδέ is a form of δέ strengthened with the particle ἤ 'truly'. The MSS are split between ἠδ' ἐπίθοντο and ἠδὲ πίθοντο (favoured by Aristarchos, who thought unaugmented forms Ionic, older, and more authentic). The former is better attested here, and, while the poet uses both augmented and unaugmented forms of this verb at the verse-end, he frequently elides the conjunction in this position before other vowels (*GH* I §§ 230–1; West I.xviii).

55–8 Harmonious commensality seems to seal the reconciliation among the Greek leaders, and the typical transitional couplet for end of feast scenes (56–7 = 1.468–9, 2.431–2, 7.320 and 323, *Od.*

16.479–80; 56 = 1.602, *Od.* 19.425) subsumes Achilleus' first described meal since Patroclos' death (cf. 27; 10–11n.; Van Wees 1992: 44–8; Sherratt 2004). **ἐσσυμένως** 'eagerly, promptly': derived from the perf. mid. ppl. of σεύω, 'I set into motion, hasten', the adverb contrasts with Achilleus' attitude (48n.) to underline his continued isolation. **δόρπον ἐφοπλίσσαντες ἕκαστοι** 'preparing the dinner, each of them …': a unique participial form of the extended formular system for meal preparation found at both ends of the verse (| δόρπά τ' ἐφλοπισόμεσθα *Il.* / | δόρπον θ' ὁπλισάμεσθ(α) *Od.*; ὁπλίσσατο δόρπον | *Od.*), perhaps recalling the injunctions to prepare meals at the end of the second day's fighting (8.503 = 9.66: 48 above ~ 8.502 and 9.65): see also 10–11n. **δαίνυντ' … δαιτὸς ἐΐσης**: the wordplay encapsulates the poem's central theme of heroic division, since the gen. formula essentialises the relationship between δαίς 'banquet' (< δαίω/-νυμι) and its correct apportionment (Sherratt 2004: 309–10). Derived from ἴσος 'fair', 'equal', ἐΐσ- is only found in the feminine, with ἐ- either a 'prothetic' vowel added to ἴσος as early as Mycenaean or resulting from a false separation of ἀσπίδα πάντοσε ϝίσην ('shield balanced to all sides') as ἀσπίδα πάντοσ'ἐϝίσην (Reece 2009: 152–6). **πόσιος**: Ion. gen. sing. (= Att. πόσεως), the standard Homeric form for i-stem 3rd declension nouns (*GH* I § 93). **ἐξ ἔρον ἕντο** 'put the desire from them': only once outside the full formula (*Od.* 24.489). ἔρος is distinguished from ἵμερος as an internal disposition towards an action, rather than an externally imposed desire requiring immediate fulfilment (13–14n.). ἕντο is unaugmented 3rd pl. aor. mid. indic. of ἵημι. **οἳ μὲν κακκείοντες ἔβαν κλισίηνδε ἕκαστος** 'they went to lie down, each to his own tent', a typical night-time dispersal formula (1.606, *Od.* 1.424, 3.396, etc., with οἴκόνδε; Létoublon 1997: 145–6). κακκείοντες = κατακείοντες, nom. masc. pl. pres. act. ppl. with apocope of κατά to fit the metre, and assimilation of κατ- to κακ-. κείω is from the same root as κεῖμαι, with 'desiderative' or 'voluntative' force (*GH* I § 215; *LfrgE* s. κεῖμαι BII, 1363.42–54). ἔβαν is athematic 3rd pl. aor. indic. (= ἔβησαν 8.343 etc.). The enclitic suffix in κλισίην-δε denotes motion towards, as in e.g. Att. Ἀθήναζε (*GH* I § 113; Bortone 2010: 129–30). The paradosis favours κλισίηνδε over κλισίην δέ; several such compounds were already established as single words in Homer (ἐνθάδε, οἴκαδε, οἴκόνδε, etc.): 136–7n. For sing. ἕκαστος after pl. ἔβαν, see 1–3n.

59–61 Achilleus' posture and groaning are natural expressions of grief, but they are also characteristic of the shade in conversations with the dead (*Od.* 11.154, 388, etc. see 62–108n.), though this pattern will not be signalled decisively until 65. **Πηλεΐδης**: particularly effective here, given the importance Patroclos' spirit will put on their shared history in

Peleus' household.　**ἐπὶ θινὶ πολυφλοίσβοιο θαλάσσης** 'on the shore of the much-sounding sea': assonance and alliteration combine with the epithet to underscore Achilleus' troubled state of mind (60), since πολυφλοίσβοιο θαλάσσης is always preferred in such contexts to its metrical equivalent θαλάσσης εὐρυπόροιο (1.34, 2.209, etc.; Friedrich 2007: 127–8). Unhappy, isolated figures often frequent the shore of the Greek camp, usually to complain or invoke a deity's aid (1.34, 348–50, etc.; Kurz 1966: 117).　**κεῖτο** 'he lay': readily applied to corpses, but Achilleus is several times found thus beside his ships in angry isolation, a sense increased by the verb's run-over hyperbaton (Kurz 1966: 13–15, 39–42).　**βαρὺ στενάχων** 'deeply groaning': a poignant contrast with Achilleus' first use of this formula (1.364): unlike his loss of Briseis, this one cannot be made good.　**πολέσιν μετὰ Μυρμιδόνεσσιν:** the adjective shows a metrically convenient alternative for πολλοῖσιν, and belongs to the original 3rd declension of πολύς, preserved alongside the o-stem declension (*GH* I §§ 94, 117). For the 'artificial' dative plural Μυρμιδόν-εσσιν, see Intro. § 3.1.2.c.iii (the expected form Μυρμίδοσιν is unattested in epos: *GH* I § 87).　**κλύζεσκον** 'kept washing on': the 'iterative' action of verbs in -σκ- is reinforced here by the neuter plural subject (typically Homeric: 15–16n.), and parallels Achilleus' groaning 'to strengthen his psychological expression' (Elliger 1975: 68).

62–108 First Night. Achilleus' encounter with Patroclos' shade hastens the beginning of Patroclos' actual funeral and, coming at night after a series of (preview) funerary rituals (4–34n.), is paralleled in Iris' visit to the winds at the end of the next day (192–225n.); despite Thetis' protection of the corpse (19.38–9), the poet nods to the extraordinary length of Patroclos' *prothesis* and the state of the corpse (Intro. § 2.1). It also looks back to the Dream sent by Zeus to Agamemnon (2.16–47), reinforcing the large-scale ring composition which couples Books 1–2 with Books 23–4 around the poem's four days of battle (Intro. § 1).

The episode uniquely combines two typical sequences: (1) (*dream*) *visitations*, in which absent characters appear to and converse with sleeping figures (2.16–47, 24.679–94, etc.; Arend 1933: 61–3; Kessels 1978: 25–173, esp. 53–8; Lévy 1982: esp. 28–9, 37–8; Morris 1983; Walde 2001: 32–42; Khoo 2019: esp. 564–9); and (2) *conversations with the dead*, in which a figure encounters one or more spirits in Hades (*Od.* 11.51–83, 84–9/152–224, 90–151, etc.; Tsagarakis 2001: 26–37). The combination is natural, since death is commonly associated with sleep and dreams in early epic (Moreux 1967, Cousin 2015), and it throws great emphasis on the near-death state of Achilleus himself throughout the last third of the poem, and on the nature of his relationship with Patroclos (Gazis 2018: 47–76).

Some scholars connect this episode with the encounter between Gilgamesh and Enkidu's ghost (*Gilgamesh* SBV XII; West 1997a: 340–7, Clarke 2019: 231–301), but the shared elements are all typical in Greek epic, and polygenesis remains a more likely explanation (see generally Davies 2023); also above, 17–18n., and Intro. § 2.1, n. 36.

62–4 62 = *Od.* 20.56 (another *visitation*). The description of Achilleus' troubled sleep is resumed at 231–2 (n.) and 24.3–22, making clear that the coming funeral processes achieve little emotional resolution (Macleod 1982: 85).   **λύων μελεδήματα θυμοῦ** 'releasing the cares from his *thymos*': this formula denotes the onset of sleep immediately before its termination, but without alleviating the concerns on the coming day (*Od.* 20.56, 23.343; cf. *Od.* 4.650). Conventionally translated 'soul' or 'spirit', θυμός here represents Achilleus' consciousness *tout court*. Probably related to Lat. *fumus* 'smoke' (*EDG* 564), and elsewhere said to be located in the chest, it is a principal motivational force in the cognitive and emotional apparatus of Homeric humans, especially 'associated with strong feelings and compelling thoughts' (Graziosi and Haubold 2010: 89; see Clarke 1999: 61–126).   **νήδυμος** 'sweet': a linguistically 'false' formation, since ἥδυμος comes from ϝήδυμος (cf. ἡδύς), and is caused by (pre-Homeric) loss of *digamma* and subsequent use of ν mobile to cure the resulting hiatus: i.e. ἔχε ϝήδυμος > ἔχεν ἥδυμος > ἔχε νήδυμος (2.2 etc.; Reece 2009: 40–5).   **φαίδιμα γυῖα** 'gleaming/glorious limbs': despite its apparent positivity, this formula underlines Achilleus' emotional state, for it is always used of a defensive, defeated, or fearful character (Sacks 1987: 105–51, esp. 113–14): see 569 (ἰσόθεος φώς), 778–81nn.   **Ἕκτορ' ἐπαΐσσων:** though ἐπαΐσσω can take an accusative object, the dative (i.e. Ἕκτορι) is universal in aggressive contexts (Leaf II.475).   **προτὶ Ἴλιον ἠνεμόεσσαν** 'towards windy Ilios': this formula well summarises Achilleus' triumphant *aristeia*, despite the hero's rather circuitous route over the plain, since it is usually applied to Trojan withdrawals. προτί and ποτί are Aeolic forms of Attic-Ionic πρός, and the latter has replaced the former in almost every possible case (Janko 1979; *GH* II § 191). Though not restricted to Troy, ἠνεμόεσσαν is particularly suitable, given the city's elevation over the Hellespont and its strong air currents (Korfmann 1986: 7–8); its first syllable has been metrically lengthened (as e.g. ἠνορέη 'manliness' < ἀνήρ; *GH* I § 43).

65 ἦλθε δ' ἐπὶ ψυχή 'and there came to (him) the shade': this *conversation* formula (*Od.* 11.84, 90, 387, etc.) establishes the pattern and draws together the varied negative hints of death in the scene hitherto: 59–61, 62–4nn. ἐπί is here a preverb, i.e. 'to (him)'. West accents ἔπι in anastrophe

(39–41n.), against the MSS and the Herodianic rule that an intervening word (δ') cancels out such recession (Vendryès 241; Probert 2003: 127). ψυχή is derived from ψύχω 'I breathe' (*EDG* 1672); the 'breath' or 'spirit' can leave the body permanently at death or temporarily at swooning, and 'go down' to Hades and survive there (Clarke 1999: 53–60, 129–228). Patroclos' ψυχή is capable of some understanding; it retains memory and the capacity for speech, is fallible in its self-evaluation (87–8n.), and lacks only physical substance (103–4n.).   Πατροκλῆος δειλοῖο: the remarkable succession of heavy syllables in this repeated phrase is very suitable for the context of Patroclos' doom; otherwise, he has very few formulae and seems to exist primarily to die (Kahane 1994: 109–11, 138–41). This need not mean that he is the poet's invention (as some Neoanalysts argue), rather that his main function as Achilleus' companion (89–90n.) is reflected in his traditional diction (Kakridis 1949: 88–92; Janko 312–14; Willcock 2004: 59–60): also 8–9, 15–16nn. The association between the formula and the noun ψυχή will recur (104–6, 221), as this theme also moves to a crescendo (218–21n.).

66–8 The spirit's form underlines the bond between the men, since *dream* visitants usually have a close relationship with the sleeper. Its physical likeness to Patroclos fulfils the conversation's typical link between spirit and living counterpart (*Od.* 11.52–4, 86, etc.), which will be an important theme in the speech.   μέγεθός τε καὶ ὅμματα κάλ' ἐϊκυῖα | καὶ φωνήν 'like in/as to his great size and fair eyes, | and to his voice': accusatives of the 'internal object' or 'respect' with ἐϊκυῖα. Impressive size and physical beauty are important for Homer's mortals, and so 'fair eyes' need not have a specifically erotic import here (nor *Od.* 1.208, *HDem.* 194, 387, but cf. *HAphr.* 156): 77–91n.   ἐϊκυῖα 'likened': fem. ppl. of perf. ἔοικα 'I am like', from the zero grade of the stem, as e.g. ἰδυῖα versus masc. εἰδώς, with indic. οἶδα (*GH* I § 202); cf. 262–3n. Only here and at *Od.* 5.338 is the *digamma* before this form neglected; some editors print a resolved εἰ-, but ἐϊ- is the reading of the MSS, and the syllable never appears in arsis, where resolution would be necessary (cf. 17–18n.).   περὶ χροΐ εἵματα ἔστο: if clothes make the man (cf. *Od.* 6.29–30), this formula stresses the relationship between a character's appearance and narrative circumstance (*Od.* 11.191, 16.457, etc., *HAphr.* 64, 171, *Cypria* fr. 4.1 B), underlining the tantalising distance separating the shade's past substance from his friend's present. χροΐ is dat. sing. of χρώς 'skin', though Homer also uses a stem χρωτ- (only in washing contexts: 10.575, *Od.* 18.172, 179) which was later generalised (*GH* I § 90; also *HG* 90–2 for other Homeric 'heteroclites'). The hiatus before εἵματα and ἔστο results from *digamma* loss (both < ϝέννυμι: *GH* I § 54), and the *figura etymologica* 'clothed in clothing' is one of the most common and productive in the tradition (5.905, 16.670, 680, etc.: Clary 2009: 261–3).   στῆ δ' ἄρ' ὑπὲρ κεφαλῆς καί μιν πρὸς μῦθον ἔειπεν: this *visitation* formula (2.59, 24.682, *Od.* 4.803, etc.) establishes the pattern alongside that of the conversation, and helps to recall the parallel Dream sent to Agamemnon by Zeus. The coming note of rebuke is clear from πρὸς μῦθον ἔειπεν, a speech-introduction hemistich typical for such contexts (Kelly 2007a: 275–7). The form ἔειπεν = ἔ-ϝειπ-εν (Att. εἶπεν), i.e. augment + redupl. 2nd aor. stem (*ϝειπ-) + thematic vowel + ν mobile.

69–92 The shade's speech is passionate, urgent, and pathetic, perfectly encapsulating the two men's past relationship, current separation, and imminent reunion. It is carefully constructed in an A–B–A ring, in which commands for burial (71–4/82–92) surround and emphasise a central section focusing on the facts of death (75–81; Lohmann 1970: 28). The two A sections underline the parallel between the houses of Hades (71, 74, and 76) and Achilleus (84, 86, and 89) as Patroclos' destinations, and so draw Achilleus structurally closer to his doom. Each section is marked by its own vocative address to Achilleus (69, 80, 83) and by internal ring composition, where πύλας Ἀΐδαο (71) is resumed by εὐρυπυλὲς Ἄϊδος δῶ (74), λελάχητε (76) by λάχε (79), and ὀστέ᾿ ... | ἀλλ᾿ ὁμοῦ (83–4) by ὀστέα ... ὁμὴ σορός (91). This latter section, the longest of the speech, also has an inner ring (ὑμέτερόνδ᾿ 86 (see n.)/ἐν δώμασιν 89), reinforced by necessary run-over at 85–6 and 89–90 (also 75–6n.), expressing the shade's emotional investment in their shared past (Bakker 2005: 52–5). Constant first-person pronouns (69, 70–3, 75–6) reinforce this impression.

69–70 εὕδεις 'you are sleeping': an abrupt opening with asyndeton, typical of this *visitation* formula (2.23 = 60, *Od.* 4.804; cf. the gentler 24.683), immediately sets the rebuking tone that will spur the sleeper into action (2.23–5, 24.683–4, etc.).   λελασμένος ἔπλευ 'you are forgetful of me': a periphrastic construction (~ λέληθας), λελασμένος is the perf. mediopass. ppl. of λανθάνω, and ἔπλευ the 2nd sing. 2nd aor. indic. of πέλω/πέλομαι 'I become/am'. The aorist of this verb frequently expresses a present meaning (*GH* II § 272), complemented here by the participle's stative sense (Bentein 2016: 107–14). West restores both ἔπλε(ο) and μεο in the next verse on the basis that -ευ is a fourth-century Ionic contraction of -εο, but it is very well attested in our MSS and there is much earlier, sixth-century, evidence for it (*GHS* 80–1 n. 25; Passa 2001).   ἀκήδεις 'you did not neglect': unaugmented imperf. indic., i.e. 'you did not neglect me when alive, but (you do) now that I am dead'.

71–4 The spirit expresses the notion, rare in Homer, that the soul's entry into Hades requires prior cremation and burial (cf. the similar state of Elpenor, *Od.* 11.51–4, though his request for burial is differently motivated). Usually the ψυχή leaves the body and enters Hades without further ado (e.g. 1.2–4, 16.855–7 = 22.361–3, 482–3, *Od.* 24.1–204, etc.). Stressing the mainly social functions of the funeral rites, Clarke 1999: 188–9 suggests that these two examples are concerned more with preventing ghostly acts of vengeance, but, since the epic world is a traditional amalgam, Homer's eschatology is 'notoriously liable to exhibit inconsistencies and contradictions' (West 2001a: 266; see Wender 1978: 21–33; Sourvinou-Inwood 1995: 56–66; Gazis 2018: 1–46).   ὅττι τάχιστα 'as swiftly as possible': Patroclos' distress is clear, since this formula accompanies urgent instructions where the speaker's mood is heightened by self-interest, and may be marked by impatience or annoyance (4.193, 9.659, 15.146, 22.129, etc). ὅττι is the adverb (acc. neut. sing.) of the indef. relative pronoun ὅστις, here with unusual preceding hiatus (only 15.227, *Od.* 10.44, 19.403 – all sense pauses).   πύλας Ἀΐδαο 'gates of Hades': widespread in the ancient world, this proverbial epic image provides Hades with the epithet πυλάρτης 'gate-keeper/ -fastener' (cf. also 11.491, 16.696); also 74 (εὐρυπυλές). Olympos, Tartaros, the sun, and dreams also have πύλαι (*LfrgE* s.v. B4–8, 1637–8; Cerri 1995: 437–52, esp. 439, Tasso 2013).   περήσω 'I want to cross': 1st sing. aor. subj. of περάω in a 'voluntative' sense, used paratactically in an urgent asyndeton – i.e. 'bury me as quickly as possible, I want to cross' (Willmott 2007: 53–112, 194–7).   εἴδωλα καμόντων 'images of dead men': in apposition to ψυχαί (as also *Od.* 24.14; cf. 11.476; 103–4n.). This formula is unsurprisingly redolent of death; though an εἴδωλον is a likeness of a person, living or dead, καμόντων (masc. gen. pl. 2nd aor. act. ppl. of κάμνω 'I grow tired') is confined to the latter (cf. also 3.278; Clarke 1999: 195–205, 194 and n. 74).   ποταμοῖο: i.e. the Styx.   ἀλάλημαι 'I am a wanderer': 1st sing. perf. indic. mediopass. of ἀλάομαι, the perf. expressing a present condition to underline Patroclos' dire situation, since wandering is rarely a positive activity in early epic, even for the living (Montiglio 2005: 24–6, 45–61).   ἀν' εὐρυπυλὲς Ἀΐδος δῶ '[throughout] the broad-gated house of Hades': this formula conveys the immense size of the underworld, denoting the area in general terms; there is thus no need to argue that ἀνά means 'up and down the edge of' (Clarke 1999: 212 n. 102). The final syllable of εὐρυπυλές is lengthened solely by its princeps position. Ἀΐδος is an athematic gen. sing. of Ἀΐδης which provides a useful metrical alternative to thematic Ἀΐδαο (19–20n.). For the expressions Ἀΐδος δῶ/Ἀϊδόσδε, see 136–7nn.

75–6 This unique request is 'a gesture ... of affection and farewell' (Richardson 173; cf. *Od.* 18.258) foreshadowing Achilleus' pathetic attempt to embrace his friend's spirit (99–100; Lateiner 1995: 38, 68–9), and perhaps symbolising the pledge to act which the shade seeks (as, e.g., Soph. *OT* 1510; Mazon 1940: 257); the failure to grasp is yet more poignant when one remembers that even gods in disguise can take Achilleus' hands (21.286). Verse 76 violates 'Hermann's Bridge', the observation that there is usually no word division in the fourth biceps (*GM* 37–8; Intro. § 3.2). Schein 2016: 101, 114 suggests that this and other examples in this book (306, 760; cf. also 587, which he does not include) are poetically motivated, increasing the audience's emotional engagement with the content (see now Sansom 2025).   τὴν χεῖρ': the demonstrative has a weak sense, approaching that of an article (*GH* I § 129, II § 243), but it captures the notion 'that hand (of yours)', looking forward to Achilleus' failure to grasp him (99).   ὀλοφύρομαι, οὐ γὰρ ἔτ' αὖτις 'I mourn, because not any more hereafter': modern editors generally punctuate with a colon or full stop after the verb, linking it with the previous request and interpreting as 'I beg you' *vel sim.*, though there is no Homeric parallel for this meaning (Richardson 173; *LfrgE* s.v. B1c). Aristarchos neatly thought ὀλοφύρομαι a short vowel subjunctive 'so I may lament', presumably to ease the transition to a new thought after the elision, but cf., e.g., 1.52 for elision at a full stop, and the striking asyndeton gives a pathetic touch here.   νίσομαι 'I (am going to) return': necessary run-over emphasises the sadness, and is the first in a series of such run-overs in this speech (77–8, 78–9, 80–1). The verb shares the same stem (*nes-*) as νόστος 'return', so that the spirit's statement mirrors Achilleus' decision to die in Troy and lose his *nostos* (9.410–16 etc.; Bonifazi 2009): also 80–1n.   ἐπήν με πυρὸς λελάχητε: λελάχητε is 2nd pl. redupl. aor. subj. of λαγχάνω, with a transitive sense ('give someone his/her portion'), taking an accusative of the person and a genitive of the thing (Perpillou 1996: 166–78, esp. 176–7): see 77–9n. for another construction.

77–91 This passage is quoted in Aischines' *Against Timarchos.* § 149 (published some time after the trial itself in 346 or 345 BCE) to show that the relationship between Achilleus and Patroclos was of a higher level than the liaisons with which Timarchos was successfully smeared. In fact, Aischines is anticipating here the opinion of an anonymous general who was to speak on Timarchos' behalf (§ 132), though he does nonetheless grant that Homer intended them to be seen as lovers, a consistent theme in the reception of this relationship in antiquity (e.g. Aisch. frr. 228–9 Radt, Pl. *Symp.* 179e–180a; Xen. *Symp.* 8.21), 'but concealed their love and the proper name of their association' (§ 142: Fisher 2001: 288–90;

Fantuzzi 2012: 187–91): also 66–7n. Scholars cannot agree on the position in the *Iliad*: though Homer is well aware of homoerotic desire (e.g. 5.265–9, 20.231–5), the most we can say with certainty is that their association is more intense than any other in the poem, like everything connected with Achilleus in the *Iliad* (cf. also Clarke 1978; Fantuzzi 2012: 191–8; Warwick 2019; Austin 2021: 32–49; Lesser 2022: 196–201); for what it is worth, a parent–child simileme frames their relationship in the second half of the poem (222–5n.).

Aischines' quotation shows several differences from the Homeric vulgate, but the changes are more likely variants, driven by contextual purposes within the speech and/or the usual transmission dynamics of the ancient world, than evidence for the multiform model of Homeric composition (Intro. § 4; Appendix).

77–9 βουλὰς ἑζόμενοι βουλεύσομεν: the etymological figure βουλὰς βουλεύ- is split only here in Homer (9.75, 10.147, 327, 415, etc.: Clary 2009: 250–1), specifically to accommodate the ppl. and stress the fact that their councils took place φίλων ἀπάνευθεν ἑταίρων. On their inseparability, see e.g. 9.190–1, 19.315–18 (Macleod 1982: 125). **Κήρ** 'Doom': an anthropomorphic death-deity assigned to someone at birth, but more usually a synonym for death or even disaster leading to it (Dietrich 1969: 240–8; Clarke 1999: 231–63). No editor prints Κήρ with a capital letter here, but other figures are always so personified in this context (20.127–8, 24.209–10, etc.). **ἀμφέχανε** 'gaped around': a threatening hapax in early epos, its necessary run-over underlining the simplex verb's association with death, whether in wishes to that end (Kelly 2007a: 184–5) or in describing the appearance of the corpse's open mouth (16.350 etc.; *LfrgE* s. χανεῖν B2, 1138). **ἥ περ λάχε γεινόμενόν περ** 'which really was my lot when I was born': the unique repetition in the same clause of enclitic περ, which originally stressed 'superlativeness' and only later acquired a concessive meaning (Bakker 1988: esp. 271–6), encapsulates the irony of death's presence at the moment of birth. λάχε is an unaugmented 3rd sing. 2nd aor. indic. of λαγχάνω (76) which rarely takes a personal object for the lot gained by the subject (*HHerm.* 430), and so emphasises the agency of personified Κήρ (75–6n.). γεινόμενον is a metrically lengthened form of γενόμενον, masc. acc. sing. 2nd aor. mid. ppl. of γίγνομαι, construed with ἐμέ from the previous clause.

80–1 The spirit tells Achilleus, albeit with less detail, what he already knows from his mother (9.410–16, 18.95–6) and Hector (22.356–60), in one of several explicit predictions of his death in the poem's last third (Burgess 2009: 43–55). Unlike in those cases, however, Achilleus immediately agrees to do as he is bid (95–6).   μοῖρα: a 'share' or 'lot' of several sorts naturally extended into matters of mortality, as here, where it is the hero's death day (Dietrich 1965: 59–90, 194–231, esp. 200–1; cf. Sarischoulis 2008: 57–9).   θεοῖς ἐπιείκελ' Ἀχιλλεῦ: this formular address contrasts powerfully with the foretelling of his death (Amory Parry 1973: 221, Shive 1987: 111–14). Confined to Achilleus in Homer (in Hesiod of other mortal sons of goddesses), and always used in speeches reminding him of his past actions or thoughts (9.485, 494, 22.279, 24.486, *Od.* 24.36), the phrase plays on the sounds in ἐπιείκελ' and Ἀχιλλεῦ (like the related address θεοείκελ' Ἀχιλλεῦ: Rank 1951: 42–3). Kanavou 2015: 29–35 discusses many other examples (with e.g. ἀχλύς, ἄχος, χιλός, etc.): also 136–7, 222–5, 226–8, 255–7nn.   τείχει ὕπο Τρώων 'beneath the wall of the Trojans': this formula may allude to the famous battle over Achilleus, since it elsewhere describes the struggle for a warrior's corpse. ὑπό + dative has local sense here ('right by' or 'beneath'), and the recessive accent in anastrophe after τείχει.   εὐηγενέων 'noble': a positive conception of the Trojans aggrandises Achilleus by flattering his killers, and fits Homer's even-handed portrait of them elsewhere. The variant εὐηφενέων 'wealthy' is adopted by many modern editors, but it is only found in the scholia and may have originated in a fifth-century conception of the Trojans as wealthy Easterners (Sanz 1999).

82 ἄλλο δέ τοι ἐρέω 'and another thing will I say to you': Patroclos' true purpose is to start the burial process, since this formula is usually coupled with σὺ δ' ἐνὶ φρεσὶ βάλλεο σῆισιν to guarantee the request's fulfilment (1.297, 4.39, 5.259, 9.611, etc.; Janko 376), which is the very form of this verse in Aischines' quotation (Appendix).   αἴ κε πίθηαι 'in the hope that you (will) obey': αἴ κε + subj. expresses the purpose of its main clause in situations of 'uncertainty about the realization of the purpose' (Wakker 1994: 365–79, at 377), but Homer uses this collocation only where the particular instruction follows, and the speaker has greater conciliar authority (presumably granted here by Patroclos' death, as it was at the moment of his demise, 16.843–57). πίθηαι is uncontracted (< *-ησαι) 2nd sing. 2nd aor. mid. subj. of πείθω.

83–4ᵃ Here expressing the characters' unique closeness in the epic tradition (cf. *Od.* 24.73–9, where their remains are mixed and kept separate from those of Antilochos), multiple burials of a variety of types (inhumation, cremation, or a combination of the two) are far from unknown in the Bronze Age (C–M 93–4, 123; Gallou 2005: 112–14) and Protogeometric period (Lemos 2002: e.g. 166 on Lefkandi), though one observes across the Greek world a general transition 'to single burial after 1100' (Morris 2000: 200; see Lemos 2002: 151–90, esp. 189): also Intro. § 2.1; 91–2n.   μή ... τιθήμεναι 'do not place': μή + infin. expresses prohibition. τιθήμεναι is a metrically lengthened form of τιθέμεναι (= Att. τιθέναι) to avoid an unmetrical succession of three light syllables.

84ᵇ–90 The spirit recalls their shared history: the youthful Patroclos was brought by his father to Peleus to escape the consequences of murder. The story reinforces the request for burial, but also claims the conciliar authority typical of these figures ('metanasts', from μετανάστης 'migrant') who, after being attached to another man's household, act as advisors to the primary heir in the father's absence. Aside from Phoinix and Theoclymenos, Homeric examples include Lycophron (15.429–32, 437–39), Tlepolemos (2.661–70), Medon (2.727–8, 13.694–7 = 15.334–6), and Odysseus' 'Cretan' (*Od.* 13.258–86). Epeigeus (16.570–6) is another to have sought refuge with Peleus, who had himself suffered exile more than once (West 1985: 162–4). Their dependent status is clear from Achilleus' claim that he has been treated by Agamemnon as an 'unvalued/-able metanast' (9.648, 16.49), and the theme will be recalled when Priam's arrival at Achilleus' hut is described with a simile which puts him in the position of an exile arriving at the house of a 'rich man' (24.480–3: Brügger 2009: 171–2: see Martin 1992; Nünlist 2009; Alden 2012).

84–6 Distress at exile is emphasised by necessary run-over of ἤγαγεν, resumed by the description of the killing (λυγρῆς).   ἐτράφην 'I was raised': 1st sing. 2nd aor. pass. indic. of τρέφω, with unusual 'Attic' correption of the first syllable (Intro. § 3.2). The 1st sing. responds well to the speech's intensely personal and emotional emphasis (69–70n.; Richardson 174–5), but especially to the autobiography which follows, and is thus preferable to the variant ἐτράφημεν 'we were raised' or the emendation τράφομεν (intrans. aor. act. with a pass. sense) favoured by some modern editors (Van der Valk 1963–4: II.329–31), both of which look like an attempt to remove a supposed awkwardness after ὁμοῦ (Aischines' impossible ἐτράφεμεν was corrected by Scaliger to ἐτράφομεν: Appendix).   τυτθὸν ἐόντα 'being a little (child)': this detail underlines their closeness, for speakers use this formula to spur another to avenge or preserve a disrupted or otherwise unusual parental relationship (6.222, 8.283, 11.223, etc.: Kelly 2007a: 277–8, Pratt 2009).   Μενοίτιος: see 24–6n.   Ὀπόεντος: Opoeis in Locris (Classical Opus: *BA* 55, E3) is listed in the Catalogue of Ships under the command of Aias son of Oileus (2.531), and was Patroclos' original home (Kramer-Hajos 2012: 100–2). Menoitios is still in Phthiē when the war begins (11.765–90), but Achilleus mentions a vow to return Patroclos to Opoeis (18.324–7), perhaps assuming that the penalty for the murder can be paid (cf. 9.632–6); Peleus' household was traditionally a haven for such figures (84ᵇ–90n.).   ὑμέτερόνδ' 'to your (sc. house)': the suffix -δε (55–8n.) is frequently attached to possessive adjectives in this context, sometimes with a noun (16.445, Od. 14.424; GH I § 113). The ellipsis is made easier by 84 above, and by the formula ἡμέτερον δῶ 'to our house' (Le Feuvre 1997).

87–8 The youthful murder recalls Patroclos' progressive loss of self-control in battle (16.744–60, 626–31: Reinhardt 1961: 347–8), and prepares for the games, where similarly non-lethal competition continually threatens to tip over into violence.   ἤματι τῶι ὅτε 'on that day when': this formula focuses attention on the murder and suggests the gruesome symmetry that, as one killing began their friendship, so another will reunite them (cf. Od. 11.465–7; Kelly 2007a: 344–6); also 69–92n. for more parallels between the houses of Hades and Achilleus.   παῖδα ... Ἀμφιδάμαντος: Σ T 86a1 offers Cleisonymos, Aianes, or Lysandros as the child's name, while the father's is reasonably common (e.g. 10.268ᵍ); West 1966: 43–5 and 1978: 321 links him with the Amphidamas at whose funeral games Hesiod competed (WD 650–62, also part of a wider metanastic narrative 618–92). A direct interaction between Homer and Hesiod is possible, but it is equally likely that Hesiod knew much more Trojan War material in which Patroclos and Achilleus were closely paired (65n.).   νήπιος 'fool (that I was)': an apt criticism since, although the word may be a negatived form of ἤπιος 'gentle'/'well-disposed' (EDG s. νήπιος 1016–17), someone so judged in Homer seems to suffer primarily from deficient understanding, not infrequently from being a child (Ingalls 1998; Di Benedetto 1998: 26–32; Kelly 2007a: 205–8; Edmunds 1990).   οὐκ ἐθέλων ... χολωθείς 'not willingly ... in anger': unconvincing excuses, since the murder lacks the strong external constraint elsewhere linked with the first assertion (4.300, 6.165, etc.; cf. Od. 22.31) and the usual range of contexts for the second (21–3n.).   ἀστραγάλοισι 'at/over the bones': the ἀστράγαλος is an anklebone from calves, sheep, or goats used in a children's game described by Plato (Lysis 206e), and amusingly played between Ganymedes and Eros in Apollonios (Arg. 3.117–55; see Laser 117–22). It also denotes the human neck vertebrae, only mentioned in Homer when being broken (14.466, Od. 10.560, 11.65).

89–90 ἱππότα Πηλεύς: ἱππότᾰ may be a voc. retained *metri causa*, since ἱππότης would not fit into the verse, to allow an originally voc. formula to be used in the nom. case (*WHS* 34–5, esp. 37–8; cf. Moreschini 1984: 341–2, for whom it is a 'very old' nom.). This would suggest that Peleus was prominent in pre-Homeric epic, frequently addressed by poets and their characters. Restricted to heroes of the pre-Trojan War generation (Delebecque 1951: 164–5), the epithet is well justified, given Peleus' immortal team (276–8n.). That reminiscence underlines once more the theme of Achilleus' mortality.   **σὸν θεράποντ᾽ ὀνόμηνεν** 'named (me) your retainer': beyond the fact that this act leads eventually to Patroclos' death, the expression itself recalls the formula φίλον τ᾽ ὀνόμηνεν ἑταῖρον, which is only used for dead – or by dying – figures (10.522, 16.491, 23.178, 24.591: Kraus 1987: 25–7): see 178n. The θεράπων 'retainer' is a subordinate warrior not always clearly differentiated from the ἑταῖρος 'comrade' (6–7n.). He is an independent figure with his own subordinates and/or the charioteer for a more powerful man (Greenhalgh 1982; Krischer 1992; Hellmann 2000: 117–19). Drawing on the word's probable pre-Greek origin (*EDG* 541), and on earlier correlations with Hittite *tarp[an]alli* and *tarpassa* 'substitute, attendant', some scholars suggest that Patroclos was Achilleus' 'ritual substitute' or scapegoat, whose death through sacrifice saves the endangered king and his community (e.g. Nagy 1990a; Clarke 2019: 244–9; *contra*, decisively, Rutherford 2020); for the similar term ὀπάων, see 358–61n.

91–2 σορός 'funerary container': this item is specified as an ἀμφιφορεύς in 92, a verse modern scholars suspect was interpolated from *Od.* 24.73–4 (δῶκε δὲ μήτηρ | χρύσεον ἀμφιφορῆα). This is 'the only place where an ancient athetesis corresponds to an omission in a prearistarchean papyrus' (S. West 1967: 171), and Σ A argues both that it would be an 'illomened' gift from a mother and that λάρναξ is used 'in other cases' (citing 24.795; Haslam 1991: 36–7 and n. 4; Richardson 176–7). Yet 92 is otherwise universally attested (even being dislodged and recast as 83a–b in Aischines' quotation: Appendix), and Achilleus is doomed to an early death throughout the poem, as his mother well knew; Σ bT sensibly suggest that it was originally filled with wine and only later judged suitable as a funerary vessel. Indeed, the ἀμφιφορεύς was used as a casket both in the *Odyssey* and throughout the Greek world in the Protogeometric and Archaic periods (Kurtz and Boardman 1971: 70–2, 74; Lemos 2002: 152–5, 163, 182–4).   **ἀμφικαλύπτοι** 'may it conceal': independent opt. of wish (*GH* II § 315), and ὥς is to be taken with καί ('so also') rather than as a conjunction. Misinterpretation as a purpose clause probably led to subj.

ἀμφικαλύπτηι in Π 12 (S. West 1967: 171).   **χρύσεος ἀμφιφορεύς:** pre-sumably given when Achilleus set out from home (Σ bT), the vessel is else-where described as Dionysos' gift and Hephaistos' work (*Od.* 24.73–6). Its grandness matches its unique purpose, and it recalls the divine panoply as a valuable present from Thetis vitally connected with her son's death. The bones will actually be stored temporarily in a φιάλη (243–4n.) in Achilleus' tent until the joint burial (252–4; *Od.* 24.76–7; cf. Petropoulou 1988).   **πότνια μήτηρ** 'queenly mother': πότνια is an august term linked with IE words for 'goddess', and was originally the fem. of the root in πόσις 'lord, husband' (*EDG* s.v. 1226–7). Aside from Thetis, this for-mula usually denotes mortal women (cf. *Od.* 12.134, *HDem.*39) and so essentialises her maternality, perhaps even weakening her divine stature: she is constantly depicted in the *Iliad* in a state of sorrow because of her short-lived son, and the notion that divine mothers of mortal children were compromised in some way by that fact contributes e.g. to Aphrodite's shame at Aineias' conception (*HAphr.* 247–55; Faulkner 2008: 10–18).

93–8 Achilleus' final speech to the spirit opens with a redundant ques-tion (94–6n.) before agreeing to the instructions and suggesting a final embrace. The intimate repetition of the 1st pers. pronoun recalls the preceding speech (69–92n.).

93 **τὸν δ' ἀπαμειβόμενος προσέφη πόδας ὠκὺς Ἀχιλλεύς:** a typical response introduction, each hemistich being itself a formula; the first is used when the speaker is trying to reassert authority (Kelly 2007a: 281–5), and the second shows one of Achilleus' 'distinctive' epithetal expressions (Parry 1971: 88–93) to reflect his traditionally encoded speed, a feature known to but not emphasised by Homer (20.89–93, 188–90, 21.599–601, 22.7–24, etc.; Foley 1991: 139–43; Burgess 2009: 14–15): see also 140–4, 217–18, 249nn.

94–6 The opening question seems to ignore the shade's speech and may suggest Achilleus' groggy state (hence Π 12's explanatory plus-verse 93a ἡδὺ μάλα κνώσσων ἐν ὀνειρείηισι πύληισιν ~ *Od.* 4.809: S. West 1967: 172), but it reflects the combination of *visitation*, where the visitor speaks first, with *conversation*, where he or she is questioned first (*Od.* 4.809–10, 11.57–8, 91–4, 154–62, etc.: 62–108n.).   **τίπτε** 'why ever?': synco-pated from τί ποτε, used to introduce a variety of surprised and/or indig-nant questions, but rarely found in responses (1.202, 6.254, 7.24–5, etc.: 62–108n.).   **ἠθείη κεφαλή** 'familiar head': 'the address of a young man to an elder' (Σ A 94) and a particularly intimate combination, since ἠθείη is derived from ἦθος 'custom' and applied to close kin (Bettini 1988:

165; Clarke 1999: 172–8, esp. 174 n. 29).   **εἰλήλουθας:** 2nd sing.
perf. act. indic. of ἐλθεῖν (= Att. ἐλήλυθας), with εἰ- metrically lengthened
from ἐ- to accommodate an 'antispastic' (◡ – – ◡) word, and -ου- rather
than -υ- also *metri gratia* (*GH* I §§ 44, 202; *WHS* 344–5; cf. ἀπελήλῦθα
etc.).   **ἐκτελέω** 'I will thoroughly complete': ἐκ- underlines the sense
of completion (Waanders 1983: 43–7) in an example of 'parechesis' (ech-
oing of one word by another, similar-sounding one) after ἐπιτέλλεαι, stressing Achilleus' sense that the shade's order is necessary (cf. *Od.* 11.294–5
= 14.293–4 ἐξετελεῦντο | περιτελλομένου: Hackstein 2007, Tsitsibakou-
Vasalos 2007: 27–96).

97–8 ἆσσον: see 8–9n.   **μίνυνθά περ** 'for a very (περ) short while':
on the particle's superlativing function, see 77–9n., though here its effect
is possibly concessive (*contra* Bakker 1988: 246–9).   **ἀμφιβαλόντε:**
nom. masc. dual aor. act. ppl. of ἀμφιβάλλω, here 'I embrace' with personal
object ἀλλήλους (98: cf. 24.588, *Od.* 8.455, etc.). The dual is used with pl.
principal verbs in these contexts to stress the relationship between the
two men (*Od.* 11.211–12, where 212[b] = 23.97[b], 21.223; more generally
5.847–8 etc.), and so is preferable to the variant plural reflected in the
majority of MSS, which often try to regularise Homer's duals.   **ὀλοοῖο
τεταρπώμεσθα γόοιο:** 10–11n. The notion that the object of the γόος (13–
14n.) could participate in it is a pathetic adynaton, resuming the theme of
the grieving shade (75–6n.), its desperation reinforced by anacolouthon
after στῆθι and the concluding, heavy, four-word verse (39–41n.).

99–101[a] This failed embrace underlines existential distance, as in other
conversations (*Od.* 11.204–24, 387–94), but also their closeness, since
embraces between the living are usually reserved for members of the same
family (*Od.* 16.214, 17.38, 19.415–17, 23.207–8, etc.; cf. *Od.* 16.20–1;
see Lateiner 1995: 58, 69; cf. Purves 2019: 158–9).   **ὠρέξατο χερσὶ
φίλησιν** 'he reached out with his hands': Patroclos, Achilleus (24.506),
and Hector (22.37, 24.743) are connected once more (Intro. § 1, n. 19)
by this gesture of supplication, generally directed to mortals within a
request (also *Od.* 11.392, 12.257, 17.366) or to gods during prayer (1.351,
15.371, *Od.* 9.527; cf. *HDem.* 15).   **ἠΰτε καπνός** 'just like smoke': the
image may evoke here the spirit's insubstantiality and its stress on cremation. Σ bT invoke slightness, and likeness to wind and movement, while
reporting the objections of Zoilos, the fourth-century 'Homeromastix' or
'Homer-whipper', that smoke is borne upwards. Otherwise unmentioned
in Homeric funerary discourse, smoke connotes destruction (8.183,
9.243), esp. in similes, where it is connected with Achilleus' violence in a
thematic run culminating pathetically at this moment of failure (18.110,

207, 21.522; cf. 22.149–50: Graz 1965: 80–1, 85–6, 250; Ready 2011: 42–8).   ᾤχετο 'it went' or 'it was gone': 3rd sing. imperf. indic. mid. of οἴχομαι. This verb frequently has a perfective sense 'I am gone', which is possible here (as 577), and would underline the pathos of the situation, since the shade was already gone as Achilleus tried to grasp it.   τετριγυῖα: fem. nom. sing. perf. act. ppl. of onomatopoeic τρίζω 'I chirp'/'I squeak', an inarticulate sound made by spirits (*Od.* 24.5, 7, and 9), birds (2.314), and the straining backs of the wrestlers (23.714), all in fairly trying situations (Tichy 1983: 64, 69–70, 121–2, 126; Perpillou 1996: 15; Heath 2005: 391–2).

101ᵇ–2 ταφὼν δ' ἀνόρουσεν 'and astonished he leapt up': this typical reaction to a close friend's unexpected but welcome arrival signals another thematic completion, here of Achilleus' previous reactions to embassies, and his decisions (9.193, 11.777; cf. *Od.* 16.12; Kurz 1966: 70–9; Lateiner 1995: 45–6); see Intro. § 1, p. 9 for other culminating themes.   **ταφών:** masc. sing. nom. 2nd aor. act. ppl. related to τέθηπα (perf. act. indic.), with no present stem (*WHS* 237–42, esp. 241).   **χερσί τε συμπλατάγησεν, ἔπος δ' ὀλοφυδνὸν ἔειπεν** 'and he clapped together (with) his hands and spoke a grieving word': hands usually strike other parts of the same person, esp. in mourning (18.30, 123, 22.33, 77), and this singular action recalls πεπλήγετο μηρώ | χερσί καταπρηνέσσ', ὀλοφυρόμενος δ' ἔπος ηὔδα (15.113ᵇ–14 = 397ᵇ–8 = *Od.* 13.198ᵇ–9; cf. *Il.* 12.162–3, 16.124–5: next n.), a formula which accompanies reactions to disturbing news or events, especially 'to foreshadow Patroclos' imminent death' (Lowenstam 1981: 32). The second hemistich by itself connotes grief driven by separation from a loved one (5.683, *Od.* 19.362). Because ϝέπος here can be restored by omitting preceding -ν (and is observed in the *Od.* example), this expression may be an older complement of the less common ὀλοφυρόμενος δ' ἔπος ηὔδα, which always neglects the *digamma* (Hoekstra 1965: 65–6); for the form of ἔειπεν, see 66–8n. The idiom 'say a word' in a variety of forms is a particularly common *figura etymologica*, but not for that reason an empty rhetorical strategy (Clary 2009: 134–40, 267–70, esp. 135).

103–4 An old crux, since Achilleus denies that spirits possess φρένες straight after this one has shown a capacity for thought (104 cannot simply be deleted, given its attestation, but it would solve the problem: West 2001a: 268). Σ offer a number of solutions: (i) intrusion from *Od.* 10.492–5, where Teiresias' spirit alone retains φρένες; (ii) φρένες refers only to the actual organ (see below); (iii) spirits of the unburied retain φρένες until cremation (cf. *Od.* 11.51–83); (iv) Achilleus is commenting negatively on the shade's erroneous impression of his neglect; (v) οὐ πάμπαν means 'not entirely' rather than 'not at all' (Van der Valk 1963–4: I.540–2). Failed embraces (99–101) typically reflect on physical insubstantiality (*Od.* 11.219–20, 393–4), so (ii) and (v) are the likeliest solutions, since (iv) does not account for the rest of the speech (cf. γάρ 105), and (i) and (iii) try to smooth out Homeric eschatology, which can deny or allow spirits speech and thought when needed (e.g. *Od.* 11.218–22 against 11.385–564, etc.; Sourvinou-Inwood 1995: 76–94; Clarke 1999: 157–228; West 2001a: 267–8). For the statement's gnomic character, see Lardinois 1995: 107–9, 130–1.   ὦ πόποι 'oh dear': onomatopoeic opening exclamation for speeches with a surprised realisation (1.254, 2.157, 272, etc.; Kelly 2007a: 220–3).   ἦ ῥά τίς ἐστι 'really, then, there is someone': in apposition to ψυχή καὶ εἴδωλον in the next verse (i.e. 'it is really the case that there is someone in the house of Hades – a spirit and an image ...', etc.), and in agreement with ψυχή as 'the closer subject' (*GH* II § 24), rendering unnecessary the variant τί 'something'/'in some way', for which Dué 2001b = 2019: 55–66 compares Propertius 4.7.1 *sunt aliquid manes*, but which looks like an attempt to smooth out a superficially awkward phrase.   καὶ εἰν Ἀΐδαο δόμοισιν: 19–20n.   ψυχή καὶ εἴδωλον: 65, 71–4nn. The collocation (as at 72) indicates the combination of *visitation* (where εἴδωλον is more usual) and *conversation* (where ψυχή is).   φρένες οὐκ ἔνι πάμπαν '*phrenes* are not within at all': the φρήν or (more usually) φρένες are an organ in the chest (16.481, *Od.* 9.301) and also the human rational/emotional processes (Clarke 1999: 66–79: also 62–4n.). ἔνι is used absolutely, the anastrophe indicating ellipsis of ἐστί/εἰσί (14.141, 216, etc.; *GH* II §§ 3, 141; Probert 2003: 138); for -ι see 45–7n. The intensive compound πάμπαν 'not at all' (πάν + πάν) most commonly strengthens a negative, underlining Achilleus' absoluteness; less often it means 'not entirely' (e.g. 13.177), in which case he would be asserting physical absence and yet a capacity for thought (Thesleff 1954: 220; *HW* 105–6).

105–7 παννυχίη 'all night': looking to the emphatically delayed ψυχή in 106, such actions typically set the scene for a corresponding, nocturnal episode, but Achilleus again uses traditional units in a novel manner, looking back to rather than introducing that episode (Kelly 2007a: 356; 217–18n.).   **Πατροκλῆος δειλοῖο:** 65n.   **ἐφεστήκει γοόωσά τε μυρομένη τε** = 6.373 (Andromache), perhaps linking once more the fates of Hector and Achilleus through their dependants' grief (Intro. § 1 with n. 19). The 'redundancy' in γοόωσά τε μυρομένη τε is typically Homeric, facilitating versification and retaining attention on the (already emphasised) noun (1.196 = 209, 2.374 = 4.291, etc.; O'Nolan 1978):

also 38n. γοόωσα is fem. nom. sing. pres. act. ppl. of γοάω, by diectasis from contract γοῶσα (*GH* I § 31f.).   **μοι ἔκαστ':** light scansion of -οι shows neglect of *digamma* (1–3n.).   **ἔϊκτο** 'he was likened': unaugmented (< *(ἐ)ϝέϝικτο) 3rd sing. mid. pluperf. indic. of perf. ἔοικα 'I am like' but with neglect of initial *digamma*; cf. the augmented form ἤϊκτο (*Od.* 4.796 etc.).   **θέσκελον** 'wonderfully': originally a 'godly drive/command' (θεσ- + κέλομαι: *EDG* 543), a meaning which might be seen in some Homeric contexts (3.130, perhaps *Od.* 11.610; but cf. *Od.* 11.374), and in Hesiod (frr. 195.34 = *Scut.* 34, 202.96 M–W). Only here in epos is it used without ἔργα.

108 τοῖσι δὲ πᾶσιν ὑφ' ἵμερον ὦρσε γόοιο 'started to rouse (in them all) a desire for lamentation': by specifying the dative object rather than a genitive source for it (Beck 2005: 141), this formula achieves the group generalisation picked up in the following verse, and connects Thetis' opening lament (23.14: 13–14n.) with Achilleus' hair-dedication to Spercheios later in this book (152–3n.), which is similarly connected to an expression marking day's start or end (109 ~ 154) and a funeral instruction carried out by Agamemnon (112–13/155–62); see also 154–5n. ὑφ' is adverbial, emphasising the initiation of the action (*GH* II § 203).

109–225 Second Day. This is the first of the standard two days of the funeral sequence (Intro. § 2.1). The Greeks begin to fulfil Achilleus' earlier instructions (49–51), constructing the pyre (110–28) and carrying Patroclos' corpse to the burial site (128–39) before Achilleus rededicates a lock of his hair to his friend (140–53). The pyre is built (155–64) and eventually lit, after Iris' intervention and voyage to the winds (192–225).

109–10ª When in the form of an independent clause introduced by μέν or δέ, Homer's expressions for dawn enact or follow through on the substance of a preceding nocturnal episode (Kelly 2007a: 67–8; cf. *Od.* 3.1–3, 5.1–2, etc.). Unnecessarily run-over ἀμφὶ νέκυν ἐλεεινόν (110) resumes the current theme.   **ῥοδοδάκτυλος Ἠώς** 'rose-finger Dawn': the epithet refers either to the sun's rays resembling a splayed hand or (more likely) dawn's appearance as a band across the horizon (West 1966: 311–12; Janni 2011). This beautiful phrase more usually occurs in ἦμος δ' ἠριγένεια φάνη ῥοδοδάκτυλος Ἠώς, and it is a familiar marker of Homeric poetry even today, as in Terence Malick's *The Thin Red Line* (1999: Hesk 2015: see Létoublon 1997; Radin 1988).

110ᵇ–26 The Greeks cut down and gather wood for the pyre. Two framing passages (110–16/120–6) form a ring around the description of the tree felling (117–20), which is thus emphasised and itself marked by three consecutive necessary run-overs in 119–21 (118–21ᵃn.). Covering the journey to and from Ida's foothills, the frames are in five parts: [A] order given by major Greek (110–12 Agamemnon ~ 125–6 Achilleus); [B] Meriones' command (112–13 ~ 123–4; 113 = 124); [C] men (114–15 ~ 123; ὑλοτόμους 114 ~ ὑλοτόμοι 123); [D] mules (115 ~ 121–2); [E] men and mules (116 ~ 120–1): see 111–16n. for another ring within the first framing passage.

110ᵇ κρείων Ἀγαμέμνων: this formula and the expanded εὐρὺ κρείων Ἀγαμέμνων show that power is traditionally associated with Agamemnon (κρείων 7×/εὐρὺ κρείων 1× for Poseidon; Whallon 1969: 2–5; Kanavou 2015: 44–5). That authority is undermined here when Agamemnon is replaced by Achilleus in the corresponding element of the passage's ring (125–6): see 35–58n.

111–16 Another ring structure, focusing attention on Meriones (112–13n.), within the overall ring's first frame: [a] mules 111; [b] men 111–12; [c] Meriones 112–13; [b] men 114–15; [a] mules 115.

111–12 οὐρῆας 'mules': of uncertain derivation (*LfrgE* suggests οὖρον 'distance to marker in a field'), this term is chosen over ἡμιόνους (cf. 121) for its rhyme with ἀνέρας. Combining the virtues of mixed equid parentage – strength, endurance, speed, and (relative) elegance – the mule is used in Homer and later literature for both prestige and mundane tasks (24.265–80, 17.742–3). Central to farming (Hes. *WD* 46), they were valuable enough to be offered as a prize in the games (23.259–61, 654–5: see nn.; Richter 1968: 76–80; Griffith 2006a: 229–39, 2006b: 336–52).   **ἀνέρας:** ἀνήρ has two stems in epos, the more frequent ἀνδρ-(ἄνδρα, ἀνδρός, etc.) and ἀνερ- (ἀνέρα, ἀνέρος, etc.), the latter always with ἀ- (*GH* I § 92: Intro. § 3.1.2.c.viii).   **ἀξέμεν:** 49–51n.   **κλισιῶν:** instead of the usual κλισιάων (found here in one medieval MS), this sole Homeric example of the 'later' gen. pl. form of this word (original -ᾱ(σ)ων gives Aeol. -άων and Ion. -ήων > -έων > Att. -ῶν) is 'normally found after -ι' in a few other nouns (*GH* I § 25), and sometimes considered an Attic feature (Intro. § 3.1.1).   **ἐπί ... ὀρώρει** 'he rose up (for)' *sc.* the task': 3rd sing. plpf. act. indic. of ὄρνυμι (cf. ὄλωλα < ὄλλυμι; *GH* I § 201). Meriones' role is emphasised, since only here does a named individual serve as the subject of the (plu)perf. forms of this verb. The form is often linked with ἐπί-ουρος 'guardian' (13.450) as though from ὄρομαι (*Od.* 3.471, 14.104) to mean something like 'supervised' (*GH* I § 202; cf. Meister 1921: 20 and n. 1), but other forms of ὄρνυμι routinely have the required meaning, esp. in the games (e.g. 288, 290, 689, etc.): 112–13n.

112–13 As Patroclos to Achilleus (89–90n.: Clay 1983: 84–5), Meriones is Idomeneus' θεράπων (and his ὀπάων: 358–61n.), fighting together with the Cretan leader in Book 13 but increasingly independent of him as the poem progresses (Erny 2020: esp. 208–11; Camerotto 2010: esp. 5–6). Structurally and thematically foregrounded (111–16n.; see also below), Meriones' role here extends his attendant functions elsewhere (9.80–4, 10.57–9, 196–7, 19.238–40) and recalls the simile of 17.742–3, where he and Menelaos, carrying Patroclos' corpse from the fray, are compared to mules dragging a tree trunk from a mountain (Σ T 111b); cf. also 16.632–5, where a woodcutting simile describes him returning to the fray with Patroclos after the latter had rebuked him for flyting (16.626–31), while Σ AT 113 add that Crete, Meriones' home, is 'mountainous and tree-bearing', making him a natural choice for this task. We are thus prepared for his participation in the games, where he comes second last in the chariot race, defeats Teucros at archery, and receives a superior prize to Agamemnon's in the spear throwing (450–5n.).   **Μηριόνης, θεράπων ἀγαπήνορος Ἰδομενῆος** = 124 (110ᵇ–26n.), in emphatically delayed runover reinforced by the four-word verse (39–41n.). This honorific whole-verse expression (thrice, all in this book) may seem ill-suited to an otherwise second-tier character, but his formulae are prominent in this part of the poem (528–9n.) and of great antiquity (see 358–61n.; Janko on 13.249–50, 78–9; Kanavou 2015: 53–4; Erny 2020: esp. 208–11). His name may originally derive from Hittite *maryannu* 'chariot-warrior' (West 1997a: 612) or else from a skill in running (< μηρός + ὀνίνημι: Mühlestein 1987: 43n.), but he largely drops out of the poetic tradition after Homer (Webber 2018: 39–45). Friedrich 2007: 107 plausibly suggests that this formula replaces Μηριόνης ἀτάλαντος Ἐνυαλίωι ἀνδρειφόντηι because of the non-martial context. The epithet ἀγαπήνωρ 'beloved of men/man loving' is used only in epos and only to qualify second- (or lower) rank heroes; it is the name of the Arcadian leader in the Catalogue (2.609), whose grandfather Lycourgos appears in Nestor's story of Pylian/Arcadian hostility (7.133–55), and whose father Ancaios was an Argonaut killed in the hunt for the Calydonian Boar (Latacz at al. 2003: 197).

114–15 πελέκεας: always trisyllabic in Homer, with -εα- one, heavy syllable in synizesis (*GH* I § 16); for the axes, see also 850–1n.   σειράς: ropes to drag the tree trunks.

116 Remarkably sonant verse, with repeated α and internal rhyme underscoring the dactylic rhythm, perhaps expressing 'the sound of the stamping feet' (Leaf II.480, sceptically; Packard 1974: 247; Stanford 1981: 129 with n. 3).   ἄναντα κάταντα πάραντά τε 'upwards, downwards, sideways': all hapax in epos, with the suffix (adv. ἄντα 'over, against') strengthening the simple adverbs in each case (*WHS* 355–6, 363–4); for similar repetitions, see βριήπυος ὄβριμος Ἄρης (13.521), τριχθά τε καὶ τετραχθά (*Od.* 9.71), Προΐωξίς τε Παλίωξίς τε (*Scut.* 154; Rank 1951: 29–30). This verse was parodied in Matro's *Attic Dinner* (fr. 1.46 Sens–Olson) to describe the cook's progress through the diners, holding serving trays.

117 The foothills of Mt Ida (Turkish *Kazdağı*), whose name means 'timber, forest' (*EDG* s.v.), have a locative formula Ἴδης ἐν κνημοῖσι (2.821, 11.105, 21.449); they are still heavily wooded and verdant today (Rix 2002; Höhfeld 2009: 77–90, esp. 81–9; Ellis-Evans 2019: 57–108). Given the mountain's centrality to Trojan history and wealth (Mackie 2015), the Greeks' use of its wood symbolises their control over the city and its future.   **πολυπίδακος Ἴδης** 'of many-springed Ida': this particularised formula is explained by the 'many rivers flowing from' the mountain (Strabo 13.1.43), and remains accurate (Cook 1973: 306). An o-stem form πολυπιδάκου is found in some MSS and in other early texts is the more favoured reading, e.g. *HAphr.* 54. It may be authentic, since 'thematism' is common in epos (e.g. δάκρυον nom. sing. < δάκρυα nom. pl. < δάκρυ nom. sing.; *HW* 157–9; Faulkner 2008: 138–9).

118–21ᵃ The felling (or falling) of trees is a common image in Homeric similes for the deaths of young men (Scott 1974: 70–1; 2009: 21–2). It is doubly fitting here, where the trees become the funeral pyre consuming Patroclos and the Trojan youths. Emphasised by the passage's ring structure (110ᵇ–26n.) and necessary run-overs in 119–21, the 'simileme' intrudes into the main narrative to form the climax of this important thematic run (Intro. § 1.2, pp. 9–10 for others). Staccato parataxis of ταὶ δέ, τὰς μέν, and ταὶ δέ connects closely with the remarkable, triple necessary run-over of τάμνον, πῖπτον, and ἔκδεον to move swiftly from one clause/subject to the next (cf. ἐπειγόμενοι 119 and ἐλδόμεναι 122), as the ring's central action progresses hurriedly into the journey back to camp.   **δρῦς** 'oaks': the original form of the acc. pl. (< *-υνς), later generalised to δρύας under the influence of other 3rd declension nouns (cf. νέκυς/νέκυας; *GH* I § 95).   **ταναήκεϊ χαλκῶι** 'with the keen-edged bronze': verse-end formula connoting death in battle and so adding to the simileme effect (7.77, 24.754, *Od.* 4.257; Bakker and Van den Houten 1992).   **ταὶ δὲ μεγάλα:** ταί is the nom. pl. fem. demonstrative pronoun, an Aeolic form preserved in Homer for metrical reasons (here avoiding hiatus after ἐπειγόμενοι) alongside later Ionic–Attic (and Lesbian) οἵ/αἵ (Intro. §§ 3.1.1.b, 3.1.2.a.ii). The final syllable of δέ is heavy as though before *μμέγα, but without any linguistic justification for the double consonant (*GH* I § 70; Intro. § 3.2). Accepted by Aristophanes of Byzantium (but not Aristarchos), this kind of gemination reflects the influence of performance practice on consonants (mostly λ, μ, ν, and ρ) which were considered to 'make position' for a preceding syllable, and is often found written out in the papyri and even in some medieval MSS (West I.xxvi): see 196–7, 203nn.   **πίπτον:** this is the accentuation found in the MSS, but some papyri have the reading πεῖπτεν, so modern editors generally print as πῖπτον (West I.xxi).   **ποσσί:** regular dat. pl. for πούς (stem ποδ- > *ποδ-σι), which (like many consonant-stem nouns in Homer) also shows the artificial πόδ-εσσι (see Intro. § 3.1.2.c.iii).

121ᵇ–2 δατεῦντο 'they divided': the mule teams spread out to distribute the territory amongst themselves, as often more literally with this verb (*LfrgE* s. δατέομαι 1c, 224), but there may also be a metaphoric reflection of hooves cutting up the earth (cf. 20.394) or divergent tracks on its surface (Σ AbT 121; Borecky 1965: 15–22, esp. 18ff.).   **ἐλδόμεναι** 'longing for': (ἐ)έλδομαι, like several verbs of 'aiming at' or 'seeking to achieve' (ἀντιάω, ὀρέγομαι, etc.), usually takes a genitive, as here (*GH* II §§ 64, 55 R iv).   **ῥωπήϊα πυκνά** 'thick brushwood': another formular expression (cf. 21.559) for the rich flora of Ida (117n.), suggesting the funeral's ominous peace, since ῥωπήϊα are elsewhere places of death (13.199), concealment (21.559), or ambush (*Od.* 14.473).

123–4 124 = 113 (112–13n.). For Μηριόνης, West prints ὀτρηρός 'attentive', found wrongly spelled only in one, often eccentric, papyrus (Π 12); this reading was obviously influenced by the formular association between the adjective and the noun θεράπων (*Od.* 4.123, 217; cf. 1.321, *Od.* 1.109), and driven by a desire to avoid repeating the name so soon after 113, but this kind of variation is entirely alien to the Homeric aesthetic.   **ὑλοτόμοι** 'wood-cutters': a noun, not an adj. as in 114. This shift was a source of ancient disquiet, with e.g. Π 12 reading ὤμοισιν instead, but Richardson 181 correctly invokes ring structure (110ᵇ–26n.) to support the majority reading.   **φιτρούς** 'beams': the term is in Homer associated only with funeral pyres and related constructions (12.29, 21.314, *Od.* 12.11). Preserving this association, it occurs next in Bacchyl. 5.141–2 to denote Meleagros' fateful log (Cairns 2010: 83–4).   **ἀνώγει** 'he ordered': elsewhere this form is frequently 3rd sing. pres. act. indic. of a thematic present ἀνώγω, which was derived from perfect ἄνωγα (e.g. 6.439. 7.74, etc.; Ruijgh 1957: 128–9), but here it is an unaugmented pluperf. functioning as a simple past tense; also 158–60n.

125-6 These lines close the ring to return to the Greek camp (~110–12), with mirrored necessary run-over of the command verb (φράσσατο ~ ὤτρυνε 111), though this time Achilleus gives the instructions, as he will do again to the Myrmidons carrying Patroclos to the pyre (138–9). New foundations will be needed for the tumulus (245–8 and 255–7 with nn.; also 7.435–7) which, returning to the spirit's request for co-burial (82–92), will serve for them both.   ἐπὶ σχερῶι 'on the shore': usually printed as adverbial ἐπισχερώ (< ἔχω) and taken to mean 'in order' or 'side by side' (*WHS* 355), the expression only describes actions on the shore-line in contexts of death or mourning (11.668, 18.68), and is a misinterpreted locative which has some MS support but was later confused with σχερός 'succession', 'order' (Pindar, *Nem.* 1.69, 11.39, etc.; Janko 1979; Perpillou 2005: 267–74, esp. 271).   ἠρίον 'grave monument': the etymology of this Homeric hapax is unexplained (*EDG* 526). Referring to function and not phsyical form, ἠρίον is found on several Attic marble discs used as grave offerings, and on the late sixth-century funeral *stele* of Archedamos at Delphi (Jeffery 1990: 271, 277 no. 33, with 411 pl. 52; Roller 1981a: 3–5, Sourvinou-Inwood 1995: 125–8, 156–8), and it is commonly deployed in Hellenistic verse (Hollis 2009: 264). Homer also uses the term στήλη for such markers (11.371, 17.434, *Od.* 12.14–15). Stone monuments of this sort were used as actual race markers in funeral games in the late Archaic period (McGowan 1995).   ἠδέ οἱ αὐτῶι 'and for (him) himself as well': hiatus after ἠδέ is obviated by original *digamma* before οἱ (*GH* I § 55: Intro. § 3.2), dat. masc. sing. of the 3rd pers. pronoun, itself light in correption before reflexive αὐτῶι (*GH* II § 234). Unaccented (and so unemphatic) οἱ is the majority reading here, but Achilleus' agency and future burial with Patroclos is a constant theme in this passage, and could support the accented form οἷ.

127-39 The Greeks bring the wood and set up the pyre after the Myrmidons in procession bring Patroclos' corpse. The abbreviated mass arming scene and formal procession parallels the earlier driving around Patroclos' tomb in the pre-funeral preview (14–16; see 4–34n.), and initiates the *ekphora* (13–14n.), which brings the corpse to its place of cremation and/or interment (though there is to be some delay in Patroclos' case). For artistic and material evidence, see Andronikos 1968: 43–51; Kurtz and Boardman 1971: 58–61 (Geometric); 78, 83 (Archaic); 144–6 (Classical); Ahlberg-Cornell 1971: 220–39 (figs 53–5).

127-8ᵃ παρακάββαλον 'they set down round about' = (unmetrical) παρακατέβαλον, with apocope and assimilation of κατ(ά) before β- (*GH* I

§ 37), reused at 683 (see also 28n.).   **ἄσπετον ὕλην** lit. 'unspeakable (amount of) wood': stressing again Ida's abundance, since the epithet in this formula, derived from the same root as ἐννέπω 'I announce' (*EDG* 153–4), denotes something too large for description, and is frequently used of earth and meat (Bakker 2015: 63–4, 70 suggests it has 'cosmic' significance). This particular collocation unsurprisingly stresses the amount of material, esp. in contexts where it is to be burned (2.455, 24.784) or is reacting to a great force (*Th.* 694, *HDion.* 10).   **εἵατ᾽** 'they sat': 3rd pl. imperf. indic. mid. of ἧμαι. -ατο reflects this athematic verb's original consonant stem *ἡσ- (i.e. *ἡσ-ντο > ἥατο), though Homer also uses ἥντο (3.153; *GH* I § 228; Intro. § 3.1.2.d.i).

128ᵇ–31ᵃ The procession around the corpse was also found in Achilleus' funeral, though once the pyre was lit (Intro. § 2.1), and is a well-known feature in artistic representations of the Geometric period (Andronikos 1968: 43–51). A four-word verse, 129 recalls 39 (39–41n.), where the Greeks attempted unsuccessfully to bathe Achilleus. The chiasmus centred around ζώννυσθαι ζεῦξαι τε in 130 throws emphasis on the delay of run-over ἵππους and the individual totality of the action in ἕκαστον.   **Μυρμιδόνεσσι φιλοπτολέμοισι:** see 5, 59–61nn.   **ὑπ᾽ ὄχεσφιν** 'beneath the chariots': purely locative (cf. 6–7n.).   **ἕκαστον:** accusative rather than dative after κέλευσε because subjects of an infinitive (ζεῦξαι), when referring to dative objects of the governing verb, may be 'raised' to the accusative (e.g. 1.541 τοι ... ἐόντα, 15.57–8 ἄνακτι ... παυσάμενον; *GH* II § 456). For sing. ἕκαστος after pl. verbs and nouns, see 1–3n.

131ᵇ–4 The leaders in their chariot teams (ἱππῆες) and the mass of infantry (πεζοί) prepare to mourn. 132ᵃ ~ 352ᵃ below (ἐς δίφρους), showing the interchangeability of acc. and dat. in this context, the latter chosen here for metrical reasons.   **παραιβάται:** lit. 'those who go beside', i.e. the warriors (cf. 11.104, 522). Used here to accommodate a word otherwise beginning with three light syllables, παραί appears both alone and in compounds (e.g. παραίφασις 2×) with no difference of meaning from παρά/ πάρ, though it was in origin a specifically locative formation (García-Ramón 1997: 48–51).   **νέφος εἵπετο πεζῶν** = 4.274 (of the Greek army). Elsewhere 'associated with death or extreme danger' (Moulton 1979: 291; cf. e.g. 16.66, 17.755; also Moreux 1967: esp. 243, 263; Cairns 2016: 32–6; 188n.), the cloud metaphor particularly captures the size of the Myrmidon host ('and its appearance and how it marches': Σ b 133–4), specified by the run-over of μυρίοι 'countless', which was used already of the Myrmidons (29) and is common in descriptions of advancing armies and similes within them (2.467–8, 4.433–6). Placement of Πάτροκλον between verb and subject enacts mimetically the introductory ἐν δὲ μέσοισι.

135–6 Looking back to Achilleus' soon-to-be-fulfilled (140–53) earlier promise (45–7n.), this almost unique action is highlighted by the run-over participle, and variously interpreted as an offering which 'delights and strengthens' the corpse since hair is a repository of power and a symbolic representation of the self (Schnaufer 1970: 163–4); as mimicry of the deceased (cf. 18.22–7, 24.160–5; Marinatos 1967: 19); a reversal of human norms and appearances, so as not to be touched by the dead's 'dangerous breath' (Andronikos 1968: 19); a symbol of separation (Sourvinou-Inwood 1995: 110), and so on. Whilst removal of hair is a typical mourning practice in Archaic literature and life (45–7n.), its offering to the dead person is usually confined to mythological contexts and hero cult (Richardson 182–3), and here prepares for Achilleus' similar offering (140–4n.; also Intro. § 2.1). **κατάεινυον** 'they totally clothed': 3rd pl. imperf. act. indic. of καταέννυμι; the tense stresses duration, and so is preferable to the variant aor. κατάεινυσαν. More often used to describe forest-covered mountains (*Od.* 13.351, 19.431, *HHerm.* 228, etc.), the striking metaphor recalls the clothes which Patroclos' spirit was wearing (23.67) and perhaps the typical funeral vestments (16.680–1, 18.352–3, 22.510–14, etc.; Brügger 2009: 209).

136–7 Mourners hold the head of the lamented figure both in Homer (24.712, 724; cf. 18.71) and in the material record from Bronze and Iron Age Greece (Huber 2001: 204–5; Brügger 2009: 244–5). **δῖος Ἀχιλλεύς:** the epithet is used of a few characters in epos, and mostly in the nominative of Odysseus and Achilleus, but its meaning is uncertain ('divine', 'heavenly', 'radiant'?), partially because of this distribution. It may have little semantic import beyond a general heroic stamp (*LfrgE* s.v. B, 313); see also 140–4n. Run-over ἀχνύμενος focuses attention on the 'paronomasia' or wordplay (Tsitsibakou-Vasalos 2007) essentialising the relationship between pain (ἀχ-) and Achilleus' name (Louden 1995: 34; Kanavou 2015: 29–35); also 80–1, 226–8, 255–7nn. **ἕταρον ... ἀμύμονα** 'excellent companion': for the noun, see 5, 6–7nn. The epithet is usually interpreted to mean 'blameless', as though from negative ἀ- and the root for 'blame' (μῶμαρ, μῶμος), though more recently it has been linked with the stem found later in ἀμεύομαι (= ἀμείβομαι) 'surpass' (*EDG* s.v.: for the old controversy over its meaning, in that it was often linked with reprehensible characters like Aigisthos, see Amory Parry 1973; Foley

1999: 211–13).   Ἄϊδόσδε 'to Hades': the expression is only here
in this position and lacks the usual verb denoting the soul's departure,
since it is uniquely viewed from a living person's perspective: again it is
as though Achilleus stretches Homer's formular resources, anticipating
his own doom. Usually paired with acc. nouns, the allative suffix -δε is
deployed with gen. Ἄϊδος (71–4n.) in the common ellipsis 'to Hades'
[house]', aided by the formula Ἄϊδος δῶ (*GH* I § 113): see 84–6n., and
200–1ᵃn. for a similar ellipsis (Ζεφύροιο … ἔνδον).

138–9 οἳ δ' ὅτε χῶρον ἵκανον, ὅθι 'and they when they came to the place
where': unique alteration of arrival formula with χῶρον for δή ῥ' (and thus
requiring unaugmented ἵκανον for an initial light syllable), emphasising
the pyre's site, though once more Achilleus is unusual in moving immediately away (140ff.), since elsewhere the introduced action remains in
the same place (e.g. 4.210–20, 18.520–9, etc.).   **κάτθεσαν** 'they
set him down': for unmetrical κατάθεσαν/κατέθεσαν, with apocope of
κατά.   **μενοεικέα νήεον ὕλην:** the epithet probably means no more
than 'desired', i.e. by the nature of the task and those who commanded it
(29n.), but Blanc 2012: 80–1 links it with the fire's μένος (175–7n.). νήεον
is 3rd pl. imperf. act. indic. of νηέω, the tense denoting the start of the
pyre's construction, to which the poet returns at 163–5.

140–4 140–1ᵃ = 193–4ᵃ, paralleling this dedication and Achilleus' prayer
to the winds (194–225) as particular marks of honour for Patroclos, and
symbols of his own status. Standing 'apart', in particular, helps to connect the two rituals (193–5n.). Achilleus' hair dedication looks back to
the Myrmidons' hair on Patroclos' chest (135–6n.), but expands its ritual
scope whilst individuating its significance; he removes a lock of his own,
promised by Peleus to the river Spercheios on his son's safe return, and
places it in his friend's hand, turning a once hopeful vow into a guarantee of imminent doom. It is characteristic of him to 'nullify vows to rivers
and disparage their ability to protect even their own sons' (Fenno 2005:
482 n. 19: 21.128–35, 184–8, 389–92: see Intro. § 2.1). Orestes similarly dedicates hair to the Inachos, and sets another lock on his father's
tomb (Aisch. *Choe.* 6–7: see Garvie 1986: 50–1). The offering of hair to
rivers was a common transitional rite in ancient myth and life, since rivers were considered nurturers of the young (Σ T 142a1; Leitao 2003:
112–26; Parker 2011: 75–6). For other votive offerings in Homer, see
6.302–3, 7.81–3, 8.203–4, 10.462–4, 10.570–1 (Seaford 2004: 54–6).
Located in Phthiotis and running into the Malian Gulf (*BA* 55, C3),
Spercheios was the father of Menesthios, one of the leaders mentioned in
the Myrmidon catalogue, by Peleus' daughter (and Achilleus' half-sister)

Polydore (16.173–8; Janko 340–1). ἔνθ' αὖτ' ἄλλ' ἐνόησε 'then in turn he thought another thing': only twice in the *Iliad* (also 193 below) but common in the *Odyssey*, this expression signals an unheralded change of course, often with following asyndeton (as here) to underline the unexpectedness of the new event (see 138–9n.). The subject (Achilleus 2×, Athene 8×) has great directive authority in the circumstances (S. West 1988: 154; De Jong 2001: 66). ποδάρκης δῖος Ἀχιλλεύς 'with foot-defending godly Achilleus': the first epithet is derived from πούς and ἀρκέω 'keep off, aid, suffice' (*EDG* 1215) and encompasses fighting on foot to defensive and offensive purpose (*LfrgE* s. ποδάρκης, 1306); cf. βοηθόος 'running to the cry for help'. For δῖος, see 136–7n. The combined expression occurs only in the *Iliad* and 7× in this book, setting Achilleus' legendary swiftness (93n.) next to his refusal to compete in the games (Whallon 1969: 14–17). ξανθήν ... χαίτην 'flame-blond ... hair': though this is not a distinctive epithet as it is for Menelaos (293–5n.), Achilleus' hair is elsewhere said to be of this colour (1.197; cf. his horse Xanthos 19.405; Nagy 1979: 209–10 suggests that it connotes immortality), a feature reproduced in the later-attested alternative name of his son Neoptolemos, Pyrrhos, given by his maternal grandfather Lycomedes (*Cypria* frr. 19, 21 B; cf., e.g., Archilochos fr. 304 W² with Swift 2019: 419; West 2013: 108). Familial allusions and references in this passage may suggest that the juxtaposition πυρῆς ξανθήν was deliberate. Sometimes used as a name (divine 6.4, 8.560, etc.; human 5.152; horses 8.185, 16.149, etc.), the adjective usually denotes human or animal hair colour in epos, and is once used of the river Hermos (*HHom.* 34.4). τηλεθόωσαν 'blooming': fem. acc. sing. pres. act. ppl. of τηλεθάω (lengthened form of θάλλω), formed by diectasis (< τηλεθῶσαν < τηλεθάουσαν): 105–7n. ὀχθήσας δ' ἄρα εἶπεν 'troubled, then, he spoke': Achilleus addresses the river-god as intimately as his own soul; this hemistich is usually elsewhere found with πρὸς ὃν μεγαλήτορα θυμόν to introduce internally directed monologues (11.403, 17.90, 20.343, etc.: Scully 1984). As with all these speeches, the association helps to suggest his coming doom and a collapsing in the divine/mortal distinction (see 144–5n.). ἐπὶ οἴνοπα πόντον '[to] the wine-faced sea': Achilleus faces thus 'since he is looking away to his fatherland and Spercheios' (Σ bT 143b; Aubriot-Sévin 1992: 126 and n. 2, 135–6). Observing original *digamma* (ϝοίν-), the famous epithet in this formula is generally taken to refer to the sea's colour in sunny reflection (dark red, purple, *vel sim.*) or its lack of brightness (*LfrgE* s. οἶνοψ, 594; Sacks 1987: 36–40; also 315–18n.), but Murray 2018: 7–8 suggests radically that it is drawn from the effects of wine's fermentation process and means 'foam-flecked'; for other explanations, see Pulleyn 2019: 157.

144–51 Explaining why he is altering the deal made by Peleus, there is rebuke in this quasi-ritualistic address (144–5n.), with its emphasis on unfulfilled reciprocity (146–8) and on the hair as votive (146, 151, 152), and its pointed reiteration of second-person pronouns (144, 146, 148, 149). There is also a sense of resignation, as the original guarantee of Achilleus' return now confirms his impending death. The speech falls into two sections, the first (a reminder of promised ritual action: 144–9) centred on vows (146–8) ringed by the failed prayer (πατὴρ ἠρήσατο Πηλεύς 144 ~ ὣς ἠρᾶθ' ὁ γέρων 149; ἄλλως 144 ~ σὺ δέ οἱ νόον οὐκ ἐτέλεσσας 149); the second comprises the resulting intention (150–1), but is joined with the first by repeating the link between return and the offering (νοστήσαντα/κόμην 145–6 ~ οὐ νέομαι/κόμην 150–1).The first section is itself a compressed example of prayer, a frequent, highly typicalised sequence in Homer (Morrison 1991; Aubriot-Sévin 1992; Pulleyn 1997; Kelly 2007a: 250–3; Hitch 2009: 83–7).

144–5 The insertion of 145 before the expected infinitive complements for ἠρήσατο fronts the condition for the promise, Achilleus' now doomed return.   **Σπερχεῖ':** though a prayer need not open with an epithet or 'hymnic' description (e.g. a relative clause giving the god's powers or location), this short address is made curter by elision and the following ἄλλως (Aubriot-Sévin 1992: 254 and n. 108, on honorific epithets). The invocation thus seems almost directed against an equal (Aubriot-Sévin 1992: 45 and n. 37: see 140–4n.), or equivalent to the cry of pain typical in ὀχθήσας monologues (Scully 1984: 13).   **ἄλλως** 'in another way': i.e. 'to another purpose', as implied in the parallel νόον οὐκ ἐτέλεσσας (149) and shading into 'in vain' (Σ A 144).   **φίλην ἐς πατρίδα γαῖαν** 'to my dear paternal land': recalling 18.101 (= 150 below, with οὐ νέομαι for νοστήσαντα) to underline the failure of Peleus' hopes, this pleonastic formular expression typically points out the distance between the individual and his *nostos* (2.140, 158, 5.867, etc.; Bonifazi 2009: 489; Briand 2015).

146–8 A rising tricolon of promises, memorably introduced by the chiastic and alliterative 146, before concentrating on the ram sacrifice (147), emphasised and expanded with unnecessary run-over (148). Either the victims' blood is poured into the river itself, not on its altar as with the hecatomb, or the victim is simply thrown into the waters (as at 21.132; Parker 2011: 75, 186 n. 85). Sheep were a common sacrificial animal at all periods, but this is a ruinously expensive undertaking, since the number fifty in this context usually comprises the whole herd, not just the rams (*LfrgE* s. πεντήκοντα 1bβ–8, 1155; Germain 1954: 21–2).   **κερέειν:** fut. act. infin. of κείρω. Like other 'liquid futures' which show *epsilon*-contract

forms (e.g. μενέω from μένω), the -έειν ending is uncontracted κερέ- + -ειν
(= Att. κερεῖν) and was perhaps the source of the distinctive thematic
aorist infinitive forms like βαλέειν etc., which are sometimes explained as
examples of diectasis (*GH* I § 238; Nikolaev 2013).   **ῥέξειν θ᾽ ἱερὴν**
ἑκατόμβην 'to sacrifice a holy hecatomb': literally a sacrifice of 'one hundred oxen' (or perhaps intended to result in such a number as a gift
from the gods: Puhvel 1964), the hecatomb is actually any large number of victims (*EDG* 396–7). While ἱερὴν ἑκατόμβην is the normal noun–
epithet combination, this formula uses κλειτήν for archers' sacrifices of
'firstborn lambs' to Apollo (4.102 = 120, where ἱερήν is avoided given
ἱερῆς εἰς ἄστυ Ζελείης in 103 = 121, 23.864 = 873 (see nn.): cf. also 7.450
= 12.6). Not understanding this distribution, Π 12 inserts this verse in the
later parallel scene (140–4n.) as 23.195a (S. West 1967: 183).   **παρ᾽**
αὐτόθι 'right by there': picked up by ἐς πηγάς (148). αὐτόθι = αὐτοῦ, with
locative suffix -θι, intensified by adverbial παρά expressing proximity (*GH*
II § 170).   **ὅθι τοι τέμενος βωμός τε θυήεις** 'where you have your pre-
cinct and fragrant altar': the only *temenos* in the poem where a sacrifice is
actually narrated (Hitch 2009: 69–70), the location adds to the rebuke,
since this formular idiom is elsewhere followed by the god's activity at this
site, and serves as a reminder of the honour paid there (8.48, *Od.* 8.363;
HAphr. 59; Kelly 2007a: 100–1). The 2nd pers. τοι (19–20n.), with ellipsis
of 'is', shows that, for Achilleus, the river has failed to live up to its part of
the deal, and he will deprive it of further honour in his turn.

150 = 18.101, where Achilleus expresses to Thetis his desire to avenge
Patroclos, connecting once more her prospective lamentation for
Achilleus with his actual γόος for Patroclos (Kelly 2012: 246–54).

151 Πατρόκλωι ἥρωϊ: the common noun ἥρως means little more than
'warrior' or 'man of status' in epos (*LfrgE* s. ἥρως, 939) and is unlikely to
refer to a hero cult in the Archaic period, whether Homer knew the institution or not (cf., e.g., Currie 2005: 48–57; Nagy 2012 and often; Deioudi
1999; Clay 2025): also 188–91n., and Intro. § 2.1.   **φέρεσθαι** 'for
carrying': pres. mid. infin. of φέρω used in what we term a 'result/final'
function, a very old capacity of the infinitive 'to complete the main verb,
expressing sometimes the result of the action and sometimes its purpose'
(*GH* II § 441). This form is found only in this position and in the *Iliad*
only in contexts of death (16.671 = 681, 21.120, 24.581) or imminent
doom (11.798).

152–3 -οιο homoioteleuton (as also 154) underlines the connection
between the placing of hair in Patroclos' hands and the consequent

lamentation.   ὡς εἰπών: this very common speech-closing formula
is chosen instead of the usual ὡς φάτο· τοῖσι δὲ πᾶσιν ὑφ' ἵμερον ὦρσε γόοιο
(see 108n.) so as to split the usual action over two verses (Beck 2005:
72–3), because the poet wished to retain the focus on Achilleus' dramatic,
run-over, act in 153 (Hoekstra 1965: 105–7).

154–5 Recalling the language of 109–10 at the day's start and so closing its
preliminary funeral processes (108n.), this contrafactual conditional sentence ('and now A would have happened, had not X ...': Morrison 1992;
Kelly 2007a: 128–32) strengthens the lamentation by intimating that its
continuation could have delayed the funeral beyond the usual two-day
span, a similar concern to that expressed by Patroclos' spirit (69–71). The
same syntax will be used for the Trojan women's initial lamentations for
Hector (24.713–15), interrupted by Priam to allow the funeral to proceed.
Line 154 = *Od.* 16.220, 21.226. Both occasions are emotional reunions
between Odysseus and members of his household, and suggest an association between lasting emotion and narrative retardation. Expressions for
day's end are more common and formular in the *Od.* (Radin 1988; De
Jong 2001: 42), but every such passage in the *Il.* is followed by a nocturnal episode (Kelly 2007a: 349–51): also 105–7n. Word placement in 155
mirrors the reversal in authority (35–58n.), as Achilleus literally surrounds
Agamemnon.   φάος ἠελίοιο: suitable more broadly for the present circumstance, given the common metonymic use of this formula for 'life',
and the general association between light and safety (Durante 1971–6:
2.116–18; Lossau 1994). For another form of φάος, see 226–8n.   εἶπε
παραστάς: continuing the tension, this expression is related to the 'stood
beside' idiom (Kelly 2007a: 272–5) and goes beyond connoting 'a certain
familiarity' (Kurz 1966: 95) to frame the following speech as critical or otherwise qualified in its support of the addressee, who proceeds to perform
the suggested action (6.75, 12.60 = 210 ~ 13.725, 23.617, etc.; cf. 20.375).
The examples in Book 23 are the only ones in the poem not addressed
to Hector. West prints minority variant Ἀγαμέμνονα because Ἕκτορα is the
object on several occasions (12.60, 210, 13.725, 20.375), but he is also
addressed in the dative case (6.75; cf. also *Od.* 16.338).

156–60 Achilleus gives another set of orders to Agamemnon (49–53
~ 110–12), this time fulfilled immediately: the army is to be dismissed
(158–9 ~ 162) while the closest companions construct the pyre and perform a series of ritual acts (159–60 ~ 163–7). Formally courteous but
potentially critical (156–7n.), the speech alludes to an earlier instruction given against his wishes (158–9) and closes with a subversive pun
(158–60n.).

156–7 Outlining an addressee's great power before giving instructions can make implicit criticism more palatable (e.g. Nestor to Agamemnon 9.69–75, 96–102), perhaps suggesting that Achilleus, entirely without cause, is trying to intimate that Agamemnon is responsible for the funeral's delays (see 9.32–9, 225–8, 12.211–14, 24.543–8; Scodel 2008: 49–73). **Ἀτρεΐδη** 'son of Atreus': the voc. of the patronymic adjective may signal Achilleus' awareness of social distance (Brown 2006: esp. 28–34), but its use without further qualification has an intimate tone often linked with rebuke or reproof of various degrees, particularly noticeable whenever Achilleus uses it (1.59, 232, 19.56; for other speakers, cf. 1.282, 2.225, 242, 284, etc.). On the patronymic itself, see Kanavou 2015: 47–8; Higbie 1995: 44–7; also below, 890–1n. **γόοιο μέν ἐστι καὶ ἆσαι** 'of lamentation it is possible *really* (καὶ) to have one's fill': looking forward to Achilleus' address to Priam (24.549–51; cf. 1.586, 5.382) but not yet showing that he has internalised the lesson about limits, this statement is typical of third-person *gnōmai* generally deployed between social equals (Lardinois 1995: 95–9, 104–5; 2000: 645–8). Some MSS and editors print μέν ἐστι (viz. with the verb as an enclitic), yet it should be accented to express 'existence or possibility' (Probert 2003: 145–6; cf. Vendryès 108–10). ἆσαι is the aor. act. infin. of ἄω 'I eat my fill'; this verb's metaphors cluster around Achilleus towards the poem's end, extending to his abstention from food, but here it plays more upon his following injunction to the opposite purpose (Moulton 1979: 288–9).

158–60 σκέδασον καὶ δεῖπνον ἄνωχθι | ὅπλεσθαι = 19.171–2, where Odysseus on Agamemnon's behalf overrides Achilleus' desire to fight without eating. This parallel resumes the reversal of authority theme (35–58n.); for ὁπλίζω in this context, see also 55 above. ἄνωχθι is 2nd sing. imp. act. of perf. ἄνωγα, with stem -γ assimilated to -χ before -θι (the athematic imperative ending, as e.g. ἴθι, ἴσθι): 123–4n. **κήδεος** 'to be cared for': probably nom. sing. = κήδειος (19.294) on the analogy of e.g. σιδήρεος/ σιδήρειος, rather than the view of 'some' ancient grammarians that it is a gen. of κῆδος (Σ A 23.160a¹), i.e. the corpse is 'of/for care' (*GHI* § 64; cf. Mawet 1979: 361–2; Ruijgh 1967: 213–14). **παρὰ δ' οἵ τ' ἀγοὶ ἄμμι μενόντων** 'and let those who are leaders remain by us': undermining his formal courtesy, Achilleus puns on Agamemnon's name by placing himself in its middle, a point reinforced by the poet's ἄναξ ἀνδρῶν Ἀγαμέμνων (49–51n.) in the next, homoioteleutic, verse (Kanavou 2015: 44–5). οἵ τ' ἀγοί is read by most MSS, Aristarchos, 'and nearly everyone' (Σ A c¹) as ταγοί 'commanders', but that word is next attested in the fifth century (Aisch. *Pers.* 23) with long α (here impossible), while ἀγοί is formular in this position. The relative clause is introduced, as often, by 'epic τε' and suffers ellipsis of εἰσί (Probert 2015: 301; *pace* Ruijgh 1971: 431).

162–4 νῆας ἐΐσας 'evenly balanced ships': the epithet in this formula, one of many in the extensive Homeric system for ships (Parry 1971: 109–13; Gray 1974: 93–8), refers to the vessels' fine engineering and stability on the water (Kurt 1979: 42); for its form, see 55–8n.   **κηδεμόνες:** lit. 'those who have concerns' for someone. Restricted to family or, as here, retainers (cf. 674 for a similar idiom) as defined by 159–60.   **μένον καὶ νήεον ὕλην** 'they stayed and piled up the wood': completing the action begun at 139, this expression illustrates the poet's play on his own parallels, as one phrase (μενοεικέα) produces another (μένον καί) with a similar sonant profile, but different meaning and syntactical function.   **ἑκατόμπεδον ἔνθα καὶ ἔνθα** 'one hundred feet square': this huge pyre will serve as foundation for the later, even larger, tumulus (245–8n.). Only here in epic (and not again until Pindar, *Isthm.* 6.22), ἑκατόμπεδος is used to describe a variety of large structures and spaces, and may have been idiomatic for the Archaic temple to Athene in Athens as early as the sixth century (Langdon and Van Rookhuijzen 2024). The common expression ἔνθα καὶ ἔνθα literally means 'there and there', i.e. in two directions or square in the context of man-made objects, as e.g. *Od.* 7.86, 10.517 (~ 11.25), etc. (*LfrgE* s. ἔνθα, B II 1a, 591; Livingstone 2014: 87–8).

165 ἐν δὲ πυρῆι ὑπάτηι νεκρὸν θέσαν 'and on the top of the pyre they set the corpse' = 24.787, of Hector immediately before the fire is lit.   **ἀχνύμενοι κῆρ** 'pained at heart': κῆρ is an acc. of respect, giving the location of the grief, and the act itself is a direct expression of sorrow, unlike those qualified by the similar ἀχνύμενός περ, which denotes persistence despite grief (Kelly 2007a: 162).

166–76 The sacrifice develops its preview scene (29–34n.), linking once more with Phoinix's story (9.466–8) and reserving wine for later libations (196–7, 218–21). Though of fewer types than in the earlier scene, the offerings move beyond the usual options to include four horses (171–2), two of Achilleus' nine table dogs (173–4), and the twelve Trojan prisoners (175–6), with jars of honey and oil added (170–1). Scholars are divided as to whether these items were intended for use in the afterlife (cf. 50–1), additional sources of fuel, or symbols of the dead man's past, destroyed along with his corpse (Vermeule 1979: 58–62; Gallou 2005: 101–4). The whole ritual is unusual, perhaps because it is to be viewed as 'chthonian' (Intro. § 2.1): though the animals are prepared as for a sacrificial meal, there is no such feast here (4–34n.), and Achilleus does not allow the fat to burn off as savour to the gods but uses it to cover Patroclos' body instead, presumably to accelerate the fire (Schnapp-Gourbeillon 1982: 82 = 2017: 86). This is not an entry in a contemporary sacrificial calendar, of course, but a heroic imagining of an extraordinary and individual version from the mythical past (Ekroth 2002: 254–6).

166–7ª 166 = 9.466, connecting the sacrifices involving Achilleus' two advising metanasts, i.e. that from which Phoinix escaped and the one marking Patroclos' death.   ἴφια μῆλα 'strong sheep': usually verse-end and always linked with βοῦς, the epithet is derived from the adverb ἶφι (= Myc. *wi-pi*, related to Latin *vis* 'strength') 'mightily': 6–7n.   εἰλίποδας ἕλικας βοῦς: formula employed usually in contexts of sacrifice, but the precise meaning of both epithets is uncertain. The former perhaps denotes an ambling or shuffling gait (< εἴλω/εἰλέω) and the latter may describe curling horns or, less probably, sleekness (< ἕλιξ). Le Feuvre 2015: 445–80 reviews the options, and suggests 'on hooves which pivot (εἰλίποδας) whilst they make spirals/turns (ἕλικας)'.   ἔδερόν τε καὶ ἄμφεπον 'they skinned and attended to': usually linked with sacrifice and always a following meal (7.316, *Od.* 8.61, *Od.* 19.421: Intro. § 2.1). In this precise form the expression is used again only in the meal Achilleus offers to Priam (24.622), which may be previewed here. ἄμφεπον is 3rd pl. imperf. indic. act. of ἀμφιέπω, with elision of final -ι (cf. ἀμφίεπον 24.804).

167ᵇ–9 From now on, Achilleus performs all the ritual acts, beginning with covering Patroclos in animal fat so as to facilitate burning (8.240; *Od.* 17.241: Intro. § 2.1), which also explains his arrangement of the skinned bodies around the pyre (Σ bT 169a). Fat is later used to protect the bones (23.243 > 253: 243–4n.).   μεγάθυμος Ἀχιλλεύς 'greathearted Achilleus': the sole Homeric use of this metrical equivalent for the common formula πόδας ὠκὺς Ἀχιλλεύς (93n.) avoids repeating πόδας (169), whether or not the poet was motivated to avoid an 'unpleasant collocation' (Combellack 1976: 54), the adjective suggesting the importance of his θυμός as 'spirit' or 'anger' in this context (Friedrich 2007: 82–3).   ἐς πόδας ἐκ κεφαλῆς 'to the feet from the head' = 18.353ª, where the Greeks lay the recently recovered Patroclos on a bier and cover him with a cloth (cf. also 16.640, of the poor state of Sarpedon's corpse).

170–1 Oil and honey are combined again in Achilleus' own cremation (*Od.* 24.67–8), the former as an accelerant and the latter to ameliorate the odour (Eustathios 1294.13–16 = Van der Valk IV.705.19–22; *LfrgE* s. ἀλείφατος, 466). Σ T 170–1a1 suggest that the fluids boil up and then 'pour forth' on to the corpse as it is consumed by the flames, though unburnt oil flasks and wine jars were also a common funerary offering well beyond the Classical period (C–M 119). In Homeric funerals, oil may also serve as a cleansing agent (24.45), an embalming fluid (18.351, for Patroclos), and a bone preservative (*Od.* 24.73; Zanni 2008); cf. 185–7n.

171–2 These horses are probably killed first rather than placed alive on the pyre, as when the Trojans let down live creatures into Scamandros' streams (21.130–2), a kind of dedication attested in cults of Poseidon and Helios (Georgoudi 2005). Horses were not commonly sacrificed by Greeks in the Archaic and Classical periods, though there is some Bronze and early Iron Age evidence for the practice, including the spectacular tomb at Lefkandi (Lemos 2002: 166) and the seventh-century royal cemetery at Salamis on Cyprus (Andronikos 1968: 85–7; Kosmetatou 1993; Gallou 2005: 99–101; Platt 2017: 90–101). πίσυρας: Aeolic for τέσσαρας (2.618, 5.271, etc.). The number may suggest an awareness that the victim is unusual, since Homer rarely groups horses thus (5.271, 8.185, 11.698–702, 15.680: Janko 302); it may reflect knowledge of historical practice, with sacrifice of multiple horses attested from the tenth (Lefkandi) to seventh (Cyprus) centuries (Reese 1995: 36, 38–9). ἐριαύχενας ἵππους 'striking?-necked horses': the epithet is variously connected with length, height, or strength (Willi 1999: 96–7 opts for the height that comes with the stance of a proud horse), but the formula suggests either the sacrifice's individual nature or the ritual's inefficacy from Achilleus' perspective (1–3n.), since teams so described elsewhere fail to fulfil the envisaged action (10.305, 11.159, 17.496, etc.; Delebecque 1951: 152–3): also 26–7, 530–1nn. ἐσσυμένως: 55–8n. μεγάλα στεναχίζων: West reads with some MSS στοναχίζων, but several verbs (here στενάχω) form derivatives in -ίζω (e.g. αἰτέω > αἰτίζω, ἀλέγω > ἀλεγίζω, etc). The minority reading would have been influenced by the noun στοναχή (13×) or the verb στοναχέω (18.124), especially since στεναχίζω is very rare after Homer (*GH* I § 159; *WHS* 299 hesitantly; Tichy 1983: 194–5). The formula ἀδινὰ στεναχίζων is probably the model here, the alteration evoking the magnitude of Achilleus' groaning rather than its emotional intensity or duration (Kaimio 1977: 25); also 222–5n.

173–4 The only asyndetic introduction in this catalogue draws attention to the fact of selection, perhaps because Achilleus does not want to lose his whole pack (see below). Reversing Patroclos' own feared treatment by Hector (17.255) and underlining the contrast with Hector's intended fate, the dog sacrifice may have a purificatory purpose (Day 1984: 26–7; Ekroth 2014: 339–41), but it also seems important that they are table dogs, symbols of Patroclos' past life, as in Odysseus' remark that such animals were kept by their masters 'for the sake of splendour' (*Od.* 17.310; Steiner 2010: 120; Perpillou 2004: 91–2; cf. also 22.69). Nine dogs are linked with four shepherds on the Shield (18.578), but the number is typical for animal groups (Germain 1954: 17).   τῶι γε ἄνακτι: dat. of possession with ἦσαν, referring probably to Achilleus rather than Patroclos (so also Eustathios 1294.17–20 = IV.706.1–3 Van der Valk), as demonstrative + γε usually denotes a prominent character/thing from the immediately preceding narrative (e.g. 2.577, 5.794, 9.894, etc.; Bertrand 2010: 207; 2015; *contra* Richardson 173).   δειροτομήσας: 21–3n.

175–7 175 = 181, as Achilleus confirms his intention to burn the victims, but not to bury Hector: 179–83n. The (twice-promised: 18.333–7, 23.19–23n.) sacrifice of the Trojan youths is noticeably hurried: after the progressively larger syntactical pattern in the previous dedications (finite verb + participle: 170–1ᵃ/171ᵇ–2/173–4), the poet omits a separate finite verb and moves straight to his comment in 176. The evidence for human sacrifice in Greece is debatable (Andronikos 1968: 82–4; Georgoudi 1999; Gallou 2005: 105–12; cf. Stampolidis 1995 for a possible eighth-century example in the context of a large funeral pyre), but it is both widely attested in Greek mythology and plays a central role in the Trojan War tradition, from Iphigeneia to Polyxena, even if it is nowhere else mentioned in Homer (Hughes 1991: 49–56; Van Straten 1995: 113–14; Ekroth 2002: 255–6). While explicit condemnation would be alien to the general distance the poet maintains from his narrative, there is an unease throughout this passage (Schnapp-Gourbeillon 1982: 83; Hitch 2009: 194–5).   κακὰ δὲ φρεσὶ μήδετο ἔργα 'and he devised ill deeds in his mind' = 21.19ᵇ, as Achilleus leaps into the river to continue his slaughter of the Trojans. Without expressing an explicit moral judgement on the poet's part (see 24–6n. on ἀεικέα μήδετο ἔργα, where the deeds in question are similarly unseemly to suffer rather than to inflict), the hurried syntax underlines the horror involved.   ἐν δὲ πυρὸς μένος ἧκε σιδήρεον 'and he cast on (it, *sc.* the pyre) the iron-like power of fire': this striking, almost oxymoronic expression represents both Achilleus' special status and the fire's personalisation, since μένος 'power' is derived from an IE root denoting mind and desire (*EDG* s.v. 930–1), and its despatch is usually reserved for gods acting on humans (Dodds 1960: 8–10). The collocation πυρὸς μένος is here uniquely qualified by an iron metaphor otherwise applied to the μένος only of Achilleus (20.372) and Odysseus (*Od.* 12.279–80; Graz 1965: 285–94).   ὄφρα νέμοιτο 'so it would consume': previewing Achilleus' metaphoric figuration of feeding fire (182–3), the subject is understood from πυρός, and νέμοιτο is 3rd sing. pres. mid. opt., though 2.780 (ὡς εἴ τε πυρὶ χθὼν πᾶσα νέμοιτο) may suggest a passive sense, in which case the subject would be the pyre (understood in the main clause as the indirect object of ἧκε; Jankuhn 1969: 86–7); cf. 6.195.

178 ὤιμωξέν τ᾽ ἄρ᾽ ἔπειτα, φίλον δ᾽ ὀνόμηνεν ἑταῖρον: these two hemistichs are formular both separately and together (= 10.522, 24.591). The first denotes heartfelt grief but only occurs here in a formal funeral (15.397, *Od.* 13.198: 101ᵇ–2n.); the second marks promises made to, or about, the dead (16.491): see 89–90n.

179–83 Achilleus repeats his earlier promise (179–80 = 19–20; 181–2 ~ 22–3; 182–3 ~ 21: see 19–23n.), but the order of threats is here reversed to introduce the imminent attempt on his enemy's corpse (184–91), and neither task will be straightforwardly achieved. On the sense of χαῖρε 'take joy in me, ... for', see 19–20n. At 180 West prints the variant τετελεσμένα, ὥς περ ὑπέστην, found in a minority of MSS, several old papyri, and the A scholia, but the promise is not yet enacted (suggesting a future interpretation for τελέω: 19–20n.). Line 181 = 175 (see n.), now with run-over demonstrative τούς introducing the clause in 182 which takes the place of a verb of killing: tr. 'twelve noble sons of the great-hearted Trojans, | all these the fire will consume with you' (Mazon 1940: 258–9). Such 'left-dislocation' of an element into the first position of its sentence isolates and emphasises the main topic of thought, continuing the unease surrounding this sacrifice (175–7n.; Bakker 1997: 101–5; Alexiadou 2005). The figuring of fire as devouring (twice) in 182–3 further links the very different treatment of the two men whose burials lie in Achilleus' power, but seeking in Hector's case to reify the metaphor.   **ἐσθίει** 'is (very soon going to be) eating': the pres. tense is employed 'to show the imminence of the future action' (*GH* II § 282).   **δαπτέμεν** 'for lacerating': this result/final use of the infinitive (151n.) pointedly recalls Hector's dying plea not to let the dogs καταδάψαι his corpse (22.339; cf. *Od.* 3.259; Tichy 1983: 113 n. 102). δάπτω is predicated elsewhere of wolves and lions in similes (11.481, 16.188–9), and also metaphorically of spears (5.858ᵇ = 21.398ᵇ, 13.831). Though the -μεν(αι) infin. ending was originally athematic, its compositional usefulness helped extend it to thematic verbs as well (cf., e.g., ἐλθέμεν 197, διδασκέμεν 308, etc.: *GH* I § 237).

184–91 With parallel syntax (demonstrative pronoun + action + negative purpose clause), the poem's two most prominent pro-Trojan deities mirror Thetis' similarly motivated tendance of Patroclos' corpse (19.38–9) by protecting Hector from Achilleus' threats, as they had combined to rescue Aineias from Diomedes in Book 5. Apollo has already washed and anointed Sarpedon (16.667–70 ~ 678–80), and he will continue his defence of Hector (24.18–21; cf. also 24.411–23): see 185–7n. for Aphrodite's involvement. Hunter 1996: 133–4 connects this scene and 19.37–9 with Theoc. 15.106–8.

184 ἀπειλήσας 'vowed': for the threat implied here, see 862–4n. **ἀμφεπένοντο** 'they busied themselves around': this usually healing or supportive verb is not quite as grimly ironic as when the eels and fish attend to Asteropaios (21.203), since the action is prevented.

185-7 187 ~ 24.21, where Apollo continues to protect Hector's corpse from Achilleus' attentions (18–21), another sign of the fruitlessness of Patroclos' death ritual as far as he is concerned (1–3n.). **Διὸς θυγάτηρ Ἀφροδίτη:** this formula is chosen to remind the audience of Zeus's distant but still normative control over human affairs, in preference to the erotic potential of the metrically equivalent expression φιλομμειδής Ἀφροδίτη (Boedeker 1974: 18–42; Friedrich 2007: 111–12; Pirenne-Delforge 1994: 310–12; Bouchard 2015). This filiation contrasts with the Hesiodic genealogy (*Th.* 191–206), where Aphrodite is born from the foam on the sea from Ouranos' genitals and so predates Zeus (Pirenne-Delforge 1994: 312–18). **χρῖεν ἐλαίωι | ἀμβροσίωι** 'anointed with oil/ambrosial': a mark of great respect. Though rose oil is only mentioned here in epos (see Hoekstra 1965: 143 for a Mycenaean parallel), anointing with oil is a typical element in bathing or cleansing scenes and will happen to Hector once more in Troy (24.587). Ambrosia(l oil) is applied to gods in divine scenes (14.170–2, *Od.* 8.364–5, etc.) or to mortals by divine agents, either to beautify the living (*Od.* 18.193–4) or preserve the dead (16.670 ~ 680, 19.38–9; Laser 1983: 142–4, 160–2; Zanni 2008). Aphrodite's role here is doubly natural, given her Trojan affiliation and prominence in beautification scenes (also 3.374–425; *Cypria* frr. 4–5 B; Boedeker 1974: 41–2; Faulkner 2008: 19, 144–5). ἀμβροσίωι means literally 'not-mortal' (ἄ-μβροτος), denoting 'anything ... infected by the charisma of the deathless gods' (Pulleyn 2006: 67), the quality emphasised by its common run-over position (14.172, 18.193, etc.; Pirenne-Delforge 2018: 144–5). **ἀποδρύφοι** 'to tear off': 3rd sing. pres. act. opt. related to ἀποδρύπτω, the more distant mood, already standard in secondary sequence in Homeric purpose clauses (*GH* § 400), perhaps expressing her conception of the action's unreality (Willmott 2007: 153–74). The form is commonly now viewed as present, which better fits the continuous process envisaged (*BDAG* 248; Leaf II.485). This verb can also be used of the cheeks in mourning (2.700, 11.393), and of the damage done to various parts of humans by rocks (*Od.* 5.426, 434–5), spears (16.323–4), and the ground (23.395 (394–7n.)). **ἑλκυστάζων:** rare verb (only here and 24.21), an intensified derivative of ἕλκω (not frequentative, as at *LfrgE* s.v.) formed like νευστάζω < νεύω by treating -τάζω (originally derived from nouns in -της like ἀγυρτάζω < ἀγύρτης) as a productive suffix (*WHS* 297–8).

188–91 τῶι δ' ἐπί 'and upon him': matching τὸν δ' (184); for the accent of ἐπί, see 65n.   κυάνεον νέφος: whether 'dark' or 'blue' (852–5ᵃn.), κύανος is a threatening colour, especially in clouds (Moreux 1967: 262–3; Irwin 1974: 84–96; Griffith 2005; 131ᵇ–4n.). This usually feminine idiom (νεφέλη) is often linked with death and danger (16.66, 20.417–18 = *Od.* 12.74–5, etc.), but here darkness hides the corpse from the sun, as Apollo rescues Aineias from Diomedes (5.345; Morrison 1999: 136–7; Kakridis 1971: 89–103, esp. 95–6).   Φοῖβος Ἀπόλλων: the first element in Apollo's most common nominative formula is frequently used by itself as his name, yet its origin is obscure. Once thought to refer to a separate deity, or to mean 'bright' in reference to the god's un-Homeric association with the sun (*pace* Moreau 1996), the adjective is now generally taken to mean 'pure' or 'clear' (Σ D *Il.* 1.43: *EDG* 1582–3; Detienne 1998: 137, 211–12; Graf 2008: esp. 121–3; Bonnell 2019: 109–10). Homer makes a link with φόβος 'rout' at 17.118 (Rank 1951: 71–2). The second element's origin remains unexplained (e.g. Nagy 1994 links it with ἀπειλή 'promise, threat', but see *EDG* s. Ἀπόλλων).   οὐρανόθεν πεδίονδε: perhaps an underrepresented formula (cf. 8.21); οὐρανόθεν combines stem οὐρανό- and separative suffix -θεν 'from', making a form elsewhere equivalent to gen. οὐρανοῦ and coupled with (pleonastic) ἐξ or ἀπό (*GH* I § 109; Lejeune 1939: 78–80); also 21–3n. πεδίονδε 'to the plain' is one word: see 55–8n. (κλισίηνδε).   ὅσσον ἐπεῖχε νέκυς 'as far as the corpse extended': reminiscent of the later language of hero cult (cf. Henrichs 1993: 171–2 on κατέχω), though it is debatable whether the institution is actually present or foreshadowed in the Homeric poems (151n.). ἐπεῖχε is 3rd sing. imperf. indic. act. of ἐπέχω 'I hold to/over' and thus 'I extend/cover', as e.g. at 21.407, 23.238.   σκήλει(ε) 'dry up': 3rd sing. aor. act. opt. of σκέλλω (the origin of English 'skeleton') with the standard distancing optative in a negative purpose clause again intimating the unreality of the action (185–7n.), and therefore preferable to the variant subjunctive σκήλη(ι). As with ἤγγειλα < ἀγγέλλω and στεῖλα < στέλλω etc., the expected aorist stem is σκειλ- (restored here by Fick), so this form is either an early scribal error connected with the common ει/η confusion in the MSS or derived from an otherwise unknown *σκάλλω (*GH* I §§ 8–11; *WHS* 249, 289).   ἀμφὶ περί 'around about on all sides': περί gives universalising precision to ἀμφί (cf. 2.305, 21.10, *Od.* 11.609).   χρόα ἵνεσιν ἠδὲ μέλεσσιν 'flesh on the sinews and limbs': whether related to ἴς 'strength' or not, this ἴς (with initial *digamma* obviating hiatus after χρόα) is a purely physiological term (*EDG* 598–9).

192–225 In the second of Achilleus' (initially) fruitless intentions (179–83n.), Patroclos' pyre will not light until Iris conveys Achilleus' prayer to the winds Boreas and Zepyhros. This parallels the visit of Patroclos' shade in its positioning at day's end after a series of funeral rituals, both episodes involving the travel of non-mortal figures to move the funeral along (62–108n.): 217–18n. In keeping with his extraordinary status, Achilleus is the only mortal to have a prayer conveyed to the addressee by another god, but, unlike with Thetis and Zeus in Book 1, there is little explicit focus on the relationship between the deities. Kakridis 1949: 75–83 argued that this scene was drawn from an appeal from Zeus to the winds to light Achilleus' own pyre, overcoming their reluctance to do so because he had killed Memnon their brother (*Th.* 378–80), but there is no early evidence for such an event (Burgess 2009: 91; cf. Quint. Smyrn. 3.699–702). Some scholars have detected a generally humorous sensibility here, and Homer's gods frequently move in more relaxed mode to bring out their essential difference from the 'deathly' seriousness of human life (Griffin 1980: 179–204; Coventry 1987: 178–80). There may, moreover, be erotic undertones to the relationship between Iris and Zephyros (198^b–9n.: also 193–5, 201^b–3, 208–11nn.).

192 τεθνηῶτος 'dead': masc. gen. sing. perf. act. ppl. of θνῄσκω; Homer generally forms the perf. act. ppl. by adding -(ϝ)ώς -υῖα -ός straight onto the perfect stem without -κ- (as in ἑσταώς, βεβαώς, τετληώς, etc.). The internal hiatus -ηω- is caused by loss of that *digamma*, and elsewhere with this verb appears with both -ηο- and -εω- (*Od.* 19.331; see *GH* I §§ 204–5; *WHS* 346–7).

193–5 193–4^a = 140–1^a (see 140–4n.). Going or standing 'apart' here highlights Achilleus, attracting the god's attention before the prayer (1.35, *Od.* 2.260–1, cf. 6.301: Morrison 1991: 147–8 'gesture'; Aubriot-Sévin 1992: 126–8 and n. 7). On Π 12's 195a (ἀρνῶν πρωτογόνων ῥέξειν κλειτὴν ἑκατόμβην), see 146–8n.   **Βορέηι καὶ Ζεφύρωι:** another acephalous verse (1–3n.) with -έηι one heavy syllable in synizesis. Some modern editors read a mixed Ionic–Attic Βορρῆι *vel sim.*, but it is hard to see why this would have been altered to the more metrically difficult form (*GH* I § 45; cf. Wyatt 1969: 221). Boreas is the violent north wind, Zephyros the speedy and (in the *Iliad*) largely negative west (Neuser 1982: 27–30). Each has an extensive sexual history (Vermeule 1979: 157, 168–9), but their collaboration runs counter to the prevailing NE winds sweeping down the Trojan coastline (Korfmann 1986: 6–8) and is closely paralleled at 9.4–7, perhaps a deliberate connection between Patroclos' death and the Greeks' low point before the embassy to Achilleus, and the poet's desire to include Zephyros (cf. Hes. *Th.* 379, 870 for their genealogical link with Notos, the south wind; also *Od.* 5.295–6; see 198^b–9n.).   **ὑπίσχετο** 'he was/

started promising': repeated in Iris' relay (209), though we never witness its fulfilment. Postponed offerings of the *da ut dem* sort are common-place in prayers (Pulleyn 1997: 17–18; Kelly 2007a: 250–1). ὑπίσχετο is 3rd sing. imperf. indic. mid. of ὑπ-ίσχομαι (cf. *LfrgE* s. ἴσχω, 1257). The imperfect is better attested than aorist ὑπέσχετο (S. West 1967: 183) and, with ἤρᾶτο (194) and λιτάνευεν (196), expresses the start of the process by which the promises are made and the whole act succeeds (cf. aorist ἦλθ(ε) 199; *GH* II § 286).   ἱερὰ καλά 'fine holy things' = animal sacrifice, as at 11.727, *Od.* 4.473, etc., but only here and at 209 in Homer does this formula lack a form of ἔρδω (cf. Faulkner 2008: 181).

196–8ᵃ Looking back to Achilleus' extended libation for Patroclos' safe return (16.220–54) and forward to the final libation directed to Patroclos himself (218–21), this kind of offering is a typical but not universal ele-ment in Homeric prayer, frequently occurring during or alongside the utterance, as καί 'also' makes clear (3.295–6, 16.225–54, 24.306–14; Arend 1933: 76–8; Burkert 1985: 70–3); also 218–21n.   χρυσέωι δέπαϊ: the *depas* is conventionally golden in a divine context (4.3, 24.101, etc.), but generally a mark of wealth and power (6.220, 24.284, *Od.* 3.41, etc.); cf. 218–21n. The final syllable of δέπαϊ (dat. sing. of δέπας) is rendered heavy before λιτάνευεν because the verb is treated as though it once began with *λλ-; cf. ἐλλιτάνευε (22.414) etc. (*GH* I § 70): see Intro. § 3.2.vii.b.   φλεγεθοίατο νεκροί 'that the corpses might burn': 3rd pl. pres. pass. opt. of φλεγέθω (< φλέγω; cf. τελέθω < τέλλω, θαλέθω < θάλλω, etc.: *GH* I § 153); for the -ατο ending, see Intro. § 3.1.2.d.i; also 233–5n. There is little to choose between νεκροί and the variant νεκρόν, as the verb could equally be passive or middle (though not elsewhere in Homer): the latter keeps the focus on Patroclos, the former reminds us of the other sacri-fices (and may also be reflected in ὕλην τε σεύαιντο, known to Didymos; see Van der Valk 1963–4: II.580–1).   σεύαιτο καήμεναι '(and so the wood) would hasten to burn': σεύαιτο is intrans. 3rd sing. aor. mid. opt. of σεύομαι/ἔσσευα, καήμεναι aor. pass. infin. of καίω, used result/finally ('for burning'; see 151n.).

198ᵇ–9 ὠκέα δ' Ἶρις: the adverbial reading ὦκα, only found in Π 12 but already conjectured by Bentley to avoid neglect of *digamma* before Ἶρις (S. West 1967: 183–4), looks like the *lectio facilior*, but the alteration of an otherwise universal formula is surely an easier step, since *digamma* is neglected before this word at 5.353, 365. Absent from the *Odyssey* (though cf. 18.5–7), Iris in the *Iliad* is both the gods' devoted messenger and the poet's fortuitous facilitator (Erbse 1986: 54–65; Nieto Hernández 1995; Kelly 2007a: 322–4; Pisano 2017). An association with the rainbow

(11.27, 17.547) as a bridge between heaven and earth is reflected in her Hesiodic parentage (*Th.* 265–9), making the Harpies her sisters and suggesting a link with wind which was early configured in erotic terms: Alcaios fr. 327 makes Eros the son of Iris and Zephyros, who in Homer sires a horse with the Harpy Podargē (*Il.* 16.150). This background may be felt here (192–225n.).   μετάγγελος 'messenger': this minority reading is preferable to μετ' ἄγγελος, which is more plausible at 15.144 (ἥ τε θεοῖσι … ἀθανάτοισι), where μετ[ά] could be postpositive to θεοῖσι but has no conceivable meaning here. That case might explain the compound's origin, but not its usage in epos (see *HDem.* 441; Hes. fr. 204.58 M–W; *HW* 69).

200–1ᵃ Olympian deities are often gathered together (1.533–4, 11.75–7, etc.: Griffin 1980: 179–204; Myers 2019), but lesser gods can be so assembled (18.37–51, *Od.* 10.8–11, 60–1), and this congregation underlines Zephyros' significance and Achilleus' exceptionality as the object of Iris' mission (Aloni 1998: 97). The mood contrasts powerfully with the funerary meal just seen in the Greek camp. For similarly timed arrivals, cf. 24.472–6, *Od.* 1.106–12, 3.31–5, etc.   Ζεφύροιο … ἔνδον: for gen. + ἔνδον meaning 'in the house of', cf. 20.13.   δυσαέος 'ill-blowing': uncontracted masc. gen. sing. from δυσαής. Fittingly (193–5n.), Zephyros is thus described at *Od.* 5.295 and 12.289.   εἰλαπίνην δαίνυντο 'were feasting (at) a revel': for the use of the 'internal' acc., see 29n. εἰλαπίνη means 'no more than generic feasting or reveling in company' (Sherratt 2004: 310), within the broad category of δαίς (*Od.* 1.225–6), but distinguished from a wedding feast (γάμος *Il.* 18.491), a communal gathering (ἔρανος *Od.* 1.226, 11.415), and a mere drinking party (*Od.* 2.57; see also Van Wees 1992: 44–8).

201ᵇ–3 The winds' enthusiastic welcome is typical (1.533–4, 15.85–6, *Od.* 1.118–22, *HAp.* 3–4: Reece 1993: 19), though nowhere else do all the gathered figures call the entrant to them individually. Σ T 202 suggested their reaction was linked to Iris' sexual relationship with Zephyros (192–225, 198ᵇ–9nn.) 'and perhaps drunken desire' (see Hunter 2021: 713–15). Conviviality strengthens the contrast with the mortal situation, and links Iris and Achilleus (23.43–7) as refusing to indulge in social behaviour; cf. 208–11n. for her assumption of his perspective.   βηλῶι ἔπι λιθέωι 'upon the stone threshold': βηλός is used in epos only for divine thresholds (1.591, 15.23; cf. 5.734 = 8.385) and later reinterpreted as a word for 'heaven' (*HW* 33). ἔπι is accented thus in anastrophe, and its final syllable is heavy because λιθέωι is treated as though it once had initial λλ- (written thus in Π 12; *GH* I § 70; Intro. § 3.2): 118–21ᵃn.   τοί:

Aeolic form of the nom. masc. pl. demonstrative pronoun, chosen here
to obviate hiatus after λιθέωι (Intro. §§ 3.1.1.b, 3.1.2.a.ii).   κάλεον ...
ἕκαστος: see 1–3n.

204–11 Iris begins with a refusal of hospitality to avoid delaying the communication of Achilleus' prayer (205–7n.), while the relay of that prayer
itself suggests an imperative context (208–11n.) reflecting her role in the
poem (198ᵇ–9n.).

204–5 ~ 11.647–8, Patroclos' refusal of Nestor's invitation to rest. Since
the old man then suggests the approach to Achilleus, this once more links
earlier turning points in the story with Patroclos' death ritual; for similar but differently worded refusals, cf. 6.360 (Hector to Helen), 24.553
(Priam to Achilleus).

205–7 Iris' desire to attend a sacrifice with the other gods amongst the
Aithiopes deliberately looks back to Book 1, where the gods' absence
there delayed Thetis' visit to Zeus (1.423–7). Kakridis 1949: 79 well terms
them 'a convenient refuge for the gods'. Hera also claims, falsely, to be
journeying there when she seduces Zeus (14.200–1, 301–11); Σ bT 206a
suggest that Iris 'lies to be delivered from those annoying her, since yes-
terday (the gods) were watching the battle, and tomorrow will be arguing
over Hector'. Yet Athene and Hera intervene in the Greek camp (1.55–6,
194–23) despite their distant sojourn and, though there may be some sexual awkwardness here (192–225, 198ᵇ–9nn.), the veracity of Iris' claim is
secondary to the poet's need to get the winds moving immediately, rather
than delayed in a hospitality scene.   Ὠκεανοῖο: Ocean, the earth-en-
circling body of water located at the very ends of the known world, was
inter al. the father of rivers (21.194–7), and the abode of sun and stars
(7.422, 19.1, etc.) as well as of 'fantastic' races (1.423–4, 3.5–6, *Od.* 11.13;
Romm 1992: 12–26; *LfrgE* s.v., 1332–5).   Αἰθιόπων: the term was
interpreted by the ancients as meaning 'with burned faces' (< αἴθω + ὄψ:
S. West 1988 on *Od.* 1.22: 75). The Aithiopes were held with some impre-
cision to live at the earth's ends, where they enjoyed close relations with
the gods (1.423–4, *Od.* 1.22–5, 5.282–7). They were early associated with
the East (the goddess Dawn is the mother of their king Memnon: Hes.
Th. 984–5), and then with a region to the south of Egypt (cf. *Od.* 4.84;
Lesky 1959; Beekes 1995). They were important Trojan allies in the rest
of the tradition, with Achilleus' slaying of Memnon the main event of the
Aithiopis (Rengakos 2015).   ἑκατόμβας: 146–8n.   μεταδαίσομαι
ἱρῶν 'I will dine with (them) from the sacrifices': several Homeric passages suggest the persistence of the idea that the gods physically partake

in the sacrifice (cf. 1.423–4, 9.535–6; Kirk II.10–13; Kelly 2007a: 403–4). ἱρῶν = ἱερῶν (194–5n.), a Lesbian feature (Wathelet 1970: 356–7), and a 'partitive' gen. (i.e. to denote a portion of a larger whole), as often with verbs of eating and drinking, since μεταδαίνυμαι elsewhere takes a dative of those 'with whom' (22.498, *Od.* 18.48; cf. 19.299).

208–11 Reframing Achilleus' prayer gives it the air of a command, the usual context for the relaying of information like this (Kakridis 1971: 76–88; De Jong 1987a: 179–85, 241–3; Kelly 2007a: 325–9). Iris is naturally a frequent relayer (e.g. 8.416–22, 11.202–9, 15.176–8; 198ᵇ–9n.), but there is minimal verbatim repetition of the prayer: 208–9 ~ 194–5 (209ᵇ = 195ᵇ); 210–11 ~ 197–8 (καήμεναι 198, 210). This latter recasting in particular indicates that she has assumed and extended Achilleus' perspective in focusing on Patroclos (as with his run-over name in 211) rather than the plural νεκροί (197), and in describing the grief for him felt by the whole Greek army.   **κελαδεινόν** 'clamorous': a fitting epithet for Zephyros (so Σ bT 208; 193–5, 200–1ᵃnn.; cf. *Od.* 2.421). It is more usually used of Artemis, reflecting the sound of the hunt (dogs Σ D 16.183; beasts bT 16.183) and/or the female choruses she led and was honoured with (bT 16.183; Marseglia 2015); its application to Zephyros may be an attempt to desexualise her visit (192–225, 198ᵇ–9nn.), but it may equally evoke the mythological rapes associated with Artemis' dances (16.181–3, *HAphr.* 118), as well as their ritual function before marriage (Ellinger 2009: 56–62; Budin 2016: 48–68, 81–96).   **ἐλθεῖν ἀρᾶται:** necessary run-over delays the main verb and allows a closer juxtaposition of the prayer's originator and its actual addressees in 208.   **ὄρσητε:** 2nd pl. aor. act. subj. of ὄρνυμι, transitive and subj. rather than the original optative forms of 197–8, because the principal verbs are now in the present, reflecting the greater proximity of Iris' direct report.

212–13 ἀπεβήσετο: reserved for divine departures, 3rd sing. aor. mid. indic. of ἀποβαίνω, another 'mixed aorist' form showing the sigmatic stem together with thematic endings (*GH* I § 199; Roth 1990: ch. 3): also 38n.   **τοὶ δ᾿ ὀρέοντο** 'and they arose': for the Aeolic demonstrative τοί, see 118–21ᵃn. ὀρέοντο is 3rd pl. imperf. mid. indic. of ὄρνυμι, a thematised form of athematic ὄρνυντο (23.131); for its (heavily debated) origins, see Latacz et al. 2003: on 2.398, 120.   **ἠχῆι θεσπεσίηι:** derived from the same roots as θεός and ἐν(ν)έπω 'I tell', the epithet in this formula means 'announced/reported by god', fitting the kind of noise made by an aggressive crowd acting under divine influence or support, where this expression is typically applied (8.159, 12.252, etc.: Kelly 2007a: 186–7, adding *Od.* 3.150, 11.633). Pseudo-Plutarch quotes this verse with πνοιῆι ὕπο λιγυρῆι (*De Hom.* 2.108), an obvious conflation from 215 (see Appendix for more examples of this kind of thing).

214–16 With only one (unnecessary) run-over (215), the staccato parataxis of their journey adds to the impression of speed.   **αἶψα ... ἵκανον:** formular collocation to denote a very swift journey. Usually the two words are separated by δέ and/or ἔπειτα, and so interposed πόντον here necessitates light scansion of unaugmented ἵκ-.   **ὦρτο:** 3rd sing. aor. mid. indic. of ὄρνυμι, like other verbs with stems ending in a guttural (κ, γ, χ) or liquid (λ, ρ) using what appears to be an old athematic form (as e.g. μίκτο < μείγνυμι, ἆλτο < ἅλλομαι, πάλτο < πάλλω) in an intransitive sense; Homer also uses thematic ὤρετο, etc. (*GH* I § 183); also 212–13, 231–2nn.   **πνοιῆι ὕπο λιγυρῆι** 'beneath the clear-/strident-whistling breeze': giving a sense of 'under the direction of', ὕπο is accented in anastrophe, and its final syllable is heavy because λιγυρῆι is treated falsely as beginning with a double consonant (in Π 12): see Intro. § 3.1.1.b. This may be an underrepresented formula (13.590; cf. 5.526), the epithet denoting clarity or shrillness (Kaimio 1977: 42–7, esp. 45).   **Τροίην δ'ἐρίβωλον** 'fertile Troy': not just the city but the whole Troad, the fertility of whose alluvial plain was enshrined in this formular expression (Létoublon 2003: 29–30, 40–2; Trachsel 2007: 12–27), though progressive silting by the Scamandros towards the current coastline on the Dardanelles would have made the area marshier than today's well-drained and verdant arable, which is the result of post-WWII engineering (Korfmann 1986: 9 and n. 18; cf. Riehl 1999: 1–6; Kraft et al. 2003). The epithet literally means 'deep clod' (with intensifying ἐρι-: Willi 1999), alternating with the oblique cases of the consonant-stem form ἐριβῶλαξ in the verse's first half to create a complementary system.   **ἴαχε:** 3rd sing. imperf. act. indic. of ἰάχω, with elision of δέ showing the neglect of initial *digamma* in ϝίϝαχε (*GH* I § 54). The poet resumes and confirms Achilleus' personification of the fire: 175–7, 179–83nn.   **θεσπιδαὲς πῦρ** 'god-kindled fire': this formula's epithet is derived from the same roots as θεός (see θεσπεσίηι 212–13n.) and δαίω, and always refers to fire directly lit or indirectly driven by a god (Graz 1965: 104–8). Underlining the importance of this event for both Patroclos and Achilleus, the theme culminates in this last Iliadic occurrence of the formula, referring earlier to the fire hurled on the ships and the Greek camp (12.177, 441, 15.597), the damage inflicted by Achilleus (20.490), and Hephaistos' flame (21.342, 381): see 26–7n. for other such thematic runs in this book.

217–18 παννύχιοι ... πάννυχος: again the poet deploys this usually introductory element to summarise the nocturnal episode, as at 105 (see n.), reinforcing the parallel between the shade's visit to Achilleus and Iris' trip on his behalf: see 192–225n. **πυρῆς ἄμυδις φλόγ' ἔβαλλον:** the winds were either 'striking the flame(s) together' (LSJ s.v. ἄμυδις II, 87), or 'together striking the flames' (*LfrgE* B1b, 643). The latter has an easier sense, while the position of ἄμυδις perhaps favours the former, but either construction has martial connotations (214–16n.). πυρῆς is either possessive or partitive gen. 'on (part of the) fire' frequent with verbs of touching or reaching, as e.g. νέκρους πυρκαϊῆς ἐπινήνεον (7.428). **λιγέως** 'keenly'/'shrilly': picking up λιγυρῆι (215), this adverb fittingly combines its usual mourning associations with the winds' sound (Kaimio 1977: 42–8), and elsewhere λιγέων ἀνέμων occur in threatening contexts (13.334, 14.17, etc.). **ὠκὺς Ἀχιλλεύς:** only in the *Iliad*, this shorter form version of πόδας ὠκὺς Ἀχιλλεύς (93n.) once more evokes his legendary speed, perhaps picking up on the winds' movement but also contrasting with his purposeful lack of movement. This particular shortening occurs elsewhere only in killing contexts (19.295, 21.211, etc.), an association which may draw together this final ritual with the earlier sacrifices.

218–21 Completing Achilleus' earlier libations for Patroclos (16.200–5, 23.196–7 (196–8ᵃn.)), the long-delayed main verb in 220 adds greatly to the sense of deliberation displayed in drawing the wine from the mixing-bowl into the cup. Drink offerings to the dead are a standard element in the material record from the Mycenaean period onwards, though, as with many other grave goods, it is unclear whether they were intended to nourish the dead or mark their separation from the living (Sourvinou-Inwood 1995: 70–92; Gallou 2005: 83–5, 87–97). Line 221 is another four-word verse (39–41n.), entirely spondaic (Intro. § 3.2, n. 134), rhythmically heavy, harsh with guttural/sibilant alliteration, and culminates the earlier combinations of ψυχή + Πατροκλῆος δειλοῖο to open and close the shade's visit (65, 104). Achilleus' sad, deliberate action aims to recall that physical presence. This very rare rhythm is particularly fitting here, since the spondee was later named for its use in libations (σπονδαί: *PMG* 941, 968 = Terpander frr. 3 and 8 Gostoli), and there is no reason to emend to Πατροκλέρεος δεελοῖο to avoid the rhythm (Pye 1964: 2–3; Edwards 1987: 117–18). **χρυσέου ἐκ κρητῆρος:** the κρητήρ is a large vessel from which the mixed water and wine was poured into cups, and a mark of great status: the only other golden example in epos belongs to Zeus (*HAphr.* 206), while silver is more common (741–3n.). -έου is two light syllables, -ou light by epic correption. **ἔχων δέπας ἀμφικύπελλον:** an apparently tautologous formula, since δέπας and κύπελλον both mean 'cup' in epos (for the system, see Paraskevaides 1984: 79–80). The compound may mean 'cups on both sides', referring to the so-called 'double cup' familiar from Mycenaean finds (Arist. *Hist. an.* 624a; cf. ἀμφί-αλος, ἀμφί-κομος, etc.: *WHS* 187–8; Bowie 2013: 106), or 'with handles on both sides' (Bruns 1970: 25–6, 42–5; Bloedow 2007). Some MSS and modern editors read ἑλών 'taking up', and the aorist is possible here and at 220 (ἀφυσσάμενος) to express subordinate actions prior to the pouring (χέε 220), but the scene's stress on the continuous nature of the libation (222–5n.) favours the majority reading. **οἶνον ἀφυσσόμενος χαμάδις χέε:** χέε is uncontracted, unaugmented 3rd sing. imperf. indic. act. of χέω 'I pour'. This 'pour to the ground' idiom falls in contexts expressing mortality or fear thereof (6.147, 7.480), and may specifically recall the situation of Book 7 (οἶνον δ' ἐκ δεπάων χαμάδις χέον), when the plan of Zeus was yet to be felt and the libationers were warding off their fears. ἀφυσσόμενος denotes transferring or 'drawing off' the wine from the κρητήρ to the cup; on the variant aorist see above. **δεῦε δὲ γαῖαν** 'wetted the earth': evokes the memory of Patroclos' death in battle, since this formula always elsewhere denotes a victim pouring blood or brains onto the earth (13.655, 21.119, *Od.* 9.290): 15–16n. (δεύοντο ψάμαθοι).

222–5 Another simileme culmination, this time of the parent–child group which has articulated the relationship between the two (9.323–7, 16.7–11, 17.4–6, 132–7, 18.56–7 = 437–8; Mills 2000; Pratt 2007: 34–8, esp. 37; Moulton 1977: 99–116): see Intro. § 1, p. 9 for other such runs. The image contributes to the more general theme of the 'bereaved father' (Griffin 1980: 123–7; cf. Stoevesandt 2004: 128–34) by looking forward to Priam and his son's corpse in Book 24, joining the narratives of Patroclos, Achilleus, and Hector in yet another way (Intro. § 1 with n. 19). The simile layout is very clear: introduction (222) matches conclusion (224) in structure, rhythm, and phrasing, enclosing unnecessary run-over and relative clause extension (223), while the rhyming present participles καίων, ἑρπύζων, and στεναχίζων combine in asyndeton to heap up and elongate Achilleus' grief (Edwards 25–8). **οὗ παιδός** 'for his son': a 'genitive of cause' after ὀδύρετο (as e.g. 22.424), especially common to denote the source with verbs of anger and grief (*GH* II § 81); οὗ is masc. gen. sing. of the possessive adjective ὅς (< *σϝός; *GH* I § 55). **νυμφίου** 'bridegroom': run-over focuses attention on the son and his recent marriage. Σ bT 222–3 astutely note that a newlywed νυμφίος does not yet have male children (cf. *Od.* 7.64–6), depriving the father figure of grandchildren as well. The simile thus implicates (i) Peleus and Achilleus, since Neoptolemos will die shortly after the end of the war, (ii) Menoitios and Patroclos himself, *and* (iii) (less directly) Priam and Hector, for Astyanax will be murdered when Troy is sacked (Nannini 2003: 100–1). **ὅς τε ... ἀκάχησε:** perhaps resonating with Ἀχιλεύς in the next verse (80–1n.), the aorist tense is 'gnomic' to express a general truth, as often in similes (cf. 432 below). Though it cannot be translated, 'epic τε' helps to mark that timeless quality; its original connective function may suggest the relative pronoun has a demonstrative force 'and he' (Ruijgh 1971: 360–72).   ἑρπύζων: later matched by Priam's self-abasement (24.162–5), crawling is an action of extreme grief (*Od.* 1.193, 13.220; Lateiner 1995: 33–4; Pulleyn 2019: 160–1). The verb is derived from ἕρπω with an 'expressive' suffix, seen also e.g. in ἀτύζω 'I cower in fear' and several onomatopeic verbs like τρύζω and ὀλολύζω (*WHS* 291–7; Tichy 1983: 112–13, 131–50, 160).   ἀδινὰ στεναχίζων 'groaning repeatedly': ἀδινά (17–18n.) replaces μεγάλα (172) to emphasise continuity over scale. On the minority reading στοναχίζων, see 171–2n.

226–57 Third Day (to 897). The funeral's second day begins with a 'ritual' expression for dawn, while the gathering of the remains and construction of the tomb in this passage are extended (~ 7.435–41, 24.788–801; also *Od.* 24.71–92 for Achilleus' funeral), underlining once more the episode's importance and looking forward to the second event of the day, the games themselves (257ᵇ–897n.).

226–8 228 ~ 9.212 (αὐτὰρ ἐπεὶ κατὰ πῦρ ἐκάη καὶ φλὸξ ἐμαράνθη), where Patroclos stokes the fire before cooking on the embers.   ἦμος/ τῆμος 'at the time when …/then …': much more common in the *Odyssey* (109–10ᵃn.), dawn expressions of this correlative sort signal transition within a ritual activity (1.477–8, 7.433–4, 24.788–9: Kelly 2007a: 67–8, 111), here the progression to the funeral's second and final day (Radin 1988; Létoublon 1997).   Ἑωσφόρος 'dawn-bearer': stressing the significance and scale of the coming day's events, the morning star uniquely co-performs the function of his mother Dawn (*Th.* 381; cf. *Od.* 13.93–4, with 2.49, 11.2, 19.2, etc.; Dicks 1970: 32, 123–4, 145–6), underlined by wordplay in φόως ἐρέων 'to announce light' (as at 2.49): see 80–1, 136–7, 255–7nn. Both figures are therefore capitalised in this passage. One heavy syllable in synizesis, Ἑωσ- is an Ionic compound showing post-quantitative metathesis -εω- alongside the simple nouns retaining the older -ηο- (ἠώς/ἑωθινός, ληός/λεωφόρος), not an Atticism (as at Wackernagel 1916: 100–7; *GH* I §§ 3, 28).   φόως 'light': formed by diectasis from φῶς (< φάος), a contracted form not found in Homer (*GH* I § 34; Wyatt 1994: 139–40). Light represents safety and life (154–5n.), and this day will witness the communal activity affirming the resumption of social normality after a funeral (Intro. § 2.1).   ὅν τε μέτα … κίδναται 'after whom … spreads': 'epic τε' is frequently found introducing descriptions of nature, 'especially periodical or permanent phenomena' (*GH* II § 352). Occupying its usual second position, it forces the preposition/preverb further from its relative referent (Ruijgh 1971: 373). Aorists and imperfects are more common in these ἦμος/τῆμος correlations than the presents κίδναται and εἶσι (226), which here underline the distance between divine and human worlds (cf. the past tenses in 228) and its extension into the world of the external audience: tr. 'at a time when ... always happens'.   **κροκόπεπλος ... κίδναται Ἡώς** 'saffron-robe ... Dawn': usually joined at the verse-start, the noun and its epithet are notably separated here, the poet adding another verse-end formula (κίδναται Ἡώς) to contrast the cyclical spread of morning light with the flame's extinction (Macleod 1982: 32, 47–8).   **ὑπεὶρ ἅλα:** metrically lengthened form of ὑπέρ only found in this expression and some compounds (ὑπείροχος, ὑπειρέχω) to avoid an unmetrical sequence of four light syllables (*GH* I § 44); cf. 23.637 (ὑπειρέβαλον). The alternation ὑπέρ/ὑπεὶρ was probably helped by analogy with ἐς/εἰς and common expressions like εἰς ἅλα, where the noun requires a heavy preceding syllable (Ruijgh 2011: 284–5).   **κίδναται** = σκίδναται, 3rd sing. pres. indic. of σκίδναμαι (related to Att. σκεδάννυμι), with *sigma* omitted to avoid making the final syllable of ἅλα heavy (*GH* I § 47; Shipp 1972: 43). For other 'biforms' with optional initial *sigma* (e.g. σῦς and ὗς), see Reece 2009: 57–70, esp. 61–3.

229–30 The winds return home: cf. 9.5 (with 193–5n.). The metaphor of the sea's groaning as the winds pass resumes Achilleus' grief (225 etc.), underlined by the link between simplex στένω and actual or figurative lamentation (10.16, 18.33, 20.169, 24.776, etc.).   **ἔβαν οἶκόνδε νέεσθαι** 'they went to go homewards': a pleonastic infinitive common after verbs of movement (38n.), the οἶκόνδε νέεσθαι formula suggests here a contrast with the lost *nostoi* of both Patroclos and Achilleus (Bonifazi 2009: esp. 490 and n. 27); for οἶκόνδε as one word, see 55–8n.   **οἴδματι θυίων** 'raging with/in its swell': always in epos of bodies of water, usually the sea but most recently Scamandros in his battle against Achilleus (21.234). A minority of good MSS read (perhaps Aeol.) θυίων rather than θύων, adopted here because -υι- re-entering the paradosis is harder to imagine than later normalisation to -υ- (*GH* I §§ 20, 177; *EDG* 527).

231–2 Achilleus' eventual sleep (cf. 217–18) recalls his earlier troubled rest (59–62), the last time he was denoted in this book by verse-initial Πηλεΐδης (59–61n.). The language used of his movement suggests a death-like state.   **ἑτέρωσε** 'to the other side, away': formed by adding the allative suffix -σε (as e.g. in κεῖσε, πόσε) to ἑτέρω- (as in ἑτέρωθι, ἑτέρωθεν: *GH* I § 113; Lejeune 1939: 212, 259–60), and usually coupled with the verb κλίνω (13.543, *Od.* 22.17) to denote death.   **λιασθείς** 'staggered away': masc. nom. sing. aor. pass. ppl. of λιάζομαι, a verb hard to define, but with connotations of weakness or sickness manifest in downward/lateral motion (Fränkel 1924: 275–7; Stefanelli 2004).   **ἐπὶ δὲ γλυκὺς ὕπνος ὄρουσεν** 'and sweet sleep rushed upon (him)': evoking Achilleus' earlier repose in this book (νήδυμος 62–4n.), γλυκὺς ὕπνος jars with its usually troubled context (and perhaps with the generally hostile connotations of the verb: see *LfrgE* s. ὀρούω, B II 5): whatever rest he gets will be insufficient (1.610, 2.71, *Od.* 2.395, etc.; Foley 1999: 231–2); cf. 62–4n. (φαίδιμα) for a similar disjunction. ὄρουσεν is 3rd sing. aor. act. indic. of ὀρούω, related to ὄρνυμι (see also 214–16n.).

233–5 As Achilleus earlier awoke in astonishment at the dream's departure (100–2), here he is stirred by the approach of the other leaders. His isolation is clear from the aggressively freighted vocabulary describing their onset.   **οἳ δ' ἀμφ' Ἀτρεΐωνα** 'and those around Atreus' son': the place of gathering focuses on Agamemnon's authority, but need not imply a permanent coterie (cf. 3.146, *Od.* 22.21).   **ἀολλέες ἠγερέθοντο** 'were gathered all together': for the form of the adjective, see 12n. ἠγερέθοντο is 3rd pl. imperf. indic. of ἠγερέθομαι, derived from ἀγείρω (as e.g. ἠερέθονται < ἀείρω, θαλέθω < θάλλω: see 196–8[a]n.) and with a quasi-aoristic sense looking to the action's completion (*GH* I § 153; Wyatt 1969: 107–11).   **ἐπερχομένων:** the ppl. elsewhere in the poem is always the object of μένω denoting resistance to an advance (1.535, 8.536, etc.; cf. *HAp.* 3–5; Kelly 2007a: 362).   **ὅμαδος καὶ δοῦπος:** ominous sounds for the individual who hears them, either war (9.573) or the gathering of comrades with disastrous consequences (*Od.* 10.556). Originally meaning 'battle' (cf. Sanskr. *samád-*), ὅμαδος denotes groups of men and/or their noise most often in war, whilst δοῦπος expresses the 'collision of two objects' (Kaimio 1977: 79–80) across a wider but still aggressive spectrum, again frequently linked with combat (Tichy 1983: 96–7, 191–4).   **ἕζετο δ' ὀρθωθείς** = 2.42[a], where Agamemnon wakes from Zeus's false dream. Perhaps an underrepresented formula, it furthers the parallels between the two days in the poem's macrostructure (Intro. § 1, scheme on pp. 3–4) and underlines Achilleus' assumption of Agamemnon's dominance (35–58n.). It is not clear whether ὀρθωθείς means he sat 'upright' in his bed (~ ὀρθός) or 'he stood', but the latter may be preferable if this is a precursor to Achilleus' announcements before most events (viz. στῆ δ' ὀρθός etc.: 271–3n.; Bannert 1988: 146–7).   **σφεας** 'them': masc. acc. pl. of the enclitic 3rd pers. pronoun (Homer also uses σφας, σφε: Intro. § 3.1.2.a.i), one heavy syllable in synizesis.   **πρὸς μῦθον ἔειπεν:** 66–8n.

236–51 The speech gives the final instructions for Patroclos' death ritual, as does Nestor after the duel between Aias and Hector (7.327–44; 236n.), while the instructions for Hector's funeral are split between the camp (24.656–70) and Troy (777–81), in which process Achilleus is once more dominant. Unlike for the other funerals, however, there is no sense here that a formal truce is required (7.342–3, 24.709–81). Several run-overs, both necessary (239, 242, 244, 247–8) and adding (238, 240, 246), suggest the speaker's perturbed emotional state.

236 = 7.327 (Nestor), 385 (Idaios), both from speeches concerned with funeral processes, unlike those introduced by the equivalent expression Ἀτρεῖδη τε καὶ ἄλλοι ἐϋκνήμιδες Ἀχαιοί (23.272, 658; see nn.); we may be intended to recall specifically the funeral in Book 7 rather than funerals generically: Intro. § 1.   **Ἀτρεΐδη:** 156–7n.   **ἀριστῆες Παναχαιῶν:** the compound in this formula = πάντων Ἀχαιῶν, denoting all the contingents present on the expedition, and does not suggest a conception of Panhellenic unity (2.404, 7.73, 7.159, etc.; Nagy 1979: 5–9; Hall 2002: 130–4; Ross 2005; Webber 2023).

237–8 ~ 250–1 below, = 24.791–2, once more connecting the poem's closing funerals (Di Benedetto 1998: 297–8). Dousing the flames with wine resumes the accompanying libations, but also finds parallels in Hittite burial customs (West 1997a: 398–9; cf. Rutherford 2008: 229–31). Wine vessels are common in Greek death ritual of all periods (Schnapp-Gourbeillon 1982: 81; C–M 115; Gallou 2005: 93–8).   **κατά** 'completely': preposition/preverb emphasising fulfilment (*GH* II § 158).   **σβέσατ':** 2nd pl. aor. act. imp. of σβέννυμι 'I quench'.   **αἴθοπι οἴνωι:** this formula is found in the dat. only here, 250 below, and in the parallel passage (above). Hiatus depends on (ϝ)οίνωι. The meaning of αἴθοψ is disputed between 'blackened' and 'gleaming' (< αἴθω: Hainsworth 1988: 338; also 205–7n.); the latter would resonate well with the present emphasis on light and fire, the former with the fire's effect.   **πᾶσαν, ὁπόσσον ἐπέσχε πυρὸς μένος** 'all of it (i.e. the pyre), as far as the fire's strength reached/extended': alternation of repeated plosives and onomatopoeic sibilants complements the fire's reach (and perhaps the sound of its hissing extinction?). For the sense of ἐπέσχε, see 188–91n.; for πυρὸς μένος, see 175–7n.

239 ~ 24.793 (see 237–8n.); fulfilled in 252. The sombre precision of the act is emphasised by the four-word verse which, like many such verses, is marked by the presence of a name (39–41n.).   **Πατρόκλοιο Μενοιτιάδαο:** this formula is only linked with Patroclos' victims (16.420,

434, 452, 21.28) or his own death (16.760 nom., 18.93, *Od.* 24.77); for the patronymic, see 24–6n.

240–2 διαγινώσκοντες 'distinguishing': -γῑν- is a common form in the MSS, representing a simplification of γιγν- with compensatory lengthening (*GH* I § 4). The reading -γιγν- in some good MSS and Π 9 is an attempt to restore the metre: see also 318 (περιγίνεται), 505 (γίνετ'). **ἀριφραδέα δὲ τέτυκται** 'and are made very clear to see': 'very' is the sense of the prefix ἀρι- (as in e.g. ἀρίγνωτος, ἀριπρεπής: Willi 1999), while the adjective's final α is rendered heavy in the princeps position. This may have influenced the adverbial form in Π 12 ἀριφραδέως γάρ ἔκειτο (S. West 1967: 187). ἀριφραδής is only elsewhere used for the revelation of σήματα 'signs'/'tokens', extended here to the process of constructing a σῆμα 'tomb'. τέτυκται is 3rd sing. perf. pass. indic. of τεύχω 'I make (ready)'. **τοί:** 118–21ᵃn. **ἄνευθεν** 'apart': formed from adverb ἄνευ + separative suffix -θεν, this word may be placed before or after its noun (in the gen.) (2.27 = 64, 5.185 etc.; Lejeune 1939: 336–8). **ἐπιμίξ ἵπποι τε καὶ ἄνδρες:** this formula, for deadly confusion driven by one person (11.525, 21.16), also looks back to its last usage in Achilleus' *aristeia*, during the slaughter in the river, shortly before he takes the prisoners (21.26–32) whose bodies are here denoted. The different context forces the further disturbing detail that 'it is neither possible nor necessary to distinguish [the] respective bones' of animals and men (Schnapp-Gourbeillon 1982: 83), in a marked contrast with Patroclos' remains. Platte 2017: 98–9 discusses this passage as an example of heroic 'hippomorphism', viz. equating heroes with horses.

243–4 243 ~ 253. The covering of the bones with fat and temporary placement in a golden vessel recalls, but does not fulfil, the shade's instructions (91–2n.) and the initial smearing of the corpse (167ᵇ–9n.), and is designed to preserve the remains until Achilleus' burial (Petropoulou 1988: 487): see also 245–8, 250–4nn. **χρυσέηι φιάληι:** -εηι is one heavy syllable in synizesis, which Π 12 avoids by reading χρυσῆι (Homer never uses the contracted form in this position, and the uncontracted form is typically deployed in this position for vessels: *Od.* 6.79, 215, *Th.* 785). Temporary storage for Patroclos' bones (91–2n.), the φιάλη was a broad, shallow pan or bowl with handles (Bruns 1970: 19, 38–9), found in Homer only in this book, here and as the last-placed prize in the chariot race (270 ~ 616: 269–70n.). It is attested as a grave good in its own right from the Protogeometric period onwards (Andronikos 1968: 30, 73; Petropoulou 1988: 490–1). **δίπλακι δημῶι** 'with double (layer of) fat': a sign of particular care, since the epithet (< πλέκω 'weave') is usually applied to tapestries and cloaks, where its double layering suggests abundant resources (3.216, 22.241, etc.; De Jong 2012: 175; Marinatos 1967: 9–10). **θείομεν** 'let us place': 1st pl. aor. act. subj. of τίθημι = θέωμεν, the result of quantitative metathesis (ηο > εω) from original *θήομεν, with ειο a compromise stage between the two (*GH* I §§ 2, 28): also 486 below. **εἰς ὅ κεν αὐτὸς ἐγών ... κεύθωμαι** 'until I am myself (forever) concealed': the temporal construction indicates fulfilment, and so usually takes a punctual aor. subj. (hence presumably Π 12 κλεύσωμαι), but the present aptly expresses the duration required (*GH* II § 390). κεύθωμαι is 1st sing. pres. mediopass. subj. of κεύθω, read by the majority of MSS and confirmed at least for the fifth century by Sophocles (*Aias* 634–5 κρείσσων γὰρ Ἅιδαι κεύθων ὁ νοσῶν μάταν: Wackernagel 1916: 164; Finglass 2011: 324–5). Σ T 244c reports an unknown form κλεύθωμαι, syncopated from κελεύθωμαι 'make a journey' and printed by West (though as 'I am subject to': 2001a: 126–8). The epenthetic ν in ἐγών avoids hiatus, and is an Aeolism in the epic dialect (Wathelet 1970: 285–6).

245–8 Achilleus limits the honouring of Patroclos by prescribing the tomb's dimensions, as he does other matters (cf. 16.83–90, 22.331–5). Based on a hundred-square-foot pyre (162–4n.), it is an impressive edifice. Petropoulou 1988: 491–5 suggests a diameter of 42.5 m = 140 ft which compares with a range of ancient funeral structures, including the *herōon* at Lefkandi (150 × 46 ft: De Waele 1998: 381), the largest of the Bronze Age tumuli, e.g., at Hexalophos in Thessaly (diam. 90 ft: Müller 1989: 38), the Geometric and Archaic examples at Vergina in Macedonia (Andronikos 1968: 112–13), the Classical mounds at Duvanli in Thrace (Petropoulou 1988: 494), and the largest of those in the Troad and the Granicus valley (Rose 2014: 73–5, 116–17; Andronikos 1968: 107–14). Despite its size, the tomb is envisaged here as a temporary cenotaph, like the permanent structures honouring the absent dead (*Od.* 1.289–91 ~ 2.220–2, 4.583–4), and its later expansion is narrated in the *Odyssey* (24.80–4): see 162–4, 243–4, 250–4nn. **ἄνωγα:** for the form, see 158–6on. **ἐπιεικέα τοῖον** 'just seemly enough' (*sc.* for someone of Patroclos' status): τοῖον is an adverbial accusative meaning 'to such an extent', 'just so' (*Od.* 3.321, 15.471, etc.). **καὶ τόν** 'this very one': καί specifies the demonstrative, connecting it with the previous sentence. **τιθήμεναι** '[let them/you] make/set': pres. act. infin. used as imperative, either in the 3rd person (rarely in Homer) or the 2nd person anticipated from the following relative clause (*GH* II § 460). Less direct than the imperative, the imperatival infinitive denotes 'actions which are elements of a particular procedure' (Allan 2010: 225), subordinating the tomb's final construction to the immediate honouring of Patroclos. **οἵ κεν ... | ...**

λίπησθε 'all you who … will be left': with or without the modal particles ἄν/κε, the subjunctive in a relative clause expresses generalisation, indefiniteness, and/or futurity, like a conditional protasis (Willmott 2007: 184–90, 233; Probert 2015: 83–97). λίπησθε is used in the passive sense 'be left behind' = 'survive'. ἐμεῖο | δεύτεροι 'following *or* after me': derived probably from δέω/δεύω 'I lack' (*EDG* 319–20, 321–2), δεύτερος is here uniquely – but naturally, given its comparative form – construed with a genitive noun, as in e.g. ἐμέο πρότερος (10.124), σεῦ ὕστερος (18.333; *GH* II § 224; Mørland 1948: 161). ἐν νήεσσι πολυκλήϊσι 'in ships with many oar tholes': here Achilleus views negatively the general Greek situation after his death, since groups associated with this formula are envisaged in defensive posture (2.74, 175, 13.742, etc.; cf. also Hes. *WD* 817). The epithet refers technically to the tholes in which the oars rested, but was early extended to the seats and so the number of rowers, probably through misunderstanding of the formula ἐπὶ κληῖσι καθῖζον (so Σ D 2.74: 'their seats are called κληῖδες'; Kurt 1979: 68–9, 141–3; Le Feuvre 2015: 408–11).

249 ποδώκεϊ Πηλεΐωνι: again evoking speed whilst Achilleus remains still (93n.), this usually acc. formula is found in the dative only here and at 24.458 (35–7n.).

250–4 Achilleus' injunctions are carried out: 250–1 ~ 237–8; 252–3 ~ 239 and 243 (see nn.). Line 254 ~ 18.352 (ἐν λεχέεσσι), after Patroclos' body is bathed for the first time. Not explicit in the instructions, this is the last we hear of the remains until Achilleus' burial (*Od.* 24.73–7), where they are interred in the same vessel (91–2n.). They are imagined as staying in Achilleus' hut until that moment, which explains the care taken over their preservation as opposed to the simple enfolding of Hector's bones in a purple robe before burial (24.795–6); for historical evidence of covering with cloth in Greek contexts in the early Archaic period, see Margariti and Spantidaki 2020 (Lefkandi), and Kolonas et al. 2017: 536–7 (Stamnos in Aitolia); for parallels with Hittite burial customs, see Intro. § 2.1. ἑτάροιο ἐνηέος 'of the gentle companion': uncontracted gen. sing. masc. of 3rd declension ἐνηής 'gentle', etymologically obscure and used in epos mostly in the acc. and gen., usually with ἑταῖρον/ ἑτάροιο of Patroclos (cf. 17.670; also of lovemaking in Hes. *Th.* 651, *Theb.* fr. 2.9 B). Only here of this figure in Homer outside character speech, suggesting either the poet's assumption of Achilleus' perspective (42n.) or focalisation through the mourners; on ἑταῖρος/ἑτάρ-, see 5, 6–7nn. Though his behaviour during Book 16 does not generally bespeak a gentle soul, 'Patroclos's gentleness is unique in the language of the poem'

(Edwards 127; e.g. 11.814–48, 17.670–2: Taplin 1992: 234–7; Zanker 1994: 138–40).   ἄλλεγον 'they picked (them) up' = ἀνέλεγον, 3rd sing. imperf. act. indic. of ἀναλέγω, with ἀνά suffering apocope and assimilation of ν- (cf. 21.321 ἄλλεξαι: 462–4n.).   ἐν κλισίηισι δὲ θέντες: plural κλισίαι can denote the whole camp (1.487, 11.834, etc.) and a leader's contingent within that space (1.306, 2.226–7, etc.), but also just one tent, which may be a very large structure (cf. 24.448–56: 9.669, 12.1, 13.256, etc.). The variant ἐν κλισίηι δ' ἐνθέντες is therefore unnecessary. Petropoulou 1988 argues that κλισίηισι in fact denotes the tomb, and that Patroclos' bones were in fact buried, but there is no Homeric parallel for this usage.   ἑανῶι λιτί 'with fine covering': both words are generally adjectives, and of uncertain meaning. The second (only acc. or dat.) is usually taken as 'smooth' or 'plain' and, when a noun, used as a protective covering for reused items (chariot 8.441; chair *Od.* 1.130); unlike Hector's purple robes, it may here help to foreshadow Achilleus' future interment. This is clearly quality material, since ἑανός (distinct from the noun ἑανός 'dress' < ἔννυμι) is applied to Athene's robe (5.734, 8.385) and the tin on Achilleus' greaves (18.613). For other interpretations, including 'strong', 'luxurious', 'bright', etc., see Σ D 5.734, 18.613 (Marinatos 1967: 11, 41–2; Pulleyn 2019: 143–4; also Faulkner 2008: 146–8).

255–7 255 is notably chiastic, with four-syllable past-tense verbs surrounding and emphasising the assonant σῆμα θεμείλιά τε. Some have suggested that the swift transition between funeral and games mid-verse in 257 betrays the separateness of the funeral and the inauthenticity of the games (an 'afterthought': West 2011: 411, also 399), and were inclined to follow 257 straight with 24.4 (αὐτὰρ Ἀχιλλεὺς 257[b] = 24.3[b]), but there is no MS which lacks this episode, it was early reflected in the artistic discourse (Intro. § 2.2), and there are no good grounds to doubt either its authenticity or its importance to the poem.   τορνώσαντο 'they measured off': the verb is derived from τόρνος 'turning lathe/compass', and implies the tomb's circular construction (so Σ D 23.255; cf. *Od.* 5.249; Petropoulou 1988: 491).   θεμείλια 'foundations': either metrically lengthened (< neut. pl. adj. θεμέλια < τίθημι) to avoid a sequence of four light syllables (*GH* I § 44) or, less likely, an adaptation of Cretan θεμήλιον (Wyatt 1969: 105 n. 1). Though temporary, the tomb is still sizeable (162–4, 245–8nn.), since this word is used in epos only of the wall around the Greek camp (12.28; also constructed from a tomb) and the foundations of Apollo's temple (*HAp.* 254, 294).   χυτὴν ἐπὶ γαῖαν ἔχευαν 'they heaped upon (them) heaped earth' = *Od.* 3.258[b], and probably an underrepresented formula; cf. χυτὴ κατὰ γαῖα καλύπτει (6.464, 14.114). χυτήν is emphatically etymologised by ἔχευαν/χεύαντες (257), and is either pleonastic or proleptic, i.e. 'so that it was heaped'/'into a heap' (Sourvinou-Inwood 1995: 122–5; Clary 2009: 140–1).   χεύαντες δὲ τὸ σῆμα πάλιν κίον = 24.801, pairing Greek games and Trojan feast. Approaching an article, the demonstrative here still retains something of its original sense 'that', pointing the audience back to the tomb just constructed (*contra GH* II § 243).   κίον 'they were leaving': usually classed as a 3rd pl. aor. act. indic. (of a verb with no present tense), though the Greeks do not actually leave the scene (Willcock 1984: 302). Richardson 200 suggests a 'regular phrase', but this verb is one of several in epos reanalysed as though it had a present tense (*GH* I § 187), and so its aorist forms can have an imperfect sense (2.509, 22.461, etc.; Létoublon 1989: 85–92). Here it sets an ongoing process of departure at the same time as Achilleus establishes the games (ἔρυκε … ἵζανεν 258, ἔκφερ' 259).

257ᵇ–897 THE FUNERAL GAMES

The events to commemorate Patroclos' funeral take up the rest of the book. For the wider phenomenon in art and literature, and the position and reception of Homer's games, see Intro. § 2. The narrative sequence in Book 23 comprises eight separate contests (Table 2), set in an order not precisely reflected in what little we know or can reconstruct of early Greek literature (Table 3). Despite considerable variation there, the boxing, wrestling, and running events seem to have formed a stable core in early epos, as in Nestor's story of his youthful triumphs (23.630–42 at 634–6), and Odysseus' challenge to the Phaiacians ἢ πύξ ἠὲ πάλῃ ἢ καὶ ποσίν (*Od.* 8.206; cf. also 103 πύξ τε παλαιμοσύνῃ τε καὶ ἅλμασιν ἠδὲ πόδεσσιν and 246; and *Scut.* 301 πύξ τε καὶ ἑλκηδόν: Bannert 1988: 148–51). The swapping of the chariot race with the spear throwing in Nestor's reminiscence may reflect the rhetoric of that passage (638–42n.), as may the placement at the end of the running in Achilleus' mini-catalogue of events which precedes it (621–3n.): see 262–652n. Ancient readers noted this sequence: Aristarchos thought it proved that the author of the *Iliad* and *Odyssey* was the same person (Σ A 23.621), while Plutarch has his characters justify it firstly in terms of 'the customs' of Homer's time, but then by military necessity, as it mirrors the course of action in a fight, and so places running after the contact events (*Mor.* 639a–640a).

Connections between the events in Book 23 are many and varied, ranging from repeated actions and phrasing to shared participants, and they are interlaced in complex ways that defy easy schematisation. Some events are naturally more closely related than others, as e.g. the chariot and running races (740–97n.), and the boxing and the fight in armour (798–825n.) or the boxing and the wrestling (700–39n.), and they may

Table 2 The Funeral Games in the *Iliad*

Event	Prizes	Standing order	Results
1. **Chariot race** (262–652)	(1) woman/tripod; (2) horse; (3) cauldron; (4) 2 gold talents; (5) urn	(1) Eumelos; (2) Diomedes; (3) Menelaos; (4) Antilochos; (5) Meriones[a]	(1) Diomedes; (2) Antilochos; (3) Menelaos; (4) Meriones; [(5) Nestor]; Eumelos DNF (extra breastplate)
2. **Boxing** (653–99)	(1) mule; (2) cup	(1) Epeios; (2) Euryalos	(1) Epeios
3. **Wrestling** (700–39)	(1) tripod; (2) woman	(1) Aias; (2) Odysseus	draw? (equal division?)
4. **Running** (740–97)	(1) silver *kratēr*; (2) ox; (3) half-talent gold	(1) Aias *meiōn*; (2) Odysseus; (3) Antilochos	(1) Odysseus; (2) Aias; (3) Antilochos
5. **Fight in armour** (798–825)	(1) Sarpedon's armour (split); (extra) sword	(1) Aias *meizōn*; (2) Diomedes	draw? (extra prize to Diomedes)

[a] A lot then determines the competing order: Antilochos – Eumelos – Menelaos – Meriones – Diomedes.

Event			
6. **Iron throwing** (826–49)	(1) iron	(1) Polypoites; (2) Leonteus; (3) Aias; (4) Epeios[b]	(1) Polypoites
7. **Archery** (850–83)	(1) 10 axes; (2) 10 half-axes	(1) Teucros; (2) Meriones[c]	(1) Meriones; (2) Teucros
8. **Spear throwing** (884–97)	(1) spear; (2) tripod[d]	(1) Agamemnon; (2) Meriones	no contest: (1) Meriones; (2) Agamemnon

[b] Competing order: Epeios – Leonteus – Aias – Polypoites.
[c] A lot then determines the competing order: Teucros – Meriones.
[d] In this contest, neither the poet nor Achilleus specify which prize is for which places (884–97n.).

Table 3 Event order in early epos

Patroclos' games 23.257–897	Nestor's games 23.630–42	Scherian games *Od.* 8.109–30	Achilleus' games Apollodoros, *Epit.* 5.5
1. Chariot	5. Chariot	–	1. Chariot
2. Boxing	1. Boxing	5. Boxing	–
3. Wrestling	2. Wrestling	2. Wrestling	–
4. Running	3. Running	1. Running	2. Running
5. Fight in armour	–	–	–
6. Iron throwing	–	4. Discus	3. Discus
7. Archery	–	–	4. Archery
8. Spear throwing	4. Spear throwing	– 3. Leap	–

also connect with episodes outside Book 23, as e.g. the fight in armour and the many duels of the *Iliad* (798–825n.). Other events link up more directly because of proximity, as with the use of text-internal analepsis in the source of the prizes for both the running race and the fight in armour (740–51, 798–800nn.).

There does, however, seem to be a grouping based around the contrast between multiple and two contestants:

I   1. Chariot Race   Group (5 contestants)
     2. Boxing   2 contestants
     3. Wrestling   2 contestants

II   4. Running   Group (3 contestants)
     5. Fight in armour   2 contestants

III 6. Iron throwing   Group (4 contestants)
     7. Archery   2 contestants
     8. Spear throwing   2 contestants

In this scheme, the headline event (1, 4, 7) for each group is obviously set off from the others, while the closing event (3, 5, 8) is marked by an intervention from Achilleus which falls progressively earlier each time: he announces a draw in the wrestling and suggests even division of an inherently uneven prize (735–7n.), he allows the crowd to stop the fight in armour before someone gets hurt and again struggles with the issue of division (809–10n.), and he shuts down the spear throwing before it even begins (884–97n.). It is as though his actions during and after the chariot race (448–99, 534–41, 566–613nn.) are now being matched and replayed throughout the games, in progressively greater stages of imposition. No scholar will ever come up with the same structural division as another; for a different analysis of the last seven events, in which three episodes of c. 50 verses are followed by three of c. 30 verses before the final very abbreviated one, see Bannert 1988: 147–8. On the doubts raised by some modern scholars over the authenticity of Events 5–7, see 798–897n.

Each episode proceeds in a standard way, with four fixed stages and one floating element (crowd reaction: Table 4): (A) the prizes are set out and the contest identified; (B) contestants stand (and sometimes draw lots for the competing order); (C) the competition is narrated; (D) prizes are awarded and any disputes settled (Köhnken 1981: 131; Scott 1997: 216–18; Minchin 2001a: 43–53; Kelly 2017: 88–92). Each contest begins and ends with the prizes, their presentation and distribution, showing the centrality to the process of the τιμή which they represent, as we will see throughout the commentary (on the multiple prizes for each contest but the iron throwing, see 259–61n.). Secondly, the crowd's reaction or participation is found in every event except the final one (abbreviated in other ways as well: 884–97n.), but in no fixed form or position within the scheme: they react with silence after Epeios' challenge in the boxing before the event has started (676), they marvel at the competitors advancing into the contest area before the fight in armour (815) and at their actions in the wrestling during the contest (728) and at the effect of Merones' shot in the archery (882), they approve of Achilleus' suggestion at the end of the chariot race (540) and shout in Odysseus' favour during the running (766–7) and at Teucros' shot in the archery (869), they laugh at Epeios' effort during the iron throwing (840) and at Aias' rueful speech after the running (784), and they even take over the agōnothetēs' role entirely in stopping the fight in armour before someone gets seriously hurt (822–3). Each reaction has a purpose in its context (see nn.) but the point here more is that this is a floating typical element, and that the laos is heavily invested in the process and outcome of the events (see, differently, Elmer 2013 and Ready 2023: 100–10).

This floating element shows how flexibly and imaginatively the poet treats this basic structure, for into it he weaves all his other tricks as well, including competitors' speeches (and quarrels) at any stage but the first; he can use lots to separate the standing order from the competing order, as before the chariot race (352–7n.) and the archery (861–2n: cf. the unannounced reordering before the iron throwing 836–8n.); he can

Table 4 The typical structure of the events

A. Prizes set out and contest announced
B. Contestants stand
C. Contest
D. Prizes distributed
+. *Crowd reaction*

1. Chariot	2. Boxing	3. Wrestling	4. Running	5. Fight	6. Iron	7. Archery	8. Spear
A 262–87	654–63	700–7	740–53	798–810	826–35	850–8	884–6
B 287–361	664–84 *+ silent* 676	708–9	754–7	811–15 *+ marvel* 815	836–9	859–62	887–8
C 362–533	685–98	710–37 *+ marvel* 728	758–79 *+ favour* 766–7	816–21 *+ stop* 822–3	840–7 *+ laugh* 840 *+ shout* 847	862–81 *+ cry out* 869 *+ marvel* 882	–
D 534–653 *+ approve* 540	699	738–9	779–95 *+ laugh* 784	824–5	848–9	882–3	889–97

vary the size and nature of the competition narrative from panoramic summary (as in the outward leg of the chariot race 362–72n.) to individual, narrativised episodes (again in the chariot race, with the encounter between Menelaos and Antilochos at 401–47, or in the wrestling, with Aias' offer to Odysseus at 722–3), and so on. Typicality is never a straitjacket, and the variation and suspense within each contest is considerable, as the poet constantly plays with the audience's expectations (see esp. Lohmann 1992: 307–9; Grethlein and Huitink 2017; Scodel 2021; Ready 2023: 196–210).

Perhaps the most noticeable aspect of this is the fact that the victors of the individual events are not those one would expect at the start of the contest: both figures touted as 'second best after Achilleus' (2.761–70) in chariot team (Eumelos) and self (Aias) have a dreadful time: Eumelos comes last in the chariot race, and Aias comes off second best or worst in the wrestling, fight in armour, and iron throwing; the rank professional and otherwise unmentioned Epeios wins the boxing against an experienced warrior with an athletic pedigree; Odysseus defeats proven runners in the lesser Aias and Antilochos; Teucros' archery across the poem is more impressive than Meriones'; and Agamemnon should have the measure of the latter in throwing a spear. Expect the unexpected, in other words, though for other reasons why Eumelos and Aias fare so poorly, see 288–9, 708–9, 798–825nn. For the relationship between these results and those at Achilleus' funeral games, see Intro. § 2.2.

258 αὐτοῦ: i.e. near the site of the tomb, from which they were starting to depart.   **ἀγῶνα** 'assembly': properly of any gathering (< ἄγειν), here it refers to those watching the competition, elsewhere to the place of competition (273, 847) and the contests themselves (531, *Od.* 8.259, *HAp.* 150; Laser 11–13).

259–61 All the items listed here make an appearance in the games, but, as typically with catalogues, the list is neither exhaustive nor precise (perhaps why Aristophanes and Aristarchos athetised the lines: see Erbse ad loc.): despite the plural (260), only one horse, mule, and ox are awarded (265–6, 654–5, 750); some later prizes are not mentioned at all (e.g. silver *krētēr*, gold talents, cup); nor are the items particularly evocative of contests, since the pairings (cauldrons–tripods, horses–mules, women–iron) occur in a wide range of contexts (see nn.). Instead, the catalogue generally encapsulates the contest for τιμή which these items represent, with many of them representative of the material *xenia* networks and wider social values found throughout the Homeric world (Laser 79–81; Papakonstantinou 2002; Brown 2003: 127–33). That he has so many

things to give away reflects well on Achilleus' resources, as does the practice of having prizes for almost every contestant (except the iron throwing), a feature quite anomalous in the historical athletic tradition, though
there is some limited evidence for lower-placed prizes at a variety of festivals (Crowther 1992) and for multiple prizes in chariot races as depicted
on vases (McGowan 1995: 625–8). Homer's literary heirs generally followed his lead in this regard (Willis 1941: 409–17), but in Book 23 it
throws yet more relief on Achilleus' authority and power in this portion of
the poem, rather than simply reflecting what happened at actual funeral
games (as, e.g., Decker 1982–3).　　**νηῶν**: metonym for the camp (Σ
bT): see 1–3n.　　**ἄεθλα** 'prizes': though the etymology is uncertain,
ἄεθλον (and derivative ἀέθλιον) is a variant form for ἄεθλος 'effort, struggle, battle' denoting the prizes on offer in athletic or musical contests
and, in the plural, funeral games *in toto* (e.g. 23.631, *Od.* 24.89, *WD* 654;
Nagy 2021: 24). Contest is not meant to be easy; cf. the Attic adjective
ἄθλιος 'wretched'.　　**βοῶν τ' ἴφθιμα κάρηνα** 'strong (heads of) cattle':
nowhere else in Homer is the adjective applied to anything other than a
human being or a god (cf. 17.749 of rivers), but this expression denotes
Apollo's stolen herd in the *HHerm.*, suggesting an underrepresented formula (Thomas 2020: 202). More frequently used of the high points of
cities and mountain ranges, this κάρηνα idiom is an archaic survival in
Homer, expressing the 'centre of the life-force' (*LfrgE* s. κάρηνα, 1334) in
humans alive (11.158) and dead, and in horses (9.407; Nussbaum 1986:
168–71); also 94–6n.　　**πολιόν τε σίδηρον**: the epithet is difficult to
define; it denotes a bright grey or dull white colour, elsewhere being used
to describe the sea and the hair of old people (*LfrgE* s.v., 1343–5). Iron is
a typical heroic resource (6.48 = 10.379 = 11.133 = *Od.* 21.10 ~ 14.324)
for trade or barter (7.473, *Od.* 1.184), to be worked into a range of practical items and even weapons (30–3n.); in these games, it is used for the
iron throwing (826–7), and for the axe-heads in the archery (850; cf.
4.485), a feature also found in the *Odyssey* (21.3, 81, 24.168): 832–5n.;
Canevaro 2018: 11–12 suggests the link between women and iron recalls
the role of the former in causing the Iron Age (*WD* 174–201).

261 = 9.366, where Achilleus states his intention to lead home to
Phthiē the spoil he has taken in Troy – a nice contrast with his current
determination.

262–652 Event 1. Chariot Race. The first, and by far the longest and
most complex contest, the chariot race shows every element in the event
sequence (257[b]–897n.); each of these is far more detailed and full than
its corresponding feature in the other contests, but the poet also achieves

monumental scale by inserting several exchanges – between Nestor and Antilochos before the start (303–50); between Menelaos and Antilochos (425–47) and Idomeneus and Oilean Aias (450–99) during the race; and between Achilleus and Antilochos (535–62), Menelaos and Antilochos (566–613), and Achilleus and Nestor (615–52) after it finishes. This allows a variety of perspectives on the action, from the narrator's overall omniscience to the uncertain summary of the race by Idomeneus (448–72), and we move regularly from the views and agencies of the participants to the internal audiences (C–G 12; Grethlein and Huitink 2017). In terms of its structure, Lohmann 1992: 295 persuasively sees three sections:

1. Before the race (257–361)
   A¹ Catalogue of prizes and drivers (257–304)
   B¹ Nestor's first 'expert-speech' – prediction (304–50)
   C¹ Starting order and start (351–61)
2. The race (392–498)
3. After the race (499–650)
   C² Finishing order (499–534)
   A² Division of prizes (523–624) – retrospection
   B² Nestor's second 'expert-speech' (625–50)

The scheme does not capture the permeability of the boundary between C² and A², the race and the distribution, since the contestants claim their prizes as they finish, and so their (and the crowd's) reactions can be interchanged whilst other competitors have yet to cross the finishing line, as also again in the running race (see Stanley 1993: 224–30 for a more complex arrangement). Nonetheless, the care and deliberation of the poet is clear, as is the greater scalar importance of the *après course*. Recent analyses include Clay 2007; Minchin 2001a: 49–70; Purves 2011 (= 2019: 67–91); Elmer 2013: 189–97; Grethlein and Huitink 2017: 74–85; Scodel 2021: 59–61; Ready 2023: 101–4.

Chariot racing, either with two- or four-horse teams, and equestrian events more broadly were prominent in Greek athletic competitions of every age (Laser 26–32; Olisová 1989; Miller 2004b: esp. 75–82; Mann and Scharff 2020). The most famous of the many artistic representations of this and other races in the Archaic period (see Friis Johansen 1967: 86–92; Roller 1981b; Laser 26–32; Moore 2016) is the magnificent François Vase (Fig. 2; *LIMC* s. Achilleus 493), whose largely different cast (Odysseus, Automedon, Diomedes, Damasippos, and Hippothoon – neither of the last two are known to Homer, though several Iliadic characters are called Hippothoos) could reflect an alternative tradition, poetic or otherwise, or even the artist's 'mistake' (Wachter 1998; Finkelberg 2017: 33–5). For what it is worth, beneath the team of Damasippos we

see a tripod, beneath the team of Hippothoon a cauldron; the latter is
the prize for third place in Homer (267–8), the former is added to a
woman to comprise the prize for first place (263–5), but there is another
tripod on the extreme right of the vase's panel, next to the labelled figure Achilleus, which is generally understood to represent the prize for
first place. Not much in these terms can be made of another depiction of
the race, on the almost equally renowned Sophilos *dinos* (Fig. 3; *LIMC* s.
Achilleus 491), where the painter signs the image and labels it 'Patroclos'
games' (in retrograde ΑΛΤΑ ⋮ ΣΥΛϘΟΡΤΑΠ), but not enough remains of
the name above the only visible team to tell. Achilleus appears on both
vases in the ἀγωνοθέτης role so prominent in Book 23. However these
depictions interact with the *Iliad*, the event itself was well known by the
early sixth century BCE (257[b]–897n.). It should also be noted that, in
common with many depictions of chariot racing from the end of the seventh century BCE onwards, the teams on these two artefacts comprise
four horses, not two as in Homer (though he does know of four-horse
teams in racing contexts: 11.698–702, *Od.* 13.81). This may be a con-
scious archaism (Scanlon 2004: 63–89), but the two-horse teams reinforce the link between combat and games, a desire seen e.g. in the fight
in armour (798–825n.) or in the mere fact that many prizes are spoils of
war (Grethlein 2007b: 158–9); alternation between two- and four-horse

2 The François Vase (Florence, Mus. Archaeol. 4209; *LIMC* s.
Achilleus 493)

3 The Sophilos *dinos* (Athens, Nat. Mus. 15499; *LIMC* s. Achilleus 491)

teams is also found throughout extant Archaic depictions of the funeral games for Pelias (Roller 1981b: 110).

Aside from references to other chariot races in these contexts (23.638–42), the similes comparing Achilleus to a 'prize-winning horse with his chariot' (22.21–4) and his pursuit of Hector to a chariot race (22.158–66), and his own intimations about other such contests (23.274–8), all show that this event was well known in the epic world. The long literary reception specifically of our episode, however, begins with the messenger speech in Sophocles' *Electra* (680–763), which tells of Orestes' supposed death in a chariot race closely modelled on this one (Davidson 1988; Johnston 2021), but Aischylos' *Glaukos Potnieus* also featured a crash in the chariot race at Pelias' funeral games (fr. 38 Radt; also Larmour 1999: esp. 99–108 for the dramatic reception of this event generally, and García Romero 2001: 75–85 for its influence on the paroemiographers). The theme proved most lasting in epic (cf. Verg. *Aen.* 5.114–285 (ships); Stat. *Theb.* 6.296–549, Sil. Ital. *Punica* 16.312–456; Quint. Smyrn. 4.500–44; Nonn. *Dion.* 37.116–84; cf. Lovatt 2019).

The placement of the chariot race as the first event in Book 23 calls for comment: there is some evidence that this event was often last, as in Nestor's recollection of Amarynceus' games (638–42n.), in Pelias' funeral games as depicted on the Chest of Cypselos (Pausanias 5.17.9–10), and in Quintus Smyrnaeus (where it is followed by a horse race). On the other hand, Nonnos mirrors Homer, as does Apollodoros' record of Achilleus' funeral games, and perhaps Apollonios in his scattered references to athletic events (Lovatt 2019: 431–2). This order is also, for what it is worth, found in Vergil, Statius, and Silius Italicus. Given how much of the early tradition of funeral games has been lost, it would be unwise to assume too much about where Homer's audience expected such an event to occur, and how far they expected contemporary practice to be reflected in the world of epos; the positional and scalar prominence of the chariot race here reflects above all the importance accorded to the horse team as an index of heroic identity in general and *Achilleus'* status in particular (cf. 2.761–70; 276–8n.), as well as the significance of Patroclos' relationship with the team (280–2n.) and thus his abiding importance to the *Iliad*'s closure.

262–70 The prizes for each place are specified in order; the level of detail is unparalleled in the other contests, and only partly because they have fewer competitors. Each entry has a form of τίθημι, the prize itself, and the place for which the prize is awarded. Variation in scale and syntax avoids monotony, every item developing the pattern of the previous one: in 263–5 chiasmus of the order verb/prize/place connects first and second (further described in 266); the third entry (267–8) partly mirrors the second in syntax – though with verb between epithet and prize (ἄπυρον κατέθηκε λέβητα |) – and in scale, with a separate descriptive verse (268); the fourth, reduced to a single verse (269), pushes the verb fully into second position between place and prize; and the fifth, also in a single verse (270), swaps verb and prize. For similar care in varying catalogue construction, see 352–7n. Sauge 1994: 34–5 notes that these prizes are a 'rather parsimonious' reflection of the gifts offered by Agamemnon (9.243–7), with the addition of the φιάλη underlining its contextual significance in holding Patroclos' remains (243–4n.).

262–3 ἱππεῦσιν … ποδώκεσιν: foregrounds the importance of this event to the competitors. Σ T mentions a variant ἱπποῖσιν, since the epithet more naturally refers to horses (as at 17.614, 23.376, etc.), but displacement the other way is hard to imagine, and the transfer from team to drivers is not difficult (cf. 287 ταχέες … ἱππῆες).   πρῶτα 'first of all': i.e. the prizes as a whole, not the first prize in the next verse.   θῆκε: the aorist signals the beginning of punctual narrative, after the continuative imperfects above. Necessary run-over from 262 connects the first prize(s) with appositional ἀγλά᾽ ἄεθλα, and marks it as the most important in the list. Heyne supplied τ᾽ after γυναῖκα to make clear the transition, and to avoid hiatus before ἄγεσθαι, but neither is necessary.   ἀμύμονα ἔργ᾽ εἰδυῖαν 'knowing noble works': Σ A 263–4a and Eustathios 1299.30–3 (IV.723.21–5 Van der Valk) discuss whether ἀμύμονα applies to the woman or the tasks, but the phrase always elsewhere qualifies women in the plural (9.128, 19.245, etc.), and so the adjective is surely neuter; the minority reading ἀμύμονας in some passages is obviously influenced by this case (and ignores otherwise universal (ϝ)ἔργα in this formula; Hainsworth 75); for the meaning of the epithet, see 136–7n. ἔργ' εἰδυῖαν is the reading of the MSS and preferable to ἔργα (ϝ)ἰδυῖαν printed by some editors (Intro. § 4, pp. 55–6). The ability to perform household tasks was a desirable female quality, weaving principal among them (e.g. 1.331, *Od.* 20.72, *HAphr.* 14–15; Pantelia 1993; Felson and Slatkin 2004; Canevaro 2018: esp. 271–2).

264–5ª Run-over τῶι πρώτωι combines with ω-assonance (Packard 1974: 250) to underline the chiasmus (262–70n.) connecting first and second place, perhaps foreshadowing the importance which the second prize will have in the quarrels at the end of the race.　　　**τρίποδ' ὠτώεντα:** found only in the context of funeral games in epos, the epithet is derived from the word 'ear' (contracted ὠτ- < οὐατ-) and refers to the handles soldered on the bowl. Whether a vessel with three supports and handles (as here) or a three-legged stand for a separate vessel (Bruns 1970: 37–8), a tripod is a common prize in epic games (11.700, 23.702, *WD* 657), but the exceptional value of this item is clear from its unusually long epithet. This particular example was given an inscription by the fourth-century BCE philosopher Phainias of Eresos (fr. 11.29–33 Wehrli), who claimed to have seen it in Delphi: that inscription sourced the item tantalisingly to the Antenorid Helicaon, who was wounded but rescued by Odysseus in the *Little Iliad* (fr. 12 B) because of his father's piety and hospitality.　　　**δυωκαιεικοσίμετρον** 'twenty-two measure': the formation is only matched in Homer by Aias' pike (δυωκαιεικοσίπηχυ 15.678), though cf. Hector's spear (ἑνδεκάπηχυ 6.319 = 8.494: Bassett 1919: 219; Edwards 1987: 123). Sometimes used to denote a measuring tool (12.422 etc.), a μέτρον is an unspecified unit of goods or distance. This bowl is very large among the prizes offered in the games, considering the cauldron's four measures (268) and the mixing-bowl's six (741); cf. the twenty measures of water in Maron's mixing-bowl (*Od.* 9.209), the twenty of barley groats sufficient for Telemachus' whole crew (*Od.* 2.355), and the thousand of wine gifted to Agamemnon and Menelaos by Euneos (7.471–2) – οἰνοβαρές indeed (1.225).

265ᵇ–6 ἑξέτε' ἀδμήτην 'six years old, hard to tame': the latter word should mean 'not (yet) harnessed', and is applied only to female animals in epos – horse, cow (10.293 = *Od.* 3.383), mule (23.655, *Od.* 4.636–7); cf. παρθένωι ἀδμήτηι in *HAphr.* 82 (ἀδμήτην at 133), and the formula παρθένος ἀδμής (6.109, 228, etc.). This is a long time to leave such a valuable animal alone: Van Leeuwen neatly redivided the words as ἑξέτεα, δμήτην 'six years old, tamed', but the latter form is otherwise unknown in Homer (Rank 1951: 83). The explanatory relative clause at 655 (see 653–6n.) suggests the meaning, at least in these two cases, of 'untameable' or 'hard to tame' (Delebecque 1951: 160; Mawet 1979: 242). On the high value of a mule in the epic world, see Griffith 2006a: 239.

267–8 ἄπυρον 'not fired': whether not yet used (Σ D 267) or not to be used on the fire ('as a votive' Σ T 702; Ap. Soph. s. ἀπύρους τρίποδας, 40.32–4 Bekker), though Athenaios 11.103.18–21 (citing 23.885) distinguishes vessels made for heating water and for holding cold water or wine. The image is picked up in λευκὸν ἔτ' αὔτως 'still white as it was', i.e. not blackened by use: see 884–6ⁿ. for another prize cauldron.   **καλόν:** this adjective is frequently used in this run-over position to introduce item descriptions, as again for the extra prize in the fight in armour (808). Such items frequently symbolise their possessor (e.g. 5.194, 9.187: Bertrand 2017: esp. 17), and the awarding process for both these items is subject to Achilleus' personal, and perhaps less than ideal, interventions (534–41, 809–10nn.).   **τέσσαρα μέτρα κεχανδότα** 'containing four measures': the same idiom describes the κρητήρ given as first prize in the running race (741–3n.); however large a μέτρον is, this item is neither as large nor as valuable (264–5ⁿn.). West prefers τέσσερα (read in some other passages) against the MSS' τέσσαρα as an Atticism (Wackernagel 1916: 13), but these forms cannot be emended out of the paradosis (cf. also 705 τεσσαράβοιον below). κεχανδότα is masc. acc. sing. perf. act. ppl. of χανδάνω (cf. ἑαδότα from ἀνδάνω: WHS 345–6), the tense expressing a present and continuing state (see Hackstein 2002: 180–1).

269–70 The fourth prize indicates that the Homeric 'talent' was worth less in the epic world than later (so Aristotle fr. 164 Rose and Σ AbT; Brown 1998: 166–7; Mayhew 2019: 123–42: Macrakis 1984 suggests an exchange rate in Homer of one ox = one talent). Unworked metals like gold and silver have great symbolic status in epos, but no precise exchange value (Brown 1998; Nicolet-Pierre 2006; Seaford 2004: 23–34, esp. 31–2). The same sum is offered in the trial scene on Achilleus' shield for the 'most direct' judgement (18.507) and as payment for Aigisthos' spy (*Od.* 4.526). Larger denominations are always tendered along with other items, e.g. ten in Agamemnon's reparations list (9.122 = 264; cf. 19.247), Hector's ransom (24.232), and Menelaos' gifts from Polybos (*Od.* 4.129); cf. also *Od.* 8.393, 9.202 = 24.274. For the diminutive 'half-talent' offered

in the running race below, see 750–1n.   ἀμφίθετον φιάλην: 243–4n.
The same epithet is used of this fifth prize again at 616, and was taken in
antiquity to refer *inter al.* to the vessel's ability either to be set down 'on
all sides' (Σ A) or to be picked up 'with handles on both sides' (Σ bT; for
more options, see Athen. 11.103).

271–86 Achilleus' first speech is a little longer than his other such invi-
tations (658–63, 707, 753, 802–10, 831–5, 855–8); it begins with a typically assertive claim about the superiority of his team and the inevitability
of their success were he to compete (272–8). Between the standard elements of naming the prizes (272–3) and encouraging the participants
to come forward (283–4), he explains his withdrawal from competition
as a mark of grief for Patroclos, though he only details the effects and
cause of this emotion from the horses' perspective (279–84), not his own.
Nowhere is his friend named, another pathetic effect. Speeches of this sort
about one's own athletic prowess always have a tone of self-justification,
like Nestor's after the chariot race (625–50n.), Epeios' before the boxing
(664–75n.), and Odysseus' during the games on Scheria (*Od.* 8.202–33) –
the speaker responds to a challenge related to a specific event or athletic
ability as a whole, and wider non-participation is a problem that needs to
be addressed.

271–3 271–2 = 657–8, before the boxing, joining the first two episodes
closely.   στῆ δ' ὀρθὸς καὶ μῦθον ἐν Ἀργείοισιν ἔειπεν: this formula
appears only in this book, usually to introduce a new contest (271, 657,
706, 752, 801, 830; Edwards 1970: 14–15; Beck 2005: 234): see 456, 785–
8nn. for the exceptions. The first six contests (i.e. all except archery and
spear throwing) are so introduced. Though not deployed in the Scherian
games of the *Odyssey* (which lack the narrativity of these events), the role
of the ἀγωνοθέτης must have been traditional; it is unlikely that this verse,
which is the only time epos splits the common verse-end formula μῦθον
ἔειπεν (cf. the variant reading *HHerm.* 366), was created specifically for the
Iliad (cf. *Od.* 18.241 οὐδ' ὀρθὸς στῆναι of the defeated Iros; Bertrand 2010:
569–72, esp. 570 on Sanskrit parallels for στῆ δ' ὀρθός).   Ἀτρεΐδη τε
καὶ ἄλλοι ἐϋκνήμιδες Ἀχαιοί: as opposed to its funerary equivalent Ἀτρεΐδη τε
καὶ ἄλλοι ἀριστῆες Παναχαιῶν (236n.), this whole-verse formula combines
several formular elements (such as ἐϋκνήμιδες Ἀχαιοί) to introduce claims
which will give rise to immediate consternation (1.7, 23.658; see 657–8n.):
Achilleus' statement on his superiority in this first part of the speech is not
intended to go down peaceably. The disyllabic scansion of ἐϋ- reflects the
derivation of ἐϋ/εὖ from the adj. ἐΰς/ἠΰς 'strong, good'.   ἱππῆας ...

δεδεγμένα 'awaiting the horsemen': δεδεγμένα is neut. nom. pl. perf. mid. ppl. of δέχομαι; its application to an inanimate object is rare, emphasising the prizes.   ἐν ἀγῶνι: 257ᵇ–8n.

274–6 Aside from hinting at the typicality of funeral games in the somewhat elliptical ἐπὶ ἄλλωι (257ᵇ–897n.), the claim not only reflects his opinion of himself, but also locates that thought in the minds of his audience (ἴστε γάρ).   κλισίηνδε: 55–8n.

276–8 The team's status and origin reflects Achilleus' authority, as in other cases where speakers use this 'how far (ὅσ[σ]ον) X is Y' idiom, with X either being or belonging to the speaker, and Y a superior quality (1.186, 1.516, 23.890–1n., etc.; Kelly 2007a: 78–9). He makes a similar claim about Agamemnon's skill at spear throwing before the final contest (890–1n.), but there includes himself within the knowledgeable group. There is no contradiction between his story and Zeus's earlier claim that 'we gave' the horses to Peleus (17.443–4; cf. 16.867), where the gods are corporately responsible for the gift. Moreover, as the god frequently given the epithet 'Hippios' (Σ T 277b), Poseidon is the most appropriate source; for the same combination (Zeus and Poseidon) in similar circumstances, see 306–8n. The offspring of Zephyros and Podargē (16.148–51), Peleus' immortal horses Xanthos and Balios were probably given at his wedding to Thetis, and said to be the best in Troy (2.769–70). They were capable, briefly, of speech (19.408–17; Schein 2002 = 2016: 11–26).   ἐγγυάλιξεν: unaugmented 3rd sing. aor. act. indic. A few -ιζω verbs in epos have aorists in -ξα rather than -σα, with epos extending the pattern beyond those verbs with guttural stems which should conjugate in that way (e.g. μαστίζω, aor. ἐμάστιξα: stem μαστιγ-: GH I §§ 159, 194; WHS 298–300). Derived from γύαλον 'hollow of the hand' and linked with ἐγγύη 'pledge', ἐγγυαλίζω usually denotes divine concessions or guarantees to humans; mortals make permanent concessions, either of life itself (17.613) or the duties of the host (Od. 16.66): for Achilleus, inheritance is an adoption of his father's authority and his divine favour.

279 ἀλλ' ἤτοι μὲν ἐγὼ μενέω 'but then, while I am determined to stay …': a typical statement of the speaker's inaction (11.317, 16.239, 19.308, 20.22, Od. 5.362, 16.132) which actually underlines his power to reserve for himself the crucial participation (Sauge 1994: 9–10 n. 8). Only here is that action extended to another subject (the horses), which then becomes the emotional focus of the next verses. ἀλλ' breaks off the previous description, ἤτοι clarifies the current state of affairs, and μέν foreshadows the contrasting participation of, as yet, unnamed others (1.140,

4.13, 4.62–3, etc.). The resumptive δέ is strikingly postponed until 285, throwing great emphasis on the horses' suffering: cf. 48n. (ἀλλ' ἤτοι νῦν μέν). **μώνυχες ἵπποι:** 6–7n., but also 293–5, 373–4nn.

280–2 Patroclos' care goes well beyond Homer's usual descriptions, which are largely limited to feeding (2.383, 5.776–7, 23.411–12, etc.). Andromache is similarly unusually dutiful towards Hector's team (8.186–90). For his gentleness, underlined here by run-over, see 250–4n.; Edmunds 1990: 15–33 suggests that characters labelled ἤπιος are not just 'kind' but also facilitators, making him a 'link between (the horses) and their military function' (29).   **σθένος ἐσθλόν:** though this combination is found nowhere else in epos, σθένος is by far the majority reading (including two early papyri) and related to a periphrasis denoting the person (σθένος + gen.: 13.248, 18.486, etc.: 826–7n.; also 717ᵇ–20n.). It is preferable to variant κλέος, usually chosen by modern editors since κλέος ἐσθλόν is common and sometimes adjudged 'more emotive' (Richardson 206; cf. Σ T), because κλέος is not lost at death, and the alteration of a unique collocation to an established, if inapposite, idiom is easier to imagine.   **ἀπώλεσαν** 'they (have) lost': 3rd pl. aor. act. indic. of ἀπόλλυμι (as at 18.82, 18.460, *Od.* 2.46, etc.), not 'destroyed'. Despite his earlier rebuke (19.399–403: cf. 404–17 for response), Achilleus implies not that the team is responsible for Patroclos' death, but that their grief renders them unable to participate.   **ὅς σφωῒν:** the relative is better attested than demonstrative ὅ, which was Aristarchos' choice and usually preferred by modern editors as 'more euphonious' (Richardson 206); for this cluster, however, see 2.687 τίς σφιν, 15.146 Ζεὺς σφώ, and for 'overlengthened' syllables before σφ-, 4.162, 10.422, 11.128, 12.366, etc.   **ὑγρὸν ἔλαιον:** a high level of care, since this formula always occurs in luxurious contexts, the oil anointing humans (*Od.* 6.79 ~ 215) or a god (*HHest.* 3), or being used to clean cloth (*Od.* 7.107; Zanni 2008).   **χαιτάων:** gen. after κατέχευε, 'poured down over their manes'; cf. 765 (κάδ ... κεφαλῆς χέ'). For χαίτη in this sense, see 6.509 = 15.266, 17.439, 23.284, etc.   **ὕδατι λευκῶι:** another sign of great care, since the epithet denotes clarity and purity (Irwin 1974: 196–8), and the formula is otherwise confined to otherworldly (*Od.* 5.70) or idealised contexts (*WD* 739). The υ in ὕδωρ, in all its forms, can be either long (as here) or short (2.825, 850, 3.270, etc.) as required.

283–4 Recalling 17.426–40, the horses' grief is structured in an A–B–A pattern around the highlighted image of their manes lowered to the ground (ἑσταότες πενθείετον ~ ἕστατον ἀχνυμένω κῆρ), but the verb of grieving is altered and the participle and finite verb are swapped (Mawet 1979:

291, 324); cf. also 19.405–6. The central image is a striking reversal of Patroclos' care, recalling not only the human mourning practice of pouring dust over the hair (Edwards 106), but also the despoliation of both Patroclos and Hector, hair and head befouled, lying in the dust (16.795–6 helmet; 22.401–4, esp. 403 πάρος χαρίεν, τότε δέ, etc.; Schein 2002: 200 with n. 24 = 2016: 20, n. 25).   **ἐρηρέδαται:** 3rd pl. perf. mid. indic. of ἐρείδω 'I lean/prop' (again at 329): lengthening reduplication ἐρ-ηρ- (like κατ-ερήριπεν < κατ-ερείπω, ὀρώρεται < ὄρνυμι) of the short stem -ερεδ- (like λέλασται < λήθω, ἐκέκαστο < καίνυμαι) + -αται usual for consonant-stem verbs (127–8ᵃn.). The idiom 'leant on the ground' (ἐρείδω + οὖδας) is otherwise only found in the death formula ὃ δ' ὕπτιος οὔδει ἐρείσθη (7.145, 11.144, 12.192), a suggestive resonance here.   **ἀχνυμένω κῆρ:** 165n.

285–6 Expected since 279 (see n.), transitional δέ completes the contrast between Achilleus' inaction and the other Greeks' participation.   **στέλλεσθε** 'make yourselves ready'.   **ἵπποισι(ν) ... καὶ ἅρμασι κολλητοῖσιν:** whether in hendiadys or not (i.e. 'chariot yoked with its team'), this formular combination (4.366, 11.198, *Od.* 17.117) marks preparatory journeys (or intentions thereto) prior to great achievement, as frequently in the *Catalogue of Women* in the context of leading away the bride (i.e. before the begetting of children: frr. 26.36, 58.7, 180.15 M–W, etc.). This perfective form of the 'trusting' idiom is applied to chariot riding only here and at 319 (cf. also 4.303 ἱπποσύνηι ... πεποιθώς), but elsewhere to a wide range of factors such as resources, weapons, physical strength, portents, etc. κολλητός 'joined together' always describes wooden composites subject to repeated, heavy stress – chariots, Aias' pike (15.678: 264–5ᵃn.), and door panels – joined together by pegs or glue (Plath 1994: 172–6).

287–351 Charioteers arise. Into the usual 'standing' sequence, where competitors rise in a certain order, the poet inserts a long exchange between Nestor and Antilochos (303–50), who stands fourth for the contest, before the sequence resumes with Meriones as fifth (351). The standing order (Eumelos, Diomedes, Menelaos, Antilochos, Meriones) does not reflect the starting order, which is obtained by casting lots (352–7n.), but mirrors the result one might expect, which will in many respects be overturned: Eumelos' horses are among the very best in Troy (288–9n.), and linked with Diomedes' as the two teams to beat, first by Nestor (346–8) and then by Antilochos (404–6). Menelaos' pair is linked with Laomedon's divine stock (296–300n.); while Antilochos' horses are explicitly labelled by Nestor as 'the slowest' (309–12), and Meriones' team is given no separate description or consideration at all. Menelaos, who will hold the same position in the starting order (293 ~ 355) will actually come third, and Meriones last of those to complete the race in good order.

287 Πηλεΐδης: the patronymic provides a suitable resonance after the team's description (17–18, 276–8nn.).   **ταχέες … ἱππῆες:** cf. 262–3n.   **ἄγερθεν:** unaugmented 3rd pl. aor. pass. indic. of ἀγείρω, with -εν (Aeol.) rather than -ησαν (Attic-Ionic: Intro. § 3.1.2.d.i).

288–9 Introduced in the Catalogue of Ships as the fastest after Achilleus' divine team (2.763–7), Eumelos' mares were tended by Apollo during his year of service to Admetos, Eumelos' father (and son-in-law of Pelias, Alcestis' father), and were apparently victorious in Achilleus' funeral games narrated in the *Aithiopis*, while Admetos had competed in the same event in Pelias' funeral games (Davies and Finglass 2014: 217–18): see Intro. § 2.2. Formidable adversaries, therefore, they foreshadow the coming encounter between Athene and Apollo as the patrons of the most likely victors: see below on ἄναξ ἀνδρῶν, 290–2n. With no role in the fighting (like Epeios: 670–1n.), Eumelos himself appears only here and in the Catalogue of Ships as the leader of the contingent from Pherai (2.713–15, 763–7), whilst his unfortunate fate here contrasts mightily, perhaps deliberately, with his later triumph in Achilleus' games (257b–897n.). Given the character's background in epos, he may well be 'favoured to win' (Scodel 2021: 60), but his defeat at the hands of Diomedes matches that of Telamonian Aias in the fight in armour (708–9, 798–825nn.) as an example of Achilleus' Iliadic *Doppelgänger* overcoming figures ranked traditionally as second only to him (290–2n.); Libanius wryly noted that the poet was being 'playful' here (*Encomium* 1.16), but it is more likely that he was asserting his poem's distinctive position within the tradition.   **ὦρτο πολὺ πρῶτος:** emphasised by the delay of μέν, his eagerness is understandable, but the 'far the first' idiom intimates questionable success in the ensuing venture (2.702, 7.162, 8.256, *Od.* 1.113, etc.: Kelly 2007a: 258); for ὦρτο, see 214–16n.   **ἄναξ ἀνδρῶν:** the application of Agamemnon's distinctive epithet formula (49–51n.) to Eumelos contributes to the growing rivalry with Diomedes (35–7n.): see also 354 (κρείων) below.   **ἐκέκαστο:** 3rd sing. pluperf. mid. indic. of καίνυμαι 'I excel/am distinguished'. The tense underlines his contemporaries' acknowledgement of Eumelos' superiority as a settled fact.

290–2 Diomedes' team was taken from Aineias (5.265–72), an episode similarly marked by Athene's help and Apollo's hindrance: cf. 377–8n. The latter's rescue of Aineias reinforces his support for Eumelos, and his

opposition to Diomedes.   τῶι δ᾽ ἐπί: 'and after him': see 65n. For
other 'standing' catalogues similarly structured, and also with 'far the
first' idioms, see 7.163–7 (NB 163 = 290 here), 8.262–5; cf. 17.256–61.
These parallels especially with Book 7 might suggest a deliberate reminiscence of the duel between Hector and Aias, and the Greek counterattack
on the second day, as combat events introduced by a speech from Nestor
and lacking Achilleus' direct participation (Bannert 1988: 131–5). The
starting order below will also use this structure for the third (Menelaos)
and fourth (Meriones) starters (355–6n.).   Τυδεΐδης 'son of Tydeus':
patronymic of Diomedes, whose father was one of the most prominent
heroes of the pre-Trojan War generation, a participant in the expedition of the Seven against Thebes (see Barker and Christensen 2011). He
is often invoked in the *Iliad* as a standard to which Diomedes is compared, with increasing levels of succcess (Andersen 1978: 34–40; Pratt
2009; O'Maley 2018). For -εῖ-, see 17–18n.   κρατερός Διομήδης: the
epithet is not confined to Diomedes, but applied mostly to him in the
Iliad; related to κράτος ~ κάρτος (see Breuil 1989) and with a less common
form καρτερός, it means both 'steadfast' and 'mighty' (Van Beek 2022:
189–236). Diomedes' name was formed from Διο- and μήδομαι ('planner
like *or* dear to Zeus' *vel sim.*), and he was the leader of the contingent from
Argos (2.559–68) but originally Aitolian through his father (23.471). He
is one of the most important figures in the *Iliad*, the driving force on the
first and second days of fighting, a participant in the *Doloneia*, and an
obvious *Doppelgänger* of Achilleus – young, powerful, especially favoured
by Athene, and stopped by Paris (11.369–400: see Wehr 2013: 15–136).
Last seen limping to the assembly called by Achilleus (19.47–9; cf. 16.25),
his wound is conveniently forgotten here. Diomedes' prominence in the
funeral games reflects this doubling function: he wins the prestigious
chariot race over Eumelos, and seems to come up trumps against Aias
in the fight in armour – both figures named as the second best in their
respective fields after Achilleus (2.761–70) – and only suffers reversal in
the form of his surrogate Euryalos in the boxing. After the events of the
Iliad Diomedes teamed up with Odysseus to steal the Palladion from Troy
and was one of the heroes in the wooden horse (*Od.* 4.280–1). Upon his
return to Argos, he was compelled to leave home because of his wife's
unfaithfulness and settled in Italy (Andersen 1978; Higbie 1995: 87–101;
Pratt 2009; Barbara 2023).   ἵππους … ὕπαγε ζυγόν 'led the horses
beneath the yoke': ζυγόν is an accusative of direction, with ὑπ- directing
the action under the yoke (*GH* II §§ 55, 213; cf. 16.148, 24.279, 294
below; and Plath 1994: 304–5). Homeric 'tmesis' may preserve a stage
where preverbs had not yet been attached to compounds as prepositions
(Intro. § 3.1.2.d.iv), but the poet clearly (also) used them as equivalents

to compound verbs (cf. 294, 300 below). ἀπηύρα: 3rd sing. aor. indic. act. Originally an athematic aorist (as 2nd sing. ἀπηύρας and ppl. ἀπούρας), these forms were reinterpreted by bards as imperfects as though from thematic ἀπαυράω, to give forms like 1st sing. and 3rd pl. ἀπηύρων, but an aorist meaning is needed here (*GH* I § 168).   οὕς ... | Αἰνείαν: the run-over underlines the reminiscence of the team's capture, and so Diomedes' achievements in Achilleus' absence. The double accusative, of the person affected and the item, is typical with verbs of removing (*GH* II § 52).   ὑπεξεσάωσεν: 3rd sing. aor. act. indic. From the root *σάϝο-'safe', the verb has a complicated system in epos, including a range of forms derived from contracted and uncontracted stems of various sorts (σαο-, σα-, σο-, σοο- (*GH* I § 173) – all of which show the poetic importance of the theme. ὑπεκ- literally denotes removal 'out of/from beneath' something, and implies Diomedes as the source of that danger; tr. 'saved (A.) from him' (see Garvie 2009: 210, on Aisch. *Pers.* 453 ὑπεκσώιζοιεν).

293–300 The long description of Aithē's origin (295ff.) emphasises Menelaos' dependence on Agamemnon's resources (evoked anyway by Ἀτρεΐδης 293) more than their brotherly devotion (so Σ bT 295c); compare Paris borrowing Lycaon's breastplate (3.332–4 with Σ bT 333a). It also looks forward to the prominence she will have in Antilochos' mind during the race (407–9, 431–3nn.). For the fraternal theme in archaic poetry, see Swift 2018.

293–5 293 ~ 356 (see 355–6n.). The structure of 295, with names bookending the central repeated possessive expressions, underlines Agamemnon's ownership. Horses are infrequently named in Homer (though more likely than other animals to be so honoured in later antiquity), and in the race none outside this team. Speed and appearance are typical reference points: Αἴθη may mean 'brown' or 'dark' (Edgeworth 1983) or 'gleaming' with reference to the glossy coat (Beekes 1995: 16; cf. 2.838–9), while Πόδαργος denotes 'swift of foot' (30–3n.). Both names are used of Hector's team (Πόδαργε καὶ Αἴθων 8.185), and Podargē was the Harpy mother of Achilleus' horses Xanthos and Balios ('Bay' and 'Dapple': 16.150, 19.400). A lack of imagination in this regard is typical of Greek literature; for 'Bay', e.g., see Alcman fr. 25 *PMGF*, Stes. fr. 2 F, etc., and Delebecque 1951: 146; Calder 2011: 44–5. The team's mixed gender is unusual in epos (for *melos* and tragedy see Finglass 2007: 313): Σ bT 295b suggests that it reveals Menelaos' skill in overcoming the sexual tension between the horses, and invokes the example of Helios' two male and two female horses to show there is no difference in 'virtue and speed' between the sexes; cf. the quality of Eumelos' all-female pair

(288–9n.; Hainsworth 287).   **ξανθὸς Μενέλαος:** the distinctive epithet for Menelaos is otherwise applied in epos to Meleagros, Rhadamanthys, Polyneices, and Ganymedes, figures from the previous heroic generation, many of whom are betrayed by their close kin. For the basic meaning of the word, see 140–4n. Stelow 2020: 32–3 suggests it signposts his special relationship with the gods; cf. also 355–6n. for a more warlike side to his epithet profile. As the cause of the war and husband of Helen, Menelaos is obviously one of the most important cast members in the poem, though his performance in the games continues the theme that he is somehow a less than, or differently, impressive figure than his brother (Hohendahl-Zoetelief 1980: 143–83; Willcock 2002; Kanavou 2015: 46–8; Castiglioni 2020; Stelow 2020).   **διογενής:** derived from Ζεύς (διο-) and γίγνομαι, this epithet is never applied to Zeus's children in epos, any more than διοτρεφής denotes his actual involvement in a character's raising (581–3n.), and is instead used as an honorific largely for βασιλῆες without divine parents – Odysseus, Aias, Patroclos, Menelaos, and Agamemnon (though twice of Achilleus; *EDG* s. διογενής; *LfrgE* s.v. B, 308).   **ὑπὸ … ζυγὸν ἤγαγεν** ~ 300 below (ἦγε); cf. ὕπαγε ζυγόν (291 above).   **ὠκέας ἵππους:** though it occupies the same position as μώνυχας ἵππους (6–7n.), this formula allows a wider range of conditions before it, i.e. short or long vowels either in correption or not, and consonants without rendering the immediately preceding syllable heavy (as μώνυχας would; Delebecque 1951: 149–50; Platte 2017: 31–2): also 373–4n.

296–300 Coming to Troy was not universally attractive: the Cypriot Cinyras gave Agamemnon a breastplate upon hearing of the expedition (11.20–3), and Odysseus was later held to have feigned madness to remain on Ithaca (*Cypria* arg. 30–4 B), while the Corinthian Euchenor avoided 'the fine of the Achaeans' by coming (13.669). On Echepolos, Aristotle well observed that it was better to get a good horse than a useless man (fr. 165 Rose), while Σ T report that he was the ruler of Sicyon in Agamemnon's day (Wathelet 1988: 558–60). Yet (i) Echepolos is also the name of the poem's first victim, killed by Antilochos (4.458); (ii) 'Hold-foal' is a suspiciously suitable *ad hoc* name (despite n. below on εὐρυχόρωι Σικυῶνι); (iii) and the patronymic Ἀγχισιάδης so soon after 291–2 readily evokes Aineias' father *and* his impressive team. Indirectly, the poet intimates the quality of Menelaos' pair and its coming role in the race (see 344–8n. for another such implication). The digression is clearly introduced and demarcated (τὴν Ἀγαμέμνονι ~ τὴν Ἀγαμεμνονέην), looking toward the concluding demonstrative at 300.   **ὑπὸ Ἴλιον ἠνεμόεσσαν** 'beneath the walls of windy Troy': 62–4n. προτί is replaced in this formula (49–51n.) because it could not fit into its usual position after ἔποιθ'. ὑπό + acc. denotes travel to

the foot of an elevated place (*GH* II § 213): also 290–2n.   εὐρυχόρωι
Σικυῶνι: Sicyon (*BA* 57, E4; 58, D2) is part of the Mycenaean contingent
in the Catalogue (2.572), the first seat of King Adrestos, who owned the
divine horse Arion (23.346–7; 344–8n.) and thus a suitable origin for this
kind of gift (Visser 1997: 162–3). The epithet is applied to both cities and
regions (2.498, 9.478, *Od.* 4.635, etc.). It originally meant 'with a broad
dancing-place' (< χορός; cf. 18.590–2, *Od.* 8.260), though pre-Homeric
bards had reinterpreted it to mean 'of broad area' (i.e. < χῶρος; cf. Visser
1997: 124–5).   **δρόμου ἰσχανόωσαν** 'aiming for the race(track)':
West prints the minority reading ἰχανόωσαν, from ἰχανάω 'I am eager', first
attested in Herodas 7.26 and related to ἰχαίνω (Callim. fr. 178.22 Pf.),
because ἰσχάνω 'I hold, restrain' and its α-contract ἰσχανάω (both derived
from ἴσχω: 465–8n.) does not seem apposite here (or at 17.572, *Od.*
8.288). This is no doubt a neat solution, but the required forms are first
attested in the Hellenistic period, and 17.572 (ἰσχανάαι δακέειν; one medieval MS reads ἰχ-) shows the bards felt that this verb could mean something like 'aiming for', perhaps by analogy with the way in which ἔχω,
which is sometimes synonymous with ἴσχω (Giannakis 1997: 147–8), can
mean 'hold back' but also 'hold course' or 'aim for' (16.378, 23.422).
δρόμου is a partitive gen. frequent after verbs of desire or achieving (*GH* II
§ 64). Like ἀγών above (257[b]–8n.), δρόμος (< δραμεῖν) can denote both the
event (768) and its location (321: see nn. and Bell 1994).

301–50 Antilochos and Nestor. In this, the largest entry in the catalogue
of entrants, the poet sets the stage for the prominence Antilochos will
enjoy in the race and its concluding quarrels.

301–4[a] The fourth competitor is introduced differently, with an ordi-
nal rather than τῶι δ' ἐπί (290, 293) and a varied expression for preparing the team (for the unique phrasing ὡπλίσαθ' ἵππους, cf. Hes. fr. 30.4
M–W); both features are retained for the fifth competitor (351n.). The
sequence of 301 – Antilochos/horses – is repeated in 302–3/303–4.
Seemingly unnecessary at such a late stage in the poem, the whole-verse
'introductory' genealogy in 302 is marked by -ος rhyme and looks forward to his importance in this race and the games generally. But father is
more prominent here than son, with a run-over patronymic (303), and
so the introduction is also preparing for his speech. Antilochos has only
one noun–epithet formula that is not patronymic in some form ('Αντίλοχος
μενεχάρμης: 418[b]–19n.), his name usually being placed at the start of the
verse without epithets. This reflects the fact that his story is inextrica-
bly bound up with his father, since he dies protecting Nestor from the
Aithiopian hero Memnon (*Aithiopis* arg. 12–14 B; Pindar, *Pyth.* 6.28–42),

and his very name Ἀντί-λοχος may mean '(he who) fights and dies "in the place of his father"' (Mühlestein 1987: 54). As Patroclos recedes from view, he becomes increasingly important to Achilleus (23.555; *Od.* 24.77–9), and Neoanalysts have argued that he was, to varying degrees, the model for Patroclos (cf. Kelly 2006; *contra* Currie 2016: 247–53).   ἐΰτριχας: the epithet (see 13–14n.) increases the contrast with the mourning demeanour of Achilleus' team: 283–4n.   Νέστορος ἀγλαὸς υἱός: longer, mobile version of the usual patronymic formula Νέστορος υἱός: see 540–2n. for another.   Νηληϊάδαο 'of the son of Neleus': Nestor has another common patronymic, Νηλήϊος, suggesting an extensive traditional background for the father as well, who was the son of Poseidon by Tyro (*Od.* 11.235–59; Higbie 1995: 48–9, 112–13, 122–4); for the very rare short form Νηλεΐδης, see 652n. As leader of the Pylian contingent (2.591–601), Nestor is one of the principal Achaean chieftains in the *Iliad*, respected for his age and advice rather than his current military capacity, and with a personal history extending deep into epic legend. The *Iliad* alone mentions entanglements with the Centaurs (1.260–73), the Arcadians (7.132–57), the Epeians (11.670–761), and Heracles (11.689–93); together with his reminiscence about the funeral games for Amphidamas later in this book (629–43n.), these stories provides a sustained para-narrative for the course of the *Iliad* itself (see esp. Alden 2001: 77–111, and more generally Erbse 1993b; Dickson 1995; Brillante 1996; Roisman 2005; Kanavou 2015: 63–7). For Pylian tradition more generally, see Zanetto 2017.   Πυλοιγενέες 'born at Pylos': this reading (sixth-century Π 9 and several good MSS) is preferred to the majority reading Πυληγενέες, since its first element is an authentic locative unlikely to be interpolated (like e.g. οἴκοι; cf. ὁδοιπόρος, ὀλοοίτροχος, etc.: *WHS* 220; cf. 2.54). 'Some write παλαιγενέες' (Σ bT 303), but this is drawn from the later statement about the horses' age (445) and has no other MS authority.   ἵπποι | ὠκύποδες: the epithet is applied only to horses in epos, and this formular collocation usually extends over the verse-end. It jars slightly with the isometric description of the team in 309–10, though epic horses, like heroes, are always superior to those of the poet's day (Delebecque 1951: 151).

304ᵇ–5 ἄγχι παραστάς: a good expression to introduce Nestor's instructions, since one can be so qualified usually when taking a supportive position, but with the intimation that the supported figure will have to do something more off their own bat (7.188, 17.338, *Od.* 16.338, 20.190; cf. 16.114, *Od.* 9.345, but Odysseus is pretending such a stance).   εἰς ἀγαθὰ φρονέων: Nestor's conciliar standing is clear: the 'thinking good things' idiom occurs in persuasive contexts, usually applied to the advisor, and always to a right-thinking figure (6.162, 24.173, *Od.* 1.43; Graziosi and Haubold 2010: 123). Σ A 305a wonder whether εἰς ἀγαθά is to be taken with μυθεῖτ᾽, φρονέων, or both. Formular integrity suggests φρονέων, and word order μυθεῖτ᾽ (cf. εἰπεῖν εἰς ἀγαθόν 9.102) – so both: 'he spoke his thoughts for the best'.   **νοέοντι καὶ αὐτῶι:** like others flattered that they 'know even in themselves', i.e. already, Antilochos does not need the advice (1.577, 24.560, *Od.* 21.257, *WD* 202: West 1978: 205–6). His equestrian status relies partly on family tradition, but Antilochos also possesses a suitable divine ancestry (Poseidon as great-grandfather: *Od.* 11.254–5) and its consequent favour; see also 306–8, 785–8nn.

306–48 Nestor is well qualified to speak: aside from genealogy, the old epithet ἱππότα (89–90n.) is applied to him more than anyone (+ Γερήνιος), and he speaks elsewhere on chariot tactics (4.301–9, 11.711–61) and races (11.698–702), and he will return to the themes after the race (23.638–42n.; Roisman 1988, 2005; Martin 1989: 101–13; Stocking 2023: 117–25): also 301–4ᵃn. The speech is structured in a ring around the σῆμα used as the race's turning-post:

A¹ Antilochos' prospects (306–12)
B¹ instructions to act intelligently (313–18)
C¹ general advice for the charioteer (319–25)
D   the σῆμα (326–33)
C² particular advice for the charioteer (334–43)
B² instructions to act intelligently (343)
A² Antilochos' prospects (344–8)

A focuses on Antilochos' skills and prospects, moving from a pessimistic to an optimistic view as the addressee takes on the lessons involved. Direct exhortation to intelligent strategy introduces (313) or comprises (343) B, and then Nestor progresses from general to particular instructions in C. The thematic movements between the corresponding elements suggest a conciliar effect, as the lessons involved are applied: thus general becomes particular in C² because the principle is (assumed to have been) accepted, and the chances of success in A² depend on the truth of everything which has been asserted hitherto (Lohmann 1970: 15–18; 1992: 305–6; Bannert 1988: 131). Richardson 208–9 rightly suggests that the speech mimics the course of the race, with the σῆμα at its centre and Antilochos triumphant – in a sense – at its end, but he will pass his particular rival *after* the turning-post (Roisman 1988; *contra* Gagarin 1983), and so the poet is enlivening his narrative through misdirection (Visa-Ondarçuhu 1999: 27–8; Scodel 2021: 60–1): see also 373–532n.

The central placement of the σῆμα as a νύσσα 'turning-post' responds to the funerary context, with the irony of an unknown warrior's tomb (331) contrasting with the certainty of *kleos* for Patroclos and Achilleus, and boosting the memorialising power of the *Iliad* (327–8, 331–3nn.; Nagy 2012: 53–4 considers it an allusion to hero cult: 151n.). It also connects the world of the poem with the audience's present, as they increasingly turned in the eighth to seventh centuries BCE to these sites as *topoi* of the heroic past (Antonaccio 1995b; Ainian 2016; for the many other σήματα on the Trojan plain, see 45–7n.) and the slightly later attested use of stone markers in races at funeral contests (McGowan 1995; McAuley 2024: 162–4). Both Plato and Xenophon quote from this speech: the former in the course of Socrates' demonstration that a charioteer would best be able to criticise the accuracy of Homer's words because of his knowledge of the τέχνη involved (*Ion* 537b); the latter as an example of the technical information which Homer can provide (*Symp.* 4.6; Murray 1996: 20–1, 126; Yamagata 2012: 146–7). Sophocles' *Electra* also contrasts the fortunes of Orestes in the false messenger speech with Nestor's advice here: Orestes falls precisely at the turning-post (*El.* 720–2, 741–5), because he fails to heed the kind of advice Nestor gives (see Johnston 2021: 4–5). For Ovid's reworking of 316–18, see n.

306–12 Chiasmus (driver–team/teams–drivers) articulates a positive/negative contrast between its elements: [A¹] Antilochos' advantages (306–9) – [B¹] his horses' failings (309–10)/[B²] others' horses' advantages (311) – [A²] other drivers' failings (311–12). This allows Nestor to assert the need for his advice, despite Antilochos' acknowledged excellence, centred upon μῆτις.

306–8 Line 306 represents another violation of Hermann's Bridge (75–6n.), as quite frequently with this combination of περ + participle (Sansom 2025: 8–9). The subjects of ἐφίλησαν are delayed until the start of the next verse, and so emphasised: Poseidon is invoked because of the equine connection (next n.) and his genealogical role in the Pylian royal line, while Zeus stands for divine authority *in toto* (hence the pl. verbs at the end of 306 and 307: next n.). Both are evoked indirectly at the speech's end (344–8n.), further underlining its overall ring structure.   **ἐδίδαξαν:** Poseidon is particularly the 'horsey god' (Σ A 307a) here, since deities frequently 'teach' a mortal a proficiency in their central province, as e.g. the Muses bards (*Od.* 8.481, 488, *Th.* 22): see *WD* 64, 662; *HAphr.* 12, 15. Yet one should not read ἐδίδαξεν (as Aristarchos and some MSS do: Schironi 2018: 331 n. 291), since the particular gift is connected to the general picture of divine favour, and the deities go closely together in sections A¹ and A². **οὔ τι μάλα χρεώ** 'not much need (at all)': χρεώ always scans as a heavy syllable in synizesis (χρείω at 10.72 is disyllabic). It is derived from the originally instrumental noun χρή, and can be followed by a dependent genitive of the thing needed and/or an accusative of the person (9.75), with or without a further infinitive, or just with the infinitive alone (as here; Shipp 1972: 31; Lynn-George 1988: 124–9). This is the only negatived example of the μάλα χρεώ idiom, which usually stresses the great necessity weighing on the participants (9.75, 197, 10.172, 11.409, 18.406), resuming the rhetorical flattery of νοέοντι καὶ αὐτῶι (304ᵇ–5n.).

309–10 Antilochos' situation matches the good charioteer's below (322–3): 322–5, 326nn. The heavy rhythm of 310 complements its sense.   **περὶ τέρμαθ' ἑλισσέμεν:** τέρμα denotes a limit set in contests, whether a turning point (as here) or the finishing line (Laser 27, 33). Nestor will focus on getting the chariot around this mark, and Idomeneus (465–6) will wrongly attribute the change in leadership to Eumelos' failure in this manoeuvre.   **ἵπποι | βάρδιστοι:** 301–4ᵃn. Menelaos comments unkindly on the age of Nestor's team (442–7n.), and they are called βραδέες by Diomedes when he rescues him (8.104). The poet makes the same charge, in his own voice, of Meriones' team (530–1n.). βάρδιστοι = βράδιστοι, superl. of βραδύς, with metathesis (cf. κάρτ-/κράτ-; 290–2n.) allowing the word to appear in the first position of the verse (*GH* I § 10).   **θείειν:** pres. act. infin. of θέω, with metrical lengthening of the first syllable (cf. θέειν 2.183, 11.617, etc.); it is epexegetic after βάρδιστοι, 'slowest at/for running', the only way in which this form is used in Homer.

311–12 **ἔασιν:** 3rd pl. pres. indic. of εἰμί. Homer uses both Attic-Ionic εἰσίν (1.153, etc.) and this form, with -ᾱσι(ν) probably derived from the perfect tense (e.g. πεποίθᾱσι 4.325) but later extended in Attic into διδόᾱσι, τιθέᾱσι, etc. (*GH* I § 224).   **ἀφάρτεροι:** this hapax is drawn from the adv. ἄφαρ 'suddenly/forthwith' (as ὑπέρτερος from ὑπέρ), and does not appear again until the third-century Dionysius (fr. 19[b].2 Benaissa). The usual translation here is 'swifter', but the -τερος suffix originally expressed 'opposition or distinction' (as in, e.g., ἡμέτερος), and its basic function in Homer is 'separative, not necessarily comparative' (*GH* II § 233): Nestor's point is that others' horses are speedy, whilst Antilochos' are not.   **πλείονα ἴσασιν:** a mark of extraordinary skill despite his youth, since the 'know more' idiom is elsewhere explained by greater age (13.355, 19.219, 21.440; cf. *Od.* 7.156–7, 12.188; Janko 91–2). Antilochos will concede in precisely these terms when facing an enraged Menelaos at the race's end (587–8n.).

313–18 Picking up μητίσασθαι, the poet now develops the theme of μῆτις 'cunning intelligence', with *figura etymologica* and emphatic anaphora. For μῆτις in early Greek culture, see Nagy 1979: 45–9, though the reductive cliché that the *Iliad* is a poem of βίη as opposed to μῆτις is thoroughly qualified here, as Achilleus' closest surviving friend is subjected to an extended sermon on the values of the latter – 'things which seem to be a matter of strength actually need skill' (Σ bT 315; Purves 2011: 534–5 ~ 2019: 78). In fact, the Homeric *basileus* must be able to access and combine both qualities so as fulfil the requirement μύθων τε ῥητῆρ' ἔμεναι πρηκτῆρά τε ἔργων ('to be a speaker of words and a doer of deeds' 9.443); Nestor may 'overvalue' μῆτις here (Dunkle 1987: 4), but that is because the requisite physical quality is lacking and requires compensation. In the end, Antilochos' different μῆτις will get him into trouble.

313–14 313 ~ 343 (306–48n.).   ἀλλ' ἄγε: with or without δή and/or σύ, this is a common means to break off (ἀλλ') before entreating a new course of action. The pres. act. imp. ἄγε/ἄγετε is used in Homer only with the sense 'come on' (49–51n.), and it prepares for a further order or exhortation.   φίλος: epos will use a nominative as a vocative (notably with οὗτος), esp. where it affords a metrically useful alternative (4.189, 21.106, 23.343, 627, etc.; *GH* II § 45).   παρεκπροφύγῃσιν: 3rd sing. aor. act. subj. (= -φύγῃι) using the athematic ending -σι (*GH* I § 219). The verb is never again found in Greek literature, and the 'triple' compound (*GH* II § 214) παρεκπρο- animates the prizes as figures evading danger (i.e. Antilochos), just as ὑπεκπροφεύγω denotes escape from a literally or metaphorically overhanging threat. The movement – to the side (παρ-), away (-εκ-), and forward/in front (-προ-) – reflects that of an overtaking team, precisely what Antilochos must avoid (345–8).

315–18 While parents typically use *gnōmai* to advise their children (e.g. 9.256, 18.128–9, etc.), Nestor is a proficient exponent of the form, in keeping with his rhetorical status (1.274, 278–9, 9.57–8, 63–4, etc.; Lardinois 1995: 85, 133–4, 142–5; Pratt 2009: 149): also 301–4ᵃ, 306–48nn. This example is an ascending tricolon, leading into the two further *gnōmai* which make up the next section of the speech (319–25n.): woodcutter (315), helmsman (316–17), charioteer (318, developed in 319–25). The first two have an indirect connection with Patroclos: the former already appeared in this book (114–16) and in a simile describing him and Meriones (16.633–6), while the winds against which the helmsman struggles (317) recall the episode with Zephyros and Boreas. Patroclos himself is a natural parallel for the third professional, the charioteer, who is apposite for the rest of the speech and the race. These reflections together recall his failure in μῆτις, when he forgot Achilleus' instructions (16.686–7). For other such triplications, see 1.266–7 (κάρτιστοι), 2.382–4 (εὖ), 2.671–3 (Νιρεύς), WD 317–19 (αἰδώς), 578–80 (ἠώς); cf. also 9.464–9 (πολλ-; West 1978: 236; Fehling 1969: 166, 184–5). The opening proverb in 315 is striking, with verse-initial μῆτι balanced by βίηφι at verse-end, especially as βίη is elsewhere the ability in which one is judged ἀμείνων (1.404, 11.787, 15.139; also Solon fr. 37.4 W²), while the helmsman's struggle is reinforced by ν-consonance and necessary run-over. Ovid, *Ars am.* 1.3–4 reworks the second and third images here (*arte citae veloque rates remoque moventur* | *arte leves currus*) before intruding his own third (*arte regendus amor*).   **μῆτι:** the heavy scansion of -ι throughout may reveal an older -ιι (*GH* I § 93).   **βίηφιν** 'by force' = βίηι (Intro. § 3.1.2.c.ix; *GH* I §§ 104–5).   **οἴνοπι πόντωι:** dative declension of the well-known formula (140–4n.).   **ἡνίοχος ... ἡνιόχοιο:** emphatic repetition of this sort is typical in agonistic contexts; cf. ζηλοῖ δέ τε γείτονα γείτων (*WD* 23); καὶ κεραμεὺς κεραμεῖ κοτέει καὶ τέκτονι τέκτων, | καὶ πτωχὸς πτωχῶι φθονέει καὶ ἀοιδὸς ἀοιδῶι (*WD* 25–6: West 1978: 147; Lardinois 1995: 54 with n. 66). The syntax continues chiastically into the following description of the two charioteers, the latter described in 319–21, the former in 322–5.   **περιγίνεται:** see 240–2n.

319–25 Two *gnōmai* (319–21/322–5) develop the comparison between charioteers in 318 through a negative/positive contrast (Lardinois 1995: 50). Aside from the obvious μέν/δέ progression, ἀφραδέως ... | ... οὐδὲ κατίσχει (320–21) is reversed in ἀλλ' ἔχει ἀσφαλέως (325). The unsuccessful driver relies only on the qualities of his horse and chariot and does not control them properly, leading to undisciplined racing, while the successful driver looks for the turning point and holds close to it, maintains a firm control over his team, and keeps his eye on the competition. His superiority is clear also from greater elaboration, with four actions in five verses opposed to three in three; on his equivalence with Antilochos, see 309–10, 322–5, 326nn.

319–21 ἀλλ' ὅς: ΑΛΛΟΣ was thus divided by the majority of ancient critics and MSS, looking forward to ὅς δέ below (322), and making 321 the main clause introduced by apodotic δέ (*GP* 178–9), as in a very similar gnomic context at 9.508–11 (twice: ὅς μέν τ' αἰδέσεται ... | τὸν δὲ μέγ' ὤνησαν ... | ὅς δέ κ' ἀνήνηται ... | λίσσονται δ' ἄρα κτλ.). ἀλλ' is thus adversative after the praise of μῆτις (cf. 320 ἀφραδέως) in the preceding verses (*pace* Leaf II.494): tr. 'but the one who, trusting in his horses and chariot, rounds the turn here and there, his horses wander over the track and he does not restrain them' (Mazon 1940: 260). ἄλλος (West, Richardson) makes less pointed sense ('another man, trusting ...' etc.), and its best parallel (11.636–7) is not in a gnomic context. For the (often insufficient) 'trusting' idiom, see 28–6n. The run-over rhyme in πεποιθώς | ἀφραδέως and the delayed position of ἑλίσσεται underline the unwisdom of this strategy.   ἐπὶ πολλόν 'over a great space'. The thematic neut. acc. sing. is a metrically useful alternative to athematic πολύ (*GHI* § 117).   ἑλίσσεται ἔνθα καὶ ἔνθα ~ *Od.* 20.24, 28, Odysseus' turning in bed as he plans his revenge; cf. *HAp.* 361, of the snake's death-throes. Here probably circular rather than square in conception, ἔνθα καὶ ἔνθα (146–8n.) conveys an obviously inappropriate lack of direction and control.   πλανόωνται: 3rd pl. pres. mid. ind. of πλανάω, by diectasis < πλανῶνται < πλανάονται.

322–5 The good charioteer resembles Antilochos (309–10), and watching for the turning-post will be central to Nestor's injunctions below (334–43): cf. 326n. The fronting of the relative clause and the generalising sense of κε + subj. are frequent in gnomic contexts (Lardinois 1995: 52 with n. 54).   κέρδεα εἰδῆι: this idiom is usually associated with Odysseus (23.709, *Od.* 19.285–6) and those linked with him (*Od.* 2.88, 13.296–7). κέρδος and its derivatives have a wide semantic range in epos, from 'profit' to 'acts of cunning/caution' in its pursuit, with the common aim of securing advantage over one's competitors (De Jong 1987b; Cozzo 1988: 13–20). For the easy association between κέρδος and μῆτις, see e.g. *Od.* 13.288–9. The issue will return at 515 (see 514–16n.).   βοέοισιν ἱμᾶσιν: here referring to the reins (as at 22.397, where Hector is lashed to his chariot). The ἱμάς can serve several purposes – a helmet chin-strap (3.375), boxing-glove bindings (23.684), the thongs of a bed-frame (*Od.* 23.201), even Aphrodite's girdle (14.214). Leather is used in epos for a range of heavy-utility items, from shield-straps and coverings to arrowstrings, shoes, and ship's cables (Humphrey et al. 1998: 346–7, 267–71).   ἔχει 'drives': for this common sense of the verb, see 398 ~ 423, 401, etc.   τὸν προύχοντα 'the one in front': pres. act. ppl. of προέχω, intransitive and contracted as usual in epos for this verb (22.97, 23.453, *Od.* 3.8, etc.; cf. *Od.* 12.11 προέχ'). Modern editors (but not West) like to print προὔχοντα here (and elsewhere), with the coronis marking the crasis between πρό and ἔχω, but it is a minority reading here, and may represent post-Homeric convention (*HG* § 377, *GHI* § 35).

326–33 Aside from falsely suggesting a narrative prominence in the coming race, which the poet furthers by making Antilochos winner of the starting-order lot and so positioned closest to it (352–7, 358–61nn.), Nestor's description of the turning-post makes it the most well-defined σῆμα in the *Iliad* aside from Patroclos' tomb (45–7, 326nn.). For the late Archaic use of stone markers as turning-posts in actual funeral contests, perhaps in an attempt to appeal to the authority of epic, see McGowan 1995.

326 = *Od.* 11.126, of the crucial question about the winnowing fan in Teiresias' instructions to Odysseus. In this very common type of positive/negative contrast (Tzamali 1997: 131–3), οὐδέ σε λήσει recalls οὐδέ ἑ λήθει (323) to reinforce Nestor's equation of Antilochos with the good driver. When the young man describes a similar strategy to his team in the same terms (οὐδέ με λήσει 416), the process is complete.   **σῆμα ... ἀριφραδές:** for the epithet, see 240–2n. This collocation places the σῆμα right at the heart of Nestor's instructions, since it always relates to the revelation of key 'tokens' between interlocutors, including physical markings (*Od.* 21.17, 23.73, 24.329) and crucial events (*Od.* 11.126, 23.273) and items (23.326, *Od.* 23.225; for the wider semantics, see Foley 1999; for an argument that it alludes to hero cult, see Nagy 2012: esp. 53–4; cf. 151n.). The clarity of its appearance contrasts with the uncertainty of its origin.

327–8 The wood's suspicious failure to rot bestows a conveniently uncertain longevity (see below, and 331–3n.) reflecting the object's memorialising potential, especially since line-final ὄμβρος may rot ships (*WD* 625) and bones (*Od.* 1.161; cf. *Il.* 11.395). Σ bT invokes Theophrastos' views about which types of wood 'do not decay by nature', e.g. the elm when exposed to air, or the oak under almost any conditions, except in the sea (*Hist. plant.* 5.4.2–3). Hippias of Thasos (86 B 20 D–K) ingeniously, but unnecessarily, suggested reading οὗ 'part of which' for οὐ, in any case failing to explain why only part of it was rotten (Cassio 2002: 125; Probert 2006: 16–17 with n. 4). The material is nonetheless suitable: an oar is used for Elpenor's grave marker (*Od.* 11.77–8 > 12.8–15).   **ὅσον τ' ὄργυι':** 'as far as a fathom': derived from ὀρέγω 'I reach', an ὄργυια is a measurement produced by extending the arms, which Hdt. 2.149.3 puts at 6 feet; the same expression is used of the olive stake (*Od.* 9.325) and a rope used to bind a slain deer's feet (*Od.* 10.167).   **ἢ δρυὸς ἢ πεύκης:** doubt over the material matches the poet's uncertainty over the original function of the σῆμα (331–2), and contrasts with the earlier detailed description of Patroclos' pyre and tomb. Oak and (mountain-?)pine are elsewhere in epos linked in contexts of destruction (11.494–5, *Scut.* 376, 421), and while the former provides material for worked items (stakes *Od.* 14.12, lathe *Od.* 14.425, ploughstock *WD* 436), other varieties of pine (i.e. πίτυς; πεύκη is only used with δρῦς as above) are used only for ship timbers (13.390 = 16.483 simile) and building material (*Od.* 9.186; see generally Meiggs 1982: 108–15, and Markwald 1986: 174–5 n. 2 for the types of pine tree).

329–30 Verse structure in 329 mirrors the object's (as does the description of the surrounding area in 330), with words denoting/qualifying the two stones (λᾶε) around the wood (τοῦ ἑκάτερθεν). Both adjective (λεῖος) and noun (ἱππόδρομος) suggest that this is not the first race around this particular σῆμα.   ἐρηρέδαται 'are fixed' either '(into the ground)' or '(around the σῆμα)'; for the form, see 283–4n. Plural verb with a dual subject is common (*GH* II § 34).

331–3 331 ~ 7.89, where Hector imagines some future traveller seeing the tomb of his victim; for other such marks, see 45–7n. The original function is unclear to Nestor, but emphatically ancient (πάλαι/προτέρων) nonetheless; nicely balanced with anaphora of ἤ, either explanation helps to connect this contest with the past, whether celebrating the dead figure or hosting earlier races (Grethlein 2008: 31).   κατατεθνηῶτος: 192n.   τό ... νύσσα τέτυκτο 'it was set as a turning-post': τό is demonstrative, with νύσσα in apposition. τέτυκτο is 3rd sing. pluperf. indic. pass. from τεύχω (see 455 below).   ἐπὶ προτέρων ἀνθρώπων: this formula elsewhere distances the world of the speaker (5.637, 791, *Th.* 100) from the past (cf. 789–91ᵃn.), a connection furthered by καὶ νῦν, a common means of transition to the present, which here focuses on Achilleus' determinative authority in choosing the landmark, and his traditional speed; cf. his actions below (358–61n.).   ποδάρκης δῖος Ἀχιλλεύς: 140–4n.

334–43 The earlier negative/positive contrast is here reversed, with positive reasons for the instruction (334–40) preceding the dispreferred outcome (340–3). The first segment (334–40) is constructed in a ring (ἐγχρίμψας ~ ἐγχριμφθήτω/ἀριστερά ~ ἀριστερός) suggesting the importance of the right-hand horse (336–7) in the manoeuvre. The second segment (341–3) mirrors the syntax of the final instruction, matching its purpose clause with a negative purpose clause. The frequent imperatival infinitives in this passage are typical of practical instructions, each being a 'signal that the various actions should be viewed as necessary elements of a larger procedure which eventually will lead to a successful completion of the chariot-race' (Allan 2010: 212–13, at 213).

334–6ᵃ The driver does not only direct the team with the reins, but uses his own position in the chariot. By leaning a little (ἦκα) towards the left of the team (ἐπ' ἀριστερὰ τοῖιν) he draws them closer to the turning-post.   τῶι ... ἐγχρίμψας 'bringing the chariot (ἅρμα) near to this', i.e. the τέρμα. The verb is more usually mid. or pass. in epos, as at 338.   ἐλάαν: pres. act. infin. of ἐλάω, related to ἐλαύνω (cf. its 'Attic future' ἐλῶ -ᾶις -ᾶι), formed by diectasis (ἐλάαν < ἐλᾶν < ἐλάειν) and used as an imperative.   κλινθῆναι: aor. pass. infin. of κλίνω: 'be inclined/ lean'.   ἐϋπλέκτωι ἐνὶ δίφρωι: with a more common form in ἐϋπλεκής (436, *Scut.* 306, 370), the epithet refers to the 'basket-weave' construction of the car (Plath 1994: 228–31). The MSS are almost unanimous in this reading, and the poet could have used the more common ἐϋξέστωι (cf. 16.402, *Od.* 17.602, 24.408), found in MS D (tenth century) and quoted for this passage in Plato (as κλινθῆναι δὲ καὶ αὐτὸς ἐϋξέστωι ἐνὶ δίφρωι) and Xenophon (though gen. for dat.); these are all probably misquotations influenced by the more familiar adjective (cf. also 24.275, 578, 590 with forms of ἀπήνη; Labarbe 1949: 93–100; Lohse 1964–7: 264–5; Mitscherling 2005; also Appendix).

336ᵇ–7 The driver must goad the right-hand horse whilst shouting at it and giving it free rein.   κένσαι: aor. act. infin. (and the only Homeric form) of κεντέω; for the derived term κέντρον, used indiscriminately with other words for devices to spur the horses, see 429–30n.   ὁμοκλήσας: there are some traces of a smooth breathing for this stem in epos (variant 20.365; Hes. *Scut.* 341) which has been 'normalised' through misassociation with ὁμός etc. (*EDG* s. ὁμοκλή, West I.xviii, who prints ὁμο-), but the MSS favour aspiration. The verb denotes an aggressive, threatening cry, as in the speeches of Menelaos and Antilochos to their teams during the race (402–16, 442–6), both of which close with the expression ὡς ἔφαθ', οἳ δὲ ἄνακτος ὑποδδείσαντες ὁμοκλήν (417 = 446: 417–18ᵃn.).   εἶξαί τέ οἱ ἡνία χερσίν 'and yield to him the reins with your hands': reins are more typically grasped, held, or dropped to the ground in Homer; the manoeuvre envisages greater directional freedom for the right-hand horse to follow a wider course around the turning-post as it reacts to the charioteer's cry, presumably whilst avoiding ill-discipline (319–20).

338–40ᵃ We return to the left-most horse, skirting close to the turning-post.   ἐγχριμφθήτω 'let him be brought near to': 3rd sing. aor. pass. imp., recalling ἐγχρίμψας (334).   πλήμνη: the hub of the wheel (κύκλου), derived from an IE stem meaning 'part that turns about the axle' (Waanders 1992; cf. 5.726, *Scut.* 309: Plath 1994: 342–5).   δοάσσεται 'seem, appear': 3rd sing. aor. mid. 'short vowel' subj. after ὡς ἄν to introduce a purpose clause. Drawn perhaps from a stem related to δῖος (*EDG* s. δέατο), the verb is only otherwise found in epos in the expression ὧδε δέ οἱ φρονέοντι δοάσσατο κέρδιον εἶναι (13.458, 14.23, 16.652, etc.), which reinforces the positive connotations (or at least intentions) of Nestor's advice.   ἄκρον 'surface': *sc.* νύσσης.   κύκλου ποιητοῖο: notably separated from πλήμνη to underline the juxtaposition with λίθου as the object the wheel must avoid.

340ᵇ-1 The disfavoured outcome in 341 is reinforced by colon-ending rhyme in disyllabic aorist subjunctives (τρώσῃς/ἄξῃς), with noticeable α-assonance in the second colon.　　**ἀλέασθαι:** aor. mid. infin. of ἀλέομαι, frequently used in admonitory contexts in epos (605, *WD* 734, 780; imp. *Od.* 4.774; cf. *Od.* 9.411, 16.447, etc.).　　**ἅρματα:** the plural is frequently used for single chariots (as with ὄχεα) because they are made up of several parts (*GH* II § 39; 503-4n.).　　**ἄξῃς:** 2nd sing. aor. subj. of ἄγνυμι.

342-3 χάρμα δέ: this expression stands in parechesis (for the term, see 94-6n.) with θ' ἅρματα and helps to connect the outcome in 341 and its summation in the contrasted halves of 342, with colon-ending assonance (τοῖς ἄλλοισιν/σοὶ αὐτῷ). Repeated in Antilochos' rebuke to his horses (407-9n.), the avoidance of ἐλεγχείη 'reproach' is a powerful motivation, related in circumstances of imminent failure to the subject's very self-conception (22.100, *Od.* 14.38 with Bowie 2013: 170-1, 21.255; Cairns 1993: 65-8). Run-over ἔσσεται is emphatic (as again at 412: see n.), especially because the copula can be readily omitted. ἀλλά, φίλος recalls ἀλλ' ἄγε δὴ σύ, φίλος (313). The injunction is strengthened by plosive alliteration within words of increasing length (φίλος/φρονέων/ πεφυλαγμένος).　　**φίλος:** 313-14n.　　**πεφυλαγμένος εἶναι** 'be on your guard': perf. mid. imperatival infin. (also *WD* 706) almost equivalent to the simple imperative φυλάσσεσθαι, but more emphatic because of the periphrasis and the perfect participle implying the enduring nature of the lesson (e.g. *Od.* 11.443, *WD* 616, 641; Bentein 2016: 107-13, esp. 107-8). Nauck deleted 343, in which case West 2001a: 270 would print χάρματα in 342 to strengthen the parechesis and make the verse fully appositional; but this would leave 344 without a sufficient introduction, and there is no MS warrant for the deletion.

344-8 This focus on 'rounding the turning-post' in a good position is/becomes proverbial for 'returning to the start' and winning (García Romero 2001: 78-9), and keeps building up the expectation that this is to be the crucial event in the race. Zeus and Poseidon are indirectly evoked (but in reverse order from 307), since Poseidon was the father of Arion (Σ T 347) and Zeus gave divine horses to Laomedon's father, Tros (5.265-7): 306-8n. The descendants of these horses are now Diomedes' team, taken from Aineias on the poem's first day of battle, the product of Anchises' secret breeding from Laomedon's team, originally given by Zeus to Tros in compensation for the rape of Ganymedes (5.265-72). Laomedon denied Apollo and Poseidon their wages for building Troy's walls (21.441-57), and then refused Heracles' payment for ridding the city of the beast they sent in revenge (20.144–8); this led to his sack of Troy (Lang 1983; Alden 2001: 158–60; Bär 2018: 33–43).   παρεξελάσηισθα: 2nd sing. aor. act. subj. using the athematic personal ending -σθα (= παρεξελάσηις), as commonly in the 3rd person -ηισι (Intro. § 3.1.2.d.1 and n. 115).   οὐκ ἔσθ᾽ ὅς κε 'there is no-one who would': this idiom, with the subj. (21.103, *Od.* 6.201–2), opt. (22.348), or fut. indic. (*Od.* 16.437–8), conveys certainty in an opinion or prediction. Such statements are not always correct (22.438, *Od.* 16.437–8), and Antilochos is almost overtaken by Menelaos' team, which is inferior to Arion and Diomedes' prize-winning horses.   ἔληισι ... παρέλθοι: ἔληισι is 3rd sing. aor. act. subj. (= ἔληι: Intro. § 3.1.2.d.i and n. 115). The alternation from subjunctive to optative (the minority reading παρέλθηι tries to regularise the sequence) indicates Nestor's view that there is a greater chance of being caught than of being passed (*GH* II § 365 cautiously). The latter's relative unlikelihood is extended into the hyperbolic οὐδ᾽ εἰ protasis (346), since such qualifications are generally deployed more often with optative than subjunctive and for events so remote as to be virtual contrafactuals (2.489, 8.478, 9.379, 385, 445, etc.; De Jong 2001: 112).   Ἀρίονα δῖον: this famous horse was the offspring of Poseidon and Demeter (or an Erinys or a Harpy), and served several masters in heroic myth. He was victor in the chariot race at the first Nemean Games established by the Seven when they campaigned against Thebes, he saved his then-owner Adrestos from that expedition (next n.), and he drew Heracles' chariot in his fight with Ares (*Scut.* 120; Σ T 347; *Theb.* fr. 8 B; Cingano 2005: esp. 141–2). There was some ancient variation in the spelling of his name (Pfeiffer 1949–53: I.214, on Callim. fr. 223), a common -ει- version leading to δῖον being replaced by πῶλον ('horse') in some MSS, presumably because ἀρείονα was read as a comparative, which thus required a noun (and perhaps also because δῖον was seen as otiose with the second half of 347).   Ἀδρήστου: Adrestos was originally king of Sicyon (2.572), where he enjoyed later cult (Finkelberg 2005: 81–2), but he became king of Argos and was the only survivor of the first expedition against Thebes, being saved there by Arion (above). Eventually he led the Epigonoi ('Successors'), sons of the original Seven, in their successful sack of Thebes. He was father-in-law of Tydeus and his son Diomedes, and his Sicyonian link recalls the origin of Agamemnon's horse Aithē (295–9), suggesting here another indirect allusion to Menelaos' team (as at 296–300n.). Thus 346–8 foreshadow, implicitly and explicitly, Antilochos' main rivals in the race (as he acknowledges at 404–9), linking the team with which he will vie for second place (346–7) with Diomedes' victorious horses (below). Adrestos is also the name of Eumelos' father, adding another level to the allusion.   ἐκ θεόφιν: the preposition/preverb makes clear the genitive function of -φι in this phrase (as also Hes. *Th.* 871: Intro. § 3.1.2.c.ix), but the word is more often dative in the formula θεόφιν μήστωρ ἀτάλαντος (cf. 17.101, where ἐκ θεόφιν means almost 'with the aid of the god': *GH* I § 107). **γένος:** acc. of respect 'as to his origin', as commonly in genealogical contexts (cf. 5.896, 6.180, 14.113, etc). **οἳ ἐνθάδε γ' ἔτραφεν ἐσθλοί** 'who were, after all (γ'), raised here (to be) excellent' ~ 21.279, of Hector (ἔτραφ' ἄριστος), with γε underlining the horses' familiarity with the terrain as a(nother) reason for their quality. The intrans. 2nd aor. of τρέφω is firmly established in epos (1.251, 266, *Od.* 10.417; *GH* I § 186) and seems the best way to account for most of the variants – the majority's very rare τέτραφεν would be a mechanical misreading of Γ as Τ.

349–50 Again Nestor is more prominent (301–4ᵃn.). **Νηλήϊος: 301–4ᵃn.** **ἑκάστου πείρατ'** 'the limits of each thing': πεῖραρ is generally a border or limit in a variety of contexts, both material (the earth) and metaphorical (death, victory, toil), but it is also used in epos to denote ropes and cables (~ πεῖσμα; *LfrgE* s.v. B 11, 1106). The poet's view of the speech's authority is nonetheless clear, since to possess/bestow 'πεῖραρ of X' is to have mastery over it (7.102, 18.501, etc.; Bergren 1975: esp. 20–1, 41–3; Nothdurft 1978).

351 For the typology of Meriones' entry in the standing order, see 301–4ᵃn. This, the shortest and least emphasised, entry befits the character's minimal role in the race (see 355–6, 528–31, 614–15nn.).

352–7 Recasting of standing into starting order also happens in the iron throwing and archery (826–49, 850–83nn.), but there is no lot deployed in the former to achieve the new order. Only Menelaos retains the same position (third), which is also his finishing-place. The new order foregrounds the three figures (Antilochos, Eumelos, Menelaos) most involved in the quarrels closing the race, and arouses interest in the event by linking Antilochos' 'slowest' team with the traditionally fastest (Eumelos), and separating the two divinely supported teams and closest rivals (Eumelos, Diomedes). Variety (cf. 262–70n.) is achieved by using different expressions for the first and second starters (353–4; moving also from the κλῆρος to the human as subject), omitting the verb with the third (355), deploying for the fourth (356) the same introductory phrase as for the third but reusing the verb from the second, and reusing for the fifth the larger expression (λάχ' ἐλαύνεμεν) from the fourth. The poet proceeds in a ring, with run-over marking the first and final starters (353–4, 356–7), which means that the second and fifth starters do not fill their verses (354, 356), and only the central figure (Menelaos) is allotted a whole verse (355).

The many adverbs (ἀνά, ἐν, ἐκ, μετά, ἐπί) give a vivid impression of the actions and their sequence until the final αὖτε (356).

Lots are widely used in epos to determine participants or the order of participation; the first striker in the duel between Menelaos and Paris (3.314–25), the identity of Hector's opponent (7.170–99), and the first contestant in the archery below (861–2n.); cf. 24.400 for a (fictitious) filial lot to choose who comes to Troy, and *Od.* 14.208–10 for an inheritance (cf. also 15.187–93, *Od.* 9.331–5, 10.206–7, Hes. *WD* 37–9: Demont 2000, and the *Klêros Project* (https://kleros.org.il)). The typical sequence has (1) lots cast into a helmet; (2) participants/onlookers pray; (3) lots shaken; and (4) one lot 'leaps out' or is drawn. Prayer is omitted here perhaps because the hopes and expectations of (some of) the participants have already been set out; for its role in the archery, see 861–2, 862^b–4nn. In the context of this race, the lot seems to suggest that Antilochos is given the position closest to the turning-post (358–61n.), a considerable advantage which resumes Nestor's lengthy focus on that item (326–33n.) and continues the poet's misdirection that this will be the crucial factor.

352–4 The bookending of names in 353 underlines the relationship between Achilleus and Antilochos (cf. 576 for another example to opposite effect), while the run-over of the latter's name in 354 after the patronymic once more foregrounds Nestor's role: 301–4^{a}n. Note the strong sense of motion provided by the adverbs ἐν and ἐκ (Hutchinson 2020: 39).   ἐν δὲ κλήρους ἐβάλοντο ~ *Od.* 14.209, Odysseus' fake story about paternal inheritance. Possibly from κλάω 'I break off', the κλῆρος is a piece of wood or pottery on which marks can be made for use in a lot (7.174), and by extension a piece of land won in the process (cf. Eng. 'allotment'). The helmet into which the marker is placed is omitted, but cf. 3.316, 7.176, 182, *Od.* 10.206, etc.   ἐκ δὲ κλῆρος θόρε: idiomatic for the successful lot (cf. ἐκ δ᾽ ἔθορε κλῆρος 7.182 = *Od.* 10.207), θόρε is 3rd sing. aor. act. indic. of θρώσκω.   κρείων Εὔμηλος: Eumelos is again (288–9n.) graced with Agamemnon's distinctive epithet (110^{b}n.).

355–6 τῶι δ᾽ ἄρ᾽ ἐπ᾽ ... | τῶι δ᾽ ἐπί: 290–2n.   Ἀτρείδης δουρικλειτὸς Μενέλαος: the epithet in this formula is distinctive of Menelaos (cf. Τυδεΐδης δουρκλειτὸς Διομήδης 11.333) and means 'famed with the spear'. It is formed directly from κλε- (*WHS* 21), unlike its semantic equivalent δουρικλυτός, which is derived from κλύω and has a much wider distribution. Menelaos is not especially powerful in the surviving traditions (Stelow 2020), though his epithet distribution – with many words for 'warlike' *vel sim.* (Rousseau 1990) – suggests a more impressive prehistory than we can see (Willcock 2002): above, 293–5n. At least he gets a full verse here, unlike Meriones (351n.).

356–7 The only item in the catalogue marked by necessary run-over (352–7n.) is reserved for the (eventual) winner.   λάχ' ἐλαυνέμεν 'he drew the lot for driving': the infin. is result/final (151n.).   ὄχ' ἄριστος 'outstandingly the best': the adverb ὄχ(α) is formed from the adj. ἔξ-οχος (cf. ἐξ-έχω 'I am pre-eminent'), and found in Homer only with a form of ἄριστος (*HW* 133–6). Only here is this common combination coupled with a participle, elsewhere having its own finite verb (2.761, 3.110, etc.) or being simply appositive (1.69, 5.843, etc.), where it is always qualified by a genitive; the required notion is inferred here from the catalogue.

358–61 358 = 757 (start of the running race). After choosing the landmark referred to by Nestor (329–32), Achilleus now points it out to the drivers and sets Phoinix there as a referee, another misdirection as to the importance of this part of the course (306–48n.), 'in case someone tries to turn within the track' (Σ bT 353–7), i.e. before the σῆμα. His greater age doubtless part of his suitability as judge (Preisshofen 1977: 22), Phoinix's last major appearance was in the Embassy, though Athene takes his form when appearing to Menelaos (17.555–68), and he is one of the group comforting Achilleus (19.310–13). By now, he has clearly returned to his position within the Myrmidon camp (9.606–22, 658–62; cf. 690–2), and he is paired with Patroclos, a metanast like him, as one of Achilleus' two closest advisors (cf. 29–34, 84b–90, 166–76nn.).   μεταστοιχεί: more likely 'in a row beside one another' than 'behind one another' (so Σ AbT 358); cf. τριστοιχεί 'in three rows' (10.473). The latter would be a more obvious handicap, though the term is clearly understood in the former sense in the foot race (757). The lot therefore determines track position closest to the side of the turning-post (Richardson 213; cf. Schironi 2018: 286). The MSS are divided between -εί and -ί, but the former is better attested and preserves the original locative sense (*WHS* 366).   ὀπάονα: somewhat like the more common term θεράπων (89–90n.), an ὀπάων is a retainer, who may in turn have his own ὀπάων (17.610–11; Greenhalgh 1982: 84–6; Alden 2012: 123–4). Derived from ἕπομαι (*EDG* s.v.) and already a personal name in Mycenaean, the word is applied usually to Meriones, adding to the intimations of his antiquity (112–13n.; Erny 2020: 209–19).   μεμνέῳτο δρόμου '(so that) he might be mindful of the track/race': 3rd sing. perf. mid. opt. of μιμνήσκω, probably by metathesis from μεμνήοιτο (*GH* I § 28). West's emendation to the older, athematic μεμνῆιτο has no MS authority, and the thematic forms continue in later Greek (Hackstein 2002: 25–6). Aristarchos' reading δρόμους has some MS authority but is unexplained in the scholia; the genitive makes perfect sense (*LfrgE* s. μιμνήσκω B 4aγ; for the equally plausible accusative, 4b). Unless he was trying to strengthen the chiasmus in 361 (cf. Schironi 2018: 154–7), perhaps he thought Phoinix was to concern himself with the course taken by each team, rather than the race as a whole.

362–532 The race has two stages, the first (362–72) to the turning-post on the plain (cf. 359) and the second (373–532) back towards the shore. The wall around the camp is not mentioned, but there is no need to follow Aristarchos' belief that the turning-post is within the walled area (Σ bT 365); as Aristotle noted, 'the poet who made [the wall] up also made it vanish' (fr. 162 Rose = Strabo 13.1.36; Boyd 1995; Porter 2011). Purves 2011: 533–4 (~ 2019: 76–7) nicely suggests that the course of the race 'corrects' the error of Patroclos, who simply ran on to the city walls, and his doom.

362–72 The excitement of the outward leg is underlined by a great deal of run-over, though no individual episodes are described in the course of the 'panoramic' view: Grethlein and Huitink 2017: 75. The sequence of images works in a rough ring (as once more at the end of the race: 499–513n.): [A] drivers and horses (362–5, 369–72), [B] dust (365–6, 372), [C] chariots (368–9).

362 ἄρα: the minority reading ἅμα is preferred by modern editors, since it often reinforces πάντες ('all at the same time') and seems to have been read by Sophocles (*El.* 711–13 οἵ δ' ἅμα | ἵπποις ὁμοκλήσαντες ἡνίας χεροῖν | ἔσεισαν: Davidson 1988: 65–6), but this would be the only Iliadic instance of οἵ δ' ἅμα πάντες (4× *Od.*), and the majority's ἄρα is perfectly idiomatic and sensible ('and they, then, all of them': 3.95 = 7.92, etc.). The change would perhaps have been motivated to remove any ambiguity in μεταστοιχεί (358–61n.).

363–4ᵃ The neat doublet (verb + instrumental dative) and closing rhyme (ἱμᾶσιν ... ἐπέεσσιν) add to the sense of unity in 363.   **ἱμᾶσιν:** these may be different items from the μάστιγας, i.e. the reins, but ἱμάσθλη means 'whip' (*LfrgE* s. ἱμάς 2b, 1191), and Homer's terminology in these matters is imprecise (Delebecque 1951: 185): also 322–5n.   **ὁμόκλησαν:** see 336ᵇ–7n.   **ἐσσυμένως:** 55–8n. The alliteration, run-over after ἐπέεσσιν and proleptic before διέπρησσον, combines with ὦκα and ταχέως to give a powerful sense of that speed; see 364ᵇ–7n.

364ᵇ–7 ὦκα διέπρησσον πεδίοιο: this formula closes summaries of large-scale human advance (2.785, 3.14), adding to the synoptic impression of the first leg. The partitive genitive πεδίοιο is found in several expressions denoting space through (a part of) which movement takes place (*GH* II § 72); cf. also 372, 518 below.   **νόσφι νεῶν ταχέως:** the track stretches away from, and then back to, the ships at the shore (362–532n.).   **ὑπὸ δὲ στέρνοισι κονίη | ἵστατ᾽ ἀειρομένη:** the image is picked up by κονίοντες below (372). Dust is frequently raised by the advance of armies (2.150–1, 13.336–7; cf *Th.* 706–7 of the clash) or the progress of chariots (11.151–2, 282, 17.457, 23.502), and its 'occluding' effect helps to prepare for the dispute between Idomeneus and Aias over who is leading the race, whilst also suggesting the danger of the action itself (Lather 2020: esp. 267). The expression here is very close to 2.150–1 (πόδων δ᾽ ὑπένερθε κονίη | ἵστατ᾽ ἀειρομένη), while the run-over phrase in 366 is also used of the wave raised by the river against Achilleus (21.130).   **ὥς τε νέφος ἠὲ θύελλα:** alternatives within a simile tend to augment one another rather than introduce a fundamentally new image (11.389, 12.167, 13.389–90, etc.), and storm similes can be constructed of one element (13.39) or several (4.275–82, 16.364–7; Scott 1974: 62–6 (wind similes); Nünlist 2020: 37–41); for cloud as a threatening metaphor, see 131ᵇ–4n.   **ἐρρώοντο:** 3rd pl. imperf. mid. of ῥώομαι 'I move violently', which is derived either from ῥώννυμι or ῥέω (*DELG* 981; *EDG* s. ῥώομαι 1297 suggests a link with a Hittite verb which may mean 'attack'). West emends to δὲ ῥώοντο (from Ap. Soph. 139.29 Bekker) without any MS support; cf. χαῖται ἐπερρώσαντο (1.529 = *HDion.* 14).   **πνοιῆϊς ἀνέμοιο** 'the breath of the wind': this formula is generally connotative of speed (12.307, 24.342 = *Od.* 1.98 = 5.46; cf. 16.149–50; also 19.415).

368–9ᵃ This passage is quoted twice in Dio Chrysostom's 32nd oration (*To the Alexandrians*), firstly (ch. 79–80) to compare his audience's fickle emotions with the progress of the chariots in this race – Homer's spectators were at least quiet – and secondly (ch. 82 = *Parod. anon.* fr. 8a Brandt) to open an anonymous parodic fragment which ostensibly mocks the behaviour of contemporary audiences and charioteers. As is typical of ancient παρωιδία, the second citation stitches together different Homeric verses and passages with little or no change (Brandt 1888: 100–7; Barry 1993; Hunter 2018: 24–41).   **ἄλλοτε … ἄλλοτε:** a very common epic idiom for alternation in a continuing action or state, this kind of description is often expressed with frequentative (-σκ-) verbs (18.159–60, *Od.* 5.331–2, 23.94–5, etc.). The fronting of ἅρματα is emphatic, since ἄλλοτε μέν is usually placed first in its clause, and ἄλλοτε generally first in its verse (cf. 5.595, *Od.* 23.94, Hes. fr. 33a.14–18 M–W – a remarkable case).   **χθονί …**

πουλυβοτείρῃ: the usual line-end formula χθονὶ πουλυβοτείρῃ is nowhere else separated in epos, and πουλυ- is preferred to πολυ- to avoid three consecutive light syllables.   πίλνατο: is 3rd sing. imperf. mid. indic. of the athematic verb πίλναμαι 'I move near', which is related to the adverb πέλας 'nearby' (*DELG* s.v., 873–4), and which generates a thematic πιλνάω (Edwards 1971: 110). The expression as a whole is very close to *WD* 510 (of trees laid waste by Boreas in winter).   μετήορα 'raised up': i.e. fully off the ground. Derived from ἀείρω, this word is used elsewhere of the gods suspended from Olympos (8.26), sacrifical meat dedicated on the cave by Hermes (*HHerm.* 135), and the lyre's sounds when plied by the unskilful (*HHerm.* 488; Richardson 2010: 177; Vergados 2012: 541–2) – all cases where the item in question is in an unusual situation: clearly their speed and its effect are exceptional.

369ᵇ–71ᵃ ἐλατῆρες: from ἐλαύνω and elsewhere in Homer only in the singular, and only of horses or chariot teams (4.145, 11.702, also *HAp.* 232). It later means 'cattle thief' (3× *HHerm.*; Thomas 2020: 146). Each racing chariot carries only one person, not driver and passenger as in combat.   **πάτασσε δὲ θυμός:** sound repetitions in πάτασσε and ἔστασαν underline the fearful context, where this expressively sonant verb (cf. πάταγος 'crash') is elsewhere coupled with cognitive organs (7.216, 13.282; Perpillou 1982: 264–5; Clarke 1999: 104–6).   **ἑκάστου | νίκης ἱεμένων** 'of each man | as they all strove for victory': for pl. verbs with sing. forms of ἕκαστος (again at 371–2), see 1–3n. The formular idiom 'striving for victory' (νίκης + a middle form of ἵημι, clustered all in this book) denotes the evenness of a contest directly before the narrative turns into the decisive episode(s): 718 (wrestling), 767 (running) – also just before 'the last turn' πύματον ... δρόμον (768); cf. below, 373–4n. The partitive genitive νίκης is expected with verbs of 'aiming at' or 'reaching for' (*GH* II § 64).

371ᵇ–2 To mark the end of the continuous general narrative of the first leg, the poet mirrors the opening progression from drivers' commands (363) to the horses' dusty course over the plain (364–5). Alternating οἱ and ὁ help to reinforce the concluding nature of 372.   **κέκλοντο ... ἕκαστος | ἵπποις:** repetition of ἕκαστος (cf., e.g., 1.606–7, 2.449–51, 15.660–2, etc.) emphasises the synoptic nature of the description and the universality of the action, and allows transition from the drivers to the team. κέκλοντο is unaugmented 3rd pl. aor. mid. indic. of κέλομαι 'I command', with reduplication (*GH* I § 189): see also 402 below (ἐκέκλετο).   **ἐπέτοντο κονίοντες πεδίοιο** ~ 365–6 above. This formula may be used of men (*Od.* 8.122) or horses (13.820 + οἴσουσι, 23.449

below, *Scut.* 342), and once more always before a transition away from the general description it offers. For πεδίοιο, see 364^b–7n.

373–532 The return leg is described at greater length and with greater detail than the outward, and contains all the race's individually described episodes. Some scholars (e.g. Gagarin 1983, Forte 2018) argue instead that these events occur at the turning point, while Nagy 1990b: 209 (and often) thinks they happen beforehand. But the text itself is clearly focused on the second leg (373–4, 398–400, 423–4, 462–4nn.; so also, e.g., Köhnken 1981: 143–5; Richardson 215; Visa-Ondarçuhu 1999: 27).

373–4 The resumptive ἀλλ' ὅτε ... τότε δή pivots on the turn into the last straight, with imperfects τέλεον 'they were completing' and φαίνετ(ο) 'showed itself' denoting the continuing background for the following events. πύματον ... δρόμον 'the last (part of the) track': as again in the running race (768), where it sets the scene for Odysseus' prayer and Aias' slip in the dung as they near the finishing line (773). Forte 2018 interprets the adjective differently, referring it to the 'furthermost' part of the course from the finish. ὠκέες ἵπποι: metrically but not prosodically equivalent to μώνυχες ἵπποι, this formula is declined from the more established accusative system (6–7, 279, 293–5nn.). ἂψ ἐφ' ἁλός 'back again towards the sea': some MSS read ἀφ' for ἐφ' (though not 'the majority' as reported by Σ AT 374), but the corruption hardly makes sense, and is easily explained by contextual alphatism (Rousseau 1992: 161–2 n. 10).

375–400 Eumelos versus Diomedes. As in the foot race, a leader emerges (375–6 ~ 758–9), closely followed by the second-place figure (377–87 ~ 759–67), only to be beaten by divine intervention from Athene in the latter's favour (388–400 ~ 768–84). The only major difference is the minor doublet in Apollo's prior intervention (382–7) which motivates hers, and the later reversal of the 'last portion of the track' (373–4n.) and 'all-out running' (375–6n.) motifs. Their participation here evokes their last encounter in the duel between Achilleus and Hector.

375–6 ἄφαρ δ' ἵπποισι τάθη δρόμος 'and immediately the running was strained (intensified) by the horses': i.e., they really went all out at this stage of the race. ἄφαρ links their increased effort with the turn into the home straight (*LfrgE* s.v. B1d, 1697), while δρόμος can mean both 'race-course' or 'track' and 'running' or 'pace', the sense most fitting here and below in the running race (758). For the passive of τείνω used in this context, cf. 758 below (~ *Od.* 8.121, both running races). The speed of Eumelos' team is underlined by ὦκα and ποδώκεες, a quality typically expressed with ἐκφέρω in such contexts, both for fleeing (16.368–9 ἵπποι | ... ὠκύποδες, 16.383 = 866 ὠκέες ἵπποι) and racing (758–9 ὦκα; cf. Platte 2017: 22). **Φηρητιάδαο:** either a papponymic (28n.) denoting Pheres' grandson Eumelos or a patronymic for his son Admetos, whose horses these originally were (2.763–4); cf. 11.597 (Νηλήϊαι ἵπποι).

377–8 The contrast between Diomedes' male and Eumelos' female team is underlined by isoteleuton in 376–7, and bookending 377 with τὰς ... μέτ᾽ and the unusual qualification ἄρσενες (of horses in early epos only at *Od.* 13.81, a four-horse team; cf. Platte 2017: 28). Male superiority is not assumed (293–5n.), but see 407–9n., and Diomedes is clearly about to overtake or draw level (382). Emphatic run-over of Τρώϊοι evokes once more the taking of the horses from Aineias in Book 5 (290–2n.). The polar expression reverses the order of 22.300 (νῦν δὲ δὴ ἐγγύθι μοι θάνατος κακός, οὐδ᾽ ἔτ᾽ ἄνευθεν), and hostility – or at least opposition – is normally predicated of a movement or position described as μάλ᾽ ἐγγύς (4.496 = 5.611, 7.225, 11.429, etc.); cf. *WD* 288.   **ἔσαν:** 3rd pl. imperf. indic. of εἰμί = ἦσαν without augment.

379–81 379 and 380 are quoted (in reverse order) by ps.-Demetrius (*On Style* 209–10) as examples of Homer's skill in *enargeia* 'vividness', specifically in the fact that 'no detail is omitted' (Otto 2009: 79–80).   **ἐπιβησομένοισιν ἐΐκτην** 'they both were like those about to mount upon ...' = 'they both appeared to be about to mount upon ...': though ἔοικα is more usually followed by a dative noun (with participle or not), the participle is found alone (15.90, 23.430, *Od.* 11.608, etc.). For the dual ἐΐκτην after several plurals in the preceding verses, see *GH* II § 34. The fut. mid. ppl. of ἐπιβαίνω elsewhere denotes drivers killed on the point of mounting their chariots (5.46 = 16.343). Platte 2017: 28 sees a sexual theme here.   **μετάφρενον** 'the back': Eumelos is in the lead but on the defensive, as with all those struck here (2.265–7, 5.56, etc.; Kelly 2007a: 140, adding *Od.* 8.528).   **εὐρέε (τ᾽) ὤμω:** this formula is normally found in the accusative (3.210, 227, 16.360, etc.), and its only other dual declension occurs also with μετάφρενον during Apollo's attack on Patroclos (16.791).   **θέρμετ᾽:** the singular verb agrees with μετάφρενον as the most important notion, passing over εὐρέε τ᾽ ὤμω as if in parenthesis (*GH* II § 24 R. 1). Necessary run-over underlines the image's individuality, since heat is normally linked in epos with tears, blood, and baths; cf. also *Od.* 9.376 (olive stake).   **πετέσθην:** the 3rd dual imperf. pass. indic. of πέτομαι is almost always confined to horses, and usually in the formula μάστιξεν δ᾽ ἐλάαν/ἵππους, τὼ δ᾽ οὐκ ἀέκοντε πετέσθην, where the drivers are assured of success in their mission (Kelly 2007a: 98–9). Arrival in those cases is instantaneous, whereas here one team chases another, and κεφαλὰς καταθέντε is much more active and aggressive ('set their heads down', i.e. almost touching) than οὐκ ἀέκοντε: cf. similarly 13.385 and 17.502.

382–4 The contrafactual conditional (154–5n.) resolves potentially conflicting narrative strands – Eumelos' superior reputation and Diomedes' imminent achievement in either pulling past or at least drawing even (382). The introduction of Apollo, Diomedes' opponent from Book 5 and Eumelos' family patron, raises the stakes and makes it seem as though the latter's status will win out, since the intervening action in these sentences usually succeeds in resolving the matter. Line 382 ~ 527 (… οὐδ' ἀμφήριστον ἔθηκεν: another contrafactual; see 526–7n.), where Menelaos would clearly have overtaken Antilochos, had the course been a little longer.   **ἤ:** this is the reading of all the MSS, changed by West to Fick's elided form ἤ' (for original ἠέ) wherever ἤ is not corrected before a vowel (West I.xxxi). ἠέ is guaranteed in several places (e.g. 4.74), but contracted ἤ is well established in epos.   **ἀμφήριστον:** neut. acc. sing., literally something 'quarrelled about', from ἀμφί + ἐρίζω (cf. ἀμφηρεφής < ἀμφί + ἐρέφω; *LfrgE* s.v., 660).   **Τυδέος υἷι:** this flexible formula uses a short gen. sing. found with some 3rd declension names in -εύς (e.g. Ἀτρέος/ Πηλέος), possibly caused by internal hiatus in the expected epic form -ηος (cf. Πηλῆος; Hackstein 2002: 24–5). -εος is largely limited to those nouns which also form patronymics, and these '[name] + son of' expressions may have developed to complement them (*GH* I §§ 46, 96; cf. also 677–80n.). The phrase activates the Tydeus–Diomedes theme, as the son proves his worth in an athletic achievement to rival his father's in Thebes (5.801–7), picked up again in Idomeneus' speech (470ᵇ–2n.; Andersen 1978: 142–3; Sammons 2014; O'Maley 2018).   **κοτέσσατο:** Apollo's reaction to his favourite's imminent defeat will be paralleled by Athene's more successful one (κοτέουσα 391). κότος is suitable for such acts of divine favouritism, since it is characteristically associated with vendetta (Walsh 2005: esp. 65–6).   **Φοῖβος Ἀπόλλων:** 188–91n.   **μάστιγα φαεινήν:** the epithet refers to the sheen of the leather (*LfrgE* s. φαεινός B2b, 794). The μάστιξ is also called a κέντρον below (387): 336ᵇ–7n. Whenever the driving equipment escapes the charioteer, the journey is at an end (5.582–3, 8.137, 11.128, etc.: Kelly 2007a: 163–4): cf. also 465–8n.

385–7 Diomedes' tearful reaction at the potential loss of honour will be parallelled by Eumelos (394–7). Crying is neither unheroic nor unmanly (cf. 1.357, 360, 7.426, 8.245, etc.). Men and women weep often in the

Homeric poems, from a range of emotions, including rage, frustration, loss, and fear (Arnould 1990: 52–3 *et passim*; Van Wees 1998: esp. 12; Föllinger 2009). The contrast between the sex of Eumelos' (τὰς μέν) and Diomedes' (οἳ δέ) teams is again marked (377–8n.). The former is described with a participle in indirect statement after ὅρα (emphasising reality: *GH* II § 477), and the second is raised to an independent clause with its own finite verb: Diomedes' point of view becomes the narrator's, laying great emphasis on his primary concern – the harm to his own team.   χωομένοιο: the loss is deeply and immediately felt, since χώομαι is normally directed against a specific character (cf. 1.244, 13.165: *LfrgE* s.v. B 1–11, 1291–4) and reflects 'a much more positive attitude to the obstacle' than other expressions of anger (Adkins 1970: 41).   οὕνεκα 'wherefore', 'because': causal conjunction, a contraction through crasis of the relative expression οὗ ἕνεκα 'for the sake of which'.   ἔτι καὶ πολὺ μᾶλλον 'still even much more': Eumelos' apparent advantage (from Diomedes' perspective) has only been increased by the loss of the whip, since this combination elsewhere denotes an increment directly caused by another action (22.235, 23.429 below, *Th.* 428).   οἳ δὲ οἱ: the second οἱ is the dative of the 3rd pers. pronoun used almost as a genitive ('the ones to himself' = 'his own': *GH* II § 92). The absence of the noun is unusual, but the immediate context easily supplies ἵπποι (for a similar ellipsis, see 24.399: ἓξ δέ οἱ υἷες ἔασιν, ἐγὼ δέ οἱ ἕβδομός εἰμι). Modern editors often print οἳ δ' ἑοί, i.e. the masc. nom. pl. of the possessive/reflexive pronoun ('his own'), citing the early first century CE scholar Ptolemy of Ashkelon (Σ A 387b1), but this reading has no MS support (Erbse 1960: 317 n. 1).   ἐβλάφθησαν: Homer also uses βλάβ-, the 2nd aor. pass. stem of βλάπτω (e.g. 23.461, 545, etc.).

388–9 'Nor did Apollo escape Athene's notice as he harmed | the son of Tydeus'.   Ἀθηναίην: well established in epos, the adjectival form of the goddess' name may be derived from a Mycenaean toponym (*at-a-na po-ti-ni-ja* 'mistress of/at Athens') being understood as a name which contracted eventually to the familiar 'Athene', though some scholars name the city instead from the goddess (Burkert 2011: 217–18; Pötscher 1987: 160–5).   ἐλεφηράμενος: nom. sing. aor. mid. ppl. of ἐλεφαίρω 'I harm, deceive', folk-etymologised at *Od.* 19.564–5 as linked with ivory (ἐλεφάντος | … ἐλεφαίρονται: also *Th.* 330). For the complementary use of the participle with λάθε, which in fact expresses the main idea of the sentence, see *GH* II § 475.   Τυδεΐδην: 290–2n.   μετέσσυτο: 3rd sing. aor. (or pluperf.: *GH* I § 182) mid. indic. of μετασεύομαι, which can have a hostile (21.423) or supportive (6.296) sense, as here.   ποιμένα λαῶν 'shepherd of the people': this famous formula is only here applied to Diomedes, presumably because the *Iliad* poet is generally less interested in linking him with the expression's 'failed shepherd' image (Haubold 2000: esp. 17–46).

390–1 The neat chiasmus in 390, with the importance of the restored μάστιγα reinforced by its juxtaposition to μένος, is introduced by repetition of κ in the verbs bookending the verse (δῶκε ... ἐνῆκεν). For the '*menos* complex', see 175–7n. Athene casts μένος into the team, probably for the second time, when Diomedes rounds Eumelos' disabled chariot (see 398–400n.).   **κοτέουσα** ~ κοτέσσατο (383), Apollo's intervention, giving Athene's hostility a touch of revenge (382–4n.).   **βεβήκει** 'she was already on her way': 3rd sing. pluperf. indic. act. of βαίνω, without augment (some MSS read κοτέουσ᾽ ἐβεβήκει: see West I.xxvi–xxvii). The pluperfect of verbs of motion gives the sense that the action is already complete (*GH* II §§ 297, 294). This form of the verb typically marks swift transitions from one scene to the next (1.221, 6.313, 495, 16.751, etc.).

392–3 The bookending of 392 (ἵππειον δέ οἱ ... οἱ ἵπποι) emphasises runover δραμέτην in 393, while the syntax of the opening clause is mimetic, with Athene breaking the yoke away from its epithet.   **ἵππειον δέ οἱ ἦξε:** West emends to ἵππειόν οἱ ἔαξε to preserve the *digamma* in (ϝ)άγνυμι (ἦξε is 3rd sing. aor. indic. act., contracted from ἔϝαξε), but this has no MS authority and introduces an asyndeton, to avoid which Chantraine reads δέ (ϝ)᾽ ἔαξε (*GH* I § 54). Neither change is warranted: the diachronic 'messiness' of Homeric language cannot be emended away.   **αἱ δέ οἱ** 'his (female) horses': see 385–7n. (οἱ δέ οἱ) for the construction.   **ἀμφὶς ὁδοῦ δραμέτην:** like δίχα, ἀμφίς (= ἀμφί) can be a preverb meaning 'in two ways', i.e. 'they ran separate ways along the road'; or a preposition with the genitive, i.e. 'they ran away (together) from the road' (8.444, *Od.* 14.352, 16.267; *GH* II § 127). The horses' familiarity with one another perhaps makes the latter more probable. However close the teams were, run-over δραμέτην underlines their new-found distance.   **ῥυμός:** the chariot pole, to which the yoke binds the horses (esp. 5.729–30; Plath 1994: 316–20). This is elsewhere broken by horses in their eagerness to escape (6.38–41, 16.370–1), but here the yoke breaks and the pole falls to the ground. For detailed descriptions of the tethering gear, see 5.722–32, 24.268–74 (Crouwel 1981: 67–8, 92–6, 113–14; 1992: 38–45, 88–91).   **ἐλύσθη** 'swung' (?): the particular sense of the aorist passive form of εἰλύω/ἐλύω 'I enfold, cover', more conventionally used of people (24.510, *Od.* 9.433), is uncertain (*LfrgE* s.v. B2). The form part-rhymes with ἐξεκυλίσθη in 394.

394–7 394 = 6.42, where the Trojan Adrestos is abandoned by his team and captured by Menelaos; the onomastic coincidence with Eumelos' father (344–8n.) suggests an association with the theme of chariot racing. The catalogue style of the injuries is furthered by the continuing series of aorist passives, with variation in their positions. The consequent aspiration is noticeable (esp. in 397), as is the mirroring of Eumelos' passivity in the verbs' voicing (Grethlein and Huitink 2017: 78). περιδρύφθη: in contrast with ἀποδρύπτω 'tear off' (23.187 ~ 24.21, *Od.* 5.435; cf. 5.426), περι- gives a sense of the whole area 'around about' (185–7n.). For similar injuries, see 16.323–4, *Od.* 5.426, 434–5. στόμα τε ῥῖνάς τε 'mouth and nostrils': this formula is used only to denote damage, both deadly (14.467, 16.349) and merely uncomfortable (23.777, *Od.* 5.456). θρυλίχθη: 3rd sing. aor. pass. indic. of θρυλίσσω, a very rare verb (only here and in a particularly gruesome groin wound at Lyc. *Alex.* 487) meaning 'smash' or 'cut up'. Σ bT 396 suggests that its onomatopoeia reflects the 'disorder of his shattered face' (Tichy 1983: 102 and n. 71). ἐπ' ὀφρύσι 'at the eyebrows': here ἐπί must have a local prepositional force, as at 15.102 (also + μέτωπον) and 20.151 ('on the brows' of a hill). Elsewhere in this formula for expressions of (usually divine) assent or command, ἐπί is a preverb meaning 'towards' with νεῦσε, i.e. 'nodded assent to something with the eyebrows' (9.620, *Od.* 16.164). τὼ δέ οἱ ὄσσε | δακρυόφι πλῆσθεν, θαλερὴ δέ οἱ ἔσχετο φωνή: for Eumelos, the race is over; this formula, and the run-over (first) idiom alone (*Od.* 10.247–8, 20.348–9; cf. 5.151–2), describe characters momentarily stunned (by fear, pain, or joy) as their role in the narrative is about to diminish and their agency assumed by someone more powerful. The only other Iliadic instance denotes Antilochos' reaction to the news of Patroclos' death (17.695–6). For -φι(ν) in δακρυόφιν, here simply a 'poetic' dative marker, see 6–7n. Against the MSS, West and several editors delete the ν mobile as unnecessary, but correption does occur before πλ- in Homer (e.g. 7.88, 9.360, 382, 14.468, etc.). πλῆσθεν: -θεν = -θησαν (Intro. § 3.1.2.d.i), unaugmented 3rd pl. aor. pass. indic. of πίμπλημι.

398–400 398 ~ 423. Τυδεΐδης: 290–2n. παρατρέψας ἔχε 'turning them aside, then drove': for ἔχω in this sense, see 322–5n. Diomedes first steers his team aside, then drives past, the wreck of Eumelos' chariot (not past the turning-post, as Gagarin 1983: 38, Forte 2018), the strain of the action being emphasised by μώνυχας ἵππους (6–7n.). πολλὸν τῶν ἄλλων ἐξάλμενος 'leaping out far in front of the others': ἐξάλμενος is nom. sing. aor. mid. ppl. of ἐξάλλομαι, used of aggressive priority (15.571, 17.342; cf. 5.142 for the only other form of this verb in Homer). Diomedes' clear lead is furthered by ἐν ... | ἵπποις ἧκε μένος (~ 390–1: see n.): either

Athene repeats her earlier infusion to put the issue beyond doubt or the poet refers to the earlier act before her pursuit of Eumelos.   καὶ ἐπ' αὐτῶι κῦδος ἔθηκεν = 406ᵇ below; cf. *Il. pers.* fr. 4.2 B (κυδίον' ἔθηκε). κῦδος is reputation linked with achievement and enjoyed during one's lifetime (*LfrgE* s.v. B3, 1576–7). It can be earned or bestowed, especially by gods, but these two occasions in Book 23 are its only uses with τίθημι (presumably the reason for the minority variant ἔδωκεν). For the poet's awareness of the novelty, see 405–6n.

401–47 Menelaos versus Antilochos. In some ways an unexpected clash, since they appear closely associated in several episodes (5.561–75, 15.568–92, 17.651–714: Willcock 1983) and post-*nostos* Menelaos is strangely unable to speak of the youth when questioned by Peisistratos (*Od.* 4.199–202, 203–15). Matching the prominence given Antilochos in the preparations (301–50), this mini-contest is the largest narrated episode in the race, and looks forward to the contest's third and final quarrel after its conclusion (566–613). Their imbroglio matches the last, in that the initial leader loses his advantage, though this time not by divine intervention but a little youthful skulduggery, and the poet uses more direct speech than narrative description. The passage is bookended by speeches directed to the team, first Antilochos' (401–18) and then Menelaos' (442–7); the inner structure comprises two sequences of (i) race description (418–24, 429–37) and (ii) a three-verse speech from Menelaos to Antilochos (425–8, 438–41), firstly trying to persuade and then rebuking him.

401–2 τῶι δ' ἄρ' ἐπ': cf. 355–6, where Menelaos is also named. The poet is clearly trying to build up an associative conflict over the result, as he resumes the catalogue style with the only character to maintain his (third) position in both standing and starting orders (352–7n.).   ξανθὸς Μενέλαος: 140–4, 293–5nn.   ἵπποισιν ἐκέκλετο: Antilochos' team will react successfully to his rebuke, since this formula introduces often rather critical team talks (no actual speech at *HDem.* 88 and *Scut.* 341) with that outcome (8.184, 19.399, 23.442; Kelly 2007a: 208). For its repetition after Menelaos' matching speech, see 442–7n. For the form ἐκέκλετο (3rd sing. aor. mid. of κέλομαι), see 371ᵇ–2n.

403–17 Antilochos' speech has a seemingly clear outer limit, with the syntax and some phrasing in 403 echoed in 414, though he then adds a promise to keep an eye on the team himself (415–16n.). The main body of the speech is composed of a deliberately unequal negative/positive contrast denoting Diomedes' team (404–6) and Menelaos' (407–13). The latter receives the most attention as the most likely target, and the focus on these two teams recalls the closing couplet in Nestor's speech (344–8n.). There are several more direct reminiscences of his father's instructions, though each time the figure is applied differently (407–9, 415–16, 417–18ªnn.). As in all team-exhortations in the *Iliad*, the horses are anthropomorphised (8.184–98, 19.399–403, 419–23, 23.442–7 below); the speaker freely deploys rhetorical figures generally reserved for humans, whether cajoling or threatening, and assumes reactions and attitudes much like his own (cf. also 17.426–55; Delebecque 1951: 58, Schnapp-Gourbeillon 1981: 169–78): also 403–4, 407–9nn.

403–4 ἔμβητον καὶ σφῶϊ: 'Get a move on, you two as well ...' (Richardson 216). ἔμβητον is 2nd pers. dual aor. act. imp. of ἐμβαίνω. For the emphatic sequence of imperative + καί + vocative, where καί stresses the noun ('I mean you two' *vel sim.*), cf. 1.274, 9.513, 20.104, 21.106, 23.469.   ὅττι τάχιστα: closing a second colon notably marked by staccato τ-consonance, this adverbial expression shows Antilochos is disturbed (71–4n.), and he repeats it at the end of his speech (414).   οὔ τι κελεύω: Antilochos knows the impossibility of competing with Diomedes, since speakers formally abjure giving advice in this idiom only when unnecessary (4.286, 359) or impractical (14.62); cf. 5.485, where Hector is rebuked for not acting when required.

405–6 These verses were athetised by Aristarchos (Σ A 405–6a: 'how did Antilochos know what Athene had done?'), but it is entirely typical for Homer's characters to retell the story with their own inferences (Kelly 2018), which in this case are hardly perverse: Σ bT 405–6b well invokes Aias *meiōn*'s rueful reflection on the running race (782–3), paralleled to the current contest in several ways (see 358–61, 369ᵇ–71ª, 373–4, 375–6nn.). The interwoven genitive + dative syntax of 405 allows the poet to bookend the line with Diomedes and his patron deity, and deepen their association. The careful isosyllabic chiasmus (verb + neuter noun/neuter noun + verb) in 406 surrounds and emphasises the central figure, Diomedes (ἐπ' αὐτῶι). The pleasing unity thus bestowed is reinforced by the fact that forms of ὀρέγω (in the first colon) are typically used with κῦδος (in the second: see 5.33, 225, 260, 11.79, etc.): the poet seems deliberately to signpost the novelty of his expression.   Τυδεΐδεω: -εω is one heavy syllable in synizesis. Homer also uses the 'older', disyllabic -αο genitive of this patronymic (5.281, 8.254), though this form is more common.   καὶ ἐπ' αὐτῶι κῦδος ἔθηκεν: 398–401n.

407–9 Another positive–negative contrast in 407 is supported by an appeal to avoid reproach, redirecting Nestor's injunction not to be 'a reproach to yourself' (342–3n.) in this *topos*' only application to a non-human. Reproof is underlined by the run-over name and sex specification, but fits ill with (i) the otherwise positive standing of female horses in epos (293–5n.), (ii) the fact that the team's sex is in fact mixed (431–3n.), and (iii) his own team's 'epicene' status (Hainsworth 287), viz. female at 8.113 and 11.597, masculine at 8.81, 104 (and here). This inappositeness may reflect Antilochos' somewhat uncertain justification in the way he runs the race (410, 415–16nn.).   **λίπησθον:** 2nd pers. dual aor. mid. subj. of λείπω used to mean 'do not (μή) be left behind' (*LfrgE* s.v. B4b, 1659). This form is not found again in Greek literature, but its rarity does not recommend the (equally rare) 2nd pers. pl. λίπησθε, read only in Π 13, presumably by dittography after κιχάνετε or before λείπεσθε (409), or influenced by λίπησθε in 248 above.   **καρπαλίμως** 'swiftly': the etymology of this word is unknown. Some have linked it with καρπός 'wrist' and/or an associated notion of 'turning' and others with κάλπη 'trot' (i.e. < καλπάλιμος with dissimilation; *DELG* s.v., 500).   **Αἴθη θῆλυς ἐοῦσα:** Hera is similarly labelled at 19.97, where her opposition to Zeus is obviously gendered; for the name Αἴθη, see 293–5n.   **τίη:** this interrogative denotes Antilochos' 'surprise, impatience, or indignation' (*GP* 173) with his team. The word is sometimes printed separately (τί ἤ), but there is no linguistic justification for it, and the majority of MSS have the form as printed here (West I.xxi–xxii).   **φέριστοι:** from threat to flattery. This 'apostrophe courtoise' (*DELG* s. φέρτερος B, 1188) is a superlative of the same root found in φέρω, and thus means something like 'most serviceable' or 'useful' (*sc.* in carrying, originally). Again, it is only applied here in early epos to non-humans (cf. *Od.* 9.269).

410 ὧδε γὰρ ἐξερέω, καὶ μὴν τετελεσμένον ἔσται: superficially, the following threat is confident and successful, since these predictions encapsulate a speaker's supreme confidence in his/her ability to enact the future, and they usually persuade the addressee to act as intended (Kelly 2007a: 279–80, adding *Od.* 2.187, 16.440, 17.229, 18.82, 19.487, 21.337). Nonetheless, Antilochos is still uncertain of himself, as other speakers (except Athene at 1.212; cf. *Od.* 17.229) focus on their own future intentions, not someone else's. μήν is the Attic form of the affirmative particle, which tends to be emended to Ion. μέν, the more common Homeric form. The particle's other form in Homer is Aeol. μάν, usually preferred to μέν before a vowel (Wackernagel 1916: 17–22; Cuypers 2005: 45–9). τετελεσμένον ἔσται means 'will be definitely (= in a state of having been) completed': the nom. neut. sing. perf. mid. ppl. of τελέω is used periphrastically with ἔσται to form a 'future perfect', laying confident emphasis on the finality of the future state (Bentein 2016: 107–13).

411–12 Antilochos' threat recalls the stress laid by Hector on his wife's κομιδή 'care' as a reason for his horses to make an effort now (8.186–90). For similar reminders in the human world, see e.g. 4.256–64 (complimentary), 4.341–6 (abusive). As in Nestor's earlier speech to his son (also recalled above: 407–9n.), run-over ἔσσεται is emphatic (342–3n.). **ποιμένι λαῶν**: 388–9n. **κατακτενεῖ ὀξέϊ χαλκῶι**: guttural sounds reinforce the threat. Correption of the fut. indic. -εῖ (< -έει) before a vowel is rare but not unprecedented; it is caused here by conjugation of the usual expression κατέκτανον/ἀπέκτανον ὀξέϊ χαλκῶι (*Od.* 13.271, 14.271 = 17.440); cf. also 5.558 (κατέκταθεν), 675 (ἀπόκταμεν), *Od.* 4.700 (κατάκταμεν). The prevalence of the alphatic forms may explain MS D's κατακτάνει. The alliterative verse-end formula ὀξέϊ χαλκῶι refers to the spear head.

413–14 414 ~ 403 (403–17n.). **ἀποκηδήσαντε φερώμεθα**: though the dual participle can qualify the subject of a plural verb (e.g. 1.331–2, 3.441 = 14.314, etc.), Antilochos is hardly likely to be criticising his own efforts, so it is best to understand ἀποκηδήσαντε as specifying the team's misdeed in a slight anacolouthon, i.e. 'you two being remiss, we claim a lesser prize' (as Σ A 314a recognises; *GH* II §§ 35, 470). ἀποκηδέω (= ἀκηδέω 'I have no care for', 'I am remiss') is only found here and Sophron fr. 142 Hordern. **ἀλλ' ἐφομαρτεῖτον καὶ σπεύδετον** = 8.191, in Hector's speech to his team (see 403–17, 411–12nn.). ἐφομαρτεῖτον 'come on (and) accompany me' is 2nd pers. dual pres. act. imp. (so also σπεύδετον), and the verb is only elsewhere used in epos at 12.412 (ἀλλ' ἐφομαρτεῖτε), where Sarpedon rebukes the Lycians' failure to assist his attack on the Greek wall (see 417–18ᵃn. for other links with this speech). The injunction is thus deployed where an aggressive speaker demands a similar mood from the addressee. West follows Wackernagel 1916: 70–1 (and Aristarchos) in preferring ἐφαμαρτεῖτον, since the o- form of this verb seems to be an Atticism. But there is no MS authority for this, and Atticisms should not all be emended away (Intro. §§ 3.1.1.c, 4). **ὅττι τάχιστα**: bookending repetition of Antilochos' disturbed urgency (403–4n.).

415–16 He now introduces the next stage of his plan, and the topography of the 'narrow place' to be picked up at 418ᵇ–19. The continuation of his speech beyond its apparent outer ring (403–17n.) resumes indications that he feels the need to bolster his own authority (407–9n.), given his reliance hitherto on Nestor. **ἐγών**: Homer often (but not

always) uses -ν to obviate hiatus (243–4n.).   στεινωπῶι ἐν ὁδῶι: this
formula denotes narrow places where a mightier opponent is defeated
by the area's confines, and by a trick (7.143, Nestor's story of Areithoos,
killed by Lycoorgos: Dunkle 1987: 6 n. 13; Elmer 2015: 162–4 relates it
to the narrative theme of ambush). It is declined into the nominative at
427; cf. also 514–16n.   παραδύμεναι: aor. act. infin. of παραδύω, to
be construed as complement of ταῦτα, i.e. 'a way to slip past' (*LfrgE* s.
δύνω/δύω, B II7, 360).   οὐδέ με λήσει ~ οὐδέ ἑ λήθει (323) and οὐδέ σε
λήσει (326), in Nestor's description of the good driver and his depiction
of the σῆμα (326n.): Antilochos' cunning reaches its apogee, but more
with regard to the former passage than the latter; cf. also 648–9n. for
Nestor's final use of the idiom.

417–18ᵃ ὡς ἔφαθ', οἳ δὲ ἄνακτος ὑποδδείσαντες ὁμοκλήν | μᾶλλον ἐπιδραμέτην
= 446–7, at the close of Menelaos' speech to his team (401–47n.). οἳ δὲ ...
ὁμοκλήν is used at 12.413 to introduce the Lycians' renewed advance: see
also 413–14n. (ἐφομαρτεῖτον). The geminate -δδ- in ὑποδδείσαντες reflects
original δϝ- (*GH* I § 62), was known to Didymus (Σ T), and is by far the
majority reading, though editors frequently print ὑποδείσαντες as *lectio difficilior* concealing the older linguistic feature (cf. Intro. § 4; also 425n.).
For the rough breathing in ὁμοκλήν, see 336ᵇ–7n. (ὁμοκλήσας).

418ᵇ–19 Antilochos presumably noted the narrowing of the track (415–
16n.), about which his father was silent, on the outward leg.   ὁδοῦ
κοίλης: the road is not 'hollow' like a ship, but 'deepened' or 'in a hollow', either naturally or by the water erosion described in 420–1 (*HDem.*
177; *LfrgE* s. κοῖλος B2, 1470); for later examples, see Hdt. 6.103, Thuc.
3.107.3, Dion. Hal. 2.43.4.   Ἀντίλοχος μενεχάρμης: this is his only formula aside from genealogical expressions (301–4ᵃn.). The a-stem epithet
also has a later o-stem μενέχαρμος (14.376: *WHS* 191) and means 'steadfast
in battle lust' (μένω + χάρμη), though a derivation from χάρμα 'joy' would
mean 'taking joy in staying' and would more closely encapsulate his fate
(Beck 2023: 504–5). It may have been devised for Antilochos and then
extended to others, since his traditional role did not extend far beyond
his connection with Nestor (301–4ᵃn.).

420–4 The 'breaking' (ῥωχμός) in the road is caused by gathered storm
water, which has also deepened (βάθυνε) the whole area around it (420–
1), and thus reduced the area available for two teams to run along side
by side. Menelaos directs his team to, and along, the 'narrow' (στεῖνος)
remaining part of the road (422), avoiding driving alongside his rival
(ἁματροχιάς); in response, Antilochos turns his team outside the road

(παρατρέψας ... ἐκτὸς ὁδοῦ) and aims to overtake Menelaos before the ῥωχμός.

420–2 ῥωχμός 'a breaking', 'gully': with several ancient critics, West reads instead ῥωγμός (both derived from ῥήγνυμι), against all the MSS and, e.g., Ap. Rhod. *Arg.* 4.1545 (*LfrgE* s.v., 60).   **ἔην** 'there was': combines the tense of the 'there was a person X' motif (5.9, 10.314, 13.663, etc.) with the frequent asyndeton in the 'there is a place X' descriptive motif (*Od.* 7.244, 9.116, etc.; De Jong 2001: 83). The latter is found at the start of a tale's (sub)section, heralding the topographical importance for what is to follow.   **ἀλὲν ὕδωρ** 'trapped water': ἀλέν is neut. nom. sing. aor. pass. ppl. of εἴλω 'I concentrate, gather'. The water's condition suggests that the road was naturally lower than the surrounding area (418ᵇ–19n.).   **ἐξέρρηξεν ὁδοῖο:** ἐξέρρηξεν is 3rd pers. sing. aor. indic. act. of ἐκ-ρήγνυμι. The genitive is either partitive, i.e. '(the water) broke off a part of the road', or ablatival, 'broke (it, *sc.* ῥωχμόν) away from the road'.   **ἁματροχιὰς ἀλεείνων:** Menelaos endeavours to stay in front as he approaches and enters the narrowed portion of the track. ἁματροχιά means 'running together', and it is next found in Callimachus fr. 383.10 Pf. and Nicander, *Ther.* 263, though both seem to understand the term to mean 'wheel-ruts', i.e. ἁρματροχιάς (23.505; Harder 2012: II.408–9): also 504ᵇ–6n.

423–4 423 ~ 398 (see 398–400n.): Antilochos now drives ἐκτὸς ὁδοῦ, since the track is too narrow for passing. Σ bT 420a and 423b suggest that his manouevre occurred at the turning-post, but they are trying to harmonise the narrative with the prominence of the turning-post in the lead-up to the race (352–7, 373–4nn.).   **ὀλίγον δὲ παρακλίνας ἐδίωκεν:** i.e., having turned the horses as described above, Antilochos begins (imperf. ἐδίωκεν) his pursuit. For παρακλίνω in this sense, see *Od.* 20.301, *WD* 262 (both transitive): ἵππους should be understood from the previous clause rather than reading the verb as intransitive (which may have led to the variant παρακλινθείς: Σ A 424). The minority reading παρεκκλίνας (also Eustathios 1303.11 = IV.759.2 Van der Valk) presumably sought to stress the heavy scansion of the second syllable and cancel the possibility of Attic correption. Though that phenomenon is evinced in Homer (Intro. § 3.2.v; also 394–7n.), this verb does not recur before the late fifth century.

425 Notably ABAB balanced, with two names beginning with α followed by ε-assonant past-tense verbs, the repeated δ sounds in the first colon underlining Menelaos' reaction.   **ἔδδεισε:** well supported in the MSS (including Π 13) over ἔδεισε, which is often favoured by modern editors for

the same reasons as ὑποδ(δ)είσαντες above (417–18ªn.).   ἐγεγώνει 'he
shouted loudly': γεγών- has no present stem, and the pluperfect serves as
a simple past tense (Hackstein 2002: 187–93).

426–8 The first of three, brief and urgent, speeches (439–41, 443–5:
see 438–41, 442–7nn.); Menelaos reflects his fear with short, jarring
phrases and little run-over. Line 427 recalls the formula at 416 (see
415–16n.), and so explicitly draws attention to the underhandedness
connoted.   ἀφραδέως ἱππάζεαι: the adverb recalls Nestor's depiction of the bad driver who allows his horses all over the place (320–1:
319–25n.). Menelaos thinks Antilochos is this driver, but the audience
knows otherwise. ἱππάζομαι is used here of the chariot ('you drive your
horse-team'), but later of horse riding alone (e.g. Hdt. 4.114, Ar. *Clouds*
15).   εὐρυτέρηι παρελάσσεις 'by a broader (route) you will drive past':
this is the best-attested reading, followed by optative παρελάσσαις 'may you
drive past', but West opts for the very neat εὐρυτέρη παρελάσσαι 'broader
to drive past' in Σ bT and some good MSS.   μή ... δηλήσεαι: punctuated as an independent prohibition 'do not harm', with sense-pauses after
426 and 427 (see e.g. 5.487, *Od.* 5.415, 19.11: Willmott 2007: 95, 101),
though it could also be a dependent final clause after ἀλλ' ἀνεχ' ἵππους
(426: 426–8n.), parenthesising 427 as with West.   κύρσας 'collid-
ing': nom. sing. aor. act. ppl. of κύρω 'I meet', 'touch upon', with ἅρματι
probably object rather than instrument (as κακῶι ... κύρεται 24.530: *LfrgE*
s. κύρω B1, 1597).

429–30 ἔτι καὶ πολὺ μᾶλλον: Antilochos' reaction is directly linked by
the poet with Menelaos' call to prudence (385–7n.).   κέντρωι: used
interchangeably for a variety of such implements (μάστιξ, ἱμάς, or ἱμάσθλη):
336ᵇ–7n., also 386–7.   ὡς οὐκ ἀΐοντι ἐοικώς 'as like to one not hearing' = 'as though he did not hear': comparative ὡς with the circumstantial
participle is rare (cf. *Od.* 16.21 ὡς ἐκ θανάτοιο φυγόντα) and stresses the
pretence involved (*contra* Dickie 1984: 12), since it is slightly tautologous
with ἐοικώς (i.e. almost a conflation of ὡς οὐκ ἀΐων and οὐκ ἀΐοντι ἐοικώς:
GH II § 473). For the more idiomatic participle alone after ἔοικα, see 379–
81n. (ἐπιβησομένοισιν εἴκτην).

431–3 Unusually, the narrative continues in the simile to convey the
moment of overtaking, which is not directly described (Edwards 27–8).
The athletic theme thus almost collapses tenor and vehicle, like the racing
image at 517–23 below, but unlike the same general theme at 22.162–4
(though war and athletics make a natural binary; Visa-Ondarçuhu 1999:
50–2). The active youth evokes Antilochos as the driving force behind

this situation (Minchin 2001a: 60 and n. 75), and the sudden conclusion typical of the discus (Lovatt 2019: 417). Correlative similes (ὅσσ-/τόσσ- *vel sim.*) describe the distance/extent of an action/object in the main narrative, and athletic themes are found herein also at 15.358–9 and 16.589–92 (both javelin throwers 'testing' themselves): see also below, 845–7. For other 'extent' similes, see e.g. 3.12, 5.770–2, 5.859–63, etc. (Scott 1974: 20–4). The action of 432 is underlined by three consecutive α-assonant words (αἰζηὸς ἀφῆκεν ἀνήρ): cf. 16.590 ἀνὴρ ἀφέηι ... ἀέθλωι. σσ sounds bookend 433, marking the reversal from τόσσον to ὀπίσσω and so the distance between the teams.   **δίσκου οὖρα** 'distance of a discus(-throw)': cf. δίσκουρα below, 522–3n. The discus is a standard throwing-item in games, formal or otherwise (2.774–5 = *Od.* 4.626 = 17.168, *Od.* 8.129, 186–207; Laser 58–62): also below, 826–49n. An unspecified unit of measurement, the neuter noun οὖρον (10.351, 21.405, *Od.* 8.124) is related to Att. ὅρος 'boundary marker'. The precise distance for such a throw was anywhere between 10 and 250 feet (Janko 266), but this is less important than implying a clear interval between the teams, which Menelaos will work hard to lessen (Grethlein and Huitink 2017: 79).   **κατωμαδίοιο** 'from the shoulder': cf. adverb κατωμαδόν 'from (above) the shoulder downwards', describing the motion of the driver's whip (15.352, 23.500). This is not a shot-put, but a twisting or turning of the shoulders (Laser 62) – and further blurs the tenor/vehicle distinction (431–3n.).   **αἰζηός** 'strong': both formation (also αἰζήιος) and derivation are unclear, though it may be related to Lat. *ensis* and originally have meant 'strong/handy with the sword'. Ancient folk-etymology invoked ἀεί + ζῆν, while Σ *WD* 509 suggests that it denotes 'sometimes a man, sometimes a young man' (*LfrgE* s.v., 288–9).   **πειρώμενος ἥβης** 'testing his youthful strength': this action is particularly suited to contests (15.359, 16.590: see above): cf. *Od.* 8.145, 184, 21.135 ~ 180 = 268, 394 (where Odysseus 'tries out' the bow). ἥβη is both strength and youth as its primary period, though the former aspect is more emphasised in Homer than in later authors (*LfrgE* s.v. B2, 887).   **αἵ**: despite the team's mixed sex (and the masculine form οἵ at 446), the feminine reflects Antilochos' gendered focus on Aithē (407–9n.) as the team's most prominent horse (296–300n.). Σ T 433b needlessly corrects to masculine τοί, invoking 295.

434–7 **ἑκών** 'willingly': etymologically a participle, though unrelated to any surviving Greek verb (*EDG* s.v.). *Digamma* is not observed either here or at 585.   **μή πως συγκύρσειαν** recalls μή πως ... κύρσας in Menelaos' call for caution above (428), but the poet augments his character's statement of his fear with two more to make a tricolon (436–7), the crescendo of which is stressed by necessary run-over. συγκύρσειαν balances ἀνστρέψειαν in mood and position, before the shorter run-over verb πέσοιεν (also ending at the 3b caesura) concludes the echo by shifting from the horses to their drivers.   μώνυχες ἵπποι: 6–7n.   ἐϋπλεκέας: 334–6ᵃn.   ἐν κονίῃσι πέσοιεν: his third fear is really of death, since this very common 'fall in the dust' idiom is usually applied to combat victims (4.482, 522–3, 5.585–6, 6.453, 11.425, etc.: see Lather 2020; Purves 2019: 37–53).   ἐπειγόμενοι περὶ νίκης 'eager/making haste for victory': cf. 496, and 639 (ἀγασσάμενοι).

438–41 Menelaos' parting shot to Antilochos looks forward in several ways to their quarrel after the race (below), and is marked by a calm and determined end-stopping (Hohendahl-Zoetelief 1980: 49–51). The angry staccato of short words (566–613n.) in 441 looks forward to him making good on his threat (581–5n.).   τὸν καὶ νεικείων προσέφη ξανθὸς Μενέλαος: the participle is only here found with προσέφη, though the pattern (demonstrative + participle + προσέφη) is very productive in Homeric discourse (Beck 2005: 284–5). For ξανθὸς Μενέλαος, see 293–5n.   οὔ τις σεῖο βροτῶν ὀλοώτερος ἄλλος: Menelaos' anger encompasses also Antilochos' detriment (440) as a result of the labelled behaviour, like all speakers of this 'no other + comparative' rebuking idiom (2.248, 3.365, 8.483, etc.: Kelly 2007a: 347–8, adding Od. 8.137, 9.27–8, 11.623–4, etc.).   ἔρρ᾽ 'begone!': 2nd sing. pres. imp. of ἔρρω, a verb which denotes inauspicious or ill-purposed movement, especially when used in this 'blunt and not at all elevated' manner (Macleod 1982: 135; 8.164, 9.377, 22.498, 24.239, etc.: Kelly 2007a: 190–1).   οὔ σ᾽ ἔτυμόν γε φάμεν πεπνῦσθαι 'not truly did we think you prudent': like ἐτήτυμος related to ἐτεός, the forms of ἔτυμος are elsewhere in epos explicitly contrasted with ψεύδεα (10.534, Od. 19.203 ~ Th. 27), underlining Antilochos' reputational reverse. The past tenses of φημί frequently denote a generally held but mistaken belief, expressed at the moment of that realisation (LfgrE s.v. B 13b and c, 886–97; cf. Kelly 2007a: 351–2 on ἐφάμην). πεπνῦσθαι is perf. mid. infin. of πέπνυμαι, which is probably derived ultimately from πνέω 'I breathe' and means 'I am prudent/clever'; cf. the epithet πεπνυμένος, used of Antilochos by Menelaos during their quarrel (569ᵇ–70n.; Heath 2001: 133–8, esp. 136; Clarke 1999: 84–5). His intellect has already been stressed in Nestor's speech (304ᵇ–5, 306–8nn.), and he will eventually justify his claim to the term (also 586n.).   ἀλλ᾽ οὐ μάν 'but no way (will you …)': determination abounds in this combination (5.895, 17.41, 448; not again until Soph. OC 153), where the speaker asserts an immediate determination to counteract a negative situation (Cuypers 2005: 45–7). For the Aeolic form μάν, see 410n.   οὐδ᾽ ὥς 'not even so': ancient grammarians determined that the adverb is always accented ὥς after οὐδέ and καί (Vendryes § 64 R. 2), though it is a decidedly minority reading here (Π 13) and generally, since the MSS prefer oxytone or barytone forms (as at 516 below).   οἴσῃι 'you will carry off': 2nd sing. fut. indic. mid. of φέρω. In Homer the more common ending is -εαι (< original -εσαι) and so West prints Payne-Knight's correction οἴσε' (for οἴσεαι), but the MSS provide several examples of -ηι which should not be emended away (*GH* I § 57).

442–7 Closing the ring structure of this episode (401–47n.), Menelaos encourages his horses, in another three-line speech, by reminding them of the relative deficiency of Antilochos' team. His judgement in 445 fleshes out Nestor's earlier appraisal of his son's team's worth (309–10n.), while 446–7 = 417–18 (see n.): nothing here justifies their fearful reaction, but formularity overrides any inconcinnity.   ἵπποισιν ἐκέκλετο ~ 402 (see 401–2n.), capping that earlier example to suggest victory for Menelaos' team in turn.   μή ... ἐρύκεσθον μηδ' ἔστατον 'do not hold yourselves back and do not stand (still)': 2nd pers. dual imperatives, ἐρύκεσθον pres. mid., ἔστατον perf. act. (implying a present state).   ἀχνυμένω κῆρ: 165n. Menelaos imagines his team is as annoyed as he.   φθήσονται ... πόδες καὶ γοῦνα καμόντα '(their) feet and knees will weary sooner (than yours)': the circumstantial participle with φθάνω expresses the primary idea, the finite verb the 'accessory' or even adverbial notion of anticipation (*GH* II § 475). φθήσονται takes its number from πόδες, while the complementary participle καμόντα agrees with γοῦνα. This is less unusual than it looks, since in Homer neuter plural nouns may take plural finite verbs (15–16n.). Like δόρυ, γόνυ has two declension systems in the oblique cases in epos: (i) gen. sing. γουνός, nom. pl. γοῦνα, dat. pl. γούνεσσι; and (ii) gen. sing. γούνατος, nom. pl. γούνατα, dat. pl. γούνασι. The lengthening of γουν- is metrically useful, but reflects an original ϝϝ-; cf. δουρός/δούρατος, δοῦρα/δούρατα (*GH* I § 91).   ἤ: 382–4n. The case for retention is even stronger here, since the princeps frequently permits hiatus (*GM* 39).   ἀτέμβονται: not again after Homer until Apollonios, this verb is more often found in the middle – in the sense 'to be/feel cheated of' (11.705 ~ *Od.* 9.42 = 549) and hence, as here, 'to lack' (23.834) – than it is in the active (*Od.* 2.90, etc.). Nonetheless, the connotation of cheating may be retained, viz. an ironic comment on the cheating team itself being cheated of its youth.   τάχα δέ σφισιν ἄγχι γένοντο: probably an underrepresented formula (8.117; cf. *Od.* 18.17) for combat after which the aggressor suffers a reversal. ἄγχι may be either pre- or postpositional with the genitive or adverbial and accompanying a dative, as here (*LfrgE* s. ἄγχι B1d, 2; for the blurring of these categories, cf. 8.117 Ἕκτορος ἄγχι γένοντο).

448–99 The first quarrel of the games, between Idomeneus and the lesser Aias. The poet suddenly turns the narrative away from Menelaos and Antilochos, thus delaying its resolution (Scodel 2021: 60), and directs us back to the struggle between Diomedes and Eumelos, where he had left them at 400: Idomeneus sees the horses of the former in the lead and notes that he cannot spy Eumelos' chariot anywhere; Aias immediately takes offence, Idomeneus suggests arbitration by Agamemnon, and Achilleus smooths over the trouble. This is the first test of the latter's abilities as ἀγωνοθέτης: certainly he is 'soothing and resolving public strife' (Taplin 1992: 253) in 'a remarkable reversal' (Richardson 220) from his previous behaviour, but he only does so here right after Agamemnon is invoked as a source of authority. The older man (450–5n.) is calm and reasonable throughout, Aias (473n.) troublesome and vindictive (Cairns 1993: 98). The internal audience's investment in the action is paralleled on the Sophilos *dinos* (262–652n.; Fig. 3) where, seating or standing on the tiered platform, several figures point (excitedly?) at the oncoming chariot (Laser 83–5; Moore 2016: 188–9, figs 2–4). That crowds at these events sometimes behaved badly is a commonplace in the scholia (e.g. Σ bT 491, T 497, etc.), and it is downplaying the potential of this scene too much to say that these are just 'quarrelling fans, not contestants' (Parks 1990: 90; cf. Lohmann 1992: 300–1; Minchin 2001a: 61–2).

448–9ª ~ 495–6ª (see 495–8n.); 449 ~ 372. The scene-change comprises, as typically, an individual or group looking on another involved in an action (cf. 4.1–4, 24.23, etc.: Griffin 1980: 179–204 on divine audiences; Richardson 1990: 111–13). The raising of that action to a finite verb instead of a participle or a demonstrative signalling the preceding narrative focalises the race from the internal audience's perspective and begins the transition (ἐπέτοντο κονίοντες πεδίοιο: 371ᵇ–2n.).   ἐν ἀγῶνι καθήμενοι: ἀγών is both process and place (257ᵇ–8n.). Transitions often deploy the image of the sitting group (καθήμενοι *vel sim.* 4.1, 7.443–4, 24.161, etc.).   εἰσορόωντο: 3rd pl. imperf. mid. indic., by diectasis from -ορῶντο < -οράοντο.

450–5 Idomeneus is the first to speak. The son of Deucalion (13.451–2), this Cretan leader (2.645–52) is slightly older than most of the other fighters at Troy (13.361; cf. 476–7 below), but still a formidable warrior with an *aristeia* of his own (13.241–515; Camerotto 2010; Kanavou 2015: 50–3; Erny 2020: esp. 206–8). Note the doublet ἐφράσαθ' ἵππους/φράσσατο ... ἵππον (453), each expression introducing a further description of the race (451–3, 453–5), the first focusing on a driver (452n.) and the second one of the horses (454–5n.). Idomeneus' priority is carefully justified by his position and elevation (451n.); Σ bT suggests that he is concerned for Meriones' fortunes (as, e.g., Diomedes for Euryalos at 23.681–4): 112–13n.

450–1 Κρητῶν ἀγός: only applied to Idomeneus in Homer (cf. *HAp.* 463, 525) and usually in the verse τὸν δ᾽ αὖτ᾽ Ἰδομενεὺς Κρητῶν ἀγὸς ἀντίον ηὔδα (4.265 etc.), with the term ἀγός 'leader' derived from ἄγω and usually found with preceding genitive ethnonym (mostly Cretans and Lycians): see also 482 below.   **περιωπῆι:** literally a 'look around' (περί + ὤψ): cf. 14.8, *Od.* 10.146. Perhaps this is one of the raised tumuli on the plain (45–7n.; cf. ὑπέρτατος) rather than 'a cliff or ship's prow' (Σ D 14.8), but the momentary convenience is a sufficient explanation.

452–3 Necessary run-over of ἔγνω and chiastic juxtaposition with φράσσατο reinforce Idomeneus' intellectual process, but it is unclear just whom he sees, and whose horse he identifies.   **τοῖο δ᾽ ἄνευθεν ἐόντος ὁμοκλητῆρος:** the most natural referent for this is Menelaos, whose ὁμοκλή is still fresh in the mind (446); the horse described in 454–5 would then be 'his own Podargos' (295). But the subject of Idomeneus' subsequent revelation is Diomedes (identified as the referent by Eustathios 1303.7–10 = IV.762.6–11 Van der Valk), so that the horse in question would be one of Aineias' unnamed male pair (291–2).   **προύχοντα:** 322–5n.

454–5 The details add to the trustworthiness of Idomeneus' judgement, since horses are rarely denoted by such individual features rather than typical qualities of size, speed, etc. (Delebecque 1951: 144–5). Sophilos uses white, black, and purple to give the horses of the leading chariot distinguishing characteristics (262–652n.), but allusion to the *Iliad* is unlikely.   **τόσον:** effectively strengthens τὸ μὲν ἄλλο while looking forward to ἐν δὲ μετώπωι; cf. similarly 22.322–4 (τοῦ δὲ καὶ ἄλλο τόσον μὲν ἔχε χρόα χάλκεα τεύχεα ... φαίνετο δ᾽ etc.). Translate '(it) was all over red-brown, but on its forehead ...' The unusual idiom causes the variant δέμας (Ap. Soph. s. φοῖνιξ, 164.29 Bekker) already endorsed by Apollonios, *Arg.* 4.1645 (τὸ μὲν ἄλλο δέμας: Rengakos 1993: 136–7).   **φοῖνιξ:** the noun is used as an adjective only here in Homer (the usual epic form is φοινικόεις), and denotes a dark, reddish colour frequently linked with status objects (4.141, 6.219 ~ 7.305, 15.538; Blum 1998: 32–3).   **σῆμα τέτυκτο:** elsewhere with perfect τέτυκται (22.30, *Od.* 23.1), formular integrity favours this reading over the better-attested σῆμ᾽ ἐτέτυκτο, which could have been influenced by the surrounding ε-assonant syllables.   **μήνη** 'full moon': the round shape of the σῆμα is the most immediate comparison, as at 19.374 (ἠΰτε μήνης) describing the flash of

Achilleus' shield (the only other use of the word in Homer), but visibility (cf. ἀριπρεπέα 453) and colour – conveyed by λευκόν bookending the verse – are also implied. The more common term for the moon is σελήνη, frequently found in similes (8.555, 17.367, *Od.* 4.45 = 7.84, 24.148; cf. *Il.* 18.484: Scott 1974: 22, 79–81, 120–1).

456–72 The speech is constructed in a four-tier ring:

A¹ injunctions to see, which connect his vision with his audience's (457–8)

B¹ opinion about the state of the race, viz. Diomedes' leadership, with δοκέω (459–60)

C¹ speculation about Eumelos' team (460–1)

D a contrast between his previous and current view (462–4)

C² speculation about Eumelos' team (465–8)

A² injunctions to see, which connect his vision with his audience's (469–70)

B² opinion about the state of the race, viz. Diomedes' leadership, with δοκέω (470–2)

References to the 'Argives' (456, 457 ~ 471) comprise further outer backing to the frame (Lohmann 1970: 29–30). Each second element is notably larger than the first, and the order of B² and A² is reversed so as to end emphatically, and dramatically, with Diomedes (see 473–81n. for Aias' parodic reply).

456 στῆ δ' ὀρθὸς καὶ μῦθον ἐν Ἀργείοισιν ἔειπεν: his words will lead to a contest, of sorts, as this verse always elsewhere introduces competitive events (271–3n.; Bannert 1988: 145–6; cf. Beck 2005: 237–40); cf. 488 below.

457–8 ὦ φίλοι, Ἀργείων ἡγήτορες ἠδὲ μέδοντες: another sign of reasonableness, since this honorific address is used when the speaker is openly cautious about his abilities or advice (2.79, 9.17, 10.533, etc.); cf. esp. 17.248 for Menelaos' acknowledgement of his visual limitation (252–3), and 11.816 (ἆ δειλοὶ Δαναῶν; cf. De Jong 2012: 157; Beck 2005: 225–6).   **οἶος ... ὑμεῖς:** bookending emphasises courtesy and deference, as does adverbial καί 'you too' before the latter (again at 469); cf. the very different, but similarly polite, question from Nestor on hearing the noise of Odysseus and Diomedes returning to the camp (10.533–4).

459–61 The notable οι-assonance (Packard 1974: 249) of 459 signposts the internal ring around the crucial fact – who is 'in front' παροίτεροι – with verbs on either side (for Aias' contradicting cap, cf. 480–1n.).

Anaphoric ἄλλοι and ἄλλος (460) link team and driver (similar alternation between 460–4 and 465–6). Demonstrative αἵ in 460 and relative αἵ in 461 denote Eumelos' horses ('those ones … who were') as the only all-female team in the race (293–5, 377–8nn.).   **που αὐτοῦ** 'somewhere there': looks forward to ἐν πεδίωι (cf. ἀγρῶν *Od.* 4.639–40).   **ἔβλαβεν:** 3rd pl. 2nd aor. pass. indic. of βλάπτω (see 385–7n. for the 1st aor. ἐβλάφθησαν).   **φέρτεραι:** 407–9n.

462–4 περὶ τέρμα βαλούσας: the (rare intransitive) aorist participle (cf. 639) denotes the whole act, 'as they went around the turning-post', but implies that Eumelos was in the lead at its start (465–8n.). This does not contradict 375–6, which does not say Eumelos went into the lead *only* after the turn. Leaf II.504 thinks 462–4 is inconsistent with 465–6 and could be deleted, but this would destroy the speech's careful ring structure, and Idomeneus' subsequent failure of vision is a poetic and dramatic opportunity, reflecting the dust (365–6), the gods' involvement, the distance of the σῆμα (needing a referee there: 358–61n.), and perhaps Idomeneus' modesty (Σ bT 458); cf. his certainty in 482–8.   **οὔ πηι δύναμαι ἰδέειν:** he draws attention to the limits of his knowledge, like all speakers of this idiom (3.236, 5.475, 17.643, 22.47; cf. *Od.* 12.232, with παπταίνοντι in 233), but the poet signals that this absence will require explanation and (if possible: cf. 3.326, 22.47) rectification. Aias' response is therefore even more misplaced, since it seeks to deny the absence rather than explain or fix it. ἰδέειν is aor. act. infin. of εἶδον, the verb having no present system (in Homer and later Greek this role is played by ὁράω); for -έειν, see 146–8n.   **ἄμ** = ἀνά with apocope and assimilation of -ν before πεδίον (cf. 5.87, 96, 6.71, etc.: 250–4n.).   **παπταίνετον:** 3rd dual pres. act. indic. of παπταίνω, which has been uncertainly linked with both πατάσσω and πέτομαι to imply a 'restless gaze' (*EDG* s.v., 1150–1), conveying Idomeneus' concern (Tichy 1983: 339–41; Kelly 2007a: 264–5).   **εἰσορόωντι:** for the diectasis -οω- see 448–9ᵃn.

465–8 This alternate supposition matches both Nestor's predictions about the dangers of the turning-post (465ᵃ ~ 323–4; 465ᵇ–6ᵃ ~ 309, 323ᵃ, 334; 466b ~ 340b–4) and some portions of the actual race (467 ~ 392–7; 468 ~ 433). It is reasonable but inaccurate (462–4n.), as often when characters retell the poet's narrative in a limited, partial, or incorrect manner (Kelly 2018): the audience again compares its own privileged knowledge with the characters' restricted vision. Frame (2009) thinks the story explains Nestor's race against the Molione (638–42n.), but this relies on reading a crash into Nestor's story of that event (306–48n.).   **τὸν ἡνίοχον:** τόν has a weak demonstrative sense, coming very close to being an article (*GH* II § 243), though the alternation from team to charioteer preserves something of its original meaning. **φύγον ἡνία:** 'reins flee' when the charioteer's journey is in vain, even if a following conversation is required to confirm that fact (8.137, 11.128: cf. also 382–4n. for the wider motif). **σχεθέειν** 'control': aor. act. infin. of ἴσχω, a reduplicated present related to ἔχω with more delimited meaning (as, e.g., μίμνω 'withstand' and μένω 'wait': *WHS* 262–70; Giannakis 1997: 126–212); for -έειν, see 146–8n. **οὐκ ἐτύχησεν ἑλίξας:** 'he did not succeed rounding (*sc.* the bend)'. **ἐκπεσέειν:** 146–8n. **ἐξηρώησαν ~ ἠρώησαν** (433). **ἐπεὶ μένος ἔλλαβε θυμόν:** for μένος see 175–7n., and for θυμός 62–4n. The phrase denotes the momentum carrying them away from the chariot, i.e. 'since might seized their hearts' i.e. so as to prevent control. ἔλλαβε is 3rd sing. aor. act. indic. of λαμβάνω, -λλ- reflecting an original *sl- and more common in Homer than augmented forms with -λ- (*GH* I § 69; Wathelet 1970: 184–90); Intro. § 3.2.vii.b; cf. 417–18ªn. on ὑποδδείσαντες.

469–70ª The invitation to the others' opinions – now an imperative rather than a question – is emphasised by another adverbial καί (457–8n.), and necessary run-over of διαγιγνώσκω underlines his own cognitive limitations. **ἴδεσθε καὶ ὔμμες** 'but now you *too* look': for the emphatic syntax, see 403–4n. **ἀνασταδόν:** formed with the adverbial suffix -δόν (like ἀμφαδόν, αὐτοσχεδόν, etc.), but used only elsewhere at 9.371, where the Greek leaders stand to receive the embassy on its return, and not again in ancient Greek literature.

470ᵇ–2 The conclusion is stressed by the reversal of the ring sequence, but it also postpones revealing Diomedes until the very end, heaping up honorific details beforehand – lineage, status, genealogy, typical epithet, and then finally his name, in 'artful titillation' (Grethlein and Huitink 2017: 80). The same technique is used, parodically, in Aias' reply (480–1: see n.). **Αἰτωλὸς γενεήν:** though Diomedes was himself born in, and king of, Argos (2.559–68), his grandfather Oineus was king of Calydon, a city in Aitolia, and his father Tydeus relocated to Argos and died in Thebes (14.115–20). The ethnonym is otherwise restricted to Meleagros and Thoas in the *Iliad*, and to an anonymous stranger who deceives Penelope (*Od.* 14.379), and the reference again evokes the Tydeus–Diomedes theme (Andersen 1978: 143): see 382–4, 632–3nn. **ἀνάσσει:** much better attested than, and preferable to, the variant reading ἀνάσσειν, since Homer's paratactic style often raises subordinate to principal clauses (385–7n.). **Τυδέος ἱπποδάμου υἱός:** a unique expression, splitting the common formula Τυδέος υἱός (382–4n.) and interposing ἱπποδάμοιο, normally found at the verse-end; cf. esp. ὤ μοι

Τυδέος υἱὲ δαΐφρονος ἱπποδάμοιο (4.370). Familiarity with the usual -οιο ending leads to the not unmetrical variant ἱπποδάμοιο (for the light scansion of υἱ-, cf. 1.489, 16.21, etc.).   κρατερὸς Διομήδης: 290–2n.

473–81 Aias does not even wait for Idomeneus' speech to close (as e.g. with 16.626 ὣς φάτο, τὸν δ᾽ ἐνένιπε) before replying. The ring here centres upon [C] slighting Idomeneus' age (476–7), with the outer sections [A] depicting Idomeneus as a babbler (474, 478–9) and [B] mentioning Eumelos' horses (474–5, 480–1). Again the elements in the second portion of the ring are larger, and again the order of [B²] and [A²] are reversed, this time so that Aias can end with Eumelos, as Idomeneus had with Diomedes. Capping and parody are deployed throughout.

473 τὸν δ᾽ αἰσχρῶς ἐνένιπεν 'and he abused him with shameful purpose' ~ Od. 18.321, where Melantho attacks Odysseus. ἐνίπτω (of which ἐνένιπεν is 3rd sing. redupl. aor. ind. act.) frequently introduces quarrels, and, while αἰσχρῶς denotes Aias' intention, the speech also reflects poorly on its speaker (Cairns 1993: 58–9; Beck 2005: 238 and n. 19).   'Οϊλῆος ταχὺς Αἴας: this formula deploys the genitive of his father's name to distinguish the 'Locrian' or 'lesser' Aias from the Telamonian (708–9n.) in a type of patronymic expression not frequently used in epos; perhaps it was developed from 'Οϊλῆος ταχὺς υἱός (13.701, 14.530) for those cases when Aias was not named in the first half of the verse. Zenodotos sometimes read the sequence ΟΙΛ as ὁ 'Ἰλ-, and 'Ἰλεύς is attested at an early stage in ps.-Hesiod and Stesichoros, but 'Οϊλεύς etc. is the correct Homeric form (Janko 51; cf. Nickau 1977: 36–42): 758–9n. The son is an ambivalent character, a powerful warrior, known for speedy pursuit (14.520–2) and conventionally paired with the other Aias in the dual form Αἴαντε (sometimes in the plural), which is also used for Telamonian Aias and his half-brother Teucros (Nappi 2002; cf. Kanavou 2015: 37–44; generally Kramer-Hajos 2012: 92–7). His rape of Cassandra at Athene's altar during the sack of Troy brings the goddess' wrath down on the Greeks (Od. 4.502, Alc. fr. 298 V; Il. pers. arg. 15–18 B), and he is killed by Poseidon after another poorly judged speech (Od. 4.499–511; Clay 1983: 46–52; S. West 1988: 116–17). The intervention here is characteristically ill-mannered, and he will compete unsuccessfully in the running race.

474–5 The address and opening question parody Idomeneus' more polite beginning, with no honorific expression for the addressee, and an abusive 2nd person verb substituted for the cautious and inclusive framing of 458. Aias denies that any observation is possible, given the horses' distance. The position and gender of demonstrative αἱ mirrors

Idomeneus' invocation of Eumelos' team (460; cf. 480–1 below), while scorn is effectively underlined by insistent π sounds in 475.   τί πάρος λαβρεύεαι; 'Why are you always blustering?': the present indicative is used with πάρος to refer to habitual action (1.553, 12.347, 15.257, etc.: *GH* II § 282). λαβρεύομαι is related to λάβρος 'furious', 'swift', restricted to wind and weather in Homer (2.148, 15.625, 21.271, etc.) but later used of men (e.g. Theogn. 634 W²; Zanker 2019: 148); the emphatic return to this form in 478 and then to a derived compound in 479 (λαβραγόρην) is revealingly excessive.   πολέος πεδίοιο 'through the great plain': for the sense of the genitive, see 363–4ᵃn. The older gen. sing. masc. and neut. of πολύς (and the only form in Homer: later at 521 and 562), πολέος is later replaced by the o-declension form πολλοῦ.

476–7 Anaphora of οὔτε followed by superlatives marks out this central section, as does its flagrant overturning of the usual Iliadic respect for greater age (Preisshofen 1977: 23–4): see 450–5n. for Idomeneus' background, and 587–8, 621–3, 643–5, 789–91ᵃnn. on age as a theme in Homer.   τοσοῦτον 'by so much': strengthening νεώτατος, i.e. 'by a long way the youngest'.   ὄσσε: for dual with a plural verb, cf. 329–30n.

478–9 Rank 1951: 35 relates αἰεί to an intentional play on Aias' name, but his other examples are more persuasive (i.e. the several in 16.102–9).   οὐδέ τί σε χρή: this corrective reproof underlines Aias' erroneous focus on bluster as characteristic of Idomeneus, since such rebukes are normally justified and persuasive (7.109, 9.496, 613, etc.; Martin 1989: 198–200; Andrade forthcoming).   πάρα: anastrophe indicates that παρέασι (viz. πάρεισι) is omitted, 'for there are others at hand better (*sc.* to speak)' (1.174, 3.440, 5.603, etc.; *HG* 164–5, 167). Presumably he means himself. Aristarchos athetised 479 because it was not necessary after 478, but also commented that 'it is not the deed of the better sort (ἀμεινόνων) to bluster', as though 479ᵇ was to be completed by λαβρεύεσθαι (Σ A 479a; cf. T 478b; Lührs 1992: 36–7; Schironi 2018: 209 n. 218).

480–1 ἵπποι δ' αὐταὶ ἔασι παροίτεραι, αἳ τὸ πάρος περ 'And the same horses are in front, the ones who were previously'. For αὐταί in this sense without an article, see e.g. 5.396, 12.225. Again αἵ recalls Idomeneus' speech (cf. 460), as does παροίτεραι (cf. 459), and Aias matches the climactic revelation of Diomedes (470–2) with his own, emphatically run-over, Εὐμήλου.   ἔασι: 311–12n.   αἳ τὸ πάρος περ: a punning echo of παροίτεραι, this forceful assertion denotes a past practice or custom whose continuity is at stake (5.806, 7.370, 10.309, etc.). The demonstrative τό and particle περ (77–9n.) place great stress on πάρος.   εὔληρα 'reins': hapax in Homer and very rare in later Greek, but possibly related to Lat. *lora* and probably of pre-Greek origin (*EDG* s.v.); its choice here may be a pun on Εὐμήλου.   βέβηκεν: perf. act. indic. of βαίνω, expressing continuity between the past act and its present state, i.e. 'he mounted *and* he is still there' (*GH* II § 294).

482 τὸν δὲ χολωσάμενος Κρητῶν ἀγὸς ἀντίον ηὔδα: Aias' abuse has hit home, since the troubled reaction is typical of those whose authority is challenged by (someone they see as) an upstart, and demands a response (3.413, 21.579, 24.55, *Od.* 18.25; Walsh 2005: 141–7, esp. 143–4). Something will be lacking in that reaction, however, for ἀντίον ηὔδα is reserved for characters with no nominative noun–epithet formula after the median caesurae – Telemachos, Antilochos, Antenor, etc. – when they try, generally unsuccessfully, to justify themselves (Kelly 2007a: 217–20). ἀντίον is adverbial from ἀντί and means 'opposite, over against' (*EDG* s.v.), helping the mood of self-exculpation. The speech follows a typical sequence for a rebuke, with abusive address (483) followed by criticism and a general description of the problem (483–4), and a concluding call to action (485–7; Martin 1989: 65–77; Minchin 2002: 74–82 = 2007: 27–38; Lentini 2013 more generally).

483–4 Αἶαν, νεῖκος ἄριστε, κακοφραδές: νεῖκος is acc. of respect ('in quarrel') and is coupled with the asyndetic oxymoron ἄριστε, κακοφραδές (the latter punctuated as vocative, rather than neut. acc. sing. with νεῖκος). Abuse often begins with a series of unflattering adjectives (cf. 1.225, 3.39 = 13.769, 13.824, etc), in which the regular appearance of εἶδος ἄριστε makes this an easy alteration of an abusive trope (Kelly 2007a: 245–6): West prints the majority's νείκει, pointing to other cases where a dative qualifies a superlative (9.56, 15.108, etc.), but none are as close to this idiom; it may have been designed to disambiguate κακοφραδές.   ἄλλα τε πάντα | δεύεαι Ἀργείων: 'coordinating' τε introduces a slight anacolouthon, as though the opening abuse had a finite verb (Ruijgh 1971: 830–1). δεύομαι 'I am inferior to' takes an ablatival genitive here (cf. *Od.* 1.254, 4.264: also *GH* II § 80), but usually the genitive refers to the quality, person, or thing lacking (2.128, 709, 5.202, 17.142, etc.).   ὅτι τοι νόος ἐστὶν ἀπηνής: a damning indictment, designed to get a reaction (16.35, *Od.* 18.381). Applied to people and their words in epos, ἀπηνής 'harsh' is often assumed (as πρηνής, προσηνής) to be linked with *ἦνος 'face', but its etymology is unclear (*EDG* s.v.). Penelope damns the character, fortune,

and reputation of an ἀπηνής (*Od.* 19.329–31) next to an ἀμύμων (332–4).   •
The νόος 'mind' is (largely) the intellectual drive in the Homeric mental
apparatus, the 'conclusion of the thinking process' which artciulates a
drive towards action (Clarke 1999: 120–6; Stella 2021: 95–129).

485–7 δεῦρό νυν 'here, then': δεῦρο echoes δεύεαι, and νῦν without accent
is enclitic, as very rarely in Homer (here and 10.105), to mean 'then,
now' esp. in commands; hence Photius' reading εἰ δ' ἄγε νῦν (cf. Ruijgh
1967: 57–67, esp. 64–7).   ἢ τρίποδος περιδώμεθον ἠὲ λέβητος 'let
us make a wager for a tripod or a cauldron': genitives of value (*GH* II
§§ 57–8), after 1st dual aor. subj. mid. of περιδίδωμι, unique in Homer
and rare later (an Atticism according to Wackernagel 1916: 55) and *lectio difficilior* to the variant -μεθα ἠέ (*GH* I § 229).   ἴστορα: derived
from the stem ϝιδ- 'see, know', this word means 'adjudicator' or 'witness'
(18.501), and its adjective 'skilled' or 'wise' (*WD* 792–3; cf. *HW* 277–9).
Though ἴστορα is found in two medieval MSS, and the aspiration 'is probably not original' (*EDG* s.v.), ἴστορα is much better attested.   θείομεν
ἄμφω: for θείομεν, cf. 243–4n.; for the dual with a plural verb, cf. 329–30n.
The precise specification of number here feels pointed (cf. 1.363, 7.299,
16.19, and 23.731 below).   ὁππότεραι πρόσθ' ἵπποι: sc. 'as to which
…' The indirect question is emphasised with aspiration and repetition of
π, and ἵπποι takes the central place of the contested παροίτεροι/-αι in the
previous speeches (459, 480): Idomeneus recognises Aias' capping, and
so shifts his ground. But he also refers directly to that prior speech, with
the feminine ending in ὁππότεραι (better attested than the masculine):
cf. esp. 480 above.   ἵνα γνώῃς: one of the few occasions when this
'so you know' idiom does not eventuate as foreseen (Kelly 2007a: 80–4);
the poet encourages an expectation that the episode will go further, and
Achilleus will cap this particular idiom in his own speech (495–8n.). The
optative γνοίης is better attested, but Idomeneus' threat requires the more
proximate mood.

488–9 488 = 754 (start of the running race), adding to the sense that this
exchange is a form of public competition analogous to the events themselves (456n.), and one which looks like getting as ugly as the confrontation
between Achilleus and Agamemnon in Book 1.   Ὀϊλῆος ταχὺς Αἴας:
473n.   χωόμενος: 385–7n. (Walsh 2005: 158 n. 7).   χαλεποῖσιν
ἀμείψασθαι ἐπέεσσιν: the situation is close to boiling point, since this formula denotes quarrels with definite outcomes (492 below, *Od.* 3.148;
Martin 1989: 20–2). It is capped by Achilleus. The infinitive has a result/
final meaning after ὤρνυτο '(rose …) to reply with harsh words'. -αι is not
correpted before (ϝ)ἐπέεσσιν.

490–1 Another contrafactual (154–5n.), this time summarising the inevitable result of the rising emotions in the preceding exchange. Achilleus is the natural intercessor in this context (491), but it is important that he waits until Agamemnon's introduction as a rival authority figure (486 above). He will intercede again like this during the wrestling (491 ~ 734: see 733–4n.), once more in a slightly cack-handed manner.

492–8 Minchin 2007: 35–6 analyses the speech as a typical rebuke with a four-part structure (482n.) – address (493), problem (492–3), action viewed from a broader perspective (494), and proposal (495–8) – but the problem statement is as much of an instruction as the proposal itself.

492–3 μηκέτι νῦν: the intervention will be decisive, since exhortations with this beginning always halt a preceding state of affairs and inaugurate a new one (2.435, 20.354, 24.560, etc.).   **χαλεποῖσιν ἀμείβεσθον ἐπέεσσιν:** the repetition (488–9n.) caps and closes off the possibility of actual conflict. ἀμείβεσθον is 2nd dual pres. mid. imp.   **ἐπέεσσιν, | Αἴαν Ἰδομενεῦ τε, κακοῖς:** the run-over hyperbaton of κακοῖς allows negative words to surround and reflect on both addressees. Αἴαν is unusually scanned as two heavy syllables, presumably because it often appears in this position before a word beginning with a consonant (but cf. 7.288, 13.68, 824). 493 is thus a so-called 'thin line' (στίχος λαγαρός), where a light syllable has been used in place of a heavy one, but we should not doubt its authenticity (*GH* I § 45b).   **ἐπεὶ οὐδὲ ἔοικεν:** Achilleus shuts down the quarrel, for such claims are made by speakers faced with untenable situations where their honour is directly affected, and which are thereafter reversed (1.119, *Od.* 5.212, 21.319; cf. 12.212: Dalfen 1984 analyses it more in terms of the link between one's status and deserts).

494 ~ *Od.* 6.286, where Nausicaa admits she would fault another woman consorting openly with an unknown male.   **νεμεσᾶτον:** 2nd dual pres. act. indic. of νεμεσάω, the present tense indicating (as in the *Odyssey* passage) a general, fixed attitude: 'you always find fault with another', etc. νέμεσις is a powerful social imperative in epos, a firmly held negative judgement to be avoided at all costs (Cairns 1993: 98, 76 n. 107; Yamagata 1994: 149–56).   **ὅτις τοιαῦτά γε ῥέζοι:** the optative distances the eventuality (*GH* II § 365), a conception somewhat ironic for all speakers of this phrase, since their connection with the condemned behaviour is not quite so remote as they would wish (*Od.* 1.47, 6.286, 22.315); in this case, indeed, 'Achilles *had* acted so!' (Kitchell 1998: 166). The predictable variant ῥέζῃ fails to recognise the rhetoric, and opts for more regular sequence.

495–8 495–6ᵃ ~ 448–9ᵃ: Achilleus bids them return to their state at the scene's start. Necessary run-over of ἐλεύσονται in 497 underlines the speech's essential point, spelt out in τότε δέ.   **ἐπειγόμενοι περὶ νίκης:** 434–7n.   **γνώσεσθε ἕκαστος:** 6–7n.   **ἵππους Ἀργείων:** may intimate Diomedes' team as originally described from Idomeneus' perspective (esp. 471; cf. 456–72n.), while the masculine οἵ for both first- and second-place teams points more towards neutrality.

499–513 Diomedes comes in first (499–510), and Sthenelos claims the prize (511–13). The arrival recalls the first leg of the race (362–72n.), being structured in a very similar ring using the same images, though this time the second element in each case is the more detailed: [A] driver and his horses (499–501, 506–10), [B] dust (502, 504–5), [C] chariot (503). This is a lengthy version of the usual chariot-journey arrival, and unharnessing is delayed until 513 (Kelly 2007a: 92–6).

499–502 **μάλα σχεδόν:** though not in Diomedes' individual case (536–8n.), there is a hint of trouble to come, since this type of proximity tends to be directly or indirectly aggressive (5.607, 9.304, 11.116, etc.).   **μάστι … κατωμαδόν** ~ 362. The theme will be reversed at 510 below. μάστι is an Ionic form for the more common μάστιγι, which is read here by many MSS (as μάστῑγι, against its universal Homeric scansion); cf. *Od.* 15.182 (μάστιν) and μάστιγας above (362).   **ὑψόσ’ ἀειρέσθην** ~ ἀειρομένη (366), though there of the dust raised by the horses (364ᵇ–7n.).   **πρήσσοντε** ~ διέπρησσον (364): 499–513n.   **ῥαθάμιγγες ἔβαλλον:** more ominous, since this phrase usually occurs when horses are hurling gore upon other parts of the chariot: 11.536ᵇ (Hector) = 20.501ᵇ (Achilleus) (11.534–7ᵃ = 20.499–502ᵃ); cf. Hes. *Th.* 183 (bloody drops from Ouranos' genitalia). For the dust theme generally, see 364ᵇ–7n.

503–4 These lines are quoted in Plutarch's *Moralia* 747e as an example of poetically mimetic arrangements of words, alongside two other passages describing motion (Eur. fr. 985 Kannicht, Pind. *Ol.* 1.20); Richardson 226 suggests that dactylic rhythm is the source of the mimesis, expressing the swiftness of the movements denoted (though successive light syllables are prominent in the Euripides fragment, and may lead to Plutarch's misquotation of παρεχόμενον for παρέχων in the Pindar).   **ἅρματα … χρυσῶι πεπυκασμένα κασσιτέρωι τε:** πυκάζω is used of chariots only elsewhere at 2.777 (εὖ πεπυκασμένα), where 'covered' refers to storage (cf. 14.289, *Od.* 22.488; Plath 1994: 176–80, esp. 179f.; Cairns 2016: 34 n. 28), but here it must refer to gold and tin facings/panels (cf. παμφανόωντος 509). They are not envisaged as being too heavy for relatively light vehicles like the heroic chariot, which are elsewhere described as 'decorated with bronze' (ποικίλα χαλκῶι 4.226, 10.322, 393; Plath 1994: 189–91), since these materials are linked with other metals on Agamemnon's breastplate (11.25), in the general mixture for Achilleus' new equipment (18.474–5), and each has several layers on his shield (20.271–2; for non-metallic facings and decorations on chariots, cf. Crouwel 1981: 66, 69, 70; 1992: 33, 70).   ἅρματα … ἐπέτρεχον: for the plural noun, see 15–16n. The plural here underlines the chariot's constituent elements, reflecting the description (340ᵇ–1n.).   ἵπποις ὠκυπόδεσσιν: 301–4ᵃn.

504ᵇ–6 'Nor was there much | trace at all of the chariot's running tyres behind | in the fine dust'. However hyperbolic the image, given the metal, Diomedes' triumph is clear in that does not leave a great trace in the 'fine' dust (λεπτός only here in epos with κονίη), falling in which is usually a sign of failure or death (434–7n.).   γίνετ': 240–2n.   ἐπισσώτρων: literally 'on the wheel rim' (σῶτρον) = 'tyre', referring to the metal band on the outside (Plath 1994: 332–5).   ἁρματροχιή: lit. 'chariot-running', denoting its physical imprint on the ground, the term etymologises the unique image of the moving chariot (ἅρματα … ἐπέτρεχον); that this was minimal even ἐν λεπτῆι κονίηι underlines the team's speed despite the vehicle's weight.   τὼ δὲ σπεύδοντε πετέσθην: see 379–81n. δὲ σπεύδοντε is chosen over δ' οὐκ ἀέκοντε because the team is at its journey's end (Hutchinson 2020: 52 thinks instead it is an intensified version).

507–8 Suddenly it is all over, the preceding description now resolved in Diomedes' abrupt and punctual halt (στῆ), but still in tension with the race's consequences, since the idiom μέσωι ἐν ἀγῶνι 'in the midst of the contest (area)' elsewhere refers to the start (23.685, 710, *Od.* 24.86).   ἀνεκήκιεν: 3rd sing. imperf. act. indic. of ἀνακηκίω 'well up', 'drip forth', used of human blood (7.262) or animal sweat (13.705ᵇ = 507ᵇ); cf. *Od.* 5.455. Horses usually sweat in battle, as heroes and gods do (Purves 2019: 48, 58–9), in another nod to their anthropomorphisation in the *Iliad* (2.390, 8.543 = *Od.* 4.39, 11.597–8, *Epigonoi* fr. dub. 6.1–2 B (Delebecque 1951: 54; Platte 2017: 59–71).

509 = 8.320, where Hector attacks Teucros.   παμφανόωντος: cf. 503–4n. There is no securely attested verb παμφανάω from which to form the contract παμφανῶντος > παμφανόωντος by diectasis. παμφανόων is, however, well known as an adjective, and several -αίνω verbs have an -άω form (e.g. ὁρμαίνω/ὁρμάω, ὑφαίνω/ὑφάω) to assist the formation (*WHS* 290–1, 336–41; *GH* I § 160). For this kind of expressive reduplication in the present tense, see 26–7n.

510 A rather precise and unusual detail. The ζυγόν holds the horses to the chariot pole (392–3n.).   οὐδὲ μάτησεν: the unaugmented form is better attested here, unlike the parallel phrase at 16.474. Linked with adv. μάτην 'in vain' and noun ματίη 'stupidity' (*Od.* 10.79), and perhaps from a root suggesting negative thought (*men-; *EDG* s. μάτη), ματάω is used in Homer only in a chariot context, and always with a negative to denote either the charioteer's (16.474) or the horses' (5.233) haste.

511–13 Sthenelos' presence recalls the taking of Aineias' horses (5.259–73, 319–30), and his name suggests a connection with σθένος, recognised here with the pleonastic generic epithet ἴφθιμος (cf. 19.123 for another Sthenelos, father of the similarly powerfully named Eurystheus: von Kamptz 1982: 37, 221). This Sthenelos is one of the three commanders of the Argive contingent (2.559–68) and the son of Capaneus (2.564 etc.), who perished in the first expedition against Thebes. A member of the 'Epigonoi' who did succeed in capturing that city, he rebukes Agamemnon for his false charge against Diomedes' courage (4.403–10), and, after some initial hesitation, he participates well during the latter's *aristeia* in Book 5 (see also 8.114–15, 9.48–9). The satisfying chiasmus (infinitive + objects [καὶ] object + infinitive) in 512–13 encourages us to connect the prizes and reflect briefly on the following tragedy: the unadorned γυναῖκα lacks her earlier description of value (cf. 263), and is not only juxtaposed with τρίποδ' ὠτώεντα (264–5ªn.), but even outranked by the unnamed companions (ἑτάροισιν ὑπερθύμοισι). The distinction between ἄγειν for animates and φέρειν for inanimates (Σ AT 512–13a) notes the ontological difference (Schironi 2018: 130–1, 234–5). The infinitives have the result/final sense (151n.) 'for leading/to lead away' which is common in this 'gave to comrades' idiom (1.347, 5.25–6, 10.269–70, 15.532–3, etc.; cf. also 17.698–9, Hes. fr. 25.22 M–W).   ἔλυεν: the imperfect implies that the action continues alongside Antilochos' arrival (514ff.). Though the required -ῡ- is only paralleled in epos at *Od.* 7.74, Homer can alter the lengths of this verb stem as needed (cf., e.g., λῦτο 21.114, λῦτο 24.1), as with θύω and forms of ἀλλύω (*GH* I §§ 45, 177).

514–33 The rest of the competitors finish, after which the quarrels begin. In the first section (514–27), Menelaos is noticeably the more prominent figure, and this encourages the audience to identify with the frustration he will show. The continuative tenses – imperfect and present indicatives, and subjunctives – highlight the clash with Antilochos' punctual aorist ἤλασεν (514), and the tension is resolved with a contrafactual sentence (526–7).

514–16 τῶι δ' ἄρ' ἐπ': 290–2n.   **Νηλήϊος:** 301–4ᵃn.   **κέρδεσιν,
οὔ τι τάχει γε:** somewhat as imagined in Nestor's instructions (322–5n.),
Antilochos comes in 'through acts of cunning' before Menelaos, despite
his 'lesser' team. The poet is adamant about the manner, even specifying
e contrario the κέρδεα in question, but more reticent about the ethics. The
combination οὔ τι … γε is found in comparisons where γε strengthens
the dispreferred quality (e.g. 9.108 οὔ τι καθ' ἡμέτερόν γε νόον), but this
precise form is only found with 7.142 (δόλωι, οὔ τι κράτεΐ γε), another
slightly underhanded achievement (415–16n.).   **ὥς:** For the accent,
see 438–41n.   **ὠκέας ἵππους:** 293–5n. It is surely pointed, after οὔ τι
τάχει.

517–23 Once more the poet blurs the distinction between simile and
narrative (431–3n.) to create one of the closest parallels in the poem
(Σ bT 517–21 call it a 'most naturally fitting image'; cf. Grethlein and
Huitink 2017: 81–2). The distance evoked is very small indeed, as on
the depictions of chariots in the Bronze, Geometric, and Archaic periods
(Wiesner 1968: 47, 48, 55, 67; Crouwel 1981: pls 66, 74–8; 1992: pls
21–30; Laser 23, 31). For the athletic theme and simile form (ὅσσον …
τόσσον), see 431–3n.

517–18 ~ 22.22–3 (σευάμενος ὥς θ' ἵππος ἀεθλοφόρος σὺν ὄχεσφιν, | ὅς ῥά τε
ῥεῖα θέηισι τιταινόμενος πεδίοιο), from Achilleus' advance on Troy after his
interlude with Apollo. This may help to allude to the only other image
of horses 'dragging' in the poem, the mistreatment of Hector's corpse
(22.464, 24.14–15, 51).   **τ' ἄνακτα:** while *digamma* is very often
observed before ἄναξ, cf. e.g. 2.672, 4.420, 5.546, etc.   **ἕλκηισιν:** 3rd
sing. pres. act. subj., with athematic ending (= ἕλκηι: Intro. § 3.1.2.d.i and
n. 115).   **πεδίοιο:** resumed in 521 to conclude the image; for the
genitive, see 364ᵇ–7n.

519–21 The simile's amplification starts and ends with the horse
(in the genitive case), and necessary run-over in 521 reinforces the
central point of the comparison; τοῦ refers to the horse, ὁ δέ to the
wheel.   **ἐπισσώτρου:** 504ᵇ–6n.   **οὐδέ τι πολλή** = 504 above, also
after a form of τρέχω. The reminiscence underlines the different situation even more clearly.   **μεσσηγύς:** much more common form than
μεσσηγύ, which is deployed where hiatus is not a risk (as with ἀμφί/ἀμφίς,
πολλάκι/πολλάκις, etc.; *GH* I § 40; Reece 2009: 57).   **πολέος πεδίοιο
θέοντος:** *sc.* the horse: cf. 6.506–7 (= 15.263–4), 16.393, 22.22–3 (517–
18n.), etc.; also 474–5n.

522–3 To underline Menelaos' progress, Homer reminds us of Antilochos' earlier manoeuvre to open up a lead (431–3), and the simile used there to denote the original gap (ἐς δίσκουρα ~ δίσκου οὖρα: 431–3n.). The framing λείπετ' ... λέλειπτο reinforces that improvement, while genitive Ἀντιλόχοιο is separative, common with expressions of 'to be behind' (*GH* II § 80; cf. also 483–4n.).   τὰ πρῶτα 'at first': adverbial (1.6, 6.489, 12.420, etc.).

524–5 'but he was right on the verge of catching him, for ...' Juxtaposition of the imperfects κίχανεν and ὀφέλλετο continues the sense of ongoing simultaneity in Menelaos' actions since Antilochos' arrival (514). Aithē's waxing strength is mirrored by the honorific line devoted to her ownership and beauty, which seems quietly to mock Antilochos' gendered slighting (407–9n.).   μένος ἠΰ: the epithet in this formula is from ἐΰς, but the lengthening of the first syllable is unexplained (*GH* I § 117; Wyatt 1969: 158–60). This quality can be predicated of gods instilling strength into horses (17.456, 24.442) or humans (20.80), and it is also a general mortal attribute (24.6; cf. *Od.* 2.271) – but Aithē's efforts are in vain, for common to all these examples is the sense of failure or disappointment in the action itself; for μένος, see 175–7n.   καλλίτριχος: the only time this epithet is used for a single horse, or outside a formula system, in epos (see 530–1n., adding *Od.* 9.336, 469 μῆλα).

526–7 The conditional is contrafactual, though not in the usual form (with apodosis before a negative protasis: 154–5n.) since resolution is impossible; for these two competitors the race is already over. Line 527 ~ 382, the contrafactual denoting Diomedes' imminent overtaking of Eumelos, which in turn introduces Apollo's intervention, but here the poet is more certain that Menelaos would have won (hence the ineptness of Zenodotos' ἤ for οὐδέ).   εἰ δέ κ' ... γένετο: a unique case for Homer: in protases ('if clauses'), κε is generally used with verb forms marking futurity, while the past tenses of the indicative expressing unreality are unaccompanied by a particle (*GH* II § 415). Presumably the unusual form of this contrafactual prompts this migration from the apodosis, and some role may also be played by the use of κε in the protasis of other conditionals (*GH* II § 408). It may be simpler to follow Kampmann's emendation δ' ἔτι καί.   ἀμφήριστον: 382–4n.

528–31 Meriones comes in the penultimate position, and the poet leaves us in no doubt as to the reasons why. Similarly unstressed is his entry into the race (351n.), and his claiming of the prize after it (614–15n.).

528–9 The catalogue style is established by the repetition of λείπετ' (523) and a reference to athletic distance (cf. 523 ἐς δίσκουρα).   **Μηριόνης, θεράπων ἐΰς Ἰδομενῆος:** shortened version (3×, again all in this book) of the usual whole-verse formula Μηριόνης, θεράπων ἀγαπήνορος Ἰδομενῆος (112–13n.); see also 859–60, 886ᵇ–8nn.   **δουρὸς ἐρωήν:** another athletic comparison (see 431–3n.), this time looking forward to the spear-throwing contest in which Meriones will actually win the prize by default (884–97n.). The formula is twice deployed in similes of extent (15.358, 21.251), but the action so described may be either aggressive or defensive (Janko 266): see 431–3n. δουρός is gen. sing. of δόρυ, from the more common of the two series of this noun's forms, the other and rarer being δούρατ- (*WHS* 59); cf. the declension of κάρη (43–4n.) and γόνυ (442–7n.).

530–1 Nestor makes the same charge of Antilochos' team (309–10n.), but here the poet does so in his own voice, adding the judgement about Meriones' driving skills with anaphoric superlatives.   **καλλίτριχες ἵπποι:** this formula is metrically but not prosodically equivalent to the pair ἐριαύχενες/ὑψηχέες ἵπποι: see 26–7, 171–2nn. Their impressive physicality makes an effective contrast with the horses' slowness and the quality of their driver, somewhat like Nireus, 'the most fair of all those who came beneath Troy's walls … but he was weak, and a small host followed him' (2.671–5; Shakeshaft 2019: 3–4).   **ἥκιστος:** the MSS favour this West Ionic (and later standard) form over East Ionic psilotic ἤκιστος (Σ AbT 531; West I.xvi–xvii): cf. 17–18n.   **ἐν ἀγῶνι** 'in the contest': 257ᵇ–8n.

532 πανύστατος 'very last of all': with a παν- prefix functioning as a genitive 'of all' (Thesleff 1954: 141), the word is used again in Antilochos' angry refusal to accept a reordering of the prizes (547) and of Polyphemos' ram (*Od.* 9.452) – all occasions where the position of the labelled figure is noticeably unexpected. The rarity of the term makes it a target for Apollonios' intertextual agonism (*Arg.* 1.1154, 3.268: Cowan 2021).

533 The balance of the line (2× participle + object) combines with asyndeton to emphasise the oddity: the driver, rather than the horses, drags the chariot (ἕλκων: 517–18n.) and drives the team in front of him – simultaneously acting as driver, team, *and* vehicle.   **πρόσσοθεν:** derived from πρόσ(σ)ω 'in front' and the separative suffix -θεν, this absolute hapax means 'in front of him' (cf. πρόσθεν), and underlines the singularity of the image. Zenodotos wanted to read ὠκέας, and some MSS have μώνυχας (i.e.

from 536), but these inoffensive readings would not have been changed for the unicum.

534–41 Achilleus' intervention is poorly judged, and causes the race's second quarrel (540–65n.). In effect, he commits a kind of category error, by turning the second-placed prize into a gift to be disposed entirely at his discretion (Gernet 1948: 178–81, 183–6), and his reasoning is the very one which has helped to cause the problem in the *Iliad*, viz. that the 'best' (never an uncontestable status anyway) should always and everywhere have reward commensurate with *his* judgement of that status, notwithstanding reality, the presence and power of others, or the actual outcomes (so Σ bT 536–7: see Brown 2003: 139–42; Elmer 2013: 189). Several features suggest the contentiousness and inappropriateness of his suggestion (536–8n.), but scholars are frequently more forgiving of Achilleus' action (e.g. Kitchell 1998: 166–7).

534 = 16.5, where Achilleus reacts to Patroclos' tears.   τὸν δὲ ἰδὼν ὤικτειρε: the formula heralds comforting words (always ἔπεα πτερόεντ(α) in the next verse) and actions from the observing character, directed both to the individual difficulty and the wider group (11.814, 16.5). West emends to ὤικτιρε (cf. also 548), but -ει- is universally attested in both places; though -ῑ- is reflected in inscriptions and Aeol. οἰκτίρρω (as preserved in much later authors), the Ionian bards were clearly following the example of other verbs in -αιρω and -ειρω (< *-ρjω: WHS 385–6).   ποδάρκης δῖος Ἀχιλλεύς: 140–4n.

535 = 22.377, where Achilleus addresses the Greeks after stripping Hector's corpse.   ἔπεα πτερόεντ': whether drawn from the idea that words are arrows or birds (Zanker 2019: 131–40), this famous metaphor suggests that his pitying reaction will continue the attitude towards the situation he displayed at the race's start (534–41n.: Kelly 2007a: 143–8). The idiom is usually found with προσηύδα introducing a speech directed at a named or single character (cf. 557 below); where the audience is a wider group, as here, the poet prefers to use ἀγορεύω (*contra Od.* 17.349, with variant προσηύδα).

536–8 ὤριστος: 'crasis' or mixing of ὁ ἄριστος 'the best man', a combination (demonstrative + superlative) which reflects Eumelos' failure, since this honorific is only used to qualify ἀνήρ in quasi-epitaphic circumstances (11.288, 13.433, 16.521, 24.384; cf. 17.689; Edwards 1984: 66–71; cf. Basset 2006: 113). The psilotic form is better attested here, though both MSS and critics are divided on whether to read ὤ- or ὤ-.   μώνυχας

ἵππους: 6–7n.   ἀλλ' ἄγε: 313–14n. This collocation is combined with
a form of δίδωμι elsewhere only to introduce guest-giving within a hospitality relationship, which – even though the item is explicitly termed
ἀέθλιον (only here and at 748 below in the singular: see *GH* I § 41 for
the alternation with ἄεθλον) – is obviously inappropriate here (*Od.* 8.389,
13.13, 20.296).   ὡς ἐπιεικές: Achilleus is aware that his proposal is
contentious, like all actions so labelled, but this example is unique in
Homer in being successfully denied (8.431, 19.147, *Od.* 8.389; cf. Hes. fr.
257.5 M–W; Kelly 2007a: 334).   δεύτερ' 'the second prize': a slightly
unusual plural after singular ἀέθλιον, the prize being a pregnant mare
(265–6). Some MSS remedy by reading ἀέθλια in 537, but the same idiom
in 751 (ἡμιτάλαντον δὲ χρυσοῦ λοισθήϊ' ἔθηκεν: see n.) shows the neuter
plural as a substantive meaning 'last prize' (Van Groningen 1941: 272).
Alternatively, Achilleus is imagined as anticipating the first prizes (538)
and aware of the sensitivities at play, as Σ T 538a suggest, putting it down
to some pre-existing tension with Diomedes (cf. 9.697–700 for the latter's
shrewd judgement on the former's character).   τὰ πρῶτα φερέσθω:
though the process could be stretched here (i.e. 'let him continue in his
claiming of the first prize'), the expression seems inapposite, as Diomedes
has already removed the items.   Τυδέος υἱός: 382–4n. Much is at
stake, given Tydeus' own athletic exploits (see 677–8on.).

539 ὡς ἔφαθ', οἳ δ' ἄρα πάντες ἐπήινεον: the poet marks this assent as problematic, since the group has nothing to do, whereas this formula is elsewhere deployed when (i) their further participation or action is required,
and (ii) they comprise explicitly or implicitly the *basilēes* only, which is not
the case here (7.344 = 9.710 with ἐπήινησαν βασιλῆες; *Od.* 4.673, 7.226,
etc., all with ἐπήινεον). Though the verb usually predicates automatic
enactment (cf. Elmer 2013: 34–8), the unusual form and context relate
only their endorsement of Achilleus' authority in the games; it is not necessarily a sign of best practice, as Homeric crowds are not infallible (cf.,
e.g., 2.142–55, 18.310–13).

540–65 The second quarrel, between two of the closest companions in
the poem; its resolution will depend heavily on that fact. This particular
encounter closely resembles that between Agamemnon and Achilleus in
Book 1, as an older man again attempts to remove the prize of a younger,
but that figure's reluctance also evokes Agamemnon's prior disagreement
with Chryses over his daughter (553–4n.). Antilochos' ability to read
Achilleus correctly will occur again in the running race; whilst his efforts
here result in an extra gift for Eumelos (558–62), he is more directly
awarded in the later event (785–97).

540–2 For the form of the contrafactual, see 154–5n. The juxtaposition of their patronymic expressions over the verse-end (re)connects the two figures in preparation for the resolution of the quarrel. μεγαθύμου Νέστορος υἱός: the epithet extends the usual patronymic to the medial caesura (see 301–4ᵃn.). Πηλεΐδην: 17–18n. δίκηι 'with his judgement': cf. 18.508 for this sense, more normally found in the plural in epos (e.g. 16.542, *Od.* 3.244, *WD* 221). The singular can also denote the totality of all such decisions = order, justice as a principle (as, e.g., at 16.388, *WD* 265: Allan 2006).

543–54 Antilochos' reply begins and ends defiantly, but deploys flattery as well (543–4, 551–2nn.); by not specifying the gift, he allows himself the opportunity to expatiate on Achilleus' manifold resources. Showing a keen appreciation of his friend's character, he moves from the reproved intention to an alternative good suggestion, before closing with a refusal to accede (Minchin 2001a: 65–6).

543–4 κεχολώσομαι: 1st sing. fut. mid. indic. of χολόω, with reduplication implying a lasting state (cf. e.g. κεκλήσομαι, λελείψομαι: *GH* I § 212). Antilochos threatens a 'bodily experience of anger' (Walsh 2005: 127, 127–40, 204–31). ἔπος: 'prediction' or 'promise', as often in this idiom with the verb τελέω (1.108, 14.44, *Od.* 2.272, 3.99 = 4.329, etc.). ἀφαιρήσεσθαι: an obvious allusion to the quarrel in Book 1, used at 1.161, 182, and only elsewhere in early epos at *Od.* 12.64. The related form ἀπαιρέομαι is deployed by Nestor and Achilleus of Agamemnon's intention to take Briseis (1.230, 275).

545–7 Antilochos shrewdly rephrases Achilleus' reasons before offering a counterargument. He is wrong about what actually happened, but not unreasonably so; here the gods had already been involved, and prayer has otherwise not been particularly prominent in the games (see 768–84, 862ᵇ–4nn.). τὰ φρονέων: this typical idiom for explaining a character's thought processes (2.36, 5.564, 10.491, etc.) is rarely found where one character conjectures the motives of another (8.430, *Od.* 2.116; cf. 4.361, *Od.* 7.312, 22.51), and may suggest a dovetailing between the poet's and Antilochos' views (cf. Martin 1989: 187–9; generally von Alvensleben 2022): also 42n. For πανύστατος, see 532n.

548–50 Anaphora of ἔστι/εἰσί helps to underline Achilleus' wealth, as e.g. in Thersites' differently purposed list of Agamemnon's resources (2.226–7; cf. also Odysseus at 9.227–8). It reflects the range of the items allocated throughout the games, and recalls Achilleus' own enumeration to the embassy of his economic capacities (9.364–7), but there are many such claims based around the possession of 'gold and bronze', in a variety of contexts from self-assertion to ransom request (6.46–50, 9.135–40 = 277–82, 10.378–81, 11.131–5, 22.49–51, etc.). Note the artful elaboration in this tricolon: one noun with epithet, then two nouns, then two nouns of which one has an epithet – that the latter denotes horses, precisely the issue here, is no accident.   οἰκτείρεις: 534n.   φίλον ἔπλετο θυμῶι: a sizeable minority of MSS (including an early papyrus and Σ AT 548) read φίλος here (as at 16.450), but formular usage favours the neuter, in which case the expression summarises the preceding pity and looks forward to the command in 552, as at 14.337–40. For ἔπλετο, 3rd sing. aor. mid. indic. of πέλω/πέλομαι, to be translated simply 'is', see 69–70n.   μώνυχες ἵπποι: see 6–7n.

551–2 The concrete suggestion resumes the thought of 548, and contrasts the later (ἔπειτ᾽) compensation to Eumelos with 'or even right now' (ἠὲ καὶ αὐτίκα νῦν). The reference to the people's approval counters their action at 540 (see 540–2n.), and wryly acknowledges the performative nature of such an act.   αὐτίκα νῦν: Antilochos flatters his friend with the kind of swiftness predicated in epos of, or expressed by, gods (6.308, *Od.* 5.205, 9.356, 13.364, etc.; also *HAphr.* 151; generally Erren 1970).

553–4 τὴν δ᾽ ἐγὼ οὐ δώσω: an obvious repetition of Agamemnon's refusal to release Chryseis (1.29 τὴν δ᾽ ἐγὼ οὐ λύσω: see 596–7ᵃn. for another), this also recalls Achilleus' declaration about Hector's corpse at 182–3 above (see 179–83n.), and may be compared with Paris' reported refusal to give up Helen (7.393) and Zeus's imagined failure to send his eagle to answer Priam's prayer (24.296) – all actions which do eventuate: the poet thus intimates that Antilochos may be forced to give up the mare, setting the scene for the next quarrel with Menelaos.   πειρηθήτω: 3rd sing. aor. pass. imp. of πειράω 'make trial of'. The challenge evokes Achilleus' refusal to give up anything else beyond Briseis (1.302 πείρησαι), but see e.g. 11.386, (esp.) *Od.* 8.205 for similarly phrased defiance.   ἐθέληισιν: 3rd sing. pres. subj. (= ἐθέληι: Intro. § 3.1.2.d.i and n. 115).

555–65 Achilleus engages playfully with Antilochos' heated speech, seeing himself in the youth's intransigence (Rengakos 2007: 108–9; more critically, Sauge 1994: 13) while acknowledging his sly flattery.

555–7 ὣς φάτο, μείδησεν δέ: Achilleus' smile is unique, reflecting not only their close relationship, but also that he recognises Antilochos' stratagem: this idiom occurs whenever a happy figure sees their best interests in the preceding speech, notwithstanding the varying levels of deception at play (1.595, 5.426, 14.222, 15.47, etc.; cf. Arnould 1990: 89). The explanation for this smile in the next verse is unusual in these circumstances (*Scut.* 115–16; cf. 1.595–6, 5.426–7, 14.222–3, etc.: cf. Beck 2005: 240–1). ποδάρκης δῖος Ἀχιλλεύς: 140–4n. χαίρων: though in a different sense, cf. his two earlier farewells (χαῖρε) to Patroclos (19, 179), esp. with φίλον … ἑταῖρον (178) and φίλος … ἑταῖρος here: Antilochos moves into the role, reflecting ironically on Achilleus' refusal to listen fully to Patroclos' request to lay aside his anger (16.20–35; cf. 48–63). φίλος ἦεν ἑταῖρος: more of their (hierarchical) connection, since this reflection falls where the companion seeks to help the superior (5.695, 17.577; cf. 17.642, 18.80 of Patroclos, with ὤλεθ'). ἔπεα πτερόεντα προσηύδα: unlike 535 above (see n.), this formula now signals his intention to align himself with Antilochos.

558–9 In principal clauses, κε qualifies a subjunctive to emphasise the connection of the future action with the previous clause or circumstance: '*then* (i.e. if you're really asking me to do this) will I complete this very (καί) thing' (1.137, 184, etc.: *GH* II § 311). οἴκοθεν ἄλλο 'another thing from my store': (playful?) recognition of his earlier error, as always with such offers, where the compensatory aspect is reinforced by an ἐπι-compound verb meaning 'in addition' (7.364 = 391, 23.592). οἴκοθεν in this sense = κλισίηθεν (564).

560–2 562 ~ *Od.* 8.405, of the ivory scabbard for the sword given Odysseus by Euryalos (cf. also δώσω 403). δώσω: asyndeton helps to stress the emphatic capping of his friend's refusal to yield in 553, and looks forward to the competitive giving in the quarrel between Menelaos and Antilochos (592, 610). δώσω is again employed with ἀπηύρων (290–2n.) when Achilleus sets the same Asteropaios' sword as an extra prize for the duel in armour (23.807–8) and when Agamemnon offers Briseis among the women to be given Achilleus (9.131; cf. also 128, 147, 149). A relationship between these three scenes is probable: in this respect as well, Achilleus turns the tables on his rival. Leader of the Paionians (21.154–6), Asteropaios made an abortive attack on the Greeks defending Patroclos' body (17.353–5), and is the only figure in the poem whose corpse is defiled by animals (21.203–4). His fate contrasts with Patroclos' and maintains uncertainty over what will happen to Hector's body (21–3, 184–91nn.), as well as recalling Achilleus' recent violence. For another analepsis to the poem's events in the prizes, see 740–51n. χεῦμα … κασσιτέροιο 'a pouring of tin': a valuable item, since this metal is confined to Agamemnon's equipment (breastplate 11.25; shield's ὀμφαλοί 11.34) and Achilleus' (greaves 18.613, 21.592; shield 18.565, 574, 20.271), and otherwise only in Homer of chariot facings (503–4n.). χεῦμα is derived from χε(ύ)ω 'pour', with περιχεύω elsewhere used for metalwork (*Od.* 6.232–4 = 23.159–61). The tin is either literally 'poured' or overlaid (as with the bands on Agamemnon's cuirass), and sits 'around' the object's edges (ὧι πέρι ... ἀμφιδεδίνηται; Gray 1974).   **πολέος ... ἄξιον** '(an object) worth ... much': πολέος is genitive of value; for the form see 474–5n.

563–4 ἦ 'he said' (24–6n.).   **Αὐτομέδοντι:** Automedon, also labelled a 'dear ... comrade' (555–7n.), is the driver of Achilleus' chariot (16.145–9, 19.392–7), one of his constant companions (9.209, 24.474, 625), and one of two men honoured by him 'most particularly after the dead Patroclos' (24.574–5; cf. 16.145–6). He drives the team for Patroclos and fights well in Book 17. His name means 'self-ruling', with the -μέδων element popular for charioteers (cf. two Eurymedons 4.228, 8.114; and Alcimos = Alcimedon 24.474) and heralds (Automedon *Od.* 4.675, Medon *Od.* 4.677–715; Kanavou 2015: 142).   **οἰσέμεναι:** fut. act. infin. of φέρω 'I carry'.   **ὤιχετο** 'went': see 99–101ⁿn.

[565] Lacking in most MSS, and deleted by several editors, this verse looks like a supplement to specify an explicit referent for οἱ in 564. Currie 2013: 31–2 argues that such specification is required, and the verse also has Achilleus, rather than Automedon, handing over the prize to Eumelos. Yet the passage responds well to a hierarchy of favour, and the unusual circumstance created by the agonothete.   **ἐν χερσὶ τίθει· ὁ δ᾽ ἐδέξατο χαίρων:** the whole-verse formula usually follows ὡς εἰπών, and denotes gifts which draw upon or seek to establish a longer relationship (1.446, 23.624, 797, *Od.* 15.130). It is unusual here, since the recipient is a third party to the usual statements of benefit and intention. The most common formula of the 'placed into hands' idiom, ἐν χερσὶ τίθει expresses supportive, friendly actions – prizes (624, 797), gifts (*Od.* 8.406, 15.130), cups of wine (*Od.* 3.51, 13.57, 15.120), even one's daughter (1.440, 445).

566–613 The third quarrel. No sooner has one dispute been resolved than another one begins, arising now from Antilochos' conduct during the race. Menelaos challenges the younger man's right to his prize on the basis of his dubious tactics, and the episode as a whole again replays the Book 1 quarrel in a different key, with lesser and more moderate versions of those figures now vying over their right to a prize. The risk that the issue will become 'zero sum' is avoided because both parties recognise that a short-term loss of τιμή is less important than the maintenance of their relationship (Kelly 2017: 98–101, with bibliography, adding Stelow 2020: 105–15; Stocking 2023: 135–42). Menelaos and Antilochos otherwise enjoy a positive relationship in the *Iliad* (see 5.561–75, 15.568–91, 17.651–701), so this episode reflects even more sharply on the poem's risky dynamics of competition and cooperation (Willcock 1983; 2002: 222–3; Stelow 2020: 68–9, 86–7, 102–3, 105–15).

566–85 Concerned with reputation, Menelaos appeals to public testimony and process as his remedy against Antilochos. Somewhat like Achilleus (534–41n.), he believes that the inherently better should always be better rewarded (571–2), but he also appeals to a wider consensus. The introduction to his speech (566–9) begins and ends with him, surrounding and emphasising the herald's call to silence.

566–7ᵃ Menelaos' anger at Antilochos contrasts with Achilleus' recent amusement ironically, given his frequent χόλος for Patroclos (21–3, 543–4nn.). τοῖσι ... ἀνίστατο 'stood up in their midst': for this locative-dative use of the pronoun, see 1.68 (τοῖσι δ' ἀνέστη), 101, etc. (*GH* II § 111). θυμὸν ἀχεύων 'grieving in his *thymos*': Menelaos' public appeal is foreshadowed, since characters predicated in this formula require external help (5.869, 9.612, 18.461, *Od.* 21.318, *WD* 399), while the grief itself has been long nurtured (Mawet 1979: 345–7). For θυμός, see 62–4n. ἄμοτον 'unceasingly': of uncertain derivation, this adverb is usually paired with μάομαι 'I am eager' (4.440, 5.518, 13.40, etc.), and is almost always used of powerful emotions. Its continuative sense is augmented by the perfect participle κεχολωμένος, which also recalls Antilochos' κεχολώσομαι (543).

567ᵇ–9ᵃ The intervention of the unnamed herald – possibly Talthybios, but he is closely linked with Agamemnon (39–41n.) – evokes the similar call made by Athene (in herald's guise) before Odysseus' rallying cry (2.279–82), but also Achilleus' oath on the sceptre (1.234–44). Underpinning the introduction to the speech, it also grants Menelaos the public authority reserved usually for his brother. Possession of the sceptre signals authority, the right to speak, the speech's importance (cf. esp. 18.505), and perhaps also a quasi-judicial function (Van Wees 1992: 83–4, 276–80; Unruh 2011) – all underlined by the necessary run-over of ἔθηκε and hyperbaton of ἐν. The Ithacan herald Peisenor similarly places the sceptre into Telemachus' hands (*Od.* 2.37–8), while Odysseus claims it for himself (2.185–6); for heralds more generally, see 39–41n. χερσί: there is very little to choose between this reading, found in some good

MSS and all the early papyri, and the majority reading χειρί here (cf. 10.328 χερσὶ σκῆπτρον).

569ᵇ–85 Menelaos' speech is carefully constructed, leading from his complaint (A¹) to his suggestion for remedy (A²):

A¹ address to Antilochos (570–2)
B¹ (ἀλλ' ἄγετ' ... δικάσσατε) a public appeal to leading figures for judgement (573–4)
C¹ an imagined reaction to that judgement (575–8)
B² (εἰ δ' ἄγε ... δικάσω) his own intention to issue judgement (579)
C² imagined reaction (579–80)
A² address to Antilochos (581–5)

Menelaos both aligns himself with majority opinion, for which he has high regard, and effectively replaces the need for any such process by appealing to an oath. Noting the formal rebuke structure of address, criticism, and proposal (482n.), Minchin 2002: 80 (= 2007: 35–6) ascribes the absence of a wider comment on Antilochos' behaviour to the fact that he has already provided one during the race, but here Menelaos effectively applies that broader perspective to his own solution (B²), and thus connects himself with the perspective of the internal audience.

569ᵇ–70 ἰσόθεος φώς 'godlike man': for all the reconciliation here, Menelaos is about to lose something: this formula does not 'lack a specific profile' (Latacz et al. 2003: 183) but is applied to a variety of generally lesser figures in the *Iliad* when their subordination has just been (2.565, 4.212, 9.211, 11.472, etc.) or is about to be made clear (3.310, 7.136, 11.428, etc.; cf. *Od.* 1.324, 20.124; Pulleyn 2019: 194; cf. 677 below). For the connotative disjunction, see 62–4n. (and 690 below). The epithet is confined in epos to this expression, while the more common φώς is etymologically unexplained (the sometimes touted link with φάος 'light' is not generally accepted: *EDG* s.v.).   **πρόσθεν πεπνυμένε** 'previously prudent': πεπνυμένος is the perf. mid. ppl. related to πνέω 'I breathe' (438–41n.), and it is frequently used of heralds (7.276, 278) and characters acting or speaking prudently (e.g. Antenor 3.203, 7.347, etc.). Nowhere else in epos is it so denied (but cf. 440), and the justice of the challenge is acknowledged by the poet when Antilochos replies (586n.; *contra* Elmer 2015: 164–5).   **ποῖον:** indignant interrogative, only elsewhere used in Homer to denote directly preceding statements (as in the formula ποῖον τὸν μῦθον ἔειπες at 1.552 etc.), not actions, underlining the equivalence in Menelaos' thinking between action and its report.

571–2 The mirrored syntax in the two cola of 571 links Menelaos' personal excellence and the quality of his horses, while the relative merits of the teams are established in 572 as the touchstone for the erroneous reversal (in Menelaos' eyes) at 577ᵇ.

573–4 ἀλλ᾽ ἄγετ᾽, Ἀργείων ἡγήτορες ἠδὲ μέδοντες ~ 457 (see 457–8n.): Menelaos' diffidence is qualified, and immediately delineated in 575–8. His request δικάσσετε is picked up by his own δικάσω (579). This 'public' voting mirrors the murder trial on the Shield (18.497–507), where again authoritative speakers (the 'elders') pronounce impartial decisions.   ἐς μέσον ἀμφοτέροισι 'into the open, for/on both sides': Suggesting the issue's gravity, this idiom is more usually deployed in combat (6.120, 20.159, 23.814, etc.; cf. also 3.416, 7.277), with genitive ἀμφοτέρων denoting the two opposing sides; the dative here refers to the participants, as ἀμφοτέροισιν ἐπήπυον (18.502). Aristarchos understood ἐς μέσον to mean 'impartially' (Σ AT 574): see 813–15n.   μηδ᾽ ἐπ᾽ ἀρωγῆι 'and not for favour': i.e. with regard only to the case's merits. For ἀρωγή, see especially Scamandros' hurried disavowal of further participation (τί μοι ἔριδος καὶ ἀρωγῆς; 21.360); an ἀρωγός is a protector or benefactor (8.205, 21.371, 428, etc.), a function served on the Shield's scene by the watching λαοί.

575–8 Menelaos explains his suggestion as a means to avoid reputational damage, this time using a 'potential τις-speech' to imagine someone describing the situation to his detriment (De Jong 1987a: 177–8; Kelly 2007a: 183–4). Like all such speakers (mostly Hector), Menelaos reflects on future reception of his behaviour. The framing of the two names in 576 emphasises their opposition (see 353–4 for another case involving Antilochos), but now Menelaos' horses are πολὺ χείρονες (577ᵇ ~ 572ᵇ), while the run-over of ἵπποι and its juxtaposition with intensive αὐτός further underlines their interdependence.   εἴπηισιν: 3rd sing. aor. subj. (= εἴπηι: Intro. § 3.1.2.d.i and n. 115).   Ἀχαιῶν χαλκοχιτώνων: a wonderfully sonant and evocative formula for the army, usually in the genitive but once in the accusative (10.287). Representing for many scholars one of the chief reasons to think of the Mycenaean background to Greek epos (though bronze corselets are known from the eighth century: Van Wees 1994: II.135 and n. 64), the epithet is particular to the Greeks (once of Epeians 11.694) and found in many contexts, but frequently with the common element – as here – of a public, visible performance before or by that group (1.371, 2.47 = 187, 163, 437, etc.). Like many of the epithets describing the Greeks and Trojans, it falls much more frequently in the first half of the poem than in the second (Benardete

2005: 21–2).   οἴχεται 'is gone': for the perfect tense of this verb, see 99–101ᵃn.   κρείσσων ἀρετῆι τε βίηι τε: for a similar statement of power disparity, see Phoinix's comment about the gods (μείζων ἀρετὴ τιμή τε βίη τε 9.498). The potentially negative colouring of power resumes the same theme from Nestor's pre-race instructions (313–18n.) and returns to the opening βιησάμενος. Doubtless this helps to underline 'his own superiority in βίη' (Elmer 2015: 163), but Menelaos does not wish to be thought of as using his greater power to force the issue.

579–80 εἰ δ' ἄγ(ε) 'come on, then': this common idiom introduces convinced statements of opinion and intention, or commands (1.302, 524, 6.376, etc.; *GH* II § 404). It is unusual to find two examples (581) so close together, suggesting agitation as he turns away from the appeal to other judges to issue his own.   ἐγών: 243–4n.   μ' = μοι, as at 12.211 (μοι ἐπιπλήσσεις); for other elisions of this pronoun, see 6.165, 9.673, 10.544, etc. (Intro. § 3.2).   ἰθεῖα: fem. nom. sing. of ἰθύς, *sc.* δίκη 'decision', understood after δικάσω. This very common metaphor seeks to align Menelaos with the right (see 18.508, *Th.* 85, *WD* 35, 224–6, etc.: Allan 2006).

581–5 This section of the speech (= A²: 570–85n.) is itself in ring composition:

A¹ an action requested of Antilochos (581–2)
B¹ reference to a god (581)
C¹ aor. ppl. linking driver and horses (στὰς ἵππων 582)
D   the whip (581–2)
C² aor. ppl. linking driver and horses (ἵππων ἁψάμενος 584)
B² reference to a god (584)
A² an action requested of Antilochos (584–5)

Promised during the race (441), the request for an oath (*OACG* 423; 42, 43–4, 45–7nn.) is unusual in concerning a past fact rather than (present and) future behaviour, but it is 'reasonable ... since there were no witnesses' (Σ bT 585). Odysseus similarly requests (19.175–6) and Agamemnon gives (258–63) an oath, in front of the army, that he has not slept with Briseis; cf. 15.36–46, *Od.* 14.331–3 (~ 19.287–90) for other such claims (false in both cases).

581–3 581ᵃ = 17.685ᵃ, where Menelaos summoned Antilochos to carry the news of Patroclos' death to Achilleus, combining ἄγε δεῦρο/δεῦρ' ἄγε 'come here' with εἰ δ' ἄγε 'come on then' (579–80n.). Antilochos' position connotes responsibility for his team and tactics, as elsewhere with the 'stood before' idiom (4.129, 5.107–8, 8.100, 9.193, etc.: Kelly 2007a: 141–3); Brügger 2009: 111 thinks it 'ritually determined' because he has to touch the horses, but that is no contradiction.   διοτρεφές: literally 'Zeus-nurtured', derived from Ζεύς (διο-) and τρέφω, it is applied to groups and individuals without implying any role for Zeus (or another god) in the actual nurturing (*EDG* s.v.). The vocative is used for a variety of characters, but about half of the time for Menelaos (see below, 594), yet Aristarchos athetised the verse because the epithet was 'ill-suited' to his anger (Σ A 581a; Schironi 2018: 456–7).   ἦ θέμις ἐστίν: the relative is attracted into the gender of the noun (as 2.73, 9.32, 275, etc.), underlining its importance, but it is not true that 'the following procedure is laid down by convention' (Richardson 232): see 43–4n. The claim refers immediately to the movement requested, and obviously to the oath as a whole, though oaths are nowhere else so qualified (Agamemnon's *themis* claim about Briseis at 9.132–4 = 273–6 concerned sexual congress).   στάς ἵππων προπάροιθε: formular subset of the 'stood before' idiom particularly linked with speech acts justifying the journey in question (24.286, *Od.* 15.150, *HDem.* 63).   ἱμάσθλην | ... ῥαδινήν: the 'slender' whip contrasts with the 'golden, well-made' ones of Zeus and Poseidon (8.43, 13.25). Emphasised by necessary run-over and the relative clause, the whip stands at the ring centre (581–5n.) as the symbol of Antilochos' control of his team (Griffin 1980: 26).   τὸ πρόσθεν 'before': for the use of demonstrative + adverb, adding to the item's emphasis, cf. 12.40, *Od.* 4.688, 11.629, Theogn. 911 W², and 480–1n.

584–5 Asyndeton underlines the transition to the command in 585, where ὄμνυθι is prominent in necessary run-over.   γαιήοχον Ἐννοσίγαιον 'earth-shaking (?) shake-earth': this perhaps tautologous (*EDG* s.vv.) and definitely chiastic formula is distinctive of Poseidon as a unit and as single words. The former, like αἰγίοχος, has also been thought to derive from an older verb meaning 'ride', while the latter is a more flexible synonym for ἐνοσίχθων, and more common both in total and as primary or sole denominator than γαιήοχος (hence printed here with a capital letter): cf. Janko 48; Petropoulos 2017). Poseidon is particularly suitable as the oath's guarantor, being the 'horsey god' (Σ A 307a), the progenitor of the Neleids (304ᵇ–5n.), and Antilochos' 'teacher' (306–8n.: Erbse 1986: 112–13); cf. also 276–8n. Apollo is similarly overdetermined in Book 1 (plague sender, Calchas' patron, and enemy of the Greeks: 1.86–7), and Zeus is the only other deity so singled out in Homer (43–4n.).   μή ... ἑκών: despite the factual content, μή is preferred to οὐ because ὄμνυμι usually refers to acts of will (*GH* II § 490). Menelaos has no doubt that his chariot was impeded; the only excuse is inadvertence or impotence, as always with negatived forms of ἑκών (3.66, 7.197, 8.81, etc.; Kelly 2007a: 124–5, adding *Od.* 4.377, 22.351): see further 434–7n.   **τὸ ἐμὸν δόλωι ἅρμα:** mild hyperbaton mirrors the intruder's sneakiness (cf. 20.425, 22.169, 342, *Od.* 4.387, etc.: cf. generally Markovic 2006 and Bertrand forthcoming).   **πεδῆσαι:** a widespread metaphor in epos (Onians 1956: 326–31, esp. 330 n. 3), but here with particular force, since horses are shackled at the end of a chariot journey (13.36–7), and this is also the only time a human is the verb's agent (usually gods: *LfrgE* s.v. B).

586–95 Antilochos' reply combines flattery with decrying his youthful folly, reverting from his own exceptionalism (311–12n.) to the general authority granted to age, particularly on intellectual terms (587–8, 589–90, 591–5nn.). He is clearly worried but stresses his own agency and victory (591–5n.), and thus never actually admits doing wrong (Hohendahl-Zoetelief 1980: 19–20).

586 τὸν δ' αὖτ(ε) ... πεπνυμένος ἀντίον ηὔδα: this formular introduction is mainly used to open Telemachus' speeches in the *Odyssey*, and also for some others whose names scan – ⏑⏑ – (such as Antilochos, Meriones, and Antenor), usually when saying something sensible (Heath 2001). πεπνυμένος is never used here for e.g. Idomeneus – though it could be – and it suffers substitution to accommodate other characters; thus it aptly signals that the coming speech seeks to restore the youth's reputation for being πεπνυμένος (569ᵇ–70n.), already seen in Menelaos' charge during the race (438–41n.).   **ἀντίον ηὔδα:** 482n.

587–8 The opening juxtaposition flatters Menelaos with two comparatives to Antilochos' one, and its invocation of youthful insufficiency is typical (e.g. 3.105–10, 9.57–9, 14.111–12 reversed, 19.218–19, *Od.* 7.294: Lardinois 1995: 58 with n. 81).   **ἄνσχεο** = ἀνάσχεο 'hold (yourself) up'/'endure': 2nd sing. aor. imp. of ἀνέχομαι, with apocope of ἀνά; cf. 24.518, 549. Without an accompanying vocative (as at 1.586, 5.382), this is an abrupt opening.   **πολλὸν ... νεώτερος** 'younger by far': for πολλόν = πολύ, see 319–21n. On the violation of Hermann's Bridge here, see 75–6n. It may have a stylistic effect, as being typical of a younger man's rhetoric (Sansom 2025: 10–12, 14–15).   **ἄναξ Μενέλαε:** emphatically delayed from the start of the speech, and more flattery, since he is never otherwise so labelled (49–51n.).   **πρότερος καὶ ἀρείων** 'earlier (*sc.* older) and better': always where one figure is compared unfavourably to a more famous one (Podarces → Protesilaos 2.707, 'Aithon' → Idomeneus *Od.* 19.184). Related to ἀρετή, ἀρείων (~ ἀμείνων) is the original comparative of ἄριστος, perhaps from a positive ἄρειος seen in τεῖχος ἄρειον (4.407, 15.736: *EDG* s.v.). For old age in Homer, see Preisshofen 1977: esp. 21–8; Falkner 1995: 3–51.

589–90 For other gnomic statements introduced by οἶσθα 'you know' as a strategy for overcoming social inferiority, see 15.204, *Od.* 15.20 (Lardinois 1995: 62–3). A common pairing, the νόος is the organ responsible for intellectual activity (483–4n.), while μῆτις is the quality or even physical manifestation of that activity (cf. 7.447, 15.509, *Od.* 19.325; also 315–18n.).   **λεπτὴ δέ τε μῆτις** = 10.226, where Diomedes damns the conceptual potential of one man alone on a scouting mission; he later chooses Odysseus as his companion (242–7). It is no coincidence that Diomedes is a developing youthful speaker, and Odysseus an old master (see also 591–5n.). Derived from λέπω 'peel off', and meaning 'slender' or 'light', λεπτός reverses the positive metaphor of intellectual thickness and closeness (πυκν-/πυκιν-): see, e.g., 2.55, 3.202, 208, 14.294, *HDem.* 414, etc. (Lynn-George 1988: 232–3; Martin 1989: 35–6; Zanker 2019: 148, 181–2).

591–5 Antilochos' 'emulous' initiative (Σ bT 591–2) is made clear by proceeding chiastically from the horse (ἵππον ... | ... τὴν ἀρόμην) to his act of giving (αὐτός | δώσω) and its central, necessary run-over. This is the first of four such run-overs, underlining his perturbation.   **τῶ τοι ἐπιτλήτω κραδίη:** this phrase introduces Odysseus' proposal to delay the opening of battle (19.220) after he compares himself favourably to Achilleus with regard to his greater age and wisdom. An allusion would underline the difference between Antilochos and Achilleus in analogous circumstances (566–613n.), suggesting the greater maturity of the former. Though the idiom is found elsewhere (*Od.* 1.353, 20.18, 23), endurance (τλα-) is more typically associated with the θυμός (62–4n.); cf. 1.227, 5.669, 24.48, and the formula τετληότι θυμῶι.   **οἴκοθεν ἄλλο:** the second example of this expression (558–9n.) in the race's aftermath recalls Achilleus' recent, indulgent suggestion to Antilochos; the young man learns quickly. The particle κε can appear in both protasis and apodosis of future remote conditionals in Homer, emphasising their close relationship vigorously and clearly (*GH* II § 408).   **ἄφαρ ... βουλοίμην:** (375–6n.) ἄφαρ is only here used with αὐτίκα in emphatic tautology. For other 'either/or' wishes with βουλοίμην expressing a clear preference for one of the alternatives, see 3.41–2, *Od.* 3.232–5, 11.358–9, 489–91, 16.106–7 = 20.316–17.   **διοτρεφές:** honestly answers Menelaos' somewhat ironic deployment (581–3n.).   **ἐκ θυμοῦ πεσέειν** 'to fall from your favour': strikingly serious metaphor not quite captured by the translation, since noun and verb are elsewhere combined only in deadly contexts (8.270 πεσὼν ἀπὸ θυμὸν ὄλεσσεν, 16.410 πεσόντα δέ μιν λίπε θυμός). For -έειν, see 146–8n.

596–7ᵃ In another reflection of the Book 1 quarrel, Antilochos himself hands over the mare, contrasting both with Achilleus' critical view of Agamemnon's distant participation (1.163–8, 226–8, 9.332–3, 372–3) and with the latter's transfer of recompense in Book 19 (238–49, 278–81). Necessary run-over underlines the action.   ἦ 'he said' (24–6n.).   **μεγαθύμου Νέστορος υἱός:** 540–2n. It is apt here to recall the father, and his conciliatory attitude.   **ἐν χείρεσσι τίθει:** this unique form of the supportive 'placed into hands' idiom (565n.) may recollect the return of Chryseis (1.440, 446), these two being the only times when a disputed item is led (ἄγων 1.440 ~ 23.596) to someone with a prior claim before being placed into his hand: see also 553–4n.

597ᵇ–600 One of Homer's most celebrated similes, emulated by Aischylos (*Ag.* 1391–2), Apollonios (*Arg.* 3.1019–21), and Vergil (*G.* 3.314–15). Ring composition (θυμός | ἰάνθη ... | ... θυμὸς ἰάνθη) underlines the effect (with the first example further marked in necessary run-over).   **θυμός | ἰάνθη** 'was stirred, gladdened': the verb is often understood as a metaphorical extension from 'warm' (*Od.* 10.358–9), but ἰαίνω may instead denote movement (Latacz 1966: 220–30, *EDG* s.v. links with ἰάομαι 'heal'); its usage in epos suggests at least a positive reaction (for Zink 1962: 4 n. 11, the simile 'aims at revitalising'). Menelaos' gladness is tinged with surprise, since this formula is reserved for reactions to very unexpected or unlikely events – omens (24.321, *Od.* 15.165), the returns of Odysseus (*Od.* 23.47) and Persephone (*HDem.* 435); for the wider idiom, cf. 24.119 (= 147 = 176 = 196), *Od.* 4.548–9, 6.155–6, 15.379 (Hoekstra 1965: 122).   **ἐέρση** 'dew': the reading of the better part of the MSS, and clearly read e.g. by Apollonios (above), requires an easy ellipsis of the verb 'as the dew about the ears of corn (*sc.* is warmed)'; it is preferable to the minority variant ἐέρσηι (printed by West), as ἔρσω is first attested in Nicander (*Ther.* 62, 631; Spatafora 2005: 234–5).   **ληΐου ἀλδήσκοντος:** otherwise found only in ecphrases (*Od.* 9.134, *Sc.* 288–90 with σταχύων), the deep cornfield (βαθὺ λήϊον) serves as a simile setting to underline extent of the action (2.147–8 with ἀσταχύεσσιν, 11.558–62; cf. Theogn. 106 W²), and so the depth of Menelaos' reaction. Intransitive ἀλδήσκοντος 'growing' is derived from transitive ἀλδαίνω, sharing the same root as Lat. *alo* 'I feed' (*EDG* s. ἀλδαίνω), and not found again until Theocritus 17.78.   **φρίσσουσιν ἄρουραι:** another reminder of the serious background to the quarrel, this is a remarkable extension of the verb's

usual military metaphor (4.282, 7.61–2, 13.339–40) which elsewhere
denotes literally 'hair-raising' reactions from humans (11.383, 24.775)
or animals (13.473, *Od.* 19.446, *WD* 512, 540, *Scut.* 171, 391; cf. *HArt.* 8:
Stanford 1936: 140–2; cf. Zaborowski 2002: 234–6).   **ὡς ἄρα σοί,**
Μενέλαε: as with several characters – notably Patroclos and Eumaios – the
poet directly addresses or 'apostrophises' Menelaos 7×, but the reason for
and effects of this phenomenon are debated: it is either a metrical relic
taken from dialogue (Yamagata 1989), a sign that he is a sympathetic figure (Kahane 1994: 104–13: Σ T remarks 'he is gentle even to the enemy'),
or it is intended to aid *enargeia* ('vividness': De Jong 2009: 93–7; Stelow
2020: 34–5; see also Hoekstra 1965: 138–9). Whichever explanation is
favoured, the audience is brought closer thereby to his reaction.

601–11 Menelaos' speech begins with Antilochos' name, and comprises
a ring centred upon the uniqueness of their relationship as the fundamental basis for compromise:

A¹ I will yield (ὑποείξομαι) + reason (602–5)
B   their relationship (606–8)
A² I will yield (ἐπιπείσομαι) + reason (609–11)

The quarrel is closed successfully, and it is hard to follow either
Hohendahl-Zoetelief 1980: 53, 143–4 in his largely negative characterisation of Menelaos' attitudes or Brown 2003: 142–3 in the measure of
compulsion he feels (cf. Minchin 2001a: 68–9; Stelow 2020: 114–15).

601 καί μιν φωνήσας ἔπεα πτερόεντα προσηύδα: a happy introduction to
continue the mood of that simile, as with all cases of this metaphor (cf.
557, 535n.).

602–5 Shifting temporal focus combines a semantic chiasmus (future,
past/past, future) and a doublet (νῦν + another temporal adverb). The
two structures are joined by asyndeton (604) around the positive–
negative contrast; the integrity of the first is clarified by its adverbs νῦν and
πάρος, the second by repeated αὖτε (604–5). The bookending (Ἀντίλοχε
... ἐγών ... αὐτός) in 602 underlines their association, while repetition
of ν and the ascending tricolon in 604 emphasise the end-placed absolute hapax νεοίη.   **παρήορος** 'useless': from παραείρω 'I hang beside'
in the passive (16.341), the adjective usually denotes an extra ('trace')
horse attached to the team, which is killed without permanently disabling
the chariot (16.471, 474; cf. 8.87, 16.152: Delebecque 1951: 98–101),
but it also describes a fallen warrior (7.156) with the metaphorical sense
seen here (cf. Archil. frr. 130.5, 172.2 W²; Erbse 1993a: 134–6; *contra*

HW 222–4).   ἀεσίφρων 'wrong-minded': used of Priam by Achilleus, who contrasts it with ἔμπεδος 'steady' (20.183), ἀεσί- seems to come from ἀάω, though the form should be ἀασίφρων (so the lexicographers), which is nowhere preserved in the MSS; perhaps the change was influenced by the numerous -εσι- compounds in epos (e.g. φαεσίμβροτος, ἑλκεσίπεπλος, etc.: *WHS* 192), while ταλασίφρων is largely limited to Odysseus (in the genitive).   νῦν ... νόον νίκησε νεοίη 'now ... youthfulness overcame your mind': though the aorist indicative *can* have a present sense when the verbal idea is realised in the present (e.g. 2.114: *GH* II § 272), Menelaos contrasts Antilochos' habitual behaviour πάρος with that shown during the race, and νῦν αὖτε = νῦν δέ 'but in contrast now' (cf. *Od.* 19.548–9). The alliterative expression culminates in the damning hapax νεοίη, which Antimachos seems to have read as νόημα (fr. 176 M), giving a somewhat epigrammatic sense (Matthews 1996: ad loc., 385–6).   ἀλέασθαι: 340ᵇ–1n.

606–8 Line 606 is testament to their relationship elsewhere in the poem (401–47n.); Menelaos similarly frames to Telemachos his debts to Odysseus (*Od.* 4.170), and he is concerned with his responsibility before the duel (3.97–100), though the (almost) unique end-positioning of εἵνεκ' ἐμεῖο makes a stronger point (cf. 6.523–6, *Od.* 6.155–6, *HAphr.* 247–8).   γάρ (607): anticipatory, looking forward to τῷ (609); tr. 'since'.   πόλλ' ἔπαθες καὶ πόλλ' ἐμόγησας: empathetically, Menelaos turns to Antilochos' benefit this usually first-person expression, where the speaker's sufferings justify his refusal to comply with his interlocutor's wishes (9.492, *Od.* 5.223, 8.155; cf. 8.490), implicitly figuring himself as the (wrong-headed) interlocutor. The augmented forms are better attested in the MSS.   ἀδελφεός: i.e. Thrasymedes (9.81, 10.255, 14.10–11, etc.), who survives the war (*Od.* 3.39, 414, etc.). Collocation of father and brother may look forward poignantly to Antilochos' own death; compare Menelaos' embarrassment (*Od.* 4.203–15) when Peisistratos questions him about his brother (199–202; cf. Gantz 1993: 189; Stelow 2020: 142–4;). -ε(ι)ο- is original, and the word is an adjectival formation of copulative α 'same' (with psilosis, as e.g. ἄλοχος) and 'womb' (perhaps neuter *δελφός; cf. δελφύς); Att. ἀδελφός is a shortened form (Renaud and Wathelet 2008: 126; Gainsford 2012).   εἵνεκ': this Ionic form of the (usually) postpositive is the most common form in Homer, followed by ἕνεκα and (rare) ἕνεκεν (*GH* I § 61).

609–11 τῷ 'so': looks back to γάρ (607).   ἠδὲ καί 'and also' (as at 5.822–3, 12.159–60, etc.) rather than just emphatic 'and' (as at 5.128, 7.274, etc.); for ἠδέ, see 54n. Mirroring the thought of 591–2, Menelaos agrees to calm down *and also* to give the horse. His intention is reinforced by the matching necessary run-over of δώσω (610; cf. 592) and then capping Antilochos' τὴν ἀρόμην with a blanketing ἐμήν περ ἐοῦσαν: note the emphasising particle περ (77–9n.) highlighting the possessive, which is picked up again in ἐμός.   ἵνα γνώωσι 'so (they) know': the truth of Menelaos' hope for his reputation is strongly implied, as always with the 'so that X knows' idiom (Kelly 2007a: 80–4). One is tempted to speculate, especially after the apostrophe above, that καὶ οἶδε refers to the external audience as much as the internal. γνώωσι is 3rd pl. aor. subj., an archaic form without contraction (*GH* I § 19).   θυμὸς ὑπερφίαλος καὶ ἀπηνής = 15.94, where Hera speaks to Themis of Zeus. Probably an underrepresented formula, it does not appear again until Oppian, *Cyn.* 2.455. ὑπερφίαλος ('arrogant', 'excessive') is now connected with ὑπερφυής, but the ancients linked it with φιάλη (cf. 616 below) as 'overflowing from a cup' and so uncivilised (*DELG* s.v.): fittingly, it is applied frequently to the Trojans, the suitors, and the Cyclopes (Stoevesandt 2004: 29–33). For ἀπηνής, see 483–4n.

612-13 As had Antilochos, so Menelaos hands over the horse himself, before claiming the third-placed prize (267–8), the cauldron now described simply as παμφανόωντα (see 509n.).   ἦ 'he said' (24–6n.).   **Νοήμονι**: an obvious 'speaking name' derived from νόος, chosen to reflect Antilochos' thoughtful display; another Noemon is killed at 5.678 (together with 'Prytanis'), and another is the son of 'Phronios' (*Od.* 2.386–7, 4.630–57), who provides a ship for Telemachos (von Kamptz 1982: 239; Kanavou 2015: 145–6).   **δῶκεν ... ἄγειν:** 511–13n.

614-15 Befitting his description when standing (351n.), Meriones receives the briefest mention as he claims fourth place. Run-over τέτρατος emphasises the continuity between his starting position (356) and the result. On τάλαντα, see 269–70n.

615-52 The last encounter in the chariot race resolves what to do with the last-placed prize, which should have gone to Eumelos but was left unallotted after Antilochos' first quarrel, the Pheraian already compensated from Achilleus' personal stock (555–64). It is fitting that Achilleus resolves the distributory problem he created, and also that he chooses to give the prize to Nestor, Antilochos' father, a proven charioteer and force for conciliation in Book 1. The connection between his greater age and non-participation is once more emphasised, as Nestor again uses a past narrative experience to fill the gap between consiliar and physical ability (301–4ᵃn.).

615–17 As at the start of the race (270), the fifth-place prize is described right before a speech from Achilleus, the resultant ring linking the boundaries of the race narrative.   ἀμφίθετος φιάλη: for the vessel, see 243–4n.; for the epithet, 269–70n.   ἀν' ἀγῶνα φέρων: something difficult this way comes, for prizes so introduced by this formula (all in this book) are awarded in exceptional, perhaps individual, circumstances (799, 886: see 798–800, 884–6ᵃnn.).   καὶ ἔειπε παραστάς: as always with this framing idiom (154–5n.), Achilleus' words are going to be less than apt.

618–23 The speech is composed in a doublet, with an extra, emphasised, element:

A¹   Let this κειμήλιον be yours (σοί … ἔστω: 618–19)
B¹   since (γάρ) you will not see Patroclos again (619–20)
A²   I give you this ἄεθλον (τοι τόδ': 620–1)
B²   since (γάρ) you will not compete in the games (621–3)
C   since (γάρ) you are old (623)

B¹ and B² create a somewhat tactless parallel between Patroclos and Nestor as non-participants, in the latter's case because of his great age, which is even more pronounced from sitting outside the doublet (C); the two necessarily run-over future indicatives ὄψει and θεύσεαι complete the link. Like his other interventions, Achilleus' words are not entirely apposite (615–17, 621–3nn.), though it is perhaps harsh to think of them as ironically directed at Nestor's responsibility for sending Patroclos into battle (Sauge 1994: 15–18), and they will draw a mild correction (cf. Hohendahl-Zoetelief 1980: 115–20; *contra* Richardson 236: 'dignified and sad').

618–20 τῆ νῦν 'here/take it now': very rare after Homer, the instrumental of the demonstrative pronoun is always used in epos with an imperative when handing over the item to be used (14.219, 24.287, *Od.* 5.346 etc.). West follows Platt in accenting νυν (i.e. treating it as an enclitic; see 485–7n.), plausibly but with no MS authority.   κειμήλιον ἔστω: this idiom is elsewhere deployed when the gift it denotes is rejected as untimely (*Od.* 1.312, 4.600), suggesting a further inappropriateness in the situation. This suits well its use in Xenophanes' critical list of athletic benefits (fr. 2.9 W²). Derived from κεῖμαι and frequently used (in the plural) with it (cf. 6.47, 11.132, etc.: Clary 2009: 264–5), κειμήλιον is an item of treasure indicating the wealth and importance of the possessing household (e.g. 11.132–3), and acting as a reminder of its willing or unwilling source (9.330–1, 18.288–92, etc.; Scheid-Tissinier 1994: 41–3; Bichler 2007).   τάφου 'funeral': 29n.   μνῆμ' ἔμμεναι: Achilleus' ascription of the μνῆμα to Patroclos and his funeral shows the extent of their

attachment, since the μνῆμα is elsewhere an object directly representing
the person giving it (*Od.* 15.126, 21.40: Simondon 1982: 81–5). The
infinitive is result/final after κειμήλιον, 'a treasure ... to be a memory of'
(151n.; *GH* II § 442).   **οὐ γὰρ ἔτ':** recalls the shade's similarly run-
over sadness at the thought he would never return (75), and Nestor will
pick up on it (627).   **ὄψει:** the usual 2nd sing. mid. (primary) ending in Homer is -εαι, though contracted -ηι is found before vowels and is
a variant here. West follows Payne-Knight in printing an elided form ὄψε'
(= ὄψε(αι)), but -ει is very solidly attested here (as e.g. at *Od.* 12.101; cf.
also πειρᾶι at 24.390, 433).

621–3 αὔτως 'just so': run-over emphasises the connection between
Patroclos and Nestor, viz. in their inability to compete (expanded in
the γάρ clause). The noticeable variation in the events' expression contrasts with anaphoric (οὐ)δέ and the repeated, closing future indicatives.
Necessary run-over of the last event, running (623), fits well with the
stress on age in the course of that event (see 789–91[a]n.); an even older
Odysseus is reluctant to compete ποσίν on Scheria (*Od.* 8.231–3; cf. the
silence on his running skills at 179–81), explaining it by reference to his
experiences at sea. Reflecting a traditional sequence (257[b]–897n.), the
order of events there is almost that of the following narrative, though the
spear throwing comes last and so the running race immediately follows
the wrestling, and there is no mention of the fight in armour, iron throwing (or discus), or archery. A similar order is preserved in Nestor's story
(634–42), with spear throwing after running and the chariot race mentioned last and at greatest length. Both speakers, therefore, close their
catalogues with the event they feel makes the greatest rhetorical point in
the context.   **ἤδη γὰρ χαλεπὸν κατὰ γῆρας ἐπείγει:** however true, this
assertion prompts Nestor's rebuttal at the suggestion of his incapacity, as
always after this 'old age oppresses' idiom (1.29, 4.315, 321, *Od.* 11.196,
etc.; Kelly 2007a: 149; Zanker 2019: 80); see also 476–7, 587–8, 643–5,
789–91[a]nn.

624 ~ [565] (see n.). The gift is intended to reinforce, through remem-
brance, a future act of reciprocity (cf. *Od.* 15.130).

625–50 Another speech drawing on Nestor's youthful experiences places
him in the position of a competitor with a proven reputation, and sets
his age and incapacity next to a glittering past (see esp. Alden 2001: esp.
102–10; Minchin 2007: 254–8; also 301–4[a]n.). Nestor engages with the
themes of Achilleus' speech in reverse order (as often in Homer):

A¹ I am indeed old (626–8) [= C in Achilleus' speech]
B¹ I wish I were young (629)
C   As when I competed in funeral games (630–42) [~ B²]
B² So was I young then (643)
A² Now I am old (643–5) [= C]
D   Continue your conduct of the games (646) [= B¹]
E   So do I accept the prize (647–50) [= A¹/A²]

Thus Nestor's age becomes the driving force of this reply (A¹–A²), arranged around Amarynceus' funeral games; though gently criticising Achilleus' implication (618–23, 626nn.), he closes with a gracious wish for the young man's fortune. On the internal structure of B² and A², see below, 643–5n. The circumstance calls forth this assertive reminiscence, as with all litanies of athletic prowess (271–84n.).

625 = 601 (see n.).

626 ναὶ δὴ ταῦτά γε πάντα, τέκος, κατὰ μοῖραν ἔειπες: though this verse is absent in some ancient and medieval MSS, and has no A scholion, it would be too abrupt to open the speech at 627 (Erbse ad Σ bT 626; οὐ γάρ is so used only at *Od.* 8.159). Nestor's corrective attitude, within an overall frame of agreement after the speech introduction, is signalled by this opening formula (1.286, 8.146, 10.169, etc.; Kelly 2007a: 180–2, adding *Od.* 4.266, 18.170, 20.37, etc.). The usual qualification is not as clearly or immediately signalled here (i.e. with ἀλλά *vel sim.*); instead, Nestor agrees with Achilleus' judgement, but disarms its 'encoding' as an act of pity by contrasting his present with his youth (Hohendahl-Zoetelief 1980: 116). ναί is the affirmative particle 'yes', while μοῖρα in this idiom is a normative judgement about what fits the context, i.e. 'appropriately' (Battilana 1985: 42–7, esp. 45; Yamagata 1994: 105–12, esp. 107).   **τέκος:** usually vocative in character speech in Homer, this neuter noun need not denote actual filiation (3.162, 9.437, 444, 14.190, etc.), and is being replaced in epos by the prosodic (and semantic) variant τέκνον (Janko 14 n. 19; Renaud and Wathelet 2008: 99–100).

627–8 ἔμπεδα literally 'on the ground' (ἐν + πέδον: 12.12): the adjective denotes stability or solidity, physical or temporal (641–2 below), and looks forward to ἔμπεδος (629) to underline the reversal of reality and wish before the story begins.   **φίλος:** for nominative as vocative, see 313–14n.   **γυῖα ... πόδες, οὐδέ τι χεῖρες | ... ἐπαΐσσονται:** an unusual expression, since γυῖα 'limbs' (5.122, 13.61, 23.772; cf. 13.512 γυῖα ποδῶν 'joints of the feet') are usually appositive to both 'feet *and* hands' –

a combination nowhere in Homer so separated – while the idiom of 628 ('hands leaping from') is otherwise confined to theogonic contexts (Hes. *Th.* 150 = 671; cf. *WD* 148–9), however apt it is for an athlete (771–2n.). Some MSS read φίλοι to connect the appositives more clearly; Düntzer emended to ποδῶν φίλος (reflecting 13.512), while West temptingly brackets 628; but the line is present in every MS.

629–43 An impossible wish, where the speaker underlines a conviction in the present by reference to something unobtainable (Kelly 2007a: 366–7; Van Erp Taalman Kip 2012). Nestor is the subject or object of several such wishes, always using stories from his past to contrast aged incapacity with youthful prowess, and so assert his continued membership of the elite community. All these tales centre on hostility between Pylos and Elis – Nestor kills their Arcadian ally Ereuthalion (4.313–25, 7.132–58), and leads his men to victory against the Epeians themselves (11.670–762) – and suggest the existence of a specifically West-Northwest Peloponnesian tradition (Alden 2001: 89–92; Zanetto 2017). For the order of events, see 257[b]–897, 638–42nn. Nestor emerges unsurprisingly well, dominating every contest but the chariot race (Alden 2001: 102–5), and his narrative is quietly agonistic, since these successes are redolent of a previous generation (e.g. Tydeus 5.805–7) that outperforms the current one, where prizes are more widely distributed, and not even Achilleus claims to be the best at every contest (cf. 1.259–74 for a more pointed generational comparison).

629 = 7.157, 11.670, *Od.* 14.468 ~ 503, all impossible wishes, where an old(er) man seeks to gain something from his addressee (a response to Hector's challenge, Patroclos' intervention with Achilleus, a cloak for Odysseus' character) through a personal reminiscence. Line 629[b] = 4.314[b], where there is no such benefit.   **ἡβώοιμι:** 1st pers. sing. pres. act. opt. of ἡβάω, with diectasis from the contracted form ἡβῷμι (7.133: < *ἡβά-οιμι; *GH* I § 31). Unlike in later usage, the optative is deployed in Homer for wishes even when they cannot be realised (*GH* II § 318).

630–1 Bouprasion was clearly an important city in the region of Elis (2.615, 11.756), but its precise location is unknown (*BA* 58, A2 (Elis): 894; Visser 1997: 566–60). Amarynceus of Elis was of varied parentage in early traditions, but his descendant Diores leads one of four Epeian contingents to Troy (2.615–24), and is killed early in the action of the *Iliad* (4.517–26). Despite the doubts of Σ bT 631 about the precise relationship between παῖδες and βασιλῆος (i.e. were they the king's own children, or does βασιλῆος imply 'for the king'?), Amphidamas' children also put out the prizes at his funeral games (*WD* 656).

632–3 Nestor's unease in this context is implied by the form of his claim (οὔ τις ὁμοῖος + dat.), for such statements are either ambivalent or unevidenced (2.553, 9.305–6, 14.521). The following increasing tricolon, together with chiastic adj. + noun/noun + adj. in 633, throws stress on the final grouping, and thus on the transregional significance of Nestor's excellence. The Aitolians are mentioned soon after the Epeians in the Catalogue (2.638–44), and their leader Thoas avenges Diores (4.527–38), but they are otherwise unprominent as a group in the *Iliad* itself, though they count among their number such traditionally important figures as Oineus, Tydeus, and Meleagros – and Thersites (Andersen 1982). Their most prominent descendant, Diomedes, is king of Argos (290–2, 470ᵇ–2nn.).

634–7 Each event before the chariot race receives one verse, conveying the same basic information but varying the syntax and the position of the defeated figure, with the first three all qualified (differently) from 4c to the verse-end. Most of the personnel are known from other stories, with some jumbling of names and traditions: the father of the otherwise unknown Clytomedes (634) is variously reported in the MSS as Enops, Phainops, and Oinops, suggesting a fragile traditional purchase (see also 14.445, 16.401). A suitable name for a wrestler (cf. ἀγκάς), Ancaios (635) is also the name of Agapenor's father, leader of the Arcadians (2.609); his origin from the Aitolian city Pleuron (cf. 2.639) picks up 633. Iphiclos (636) was also the name of Podarces' father, leader of the contingent from Phylace and Pyrasos in Thessaly (2.704–5); that he was a preternaturally quick runner (Hes. fr. 62 M–W) presumably explains the name here. These two characters later appear in stories of the Calydonian boar-hunt (Bacchyl. 5.117–20, 127–9). Phyleus (637) was the son of King Augeas of Elis, and father of Meges, leader of the Doulichians (2.625–30); Polydoros (637) is otherwise unknown (also a son of Priam killed at 20.407–18, and a daughter of Peleus at 16.175: Janko 340–1).

636–7 ἐσθλὸν ἐόντα 'valorous though he was': Nestor highlights his achievement with this typical description of a defeated or otherwise overborne figure (2.709, 13.461, 20.312, 22.176, 22.359). The epithet 'denotes noble, competent, valorous, useful, and/or beneficial' (Yamagata 1994: 192–9, esp. 194–5), a definition that neatly summarises the ideal Homeric *basileus*; for the opposition ἐσθλός/κακός, cf.

e.g. 2.265–6, 4.298–300. The participle bears its (common) concessive sense. **δουρί:** 528–9n. **ὑπειρέβαλον:** for lengthened ὑπερ-, see 226–8n.

638–42 Asyndeton and fronting of οἷοισιν underlines his discomfort at the loss, while 640 explains the Actorione-Molione's (and Nestor's) eagerness, for the chariot race is always the prestige event. The chariot race is the catalogue's last, elaborated item, the only contest he did not win, and the most valuable one (640). Its final position in the event order may well be the result of Nestor's presentation, leaving the sole exception to his athletic successes to last, rather than reflecting an actual order of competition (257ᵇ–897n.). He ascribes his loss to the advantage of the two (purported) sons of the Elean king Actor, the 'Actorione-Molione' Eurytos and Cteatos (2.621), who could drive and whip the team simultaneously, a somewhat unclear benefit (which perhaps Nestor knows: 632–3n. οὔ τις ὁμοῖος) already debated in antiquity (Σ A 638–42: Schironi 2018: 253–4). They appeared in Nestor's Pylian–Elean conflict (11.708–9), where their effectiveness was qualified by youth and they were saved – *from Nestor's onset* – by their real father Poseidon (750–2). The manner of their competition suggests they are conjoined twins, as often elsewhere in Archaic art (Ahlberg-Cornell 1992: 32–5; *LIMC* s. Aktorione, esp. 473–4, 476) and literature (Hes. frr. 17a, b, 18 M–W ~ 11 H; Ibycos fr. 285 *PMGF* with Wilkinson 2013: 209–12). Their physical bond (δίδυμοι 'twofold' 641, as αὐλοῖσιν διδύμοισι *Od.* 19.227; not 'twins' διδυμάονε 5.548 etc.) is reflected mimetically in the syntax, with each character introduced, after hiatus, at the same point in subsequent verses marked by homoioteleuton (ἡνιόχευεν/κέλευεν), and the action of the first verse repeated at the start of the next. For the noticeably long and very emphatic repetition ('epanalepsis') of ἔμπεδον ἡνιόχευ[εν], see 20.371–2 (καὶ εἰ πυρὶ χεῖρας ἔοικεν, | εἰ πυρὶ χεῖρας ἔοικε) and 22.127–8 (τῶι ὀαριζέμεναι, ἅ τε παρθένος ἠΐθεός τε, | παρθένος ἠΐθεός τ᾽ ὀαρίζετον ἀλλήλοιιν), both cases where Hector speaks about Achilleus (Fehling 1969: 183–6, esp. 185): Nestor clearly feels that the Actorione-Molione were his chief opponents. For a very different interpretation and supplementation of this story by reference to Pylian and IE myth, and which makes this episode the key to all the other chariot contests in this book, see Frame 2009: 131–72. **πλήθει πρόσθε βαλόντες** 'by their number, casting (their horses) in front': the phrasing recalls Menelaos' complaint against Antilochos (πρόσθε βαλών 572), and sets apart the sinned-against father and his sinning son. Unusual in Homer (who prefers πληθύς to πλῆθος), πλήθει alludes to their conjunction; in antiquity the word was variously interpreted as referring to more than one chariot, the race officials' favour for the twins at the start, or the crowd's support for them to compete as one (Σ A and Schironi 2018: 253–4).   **παρ' αὐτόφι** = παρ' αὐτοῖς 'for them', i.e. the horses (638), with αὐτόφι = dative (an easy extension of the -φι ending: *GH* I § 108) and much better attested than variant παρ' αὐτόθι 'there' (West).

643–5 Nestor closes with alternating present and past, old and young (625–50n.): so once (ποτ(ε)) was I (A¹ 643), now (νῦν αὖτε) the young should compete (B¹ 643–4), while I must yield to age (B² 644–5), but then (τότε δ' αὖτε) I was foremost (A² 645). Here A¹ and A² are confined within their verses, and B¹ is held together by ω-assonance extended into 644, while (further) necessary run-over of πείθεσθαι (645) underlines his sense of loss in old age in B².   **ἔον:** rare 1st sing. thematic imperf. of εἰμί, a form for which Homer has several alternatives (ἦα, ἔα).   **ἀντιοώντων:** 3rd pl. pres. imp. act. of ἀντιάω, with diectasis (< ἀντιώντων < ἀντια-όντων).   **γήραϊ λυγρῶι:** this distancing formula, normally applied to old men separated either from their children or their youth (5.153, 18.434; cf. 10.79), stresses the gap between them (cf. 587–8, 621–3, 789–91ᵃnn.; Zanker 2019: 80).

646–7 ἀλλ' ἴθι: the poet signals the end of the theme, and the event, with a transitional expression usually followed by an imperative (or equivalent) to introduce a departure (normally the addressee's) to fulfil the command (1.32, 2.163 = 179, 3.431, 4.362, 10.52, etc.).   **σὸν ἑταῖρον:** 6–7n.   **κτερέϊζε:** etymologically unexplained, κτέρεα are gifts for the dead, often found as an internal accusative with κτερ(ε)ίζω 'conduct the funeral' (24.38, *Od.* 1.291, 2.222, etc.). For the current construction, with the dead person as direct object, see 11.455, 18.334, 22.336, 24.657, etc. (with Hoekstra 1965: 142–3 for a developmental narrative).   **πρόφρων δέχομαι:** Nestor hints that he is doing Achilleus a favour; ὑποδέχομαι is more usual with this adjective in epos, referring to acts of hospitality (9.480, *Od.* 2.387, 14.54, etc.) or divine help (*HDem.* 226, Hes. *Th.* 419), while πρόφρων 'is used especially of a favourable deity' (Richardson 1974: 228).

648–9 Nestor now responds to Achilleus' earlier characterisation of the gift as a μνῆμα for Patroclos (619) by reconfiguring that act of memory on himself, in a very subtle rebuke that asserts his worth despite his age. Note especially the close sonant mirroring of the two cola in 649 around the notion of τιμή. The phrasing is compressed, and scholars have wrongly sought to delete 649 or read it as parenthetical to 648 (cf. Ruijgh 1971: 408).   **μευ:** this contracted form is light by correption before ἀεί (itself rare next to αἰεί in Homer).   **μέμνησαι:** intervocalic *sigma* in the

2nd pers. mediopass. primary endings is rare in epos (generally -εαι/-ηαι or contracted -ηι: *GH* I § 227; Intro. § 3.1.2.d.i). Elsewhere the poet uses both μέμνηαι (which West prints) and μέμνηι, but μεμνήσαι is by far the best attested of the variants, and the restoration (less likely retention) of -σ- in the perfect middle is paralleled in Homer (δεδάκρυσαι 16.7) and standard in later Greek.   **ἐνηέος:** uncontracted gen. sing. of the adjective ἐνηής (as at 252 above), otherwise only applied to Patroclos. The transfer of his typical quality (250–4n.) to Nestor is meaningful: the old man equates himself with the honorand in a different way from that Achilleus used above (625–50n.; cf. Grethlein 2007b: 168–9).   **οὐδέ σε λήθω** 'nor do I escape your notice': a lightly strained tone is bestowed by this particular form of the common idiom when a speaker vocalises a previously latent and troublesome theme (1.561, 10.279, 24.563, *Od.* 19.91). λήθω = λανθάνω, formed straight from λαθ- without the -άνω suffix (cf. κεύθω = κευθάνω: *GH* I § 147). Nestor also caps his own and his son's earlier use of the third-person form of this idiom (323, 326, 416: see 326, 415–16nn.) as progressive stages in the dynamic between his advice and Antilochos' partial deployment of it.   **τιμῆς ... τετιμῆσθαι** 'the honour (which it is right for me) to have been honoured with among the Argives': genitive τιμῆς after οὐδέ σε λήθω as a verb of remembering ('you do not forget my honour' *GH* II § 66) or because of 'reverse attraction' into the case of the relative pronoun ἧς (genitive of value after τετιμῆσθαι: *GH* II § 71; Probert 2015: 178). The perfect tense expresses Nestor's framing of his honour as an acquired *and* continuing state, the whole reinforced by the notable τιμ- polyptoton, an unusual example of *figura etymologica* with a genitive (cf. γούνων γουνάζεο 22.345; Clary 2009: 114–16).

650   The necessity of marking τιμή is continued and underlined here, since benedictions of this sort tend to occur in contexts of exchange, where the speaker requires something from the addressee (see 1.18–19, *Od.* 6.180–1, 7.148, 8.410–11, etc., *HAp.* 466, *HDem.* 135–6 with Richardson 1974: 190–1).   **τῶνδ' ἀντί:** for postpositive ἀντί, see 8.163, 13.447, 14.471, etc.   **μενοεικέα:** 29n.

652 αἶνον: an αἶνος is a speech or story (frequently a fable) with an ulterior motive or hidden meaning, as Σ bT recognise (see 23.795, *Od.* 14.508, *WD* 202; Archil. frr. 174.1, 185.1 W²). Adrados 1997–2003: 5–6 focuses more on connections with αἰνέω to define it as 'a persuasive story'. The poet thus signals Nestor's veiled correction of Achilleus, though Richardson 240 plausibly sees it signalling the old man's praise of himself (cf. Alden 2001: 30–3, Van Dijk 1997: 79–80).   **Νηλεΐδαο:** the only example of the shortened patronymic Νηλεΐδης in archaic epos (next in Choerilos fr. 13a.5 B), with Homer elsewhere preferring the longer Νηληϊάδης or Νηλήϊος (301–4ᵃn.), neither of which would fit the metre here. For this alternation within a patronymic system, see Achilleus' very common Πηλεΐδης/Πηληϊάδης (Πηλήϊος is not deployed in the same way).

653–99 Event 2. Boxing. The first of the remaining contests will end in a clear victory for the first-rising competitor Epeios, and requires no intervention. Competitors and prizes are somewhat less impressive than in the preceding and following contests, and the fight itself is like the brawl between Odysseus and Iros (*Od.* 18.1–123) in that it focuses more on the initial speeches than the actual combat. Of recent discussions, cf. esp. Ready 2023: 104–7. The typical four-part event structure (257ᵇ–897n., Table 4) is weighted heavily in favour of the second stage, the standing of the contestants, since Epeios' prospective claim on the prize replaces his actual taking it in the fourth stage, where the poet focuses instead on the actions of Euryalos' companions.

   Homer's was the first of many later literary treatments of boxing, in which by contrast the violence of the conflict is foregrounded and the course of the fighting itself narrativised (Theoc. 22.27–134, Ap. Rhod. *Arg.* 2.1–97, Verg. *Aen.* 5.362–484, Stat. *Theb.* 6.729–825, Val. Fl. *Arg.* 4.141–293, Quint. Smyrn. 4.284–404, Nonn. *Dion.* 37.485–545; Crowther 1999). Aside from being one of the standard core of events (257ᵇ–897n.), and its centrality to the mythological profile of Polydeuces (3.236–8), boxing's early imprint in Greek literature is evident *inter al.* in Anacreon's figuration of Eros as a boxer (346 fr. 4, 396 *PMG*), in the several Pindaric odes dedicated to boxers (*Ol.* 7, 10, and 11) and victors in the pancration (*Isthm.* 8, *Nem.* 5), in tragedy (e.g. Soph. *Trach.* 441–2) and mime (Sophron fr. 4.16 Hordern: see generally Fiedler 1992; Weiler et al. 1995: esp. 265–6; Larmour 1999: 117–19; García Romero 2001: 31–73; Nicholson 2014). This was a very popular and visible sport right throughout the ancient world (Laser 37–48; Poliakoff 1987: 68–88; Miller 2004b: 51–7; Nakamura 2019).

653–6 Setting up the prizes is straightforward: first prize named first (without place label) over two verses, second prize named second and place labelled in just one verse. The relative prominence here, and much else, is reflected in Achilleus' speech and Epeios' boast (see 658–63, 664–6, 667–9nn.).   ἀλεγεινῆς 'causing pain' (ἄλγος): mostly used for negative or threatening events (battle, distressing messages, etc.), the adjective reminds us of the potential for loss and physical harm in athletic activity. It is applied to the next event, the wrestling (701, *Od.* 8.126), where the expression θῆκεν ἄεθλα is also found, creating a link which will be developed below (Mawet 1979: esp. 230): 685–7n.   ἐξέτε᾽ ἀδμήτην = 266ᵃ (see 265ᵇ–6n.), describing the second prize in the chariot race, the horse pregnant with a mule. The following relative clause seems to gloss the epithet as 'untameable' rather than 'untamed' (Rank 1951: 82–3), though one could take ἀδμήτην in its usual sense: 'in its mature vigour it does not yield to the yoke' (Σ T 654).   νικηθέντι 'for the loser': also at 704, another link with the wrestling.   δέπας ἀμφικύπελλον: 218–21n.

657–8 = 271–2 (see 271–3n.). The opening address Ἀτρεῖδη τε καὶ ἄλλοι ἐϋκνήμιδες Ἀχαιοί connotes consternation arising from the claims to come, but here that consternation will come in Epeios' speech and self-presentation, underlining further the unusual nature of his participation (see 664–75, 664–6nn.).

658–63 Achilleus' speech mirrors and augments the poet's description of the prize setting in progression and language, with naming of the contest (659–60 ~ 653) naturally followed by delineation of the first (660–2 ~ 654–5, with 662ᵃ = 654ᵃ) and second (663 ~ 656) prizes (von Alvensleben 2022: 102; see 42n.). This will be repeated, with variation, by Epeios (664–7, 667–9nn.). Line 659 = 802, before the fight in armour.   ὥ περ ἀρίστω: dual relative clause, with verb 'to be' omitted, and with emphatic περ (77–9n.).   πύξ μάλ᾽ ἀνασχομένω πεπληγέμεν: lit. 'raising (them) up, to strike hard (μάλ᾽) with the fist'. For ἀνασχομένω in this sense (cf. English 'put 'em up'), see 686, Od. 18.95. πεπληγέμεν is reduplicated aor. act. infin. of πλήσσω (GH I § 189).   καμμονίην 'steadfastness': derived from κατά and μένω (with apocope and assimilation), it denotes the 'victory that comes from standing fast' (Σ D Zs 22.257). Apollo has an early link to boxing (HAp. 149–50), which Σ D Zs 23.660 refers to the story in 'the Cyclic poets' that he killed the violent brigand Phorbas in a boxing match, an event related by Philostratos (Imag. 2.19; cf. also Plutarch, Mor. 724b; Pausanias 5.7.10; Graf 2008: 24, 30, 113).   γνώωσι: for the form, see 609–11n. This reference to public notice as some guarantee of victory is unique in these pre-contest speeches, and captures the fact that basileutic dominance must be seen.   νεέσθω: 3rd sing. pres. mid. imp. of νέω 'I return', and generally favoured by modern editors despite its inferior attestation in the MSS (which favour φερέσθω). It may be an Aristarchean emendation, since it would preserve his ἄγειν/ φέρειν distinction (511–13n.: cf. Van der Valk 1963–4: II.175), but the corruption is easily imagined the other way, with φερέσθω intruding from proximate athletic contexts (as 23.538, 809, and esp. 856; cf. also 229–30n.).   δέπας … ἀμφικύπελλον: see 218–21.

664–75 Epeios sets the pattern of the confident boxer in subsequent literary matches (Fiedler 1992: 4; Crowther 1999: 126–7), and his speech, judged 'unseemly [and] ... boastful' by Plutarch (*Mor.* 543f), culminates and combines the poet's description (653–6) and Achilleus' pre-contest speech (659–63) in both language and structure, but now in an elaborate ring: the contest is named within his expertise (A 665 ~ 653 πυγμαχίης ~ 660 πύξ) and the first prize qualified with the same epithet (B 666 ἡμιόνου ταλαεργοῦ ~ 654 = 662) in the poet's voice, and then Epeios begins with the second prize (C 667 ~ 663 ~ 656, with 667ᵇ = 663ᵇ), progresses to the first prize (B 668), and finally names the contest (A² 669) once more. This emphasises the loser in the centre of the ring, preparing for the ironic reversal at the speech's end (674–5n.) and allowing the transition to Epeios' intervening claims to pre-eminence (670–5). His claim to athletic prowess or dominance suggests an uncertainty about the audience's attitude to him, or at the very least a need to justify himself (271–84n.), though here Epeios asserts his worth *despite* the athletic skill, not because he is failing to show the full range of his competitive talents. Parks 1990: 90 analyses the speech as an example of battlefield 'flyting', with alterations of the usual pattern (killing, vaunting, etc.) for the non-lethal context; certainly the seriousness of the challenge reflects a constant theme in the 'heavy events' in ancient sources, where a determination to harm one's opponent is constantly stressed (Crowther 1999: 121–4).

664–6 ἠΰς τε μέγας τε 'strong and great': this formula is not 'mostly used of Trojans' (Graziosi and Haubold 2010: 131), but adds to the slightly unsettling sense around Epeios, since characters so labelled suffer something harmful to themselves and/or their reputation in the immediate context (2.653, 3.167, 226, 5.628, etc.; Bernsdorff 1992: 20–1). For ἠΰς, see 524–5n.   υἱὸς Πανοπῆος Ἐπειός: Epeios was the maker of the Trojan Horse (*Od.* 8.493, 11.523), and he participates also in the iron throwing, where his efforts make the Greeks laugh (839–40n.). Stesichorus fr. 200 F makes him a lowly water carrier to the Atreidai, while some later authors expanded his role a little, casting him as a leader with his own contingent (Dictys 1.17), and a participant in the planning and/ or execution of the ambush (Verg. *Aen.* 2.264, Tzetz. *Carm. Il.* 632–50, Quint. Smyrn. 12.314–35; cf. Howland 1954–5 and now Adamo 2024: 85–9). In Homer he remains a secondary figure, an example of the 'unpromising hero' whose later career was determined by his association with Odysseus (Finglass 2013: 7–13), and some see his participation here as a class-based challenge to the usual aristo-monarchic patterns of restricted excellence (Dunkle 1987: 10–11; Scanlon 2018; Dova 2020);

certainly he is the only participant in the games unmentioned in the Catalogue of Ships. In the fifth century, a tradition developed that he was a coward, as in the proverb Ἐπειοῦ δειλότερος (com. adesp. fr. 952 *PCG*), perhaps sourced in this admission about his fighting prowess. In Lucian's 'Thanatousia' on the Isle of the Blest, Epeios ties in the boxing with a certain Areios the Egyptian, but he does at least get a mention (*Ver. hist.* 2.22): only the wrestling, boxing, and poetic contests seem to have interested the narrator.

667–9 ἆσσον ἴτω: see 8–9n. for the accent. The combination of this adverb with a verb of motion need not denote an offensive movement (cf. above, 23.8–9, 44, 97), but in a context like this, it is an aggressive expression obviously redolent of life or death conflicts (1.567, 6.143 = 20.149, 22.92, *Od.* 9.300, etc.; cf. 14.247, 15.105).   δέπας ... ἀμφικύπελλον: Epeios pointedly caps the unusual splitting of this formula (218–21n.) in Achilleus' speech (663) by mirroring it.   οὔ φημι: the verb frequently means 'I declare as my belief' (*LfrgE* s.v. I 3 a), and it can be difficult to narrow the sense either to the act or the thought behind it. The negative is usually taken with the dependent infinitive 'no other man will' etc. (but see 3.342, *Od.* 7.239, 23.116).   ἀξέμεν: 'mixed aorist' infin., here with future effect (see 49–51n.).   εὔχομαι εἶναι 'I claim to be': not usually coupled with a superlative (except at 1.91, 2.82), these typically verse-end expressions represent the character's central conception of themselves, drawing on a variety of themes (genealogy, origin, general status) but only rarely on proficiency with a single skill (e.g. 5.173; Kelly 2007a: 210–11). It is unsurprising that Epeios makes a claim like this in the context, but its surprising specialism matches the following admission.

670–1 In keeping with his non-appearance in the battle (only Eumelos of the other competitors is similarly absent in the rest of the poem: 288–9n.), Epeios' candour is striking, and the specialism he relies on here may be reflected in his poor performance in the iron throwing (839–40n.). Σ AbT 670 was of the view that 'conceding the respects in which one is inferior creates trust about things one professes', though Plutarch was much less impressed by it (*Mor.* 543f).   ἦ οὐχ ἅλις 'Is it not enough?': synizesis (Intro. § 3.2) of the first two syllables gives a heavy beginning to the verse. This idiom, which usually criticises the addressee's presumption (5.349, 17.450, *Od.* 2.312, 17.376 – and next in Eur. *Andr.* 582), is untypically applied to the speaker. West 2001a: 271–2 finds the expression difficult here, but that matches the unusual nature of the admission.   μάχης ἐπιδεύομαι 'I fall short in (lit. 'of') battle': the genitive denotes removal or 'distance from' (*GH* II § 80). This particular collocation is a (too?)

candid admission, for it is elsewhere only a rebuke (17.142) or made positive in litotes (24.385; cf. 13.310).   οὐδ' ἄρα πως ἦν 'nor, then, is it possible that': an expression used for gnomic statements, most closely paralleled at 16.60 (Lardinois 1995: 73–4 n. 149). The indefinite adverb πως is often found as an adjectival predicate for γενέσθαι (e.g. 12.65–6, 13.114, with gnomic force *Od.* 5.103–4 = 137–8); for von der Mühll 1952: 241 n. 9, the phrase is a sign of his 'unwilling concession'. The imperfect ἦν denotes 'a process still true in the present' (*GH* II § 284), and is very often found with the consequential particle ἄρα 'then' to 'indicate what is already known' (George 2018: 253): see 11.604, 16.33, *Od.* 13.209–10.

672–3 Reminiscent of the posturing before a prize fight, the gruesome threat in 673 is certainly more serious than anything with which Odysseus or Iros threaten one another (*Od.* 18.20–4, 25–31), and underlined by the colon-ending rhyme ῥήξω/ἀράξω.   ὧδε γὰρ ἐξερέω, τὸ δὲ καὶ τετελεσμένον ἔσται: Epeios is supremely confident, and he will be successful (see 410n.).   σὺν τ' ὀστέ' ἀράξω 'I will smash up his bones (i.e. skull)': for σύν as preposition/preverb emphasising the resulting confusion, see 465–8n. ἀράσσω is almost always used with such a word, and this formula is only found in deathly contexts, caused by large objects (12.384 boulder, *Od.* 5.426 wave, 12.412 mast and sail); cf. 16.324.

674–5 The opening image, where the loser 'will carry off' (οἴσεται 667) the cup, is transformed ominously into the supporters who 'will/are to carry him out' (ἐξοίσουσιν) of the contest (perhaps an etyomological play on *ekphora*, Oliver Thomas suggests to me). The reminiscence of 159–60 and 163 (κηδεμόνες ... αὖθι μένον), where the κῆδος was Patroclos' corpse (see Martin 2023: 97 n. 1), adds to the threat, as does the number of those (ἀολλέες: 12n.) required to do the job; for the κηδεμόνες, see 162–4n. κε is commonly found with a future indicative in relative clauses with a final sense (*GH* II §§ 332–3).   ἐμῆις ὑπὸ χερσὶ δαμέντα: more unpleasantness, since this idiom is usually deployed in fatal contexts (2.860 = 874, 3.352, 10.452, etc.; cf. esp. 20.143). ὑπό (lit. 'under') + dative approaches an instrumental sense, i.e. 'under the effects of', especially with the mediopassive forms of verbs like δάμνημι, and ὄλλυμι; tr. here 'beneath' (*GH* II § 208; Aliffi 2002).

676 ὡς ἔφαθ', οἱ δ' ἄρα πάντες ἀκὴν ἐγένοντο σιωπῆι: ἀκήν is an adverb, whether a contracted form of ἀκέων or from nominal ἀκή ('silence', first attested in Moschos), but here adjectival and closely bound to σιωπῆι to mean '(they became) silent ... in silence'. The only time in the games that contestants hesitate to compete, this formula marks indecision after

a strong statement or dangerous challenge. In accepting it, the respond-
ent can be labelled as 'alone' or 'late' (as at 677 below) to underline his
individuality and courage (e.g. 3.95, 7.92, 10.218, 10.313, *Od.* 16.393),
but we note that Euryalos does not give a speech here, as would be usual
(Person 1995; Kelly 2007a: 85–8; A. Porter 2011: 503). This is also the
earliest of the crowd reactions in the event structure across the games
(257ᵇ–897n.), reflecting the extraordinary nature of Epeios' speech.

677–80 Euryalos is the third leader of the Argive contingent after
Diomedes and Sthenelos (2.563–6, 566 = 23.678), with a small catalogue
of victims (6.20–8). His paternal uncle was the Argive leader Adrestos,
and in some sources he was one of the Epigonoi who sacked Thebes,
reversing his father's failure there (see below) just as he reverses his success here in athletic competition (Kullmann 1960: 90, 148–50; Gantz
1993: 523–4). His name is derived from ἄλλομαι or ἅλς and shared by several characters in early Greek epos, including a Scherian youth and one
of Hippodameia's suitors (*LfrgE* s.v., 796–7).   ἰσόθεος φώς: predicts
Euryalos' loss (see 569ᵇ–70n.).   Μηκιστέος υἱὸς Ταλαϊονίδαο ἄνακτος
= 2.566, in the Catalogue. Son of the Argive king Talaos, Mecisteus himself has little extant myth beyond this episode and taking part in the first
expedition against Thebes (Hdt. 5.67.20; Gantz 1993: 516–17, 524). The
genitive of his name is generally printed by editors as Μηκιστῆος, an older
form almost entirely unrepresented in the MSS, which give either -εος or
-εως (both heavy syllables in synizesis). I print the former, though the latter is better attested, because it would be analogous to other such '-εος
+ son' formations in this context (cf. *GH* I §§ 46, 96; Shipp 1972: 65–8;
Janko 264, 318): 382–4n.   Θήβασδ': as the site of previous heroic
contests, Thebes is a resonant place for games, as in Tydeus' similar success on the occasion of his embassy and its violent aftermath (4.385–98;
Barker and Christensen 2019). Mecisteus' achievements seem here to
mirror those events (681–2nn.) so as to increase the connection between
Euryalos and Diomedes, Tydeus' son and his main supporter (680–1).
Unlike Diomedes, who performs well next to his father's reputation,
Euryalos will fail to live up to his.   δεδουπότος: gen. masc. sing. perf.
act. ppl. of δουπέω 'I make a heavy sound', here simply 'dead' (13.426).
The verb (and noun: 233–5n.) usually connotes violence, esp. in the common formula δούπησεν δὲ πεσών, giving rise to suggestions that the poet
knows of a tale in which Oidipous perished fighting, or 'he threw himself
from a height', or that the poet made a mistake (Σ A 679a, T 679e). Later
traditions locate his death in several places, but Thebes is understood
here and probably by *Od.* 11.275–6, where he rules on after his mother's/wife's death (Cingano 1992; Kelly 2009: 41–5).   πάντας ἐνίκα:

adding to the intimations that Euryalos will lose, this idiom is confined to athletic contexts when the application of that record in the narrative present proves more than a little tricky (4.389, 5.807, 20.410, 23.756).

681–2 The patronymic (290–2n.) reinforces Tydeus' latent presence in the context, further connecting the two cousins. δουρικλυτός: the MSS are divided over whether this is one word or two, but its components are never elsewhere split or rearranged (though cf. κλυτὸν ἔγχεϊ 21.159). It is used for several characters, unlike its relative δουρικλειτός (355–6n.). βούλετο νίκην: Diomedes' wish is bound to be upset, in the only example of this formula not applied to a deity's intervention about to be challenged or frustrated (Kelly 2007a: 223–4).

683–4 The brief equipping sequence is structured chiastically (noun – verb/verb–noun), throwing greater emphasis on the boxing bindings, and it recalls an arming scene, with πρῶτ- followed by αὐτὰρ ἔπειτα (as, e.g., at 3.330–5, 16.131–6, 19.369–73), though this is also a general trope of narrative progression (e.g. 1.386–7, 3.315–16, 6.259–60, etc.). ζῶμα: a girdle 'trailing to the feet, to prevent being nastily struck' (Σ b 683b2), though archaic depictions of the item do not show it extending that far, and Σ A 4.133a suggest it 'extended from the knees to the flanks' (bT ad loc. 'from the shins'). It seems to have been abandoned early in favour of nude competition (cf. Marinatos 1967: 12, 22–4; Visa-Ondarçuhu 1999: 29–30). This girding occurs again before the next contest, the wrestling (710–11n.), while in Odysseus' fight with Iros rags are used to cover the genitals (*Od.* 18.66–7). παρακάββαλεν: see 127–8ᵃn. Diomedes sets the girdle down on the ground for Euryalos to put on himself, as suggested by the middle participle ζωσαμένω (685); the variant περικάββαλεν in one MS is an unnecessary correction. ἱμάντας ἐϋτμήτους: for the noun, see 322–5n. These were strips of leather wound around the hands, later known as 'soft bindings' to differentiate them from 'sharp bindings' (Paus. 8.80.4), to which was attached a piece of hard leather over the knuckles (Poliakoff 1987: 68–79; Miller 2004b: 51–2).

685–7 Line 685 was quoted by Dionysius of Halicarnassos, though misidentified as coming from the wrestling match, as evidence that competitors at Greek games were not naked (*Ant. Rom.* 7.72.3–4). As in the setting out of the prizes (653–6n.), the start of the brief contest is very much like that of the next event, the wrestling, with several shared expressions (685–6 ~ 710–11) encouraging a specific connection (710–11n.). The poet focuses initially on the competitors' hands: impressive assonance and rhyme at either end of 686 (ἀντὰ δ' ἀνασχομένω ... ἅμ' ἄμφω) bookend central χερσὶ στιβαρῆισιν, an emphasis resumed in the imbalance between the two anaphoric (σύν) clauses of 687, and in the reversed positions of the noun–epithet phrases in 686–7.   **βήτην:** 3rd dual unaugmented aor. indic. act. of βαίνω. Hom. also uses βάτην (as at 710 below), since epos can preserve both long and short vowel stems in the athematic aorists (*GHI* § 180).   **ἐς μέσσον ἀγῶνα:** a typical opening, used also in the wrestling (710): see 507–8n.   **χερσὶ στιβαρῆισιν:** being μακρόχειρ and εὔπηχυς are the two first qualities Philostratos praises in a boxer (*Gymn.* 35), and hands are 'mighty' even when they're not being used, as they are here, to display physical strength. Only in Book 23 is this expression used of two people; elsewhere it is deployed of a (named) individual showing a strength most proper to them in the context (12.397, *Od.* 4.506, 8.84, 12.174, 18.335); see 84–3n. for the related expression χειρὸς ἄπο στιβαρῆς.   **ἔμιχθεν** 'were mixed': -θεν = -θησαν (287n.).

688–9ᵃ χρόμαδος: with the same suffix as many other words for sound (κέλαδος, ὅμαδος, ῥοῖβδος), this hapax was defined by the ancients variously, but obviously only with reference to this passage, as 'the sound that arises when the jaws are struck' (*Et. Gen.* B s.v.) or 'the grinding/hissing sound boxers make when they strike' (Σ AbT 688). The related verb χρεμ(ετ)ίζω is used in epos of horses whinnying in a fearful or aggressive setting (Tichy 1983: 199; Perpillou 1996: 92–4).   **ἔρρεε δ᾽ ἱδρώς:** the image raises the matter of defeat, as again in the wrestling (714–17ᵃn.), since this idiom is only found elsewhere of wounded or defensive characters (11.811, 16.109, *Od.* 11.599; cf. Mimn. fr. 5.1 W²).

689ᵇ–90 Epeios strikes with a decisive uppercut, the only described punch in the encounter.   **δῖος:** see 136–7n.   **παπτήναντα** 'looking around': masc. acc. sing. aor. act. ppl. of παπταίνω. Linking with the defeat theme raised by ἔρρεε δ᾽ ἱδρώς, Euryalos' nervous observation is definitely a defensive modality (see 691n.), as with all characters so predicated (see 462–4n.).

690–1 οὐδ᾽ ἄρ᾽ ἔτι δήν 'nor, then, hereafter for long …': Euryalos' 'fall' is immediate, since this formula marks the direct consequence of a previous action or speech, which turns out as the agent had willed it, and in each case (except *Od.* 2.36) with emphatic necessary run-over (here ἑστήκειν: 6.139, 8.126, *Od.* 2.296, 397, 17.72) ἄρα marks the continuation from the previous sentence (George 2018), ἔτι and δήν are mildly tautological (perhaps why the combination occurs only once outside this formula at *Od.* 6.33, nor after Homer until Eudocia in the fifth century CE), and the heavy

scansion of -ι reveals original δρήν.   ἑστήκειν: 3rd sing. pluperf. act.
indic., with ν mobile to avoid hiatus (as also *Od.* 18.344).   ὑπήριπε:
3rd sing. 2nd aor. act. indic. of ὑπερείπω, with intrans. meaning 'collapsed
beneath' (ὑπό).   φαίδιμα γυῖα: despite their lustrous appearance,
only defeated characters are so described (62–4n.).

692–4 The image nicely captures the effect of a really good uppercut.
The power of wind-driven water represents Epeios' inherent superiority,
while Euryalos is the typically unheroic and helpless fish (De Jong 2001:
540), saved in a unique take on the usual deadly contexts of these similes (16.406–10, 21.22–6, 24.80–2, *Od.* 10.124, 12.251–5, 22.383–8: Scott
1974: 75; Said 2012: 358–9). In the interplay of timeless aorist and continuative present indicatives, ἐκάλυψεν emphasises the safety it represents
(common in similes: *GH* II § 274): to capture the difference, tr. 'as when
a fish … is thrown up (ἀναπάλλεται: below) on the weed-strewn shore, but
a dark wave has covered it …' The concatenation of rippling (φρίξ), black
water, and sea fauna is also typical, though usually linked with Zephyros
(7.63–4, 21.126–7, *Od.* 4.402–3). Perhaps the poet's choice of the north
wind is intended to underline the hostility and destructiveness at play
(193–5n.).   Βορέω: gen. sing. Homer also uses the older Βορέαο,
which leads to this Ionic form through contraction and the usual -ηο >
-εω quantitative metathesis.   ἀναπάλλεται: either passive 'is thrown
up' or middle 'flops up' (so *LfgE* s. πάλλω): more commonly in the
active applied to a spear before it is thrown (so 'brandished', 'poised'),
this compound verb is resumed in the main narrative by the syncopated
aorist middle form ἀνέπαλτο, though this and similar forms may originally
come from ἅλλομαι by misdivision (i.e. ἔπ-αλτο > ἔ-παλτο: *HW* 60–4, esp.
63).   μέλαν δέ ἑ κῦμ' ἐκάλυψεν = *Od.* 5.353 (of Ino's return to the
sea); if formulaic, even more suggestive of Euryalos' survival. A minority
of MSS read μέγα, a common epithet with κῦμα (cf. esp. *Od.* 5.435 μέγα
κῦμ' ἐκάλυψεν), but the majority (including some early papyri) have μέλαν,
an appropriately threatening colour (Moreux 1967: 257–8) which qualifies this noun only in the parallel passage, and so a less likely source of
corruption.

694–5 Matching his mid-verse appearance in 689, Epeios once more
steps in, but this time he raises upright (ὤρθωσε) his fallen foe; cf. 7.272
for a less unexpected example. Σ bT 695 relate this to a contemporary
practice not to hit someone when they are down, Scott 1997: 221 to the
practice of sending one's enemy away for ransom, while Laser 40 n. 214
cautions against seeing a 'chivalrous gesture', thinking that Epeios merely
stops his competitor from falling – but that is surely why his companions

are at hand.　　　**μεγάθυμος:** see 167ᵇ–9n. for the denotation, though 'spirited' has a more straightforwardly positive application here.

695–9 As predicted at 674–5, Euryalos' companions remove him from the arena, and the poet expands Epeios' laconic ἐμῆις ὑπὸ χερσὶ δαμέντα into a description of his foe's dazed state, together with a contrast between the attendants' actions and their lord's passivity: αὐτοί (699) stresses that they had to because he could not.　　　**ἐφελκομένοισι πόδεσσιν** 'the feet dragging after': a striking image, reversing the usual but similarly undignified circumstance where the corpse, friend or enemy, is dragged by the foot (ἕλκε ποδός *vel sim.*) from the battlefield (4.463, 10.490, 11.258 etc.; cf. *Od.* 18.100–7, where Odysseus does this to Iros).　　　**αἷμα παχύ** 'thick(ened) blood': clots or globules, as in the later medical sense (*LfrgE* s. παχύς, B2, 1082), rather than a 'thick stream of blood' (αὐλός … παχύς … | αἵματος: *Od.* 22.18–19).　　　**κάρη βάλλονθ᾽ ἑτέρωσε:** not a healthy sign, whether the subject of the verb owns the head (8.306) or not (20.482). For ἑτέρωσε, see 231–2n.　　　**κάδ:** 28n.　　　**ἀλλοφρονέοντα** 'thinking otherwise', i.e. not mentally 'in' his surroundings (so Σ D Zˢ 698; cf. Ap. Soph. s.v., 24.7 Bekker); cf. Theoc. 22.129 (of the unconscious Amycos). Probably derived from ἀλλο- rather than Aeol. ἄλλος 'mad' (or Ion. ἠλεός), the verb is also applied to Odysseus *compos mentis*, thinking of his still captive companions (*Od.* 10.374).　　　**δέπας ἀμφικύπελλον:** 218–21n. The cup receives noticeably more attention throughout (656, 663, 667), and nothing further is said of the mule after the prize setting: the poet's interest here lies in the loser's experience.

700–39 Event 3. Wrestling. This event makes an obvious pair with the boxing, to which the audience is encouraged to relate it at every stage (setting of the prizes and description of the prizes 653–6, commencement of combat 685–7nn.), but this contest has higher-profile contestants and more valuable prizes. The event replaces Diomedes (the victor and surrogate loser in the first two contests) with his frequent partner Odysseus (the better performer here) throughout the *Iliad*, and simultaneously downplays Telamonian Aias' fortunes even beyond this poem (708–9n.). The contest has two stages: firstly they grip and try to force each other to the ground (710–20), and then they try to raise one another from the ground (721–32), presumably for a throw, whereupon Achilleus intervenes before they can go for a third round. The practice in later antiquity held that the winner had to achieve three throws over his opponent (cf. 733–4n.), but in neither of the two moves here is there a clear victor. Nonetheless, Odysseus seems to have the advantage throughout

(717ᵇ–20, 725–32, 726–8, 729–32nn.). The most prominent stage in the four-part event structure (257ᵇ–897n.) is the contest itself, returning to the proportions suggested by the chariot race, and setting the pattern for the remaining events until the spear throwing.

Beyond its prominence in the core of events (257ᵇ–897n.), wrestling had a strong mythological imprint, with Heracles a famous and famously deadly exponent (Weiler 1974: 129–52), and it proved very popular in literature: it recurs readily as a theme in early lyric (e.g. Pindar, *Nem.* 4.91–6, 7.72–4) and dramatic poetry (e.g. Aisch. *Ag.* 171–2, 1206–8; Soph. *Trach.* 517–22; cf. fr. 941.13 Radt; see Larmour 1999), Plato set his *Lysis* in a wrestling school, and among the list of Protagoras' works is an 'On Wrestling' (A 1 D–K) unrelated to the actual training manual which survives in an undated first- or second-century CE papyrus fragment (*P.Oxy.* III.466 ii: Poliakoff 1986: 161–3; 1987: 51–3; for the proverbial imprint of wrestling, along with boxing and the pancration, see García Romero 2001: 31–73). More directly, Homer's episode was the first extant of many literary matches in antiquity (Ov. *Met.* 9.1–99; Verg. *Aen.* 3.278–83; Luc. *Phars.* 4.589–660; Stat. *Theb.* 6.826–910; Quint. Smyrn. 4.215–83; Nonn. *Dion.* 37.546–613: see Mauritsch 2006); those sympathetic to Aias will be pleased to learn that Lucian corrects the result here, when Odysseus loses out in the 'Thanatousia' to the Heraclid Caranos (*Ver. hist.* 2.22). For summaries and illustrations of this enduringly popular sport, see Laser 49–53; Poliakoff 1987: 23–53; Weiler et al. 1998: 363–5; Miller 2004b: 46–50.

700–7 The prizes are set out in the usual way, with a form of τίθημι and the noun ἄεθλον (700), the naming of the contest (παλαισμοσύνης 701), the labelling of the first- and second-place prizes with participles (τῶι μὲν νικήσαντι 702 ~ ἀνδρὶ δὲ νικηθέντι 704), but with the briefest accompanying speech (707). Further variation comes in separate valuations of each prize, for the first time in these games, connected by the public worth assigned to each (703b ~ 705b). Note that the two prizes – tripod and woman – parallel the combined prize for the winner of the chariot race (263–5): this is a less valuable contest.

700–1 700ᵃ = 740ᵃ, while 700ᵇ = 653ᵇ (see 653–6, 740nn.). **δεικνύμενος Δαναοῖσι**: again performative, both introducing the Achaians' valuation in 703ᵇ and 705ᵇ, and reflecting Achilleus' need for his wealth and resources to be seen. **παλαισμοσύνης:** West prints παλαιμοσύνης, which is favoured apparently by Aristarchos (Eustathios 1325.1–5 = IV.818.7–10 Van der Valk, with note; also 1587.40–1 Culhed–Olson), is found in one papyrus for this passage, and is a minority reading at *Od.* 8.103, 126 (cf.

Tyrtaios fr. 12.2 W²). Both forms are etymologically plausible, but -σμ- has better authority (Van der Valk 1949: 145). For ἀλεγεινῆς, see 653–6n.

702–3 Unlike the ἄπυρος tripod (267–8n.) offered as part of the first prize in the chariot race, this one has been used or is made 'to be put on the fire' (ἐμπυριβήτην hapax, and rare later).   δυωδεκάβοιον … τῖον 'they valued it twelve oxen worth' ~ 705 (τίον … τεσσαράβοιον) – worthy, but not magnificent prizes. A high-value item in the rural economy, oxen are the only kind of animal used as an exchange measure in Homer, and only for valuable items (Macrakis 1984). Other examples are each of the hundred tassels on the *aigis* (100: 2.449), Lycaon's ransom (100: 21.79), the proposed compensation to Odysseus from each suitor (20: *Od.* 22.57 – also Eurycleia's price: *Od.* 1.431), Glaucos' and Diomedes' 'new' suits of armour (9 and 100 respectively: 6.236), and the cauldron in the spear throwing (1: 884–6ᵃn.). Compositional need determines τῑ- (as here, 5.536, 18.81) or τῐ̄- (as at 8.161 and 705 below: *GH* I § 48).

704–5 704ᵃ = 656ᵃ (see 653–6n.). Again the woman is nameless, with the bare functional qualification that 'she knew many works' (cf. *Od.* 2.117 = 7.111 for Athene's gift ἔργα τ᾽ ἐπίστασθαι περικαλλέα καὶ φρένας ἐσθλάς, and 262–3n. for a similar formular expression, and women's work more generally), and of low value (see previous n.; esp. *Od.* 1.431 for Eurycleia). Moreover, her exposure is clear: when something/someone is placed ἐς μέσ(σ)ον, it is a matter of claim and contestation, as with the similarly positioned ἐς μέσσον ἀγῶνα for the start of the boxing (685) and wrestling (710); cf. 573–4n. For τεσσαρα-, see 267–8n.

706–7 707 ~ 753 = 831, connecting this event with the running race and iron throwing, in all of which (an) Aias competes and comes off at least second best.   στῆ δ᾽ ὀρθὸς καὶ μῦθον ἐν Ἀργείοισιν ἔειπεν: 271–3n.   τούτου ἀέθλου πειρήσεσθον: the genitive is common after verbs of 'aiming at or seeking to reach' (*GH* II § 64), while πειρήσεσθον is 2nd dual fut. mid. indic. of πειράομαι, the reading of the majority of MSS against the minority's normalising plural πειρήσεσθε, obviously the result of contamination from 752 = 830 (with three and four contestants, respectively).

708–9 The introductions juxtapose each character's essential qualities – Aias' strength and Odysseus' cunning (Whitman 1958: 169–70). Homer does not give us a precise impression of their physiques beyond the fact that Aias is huge (3.226–7) and Odysseus relatively short (3.193–4, 210–11), but they match rather well the two ideal body types praised by Philostratos for wrestling, the 'larger than proportioned' (εὐμήκης μᾶλλον ἢ ξύμμετρος *Gymn.* 35) and the 'large in small' (οἱ ἐν μικρῶι μεγάλοι 36; on the practical limitations of his judgement, see Poliakoff 1987: 144–5).   **μέγας Τελαμώνιος Αἴας:** used again at 722 and then in the fight in armour and iron throwing (811, 842), this formula combines with Τελαμώνιος ἄλκιμος Αἴας as his major noun–epithet system in the nominative case from the 3b/3a boundaries, linking paternity with characteristic size and strength; cf. his epithet πελώριος 'huge' (3.229 etc.), and Priam's description of him 'outstanding in height and broad shoulders' (3.227). This is the first appearance in Book 23 of this 'greater' Aias (cf. 473n. for the 'lesser'), leader of the Salaminian contingent (2.557–8), son of Telamon (lit. 'shield-band') and known for his huge, 'tower' shield (7.219–23, 11.485, etc.), which is the only weapon Achilleus thinks he could wield (18.192–3). Aias has a chequered record in this book, losing the fight in armour and the iron throwing, and being held to a draw here. These 'disappointing and surprising' (Hinckley 1986: 210) results are hints at his fortune after the end of the *Iliad*, given his failure to gain the arms of Achilleus after the latter's death, and his subsequent madness and suicide (*Little Iliad* arg. 3–5 B): Kullmann 1960: 83–4: also 726–8, 798–825nn. His suicide appears early in the visual record, in the seventh century (see Greco 2002, esp. for Mycenaean origins; Zunker 1988: 133–64, esp. 141ff.; Kanavou 2015: 36–44; Bocksberger 2022: 7–75).   **Ὀδυσεὺς πολύμητις:** the nominative form in -σ- is usually found, as here, in the first part of the verse or straddling the mid-verse caesura, while the -σσ- form is much more common esp. at verse-end; this alternation is metrically very productive, whatever its linguistic origin (*EDG* s. Ἀχιλλεύς: see 782–3, 791ᵇ–3nn.). πολύμητις is used with both, and is particular to Odysseus: the formula ἂν δ' Ὀδυσεὺς πολύμητις suggests a coming exercise in μῆτις, since it is used when he rises second for a public performance in which he is an apparent or actual subordinate (3.268, 23.755): 'great' Telamonian Aias is a more probable winner in a trial of strength, and the fight will call on all Odysseus' skill (as in the story of another wrestling triumph, over the Lesbian Philomeleides, *Od.* 4.341–5 = 17.132–6). The pleonastic ἂν ... ἀνίστατο is not well paralleled (cf. *Od.* 5.260), caused here by the typical use of ἀνά + name after a verb of standing *vel sim.* in a previous verse (as at 3.267–8, 23.754–5, 836–8, 859–60, 886–8, etc.). Odysseus was last seen in the assembly preceding Achilleus' return to battle still labouring from the wound he received in Book 11 (19.47–50; cf. 11.434–8), but, as with Diomedes (280–2n.), his incapacity is conveniently forgotten here (cf. generally Stanford 1968; Rutherford 1992: 19–27; Kanavou 2015: 90–106).   **κέρδεα εἰδώς:** for the idiom – another feature, as well as μῆτις, linked usually with Odysseus or his close associates – see 322–5n.

710–11 ~ 685–6 (see 685–7n.).   ζωσαμένω: Eustathios (1326.15
= IV.821.21–2 Van der Valk) suggests plausibly that the competitors wear
the same girdle as the boxers.   βάτην: see 685–7n.   ἀγκάς 'into,
viz. by, the arms/elbow': possibly this adv. was an elided form of dat.
pl. ἀγκάσι from ἀγκών (*EDG* s.v. ἀγκύλος; cf. 5.371, 14.346, 24.227,
etc.), though this is the only example before a consonant.   χερσὶ
στιβαρῆισιν: cf. 686 (with 685–7n.).

712–13 713 = 16.213 (also a simile, sometimes considered the origin of
this expression: West 2001a: 272–3), denoting the wall of a house fitted
around with close-packed stones to keep out the winds (see Purves 2010:
342–3 on this theme in the *Odyssey*), and applied to the bristling helms
and shields of the Myrmidons. The architectural techniques are well
known from the Mycenaean period onwards (Rougier-Blanc 2005: 294–
5, 320–3), and the stress on defensive protection gives an insight into its
importance in the wrestler's mindset, where extricating oneself from an
attack is an essential skill, alongside 'the tension and strength … and the
balance' between them (Lovatt 2019: 418).   ὡς ὅτ' ἀμείβοντες 'just
like rafters': the participle means 'exchanging' or 'interchanging', and
denotes 'large beams, falling across one another so as to hold up the
roof' (Σ A 711–13; cf. 12.456 ἐπημοιβοί).   τούς τε: the demonstrative pronoun is frequently used as a relative (*GH* I § 130, II §§ 248–50),
whilst 'epic τε' is very common with relative clauses, esp. within similes,
expressing a habitual state of affairs (Ruijgh 1971: 455–6).   κλυτὸς
ἤραρε Τέκτων ~ 4.110 (the making of Pandaros' bow). Editors usually
print τέκτων, viz. an anonymous 'maker', esp. since the parallel passage
has no qualification but κεραοξόος, but κλυτός is not otherwise used of
an unnamed person and suggests here a specific figure. Such 'speaking
names' are well known in Homer, especially applied to craftsmen (von
Kamptz 1982: 260–1): indeed, we find reference to a Tecton who is the
son of the similarly usefully named 'Joiner' (5.59–60) and even a patronymic Τεκτονίδαο (*Od.* 8.114; Kirk II.60; Kanavou 2015: 148). None of
these exist beyond the immediate passage, and 'false' specificity hints at
knowledge of figures and names beyond the poet's tale (cf. 18.591–2);
for another example, see the Τυχίος responsible for Aias' shield (7.220),
who then becomes part of Homeric biography (Graziosi 2002: 158–9).
The τέκτων is one of the δημιοεργοί 'workers for the people' (*Od.* 17.383–
5; Morris 1992: 3–35). ἤραρε is 3rd sing. redupl. (and augmented) aor.
indic. act. of ἀραρίσκω (*GH* I § 190). The timeless quality of the aorist
is typical in similes, and need not refer to a specific construction rather
than the sort of thing Tecton produced.

714–17ᵃ τετρίγει: 3rd sing. pluperf. act. indic. of τρίζω, a sound otherwise confined to birds, bats, and souls, and all when under some duress (99–101ᵃn. τετριγυῖα).   **θρασειάων ἀπὸ χειρῶν:** underlines the quasi-martial nature of the contest, and the contestant's great strength, since the expression is otherwise confined in the *Iliad* to massed spear casts or defence (11.553, 571, 13.134, etc.; cf. *Od.* 5.434, again of Odysseus).   **κατὰ δὲ νότιος ῥέεν ἱδρώς** = 11.811, describing the wounded Eurypylos when he meets Patroclos. This particular collocation is not found again until Callimachos (*HDelos* 211), but 'sweat flowed' is another link with the boxing, raising the spectre of defeat (688–9ᵃn.).   **σμώδιγγες ... αἵματι φοινικόεσσαι** 'weals spotted with blood': recalls the σμῶδιξ αἱματόεσσα raised by Odysseus' attack on Thersites (2.267), denoting contusions produced by the great strength behind the grips.

717ᵇ–20 The contest is even and about to be resolved, as with other cases of the 'striving for victory' idiom (369ᵇ–71ᵃn.). Anaphoric οὔτ(ε) ... δύνατο amplifies the stalemate from both perspectives but nonetheless hints at Aias' inferiority, with three of four clauses having Odysseus as subject.   **κρατερή ... ἲς Ὀδυσῆος:** such onomastic periphrases usually denote the person as a whole, as e.g. the formulae βίη Ἡρακληείη, ἱερὴ ἲς Τηλεμάχοιο, and ἱερὸν μένος Ἀλκινόοιο, in order to underline the named figure's strength (*LfrgE* s. σθένος B1b), but here the noun seems to have its proper sense (cf. Ὀδυσῆος ἱερὴ ἲς: Hes. fr. 198.2 M–W).

721–2 A typical transitional syntax, ἀλλ' ὅτε encapsulating the preceding state of affairs and καὶ/δὴ τότε introducing the resolving action (1.493–4, 6.175–7, 9.474–5, etc.).   **ἀνίαζον** 'were grieved/weary': *sc.* at the stalemate, since 'there is nothing less pleasurable for the spectators than wrestlers to be balanced for the whole day in a contest' (Σ T 721c¹). The verb is here probably intransitive (as, in similar context, at *Od.* 4.460–1), though Aristarchos and the majority of MSS read ἐϋκνήμιδας Ἀχαιούς (Van der Valk 1963–4: II.141; West 2001a: 273). Despite being formulaic (708–9n.), μέγας reinforces Aias' reliance on his size and strength, esp. before its juxtaposition with Odysseus' qualities in 723.

723–4 Aias' speech is characteristically short. The suggestion is given the term λαβή and labelled 'customary' by Σ bT 724 ad loc., but early parallels are lacking: Pausanias' story (8.40.3, set c. 400 BCE) reporting a similar agreement between boxers is clearly exceptional, and μέσον λαβεῖν *vel sim.* was the manoeuvre whereby one competitor seized another by the middle

(Poliakoff 1987: 40–53; Miller 2004b: 48). διογενές Λαερτιάδη, πολυμήχαν' Ὀδυσσεῦ: just as 722ᵇ combines Aias' central quality with his paternity, so this whole-verse formula matches and caps that traditional idiom. The first epithet does not imply actual descent from Zeus (293–5n.), and πολυμήχανος is Odysseus' distinctive epithet (cf. also *Od.* 1.205), while the patronymic evokes a figure who exists solely for this paternal role (Kanavou 2015: 106–7). A vocative formula suggests that the bards felt a need specifically for people to speak to Odysseus; while the Homeric poems have an exceptional amount of direct speech which may not have been mirrored in the rest of the tradition, conversation would have been an important element in any story involving this character. ἤ μ' … ἤ ἐγώ σέ: the repeated syntax (ἤ + 1st pers. personal pronoun), the juxtaposition of 1st and 2nd personal pronouns, and the placement of σε at the end of its sentence makes that pronoun very pointed – and so accented as in the majority of MSS (Vendryès 94). τὰ δ' αὖ Διὶ πάντα μελήσει: might Aias succeed? Concessions in this idiom tend to fall when the speaker's interest or view of the action eventuates (5.430, 17.515, *Od.* 11.332, 17.601).

725–32 First Aias (725–8) and then Odysseus (729–32) attempt the lifting manouevre, chiastically reversing the order envisaged in 723. More attention is given to Odysseus' actions in each case.

725 δόλου δ' οὐ λήθετ': in keeping with his introduction and epithets above, Odysseus reverts to his characteristic modality, as with other transitional returns embedded in the 'did not forget' idiom (1.495, 5.319, 12.203, 393, 13.835, etc.: cf. generally Simondon 1982: 22–33).

726–8 Odysseus' fist (presumably) strikes the hollow of Aias' knee (726ᵃ with notable κ-alliteration), bringing him to the ground on his back, whereupon Odysseus promptly 'falls' onto his chest. The act is underlined by the strongly run-over κάππεσε. Line 728 = 881, immediately before Meriones lifts (ἄειρεν) the prizes for the archery. Note the vividness provided by the frequent spatial adverbs – 'from behind' (ὄπιθεν), 'beneath' (ὑπ-), 'down … backwards' (κάδ … ἐξοπίσω), 'upon … down' (ἐπί … κάπ-). ὑπέλυσε δὲ γυῖα: reflects the seriousness of the contest, since this 'loosened limbs' idiom in the active almost always signals death in combat (4.469, 11.240, 260, 16.312, etc.; *contra* 21.406; Saunders 2004: 10–11) and may be an allusion to Aias' suicide after defeat in the funeral games for Achilleus. ἔβαλ' ἐξοπίσω: this majority reading is preferable to ἔπεσ', which would refer to Aias with a not un-Homeric swift change of subject (so C–G 101), because it keeps our focus on Odysseus' agency, and the influence of ἐξοπίσω and κάππεσε makes corruption of inoffensive ἔβαλ' easier to imagine.   **θηεῦντό τε θάμβησάν τε:** 'they wondered' reactions (θάμβησαν) denote surprise and suggest a change of opinion or action (1.199, 3.398, 8.77, etc.: Kelly 2007a: 115–16), so Odysseus' success was not widely expected; for θαμβέω, see also Pulleyn 2019: 193–4. θηεῦντο is 3rd pers. pl. mid. indic. of θηέομαι 'I gaze at', frequently used (as here) with a sense of astonishment or wonder (*LfgE* s.v. B 1–2); for -ευ-, universal in the MSS, see 69–70n.

729–32 Odysseus' turn will see them both end up in the dust, with no stated advantage on either side, but again the Ithacan seems to dominate. Once more a concentration of vivid adverbs – τυτθὸν ἀπό 'a little away', ἔτ' 'further', ἐν 'in', ἐπί 'on' – directs the narrative, within a very focused area of contestation, underlined by the repetition χθονός/χθονί. Line 729 ~ 778 (with κρητῆρ' for δεύτερος), as Odysseus claims the prize in the running race. Note the emphasis: a whole verse is deployed for this attempt, unlike the interruption of Aias' turn at 725.   **πολύτλας δῖος 'Οδυσσεύς:** much more common in the *Odyssey*, this distinctive formula encapsulates the character's status as the ultimate hero of *nostos* (return) songs (Bonifazi 2009). The first epithet is only used in this phrase in early epos, and exploits the semantic ambivalence of τλάω in wavering between 'much enduring' and 'much daring' (*LfgE* s.v.; Pucci 1987: 44–9, 50–62; Kanavou 2015: 95–8). For the second epithet, used again of this character at 759, 765, 778, see 136–7n.   **ἐν δὲ γόνυ γνάμψεν** 'and he bent his (own?) knee in': the manouevre 'can only be guessed at' (Leaf II.523), despite the variety of technical terms in ancient commentary. Σ bT 730–2 report 'some' claimed that Odysseus 'clashes against' (or 'turns aside': see Erbse ad loc.) Aias' 'left leg with his right knee' so that 'they fall sideways', others that 'wearying under the strain of his weight, he rolls his competitor away with himself'; Eustathios 1327.10–13 (IV.826.6–10 Van der Valk) combines the two. No matter whose it is, γόνυ is the direct object of ἐν ... γνάμψεν (only found here), and the ambiguity doubtless led to the minority reading κάμψεν (as at 7.118).   **μιάνθησαν δὲ κονίηι:** striking phrase, only paralleled in the case of the plumes on Patroclos' fallen helmet (16.795–6, 797), though cf. 4.146 (of Menelaos' thighs stained with blood). Metrical need determines κονῑ- (as here) or κονῐ-.

733–4 This contrafactual conditional (154–5n.) shows how the narrative would have continued, into a third move, had not Achilleus intervened; another example introduces his intervention in the chariot race's first quarrel (490–1n.), which has several other links with this episode (491ᵃ = 734ᵃ, μηκέτι + imp. 492 and 735: Kirk 1978: 38). Only two moves have taken place, but the typical number in epos for a stalemate in need of external resolution is *three* (as with the fight in armour: 816–17n.), the same number of throws required for wrestling victory later in antiquity, and the very number advertised here (τρίτον) in the unrealised apodosis (Kelly 2007a: 194–7). Thus Achilleus intervenes too early (*contra* e.g. Kitchell 1998: 170); cf. also 735–7n.

735–7 End-stopping dominates; the single hard run-over (ἔρχεσθ') foregrounds Achilleus' slightly odd idea that continued competition is stopping the games from proceeding, and de-emphasises his problematic division of prizes.   **ἐρείδεσθον:** 2nd pers. dual pres. mid. imp. of ἐρείδω 'I lean, press hard'. In Homer the middle usually means 'I set myself', which is sometimes applied to launching a weapon or a blow (12.457, 16.736), and so here means something akin to 'exert yourselves' (Oliver Thomas suggests to me plausibly that it could refer to taking a solid stance). The rarity of this extension accounts for the flatter variants ἐρίδεσθον and ἐρίζεσθον. Coordinated dual and plural (τρίβεσθε) verb forms are well established in Homer (e.g. 7.279 μηκέτι … πολεμίζετε μηδὲ μάχεσθον; *GH* II § 34).   **ἄεθλια δ' ἴσ' ἀνελόντες:** it is unclear how this could happen, but the poet ignores the aftermath, as again with the same problem (this time a condition of the contest! 809–10n.) after the fight in armour (816–17, 822–3nn.). Recognising his upper hand, Σ bT report a suggestion by 'some' that Odysseus took the first prize and the second prize was held 'in common', while Eustathios 1325.54–61 (= IV.820.9–20 Van der Valk) imagines a division after the games, using the bovine valuations expressly to apportion compensation (Scodel 2008: 40). Yet the poet says nothing of this, and it may be a(nother) sign of Achilleus' inadequate performance (Kelly 2017: 102–3). Taplin 1992: 257–8 takes the impossibility of division as a sort of joke on the usual, deadly competitions in this world.

738 = 54 (see n.). As always with this verse, the narrative moves on without further comment.

739 A rather homely detail, not really paralleled after the other contests; Hephaistos does the same as he prepares to receive Thetis (18.414–16), while characters returning from combat 'cool off' sweat in the sea(breeze); cf. 10.572–5, 11.621–2, 21.561, 22.1–2).   **ἀπομορξαμένω:** nom. masc. dual aor. mid. ppl. of ἀπομόργνυμι, the compound (and simplex) used transitively (as here) and intransitively, mostly to wipe away tears (2.269, 18.124, *Od.* 8.88, 11.527, 530, 17.304).

740–97 Event 4. Running. Unsurprisingly, this fourth contest in many ways recalls the chariot race, with possibly a two-part course (see 758–67, 778–81n.), a close tussle over the lead (with the winner initially trailing), speeches involving Antilochos afterwards (and another favourable reaction from Achilleus), a bullion prize, and an intervention from Athene for one of her favourites, though the order of the shared motifs 'last portion of the track' (768–9n.) and 'all-out running' (758–9n.) is swapped. Odysseus is the victor, reflecting the earlier triumph of Diomedes and their general Iliadic pairing (see 765–7n.: Köhnken 1981: esp. 130–1; more widely, Purves 2019: 67–92). The contest stage is still the most prominent of the typical four, but only just behind the prize setting, and this event is the first to have two crowd reactions (765–7, 784), which will be the norm for the rest of the events until the spear throwing.

The three competitors appear here for the last time in the poem. Many more enter the lists for this event on Scheria (*Od.* 8.120–5; for other points of contact with that race, see 758–67, 758–9, 765–7nn.), while Nestor mentions defeating only Iphiclos at the games of Amarynceus (23.636), and Homer even dissociates the race for Hector's life from the usual prizes for running contests (22.158–61: cf. 20.408–12; Laser 32–7; Weiler et al. 2002: esp. 132–41).

Running was early identified as a representative athletic activity in literature (Tyrtaios fr. 12.1–4 W²), and a fruitful source for metaphor for both success (Eur. *El.* 883) and risky behaviour (Hdt. 8.74.1, 102.3, 140.4; cf. Larmour 1999: 99–108 for drama; García Romero 2001: 1–21 for its proverbial profile). Possibly depicted as early as a sixth-century band cup now in Basel, and on a seventh-century cup from Kommos in Crete (Intro. § 2.2), Homer's race helped to spawn many such episodes (Pind. *Ol.* 4.17–27; *Pyth.* 9.111–25; Theoc. 3.42; Verg. *Aen.* 5.286–361; Stat. *Theb.* 6.550–645; Sil. Ital. *Pun.* 16.457–526; Quint. Smyrn. 4.180–214; Nonn. *Dion.* 37.614–66), but one of its less well-known receptions is found in Libanios' description of a painting of the race in which a sorrowful Achilleus presides whilst the two Atreidai sit with sceptres and crowns, intent on the action, as Nestor speaks to them (*Ecphrasis* 3): Libanios says the image 'competes with' (ἀμιλλᾶται) the poetry, but none of the participants have any role in our episode except Achilleus, whose demeanour is much different, and as much space is given to the Atreidai's unnamed three attendants (3.3) as to any heroic character.

Foot races, over a variety of distances, were a central element in Greek athletic contests in all periods of antiquity, and their prominence was clear in the fact that running was the first kind of event established at Olympia (Miller 2004b: 31–46; Kyle 2015: 115–17; Romano 2021). Much like the current race (758–67n.), the *diaulos* or 'two-pipe' was apparently introduced there in 724 BCE (= 14th Olympiad: Philostratos, *Gymn.* 12) and run over c. 400 m (the more prestigious *stadion* was one length of the track, c. 200 m).

740–51 Prizes are set out in the usual way (τίθημι + ἄεθλα), but the first has by far the most, and most elaborate, description of any item offered in this book (741–9). Ringed by Achilleus setting the prize for speed (740 ~ 748–9), though only the closing element links it explicitly with the winner (749), the κρητήρ is explored as to its material, size, quality, origin, and trade-destination, before its presence in the camp is explained as ransom for Lycaon, an episode recalled when the newly returned prince encounters Achilleus for the second, fateful time (21.34–136). In another analepsis, Asteropaios' armour is given as an extra prize after the chariot race (560–2n.), and Sarpedon's panoply in the next contest (fight in armour), which like the current example evokes Patroclos' presence as the original claimant (Köhnken 1981: 132 and n. 9). The extended description underlines the item's huge value (see 746–7n.) and, like other object biographies in Homer, contributes an 'archaeology of the past' and diachronic depth to the heroes' world and its analogy to the audience's (Grethlein 2008: 35–43; Whitley 2013). Beautifully wrought metal bowls of this sort are known in Levantine contexts in the Iron Age and early Archaic period, and two examples have been found in Lefkandi (López-Ruiz 2021: 87–9): see 741–3, 744–5nn.

740 740ᵃ = 700ᵃ (wrestling), connecting the two events (see also 752–3 below). The ring surrounding the description is closed at 748–9 (see n.).

741–3 A high-value metal (269–70n.), silver is used for mixing-bowls (218–21n.) for Menelaos' gift to Telemachos (another Sidonian artefact, a gift from their king: *Od.* 4.614–19 = 15.114–19), in Odysseus' gifts from Maron (*Od.* 9.203–4) and in his fake tale to his father (*Od.* 24.275), and in Circe's house (*Od.* 10.356–7).   **τετυγμένον:** masc. acc. sing. perf. pass. ppl. of τεύχω 'I make', used for a variety of metal items to mean 'well made' rather than just 'made' (Müller 1974: 16), a sense amplified in 743. For the extent implied by 'six measures' see 264–5ᵃn., and 267–8n. for the μέτρα | χάνδανεν idiom (of the cauldron, third prize in the chariot race).   **κάλλει ἐνίκα πᾶσαν ἐπ' αἶαν | πολλόν:** a big claim, since extent qualifications (πᾶσαν ἐπ' αἶαν) are elsewhere used of divine influence (Eos 8.1 = *Od.* 24.695, Atē 9.506) or universal *kleos* (*Od.* 24.509), and the 'conquering in beauty' idiom is similarly superlative (of Lesbian women 9.130 = 272): see 677–8on. for the similar 'conquered all' expression. κάλλος is elsewhere in Homer applied to people, increasing the object's 'desirability' but also linking victory with the physical attractiveness of the basileutic class (Shakeshaft 2019: 6). The whole is emphasised by run-over πολλόν enabling the explanation in 743. **Σιδόνες πολυδαίδαλοι:** denoting the Sidonians' skill and/or productivity in high-quality manufacture, this compound adjective elsewhere in epos describes the wrought item ('with much ornament'; e.g. 24.597; see Frontisi-Ducroix 1975: 35–82, esp. 70; Morris 1992: 22–3). For the shift, consider city epithets like πολύχρυσος and πολύχαλκος, where having 'much' of a certain thing translates into producing it (cf. Σιδῶνος πολυχάλκου *Od.* 15.425; *HW* 132–3). The inhabitants of Sidon are famously skilful manufacturers (e.g. 6.289–91), but not sharply distinguished from 'Phoenicians' (cf. *Od.* 13.272–3 and 285–6, and next n.).

744–5 Named here for the only time in the *Iliad*, and lacking formular purchase in epos, the Phoenicians are traders and sailors with a mixed epic reputation; next to their positive depiction in Odysseus' first lying tale (*Od.* 13.272–86), compare Eumaios' kidnap (*Od.* 15.415–84) and their range of largely negative epithets (Dougherty 2001: 102–21, *contra* Crielaard 1995: 227–8). The ethnonym is Greek, derived from φοινός/ φοῖνιξ 'blood-red' or 'purple' (cf. 454–5n.), whence Lat. *Poenus* and *Punicus*, and its application to the communities of the Syrian coastline may stem from their trade in dye/dyed items or palm-dates (also termed φοῖνιξ; Wathelet 1983; Winter 1995; López-Ruiz 2021). **ἐπ' ἠεροειδέα πόντον:** adding to the history, the *krētēr*'s journey was not straightforward, for this formula is reserved for difficult and dangerous voyages (*Od.* 2.263, 3.105, 294, *HAp.* 493, etc.; cf. *Th.* 873, *WD* 620). **στῆσαν δ' ἐν λιμένεσσι** 'and they moored in the harbour': sc. νῆα, as with similar expressions (*Od.* 2.391, 12.305, etc.). Ships in epos may be drawn fully onto the shore for a longer stay or fastened offshore, a tactic designed for quick departures (14.75–9, *Od.* 4.785; see Casson 1971: 48; Kurt 1979: 187–8, 194 n. 28). **Θόαντι δὲ δῶρον ἔδωκαν:** the polyptoton (cf. 23.296–7, *Od.* 21.13: Clary 2009: 225–34) emphasises the quasi-heroic (if unexplained) behaviour of these traders, matching that of Euneus in exchanging the *krētēr* for Lycaon (NB ἔδωκεν in 746). Not an uncommon name, this Thoas is the 'godlike' ruler of Lemnos (14.230), father of Hypsipyle and grandfather of Jason's son Euneos (7.468–9), whose role in the ransom (21.40–1) is here expanded; for Homer's knowledge of Argonautic myth, see West 2005.

746–7 υἷος: athematic gen. sing. of υἱός (originally ὑύς/υἱύς), slightly more common than υἱέος in Homer, who has only one example of the common later thematic gen. υἱοῦ (*Od.* 22.238: *GH* I § 100). The genitive is typical in contexts of value and exchange (*GH* II § 71).   ὦνον ἔδωκεν 'gave as the price': the noun is often linked with slavery (*LfrgE* s.v. B2), and the phrase is used of this episode at 21.40 and of Eumaios' sale to Laertes (*Od.* 15.388, 429). Given that Lycaon specifies his price as worth a hecatomb (21.79: see 146–8n.), the cup is incredibly valuable.   Ἰησονίδης Εὔνηος: the patronymic (7.468, 471) suggests that Euneus, a good name for someone who supplies the Greek army by ship (7.467–71), may not have been a Homeric invention, especially since Lemnos had considerable purchase in the Trojan story, *inter al.* as a slave market (24.751–3; see Kullmann 1960: 270, 293–7; Kelly 2008b: 9–10).

748–9 The description closes the ring from 740: ἀέθλιον ~ ἄεθλα, and ταχυτῆτος is picked up by the relative clause (with suppressed dative antecedent) in 749, which is further unified by plosive alliteration and explicitly introduces the catalogue of prizes. The optative (πέλοιτο) with or without a modal particle (κε/ἄν) is frequent in indefinite relative clauses, expressing a less proximate view than the subjunctive, i.e. 'whoever should be …', especially but not only after past-tense principal verbs (*GH* II § 365).

750–1 The rewards for second and third are somewhat anticlimactic.   πίονα δημῷ 'rich in fat': a sign of a valuable animal (see 30–3n.). In a variety of forms, this usually line-ending and somewhat tautological formula (πίων and δημός both mean 'fat') can refer either to animal fat (δημός) or to a territory and its people (δῆμος). However the words are related (Onians 1953: 211–12 n. 9 derives the latter from the former, Ceccarelli et al. 1998 vice versa), here the expression clearly refers to the animal itself (cf. Nagler 1974: 5–9, 37–44).   ἡμιτάλαντον 'half-talent': compounded in a common way (e.g. ἡμί-ονος, ἡμί-θεος: *WHS* 189), this word is found in early epos only here and at 796 below. For the surprisingly low value of the Homeric talent, see 269–70n. Bullion prizes are offered here and in the chariot race (fourth place).   λοισθήϊ' 'the last prize': acc. neut. pl. from the adjective λοισθήϊος, used as a substantive (see δεύτερ' 536–8n.).

752–3 = 706–7 (wrestling), 830–1 (iron throwing); for 752, see 271–3n.; for 753, see 706–7n.

754–6 The competitor list opens and closes with quick runners, the poet favouring Antilochos over Oilean Aias with a verse-and-a-half of description, a patronymic formula and run-over name, and a call-back to the description of the first prize (cf. ἐνίκα 742), though the 'defeated everyone' idiom foreshadows Antilochos' failure to apply that record to this race (677–80n.; cf. 15.569–71 for his speed, and Nelson 2023: 98–100). The eventual winner Odysseus is sandwiched and qualified by the proleptically relevant πολύμητις (708–9n.), but he is increasingly favoured by the poet as the narrative proceeds (Köhnken 1981: 132–3, 135–7). Aias' eagerness directly recalls his rather unsavoury quarrel with Idomeneus (754 = 488; see 488–9n.), and prepares us for his failure; for Ὀϊλῆος ταχὺς Αἴας (and his speed) see 473n. The use of ἄν reflects the original independence of the preposition/preverb; tr. 'and up, too' (cf. also 836–8, 860); Fehling 1969: 196 differently interprets it as a 'Vermischung' of cases like 884–6 (see n.), i.e. as though following a form of ἀνόρνυμι.

757 = 358 (see 358–61n.).

758–67 There is some uncertainty over precisely what is envisaged. Like the chariot race, this could be a *diaulos* (740–97n.) in two legs around the turning-post (τέρματ') pointed out by Achilleus, with νύσσης (1) once more another word for that item (332, 338: Köhnken 1981: 133–4), or (2) denoting the starting line (Richardson 253, *LfrgE* s. νύσσα B2). If the latter is preferred, the race could also be a single, sprint lap (Σ bT 758), though 768 (= 353) would then refer to the 'very last part' of the straight, rather than the whole of the homeward leg. This is not impossible, and perhaps we could imagine that the earlier turning-post served as the starting point for this race.

758–9 Initial description matches the standing order, though the poet omits all mention of Antilochos.   **τοῖσι δ' ἀπὸ νύσσης τέτατο δρόμος** = *Od.* 8.121 (the first narrated action in that race), also followed by a simile (124–5) to illustrate the distance between the winner and the rest. τέτατο is 3rd sing. unaugmented pluperf. pass. indic. of τείνω 'was strained (taut)', stressing the result of this effort before a series of imperfects move the narrative on. The same metaphor (Moulton 1979: 290–3) also appears in the chariot race, similarly followed by line-end ὦκα δ' ἔπειτα + intransitive ἐκφέρω (375–6n.); for the meaning of δρόμος, see 296–300n. Note the heavy scansion ἀπὸ νύσσης, as though before *νυύσσης (Intro. §3.2).   **Ὀϊλιάδης:** as a significant character in epos, Aias has an -ιάδης patronmyic, though it is not often used when compared with the straight genitive Ὀϊλῆος (with or without υἱός). Zenodotos may have read ὃ Ἰλιάδης, an un-Homeric combination of demonstrative and patronymic which he favoured wherever this nominative form is found (13.203, 14.446), and which he rewrote in the other cases (12.365, 13.712: Nickau 1977: 36–42; Janko 51); also 473n.

760–3 'As when a weaving rod (κανών) is [very close to] a well-girdled woman's chest, which she draws with practised (εὖ μάλα) hand, dragging the spool (πηνίον ἐξέλκουσα) across and away from the thread (παρὲκ μίτον), and she holds it near her chest'. Precisely how this action is to be understood in detail is uncertain (Edmunds 2020: §§ 24–38 discusses the function of the various items here). Developing the metaphor from 758 (τέτατο ~ τανύσσηι), the simile is anchored to the narrative (ἄγχι ~ ἀγχόθι), marked by ring composition (στήθεος 761, 763), and closed by references to Odysseus running 'near' (ἄγχι μάλ' 760, ἐγγύθεν 763). Though not often used in similes (see 4.141–7, 12.433–6), women's work is implicated and active in τιμή competition, and – aside from how close the race is – the image underlines Odysseus' wider connections to weaving women (Calypso, Circe, Penelope; Pantelia 1993; Ready 2011: 157–8; Canevaro 2018: 55–107, 141–3). On the break of Hermann's Bridge before ἐϋζώνοιο, see 75–6n.   **δῖος Ὀδυσσεύς:** 136–7, 729–32nn.   **στήθεος:** genitive after ἄγχι (760) in the main narrative (cf. ἄγχοθι δ' ἴσχει | στήθεος).   **κανών** '[weaving] rod': in the plural this is part of a shield (8.193, 13.407), but its function in either context is uncertain (Borchhardt 1977: 4; Edmunds 2020: §§ 24–38).

763–4 The spatial adverbs of 763 continue and amplify the simile effect, the image in 764 reinforced by repeated κ and ν sounds (ἴχνια/κόνιν ἀμφιχυθῆναι) surrounding the plosive footfall (τύπτε πόδεσσι πάρος).

765–7 Like Diomedes' horses on Eumelos' back shortly before Apollo's intervention (380–1), so here Odysseus' breath strikes down (κάδ: 28n.) onto Aias' head/neck (οἱ κεφαλῆς: Σ bT comment on their relative height). The variant ἐκ κεφαλῆς (with Aristarchos) makes Odysseus 'pour the breath from his head', as though laboured (see 768–9n.). Odysseus' support from the Greeks is long-standing (cf. 2.272–5).   **δῖος Ὀδυσσεύς:** repetition of the epithet (729; cf. 136–7n.) maintains a favourable emphasis on Odysseus, in a passage where Aias remains undernamed and largely out of focus, until he slips in the dung.   **ἱεμένωι:** Σ bT read ἱέμενοι as a sign that the crowd is 'of good intent' (sc. to him), but the 'striving for victory' idiom is elsewhere confined to competitors (369ᵇ–71ᵃn.), the dative fits well with their general bias, and it prepares for their happy laughter at Aias' discomfiture (784; cf. Köhnken 1981:

136–7). Note the chiasmus so constructed, with the Greeks at either end of the sentence, and Odysseus qualified by two dative participles in the middle: their favour is clear.

768–84 The chariot race's Apollo–Athene episode is here a prayer to the latter and her speedy intervention. This is a very brief example of Homeric prayer (768–72), responding to the narrative's needs; opened and closed by standard expressions, Odysseus' prayer names the deity and gives his request, omitting any past or future actions which would justify divine intercession (though cf. 770n. on ἐπίρροθος; cf. Muellner 1976: 66 and n. 92; also 144–51n.).

768–9 Brevity befits the runner's exertion (so Σ bT), his physical strain emphasised by necessary run-over in 769.   **πύματον ... δρόμον:** the 'last (part ... of the) track' (373–4, 758–67nn.), introducing individual episodes just as in the chariot race.   **Ἀθηναίηι γλαυκώπιδι:** this dative declension of the very common verse-end formula γλαυκῶπις Ἀθήνη relies on the adjectival form of the goddess' name (388–9n.). Her distinctive epithet means either 'bright-eyed' or 'owl-eyed' (cf. γλαύξ, the goddess' bird) rather than 'grey-eyed' (< γλαυκός, of the sea; cf. 16.34; Pötscher 1997).   **ὃν κατὰ θυμόν:** thought, emotion, and even detailed internal monologues may be located 'in (one's own) *thymos*' (62–4n.), often linked with the *phrenes* (103–4n.), but only one other prayer in epos is so described (*Od.* 5.444: a swimming Odysseus to the Scherian river). These are probably silent prayers, with exertion a more likely cause than a desire to conceal the request (as envisaged at 7.194–6; see Aubriot-Sévin 1992: 153, 209 n. 39, 214 n. 61; Pulleyn 1997: 185–6).

770 The θ-consonance of this verse is unparalleled in Homer (Packard 1974), and helps to underline the request.   **κλῦθι** 'hear (me)': 2nd sing. athematic aor. imp. act. of κλύω, with first syllable metrically lengthened (but cf. Wyatt 1969: 230–1). This invocation is confined to prayers but in Homer only those to Athene, Poseidon, Apollo, and a river-god (*Od.* 5.445; see Morrison 1991: 147 and n. 10).   **θεά:** Aeolic form used in epos alongside Attic-Ionic θεός (1.516, etc.).   **ἐπίρροθος** 'helper': Athene's imagined role fits the 'consistent partisanship' (*LfrgE* s. ἐπιτάρροθος) of this term, neatly summarising their wider relationship. Though the precise nature of the relationship remains uncertain, an ἐπίρροθος/ἐπιτάρροθος is a deity who 'brings noise (ῥόθος) to help', overwhelmingly in the context of athletics or combat (cf. *WD* 560; *EDG* s.v.; Barker and Christensen 2011: 19–20).   **ἐλθὲ ποδοῖιν** 'come on your two feet': cf. *Od.* 16.6, 19.444 (ἦλθε). ποδοῖιν is dat. dual of πούς = Attic-Ionic ποδοῖν (334–6ᵃn.).

771–2 = 5.121–2, of Athene's favourable reaction to Diomedes' prayer for vengeance against Pandaros; 772 = 13.61, of Poseidon instilling strength into the Aiantes. Line 771 is a standard way to close a prayer and indicate the god's acceptance and subsequent fulfilment of the request (1.43, 457, 10.295, etc.; cf. 16.249; Muellner 1976: 17–6; Morrison 1991: esp. 148 with n. 14). Aristarchos athetised 772, since it has less of an effect on the outcome than in Book 5, but Odysseus' request gives Athene much freedom to act, her intervention in the chariot race was similarly bifocal, and it makes sense to help her favourite and harm a (future) enemy (see 473n.; also Köhnken 1981: 135–7). Παλλάς Ἀθήνη: common line-ending formula, also found line-initial as Παλλάς Ἀθηναίη, but it responds to Odysseus' prayer. Παλλάς is yet another distinctive epithet, only found once in epos without the name (*HDem.* 424; cf. 584–5n. for Poseidon's epithets), and is possibly related to παλλακή 'concubine' (*DELG* s.v., 853) and other words linked by the notion of youth (πάλλαξ, πάλλας). Later speculation centred upon the name of a companion Athene killed inadvertently (or a giant, deliberately), or from the fact that she 'brandishes' (πάλλειν) her weapons (Pl. *Cra.* 406d–407a), but it is doubtful that any of these meanings were felt in early epos (see generally Deacy 2008: 59–73; Burkert 2011: 217). πόδας καὶ χεῖρας ὕπερθεν: in apposition to γυῖα (see 627–8n.). The effect of divine–human interactions are frequently so denoted (in addition to 5.122 and 13.61 above, see 13.75, *Od.* 12.248; cf. 21.543). The importance of the runners' arm movements was well known in antiquity: Aristotle commented that they move faster 'when they swing their hands' (*IA* 705a17), while Philostratos contrasted distance runners' relative stillness with the energetic arm movement of sprinters ('as though winged' *Gymn.* 32; cf. Σ T 772d), reflected also in visual art (Laser 34–7, and Taf. 2).

773–7 The winner is the first physically to reach the prize, as in the chariot race. Mentioned three times in this passage (775, 777, 780–1) and nowhere else in epos (later in fable and tragedy), the ὄνθος 'dung' strewn about the place of sacrifice makes Aias' slip all the more humiliating, and brings vividly to life the ritual's unpleasantness. Σ AbT 777 note that he ran with his mouth open, and paid the price for his earlier abuse of Idomeneus (473–81; cf. also Σ bT 11.146a), a poetic justice seen in Pandaros' death (5.290–6), also engineered by Athene. ἀλλ' ὅτε δὴ τάχ' ἔμελλον 'but when they were right on the verge of': the god's further intervention is signalled, since this transitional syntax introduces a divine action preventing or radically altering the following infinitive's action (10.365, 11.181, *Od.* 4.514, *Th.* 468, 888, etc.).   ἐπαΐξεσθαι: the better-attested aorist infinitive is frequently used after μέλλω to refer to future time with very little distinction in meaning (*GH* II § 451), but ἀλλ' ὅτε δὴ τάχ' ἔμελλον elsewhere uses only future (or future adjacent: *Od.* 6.110) forms.   βοῶν ... ἐριμύκων: more often a line-ending formula, the sound ('deep-lowing' from ἐρι- (6n.) and μυκάομαι) recalls their sacrifice before the games (166–9), as the following relative clause makes clear; in other contexts it fuels a tension between their lowing and the need for silence (*Od.* 15.235, *HHerm.* 75, 105; Thomas 2020: 74).   πέφνεν: unaugmented reduplicated 3rd sing. aor. act. indic., related to θείνω 'strike', the aorist forms meaning 'kill' (cf. φόνος, πέφαται, etc.).   ποδὰς ὠκὺς Ἀχιλλεύς: 93n.   ἐν δ' ὄνθου βοέου πλῆτο στόμα τε ῥῖνάς τε: 'and his nose and mouth were filled inside with bovine dung': ἐν is adverbial, while the partitive genitive is usual in this idiom (i.e. 'filled up from' = 'with': cf. 17.499, 21.16, etc.; *GH* II § 62). στόμα τε ῥῖνάς τε (394–7n.) is an accusative of respect/location and πλῆτο is 3rd sing. (unaugmented) aor. mid. indic. of πίμπλημι 'I fill', not πίλναμαι/πελάζω 'I bring near to' (as e.g. 14.438).

778–81 πολύτλας δῖος Ὀδυσσεύς: 765–7n.   φθάμενος: nom. sing. masc. aor. mid. ppl. of φθάνω. This predicative participle is used where one of two figures trying to achieve the same end (frequently in combat) gets there first (cf. 5.119, 13.387, 21.576, *Od.* 19.449).   φαίδιμος Αἴας: the epithet is more usually reserved for Hector, though both Aias and his larger namesake are so qualified – but this is the only time Hector is not Aias' chief opponent in these situations, and reflects once more a disjunction between the denotation and connotation of the epithet (62–4n.).   μετὰ χερσὶν ἔχων 'holding it in the middle of/between his hands': the preposition/preverb can modify a locative dative in Homer (11.4, 184, 15.717, etc.: *GH* II § 165; for ἐν χερσίν cf. 1.14, 373, etc.), and here it inclines attention towards what he is holding, and the irony of that fact, given what he has just spat out.   μετὰ δ' Ἀργείοισιν ἔειπεν: he addresses the crowd, who have not hidden their favouritism. This way of introducing a speech to a group is typical in the second half of the verse, complementing μετὰ μῦθον ἔειπεν with the group named in the first half, and not infrequently precedes rueful acknowledgment of failure or distress (3.85, 6.375, 7.66, 9.623, 22.476, etc.).

782–3 Against the usual rule that human characters cannot identify gods and speak instead of a δαίμων, a god or gods, or Zeus (Jørgensen 1904), Aias here mirrors the poet's language (ἔβλαψε ~ βλάψεν) and recognises

the deity responsible for his misfortune, as with other *post eventum* realisa-
tions of malign influence, e.g. Hector with Athene (22.299) and Patroclos
with Apollo (16.844–9; see generally Turkeltaub 2007, though he does
not discuss this case). Aias seems careful not to name Athene, using
instead only θεά and an oblique relative clause, as though their link is
too well known (τὸ πάρος περ) to need specificity (see 789–91ᵃn.). The
comparison itself skirts with negativity, as child–parent similes focus on
protection and can undermine the martial quality of the comparandum
(4.130–2, 8.271, 16.7–11; cf. 9.323–7, 17.4–5, *Od.* 10.410–14; Kelly
2007a: 265–7; Pratt 2007); also 222–5n.   ὢ πόποι: the deficiency
thus signalled in his understanding (103–4n.) is deepened by his remem-
brance of her long-standing support for Odysseus.   Ὀδυσῆϊ: by far
the most common dative form next to Ὀδυσσῆϊ; the alternation is of obvious metrical utility, whatever its linguistic origin (*EDG* s. Ἀχιλλεύς): see
708–9, 791ᵇ–3nn.

784 = *Od.* 20.358, 21.376, both occasions where the suitors laugh at
Theoclymenos and Telemachos; 784ᵇ = 2.270ᵇ, where the Greeks laugh
at Thersites, another intemperate speaker beaten down by Odysseus
(Arnould 1990: 26, 138–40, 171–2). The Greeks do not realise the
danger represented *to them* by Aias' statement, i.e. his relationship with
Athene, since the 'sweet laughter' idiom, directed at another's misfortune
(ἐπ' αὐτῶι), connotes that misfortune as wrongly isolated from the happy
figure (11.378, 21.508, *Od.* 18.111 γελώοντες, *HAphr.* 49 γελοιήσασα).
For the consequences of Athene's anger at his rape of Cassandra, see
473n.   γέλασσαν: 3rd pl. unaugmented aor. act. indic. of γελάω; the
geminate -σσ-, usual for the aorist forms of this verb, aids in its compositional utility.

785–97 Unmentioned during the event, Antilochos comes in last and, as
in the chariot race, manages to flatter Achilleus and so gain another extra
prize. The lesson comes first (787–8), before he recounts in inverse order
the result of the race in light of that lesson (789–91) and concludes with
the rhetorical end point (791–2); the first and last stages of the speech
are marked with run-over to underline Achilleus' exceptional status with
regard to the opening lesson. This is the second time Antilochos has compared himself unfavourably in these terms (587–8n.), though he now
relates it to more divine assistance for his elders rather than their greater
wisdom.

785–8 μειδιόων: nom. masc. sing. pres. act. ppl. of μειδιάω, a metrically
expanded form of μειδάω by diectasis (< μειδιῶν < μειδιάων: *WHS* 321), rare

in epos but common later. Picking up on Achilleus' earlier smile at him (555–7n.) and perhaps anticipating a repetition of that favour, Antilochos is about to impose himself on the situation, like other characters so qualified (if more violently: 7.212, 21.491, *HDion.* 14; cf. Arnould 1990: 89–90, 140–2).　　**καὶ μῦθον ἐν Ἀργείοισιν ἔειπεν:** this second half of the formula (Edwards 1970: 14–15) used to announce each event (271–3n.) adds more to the contestation suggested by μειδιόων, which is picked up by Achilleus in his reply; cf. 456n. for another example.　　**εἰδόσιν ὔμμ' ἐρέω:** this variant on the 'know already' idiom (304ᵇ–5n.) pre-empts agreement by asserting that the audience is quite aware of the truth of what Antilochos is about to say; it is particularly close to Hesiod's introduction to the fable of the Hawk and Nightingale (νῦν δ' αἶνον βασιλεῦσ' ἐρέω, φρονέουσι καὶ αὐτοῖς *WD* 202), though Achilleus rather than the speaker labels the speech an αἶνος (794–7n.).　　**παλαιοτέρους** is the first of three comparatives, binding the conclusion (gods favour elders) closely with each of the other two contestants.

789–91ᵃ Aias' pre-eminence is limited to one verse, Odysseus' expanded to two (with 2× προτερ-) to stress his precedence; Αἴας and οὗτος are fronted to make the comparison, and the need not even to name Odysseus. The echo of προγενέστερος in προτέρης γενεῆς, despite the change in construction, further amplifies him, since the latter expression suggests not simply greater age but membership of an earlier (and greater?) generation, like Nestor (1.250–2), Heracles (5.637), or the race of heroes (*WD* 159–60; Most 1997: esp. 112–13; Nelson 2023: 173–4). For the similarly distancing effect of προτέρων ... ἀνθρώπων, see 331–3n.　　**ὠμογέροντα:** hapax, drawing on 'raw' or 'unripe' (ὠμός) to mean 'not yet an (utterly) old man'. Aristophanes of Byzantium locates this stage between προβεβηκώς 'advanced in years' and γέρων (frr. 60–3 Slater). Elsewhere in epos ὠμῶι γήραϊ is an undesirable state (*Od.* 15.357, *WD* 705; cf. 643–5n.), and Antilochos' point is that, despite his exaggerations in 790, the indeterminately aged Odysseus (scholarly views range between 30 and 40 years) is 'both old and young ... (and) can have it both ways' (Purves 2019: 79–80; also Falkner 1995: 47–51): see also 476–7, 587–8, 621–3, 643–5nn.　　**φασ':** Antilochos' disbelief is underlined by his reference to the general report (more explicitly at e.g. 5.635, 6.99–100; cf. 20.206–7), though 'they say' statements can also signpost a wider story, in this case perhaps the theme of old age in Odysseus' *nostos* (Nelson 2023: 100–1).

791ᵇ–3 The sting in the tail generalises Odysseus' superiority before excepting Achilleus from the rule.　　**ἀργαλέον δὲ | ποσσὶν ἐριδήσασθαι** 'and it is difficult/to strive (with him) in running': Achilleus'

status is particularly underlined by this typical idiom to excuse or admit
failure, because its speakers usually attempt, or enjoin others, to accept
or respond to reality notwithstanding that failure, not to provide an out-
right exception to it (12.176, 410, 15.140, 17.252, etc.). ἐριδήσασθαι (aor.
mid. infin. of ἐριδαίνω) is the best-attested reading, though both -ī- and
-ησ- have given pause and prompted emendations; the existence of -αω
forms for several -αινω verbs (ὁρμαίνω/ὁρμάω, ὑφαίνω/ὑφάω) answers the
latter concern, while variable prosody would have been aided by the
consistent placement of synonymous ἐρίζω after trochaic caesura (e.g.
παισὶν ἐριζέμεναι 21.185).   εἰ μὴ Ἀχιλλεῖ 'except for Achilleus': for
this usage, where the construction depends on the preceding clause, see
17.477, 18.193, *Od.* 12.326, 17.383, *HDem.* 78. Ἀχιλλεῖ is found only here
in epos, the usual forms being Ἀχιλῆϊ and Ἀχιλλῆϊ (Intro. § 3.1.2.c.vii) As
with the forms of Odysseus' name (708–9, 782–3nn.), the alternation is
metrically productive, though its origin is unclear. There is no reason to
emend it away (e.g. to Σ T's otherwise unattested Ἀχιλλῆι), since Homer
does contract some forms of these names in -εύς (Μηκιστῆ < Μηκιστέα
15.339; possibly Πορθεῖ < Πορθεῖ/Πορθῆϊ 14.115: see *GH* I § 96 *dubitan-*
ter).   ποδώκεα Πηλεΐωνα: this common formula is used once more of
Achilleus whilst he is not running (see 35–7, 249nn.), and in a context
where speed is praised.

794–7 797 ~ 565 (see n.) = 624. Again the poet looks to the future
beyond the end of the *Iliad*, so the interaction with Antilochos is something more than just friendly byplay.   ἀμειβόμενος προσέειπεν: the
participle more frequently introduces speeches in its compound form
(ἀπ-) with προσέφη; the present combination violates the economy of
'Achilleus responded' expressions, perhaps to bring his name more
prominently into the first half of the verse (Edwards 1970: 27). It is much
more popular in the *Odyssey*, where many (but not all) examples are in
the first person or the context of a first-person narrative (Edwards 1970:
9–10).   οὐ ... μέλεος ἐρήσεται αἶνος: picking up on the poet's pithy
κύδηνεν, Achilleus recognises the hidden purpose to the 'no vain ... tale'
(652n.; ἐρήσεται ~ ἐρέω 787), and rewards his friend by increasing the
remuneration for third place (750–1n.).   ἐπιθήσω 'I will add': for
this sense, see 7.364, *Od.* 22.62.

798–897 The last four contests of the funeral games have caused critical
consternation, usually an aesthetic response to the increasingly hurried
nature of the events ('we now leave poetry for patchwork' Leaf II.528;
Kirk 1962: 222–3; Willcock 1976: 262–3; Sauge 1994). While the spear
throwing is generally exempted (e.g. Van Thiel 1982: 577) because of

its exchange between Achilleus and Agamemnon, 'everything else is unreasonable, even incomprehensible in terms of content and expression' (Lehrs 1882: 429–30, at 429; cited in West's apparatus). The events decrease in size and sometimes therefore even in clarity as the narrative wends to its conclusion, but this is typical of Homeric structure (see e.g. Kelly 2007b on the end of the *Odyssey*, and Kelly 2012 on the recognition scene between Penelope and Odysseus). It is also true that these events stand outside what looks to have been the traditional core of boxing, wrestling, and running (257^b–897n.), but they are – with the exception of the next event, the fight in armour (798–825n.) – well attested in athletic contexts both in epos and in the Archaic period (see 826–49, 850–83, 884–97nn.). Crucially, there is no sign that any MS of the poem existed which did not contain these contests, and the careful tripartite macrostructure of the funeral games (257^b–897n.) would be harmed by their exclusion. They are, without doubt, an authentic part of Book 23 (Bannert 1988: 148–51).

798–825 Event 5. Fight in Armour. This contest bears similarities to the final one (spear throwing) in its prize setting (798–800n.), and to the third event (boxing) in several respects: Achilleus' invitation (802–4n.), the participation of Diomedes, the number of competitors, and the combat-sport risk of serious but non-lethal harm. It also recalls the wrestling, in the participation of Aias, the use of a triple-attempt motif (816–17n.), and another impossible division of prizes (809–10n.). Besides using much traditional language associated with prominent duels (see Kirk 1978: 35–9; Bannert 1988: 140–1; Myers 2019: 182–4), the episode evokes the encounter between Aias and Hector (7.244–305) in containing another triple attempt and closing with the award of a sword to the winner (805–8, 824–5nn.). Once more Achilleus intervenes, leaving the mechanics of the prizes somewhat uncertain. The action again pits Diomedes, the *Iliad*'s Achilleus surrogate (290–2n.), against the traditionally 'second-best' figure in the Greek army (2.768–70), as with Eumelos in the chariot race (288–9n.: Willcock 1973: 3–4; Hinckley 1986: 214–15). Aias' defeat matches his generally poor performance in the games and anticipates his imminent demise (802–4, 813–15nn.; cf. 708–9n.). Typical structure (257^b–897n.) once more keys a few important points: the two crowd reactions mirror the preceding event, but they are shifted earlier in the pattern so as to focus on the greater level of danger involved in this episode; the second reaction is actually an intervention which brings the event to a close (822–3n.). Danger is also clear from the relative diminution in the contest stage itself, which is aborted and only just larger than the prize-setting stage

(Table 4): had it been allowed to continue, the risks would have been too great.

Perhaps the best Iliadic illustration of Orwell's dictum that sport is 'war minus the shooting',[1] this event has no parallel in the games of early epos, and no place in later Greek athletics (some link it to the later *hoplomachia*, but this seems to have been an armed demonstration rather than actual combat: Wheeler 1982). Plutarch refers, diffidently, to an original Olympian contest of this sort (*Mor.* 675c–d), and scholars have hypothesised that it is an ancient relic of ritual combat (Malten 1923–4: 304–5; Meuli 1968: 41–50; Bierl 2019), comparing *inter al.* Etruscan, Campanian, and Roman evidence, while the Tanagra *larnax* depicts armed pairs in a possibly funeral Mycenaean context (Decker 1982–3: esp. 6–13; Mouratidis 1990: 15–16; *contra* Roller 1977: 116–18). Nonetheless, an origin in or direct influence from any historical period remains uncertain (Laser 186–7; Poliakoff 1987: 154–7; 2021: 227–8). Far from being 'the least acceptable of the games, the least authentic in the *Iliad*' (Willcock 1976: 263) or even 'a stupidity' (Sauge 1994: 5 n. 1), the event adds in several ways to Book 23's reflection on the poem and, as a context-specific addition to the 'core' (257^b–897n.), quite naturally responds to the wider military setting of the episode.

798–800 798 = 884, 799^a = 886^a, in the spear throwing. Another text-internal analepsis (740–51n.), this time to Sarpedon's death (16.462–505). As in the description of the bowl and its provenance in the previous contest, Patroclos' memory is (re)invoked. Though made up of several items, only one prize *in toto* is named, leaving the matter of its apportioning, and relative value, for Achilleus' speech (809–10n.). For anaphora of κατά over successive clauses without repeating the verb, see e.g. 7.57–8, 23.884–5, *Od.* 6.102–3 (Fehling 1969: 194–7).   δολιχόσκιον ἔγχος: only found in this common formula (cf. also δολίχ' ἔγχεα, δολιχὸν δόρυ, and δολιχεγχέας), the epithet means 'with a long shadow' (δολιχός + σκιή). τεύχεα Σαρπήδοντος (800) is in apposition to the individual items (798–9), while ἀπηύρα (800) and its synonyms frequently take a double accusative (i.e. of the person and the thing): see 808 below, and 6.17–18, 8.327, 10.495, etc.   ἐς ἀγῶνα φέρων: something irregular is afoot in the prize-giving: see 615–17n. for the expression, and 809–10n. for what goes wrong.

---

[1] 'The Sporting Spirit' (orig. publ. in *Tribune*, 14 December 1945). The whole sentence is worth quoting: 'Serious sport has nothing to do with fair play. It is bound up with hatred, jealousy, boastfulness, disregard of all rules and sadistic pleasure in witnessing violence: in other words it is war minus the shooting.' My fellow Australians will know exactly what this means.

801 = 271, etc. (see 271–3n.).

802–10 The speech begins and ends with the competitors and armour (802–4 ~ 809; cf. τεύχεα 803, 809) around the description of the extra prize (805–8).

802–4 802 = 659 (see 658–63n.). ὥ περ ἀρίστω is especially pointed, given the respective standings of the pair (798–825n.) and the metapoetic context. Line 804 is omitted by a fair number of ancient and medieval MSS – oddly, for the infinitive is clearly required after κελεύομεν (cf. 659ff.) and there is no other obvious cause (Apthorp 1980: 128–33).   **ταμεσίχροα** 'flesh-cutting': picked up in 805 (χρόα καλόν), the compound (< τάμνω + χρώς) adds -σι to the aorist stem, as e.g. in φαεσίμβροτος (φάε) and ἀλφεσίβοια (ἦλφον; WHS 191–2).   **προπάροιθεν ὁμίλου:** making clear again the performative nature of basileutic authority, this expression is used before Menelaos' duel with Paris (3.22), another episode which looks beyond the *Iliad* to place the poem in the wider context of the Trojan War: 813–15n.   **πειρηθῆναι:** aor. pass. infin. of πειράω/-ομαι 'I make trial of', construed with κελεύομεν and the genitive (sometimes dative) of the person, mostly in the context of single combat (5.220, 20.349, 21.225, *Scut.* 359); cf. *Od.* 24.240, and 553–4n. The passive form has the same meaning as the middle (*GHI* § 193).

805–8 The central element in the speech's ring is this unique addition to the prizes (its structural integrity reinforced by repetition of καλόν to describe both target and reward), picking up on the lack of clarity about how Sarpedon's set is to be apportioned. Part of the same panoply from which Achilleus made the extra award to Antilochos in the chariot race (560–2), this additional prize seems to make sense (how else to judge the winner in a case like this?), but its description is troubled (see nn.). For an example of the syntax in 805–7 – a conditional sentence referring to the future with relative protasis (ὁππότερός κε + subj.) – used in precisely this context, see 3.71–2 (= 92–3, *Od.* 18.46–9). Line 806 was athetised by Aristarchos because so severe a wound is inappropriate (Σ A 806a), while Aristophanes read a different version of 805–6; yet the line is universally attested and once more reflects on Achilleus' performance.   **φθήῃσιν:** 3rd sing. aor. subj. (= φθῇι: Intro. § 3.1.2.d.i and n. 115). For φθάνω + circumstantial participle, see 442–7n.   **χρόα καλόν:** not often found in this position, this formula usually occurs in contexts of actual or threatened harm (5.354, 858, 21.398, etc.; *contra* 14.175, though with dangerous ramifications).   **διά τ' ἔντεα καὶ μέλαν αἷμα:** the phrase appears at 10.298 and 469 as Diomedes and Odysseus proceed through the chaos

they have caused.   **δώσω:** 560–2n.   **φάσγανον ἀργυρόηλον:**
the epithet 'silver-nail' is only used in this position, either of swords or
thrones; ξίφος is more common than φάσγανον, which may originally have
denoted a more dagger-like weapon, but the terms are functionally equivalent (Foltiny 1980: 232–6, 269–71; Paraskevaides 1984: 20–2). Well represented at Mycenaean sites but rare in later periods, the nails fasten the
handle-fittings to the blade (Foltiny 1980: 237).   **καλὸν Θρηΐκιον:** for
run-over καλόν introducing object descriptions, see 267–8n. Asteropaios
hails from Paeonia, an area inhabited by an eastern Thracian tribe
(2.848–50), and Helenos kills Deipyros with a Thracian sword (13.577),
which Σ A ad loc. suggests he obtained from a local mercenary or sent for
because of its beauty (καλλιστεῦον; cf. καλόν). Known in antiquity for their
long (and later, curved) swords (Webber 2011: 47–69; Stoyanov 2015:
428–9), the Thracians are important Trojan allies throughout the poem
(2.844–5, 4.519–20, 6.7–8, etc.), with a strong link to Ares (13.301–3,
Od. 8.361; cf. 5.461–2), and a source of wine (9.72) and a valuable cup
(24.234; see Valeva et al. 2015).   **τὸ μὲν Ἀστεροπαῖον ἀπηύρων:** for
the double accusative, see 798–800n. The syntactical reminiscence reinforces the connection, as the eventual prize combines items won in combat by Patroclos and Achilleus.

809–10 Achilleus returns to the prizes already set out, but once more
(735–7n.) does not make it clear how this prize can be 'shared', before
adding a special feast for the competitors. Perhaps this is an allusion to
the meal in Agamemnon's tent after the duel between Aias and Hector
(7.311–22), and so Achilleus' attempt to claim the same kind of authority
(ἐν κλισίηισιν would refer to his own tent); the draw in that event seems
to play with the indeterminate outcome in this one (Hinckley 1986:
217–18). Nonetheless, 810 was athetised by Aristarchos as unreasonably
singling out this competition (Σ T replies that 'it should be more honoured'), while Plutarch, Mor. 736d suggests Achilleus was attempting to
soothe any ill-feeling that might have arisen during the fight. Certainly
it looks like an addition to the speech's ring (802–10n.), and the awkwardness once more reflects poorly on the agonothete.   **ξυνήϊα:** a
probable allusion to the only other example of this word in epos (1.124,
where Achilleus tells Agamemnon they no longer have 'common' stock
to compensate for the loss of Chryseis) would underline the two's role
reversal but not solve the problem: if the panoply is split according to
the division in 798–9, it is hard to see how the spear could equal the
value of the shield and helmet together. Hector's similar suggestion with
regard to Patroclos' spoils (17.229–32) is just as misguided, and doomed
to failure anyway.   **παραθήσομεν:** either 1st pl. short vowel aor. subj.

or fut. indic. (Intro. § 3.1.2.d.v), better attested than παραθήσομαι, which would focus attention on Achilleus; though it is perhaps easier to envisage the former as the product of dittography before ἐν, yet the plural effectively associates Achilleus with the group (*GH* II § 42; *contra* van der Valk 1963–4: II.625).

811–12 811 = 708, 812 ~ 290 (see 290–2, 708–9nn.) = 7.163. Both heroes are evenly matched, given a general quality and a patronymic. The basic formula κρατερὸς Διομήδης can be supplemented, as here, by the mobile patronymic Τυδεΐδης (290–2n.); cf. 472 with 470^b–2n. For μέγας Τελαμώνιος Αἴας see 708–9n.; for ὦρτο see 214–16n.

813–15 813 = 3.340, ἐς μέσον 814 ~ ἐς μέσσον 3.341, 815 ~ 3.342, all as Menelaos and Paris begin their duel. Possibly an allusion to that episode, also because θωρήχθησαν in these two episodes makes for the only indicative examples of the common aor. pass. stem of θωρήσσω in epos; just as that earlier, indeterminate duel looks to the *casus belli* and its reactivation in the plot of the *Iliad*, so this encounter enshrines the poem's decisions about Aias' status (798–825n.) and looks forward to his eventual fate: Menelaos will always fail to have his revenge on Paris, and Aias will forever be second to Achilleus or his surrogate. Line 814 = 6.120, 20.159, also before duels (Glaucos and Diomedes, Aineias and Achilleus), though here with no pre-combat exchange; the repetition could allusively suggest Diomedes' victory, and also a non-lethal outcome (like several other idioms below). **ἐς μέσον ἀμφοτέρων:** a combative idiom (573–4n.); West prints ἀμφοτέρω, since ἀμφοτέρων is less appropriate for one crowd (whatever its partisan divisions), but the much better-attested genitive looks like an 'error' brought on by the novel use of a traditional unit. **συνίτην:** 3rd dual imperf. act. indic. of σύνειμι 'I meet with' (always in combat). **μεμαῶτε μάχεσθαι:** being 'eager to fight' is naturally a positive stance in martial epos, and this is its most fixed form (participle + infinitive), which is used by the poet of characters about to participate in non-lethal combat (5.569, 6.120, *Od.* 16.171), and by characters of an opponent in order to stress their own determination (13.80, 317; cf. 22.243) or hesitation (5.244) in the face of this quality; *contra* 22.36 (of Hector before the gates of the city). **δεινὸν δερκομένω** 'glaring terribly', i.e. threateningly: both gods and mortals can be so described in the preparation for a combat encounter, reinforcing a minatory impressiveness which sits ill with the non-lethality of that fight (3.342, 11.37, *Scut.* 160; cf. Rakoczy 1996: 42–55, 95). **θάμβος δ' ἔχε πάντας Ἀχαιούς:** typical after a remarkable event with strong divine resonance (3.142, omen 4.79, epiphany *Od.* 3.372,

24.482), this reaction elevates the duel's importance. While the following encounters are never lethal, there is a strong sense of that danger
among the group (Kelly 2007a: 116–17), which here prepares us for
the crowd's intervention below (also 726–8n.). θάμβος δ' ἔχε is elsewhere
followed by εἰσορόωντας, a minority reading here, but πάντας Ἀχαιούς well
conveys the reaction's unanimity (unlike e.g. at 24.432, where few people see Priam, and 3.142 and 4.79, where both Trojans and Greeks are
named in the next verse).

816–17 ἀλλ' ὅτε δὴ σχεδὸν ἦσαν ἐπ' ἀλλήλοισιν ἰόντες: the combat is very
abbreviated, since elsewhere this duel-introducing phrase (with οἳ δ' ὅτε)
is followed by either a speech or a first spear cast (3.15, 5.14, 630, 850,
etc.). Here instead we move straight into the 'triple attempt' (τρὶς μέν ...
τρὶς δέ), where a repeated stalemate (817) is resolved by a fourth (and
here fifth) action (818ff.; see Kelly 2007a: 194–7). As in the wrestling,
the apparent stalemate requires an external intervention, and the crucial action never comes. Both ἐπήϊξαν 'leapt at' and ὡρμήθησαν 'rushed
forward' refer to attacking movements, though the latter often implies
a closer initial starting point (cf. 13.496, 526, 559, etc.). Since σχεδόν in
816 need only be relative, the fight may therefore comprise rounds of
contrasting distance and close-quarters attacks, a different process from
the three-round duel between Aias and Hector (spear cast – spear thrust –
stone). Heyne condemned 817, which avoids the slight tautology and
achieves a smoother transition to 818, but the verse is universally attested
and makes tolerable sense. The 'dyadic structure' in the repetition of
τρὶς (817) and ἔπειτα in this episode (818, 820) connects the combatants
(Di Benedetto 1998: 90–2).

818–19 Aias' action initially appears to be the stalemate's resolution,
with a strong sense of temporality (ἔνθ' ... ἔπειτα, capped by isometric
ἔπειτα in 820) and necessary run-over of νύξ'.   **ἔνθ' ... ἔπειτα:** both
in effect temporal (cf. Eng. 'there and then': 18.450, *Od.* 10.297, 12.56),
though elsewhere ἔνθα in this combination can be more explicitly local
(16.613 = 17.529, *Od.* 3.108; Brügger 2016: 267).   **ἀσπίδα πάντοσ'
ἐΐσην** 'shield balanced on all sides': for the orthography of this formula,
see 55–8n. We expect a further description of the strike's effect, as typical here (3.347, 356, 7.250, 11.434, 13.160, 17.43, 20.274, etc.), whilst
it is unusual for those so equipped to be harmed or killed in the combat (1/15×, 17.517; cf. 5.300, 11.61, 13.157, etc.): 813–15n. For other
piercing strikes (νύξε) on the shield, see 7.260 ~ 12.404 (both Aias),
16.704; cf. 11.424 (ὑπ' ἀσπίδος).   **ἔρυτο:** 3rd sing. mediopass. athematic imperf. indic. of ἔρυμαι/ἐρύομαι 'I save, protect' (cf. thematic ἐρύετο

6.403).   ἔνδοθι: i.e. the breastplate, within the shield's cover, stopped the spear-point.

820–1 Diomedes constantly watches for an opening at his opponent's neck (where Hector was fatally struck: 22.322–7), a tactic judged by the scholia 'disgraceful and envious' (bT 818–19a).   ὑπὲρ σάκεος μεγάλοιο: either looking out over his own shield (cf. *Od.* 22.279, *Scut.* 24) or aiming above Aias' shield 'at his neck' (cf. e.g. ὑπέρ μαζοῖο 4.528, 5.145, 11.108: *GH* II § 201; *LH* s. ὑπέρ B2c, 370).   κῦρε 'was trying to reach': 3rd sing. imperf. indic. act. of κύρω 'I happen upon, meet with', used conatively; for this less common sense, see *HDem.* 189, *HAphr.* 174.   ἀκωκῆι: the majority reading ἀκωκήν makes κῦρε transitive (in the sense of 'aim'?), perhaps seeking to distinguish this case from the usual dative construction, i.e. 'chance upon, meet with'. For δουρός, see 528–9n.

822–3 The Greeks' fear reflects the danger of the threatened manoeuvre, though Σ T 821 also suggests they know that Aias 'is weary from the battle at the ships, whilst Diomedes has rested'. In effect they simply follow Achilleus' pre-contest suggestion (809–10n.), once more leaving unclear how the panoply is to be divided, but their intervention here actually assumes Achilleus' authority – and so draws attention to his failure to act at the right time.   περιδδείσαντες: for -δδ-, see 417–18ᵃn.

824–5 824 ~ 7.303, 825 = 7.304, where Hector and Aias swap gifts after their duel. Allusion would underline the reversal in the latter's fortunes, especially if Homer knew the later story that Hector's gift was the sword with which Aias killed himself (Soph. *Aj.* 661–13, 815–18). Both swords are equipped ἐϋτμήτωι τελαμῶνι (only here in epos), an object with obvious resonance with Aias' father (cf. 811 Τελαμώνιος). The verses were athetised by both Aristophanes and Aristarchos for a variety of reasons – the even outcome of the fight (Σ A), the lack of a determinative wound (Σ b), and the risk that Achilleus (who was apparently seeking to resolve a private quarrel with Diomedes) would hereby incur Aias' enmity (Σ T) – but, despite the fact that the award does not match the condition sketched out at 805–6, they effectively convey Diomedes' superiority (Van der Valk 1952: 269–71; Andersen 1978: 142–4).

826–49 Event 6. Iron Throwing. This contest continues the narrative's progressive diminution in scale, though with a complete sequence of prize setting and sourcing, accompanying speech, standing order, and competing order. This is the only contest with one prize, which is itself the implement, and Telamonian Aias once more comes off second best. Again the crowd react twice, though now in the same stage (257^b–897n.), the contest itself.

δίσκος throwing was a very well-known element in later Greek athletics (Laser 58–63; Weiler et al. 1991; Romano 2021: 216–17), and occurs in the Phaiacian games (*Od.* 8.129, 186–200), is a standard diversion (2.773–5, *Od.* 4.625–7 = 17.167–9), and sufficiently familiar as to provide images for two similes in this book (23.431–3, 517–23). But the hurling of a large weight or σόλος, as here in Book 23, is less well represented in the historical and literary record, though ῥίπτασκε (827) makes it seem a typical pastime at least for Eetion. This may be the (non-Greek) origin story for the discus event as a whole (Decker 1976), and the throwing of stones is attested as one of the very oldest of human sports (Rieder 2005: 10–12). However, like the fight in armour (798–825n.), the episode is perhaps resonant less with actual athletic or historical practice and more with the immediate context of the *Iliad*, where stones are freely deployed as weapons (4.517–28, 5.301–10, 580–9, 7.263–76, 12.445–62, etc.). Later authors can use the term σόλος and δίσκος more or less interchangeably (Weiler et al. 1991: 118), and Homer's episode once more has a long, if slightly less prominent, literary afterlife (Stat. *Theb.* 6.646–728; Quint. Smyrn. 4.436–54; Nonn. *Dion.* 37.667–702; Langdon 1990; Weiler et al. 1991: 115; cf. Lovatt 2019: 431 on its absence from Apollonios).

826–7 The iron is sourced to Andromache's father, Eetion, the rich and powerful king of Thebe (Wathelet 1988: 563–9). Perhaps a call-back to the lyre taken from that city (9.186–9), which in general is a model for Troy (Kullmann 1960: 287–91; Zarker 1965), it is both another sign of Achilleus' triumphs over others (cf. esp. 'with his other possessions' 829) and a reminder of the contrasting, unresolved treatment of Hector's corpse (cf. 6.415–19). Note the underwriting of Achilleus' supremacy: his setting down of the prize and speech form the outer ring (A^1 826 ~ A^2 830), and the σόλος is described (B^1 826–7, B^2 829) and related to Eetion and his fate (C^1 827, C^2 828), placing the killer at the centre.   **σόλον αὐτοχόωνον:** a lump of iron, possibly a product of the early smelting process to be worked into other implements (833–5: Forbes 1967: 31–2 and n. 170; *contra* Sherratt 1990: 810–11). Σ A 826b differentiates it from a δίσκος (cf. *Od.* 8.189–92), because the latter is 'flat and circular, while the σόλος is round and ball-shaped', though the distinction is not always observed later. Related to χόανος 'furnace' (*WHS* 98) with diectasis of contracted -ω-, the compound's precise meaning is unknown; perhaps 'smelting there/in the same place', i.e. in Thebe (cf.

αὐτοσταδίη 'combat in the same place') or 'straight from the furnace', i.e. before working (αὐτο- = αὐτοῦ with a quasi-temporal force; *LfrgE* s. αὐτοῦ B3)?   ῥίπτασκε 'used to throw': 3rd sing. imperf. indic. act. of ῥίπτω/ῥιπτάζω, with iterative infix -σκ- (as e.g. κρύπτασκε < κρύπτω; *GH* I § 150, *WHS* 276–8).   μέγα σθένος Ἠετίωνος 'great strength of Eetion': this relatively rare kind of onomastic periphrasis (717^{b}–20n.) is confined to Ocean (18.607, 21.195) and Idomeneus (Hes. fr. 204.56 M–W): see 837 below. Eetion is also the name of another Trojan (17.575–6), an Imbrian guest-friend of Jason's son Euneos (21.42–3), and the brother of Dardanos killed by Zeus for sexual transgression with Demeter (Hes. fr. 177.8–10 M–W; Wathelet 1988: 563–71).

828–9 These verses recall Andromache's speech to Hector in Book 6 about her family's fate, with the same noun–epithet formula (+ κατέπεφνεν) when she describes her brothers' death (6.423), and ἄλλοισι κτεάτεσσι qualifying her mother (6.426), who was brought to Troy but later ransomed (6.425–8).   ἔπεφνε: see 773–7n.   ποδάρκης δῖος Ἀχιλλεύς: 140–4n.

830–1 830 = 271, etc. (see 271–3n.), while 831 = 707 (see 706–7n.), 753.

832–5 The city is here the place to acquire valuable commodities unavailable in the countryside, in one of the few nods towards a market economy in Homer (others include the 'commissariat' 7.467–75, and Lemnos as a specialised slave market (746–7n.); Edmunds 2023: 318–19; Van Wees 1992: 49–53 on the rural economy); Hesiod shows us a farmer making his plough at home (*WD* 432; cf. 407–9, 456–7 for the virtues of the domestic store). As though marking the individuality of this prize, since the others' utility or purpose needs little or no explication, Achilleus stresses its benefit in several ways: developing the common polarity between the inhabited world and the 'rich fields' (πίονες ἀγροί) motif (*Od.* 4.757, 8.560; cf. Tyrt. fr. 10.3 W²), he uses it as the passage frame (832, 835); repeating ἕξει ... παρέξει around a positive/negative contrast; emphatically adding run-over of χρεώμενος 'as he needs it'; and negating the usual time-ending formula περιπλομένους ἐνιαυτούς (see n.).   πολλόν: for the form, see 319–20n.   μιν: *sc.* σόλον.   (πέντε) περιπλομένους ἐνιαυτούς 'for (five) years that have come to an end': Achilleus uniquely replaces the new, concluding action consequent on this usually genitive formula (*Od.* 1.16, 11.248, *HDem.* 265, *Th.* 184, *WD* 386) with a denial that any such action will be necessary (834–5). περιπλομένους is masc. acc. pl. aor. mid. ppl. of περιπέλομαι 'I complete (a course)'.

836–8 The standing order is recast into a starting order, as before in the chariot race and the archery (352–7, 850–83nn.), but without the lot mechanism. It plays with the competing order/outcome in a chiastic way: the first to stand (Polypoites) wins the prize, the last stander (Epeios) competes first but comes last, and Leonteus and Aias stand and compete in the same position, though with reverse outcome (= ABCD–DBCA): see also 839–47, 844–7, 859–6onn. For ὦρτο see 214–16n., and 754–6n. for repeated ἄν in these contexts. **μενεπτόλεμος Πολυποίτης:** leader of the Lapith contingent (2.740–4), Polypoites is the son of Peirithoos (victor over the Centaurs: 1.263–8); he kills a Trojan at 6.29, and together with Leonteus stops the Trojan advance under Asios (12.127–94), later journeying home from Troy on foot (*Nostoi* arg. 8 B). μενεπτόλεμος means 'steadfast in war' (< μένω), and is used of several figures but four times of Polypoites (2× Thrasymedes, 1× Podarces, Diomedes, Polyphontes), so is perhaps not 'purely ornamental' (*LfrgE* s.v.). He is not a 'virtual unknown' whose only purpose is to encapsulate Aias' failures (Hinckley 1986: 220); for -πτ- see 1–3n. **Λεοντῆος κρατερὸν μένος ἀντιθέοιο:** the son of Koronos (2.745–6) and grandson of Caineus (1.264), Leonteus is Polypoites' companion in and beyond the *Iliad* (see last n.). This periphrasis (717ᵇ–20n.) is obviously suitable for a contest of strength but only found once with this character; other examples also place the name before the formula and an epithet to close the line (7.38, 16.189, Hes. fr. 16.9 M–W). He is the only competitor in the games to receive no prize at all (Aias and Epeios have some success in other events). **Τελαμωνιάδης:** like other major characters, Aias has more than one patronymic (for the usual Τελαμώνιος, see 708–9n.), though the -ιάδης form is only used twice in the nominative (here and 9.623) and appears most frequently in the genitive (cf. generally *WHS* 147–9). **δῖος Ἐπειός:** see 664–6n. for this character, victor in the boxing, and 136–7n. for the epithet, whose repetition in 839 helps underline the chiasmus.

839–47 As the list nears Polypoites' climactic action, each attempt in the competing order (i.e. DBCA) progresses into the next – ἧκε 840 (1) ~ ἀφέηκε 841 (2); δεύτερος αὖτ' 841 (2) ~ τρίτον αὖτ' 842 (3), ἔρριψε 842 (3) ~ ἔρριψε 845 (4) , ὑπέρβαλε 843 (3) ~ ὑπέρβαλε 847 (4) – and becomes progressively larger, with the ascending scale of achievement moving from Epeios' actions (a syllable short of a full verse: 839ᵇ–40ᵃ) to Polypoites' cast described over four (844–7).

839–40 Staccato parataxis swiftly puts Epeios out of his misery, while the Greeks' uniform laughter at his throw may reflect the careless inexpertise of his efforts (one of the explanations offered by Σ bT 840a1/2, the others being he did not throw it far or he did not set his feet apart before throwing), chiming nicely with Epeios' own estimation of his limitations before the boxing (670–1n.) and suggesting no malice in their reaction. Scanlon 2018 argues that Epeios' defeat here represents a reassertion of aristocratic primacy after the boxing, but Homer leaves the feeling behind the laughter unstated (for more obvious denigration, see 784, 865–9nn.; Adamo 2024: 88–9).   ἧκε δὲ δινήσας 'and he sent it, making it whirl': throwing a discus seems to have involved partially turning the body (cf. 431–3n. on κατωμαδίοιο) and spinning the object (*Od.* 8.189 περιστρέψας), but the weight and shape of a σόλος may not have lent itself to such a method, and there is anyway some disagreement about the precise mechanics (Howland 1954–5: 16; Langdon 1990; Weiler et al. 1991: 134–40). When stones are thrown as weapons the poet uses the expression ἧκ' ἐπιδινήσας (7.269 = *Od.* 9.538; cf. also the less aggressive ῥῖψ' 3.378, 19.268), and some turning of the body would increase the power in the cast.

841–3 ὄζος Ἄρηος: the first term of the formula, which is rarely used for major figures (cf. Iphitos in Hes. fr. 26.30 M–W; Polydeuces in *Cypria* fr. 8.2 B) but 3× for Leonteus, is probably the same as ὄζος 'branch' (hence 'scion of Ares') but does not imply a genealogical connection.   **μέγας Τελαμώνιος Αἴας:** see 708–9n.   **χειρὸς ἄπο στιβαρῆς:** this looks like being the determinative or at least a very considerable cast, since missiles or weapons despatched with this variable idiom (also στιβαρῆς ἄπο χειρός) are generally successful (14.455, *Od.* 8.189, Hes. *Th.* 692, 715 (pl.); even at 13.505 = 16.615, the effect of the spear, despite being ἅλιον, reflects the power of the throw); cf. 15.126 (and 685–7n. for χερσὶ στιβαρῆισιν).   **ὑπέρβαλε σήματα πάντων:** cf. ὑπέρπτατο σήματα πάντων (*Od.* 8.192, of Odysseus' successful cast in the Phaiacian games) with πέτεται below (846). Aristarchos athetised the verse as copied from the *Odyssey*, because πάντων should not refer to only two competitors, while on Scheria 'more people were throwing the discus' (Σ A 843). In reply, the T scholiast aptly invokes *Od.* 21.230–1.

844–7 The largest and most elaborate attempt, Polypoites' victorious throw culminates the chiasmus in several ways, combining the first thrower's 'grasping' (σόλον εἷλε; cf. σόλον δ' ἕλε 839) and repetition of the same epithet phrase (838/9 ~ 836/844), with the two 'throwing' verbs used by the third (ἔρριψε/ὑπέρβαλε; cf. 842, 843). Once more expressive of their view (257ᵇ–897n., Table 4) and for the second time in this event, the crowd presumably admires the clarity of the victory.   **μενεπτόλεμος Πολυποίτης:** 836–8n. Connecting him to the cowherd to stress difference, superiority, and the determinativeness of his throw, the simile's τόσσον clause moves from the subject of 844 to the σόλος itself.   **καλαύροπα:** the first element of this Homeric hapax is unexplained, but it seems to be a staff (ῥόπαλον) which can be thrown to separate or gather the herd (Σ b 845c); cf. Antimachos fr. 64 M (with Matthews 1996: 200–2), Ap. Rhod. *Arg.* 2.33, 4.974.   **βουκόλος ἀνήρ:** ἀνήρ/γυνή are frequently used, somewhat redundantly, in apposition to job titles and ethnic adjectives (1.144, 2.474, 4.275, 485, etc.: Russo 1994: 377–8): see also 886 below (ἥμονες ἄνδρες). The cowherd enjoys a high status among flock workers in epos, as Apollo (21.448–9), Anchises (5.313, *HAphr.* 55), and Philoitios (*Od.* 20.227, 235, etc.; Bernsdorff 2001: 50–66; Berman 2005: 232–4). They participate in similes elsewhere (13.570–2, 15.586–8), though this image is unique (Scott 1974: 79–80) and connects 'games and the reality of argicultural production' (Lovatt 2019: 417; for other similes of extent, see 431–3n.).   **δέ θ' ἐλισσομένη:** *digamma* is sometimes respected before this verb and related words (*GH* I § 54), but not invariably (e.g. 309 above), and the majority of MSS have either θ' or τ' before the participle (reflecting a somewhat ambivalent attitude to its aspiration).   **παντὸς ἀγῶνος ὑπέρβαλε** 'threw it beyond the whole area of contest': παντὸς ἀγῶνος is a genitive of separation (+ compound verb: *GH* II § 63); for this sense of ἀγών see 257ᵇ–8n.

848–9 The event begins and ends with the prize (cf. 826–7).   **Πολυποίταο κρατεροῖο:** the only example of the sole genitive form for Polypoites shows the archaic gen. sing. for masc. a-stem nouns (1st declension).   **νῆας ἔπι γλαφυράς** 'to the hollow ships': metonymic formula for the Greek camp as an end point for journeys from the battlefield, the city, even (as here) from places very close to the camp itself (see 1–3n.). The epithet is related to γλάφυ 'cavern' (*WD* 533) and refers to the cavity within the ship's frame; though it may derive from the process of hollowing out a tree beam (Kurt 1979: 33–5, esp. 35), in denotation the word is indistinguishable from the very common κοῖλος (Alexanderson 1970: 32; see 882–3n., 892 below). Whether it is ornamental in other cases, since the ships are on the shore and not carrying anything (De Jong 2012: 182), here a prize is being carried for storage and, presumably, transport home (similarly 10.531, 17.397, 22.246: esp. Ward 2019 on κοῖλος).

850–83 Event 7. Archery. The penultimate contest is once more brief but (even more) fully described, with a prize setting, accompanying speech, standing order, lot for competing order, and then the event and prize claiming. Meriones' triumph fits with his increased prominence in the

last third of the poem (see 112–13n.) and prepares for his abbreviated triumph in the spear throwing, but is still somewhat surprising after his poor
showing in the chariot race, and Teucros' consistently good performances
on the battlefield (859–6on.). Several unusual details show that the narrative is winding down (850–1, 855ᵇ–8nn.), but may also foreshadow
indeterminacies in the final contest (884–97n.), though since Aristarchos
readers and critics have found individual features hard to understand or
justify (see also 870–1, 877ᵇ–81nn.). The largest stage in the four-part
event pattern (Table 4) is once more the contest itself, with the (now
standard) two crowd reactions (869, 881) mirroring those in the previous
event in being situated at different parts of that stage.

   Like the fight in armour, archery was not a typical element in later Greek
athletics, though the Myrmidons amuse themselves τόξοισιν (2.775) and
Odysseus frames it as a contest activity of some antiquity when speaking
to the Phaiacians (*Od.* 8.214–28). For possible Mycenaean antecedents,
see Decker 1982–3; Younger 2021: 53; for Near Eastern comparanda,
Haas 1989; Wilkinson 1991; Decker 2021: 35–6, 42–3. Often said to be of
somewhat dubious status in the *Iliad*, archery is nonetheless important in
battle and epos generally (Farron 2003; Buchholz 2010: 252–9), where
it is notably represented by Odysseus' triumph over the suitors and in the
person of Heracles, whose bow is essential to the sack of Troy (e.g. *Od.*
8.225, 11.605–8; Cohen 1994; Bär 2018: 45–52; Tsagalis 2024).

   Homer's episode spawned fewer imitations than his foot race (Verg.
Aen. 5.485–544; Quint. Smyrn. 4.405–35; Nonn. *Dion.* 37.703–49), and
enjoyed a somewhat indirect reception in the mythological part of the
votive section on the first-century BCE Lindian Chronicle (B 78–87),
where Teucros and Meriones are the last-named figures from the Trojan
War, and offer quivers (the former that of Pandaros, the latter simply a silver object 'from the spoils of Troy': Higbie 2003: 91–3). This could reflect
a story about the archery at the funeral games for Achilleus (Intro. § 2.2),
and some scholars have felt that the unusual conditions of the contest
reflect an earlier version (e.g. Lovatt 2019: 416–17). The lateness of the
monument, and the fact that we do not know who else aside from Teucros
participated in that event, makes a reference to our episode more likely.

850–1 The prize setting initially recalls the σόλος, but these items are
already worked; the alliterative and anaphoric description of the axe-heads
is mirrored in Achilleus' description (855–8): von Alvensleben 2022: 110
sees a play on πελ- sounds and a link between Meriones and the μήρινθος,
suggesting a close interaction between the narrator and Achilleus. Axes
are well attested as both tools and weapons in Homer (e.g. 114 above,
13.611–18), and the standard epic item has two blades (Forbes 1967:

31–2); ἡμιπέλεκκον is not found again in Greek literature. The obvious epic comparandum is the *Odyssey*'s archery contest (21.75–6, 118–23), where the winner has to shoot through the iron axe-heads, but events of this sort have a worldwide imprint (Haas 1989; Russo 2004; Buchholz 2010: 251–2; Decker 2021).   **ὅ:** i.e. Achilleus.   **ἰόεντα σίδηρον:** compounded from ἴον 'violet' (original *digamma* obviates hiatus after τίθει) with suffix -ϝεντ- (cf. e.g. πτερό-εις, σκιό-εις, φοινικό-εις), the adjective denotes dark purple or blue (Forbes 1967: 31; Moreux 1967: 258–9 n. 121), like the much more common ἰοειδής (of the sea or water; cf. Σ A 850b, making the same link but referring instead to ἰούς 'arrows', as befits an archery contest): the expression also denotes the discovery of iron in *Phoronis* fr. 2.6 B (see Tsagalis 2017: 417–18).   **κὰδ δ':** 28n.

852–5ᵃ The arrangement is reminiscent of the turning-post from the chariot race (τηλοῦ ἐπὶ ψαμάθοις 853 ~ τηλόθεν ἐν λείωι πεδίωι 359).   **ἱστὸν δ' ἔστησεν:** a *figura etymologica* common in naval contexts (1.480, *Od.* 2.94, 9.77, etc.: Tsitsibakou-Vasalos 2007: 36; Clary 2009: 271–2).   **νηὸς κυανοπρώιροιο** 'dark-prowed ship': probably reflecting the practice of coating ships with pitch, the epithet in this usually genitive formula is drawn from κύανος, which refers in Homer to niello but is later linked with lapis lazuli or azurite crystal (Irwin 1974: 79–110, esp. 92–4; Kurt 1979: 57–60); also 188–91n. The formula helps to fill out the very productive oblique-case 'black ship' system, which otherwise lacks a genitive singular expression (except the expanded νηὸς ἐϋσσέλμοιο μελαίνης: Alexanderson 1970: 27–8).   **τρήρωνα πέλειαν:** never in epos without πέλεια, τρήρων is either an epithet meaning 'fearful' (< τρέω) or a general noun further specified by πέλεια, i.e. 'the dove, the rock-dove': cf. πολυτρήρων 2.502, 582 (Arnott 2007: 248–50, 358). For similar doubling, see e.g. συσὶ κάπροισιν (5.783), ἴρηξ κίρκος (*Od.* 13.86–7; Russo 1994: 377–8). The collocation occurs often in similes (5.778 ~ *HAp.* 114, 22.140, *Od.* 20.243), emphasising speed along with fear (cf. *Od.* 12.62–3: Scott 2009: 230 n. 71). Repeated at 855 and 874, a link with skittishness would make the bird a difficult target, which is increased by its being bound (Σ bT 855).   **μηρίνθωι** 'thread': related to the μέρμιθι φαεινῆι | ἀργυρέηι fastening the bag of winds (*Od.* 10.23–4), this word is only found in Homer in this episode, but becomes proverbial for a fishing line (Ar. *Thesm.* 928, Theoc. 21.12: Quattordio Moreschini 1984: 69–70).   **ποδός, ἧς ἄρ' ἀνώγει | τοξεύειν:** ποδός is a partitive genitive meaning 'by the foot' (11.258, 17.289–90, 24.515) while the relative pronoun, referring to the dove, is also partitive, as with other expressions of shooting or aiming 'at' or 'in the direction of' (4.100, 13.159, 17.304). The variant πόδα 'in some texts' (Σ A 854b1, 2) presumably sought to separate the two more clearly (cf. 21.453–4).

855ᵇ–8 The lack of the usual speech introduction στῆ δ᾽ ὀρθὸς καὶ μῦθον ἐν Ἀργείοισι ἔειπεν (271–3n.) rather unexpectedly puts that role on ἀνώγει (854), an uncommon usage (cf. 4.301–2) made more so by direct speech beginning, unheralded, within the verse (Edwards 1970: 20–35, esp. 27; De Jong 2022: 46 and n. 42). The line between narrator text and character speech is blurred, suggesting another confluence of perspective (von Alvensleben 2022: 109; see 42n.). The descriptions of winner and loser mirror one another in conditional syntax (ὅς ... κε + subj.) and main verb (φερέσθω ~ οἴσεται), though they reverse the object + verb order, and the oddness of the whole proposal, specifically Achilleus' foreknowledge of happenstance, struck Aristarchos (Σ AT 857) and led some modern scholars to speculate about previous versions to which they may be an allusion (Wilamowitz-Moellendorff 1916: 69; Lovatt 2019: 416–17).   **τρήρωνα πέλειαν:** 852–5ᵃn.   **οἴκόνδε:** better attested than the unobjectionable reading κλισίηνδε, and suggesting the victor's eventual return home (cf. 848–9n.); for the spelling, see 55–8n.

857–8 Line 857 deploys a balanced doublet of gen. + verb before the chiasmus in 858, with ἥσσων ~ ἡμιπέλεκκα surrounding the emphatic juxtaposition (κεῖνος, ὃ δ᾽), underlining the link between the lesser prize and the lesser man. δ(έ) in 858 is apodotic rather than connective (*GP* 177–85, esp. 177), resuming the sentence and initiating the main clause after the γάρ parenthesis. Translate 'and whoever hits the thread, missing the bird – for truly that man is the lesser – *then* he ...'

859–60 The two competitors arise, in the same order as their competition, but reverse order to their success (as in the iron throwing: 836–8n.). Teucros' introduction is impressive (see below), while Meriones' phrase has only appeared in his disastrous chariot race. For ὦρτο, see 214–16n., and 754–6n. for ἄν in these contexts.   **βίη Τεύκροιο ἄνακτος:** often paired with his half-brother Aias, Teucros is the bastard son of Telamon and Priam's sister Hesione (though Homer makes no mention of his maternity) and mainly fights with the bow in the *Iliad* (8.266–334, 12.335–435, 15.458–83; Higbie 1995: 11–12). Explicitly praised by Idomeneus as ἄριστος Ἀχαιῶν | τοξοσύνηι, ἀγαθὸς δὲ καὶ ἐν σταδίηι ὑσμίνηι (13.313–14), he is a reliable and effective performer (Ebbott 2003: 37–66). Not especially prominent in early post-Iliadic myth, he was prevented by Telamon from remaining in Salamis after the war, and so founded another Salamis in Cyprus. The onomastic idiom βίη + genitive emphasises strength (826–7n.), combining with his general reputation to make Teucros a natural favourite here, and he does win the corresponding contest in Achilleus' funeral games (Intro. § 2.2), though perhaps his traditional association with Aias (Zunker 1988: 165–6; Kanavou 2015: 39–40) influences the outcome here. **Μηριόνης, θεράπων ἐΰς Ἰδομενῆος:** see 112–13, 528–9nn. Prominent in the lead-up to the funeral (112–13n.), he was the least successful competitor in the chariot race (where this expression was last used at 528), but his fortunes are looking up (see 888, where it is next used). He fights mostly with a spear, but kills one victim with a bow (13.650).

861–2ª 861 = 3.316, in the duel between Menelaos and Paris, to determine first cast ~ *Od.* 10.206, to determine which band would investigate Aiaia. The typical lot sequence (352–7n.) is varied in this very brief example: the prayer element is recast as Teucros' failure to promise sacrifice to Apollo (and, then, Meriones' rectification: 872–3), and the casting of the lots into the helmet and their shaking are combined. **ἐν κυνέηι χαλκήρεϊ** 'in brazen helm': originally a cap made of dog-fur (Trümpy 1950: 40–1), the κυνέη in epos is synonymous with other words for helmet, and can be variously of ox-hide (10.257–9), marten-fur (10.335), or metal; it is the only term for helmets used in lots. The epithet in this formula, 'made of bronze', is compounded from χαλκ- and ἀραρίσκω, and widely used with no difference in meaning from χάλκε(ι)ος etc. (see e.g. 5.743–4, 12.183). **πάλλον ἑλόντες** 'taking up (the lots in the helmet) they shook (them)': cf. *Od.* 10.206 (πάλλομεν ὦκα).

862ᵇ–4 Beginning abruptly at the bucolic diaeresis, Teucros' shot is marked by its power (ἐπικρατέως; cf. βίη) and the necessary run-over of ἧκεν, but immediately qualified for the lack of prayer. Perhaps prompted by Apollo's association with archery (cf. 865–9n. on μέγηρε), coupled with a need to explain why the previously favoured Teucros does not win, prayer is otherwise not a prominent feature in the games (see 768–84n.; at 546–7 divine help had already been proffered and countered: see 545–7n.) but a standard element in the lot sequence (352–7, 861–2nn.); his failure to do what he ought (Aubriot-Sévin 1992: 52) is bolstered by Meriones' apparent lesson from the chariot race, that 'while human skill can improve your chances, a spectacular upset victory lies in the hands of the gods' (Clay 2007: 74). **ἠπείλησεν** 'vow': an unusual sense for this verb, normally glossed as 'threaten' or 'boast', but an extension of its basic 'make a statement about oneself' in the present and future, which devolves readily in combat into a threat, and in other contexts to a promise (23.184 combines them: *LfgE* s.v. B). Verse 864 (= 4.102, 120, 23.872) is omitted in some early papyri and good medieval MSS, possibly because it is repeated in Meriones' shot. Neither line has any ancient scholia, but to end at 863 seems too abrupt, and the offer – made even more valuable by the selection – may well be standard for an archer (4.102, 120, from Pandaros' vow – NB the close repetition: see Leaf II.864, and 146–8n., also for κλειτὴν ἑκατόμβην).

865–9 The miss resumes the order of Achilleus' statement (856), and alternates thrice from bird (865, 866, 868) to thread (866, 867, 868–9) in a repeated A–B structure that rapidly shifts from one to the other until the closing μέν/δέ contrast is capped by the crowd's reaction (see n. on κελάδησαν; Σ A 868 notes the style's vigorous 'up and down' movement). Line 866 is closely modelled on 854.   **μέγηρε** 'begrudge': 3rd sing. aor. act. indic. of μεγαίρω, literally 'I make something (too) big' i.e. for someone, and thus view it negatively. Divinities elsewhere frustrate mortal actions on this basis (13.563, 15.473; cf. *Od.* 3.55), especially when they are intimately involved with the narrative or character (cf. also 4.54, and Thomas 2020: 404–5, on *HHerm.* 465).   **γάρ οἱ:** light scansion of γάρ neglects the effect of *digamma* in (ϝ)οἱ, which is rare but not unknown in Homer (West 1978: 291 on *WD* 526).   **πικρὸς ὀϊστός** 'bitter arrow': Teucros' loss is confirmed, since this formula is used for failed shots (4.118, 134, 217, 5.99, 110, 278, 8.323, etc.; cf. *Od.* 22.8, where the reversal has a particular, deliberate effect).   **παρείθη** 'fell to the side, fell down': 3rd sing. aor. pass. indic. of παρίημι, an Homeric hapax.   **ποτί:** see 62–4n.   **κελάδησαν:** groups in epos shout thus to show approval at a proposal (8.542, 18.310, both with adverbial ἐπί), while the Greeks laugh at other competitors' discomfiture (784, 839–40nn.) and shout (in admiration?) at Polypoites' victorious throw (847: see 257ᵇ–897n. and Table 4). Teucros' failure obviously pleases them, not from *Schadenfreude* but because it was so close and sets up a final, even more difficult shot.

870–1 Presumably because the bird is in flight and he does not have his own bow, Meriones hastily grabs Teucros' to make his shot. The ancients were puzzled: Σ AT reports that Antimachos of Colophon (fr. 177 M) felt the need either to specify that it was Teucros' bow (ἐξείρυσε Τεύκρου | τόξον· χερσὶ δ' ὀϊστὸν ἔχεν πάλαι) or, less likely, to make it (probably?) Meriones' own (ἐξείλετο τόξον | χερσίν, <ἀτὰρ δὴ ὀϊστὸν ἔχεν πάλαι ...>), as did the Massilian 'city text' (ἐπεθήκατ' ὀϊστὸν | τόξωι· ἐν γὰρ χερσὶν ἔχεν πάλαι): cf. Matthews 1996: 386–7. But the vulgate makes perfect sense: as in the σόλος and (perhaps) javelin throwing, the competitors use the same implement, and the lot bestows a real advantage. Meriones' achievement becomes even more impressive, and also more connected with Apollo, who 'gave' Teucros his bow (15.440–1).   **ὡς ἴθυνεν** 'as/when [Teucros] was making his shot': this phrase been faulted for its sudden change of subject and use of ὡς to mean 'while' (Leaf II.533), but the narrative's increasing pace explains the former (if defence is needed, cf. e.g. 15.556–8 with Janko 289, and Currie 2013), and for temporal ὡς with the imperfect see 6.237, *Od.* 19.445, 24.262 (*GH* II § 375).

872–4 872–3 ~ 863[b]–4 (873 = 864): see 862[b]–4n. Note the differences: while both are marked by αὐτίκα, Meriones' action begins the verse, and is directed towards Apollo, as though he has been paying attention to the narrative.   **ἐκηβόλωι Ἀπόλλωνι:** -ωι is light in epic correction. An obviously contextually suitable formula, also because the god is so labelled when his power is exhibited and acknowledged (1.14, 21, 373, 438, 16.513), this is the first time in the book Apollo has been denoted with his 'archer' epithet system (ἑκάεργος, ἕκατος, ἑκατηβόλος). Despite the neglect of *digamma*, ἑκηβόλος probably derived from *ϝέκα- (> ἑκών) and should mean 'shooting *at will*', but the poets seem to have understood it as 'shooting *from afar*' (< ἑκάς: Bonnell 2019: 77).   **ὑπαὶ νεφέων** 'beneath the clouds' or 'from out of the clouds': both locative and separative meanings are possible (*GH* II §§ 209–10), the first marginally better because the bird would be just about to reach safety. The paradosis is divided between ὑπαί and ὑπό; the latter treats νεφέων as though it began with a double consonant (linguistically unsound, but well paralleled before this word: *GH* I § 70), while ὑπαί's scansion is regular and is better attested in parallel passages (15.625, 16.375).   **εἶδε:** the best preserved of the several variants (ἴδετο, ἴδε, ἴδε δέ), and well paralleled in this position (4.275, *Od.* 4.524, esp. 17.3; cf. 15.484, 16.818).   **τρήρωνα πέλειαν:** 852–5[a]n. An etymologising connotation of τρήρωνα (see also 875–7[a]n. on δινεύουσαν) would underline the shot's quality.

875–81 The poet's focus moves A–B–A from the target to the arrow and back, setting the arrow's fall (876–7) as a precursor to the bird's (877–81) in an increasing doublet. The passage naturally draws freely on combat phraseology (cf. e.g. *Od.* 10.157–71, 19.428–58), and Friedrich 1956: 49–52 connects it especially with the death of Polydoros (20.413–18) for the shared 'strike in the middle' theme and the use of λιάζομαι (see below), and finds here a parody of the usual *androktasia*.

875–7[a] 876[a] = *Od.* 19.453[a], the boar-hunt. The violence of the action is underlined by necessary run-over and delay of the main verb πάγη. Missiles frequently pierce (ἀντικρύ 'right through') their victims and/or their armour (3.359–60, 4.481, 5.66–7, 74, etc.), while the passive aorist forms of πήγνυμι are elsewhere reserved for missiles fixed in the ground or victims' bodies or armour (4.185, 528, 5.616, etc.: Trédé 1992: 26 and n. 4).   **τῆι** 'there': i.e. ὕψι δ' ὑπαὶ νεφέων. The *h* scholia note the reading τῆν, which looks like dittography before the participle, δινεύουσαν 'whirling about', which expands the image latent in τρήρωνα.   βάλε μέσσην: strikes 'in the middle' are usually fatal, and generally followed by a description of the wound or death (5.657–8, 13.506–8, 16.411–13, 17.309–10, etc.; cf. 16.623–5).

877ᵇ–81 The bird settles back on the mast, hangs down its neck, droops its wings, dies, and falls down. The description is detailed, and pathetic, alternating between end-stopped and heavily run-over lines (877–9, 880–1) in a mimetically unsettled manner, focusing attention on each stage in the dove's demise. The first action is, frankly, odd, and West follows Nauck in bracketing 878, but the verse is contained in all our MSS and brings the dove back to where it was tethered, just as Meriones' arrow fell at his feet with a similar lack of verisimilitude (Friedrich 1956: 51 well notes the 'complete irrationality' despite the impression of accurate if picturesque details) – hence, partly, the crowd's astounded reaction at 881 (see n.). Line 880ᵇ = 16.117ᵇ, where the head of Aias' pike falls to the ground; 881 = 728 (see 726–8n.), during the wrestling, when the audience marvel at Odysseus' reversal of the lifting manouevre (a similarly unexpected triumph, and another very skilful tactic).   ἥ ὄρνις: the Homeric demonstrative can look very much like an article, especially where it effects a contrast, directing the audience back to an earlier subject (*GH* II §§ 239–40;).   νηὸς κυανοπρώιροιο: 852–5ᵃn.   αὐχέν' ἀπεκρέμασεν 'let hang its neck away', i.e. on one side: vivid and alliterative, reminiscent in detail of Gorgythion's death (esp. 8.306–8) and Polyphemos' drunken stupor (ἀποδοχμώσας *Od.* 9.372).   πτερὰ πυκνά: strong juxtaposition with the following verb, since this collocation elsewhere describes birds very much alive in swift and vigorous action (11.454, *Od.* 2.151, 5.53; cf. Sappho fr. 1.11 V; *LfrgE* s. πυκινός, πυκνός, B 1b).   λίασθεν: 3rd sing. aor. mediopass. indic. of λιάζομαι, of downward and defeated movement in general (see 231–2n.); here perhaps 'drooped', though the range of ancient variants (λιάσθη, λιάσθην, λίασσεν) reveals some early uncertainty.   ὠκὺς δ' ἐκ μελέων θυμὸς πτάτο: this unique combination of ἀπὸ δ' ἔπτατο θυμός and ὦκα δὲ θυμός | ὦιχετ' ἀπὸ μελέων fronts the notion of speed, giving ὠκύς a quasi-adverbial force and independence ('and quick from its limbs did the *thymos* fly'). πτάτο is 3rd sing. aor. mid. indic. of πέτομαι; on θυμός as 'the breath of life', see 62–4n.

882–3 The competition closes in reverse order (859–60n.). πελέκεας: -εα- is a single heavy syllable (synizesis: Intro. § 3.2 (vi)). κοίλας ἐπὶ νῆας: this formula is a line-end alternative for line-initial νῆας ἔπι γλαφυράς (849), from whose denotation it cannot be distinguished (848–9n.; Alexanderson 1970: 32; Kurt 1979: 35–7). Gesturing towards conveyance in the ship's hold, in the form of prize-conveying, is also found with these expressions (5.26, 7.78, 16.664, 21.32, *Little Iliad* fr. 21.2 B: Ward 2019: esp. 28–30).

884–97 Event 8. Spear Throwing. By some distance the shortest, the final contest is one of the most controversial, since Agamemnon is for the first time a direct competitor and Achilleus' intervention now prevents the usually most prominent stage, the contest, (257ᵇ–897n.), from taking place at all (for his intrusions in the wrestling and the fight in armour, see 733–4, 809–10nn.). Scholarly views have differed widely on what it means for the poem and its treatment of Achilleus' wrath and character, some arguing for a peaceful rapprochement symbolic of the host's courtesy, in which he tactfully prevents a potentially embarrassing loss (e.g. Dickie 1984; Scodel 2008: 153–7), others a tense, competitive continuation of their struggle for supremacy, which Achilleus has now won by depriving Agamemnon of even a chance to display his qualities (e.g. Lohmann 1992: 314–17; Sauge 1994: 22–9; Postlethwaite 1995): see further Stanley 1993: 224–32; Stocking 2023: 163–6. This divergence reflects the fact that the poet deliberately leaves the question open, placing this episode last and omitting to give the kind of detail normal in the other contests (884–6ᵃn.), thus breaking off the hitherto close interplay between narrator and character in this situation (von Alvensleben 2022: 111–14: see 42n.). It is also the only contest with no crowd reaction whatsoever (257ᵇ–897n.), as is even more noticeable since the last four events have enjoyed two such reactions (Table 4): the λαός has receded entirely from view, and we are left with the personal contest between two men with which the poem started.

Spear-throwing contests were a staple of Greek athletics, usually as part of the pentathlon (Harris 1964: 92–7; Weiler et al. 1993; Miller 2004b: 68–73; Romano 2021: 216), and well evidenced in epos: a simile image (16.589–92); mentioned by Achilleus as a typical event (621); listed among Nestor's triumphs at Amarynceus' funeral games (637), the Myrmidons' diversions (2.773–5: cf. *Od.* 4.625–7 = 17.167–9 for the suitors), and the events at which Odysseus claims to excel (*Od.* 8.229: Laser 53–7). This kind of episode proved common, but slightly less emphasised or developed in the games of Homer's poetic successors than the preceding ones (Simon. fr. 273.1–3 Poltera; Verg. *G.* 2.527–31; Stat. *Theb.* 6.351–4; Sil. Ital. *Pun.* 16.557–74; Quint. Smyrn. 4.472–8; Nonn. *Dion.* 37.750–78).

884–6ª 884 = 798, 886ª = 799ª, from the prize setting before the fight in armour (Sarpedon's panoply). Achilleus sets down the prizes, but the type of contest is not made clear (unlike for the chariot race, boxing, wrestling, running, and archery) until the competitors stand at 886ᵇ (see 886ᵇ–8n.); we have a somewhat similar delay before the fight in armour and the iron throwing, where there is only one prize, but on each occasion an accompanying speech clarifies the situation. There is no explicit labelling of the prizes' place order (as in the chariot race, boxing, wrestling, and running), and no accompanying speech announcing the contest or specifying that order (as in the boxing, fight in armour, and archery). From the practice in the previous contests, where prizes are always set out in order of value, the spear would be for first place, and the cauldron for second (*pace* Richardson 269: see below, and Spariosu 1991: 16 n. 25).   **κατά ... κάδ ... θῆκ':** the repeated preposition/preverb looks forward to the verb, the whole set paired chiastically with ἀνέσταν ... ἄν ... ἄν (886–8).   **δολιχόσκιον ἔγχος:** 798–800n. Possibly this was the implement to be used by the contestants (870–1n.), but it is still a prize.   **λέβητ' ἄπυρον ... ἀνθεμόεντα:** for ἄπυρον, see 267–8n. ἀνθεμόεντα is derived from the same stem as ἄνθος (perhaps, as adjectives in -όεις are particularly linked with place names, by analogy with ἠνεμόεσσαν: HW 249–51) and refers to floral decorations on metalwork (*Od.* 3.440, another cauldron; *Od.* 24.274) or qualifies meadows (2.467, 695, *Od.* 12.159). The value of this vessel, one ox, is the lowest of any item so measured: the first prize in the wrestling is a tripod worth twelve oxen (702–3n.), the second a woman worth four oxen (704–5n.), while an ox is the second prize in the running race, though still worth more than the half-talent of gold for third (750–1n.; Macrakis 1984: 211–13).   **ἐς ἀγῶνα φέρων:** another signal that things are a little awry (615–17n.).

886ᵇ–8 Only now is the contest specified, as the contestants stand. The structural parallel in 887–8 (ἄν + name ending -ης to 3a, noun–epithet to verse-end) places Meriones at a traditional disadvantage, setting his subordinate status to Idomeneus next to Agamemnon's patronymic and wide-rulership, but the choice of expression also evokes his performance in the last contest (859–60n.). Reversing the preposition/preverb + verb order above, ἀνέσταν is continued by anaphoric ἄν (798–800n.).   **ἤμονες ἄνδρες:** ancestrally glossed as 'javelinists' (Σ D 886 Zs, Ap. Soph. s.v., 84.10 Bekker), the absolute hapax ἤμονες is connected with ἤμασιν below and derived from ἵημι with agent suffix -μων, as in e.g. ἡγεμών, κηδεμών, and perhaps δαίμων (*WHS* 51–2). The reading ῥήμονες (Π 9) is a misdivision of ῥ' ἤμονες, already addressed in the scholia (Σ A 886a, T 886b); for pleonastic

ἄνδρες see 844–7n.   εὐρὺ κρείων Ἀγαμέμνων: 110ᵇn.   Μηριόνης,
θεράπων ἐΰς Ἰδομενῆος: 112–13, 528–9, 859–6onn.

889 Achilleus' usual introduction στῆ δ' ὀρθὸς καὶ μῦθον ἐν Ἀργείοισιν ἔειπεν
(= 271: see 271–3n.) was abandoned in the archery (855ᵇ–8n.), and is
here replaced with a unique combination. Its very form suggests trouble
over the intercession, which falls at the earliest stage of all his actions in
the events.   τοῖσι δὲ καὶ μετέειπε: a contentious opening, since this
speech introduction for crowd address (Edwards 1970: 8–9, type 3.5;
Riggsby 1992: 103–5, type 4c) falls where the speaker is acutely aware
of potential disagreement, whether from the situation or his own standing with the group (2.336, 3.96, 3.455, 7.70, etc.).   ποδάρκης δῖος
Ἀχιλλεύς: 140–4n.

890–1 The suggestion is termed in the scholia a victory ἀκονιτί 'without
dust', i.e. actual competition (bT 892), which is quite well attested in the
historical record, and a sort of prize no less coveted by those who were
crowned without competing (Crowther 2001). How we take this description of Agamemnon's abilities is crucial to our reading of this scene and
the poem; elsewhere he is not an inconsiderable fighter (see e.g. 7.179–
80 for the general Greek view, and Porter 2019: 273–4), Σ bT 887 even
calling him 'everywhere a good javelin thrower' (cf. e.g. 3.179), but there
is a consistent sense that something is amiss. The general claim to knowledge recalls Achilleus' statement about himself before the chariot race
(276).   Ἀτρεΐδη: the patronymic alone is often found in reproving
contexts (156–7n.), and it may be suggestive that Achilleus does not use
an (easy) whole-verse honorific, as at e.g. 19.199 (Ἀτρεΐδη κύδιστε ἄναξ
ἀνδρῶν Ἀγάμεμνον). Friedrich and Redfield 1978: 281–4 characterise his
propensity to open speeches with simple vocatives as a dominating strategy.   γάρ: anticipatory of 892–4 (*GP* 69–71), to be translated 'as' or
'since', with resumptive ἀλλά (892) marking an exhortation.   ὅσον
προβέβηκας ἁπάντων | ἠδ' ὅσσον δυνάμει τε καὶ ἥμασιν 'how far you are
superior to others, | and how far in spear-throwing power (*or* powerful
spear throwing) …': an unsettling statement, which uniquely expands an
idiom (προβαίνω + gen. pers. + dat. *rei*) used of those whose prominence
leads to trouble (6.125, 16.94, *Scut.* 354–5), lending greater weight to
the unexpected closure of the second clause (next n.). The dative nouns
are linked in hendiadys, as e.g. in δύναμις καὶ χεῖρες 'powerful hands' (*Od.*
20.237 = 21.202), θάνατος … τάρβος 'fear of death' (24.152), εὐνῆι καὶ
φιλοτῆτι 'the bed of love' (3.445; see Sansone 1984). Hapax ἥμασιν is dat.
pl. (< *ἧμα) linked with ἥμονες above; ῥήμασιν in Π 453 misreads ῥ' ἥμονες
above.   ἔπλευ ἄριστος 'you are the best': also at 9.43, where Nestor

compliments Diomedes but immediately qualifies his speech's appropriateness. Allusive or typical, it is another hint at Agamemnon's subordination. The quest to be acknowledged as ἄριστος is fundamental to Homeric society, and Achilleus admits his rival's right to be considered on this level, even if only in spear throwing, recalling his scornful earlier reference to Agamemnon's claims to be 'far best of the Achaeans' (1.91; cf. 2.82). On the present meaning of this aorist indicative form, see 69–70n.; -ευ is light in correption before ἄριστος.

892–4 Achilleus couches his proposal carefully, seemingly aware of the potential for trouble and returning to his opening alternation with Agamemnon (+ γάρ), which is underlined by chiasmus (σύ γε + verb | verb + ἔγωγε) in the alliterative and assonantal 894 connecting the two men.   **ἀλλά ... ἀτάρ:** Achilleus may be acknowledging the difficulty into which he is placing Agamemnon, since ἀτάρ (almost with the sense 'though') frequently introduces strong qualification to the statement or injunction in the ἀλλά clause (1.165–6, 5.482–3, 17.691–3, Od. 12.47–9, 16.150–1, 21.230–1, 259–60, 22.51–3: GP 54–5).   **κοίλας ἐπὶ νῆας:** 882–3n. The connotation of conveyance evokes in less explicitly hostile terms some previous statements of Agamemnon's covetousness (1.122, 165–9, 231, 9.331–3).   **πόρωμεν:** the subjunctive is either voluntative 'I/we want to ...' or hortative 'let us ...' (71–4n.). The plural may simply mean 'I', or it may include the suggestion that the gathered army is involved (or implicated?) in the decision (GH II § 42), which would be a nice reversal from the situation in Book 1, where the army is clearly held liable for Agamemnon's personal missteps (1.298–300).   **εἰ ... σῶι θυμῶι ἐθέλοις:** he defers to Agamemnon's will, as elsewhere with this 'willing in (your) soul' idiom (17.488–9, Od. 14.445, 23.257–8, Th. 443, 446). The optative is better attested and less direct than the variant ἐθέλεις, in keeping with the deliberate politeness (next n.).   **κέλομαι γὰρ ἔγωγε:** an assertive flourish used with a prudent suggestion which elsewhere prompts immediate disagreement (18.254, Od. 17.400; Rutherford 2019: 149, on 18.254).

895–7 895 = 2.441, where Nestor bids him rouse the army to battle (allusion?). Agamemnon does as he is told, the reversal in authority is complete, and the prizes are (as usual) despatched in order of value (884–6ᵃn.). Richardson 271 suggests that Agamemnon, as the last-named figure, hands over the spear to Meriones, but the alternation Achilleus > Agamemnon in 895 can easily be continued in 896; indeed, αὐτὰρ ὅ γ' ἥρως suggests a subject change (as at 1.333, 488, 597, 2.50, 105, 107, etc.) most naturally referring to Agamemnon, given that 896–7 concern his

herald Talthybios (below).   οὐδ' ἀπίθησεν ἄναξ ἀνδρῶν Ἀγαμέμνων:
Achilleus gets his way, since the litotic 'did not disobey' idiom (frequently
after ὣς ἔφατ') expresses acceptance by linking directly the speaker's intention with the following narrative as its successful fulfilment (1.220, 2.166,
441, 4.68, etc.: Kelly 2007a: 152–4). This sits uneasily with the authority connoted by the noun–epithet formula (49–51n.): Agamemnon may
well remain in charge, but a point has been made.   Ταλθυβίωι:
Agamemnon's herald (1.320–1, there together with Eurybates; cf. *Od.*
19.247), whose name probably means 'with thriving strength' (< θάλλω,
θαλερός: von Kamptz 1982: 87) and was linked in antiquity with a family
of heralds in Sparta, the Talthybiadai (Hdt. 7.134–6; Kirk I.85; Murakawa
1957: 401–2); this character is on hand whenever and for whatever
required, fetching a sacrificial animal (3.118–20, 19.196–7, 250–1, 267–
8) or summoning a doctor for Menelaos (4.192–208), but he does not
go on the embassy and only acts unprompted with Idaios (Trojan herald)
to stop the duel between Aias and Hector (7.274–6; see Kanavou 2015:
141–2 on heralds' names, and 39–41n.).   περικαλλὲς ἄεθλον: a fitting
end to this portion of the narrative, the combination is used in the pl. of
the divinely sourced prizes Thetis sets out for Achilleus' own funeral (*Od.*
24.85, 91); an allusion to that event would nicely conclude the references
to the characters' futures throughout the Funeral Games.

APPENDIX

AISCHINES' HOMER

Aischines' quotation of 23.77–91 in the speech *Against Timarchos* (§ 149), the ancient context for which is given in the commentary (77–91n.), is very important to our picture of the pre-Alexandrian phase of Homer's text, and to the multiform model in Homeric studies (Intro. § 4). In particular, Dué has examined the quotation from this perspective,[1] and concludes that all the differences between Aischines' text and the vulgate are precisely the kind of thing which oral recomposition would produce in an era of competing multiforms. Nardelli, on the other hand, reviews the orator's other quotations from Homer to show that he is simply an unreliable witness, quoting in a careless and indirect manner when he is not actively making up variants and verses (somewhat like Labarbe's, Lohse's, and Mitscherling's findings on the many Platonic quotations of Homer),[2] and Efstathiou extends that generally sceptical treatment also to this passage, though he does not think slips of memory are the cause, putting it down instead to Aischines' desire to make his point about the relationship between Achilleus and Patroclos more powerfully.[3] The stakes are high, since Aischines provides us with the largest extensive quotation to survive from such an early period.[4]

Before getting to the individual cases, it must be noted, firstly, that earlier in his speech (§§ 146–7) Aischines had given a prose summary of the passage he goes on to quote (much as he does with his quotation of 18.95–9 in § 150, summarised earlier at § 145). The orator encapsulates the Book 23 passage as follows (text Budé; the particular paraphrase which relates directly to our following discussion is in bold):

καθεύδοντος δ' αὐτοῦ ἐπὶ τῆι πυρᾶι, ὥς φησιν ὁ ποιητής, εἴδωλον ἐφίσταται Πατρόκλου, καὶ τοιούτων ἐπεμνήσθη καὶ τοιαῦτα ἐπέσκηψε τῶι Ἀχιλλεῖ, ἐφ' οἷς καὶ δακρῦσαι καὶ ζηλῶσαι τὴν ἀρετὴν καὶ τὴν φιλίαν ἄξιον αὐτῶν ἐστιν. **ἐπισκήπτει μὲν γὰρ αὐτῶι, προειπὼν ὅτι οὐδὲ ἐκεῖνος ἀπέχει μακρὰν τῆς τοῦ βίου τελευτῆς, εἴ πως εἴη δυνατόν, προδιοικήσασθαι, ὅπως τὸν αὐτὸν τρόπον, ὥσπερ καὶ ἐτράφησαν καὶ ἐβίωσαν ἐν τῶι αὐτῶι, οὕτω καὶ τελευτησάντων αὐτῶν τὰ ὀστᾶ ἐν τῆι αὐτῆι σορῶι κείσεται·** ὀδυρόμενος δὲ καὶ τὰς διατριβὰς διεξιὼν ἃς μετ' ἀλλήλων ζῶντες διέτριβον, λέγει

---

[1] Dué 2001a = 2019: 66–82. The later version cites neither Nardelli 2003 nor Efstathiou 2016.
[2] Nardelli 2003; cf. Labarbe 1949; Lohse 1964–7; Mitscherling 2005. For more examples in Book 23, see 212–13, 334–6ann.
[3] Efstathiou 2016.   [4] Haslam 1997: 74–7.

ὅτι οὐκέτι περὶ τῶν μεγίστων, ὥσπερ τὸ πρότερον, καθεζόμενοι μετ᾿
ἀλλήλων μόνοι ἄπωθεν τῶν ἄλλων φίλων βουλευσόμεθα, τὴν πίστιν
οἶμαι καὶ τὴν εὔνοιαν ποθεινοτάτην ἡγούμενος εἶναι. ἵνα δὲ καὶ διὰ τοῦ
μέτρου τὰς γνώμας ἀκούσητε τοῦ ποιητοῦ, ἀναγνώσεται ὑμῖν ὁ γραμματεὺς
τὰ ἔπη τὰ περὶ τούτων ἃ Ὅμηρος πεποίηκε.

And while he was sleeping next to the pyre, as the poet says, the
shade of Patroclos stood close to him, and he shared such memories and gave such instructions to Achilleus that one can weep and
envy their virtue and their worthy friendship. **For he ordered him,
predicting that Achilleus too was not far from the end of his life, to
make any possible provision to see to it that, in the same way they
had been raised and lived together, so in death their bones would lie
in the same coffin. And in tears as he recalled their living pursuits
together, he says 'no longer shall we take counsel about the greatest
matters, as we used to, sitting with one another apart from our other
friends', because he thought, in my view, that this pledge of their
goodwill was the most desirable thing.** But in order that you hear the
poet's thoughts as he composed them in verse, the clerk will read out
to you the verses which Homer has composed about these matters.

This reveals to us the purpose of Aischines' quotation, in terms of what
he thought the speech of Patroclos' shade conveyed – to highlight the
ongoing connection between these two characters in life and death, and
the impossibility of their future deliberations together.

Secondly, it is relatively clear that Aischines' text did not contain 92
(χρύσεος ἀμφιφορεύς, τόν τοι πόρε πότνια μήτηρ ~ 83b: see below), despite
Dué's invocation of Allen's characterisation of that view as essentially an
argument from silence.[5] The verse itself would obviously have helped to
underline the closeness of the two characters as manifest in Patroclos'
desire to be buried in the same vessel as Achilleus. Indeed, as we saw, this
is precisely how Aischines characterises the quotation in the prose summary (τὰ ὀστᾶ ἐν τῆι αὐτῆι σορῶι κείσεται), and he repeats that emphasis in
his instruction to the court clerk to read out the passage (ἀναγίγνωσκε δὴ
τὰ περὶ τοῦ ὁμοτάφους αὐτοὺς γενέσθαι καὶ περὶ τῶν διατριβῶν ἃς συνδιέτριβον
ἀλλήλοις § 149). If 92 had been in his text, especially with the extra emphasis it gives to 83b, it would have been quoted.[6]

---

[5] Dué 2001a: 37 = 2019: 72. On the question of its authenticity, see 91–2n.
[6] So also, e.g., S. West 1967: 171; Richardson 174; Haslam 1997: 76. They do
not, however, consider the internal dynamics of Aischines' quotation as a factor in
their conclusion.

i. 77 οὐ γὰρ ἔτι
οὐ μὲν γὰρ **vulg.**

Opening the quotation, οὐ γὰρ ἔτι would be clumsy in the same speech so soon after οὐ γὰρ ἔτ᾽ αὖτις in 75; such a proximity is unparalleled in Homer, who avoids repeating this figure in this way. Though the quotation does not go back that far, Aischines' wording in 77 was clearly influenced by it. His earlier prose paraphrase in § 147 stressed futurity and its contrast with a previous consuetude as the really tragic aspect of this part of the speech; and it actually used the word οὐκέτι to do so. For Aischines, this was the rub, and οὐ γὰρ ἔτι makes the point more clearly and obviously than οὐ μὲν γάρ. His reading was also 'in some of the city texts' known to the Alexandrians (Σ A 23.77), which is an independent error in those texts caused by the same fact of proximity (as West hints in his apparatus). 'What for Aeschines is an error with rhetorical backing is for the MS tradition a simple error of perseveration.'[7]

ii. 81a μαρνάμενον δηίοις Ἑλένης ἔνεκ᾽ ἠϋκόμοιο

This plus verse uses the *casus belli* significance of Helen to underline by contrast the relationship between Achilleus and Patroclos, which has an obvious contextual point for Aischines' purpose.[8] The idiom and style, moreover, is not as Homeric as Dué and Di Luzio contend: though μάρνασθαι δηίοισι(ν) is used 4× at the start of the verse, the participle is not found in this or any position with that noun, nor with a dative except Σολύμοισι (6.204) – a collocation which, as with other expressions in this quotation (see below, and also on 83ab), is very Hesiodic (*Th.* 663, frr. 25.13, 33a.20 M–W). Moreover, Homer only uses the long dative plural δηίοισι(ν) (8×),[9] and δηίοις is anyway awkward after Τρώων in 81; none of the examples of μάρνασθαι δηίοις adduced by Dué 2001a: 41 = 2019: 74–5 refers to the group denoted by δηίοισι(ν) in a different case in the previous verse.

---

[7] Henry Spelman *per litteras*.

[8] See below n. 10 for the attestations of the formula and its encapsulating purposes, but note that the collocation is more frequently found with πόσις to denote either Paris (3.329, 7.355, 8.82, 11.369, 505, 13.766) or someone in the process of trying to become Helen's husband (Hes. frr. 199.2, 200.2, 204.43, 55 M–W). If this is the operative field here, then the contrast between that relationship and the one at hand is even greater.

[9] One could conclude it is elided here before Ἑλένης, according to the principle that short-form dative plurals of nouns and adjectives are in some way 'hidden' in Homeric epos, being placed before vowels or in positions where another form of the word is routinely placed (Cassio 2023: 107–10).

The second hemistich Ἑλένης ἕνεκ' ἠϋκόμοιο is paralleled at 9.339, and (again) twice in Hesiod (WD 165, fr. 200.11 M–W), in all of which it serves to encapsulate the Trojan War as a whole.[10] There is a further, noticeable sense of distance to all these passages which seems to have little point in the context of Book 23 beyond that already identified above. But, in fact, by far the closest parallel for 81a is actually found in a fragment of the fourth-century BCE historian Hereas of Megara (FGrH 486 F 2), preserved in Plutarch's Theseus (32.6–7) and describing the death of Halycos ('fr. epicum anon.' B (p. 52) = ep. adesp. fr. 8 W):

> ... τὸν ἐν εὐρυχόρωι ποτ' Ἀφίδνηι
> μαρνάμενον Θησεὺς Ἑλένης ἕνεκ' ἠϋκόμοιο
> κτείνεν ...

Though we have no way of dating this fragment, Cingano illustrates its 'Hesiodic flavour'[11] by citing WD 163 (ὤλεσε μαρναμένους μήλων ἕνεκ' Οἰδιπόδαο).[12] This verse thus looks like a supplement, drawing mostly on un-Homeric phraseology, designed to make the passage stand alone by linking it explicitly – and somewhat unnecessarily – to the whole of the war, and therefore to underline the point and integrity of the quotation.

iii.   82   σὺ δ' ἐνὶ φρεσὶ βάλλεο σῇσιν
            καὶ ἐφήσομαι αἴ κε πίθηαι **vulg**.

Again unattested anywhere else (Π 9, 23, 258 all confirm the vulgate reading), Aischines' text offers the usual closing hemistich for the formula in 82ᵃ (see n. for attestations). σὺ δ' ἐνὶ φρεσὶ βάλλεο σῇσιν is readily explained as a simple error on that basis.[13] Homer elsewhere varies this formular verse with an individual second hemistich (15.212, Od. 24.248), while

---

[10] In Achilleus' case in Book 9, he seeks to relate the current imbroglio between himself and Agamemnon to the wider, pre-existing fact of his participation in the war and its whole motivation. Hesiod uses the phrase (WD 165) to set up a self-definition of his own poetic achievements in contrast to that of heroic, narrative epos; and (fr. 200.12 M–W) to denote the activity of one of Helen's suitors, an event which obviously looks forward to the Trojan War.

[11] Cingano 2017: 316–19 (quotation from 316).

[12] Hirschberger 2004: 469–70 even classes it as Hesiodic (fr. *7 H).

[13] For another example of Aischines' formular modifications, see the treatment of 18.97 in § 150, replacing one formula (τὴν δὲ μέγ' ὀχθήσας προσέφη ποδὰς ὠκὺς Ἀχιλλεύς 4×) with another (τὴν δ' αὖτε προσέειπε ποδάρκης δῖος Ἀχιλλεύς 3×). Efstathiou 2016: 110 suggests plausibly that this was motivated by a desire to remove a potential confusion, viz. that Achilleus was angry with Thetis (to whom he is speaking); if so, this is another example of Aischines' text being designed to make more sense as an excerpt.

αἴ κε πίθη(τ)αι accompanies requests or instructions which are sure to be fulfilled, issued in circumstances where the speaker enjoys greater conciliar status (1.207, 420, 11.791, 21.293, *Od.* 1.279); this status is given to Patroclos' shade because of the fact of death (see 82n.). The individual manipulation of the whole-verse formula in the vulgate is definitely Homeric, and the quotation's return to the rather flatter formula, away from an individual configuration of it, is readily imagined in variant terms. A quoting author is at least as likely to do this as a performer.

iv. 83a   ἀλλ' ἵνα πέρ σε καὶ αὐτὸν ὁμοίη γαῖα κεκεύθηι
     83b   χρυσέωι ἐν ἀμφιφορεῖ, τόν τοι πόρε πότνια μήτηρ

This is the version of 92 in Aischines' text (see above), and these plus verses are only recorded here (and absent from the three early papyri cited in the previous paragraph covering the passage). There is nothing absolutely impossible in either verse, though the idiom γαῖα κεκεύθηι in 83a is not Homeric (though cf. ὁμοίην γαῖαν ἐρεῦσαι 18.329)[14] but found once in Hesiod (*Th.* 505); the change of construction between 83 and 83a seems unusually harsh. The only other Homeric example of ἀλλ' ἵνα with the subjunctive (17.223–4)[15] corrects two causal participles explaining Hector's reasoning (οὐ διζήμενος ... οὐδὲ χατίζων 221), while the correction of an adverbial phrase as signalled by 83a (μή ... ἀπάνευθε 83) is much more elliptical and awkward.[16]

These plus verses, Dué argues, would strengthen the ring-compositional echo with 92 (see 69–92n. on 82–92), but, given that 92 was not in Aischines' text, the ring would actually have comprised ὁμοίη γαῖα κεκεύθηι | χρυσέωι ἐν ἀμφιφορεῖ etc. (83ab) ~ ὁμὴ σορὸς ἀμφικαλύπτοι (91). So Aischines' text does largely what the later transmitted text does, but with more difficult phrasing, and using idioms and expressions not otherwise found in Homer. It also reverses the rhetorical balance of this section of

[14] Interestingly, in an earlier part of the speech (§ 144), Aischines quotes this very phrase (also with the variant ἐρεύθειν for ἐρεῦσαι); i.e. he was already thinking about the image when he came to the deployment of 23.77–91.

[15] See *Od.* 17.68 for the only Homeric examples of locative ἀλλ' ἵνα with indicative (the usual mood with locative ἵνα in general).

[16] Chantraine reviews some cases of ἵνα with the subjunctive where one could see how an originally locative sense had evolved into the more common final sense (*GH* II § 396), but none of those examples show the awkwardness of 83a. The parallels for the sequence 83–83b adduced by Dué 2001a: 38 = 2019: 71–2 (drawing on Di Luzio 1969: 84–6; cf. 110) are neither apposite nor sufficient: more precise support is needed than the simple (and very common) 'not A, but instead B' figure (and it should anyway be 'not A, but instead not-A', i.e. the opposite of A).

the speech in order to make its own opening more punchy, by taking the vulgate's triumphant and emphasised closure (91–2) and putting it at the start of the quotation; where the portions of the standard ring are close in length (ὁστέ' ... | ἀλλ' ὁμοῦ 83–4 ~ ὀστέα ... ὁμὴ σορὸς 91), Aischines' quotation makes it 3:1. Remember that the fact of burial together is one of the points which he explicitly highlighted in the earlier prose summary (οὕτω καὶ τελευτησάντων αὐτῶν τὰ ὀστὰ ἐν τῆι αὐτῆι σορῶι κείσεται), and so a greater focus on this theme at the very start of the quotation makes good sense for his purpose. In short, it benefits the strength of the Homeric passage in its fourth-century context, but reshapes to that end the rhetorical emphasis of the shade's speech in Homer.

v. 84   ὡς ὁμοῦ ἐτράφεμέν περ
         ἐτράφομεν corr. Scaliger
         ἀλλ' ὁμοῦ, ὡς ἐτράφην περ vulg.
         ἐτράφημεν v. l., τράφομεν edd.

ἐτράφεμεν is *vox nihili* corrected by Scaliger to ἐτράφομεν, and the reading is purely a function of 83ab (with which it stands or falls), since 84 no longer needs to express the contrast with 83. Whatever one's judgement on the plus verses, the plural verb seems to confirm the impression from the several later variants about the difficulty felt between the linking of ὁμοῦ and the first-person singular ἐτράφην (84–6n.). Note once more how Aischines first glossed this section: ἐτράφησαν καὶ ἐβίωσαν ἐν τῶι αὐτῶι (§ 147). For him, plurality responds better to the context of his court speech and its depiction of a strong mutual, relationship.

* * *

None of these readings, in my view, can bear the probative weight which the multiform model seeks to place upon them. They look to be precisely the kind of misrememberings and active inventions of which Aischines stands accused in many other cases, and it takes no great leap of faith or argument to interpret them as variants from an established text, whether that was done in every case by Aischines himself or was simply reflected in his text of the *Iliad* (we do not need a single, exclusive explanation for every feature, of course; two things can be true at once). Not only are these practices demonstrated in other cases by Nardelli and Efstathiou, but the orator himself, in his prose summary before the quotation, makes clear exactly what he wants this passage of Homer to achieve. Though one might assert that he viewed the passage in this way because that was how it appeared in his text, the consistent signs of awkwardness and inappropriateness in these differences suggest rather that his Homeric text has been shaped for this particular oratorical context (i, ii, iv, v), and that mistakes have also been made whilst this end was pursued (i, iii).

There are two cases where Aischines' reading has some later diplomatic support: (i) οὐ γὰρ ἔτι (77) was apparently found in 'some of the city texts' (Σ); and (iv) the absence of 92, which was 'not in all texts' (Σ bT) and missing from Π 12 (though present in Π 9, 257, 511, and h142). The former case is an obvious confluence of proximity error, while the latter verse has seemed on independent grounds to many scholars to be an interpolation (in my view incorrectly: see 91–2n.). The discussion above proposed that the insertion of 83b to replace 92 was done either by Aischines himself to make the point of his quotation stronger in its opening, or by whoever was responsible for his text in order to render the first ring in that section in the speech more emphatic. In both cases, the later support is coincidental, consequent upon the repetition of a predictable error (i) and independent doubts on the appropriateness of using an amphora as a coffin (iv).[17]

Alternance might be proposed for the presence of 81 (ii) and 83ab (iv), and the formular return to the mean in 82 (iii), but for the reasons given above, I am unconvinced. Let us, nonetheless, grant the multiform conclusion for a moment once more: even if all these differences were evidence of 'as many Homers as you please',[18] what kind of thing would this creature be? However the modes of movement are being policed or controlled, it is one which offers very delimited freedom, and one which has to respect – or at least not disregard – the detailed rhetorical structure of the text we know, and even of individual verses; minor intralinear variants are introduced, links with other parts of the storyline made more explicit (without disturbing the integrity of the other verses in the vicinity), structural patterns (over)amplified. This would not amount, as some have both feared and celebrated in equal measure, to an entirely new form of ancient composition or transmission (or composition through transmission). And in any case, it is hard to see how such stability could be achieved without the existence and authority of a fixed, written text.

---

[17] See 91–2n.
[18] The phrase comes from the title of the review of Nagy 1996a by Hayden Pelliccia in the *New York Review of Books* 44.18 (20 November 1997): 46.

WORKS CITED

Adamo, S. (2024), *Epeo, mitologia di un artigiano: economie della montagna, economia del legno nella Grecia antica*, Naples.

Adkins, A. W. H. (1970), *From the Many to the One: a Study of Personality and Views of Human Nature in the Context of Ancient Greek Society, Values and Beliefs*, London.

Adrados, F. (1997–2003), *History of the Greco-Latin Fable*, 3 vols, Leiden.

Ahlberg-Cornell, G. (1971), *Prothesis and Ekphora in Early Greek Art*, Gothenburg.

Ahlberg-Cornell, G. (1992), *Myth and Epos in Early Greek Art: Representation and Interpretation*, Jonsered.

Ainian, A. M. (2016), 'Heroes in Early Iron Age Greece and the Homeric Epics', in S. Sherratt and J. Bennet (eds), *Archaeology and Homeric Epic*, Oxford: 101–15.

Alden, M. (2001), *Homer beside Himself: Para-narratives in the Iliad*, Oxford.

Alden, M. (2012), 'The Despised Migrant (*Il.* 9.648 = 16.59)', in Montanari, Rengakos, and Tsagalis (2012): 115–32.

Alexanderson, B. (1970), 'Homeric Formulae for Ships', *Eranos* 68: 1–46.

Alexiadou, A. (2005), 'Left Dislocation (Including CLLD)', in M. Everaert and H. van Riemsdijk (eds), *The Blackwell Companion to Syntax*, Malden, MA: II.668–99.

Aliffi, M. L. (2002), 'Le espressioni dell'agente e dello strumento nei processi di "morte violenta"', in Montanari and Ascheri (2002): 409–23.

Allan, R. (2010), 'The *infinitivus pro imperativo* in Ancient Greek: the Imperatival Infinitive as an Expression of Proper Procedural Action', *Mnemosyne* 63: 203–28.

Allan, R. (2023a), 'Cola and Caesurae in the Homeric Hexameter: a Functional-Cognitive Approach to Colometry', *Philologia Antiqua* 16: 101–17.

Allan, R. (2023b), 'Homeric Enjambment (and Caesura): a Functional-Cognitive Approach', in Giannakis (2023): 69–106.

Allan, W. (2006), 'Divine Justice and Cosmic Order in Early Greek Epic', *JHS* 126: 1–35.

Allan, W., and Cairns, D. (2011), 'Conflict and Community in the *Iliad*', in N. Fischer and H. van Wees (eds), *Competition in the Ancient World*, Swansea: 113–46.

Aloni, A. (1998), *Cantare glorie di eroi: communicazione e performance poetica nella Grecia arcaica*, Turin.

Alvensleben, L. von (2022), *Erzähler und Figur in Interaktion: Metalepsen in Homers Ilias*, Berlin.

Amory Parry, A. (1973), *Blameless Aegisthus: a Study of* AMYMΩN *and Other Homeric Epithets*, Leiden.

Andersen, Ø. (1978), *Die Diomedesgestalt in der Ilias*, Oslo.

Andersen, Ø. (1982), 'Thersites und Thoas vor Troia', *SO* 57: 7–34.

Andersen, Ø., and Haug, D. (eds) (2012), *Relative Chronology in Early Greek Epic Poetry*, Cambridge.

Andrade, T. (forthcoming), '"You Must Not": Traditional Referentiality in Sappho's "Brothers' Poem"'.

Antonaccio, C. (1995a), 'Homer and Lefkandi', in Ø. Andersen and M. Dickie (eds), *Homer's World: Fiction, Tradition, Reality*, Bergen: 5–28.

Antonaccio, C. (1995b), *An Archaeology of Ancestors: Tomb Cult and Hero Cult in Early Greece*, Lanham, MD.

Antonaccio, C. (2002), 'Warrior, Traders, and Ancestors: the "Heroes" of Lefkandi', in J. M. Højte (ed.), *Images of Ancestors*, Aarhus: 13–42.

Apthorp, M. (1980), *The Manuscript Evidence for Interpolation in Homer*, Heidelberg.

Arend, W. (1933), *Die typischen Szenen bei Homer*, Berlin.

Arnould, D. (1990), *Le rire et les larmes dans la littérature grecque d'Homère à Platon*, Paris.

Arnott, W. G. (2007), *Birds in the Ancient World from A to Z*, London.

Aubriot-Sévin, D. (1992), *Prière et conceptions religieuses en Grèce ancienne jusqu'à la fin du V* siècle av. J.-C.*, Lyon.

Austin, E. (2021), *Grief and the Hero: the Futility of Longing in the Iliad*, Ann Arbor.

Bakker, E. J. (1988), *Linguistics and Formulas in Homer: Scalarity and the Description of the Particle per*, Amsterdam.

Bakker, E. J. (1990), 'Homeric Discourse and Enjambement: a Cognitive Approach', *TAPhA* 120: 1–21.

Bakker, E. J. (1997), *Poetry in Speech: Orality and Homeric Discourse*, Ithaca, NY.

Bakker, E. J. (2001), 'Similes, Augment, and the Language of Immediacy', in J. Watson (ed.), *Speaking Volumes: Orality and Literacy in the Greek and Roman World*, Leiden: 1–23.

Bakker, E. J. (2005), *Pointing at the Past: from Formula to Performance in Homeric Poetics*, Cambridge, MA.

Bakker, E. J. (2015), *The Meaning of Meat and the Structure of the Odyssey*, Cambridge.

Bakker, E. J. (2025), *Homer, Odyssey: Book IX*, Cambridge.

Bakker, E. J., and Houten, N. van den (1992), 'Aspects of Synonymy in Homeric Diction: an Investigation of Dative Expressions for "spear"', *CPh* 87: 1–13.

Baltes, M. (1987), 'Beobachtungen zum Aufbau der Ilias', *Literaturwissenschaftliches Jahrbuch* 28: 9–25.

Bannert, H. (1988), *Formen des Wiederholens bei Homer*, Vienna.

Bär, S. (2018), *Herakles im griechischen Epos: Studien zur Narrativität und Poetizität eines Helden*, Stuttgart.

Barbara, S. (2023), *Diomède outre-mer: sur les traces d'un héros grec en Occident*, Paris.

Barker, E. T. E., and Christensen, J. P. (2011), 'On Not Remembering Tydeus: Agamemnon, Diomedes and the Contest for Thebes', *MD* 66: 9–43.

Barker, E. T. E., and Christensen, J. (2019), *Homer's Thebes: Epic Rivalries and the Appropriation of Mythical Pasts*, Washington, DC.

Barry, W. D. (1993), 'Aristocrats, Orators, and the "Mob": Dio Chrysostom and the World of the Alexandrians', *Historia* 42: 82–103.

Basset, L. (2006), 'La préfiguration dans l'épopée homérique de l'article défini du grec classique', in E. Crespo, J. de la Villa, and A. R. Revuleta (eds), *Word Classes and Related Topics in Ancient Greek*, Louvain-la-Neuve: 105–20.

Bassett, S. E. (1919), 'Versus Tetracolos', *CPh* 14: 216–33.

Bassett, S. E. (1933), 'Achilles' Treatment of Hector's Body', *TAPhA* 64: 41–65.

Bassett, S. E. (1938), *The Poetry of Homer*, Berkeley and Los Angeles.

Battilana, G. (1985), ΜΟΙΡΑ *e* ΑΙΣΑ *in Omero: una ricerca semantica e socioculturale*, Rome.

Beck, D. (2005), *Homeric Conversation*, Washington, DC.

Beck, W. (2020), 'Reassessing the Scholiastic Evidence for the Cretan *Odyssey* Theory', *TAPhA* 150: 357–78.

Beck, W. (2023), 'How Did Homer's Troilus Die?', *CQ* 73: 495–507.

Beecroft, A. (2008), 'Nine Fragments in Search of an Author: Poetic Lines Attributed to Terpander', *CJ* 103: 225–41.

Beek, L. van (2022), *The Reflexes of Syllabic Liquids in Ancient Greek*, Leiden.

Beekes, R. S. P. (1995), 'Aithiopes', *Glotta* 73: 12–34.

Bell, D. J. (1994), 'The Meaning of "drómos" in Homer's *Iliad* 23.758', *Nikephoros* 3: 7–9.

Ben, N. van der (1986), '*Hymn to Aphrodite* 36–291: Notes on the *pars epica* of the *Homeric Hymn to Aphrodite*', *Mnemosyne* 39: 1–41.

Benardete, S. (2005), *Achilles and Hector: the Homeric Hero*, South Bend, IN.

Bentein, K. (2016), *Verbal Periphrasis in Ancient Greek: Have- and Be-Constructions*, Oxford.

Benzi, M. (1999), 'Riti di passagio sulla larnax dalla Tomba 22 di Tanagra?', in V. La Rosa, D. Palermo, and L. Vagnetti (eds), *Epi ponton plazomenoi: Simposio italiano di studi egei dedicato a Luigi Bernabò Brea e Giovanni Pugliese Carratelli*, Rome: 215–33.

Bergren, A. T. (1975), *The Etymology and Usage of* ΠΕΙΡΑΡ *in Early Greek Poetry*, State College, PA.

Berman, D. (2005), 'The Hierarchy of Herdsmen, Goatherding, and Genre in Theocritean Bucolic', *Phoenix* 59: 228–45.

Bernsdorff, H. (1992), *Zur Rolle des Aussehens im homerischen Menschenbild*, Göttingen.

Bernsdorff, H. (2001), *Hirten in der nicht-bukolischen Dichtung des Hellenismus*, Stuttgart.

Bertolín-Cebrián, R. (2002), 'Parallel Ideological Use of Literature and Sport in Ancient Greece', *Nikephoros* 15: 39–49.

Bertrand, N. (2010), *L'ordre des mots chez Homère: structure informationnelle, localisation et progression du récit*, diss. Paris (IV Sorbonne).

Bertrand, N. (2017), 'Le rôle de l'adjectif ΚΑΛΌΣ dans les descriptions homériques', *RPh* 91: 7–41.

Bertrand, N. (forthcoming), *A Handbook of Homeric Greek Word Order: Expressing Information Structure in Homer and Beyond*, Washington, DC.

Bethe, E. (1914–27), *Homer: Dichtung und Sage*, 3 vols, Leipzig.

Bettini, M. (1988), 'ΉΘΕΙΟΣ', *RFIC* 116: 154–66.

Bichler, R. (2007), 'Über die Bedeutung der Zimelien in der Welt der Odyssee', in E. Alram-Stern and G. Nightingale (eds), *Keimelion: Elitenbildung und elitärer Konsum von der mykenischen Palastzeit bis zur homerischen Epoche*, Vienna: 31–9.

Bierl, A. (2019), 'Agonistic Excess and Its Ritual Resolution in Hero Cult: the Funeral Games in *Iliad* 23 as a *mise en abyme*', in C. Damon and C. Pieper (eds), *Eris vs. Aemulatio: Valuing Competition in Classical Antiquity*, Leiden: 53–77.

Bird, G. (2010), *Multitextuality in the Homeric Iliad: the Witness of the Ptolemaic Papyri*, Cambridge, MA.

Bitto, G. (2019), 'Alexandrian Book Division and Its Reception in Greek and Roman Epic', in Reitz and Finkmann (2019): I.133–63.

Blanc, A. (2012), 'Étymologies grecques: formes en -εικ- (ἀεικέλιος, μενοεικής, ἐπιεικτός)', *Glotta* 88: 54–98.

Bloedow, E. F. (2007), 'Homer and the *depas amphikypellon*', in S. P. Morris and R. Laffineur (eds), *Epos: Reconsidering Greek Epic and Aegean Bronze Age History (Aegeum* 28), Liège: 87–96.

Blum, H. (1998), *Purpur als Statussymbol in der griechischen Welt*, Bonn.

Bocksberger, S. (2022), *Telamonian Ajax: the Myth in Archaic and Classical Greece*, Oxford.

Boedeker, D. (1974), *Aphrodite's Entry into Greek Epic*, Leiden.

Bohringer, F. (1979), 'Athletic Cults in Ancient Greece', *REA* 81: 5–17 (reprinted with addendum under the name F. de Polignac in T. Scanlon (ed.) (2014), *Oxford Readings in Sport in the Greek and Roman Worlds, Volume I: Early Greece, the Olympics, and Contests*, Oxford: 91–116).

Bolling, G. M. (1950), *Ilias Atheniensium: the Athenian Iliad of the Sixth Century B.C.*, Lancaster, PA.

Bonifazi, A. (2009), 'Inquiring into *Nostos* and Its Cognates', *AJPh* 130: 481–510.

Bonnell, K. (2019), *The Homeric Hymn to Apollo: Introduction and Commentary on Lines 1–178*, DPhil diss., Oxford.

Bonnell, K. (2021), review of Clarke (2019), *BMCR* 2021.02.44.

Borchhardt, J. (1977), "Frühe griechische Schildformen', in H.-G. Buchholz et al., *Kriegswesen, Teil 1. Archaeologia Homerica E 1*, Göttingen: 1–56.

Borecky, B. (1965), *Survivals of Some Tribal Ideas in Classical Greek: the Use and Meaning of λαγχάνω, δατέομαι, and the Origin of ἴσον ἔχειν, ἴσον νέμειν, and Related Idioms*, Prague.

Bortone, P. (2010), *Greek Prepositions: from Antiquity to the Present*, Oxford.

Bouchard, E. (2015), 'Aphrodite *philommêdês* in the *Theogony*', *JHS* 135: 8–18.

Bowie, A. M. (2013), *Homer: Odyssey Books XIII–XIV*, Cambridge.

Bowie, A. M. (2019), *Homer: Iliad Book III*, Cambridge.

Boyd, T. (1995), 'A Poet on the Achaean Wall', *Oral Tradition* 10: 181–206.

Bozzone, C. (2024), *Homer's Living Language: Formularity, Dialect, and Creativity in Oral-Traditional Poetry*, Cambridge.

Brandt, P. (1888), *Parodorum Epicorum Graecorum et Archestrati Reliquiae*, Leipzig.

Breuil, M. (1989), 'ΚΡΑΤΟΣ et sa famille chez Homère', in Casevitz (1989): 17–53.

Briand, M. (2015), 'Sur la formule ἐς πατρίδα γαῖαν dans l'*Odyssée*: pour une poétique du νόστος', in Dell'Oro and Lagacherie (2015): 245–60.

Brillante, C. (1996), 'Nestore Gerenio: le origini di un epiteto', in E. de Mito, L. Godart, and A. Sacconi (eds), *Atti e memorie del secondo congresso internazionale di micenologia 1991*, Rome: 209–20.

Brown, A. (1998), 'Homeric Talents and the Ethics of Exchange', *JHS* 118: 165–72.

Brown, B. (2003), 'Funeral Contests and the Origins of the Greek City', in D. Philips and D. Pritchard (eds), *Sport and Festival in the Ancient Greek World*, Swansea: 123–62.

Brown, H. P. (2006), 'Addressing Agamemnon: a Pilot Study of Politeness and Pragmatics in the *Iliad*', *TAPhA* 136: 1–46.

Brownlee, A. B. (1988), 'Sophilos and Early Attic Black-Figured Dinoi', in J. Christiansen and T. Melander (eds), *Proceedings of the 3rd Symposium on Ancient Greek Art and Pottery*, Copenhagen: 80–7.

Brügger, C. (2009), *Homers Ilias Gesamtkommentar Band VIII.2: 24. Gesang. Kommentar*, Berlin.

Brügger, C. (2016), *Homers Ilias Gesamtkommentar Band IX.2: 16. Gesang. Kommentar*, Berlin.

Bruns, G. (1970), *Kuchenwesen und Mahlzeiten: Archaeologia Homerica II Q*, Göttingen.

Buchholz, H.-G. (2010), *Kriegswesen, Teil 3. Archaeologia Homerica E 3*, Göttingen.

Budin, S. L. (2003), *The Origin of Aphrodite*, Bethesda, MD.

Budin, S. L. (2014), 'Before Kypris Was Aphrodite', in D. T. Sugimoto (ed.), *Transformation of a Goddess: Ishtar – Astarte – Aphrodite*, Göttingen: 195–216.

Budin, S. L. (2016), *Artemis*, London.

Burgess, J. (2009), *The Death and Afterlife of Achilles*, Baltimore.

Burkert, W. (1975), 'Apellai und Apollon', *RhM* 118: 1–21.

Burkert, W. (1985), *Greek Religion* (tr. by J. Raffan), Oxford.

Burkert, W. (2011), *Griechische Religion der archaischen und klassischen Epoche*, 2nd ed., Stuttgart.

Burkert, W. (2012), 'Abschluss der *Ilias* im Zeugnis korinthischer und attischer Vasen (580/560 v.Chr.)', *MH* 69: 1–11.

Cairns, D. L. (1993), *AIDOS: the Psychology and Ethics of Honour and Shame in Ancient Greek Literature*, Oxford.

Cairns, D. L. (2010), *Bacchylides: Five Epinician Odes (3, 5, 9, 11, 13)*, Cambridge.

Cairns, D. L. (2016), 'Clothed in Shamelessness, Clouded in Grief: the Role of "Garment" Metaphors in Ancient Greek Concepts of Emotion', in G. Fanfani, M. Harlow, and M. L. Nosch (eds), *Spinning the Fates and the Song of the Loom: the Use of Textiles, Clothing and Cloth Production as Metaphor, Symbol and Narrative Device in Greek and Latin Literature*, Oxford.

Calder, L. (2011), *Cruelty and Sentimentality: Greek Attitudes to Animals, 600–300 BC*, Oxford.

Callaway, C. (1998), 'Odysseus' Three Unsworn Oaths', *AJPh* 119: 159–70.

Camerotto, A. (2005), 'Cinghiali eroici', in E. Cingano, A. Ghersetti, and L. Milano (eds), *Animali tra zoologia, mito e letteratura nella cultura classica e orientale*, Padua: 117–38.

Camerotto, A. (2010), 'Storie cretesi, ovvero altre storie: tra Idomeneus e i suoi parenti', in E. Cingano (ed.), *Tra panellenismo e tradizioni locali: generi poetici e storiografia*, Alessandria: 1–40.

Canevaro, L. G. (2018), *Women of Substance in Homeric Epic*, Oxford.

Cantilena, M. (2012), 'Oralità, tradizione, testo: tre dimensioni della questione omerica', in G. Bastianini and A. Casanova (eds), *I papiri omerici: Atti del convegno internazionale di studi, Firenze, 9–10 giugno 2011*, Florence: 79–96.

Carlier, P. (2006), 'ἄναξ and βασιλεύς in the Homeric Poems', in S. Deger-Jalkotzy and I. Lemos (eds), *Ancient Greece: from the Mycenaean Palaces to the Age of Homer*, Edinburgh: 101–10.

Carter, C. (1988), 'Athletic Contests in Hittite Religious Festivals', *JNES* 47: 186–7.

Carter, J., and Morris, S. (eds) (1995), *The Ages of Homer: a Tribute to Emily Townsend Vermeule*, Austin, TX: 123–36.

Casevitz, M. (ed.), (1989), *Études homériques: séminaire de recherche sous la direction de Michel Casevitz*, Travaux de la Maison de l'Orient 16, Lyon.

Cassio, A. C. (1998), 'La cultura euboica e lo sviluppo dell'epica greca', in B. D'Agostino and M. Bats (eds), *EUBOICA: L'Eubea e la presenza euboica in Calcidica e in Occidente*, Naples: 11–22.

Cassio, A. C. (2002), 'Early Editions of the Greek Epics and Homeric Textual Criticism in the Sixth and Fifth Centuries BC', in Montanari and Ascheri (2002): 105–46.

Cassio, A. C. (2023), 'Old Morphology in Disguise: Homeric Episynaloephe, Ζῆν(α), and the Fate of IE Instrumentals', in Giannakis (2023): 107–15.

Casson, L. (1971), *Ships and Seamanship in the Ancient World*, Baltimore.

Castiglioni, B. (2020), 'Menelaus in the *Iliad* and in the *Odyssey*: the Anti-hero of πένθος', *Commentaria Classica* 7: 219–32.

Cavanagh, W., and Mee, C. (1998), *A Private Place: Death in Prehistoric Greece*, Jonsered.

Ceccarelli, P., Létoublon, F., and Steinrück, M. (1998), 'L'individu, le territoire, la graisse: du public et du privé chez Homère', *Ktèma* 23: 47–58.

Cerri, G. (1995), 'Cosmologia dell'Ade in Omero, Esiodo e Parmenide', *PP* 50: 437–67.

Chiai, G. F. (2017), *Troia, la Troade ed il Nord Egeo nelle tradizioni mitiche greche*, Paderborn.

Christesen, P., and Kyle, D. G. (eds) (2014), *A Companion to Sport and Spectacle in Greek and Roman Antiquity*, Malden, MA and Oxford.

Cingano, E. (1992), 'The Death of Oedipus in the Epic Tradition', *Phoenix* 46: 1–11.

Cingano, E. (2005), 'Il cavallo "aiutante magico" nella Grecia eroica', in E. Cingano, A. Ghersetti, and L. Milano (eds), *Animali tra zoologia, mito e letteratura nella cultura classica e orientale*, Padua: 139–54.

Cingano, E. (2017), 'Epic Fragments on Theseus: Hesiod, Cercops, and the *Theseis*', in T. Derda, J. Hilder, and J. Kwapisz (eds), *Fragments, Holes and Wholes: Reconstructing the Ancient World in Theory and Practice*, Warsaw: 309–32.

Clarke, M. (1999), *Flesh and Spirit in the Songs of Homer*, Oxford.

Clarke, M. (2004), 'Manhood and Heroism', in R. Fowler (ed.), *The Cambridge Companion to Homer*, Cambridge: 74–90.

Clarke, M. (2019), *Achilles beside Gilgamesh: Mortality and Wisdom in Early Epic Poetry*, Cambridge.

Clarke, W. M. (1978), 'Achilles and Patroclus in Love', *Hermes* 106: 381–96.

Clary, T. C. (2009), *Rhetoric and Repetition: the Figura Etymologica in Homeric Epic*, PhD diss., Cornell.

Clay, J. Strauss (1983), *The Wrath of Athena: Gods and Men in the Odyssey*, Princeton, NJ.

Clay, J. Strauss (2007), 'Art, Nature and the Gods in the Chariot Race of *Iliad* Ψ', in M. P. Paizi-Apostolopoulou, A. Rengakos, and C. Tsagalis (eds), *Contests and Rewards in the Homeric Epics: Proceedings of the 10th International Symposium on the Odyssey*, Ithaca, NY: 69–75.

Clay, J. Strauss (2011), *Homer's Trojan Theater: Space, Vision and Memory in the Iliad*, Cambridge.

Clay, J. Strauss (2025), 'Achilles Inaugurates His Cult', *G&R* 72: 38–64.

Cohen, B. (1994), 'From Bowman to Clubman: Herakles and Olympia', *ABull* 76: 696–715.

Combellack, F. (1976), 'Homer the Innovator', *CPh* 71: 44–55.

Cook, J. M. (1973), *The Troad: an Archaeological and Topographical Study*, Oxford.

Cousin, C. (2015), 'Le songe et la mort dans les poèmes homériques', in Dell'Oro and Lagacherie (2015): 103–16.

Coventry, L. (1987), 'Messenger Scenes in *Iliad* xxiii and xxiv (xxiii 192–211, xxiv 77–188)', *JHS* 107: 178–80.

Cowan, R. (2021), 'The Last Shall Be First: πανύστατος in Apollonios and Homer', *Yearbook of Ancient Greek Epic* 5: 135–65.

Cozzo, A. (1988), *Kerdos: semantica, ideologie e società nella Grecia antica*, Rome.

Crielaard, J. P. (1995), *Homeric Questions*, Amsterdam.

Crielaard, J. P. (2016), 'Living Heroes: Metal Urn Cremations in Early Iron Age Greece, Cyprus and Italy', in F. Gallo (ed.), *Omero: quaestiones disputatae*, Milan: 43–78.

Croiset, A., and Croiset, M. (1896–98), *Histoire de la littérature grecque*, 3 vols, 2nd ed., Paris.

Crouwel, J. H. (1981), *Chariots and Other Means of Land Transport in Bronze Age Greece*, Amsterdam.

Crouwel, J. H. (1992), *Chariots and Other Wheeled Vehicles in Iron Age Greece*, Amsterdam.

Crowther, N. B. (1992), 'Second-Place Finishes and Lower in Greek Athletics', *ZPE* 90: 97–102.

Crowther, N. B. (1994), 'Reflections on Greek Equestrian Events: Violence and Spectator Attitudes', *Nikephoros* 7: 121–33.

Crowther, N. B. (1999), 'Athlete as Warrior in the Ancient Greek Games: Some Reflections', *Nikephoros* 12: 121–30.

Crowther, N. B. (2001), 'Victories without Competition in the Greek Games', *Nikephoros* 14: 29–44.

Culhed, E., and Olson, S. D. (eds) (2022–), *Eustathius of Thessalonica: Commentary on the Odyssey*, 2 vols, Leiden (https://scholarlyeditions .brill.com/eooc/).

Currie, B. G. F. (2005), *Pindar and the Cult of Heroes*, Oxford.

Currie, B. G. F. (2013), 'The Genitive ΟΔΥΣΕΥΣ (*Od.* 24.398) and Homer's "Awkward" Parentheses', *JHS* 133: 21–42.

Currie, B. G. F. (2016), *Homer's Allusive Art*, Oxford.

Cuypers, M. (2005), 'Interactional Particles and Narrative Voice in Apollonius and Homer', in M. Cuypers and A. Harder (eds), *Beginning from Apollo: Studies in Apollonius Rhodius and the Argonautic Tradition*, Leuven and Paris: 35–69.

Daitz, S. G. (1991), 'On Reading Homer Aloud: to Pause or Not to Pause', *AJPh* 112: 149–60.

Dalfen, J. (1984), 'οὐδὲ ἔοικε: eine "homerische" Art, menschliches Verhalten zu beurteilen', *WS* 97: 5–26.

Danek, G. (2002), 'Traditional Referentiality and Homeric Intertextuality', in Montanari and Ascheri (2002): 3–20.

Davidson, J. F. (1988), 'Homer and Sophocles' *Electra*', *BICS* 35: 45–72.

Davies, M., and Finglass, P. J. (2014), *Stesichorus: the Poems*, Cambridge.

Davies, T. H. (2023), 'Beyond the Parallel: the *Iliad* and the *Epic of Gilgameš* in Their Macro-regional Tradition', *TAPhA* 153: 1–42.

Day, L. P. (1984), 'Dog Burials in the Greek World', *AJA* 88: 21–32.

Deacy, S. (2008), *Athena*, Abingdon.

Deacy, S. (2015), 'Gods – Olympian or Chthonian?', in E. Eidinow and J. Kindt (eds), *The Oxford Handbook of Ancient Greek Religion*, Oxford: 355–68.

Debiasi, A. (2004), *L'epica perduta: Eumelo, il Ciclo, l'occidente*, Rome.

Decker, W. (1976), 'Zum Ursprung des Diskuswerfens', *Stadion* 2.2: 196–212.

Decker, W. (1982–3), 'Die mykenische Herkunft des griechischen Totenagons', *Stadion* 8–9: 1–24.

Decker, W. (2004), 'Vorformen griechischer Agone in der Alten Welt', *Nikephoros* 17: 9–25.

Decker, W. (2012), 'Sport in Ancient Egypt', in Petermandel and Ulf (2012): 23–34.

Decker, W. (2021), 'Sport in Egypt and the Ancient Near East', in Futrell and Scanlon (2021): 31–46.

Decloquemont, V. (2023), 'Mental Paratext? Homeric Criticism in the *Progymnasmata*', *Philologia Antiqua* 16: 119–32.

Deioudi, M. (1999), *Heroenkulte in homerischer Zeit*, Oxford.

Del Barrio, M. L. (2014), 'Ionic', in G. Giannakis (ed.), *Encyclopedia of Ancient Greek Language and Linguistics*, 3 vols, Leiden: II.260–7.

Delebecque, E. (1951), *Le cheval dans l'Iliade; suivi d'un lexique du cheval chez Homère et d'un essai sur le cheval pré-homérique*, Paris.

Dell'Oro, F., and Lagacherie, O. (eds) (2015), Πολυφόρβηι Γαίηι: *mélanges de littérature et linguistique offerts à Françoise Létoublon*, Grenoble.

Demont, P. (2000), 'Lots héroïques: remarques sur le tirage au sort de l'*Iliade* aux *Sept contre Thèbes* d'Eschyle', *REG* 113: 299–325.

Derderian, K. (2001), *Leaving Words to Remember: Greek Mourning and the Advent of Literacy*, Leiden.

Detienne, M. (1998), *Apollon le couteau à la main: une approche expérimentale du polythéisme grec*, Paris.

Di Benedetto, V. (1998), *Nel laboratorio di Omero*, Turin.

Dickie, M. W. (1984), 'Fair and Foul Play in the Funeral Games of the *Iliad*', *Journal of Sport History* 11: 8–17.

Dicks, D. R. (1970), *Early Greek Astronomy to Aristotle*, London.

Dickson, K. (1995), *Nestor: Poetic Memory in Greek Epic*, New York and London.

Dietrich, B. C. (1965), *Death, Fate and the Gods: the Development of a Religious Idea in Greek Popular Belief and in Homer*, London.

Dijk, G.-J. van (1997), *Ainoi, logoi, mythoi. Fables in Archaic, Classical, and Hellenistic Greek Literature: with a Study of the Theory and Terminology of the Genre*, Leiden.

Di Luzio, A. (1969), 'Papirici omerici d'epoca tolemaica e la costituzione del testo dell'epica arcaica', *RCCM* 11: 3–152.

Dodds, E. R. (1960), *The Greeks and the Irrational*, 2nd ed., Berkeley.

Dougherty, C. (2001), *The Raft of Odysseus: the Ethnographic Imagination of Homer's Odyssey*, Oxford.

Dova, S. (2020), 'On Princes and Carpenters Boxing in Homer', *Journal of the Philosophy of Sport* 47: 362–76.

Dué, C. (2001a), 'Achilles' Golden Amphora in Aeschines' "Against Timarchus" and the Afterlife of Oral Tradition', *CPh* 96: 33–47.

Dué, C. (2001b), '*Sunt aliquid manes*: Homer, Plato, and Alexandrian Allusion in Propertius IV 7', *CJ* 96: 401–13.

Dué, C. (2019), *Achilles Unbound: Multiformity and Tradition in the Homeric Epics*, Washington, DC.

Dué, C. (2023), '"New" Philology and the Homer Multitext', *Philologia Antiqua* 16: 43–53.

Dué, C., and Ebbott, M. (2010), *Iliad 10 and the Poetics of Ambush: a Multitext Edition with Essays and Commentary*, Washington, DC.

Dunkle, R. (1981), 'Some Notes on the Funeral Games: *Iliad* 23', *Prometheus* 1: 11–18.

Dunkle, R. (1987), 'Nestor, Odysseus and the MÊTIS : BIÊ Antithesis: the Funeral Games, *Iliad* 23', *CW* 81: 1–17.

Durante, M. (1971–6), *Sulla preistoria della tradizione poetica greca*, 2 vols, Rome.

Ebbott, M. (2003), *Imagining Illegitimacy in Classical Greek Literature*, Lanham, MD.

Edgeworth, M. (1983), 'Terms for "Brown" in Ancient Greek', *Glotta* 61: 31–40.

Edmunds, L. (2023), 'A Sociology of Textile Production in Homer', *C&M* 72: 311–28.

Edmunds, S. (1990), *Homeric Nepios*, New York.

Edmunds, S. (2020), 'Picturing Homeric Weaving', in D. Elmer, D. Frame, L. Muellner, and V. Bers (eds), *Donum natalicium digitaliter confectum Gregorio Nagy septuagenario a discipulis collegis familiaribus oblatum*, Harvard (CHS).

Edwards, A. T. (1984), '*Aristos Achaiōn*: Heroic Death and Dramatic Structure in the *Iliad*', *QUCC* 46: 61–80.

Edwards, G. P. (1971), *The Language of Hesiod in Its Traditional Context*, Oxford.

Edwards, M. W. (1970), 'Homeric Speech Introductions', *HSCP* 74: 1–36.

Edwards, M. W. (1986), 'The Conventions of an Homeric Funeral', in J. Betts, J. Hooker, and T. Green (eds), *Studies in Honour of T. B. L. Webster I*, Bristol: 84–92.

Edwards, M. W. (1987), *Homer: Poet of the Iliad*, Baltimore.

Efstathiou, A. (2016), '*Argumenta Homerica*: Homer's Reception by Aeschines', in A. Efstathiou and I. Karamanou (eds), *Homeric Receptions across Generic and Cultural Contexts*, Berlin: 93–124.

Ekroth, G. (2002), *The Sacrificial Rituals of Greek Hero-Cults*, Liège.

Ekroth, G. (2005), 'Blood on the Altars? On the Treatment of Blood at Greek Sacrifices and the Iconographical Evidence', *AK* 48: 9–29.

Ekroth, G. (2014), 'Animal Sacrifice in Antiquity', in G. L. Campbell (ed.), *The Oxford Handbook of Animals in Classical Thought and Life*, Oxford: 324–54.

Elliger, W. (1975), *Die Darstellung der Landschaft in der griechischen Dichtung*, Berlin.

Ellinger, R. (2009), *Artémis, déesse de tous les dangers*, Paris.

Ellis-Evans, A. (2019), *The Kingdom of Priam: Lesbos and the Troad between Anatolia and the Aegean*, Oxford.

Elmer, D. (2013), *The Poetics of Consent*, Baltimore.

Elmer, D. (2015), 'The "Narrow Road" and the Ethics of Language Use in the *Iliad* and *Odyssey*', *Ramus* 44: 155–83.

Erbse, H. (1960), *Studien zur Überlieferung der Iliasscholien*, Munich.

Erbse, H. (1986), *Die Funktion der Götter in der Ilias*, Berlin.

Erbse, H. (1993a), 'Zwei homerische Wörter', *Glotta* 71: 130–6.

Erbse, H. (1993b), 'Nestor und Antilochos bei Homer und Arktinos', *Hermes* 121: 385–403.

Erny, G. (2020), '*Iliad* 13, Homer's Cretan Heroes, and "Cretan Exceptionalism"', *Phoenix* 74.3: 197–219.

Erp Taalman Kip, A. M. van (2012), 'On Defining an Homeric Idiom', *Mnemosyne* 65: 539–51.

Erren, M. (1970), 'αὐτίκα "sogleich" als Signal der einsetzenden Handlung in *Ilias* und *Odyssee*', *Poetica* 3: 24–58.

Falkner, T. M. (1995), *The Poetics of Old Age in Greek Epic, Lyric, and Tragedy*, Norman, OK and London.

Fantuzzi, M. (2012), *Achilles in Love: Intertextual Studies*, Oxford.

Farron, S. (2003), 'Attitudes to Military Archery in the *Iliad*', in A. Basson and W. Dominik (eds), *Literature, Art, History: Studies on Classical Antiquity and Tradition*, Frankfurt am Main: 169–84.

Faulkner, A. (2008), *The Homeric Hymn to Aphrodite: Introduction, Text and Commentary*, Oxford.

Fehling, D. (1969), *Die Wiederholungsfiguren und ihr Gebrauch bei den Griechen vor Gorgias*, Berlin.

Felson, N., and Slatkin, L. (2004), 'Gender and Homeric Epic', in R. Fowler (ed.), *The Cambridge Companion to Homer*, Cambridge: 91–114.

Fenno, J. (2005), 'A Great Wave against the Stream: Water Imagery in Iliadic Battle Scenes', *AJPh* 126: 475–504.

Fiedler, W. (1992), 'Der Faustkampf in der griechischen Dichtung', *Stadion* 18: 1–67.

Finglass, P. J. (2007), *Sophocles: Electra*, Cambridge.

Finglass, P. J. (2011), *Sophocles: Ajax*, Cambridge.

Finglass, P. J. (2013), 'How Stesichorus Began His *Sack of Troy*', *ZPE* 185: 1–17.

Finkelberg, M. (2000), 'The *Cypria*, the *Iliad*, and the Problem of Multiformity in Oral and Written Tradition', *CPh* 95: 1–11.

Finkelberg, M. (2005), *Greeks and Pre-Greeks*, Cambridge.

Finkelberg, M. (ed.) (2011), *The Homer Encyclopedia*, 3 vols, Oxford and Malden, MA.

Finkelberg, M. (2017), 'Homer at the Panathenaia: Some Possible Scenarios', in C. Tsagalis and A. Markantonatos (eds), *The Winnowing Oar: New Perspectives in Homeric Studies*, Berlin: 29–42.

Fisher, N. (2001), *Aeschines: Against Timarchos*, Oxford.

Foley, J. M. (1991), *Immanent Art: from Structure to Meaning in Traditional Epic*, Bloomington.

Foley, J. M. (1999), *Homer's Traditional Art*, University Park, PA.

Föllinger, S. (2009), 'Tears and Crying in Archaic Greek Poetry (Especially Homer)', in F. Thorsten (ed.), *Tears and Crying in the Greco-Roman World*, Berlin: 17–36.

Foltiny, S. (1980), 'Schwert, Dolch, und Messer', in H.-G. Buchholz, S. Foltiny, and O. Höckmann, *Kriegswesen, Teil 2. Archaeologia Homerica E 2*, Göttingen: 231–74.

Forbes, R. J. (1967), *Bergbau, Steinbruchtätigkeit, und Hüttenwesen: Archaeologia Homerica K*, Göttingen.

Forte, A. (2017), *Tracing Homeric Metaphor*, PhD diss., Harvard.

Forte, A. (2018), 'The Disappearing Turn of *Iliad* 23.373', *CPh* 114: 120–5.

Frame, D. (2009), *Hippota Nestor*, Washington, DC.

Frangoulidis, H. (1999), *Nonnos de Panopolis: Les Dionysiaques, Tome XIII: Chant XXVII*, Paris.

Fränkel, H. (1924), 'Homerische Wörter', in ΑΝΤΙΔΩΡΟΝ: *Festschrift Jacob Wackernagel zur Vollendung des 70. Lebensjahres*, Göttingen: 274–82.

Fränkel, H. (1926), 'Der kallimachische und der homerische Hexameter', *NAWG*: 197–229.

Fränkel, H. (1960), 'Der homerische und der kallimachische Hexameter', in *Wege und Formen frühgriechischen Denkens*, 3rd ed., Munich: 100–56.

Friedrich, P., and Redfield, J. (1978), 'Speech as a Personality Symbol: the Case of Achilles', *Language* 54: 263–87.

Friedrich, R. (2007), *Formular Economy in Homer: the Poetics of the Breaches*, Stuttgart.

Friedrich, W.-H. (1956), *Verwundung und Tod in der Ilias*, Göttingen.

Friis Johansen, K. (1967), *The Iliad in Early Greek Art*, Copenhagen.

Frontisi-Ducroix, F. (1975), *Dédale: mythologie de l'artisan en Grèce ancienne*, Paris.

Futrell, A., and Scanlon, T. (eds) (2021), *The Oxford Handbook of Sport and Spectacle in the Ancient World*, Oxford.

Gagarin, M. (1983), 'Antilochus' Strategy: the Chariot Race in *Iliad* 23', *CPh* 78: 35–9.

Gainsford, P. (2012), 'Sibling Terminology in Homer: Problems with ΚΑΣΙΓΝΗΤΟΣ and ΑΔΕΛΦΕΟΣ', *CQ* 62.2: 441–65.

Galanakis, Y. (2020), 'Death and Burial', in I. Lemos and A. Kotsonas (eds), *A Companion to the Archaeology of Early Greece and the Mediterranean, Volume 1*, Oxford and Hoboken, NJ: 349–74.

Gallou, C. (2005), *The Mycenaean Cult of the Dead*, BAR International Series 1372, Oxford.

Gantz, T. (1993), *Early Greek Myth*, Baltimore.

García-Ramón, J. L. (1997), 'Lat. *prae*, gr. παραί und Verwandtes', in A. Lobotsky (ed.), *Sound Law and Analogy: Papers in Honour of Robert S. P. Beekes on the Occasion of His 60th Birthday*, Amsterdam: 47–62.

García Romero, F. (2001), *El deporte en los proverbios griegos antiguos*, Hildesheim.

Garland, R. (1982), '*Geras thanonton*: an Investigation into the Claims of the Homeric Dead', *BICS* 29: 69–79 (= 'γέρας θανόντων: an Investigation into the Claims of the Homeric Dead', *Ancient Society* 15 (1984): 5–22).

Garland, R. (1985), *The Greek Way of Death*, Ithaca, NY.

Garvie, A. E. (1986), *Aeschylus: Choephori*, Oxford.

Garvie, A. E. (2009), *Aeschylus: Persae*, Oxford.

Gazis, G. A. (2018), *Homer and the Poetics of Hades*, Oxford.

Gehrke, H.-J., and Kirschkowski, M. (eds) (2009), *Odysseus: Irrfahrten durch die Jahrhunderte*, Freiburg im Breisgau.

George, A. R. (2003), *The Babylonian Gilgamesh Epic*, 2 vols, Oxford.

George, C. H. (2018), 'Homeric APA: an (In)consequential Particle', *CPh* 113: 241–54.

Georgoudi, S. (1999), 'À propos du sacrifice humain en Grèce ancienne: remarques critiques', *Archiv für Religionsgeschichte* 1: 41–62.

Georgoudi, S. (2005), 'Sacrifice et mise à mort: aperçus sur le statut du cheval dans les pratiques rituelles grecques', in A. Gardeisen (ed.), *Les équides dans le monde méditerranéen antique*, Lattes: 137–42.

Germain, L. (1954), *Homère et la mystique des nombres*, Paris.

Gernet, L. (1948), 'Jeux et droit (Remarques sur le XXIIIᵉ chant de l'*Iliade*)', *Revue historique de droit français et étranger* 25: 177–88.

Giannakis, G. K. (1997), *Studies in the Syntax and Semantics of the Reduplicated Presents of Homeric Greek and Indo-European*, Innsbruck.

Giannakis, G. K. (2023), *Classical Philology and Linguistics: Old Themes and New Perspectives*, Berlin.

Golden, M. (1998), *Sport and Society in the Ancient World*, Cambridge.

Gordesiani, R. (1987), *Kriterien der Schriftlichkeit und Mündlichkeit im homerischen Epos*, Frankfurt am Main.

Graf, F. (2008), *Apollo*, London.

Gray, D. (1974), *Seewesen: Archaeologia Homerica I G*, Göttingen.

Graz, L. (1965), *Le feu dans l'Iliade et l'Odyssée: ΠΥΡ, champ d'emploi et signification*, Paris.

Graziosi, B. (2002), *Inventing Homer: the Early Reception of Epic*, Cambridge.

Graziosi, B. (2007), 'The Ancient Reception of Homer', in L. Hardwick and C. Stray (eds), *A Companion to Classical Receptions*, Oxford and Malden, MA: 26–37.

Graziosi, B., and Haubold, J. (2005), *Homer: the Resonance of Epic*, London.

Graziosi, B., and Haubold, J. (2010), *Homer, Iliad Book VI*, Cambridge.

Graziosi, B., and Haubold, J. (2015), 'The Homeric Text', *Ramus* 44: 5–28.

Greco, A. (2002), 'Aiace Telamonio e Teucro: le tecniche di combattimento nella Grecia micenea dell'età delle tombe a fossa', in Montanari and Ascheri (2002): 561–78.

Greenhalgh, P. A. L. (1982), 'The Homeric *THERAPON* and *OPAON* and Their Historical Implications', *BICS* 29: 81–90.

Grethlein, J. (2007a), 'The Poetics of the Bath in the *Iliad*', *HSCP* 103: 25–49.

Grethlein, J. (2007b), 'Epic Narrative and Ritual: the Case of the Funeral Games in *Iliad* 23', in A. Bierl, R. Lämmle, and K. Wesselmann (eds), *Literatur und Religion, 1: Wege zu einer mythisch-rituellen Poetik bei den Griechen*, Berlin: 151–78.

Grethlein, J. (2008), 'Memory and Material Objects in the *Iliad* and *Odyssey*', *JHS* 128: 27–51.

Grethlein, J., and Huitink, L. (2017), 'Homer's Vividness: an Enactive Approach', *JHS* 137: 67–91.

Griffin, J. (1980), *Homer on Life and Death*, Oxford.

Griffith, M. (2006a), 'Horsepower and Donkeywork: Equids and the Ancient Greek Imagination: Part I', *CPh* 101: 185–246.

Griffith, M. (2006b), 'Horsepower and Donkeywork: Equids and the Ancient Greek Imagination: Part II', *CPh* 101: 307–58.

Griffith, R. D. (2005), 'Gods' Blue Hair in Homer and Eighteenth Dynasty Egypt', *CQ* 55: 329–34.

Groningen, B. A. van (1941), 'La parathèse grammaticale en grec', *Mnemosyne* 3rd ser. 9: 262–80.

Gurney, O. (1990), *The Hittites*, 2nd ed. rev., Harmondsworth.

Haas, V. (1989), 'Kompositbogen und Bogenschießen als Wettkampf im Alten Orient', *Nikephoros* 2: 27–42.

Hackstein, O. (2002), *Die Sprachform der homerischen Epen*, Wiesbaden.

Hackstein, O. (2007), 'La paréchèse et les jeux sur les mots chez Homère', in A. Blanc and E. Dupraz (eds), *Procédés synchroniques de la langue poétique en grec et en latin*, Brussels: 103–13.

Hackstein, O. (2010), 'The Greek of Epic', in E. J. Bakker (ed.), *Companion to the Ancient Greek Language*, Oxford: 401–23.

Hagen, H. (2005), 'ἕταρος, ἑτάρη, ἑταίρα, ἑταῖρος bei Homer', *Glotta* 81: 83–5.

Hägg, R., and Alroth, B. (eds) (2005), *Greek Sacrificial Ritual, Olympian and Chthonian*, Sävedalen.

Hainsworth, J. B. (1968), *The Flexibility of the Homeric Formula*, Oxford.

Hainsworth, J. B. (1988), 'The Epic Dialect', in A. Heubeck, S. West, and J. B. Hainsworth, *A Commentary on Homer's Odyssey, Volume I: Introduction and Books I–VIII*, Oxford: 24–32.

Hajnal, I. (1995), *Studien zum mykenischen Kasussystem*, Berlin and New York.

Hall, J. (2002), *Hellenicity: between Ethnicity and Culture*, Chicago.

Halliwell, S. (2008), *Greek Laughter: a Study of Cultural Psychology from Homer to Early Christianity*, Cambridge.

Hammer, D. C. (1997), '"Who Shall Readily Obey?": Authority and Politics in the *Iliad*', *Phoenix* 51: 1–24.

Hammer, D. C. (2002), *The Iliad as Politics: the Performance of Political Thought*, Norman, OK.

Harder, A. (2012), *Callimachus: Aetia*, 2 vols., Oxford.

Harris, H. A. (1964), *Greek Athletes and Athletics*, London.

Haslam, M. (1991), 'Kleitias, Stesichoros, and the Jar of Dionysus', *TAPhA* 121: 35–45.

Haslam, M. (1997), 'Homeric Papyri and Transmission of the Text', in Morris and Powell (1997): 55–100.

Haubold, J. (2000), *Homer's People: Epic Poetry and Social Formation*, Cambridge.

Haug, D. (2002), *Les phases d'évolution de la langue epique: trois études de linguistique homérique*, Göttingen.

Haug, D. (2012), 'Tmesis in the Epic Tradition', in Andersen and Haug (2020): 96–105.

Heath, J. (2001), 'Telemachus ΠΕΠΝΥΜΕΝΟΣ: Growing into an Epithet', *Mnemosyne* 54: 129–57.

Heath, J. (2005), 'Blood for the Dead: the Homeric Ghosts Speak Up', *Hermes* 133: 289–400.

Heiden, B. (1996), 'The Placement of "Book Divisions" in the *Odyssey*', *CPh* 95: 247–59.

Heiden, B. (1998), 'The Placement of the Book Divisions in the *Iliad*', *JHS* 118: 68–81.

Heiden, B. (2000), 'Major Systems of Thematic Resonance in the *Iliad*', *SO* 75: 34–55.

Heiden, B. (2002), 'Structures of Progression in the Plot of the *Iliad*', *Arethusa* 35: 237–54.

Heiden, B. (2008), *Homer's Cosmic Fabrication: Choice and Design in the Iliad*, Oxford and New York.

Hellmann, O. (2000), *Die Schlachtszenen der Ilias*, Stuttgart.

Henrichs, A. (1981), 'Human Sacrifice in Greek Religion', in J. Rudhardt and O. Reverdin (eds), *Le sacrifice dans l'antiquité*, Entretiens sur l'antiquité classique 27, Vandœuvres–Geneva: 195–235 (reprinted in H. Yunis (ed.) (2019), *Albert Henrichs: Greek Myth and Religion. Collected Papers, Vol. II*, Berlin: 37–68).

Henrichs, A. (1993), 'The Tomb of Aias and the Prospect of Hero Cult in Sophokles', *ClAnt* 12: 165–80.

Hesk, J. (2015), 'Terence Malick's *The Thin Red Line* and Homeric Epic: Spectacle, Simile, Scene and Situation', in A. Bagokianni and V. M.

Hope (eds), *War as Spectacle: Ancient and Modern Perspectives on the Display of Armed Conflict*, London: 313–34.

Heubeck, A. (1992), in J. Russo, M. Fernandez-Galiano, and A. Heubeck, *A Commentary on Homer's Odyssey, Volume III: Books XVIII–XXIV*, Oxford.

Higbie, C. (1990), *Measure and Music: Enjambement and Sentence Structure in the Iliad*, Oxford.

Higbie, C. (1995), *Heroes' Names, Homeric Identities*, New York.

Higbie, C. (2003), *The Lindian Chronicle and the Greek Creation of Their Past*, Oxford.

Hinckley, L. V. (1986), 'Patroclus' Funeral Games and Homer's Character Portrayal', *CJ* 81: 209–21.

Hirschberger, M. (2004), *Gynaikon Katalogos und Megalai Ehoiai: ein Kommentar zu den Fragmenten zweier hesiodischen Epen*, Munich and Leipzig.

Hitch, S. (2009), *King of Sacrifice: Ritual and Royal Authority in the Iliad*, Washington, DC.

Hodot, R. (2014), 'Aeolic Dialects', in G. Giannakis (ed.), *Encyclopedia of Ancient Greek Language and Linguistics*, 3 vols, Leiden: I.61–5.

Hoekstra, A. (1965), *Homeric Modifications of Formulaic Prototypes: Studies in the Development of Greek Epic Diction*, Amsterdam.

Höhfeld, V. (ed.) (2009), *Stadt und Landschaft Homers: ein historisch-geografischer Führer für Troia und Umgebung*, Mainz.

Hohendahl-Zoetelief, I. M. (1980), *Manners in the Homeric Epic*, Leiden.

Hollis, A. (2009), *Callimachus: Hecale*, 2nd ed., Oxford.

Hölscher, U. (1939), *Untersuchungen zur Form der Odyssee: Szenenwechsel und gleichzeitige Handlungen*, Stuttgart.

Holt, P. (1992), 'Ajax's Burial in Early Greek Epic', *AJPh* 113: 319–31.

Horrocks, G. (1997), 'Homer's Language', in I. Morris and B. Powell (eds), *A New Companion to Homer*, Leiden: 193–217.

Hose, M., Bernard, W., and Schuol, M. (2012), *Synesios von Kyrene: ägyptische Erzählungen oder Über die Vorsehung*, Tübingen.

Howland, R. L. (1954–5), 'Epeius, Carpenter and Athlete', *PCPhS* 183: 15–16.

Huber, I. (2001), *Die Ikonographie der Trauer in der griechischen Kunst*, Mannheim and Möhnesee.

Hughes, D. D. (1991), *Human Sacrifice in Ancient Greece*, London.

Humphrey, J. W., Oleson, J., and Sherwood, A. (1998), *Greek and Roman Technology: a Sourcebook*, London.

Hunter, R. (1996), *Theocritus and the Archaeology of Greek Poetry*, Cambridge.

Hunter, R. (2018), *The Measure of Homer: the Ancient Reception of the Iliad and the Odyssey*, Cambridge.

Hunter, R. (2021), 'Eustathian Moments: Reading Eustathius' Commentaries', in *The Layers of the Text: Collected Papers on Classical Literature 2008–21*, Berlin: 682–749.

Hutchinson, G. O. (2020), *Motion in Classical Literature*, Oxford.

Ingalls, W. B. (1998), 'Attitudes towards Children in the *Iliad*', *EMC* 17: 13–34.

Irwin, E. (1974), *Colour Terms in Greek Poetry*, Toronto.

Janni, P. (2011), 'ΡΟΔΟΔΑΚΤΥΛΟΣ ΗΩΣ: piccola storia di un miraggio', *QUCC* 97: 187–96.

Janko, R. (1979), 'The Etymology of σχερός and ἐπισχερώ: an Homeric Misunderstanding', *Glotta* 57: 20–3.

Janko, R. (1982), *Homer, Hesiod, and the Homeric Hymns*, Cambridge.

Janko, R. (1998), 'The Homeric Poems as Oral Dictated Texts', *CQ* 48: 1–13.

Jankuhn, H. (1969), *Die passive Bedeutung medialer Formen untersucht an der Sprache Homers*, Göttingen.

Janse, M. (2003), 'The Metrical Schemes of the Hexameter', *Mnemosyne* 56: 343–8.

Janse, M. (2020), 'Phrasing Homer: a Cognitive-Linguistic Approach to Homeric Versification', *SO* 94: 2–32.

Jeffery, L. H. (1990), *The Local Scripts of Archaic Greece*, 2nd ed., Oxford.

Jensen, M. S. (2011), *Writing Homer: a Study Based on Results from Modern Fieldwork*, Copenhagen.

Jensen, M. S. et al. (1999), 'Dividing Homer: When and How Were the *Iliad* and the *Odyssey* Divided into Songs?', *SO* 74: 5–91.

Johnston, A. (2021), '"Horse Race, Rich in Woes": Orestes' Chariot Race and the Erinyes in Sophocles' *Electra*', *JHS* 141: 197–215.

Jones, B. (2012), 'Relative Chronology and an "Aeolic Phase" of Epic', in Andersen and Haug (2012): 44–64.

Jong, I. J. F. de (1987a), *Narrators and Focalizers: the Presentation of the Story in the Iliad*, Amsterdam.

Jong, I. J. F. de (1987b), 'Homeric κέρδος and ὄφελος', *MH* 44: 79–81.

Jong, I. J. F. de (2001), *A Narratological Commentary on the Odyssey*, Cambridge.

Jong, I. J. F. de (2009), 'Metalepsis in Ancient Greek Literature', in Grethlein, J. and Rengakos, A. (eds), *Narratology and Interpretation: the Content of Narrative Form in Ancient Literature*, Berlin: 87–116.

Jong, I. J. F. de (2012), *Homer Iliad: Book XXII*, Cambridge.

Jong, I. J. F. de (2022), 'Homer', in de Bakker, M. and de Jong, I. J. F. (eds), *Speech in Ancient Literature*, Leiden: 33–55.

Jørgensen, O. (1904), 'Das Auftreten der Goetter in den Buechern ι–μ der *Odyssee*', *Hermes* 39: 357–82.

Jouanna, D. (2015), *Les Grecs aux Enfers: d'Homère à Épicure*, Paris.

Kahane, A. (1994), *The Interpretation of Order: a Study in the Poetics of Homeric Repetition*, Oxford.

Kaimio, M. (1977), *The Characterization of Sound in Early Greek Literature*, Helsinki.

Kakridis, J. T. (1949), *Homeric Researches*, Lund.

Kakridis, J. T. (1971), *Homer Revisited*, Lund.

Kamptz, H. von (1982), *Homerische Personennamen: Sprachwissenschaftliche und historische Klassifikation*, Göttingen.

Kanavou, N. (2015), *The Names of Homeric Heroes: Problems and Interpretations*, Berlin.

Karavites, P. (1987), 'Diplomatic Envoys in the Homeric World', *RIDA* 34: 41–100.

Kavvadias, G. G. (2010), 'Ἄθλα επί Πατρόκλῳ: Ἔπος και αττική εικονογραφία', in W. Walter-Karydi (ed.), *Μύθοι, κείμενα, εικόνες: ομηρικά έπη και αρχαία ελληνική τέχνη*, Ithaki: 153–89.

Kelly, A. (2006), 'Neoanalysis and the *Nestorbedrängnis*: a Test Case', *Hermes* 134: 1–25.

Kelly, A. (2007a), *A Referential Commentary and Lexicon to Homer Iliad VIII*, Oxford.

Kelly, A. (2007b), 'How to End an Orally-Derived Epic Poem', *TAPhA* 137: 371–402.

Kelly, A. (2008a), 'Performance and Rivalry: Homer, Odysseus and Hesiod', in M. Revermann and P. Wilson (eds), *Performance, Reception, Iconography: Studies in Honour of Oliver Taplin*, Oxford: 177–203.

Kelly, A. (2008b), 'The Ending of *Iliad* 7: a Response', *Philologus* 152: 5–17.

Kelly, A. (2009), *Sophocles: Oedipus at Colonus*, London.

Kelly, A. (2012), 'The Mourning of Thetis: "Allusion" and the Future in the *Iliad*', in Montanari, Rengakos, and Tsagalis (2012): 211–56.

Kelly, A. (2014), review of Bird (2010), *JHS* 134: 150–1.

Kelly, A. (2015), 'Stesichorus' Homer', in P. J. Finglass and A. Kelly (eds), *Stesichorus in Context*, Cambridge: 21–44.

Kelly, A. (2017), 'Akhilleus in Control? Managing Oneself and Others in the Funeral Games', in P. Bassino, L. Canevaro, and B. Graziosi (eds), *Conflict and Consensus in Early Greek Hexameter Poetry*, Cambridge: 93–116.

Kelly, A. (2018), 'Homer's Rivals? Internal Narrators within the *Iliad*', in J. L. Ready and C. Tsagalis (eds), *Homer in Performance: Rhapsodes, Narrators, Characters*, Austin, TX: 351–77.

Kelly, A. (2021), 'Sappho and Epic', in P. J. Finglass and A. Kelly (eds), *The Cambridge Companion to Sappho*, Cambridge: 53–64.

Kelly, A. (2022), 'Epic and Lyric', in L. Swift (ed.), *The Blackwell Companion to Greek Lyric Poetry*, Oxford and Malden, MA: 34–46.

Kessels, A. H. M. (1978), *Studies on the Dream in Greek Literature*, Utrecht.

Khoo, A. (2019), 'Dream Scenes in Ancient Epic', in Reitz and Finkmann (2019): II.563–96.

Kirk, G. S. (1962), *The Songs of Homer*, Cambridge.

Kirk, G. S. (1978), 'The Formal Duels in Books 3 and 7 of the *Iliad*', in B. C. Fenik (ed.), *Homer: Tradition and Invention*, Leiden: 18–40.

Kirk, G. S. (1981), 'Pitfalls in the Study of Greek Sacrifice', in J.-P. Vernant, J. Rudhardt, and O. Reverdin (eds), *Le sacrifice dans l'antiquité*, Geneva: 41–90.

Kitchell, K. F. (1998), '"But the Mare I Will Not Give Up": The Games in *Iliad* 23', *CB* 74: 159–71.

Kitts, M. (2007), '"Bulls Cut Down Bellowing": Ritual Leitmotifs and Poetic Pressures in *Iliad* XXIII', *Kernos* 20: 17–41.

Kitts, M. (2011), 'Ritual Scenes in the *Iliad*: Rote, Hallowed, or Encrypted as Ancient Art?', *Oral Tradition* 26: 221–46.

Kloss, G. (1994), *Untersuchungen zum Wortfeld 'Verlangen/Begehren' im früh-griechischen Epos*, Göttingen.

Köhnken, A. (1981), 'Der Endspurt des Odysseus: Wettkampfdarstellung bei Homer und Vergil', *Hermes* 109: 129–48.

Kolonas, L., Sarri, K., Margariti, C., Berghe, I. van den, Skals, I., and Nosch, M.-L. (2017), 'Heirs from the Loom? Funerary Textiles from Stamna (Aitolia, Greece): a Preliminary Analysis', in M. Fotiadis, R. Laffineur, Y. Lolos, and A. Vlachopoulos (eds), *Hesperos: The Aegean Seen from the West*, Aegaeum 41, Liège: 533–44.

Korfmann, M. (1986), 'Troy: Topography and Navigation', in W. Mellink (ed.), *Troy and the Trojan War: a Symposium Held at Bryn Mawr College*, Bryn Mawr: 1–16.

Kosmetatou, E. (1993), 'Horse Sacrifice in Greece and Cyprus', *JPR* 8: 31–41.

Kossatz-Deissmann, A. (1981), 'Achilleus', in *LIMC* 1.1: 37–200.

Kotsonas, A. (2019), 'The Iconography of a Protoarchaic Cup from Kommos: Myth and Ritual in Early Cretan Art', *Hesperia* 88: 595–624.

Kozak, L. (2014), 'Oaths and Characterization: Two Homeric Case Studies', in Sommerstein and Torrance (2014): 213–29.

Kraft, J. C., Kayan, İ., Brückner, H., and Rip Rapp, G. (2003), 'Sedimentary Facies Patterns and the Interpretation of Palaeographies in Ancient Troia', in Wagner, Pernicka, and Uerpmann (2003): 361–77.

Kramer-Hajos, M. (2012), 'The Land and Heroes of Lokris in the *Iliad*', *JHS* 132: 87–105.

Kraus, M. (1987), *Name und Sache: ein Problem im frühgriechischen Denken*, Amsterdam.

Krieter-Spiro, M. (2009), *Homers Ilias Gesamtkommentar: Band III.2: 3. Gesang: Kommentar*, Berlin and New York.

Krischer, T. (1992), 'Patroklos, der Wagenlenker Achills', *RhM* 135: 97–103.

Kullmann, W. (1960), *Die Quellen der Ilias*, Wiesbaden.

Kurt, C. (1979), *Seemännische Fachausdrücke bei Homer: unter Berücksichtigung Hesiods und der Lyriker bis Bakchylides*, Göttingen.

Kurtz, D., and Boardman, J. (1971), *Greek Burial Customs*, London.

Kurz, G. (1966), *Darstellungsformen menschlicher Bewegung in der Ilias*, Heidelberg.

Kyle, D. G. (2015), *Sport and Spectacle in the Ancient World*, Oxford and Malden, MA.

Labarbe, A. (1949), *L'Homère du Platon*, Liège.

Langdon, M. L. (1990), 'Throwing the Discus in Antiquity: the Literary Evidence', *Nikephoros* 3: 177–87.

Langdon, M. L., and Rookhuijzen, J. Z. van (2024), 'Mikon's Hekatompedon: an Architectural Graffito from Attica', *AJA* 128: 433–42.

Lardinois, A. (1995), *Wisdom in Context: the Use of Gnomic Statements in Archaic Greek Poetry*, PhD diss., Princeton.

Lardinois, A. (1997), 'Modern Paroemiology and the Use of Gnomai in Homer's *Iliad*', *CPh* 92: 213–34.

Lardinois, A. (2000), 'Characterization through *Gnomai* in Homer's *Iliad*', *Mnemosyne* 53: 641–61.

Larmour, D. A. (1999), *Stage and Stadium*, Hildesheim.

Laser, S. (1983), *Medizin und Körperpflege*, Archaeologia Homerica III. S, Göttingen.

Latacz, J. (1966), *Zum Wortfeld Freude in der Sprache Homers*, Heidelberg.

Latacz, J. (2009), 'Zur Struktur der Ilias', in J. Latacz et al. (2009), *Homers Ilias Gesamtkommentar: Prolegomena*, 3rd ed., Munich and Leipzig: 145–58.

Latacz, J. et al. (2003), *Homers Ilias Gesamtkommentar: Band II.2: 2. Gesang: Kommentar*, Munich and Leipzig.

Lateiner, D. (1995), *Sardonic Smile: Nonverbal Behaviour in Homeric Epic*, Ann Arbor.

Lateiner, D. (1997), 'Homeric Prayer', *Arethusa* 30: 241–72.

Lather, A. (2020), 'Epic Matter: Iliadic Dust, Sand, and the Limits of the Human', *TAPhA* 150: 263–86.

Le Feuvre, C. (1997), 'La form épique du nom de la maison', *RPh* 71: 217–25.

Le Feuvre, C. (2011), 'Πολλοὶ μὲν βόες ἀργοὶ ὀρέχθεον/ἐρέχθεον/ῥόχθεον: que lisaient les auteurs classiques en *Il.* 23, 30?', *RPh* 85: 61–88.

Le Feuvre, C. (2015), Ὅμηρος δύσγνωστος: *réinterprétations de termes homériques en grec archaique et classique*, Geneva.

Le Feuvre, C. (2022), *Homer from Z to A: Metrics, Linguistics, and Zenodotus*, Leiden.

Lehrs, K. (1882), *De Aristarchi studiis homericis*, 3rd ed., Leipzig.

Leitao, D. D. (2003), 'Adolescent Hair-Growing and Hair-Cutting Rituals in Ancient Greece: a Sociological Approach', in D. B. Dodd and C. A. Faraone (eds), *Initiation in Ancient Greek Rituals and Narratives: New Critical Perspectives*, London: 109–29.

Lejeune, M. (1939), *Les adverbes grecs en -θεν*, Bordeaux.

Lemos, I. (2002), *The Protogeometric Aegean: the Archaeology of the Late Eleventh and Early Tenth Centuries BC*, Oxford.

Lentini, G. (2013), 'The Pragmatics of Verbal Abuse in Homer', in H. Tell (ed.), *The Rhetoric of Abuse in Classical Literature*, Classics@ 11 (https://classics-at.chs.harvard.edu/volume/classics11-the-rhetoric-of-abuse-in-greek-literature/).

Lesky, A. (1959), 'Aithiopika', *Hermes* 87: 27–38.

Lesser, R. H. (2022), *Desire in the Iliad*, Oxford.

Létoublon, F. (1989), 'Aoristes et imparfaits des verbes de mouvement chez Homère: problèmes d'aspect et de morphologie verbale (ἤια, ἤιον, ἤλθον, et ἔκιον)', in Casevitz (1989): 77–94.

Létoublon, F. (1997), 'Le jour et la nuit: formulaire épique et problèmes de narratologie homérique', in Létoublon and Dik (1997): 137–46.

Létoublon, F. (2003), 'Ilion battue des vents, Troie aux larges rues: la représentation de Troie dans l'*Iliade*', in M. Reddé (ed.), *La naissance de la ville dans l'antiquité*, Paris: 27–44.

Létoublon, F. (2018), 'Living in Iron, Dressed in Bronze: Metal Formulas and the Chronology of Ages', *Brolly: Journal of Social Sciences* 1: 7–39.

Létoublon, F. (2023), 'The *Iliad*, a Large Scale Composition', *Philologia Antiqua* 16: 27–42.

Létoublon, F., and Dik, H. (1997) (eds), *Hommage à Milman Parry: le style formulaire de l'épopée homérique et le théorie de l'oralité poétique*, Amsterdam.

Lévy, E. (1982), 'Le rêve homérique', *Ktèma* 7: 23–41.

Livingstone, D. (2014), *Imagery of Psychological Motivation in Apollonius Rhodius' Argonautica and Early Greek Poetry*, PhD diss., University of Edinburgh.

Lohmann, D. (1970), *Die Komposition der Reden in der Ilias*, Berlin.

Lohmann, D. (1992), 'Homer als Erzähler: die Athla im 23. Buch der *Ilias*', *Gymnasium* 99: 289–319.

Lohse, G. (1964–7), 'Untersuchungen über Homerzitate bei Platon', *Helikon* 4: 3–28; 5: 248–325; 7: 223–31.

López-Ruiz, C. (2021), *Phoenicians and the Making of the Mediterranean*, Cambridge, MA.

Lord, A. B. (1953), 'Homer's Originality: Oral-Dictated Texts', *TAPhA* 84: 124–34.

Lossau, M. (1994), 'Retter-Licht (φόως, φάος) bei Homer und den Tragikern', *Eranos* 92: 85–92.

Louden, B. (1995), 'Categories of Homeric Wordplay', *TAPhA* 125: 27–46.

Louden, B. (2006), *The Iliad: Structure, Myth, and Meaning*, Baltimore.

Lovatt, H. (2019), 'Epic Games: Structure and Competition', in Reitz and Finkmann (2019): II.409–45.

Lowenstam, S. (1981), *The Death of Patroklos: a Study in Typology*, Königstein.

Luce, J. V. (2003), 'The Case for Historical Significance in Homer's Landmarks at Troia', in Wagner, Pernicka, and Uerpmann (2003): 9–30.

Lührs, D. (1992), *Untersuchungen zu den Athetesen Aristarchs in der Ilias*, Hildesheim.

Lynn-George, M. (1988), *Epos: Word, Narrative and the Iliad*, Basingstoke.

Mackie, C. J. (2015), 'Zeus and Mount Ida in Homer's *Iliad*', *Antichthon* 48: 1–13.

Macrakis, A. L. (1984), 'Comparative Economic Values in the *Iliad*: the Oxen-Worth', in A. Boegehold et al. (eds), *Studies Presented to Sterling Dow on His Eightieth Birthday*, Durham, NC: 211–15.

Macleod, C. (1982), *Homer, Iliad XXIV*, Cambridge.

Magnani, M. (2018), 'The Other Side of the River: Digital Editions of Ancient Greek Texts Involving Papyrus Witnesses', in N. Reggiani (ed.), *Digital Papyrology II: Case Studies on the Digital Edition of Ancient Greek Papyri*, Berlin: 87–102.

Malfas, P. (2008), 'Trojan Plain and Homeric Topography', in Paipetis (2008): 415–31.

Mal-Maeder, D. van (1992), 'Les détournements homériques dans l'"Histoire vraie" de Lucien: le repatriement d'une tradition littéraire', *EL* 2: 123–46.

Malten, L. (1923–4), 'Leichenspiel und Totenkult', *MDAI(R)* 28/9: 300–40.

Mann, C., and Scharff, S. (2020), 'Horse Races and Chariot Races in Ancient Greece: Struggling for Eternal Glory', *International Journal for the History of Sport* 37: 163–82.

Manolea, C.-P. (ed.) (2022), *Brill's Companion to the Reception of Homer from the Hellenistic Age to Late Antiquity*, Leiden.

Margariti, C., and Spantidaki, S. (2020), 'Revisiting the Hero of Lefkandi', in M. Bustamante-Álvarez, E. H. Sánchez López, and J. Jiménez Ávila (eds), *Redefining Ancient Textile Handcraft: Structures, Tools and Production Processes*, Granada: 401–12.

Marinatos, S. (1967), *Kleidung, Haar und Barttracht: Archaeologia Homerica I A and B*, Göttingen.

Markovic, D. (2006), 'Hyperbaton in the Greek Literary Sentence', *GRBS* 46: 127–46.

Markwald, G. (1986), *Die homerische Epigramme: sprachliche und inhaltliche Untersuchungen*, Meisenham am Glan.

Marseglia, R. (2015), 'Cur Artemis κελαδεινή nuncupetur', *RhM* 158: 206–9.

Martin, R. P. (1989), *The Language of Heroes*, Ithaca, NY.

Martin, R. P. (1992), 'Hesiod's Metanastic Poetics', *Ramus* 21: 11–33.

Martin, R. P. (2023), 'Friends, Death, and Kinship: Homeric Diction and the Semantics of Care', *Philologia Antiqua* 16: 83–99.

Matthews, V. J. (1996), *Antimachus of Colophon*, Leiden.

Mauritsch, P. (2006), 'Materialien zur Darstellung von Gewalt', *Nikephoros* 19: 57–66.

Mawet, F. (1979), *Recherches sur les oppositions fonctionnelles dans le vocabulaire homérique de la douleur (autour de πῆμα-ἄλγος)*, Brussels.

Mayhew, R. (2019), *Aristotle's Lost Homeric Problems: Textual Studies*, Oxford.

Mazon, P. (1940), 'Notes sur quelques passages du XXIIIᵉ chant de l'*Iliade*', *REA* 42: 254–62.

McAuley, A. (2024), 'Following the Local Traces of the (Argive?) Games in Honor of Hera', in S. Scharff (ed.), *Beyond the Big Four: Local Games in Ancient Greek Athletic Culture*, Münster: 143–68.

McConnell, T. (2025), *Chronology, Dialect and Style in Early Greek Hexameter Poetry*, Oxford.

McGowan, E. P. (1995), 'Tomb-Marker and Turning Post: Funerary Columns in the Archaic Period', *AJA* 99: 615–32.

Meiggs, R. (1982), *Trees and Timber in the Ancient Mediterranean World*, Oxford.

Meister, K. (1921), *Die homerische Kunstsprache*, Leipzig.

Meuli, K. (1968), *Der griechische Agon*, Cologne.

Meyer, W. (1907), *De Homeri patronymicis*, Göttingen.

Miller, S. G. (2004a), *Arete: Greek Sports from Ancient Sources*, 3rd ed., Berkeley and Los Angeles.

Miller, S. G. (2004b), *Ancient Greek Athletics*, New Haven and London.

Mills, S. (2000), 'Achilles, Patroklos and Parental Care in Some Homeric Similes', *G&R* 47: 3–18.

Minchin, E. (2001a), *Homer and the Resources of Memory: Some Applications of Cognitive Theory to the Iliad and the Odyssey*, Oxford.

Minchin, E. (2001b), 'How Homeric Is "Hysteron Proteron"?', *Mnemosyne* 54: 635–45 (= 2007: 102–16).

Minchin, E. (2002), 'Speech Acts in Homer: the Rebuke as a Case Study', in I. Worthington and J. M. Foley (eds), *EPEA and GRAMMATA: Oral and Written Communication in Ancient Greece*, Leiden: 71–98 (= 2007: 23–51).

Minchin, E. (2005), 'Homer on Autobiographical Memory: the Case of Nestor', in R. J. Rabel (ed.), *Approaches to Homer: Ancient and Modern*, Swansea: 55–72.

Minchin, E. (2007), *Homeric Voices: Discourse, Memory, Gender*, Oxford.

Mitscherling, J. (2005), 'Plato's Misquotation of the Poets', *CQ* 55: 295–8.

Montana, F. (2020), 'Hellenistic Scholarship', in F. Montanari (ed.), *History of Ancient Greek Scholarship*, Leiden and Boston: 132–259.

Montanari, F. (2002), 'Alexandrian Homeric Philology: the Form of the Ekdosis and the Variae Lectiones', in M. Reichel and A. Rengakos (eds), *EPEA PTEROENTA: Beiträge zur Homerforschung. Festschrift für Wolfgang Kullmann zum 75. Geburtstag*, Stuttgart: 119–40.

Montanari, F., and Ascheri, D. (2002) (eds), *Omero: tremila anni dopo*, Rome.

Montanari, F., Rengakos, A., and Tsagalis, C. (2012) (eds), *Homeric Contexts: Neoanalysis and the Interpretation of Oral Poetry*, Berlin.

Montiglio, S. (2005), *Wandering in Ancient Greek Culture*, Chicago.

Moore, M. (2016), 'Sophilos, Inscriptions, and the Funeral Games for Patroklos', in D. Yatromanolakis (ed.), *Epigraphy of Art: Ancient Greek Vase-Inscriptions and Vase-Paintings*, Oxford: 185–202.

Moreau, A. (1996), 'Quand Apollon devint soleil', in B. Bakhouche, A. Moreau, and J.-C. Turpin (eds), *Les astres: les astres et les mythes; la description du ciel*, 2 vols, Montpellier: I.11–33.

Moreschini, A. Q. (1984), 'Elementi micenei nella tradizione formulare: Γερήνιος ἱππότα Νέστωρ', *SMEA* 25: 337–47.

Moreux, B. (1967), 'La nuit, l'ombre, et la mort chez Homère', *Phoenix* 21: 237–72.

Mørland, H. (1948), 'Zum griechischen genitivus comparationis I', *SO* 26: 151–66.

Morris, I. (1987), *Burial and Ancient Society: the Rise of the Greek City State*, Cambridge.

Morris, I. (1999), 'Iron Age Greece and the Meanings of "Princely Tombs"', in P. Ruby (ed.), *Les princes de la protohistoire et l'émergence de l'État*, Naples: 57–80.

Morris, I. (2000), *Archaeology as Cultural History: Words and Things in Iron Age Greece*, Oxford.

Morris, I., and Powell, B. (eds) (1997), *A New Companion to Homer*, Leiden.

Morris, J. (1983), '"Dream Scenes" in Homer: a Study in Variation', *TAPhA* 113: 39–54.

Morris, S. P. (1992), *Daidalos and the Origins of Greek Art*, Princeton, NJ.

Morrison, J. (1991), 'The Function and Context of Homeric Prayers', *Hermes* 119: 145–57.

Morrison, J. (1992), *Homeric Misdirection: False Predictions in the Iliad*, Ann Arbor.

Morrison, J. (1999), 'Homeric Darkness: Patterns and Manipulation of Death Scenes in the *Iliad*', *Hermes* 127: 129–44.

Most, G. (1997), 'Hesiod's Myth of the Five (or Three or Four) Races', *PCPhS* 43: 104–27.

Moulton, C. (1977), *Similes in the Homeric Poems*, Göttingen.

Moulton, C. (1979), 'Homeric Metaphor', *CPh* 74: 279–93.

Mouratidis, J. (1990), 'Anachronism in the Homeric Games and Sports', *Nikephoros* 3: 11–22.

Muellner, L. (1976), *The Meaning of Homeric EUXOMAI through Its Formulas*, Innsbruck.

Mühlestein, H. (1987), *Homerische Namenstudien*, Frankfurt am Main.

Mühll, P. von der (1952), *Kritisches Hypomnema zur Ilias*, Basel.

Müller, D. (1974), *Handwerk und Sprache: die sprachlichen Bilder aus dem Bereich des Handwerks in der griechischen Literatur bis 400 v. Chr.*, Meisenheim am Glan.

Müller, S. (1989), 'Les tumuli helladiques: Où? Quand? Comment?', *BCH* 113: 1–42.

Müller, S. (1995), *Das Volk der Athleten: Untersuchungen zur Ideologie und Kritik des Sports in der griechisch-römischen Antike*, Trier.

Murakawa, K. (1957), 'Demiourgos', *Historia* 6: 385–415.

Murray, O. (2018), 'The History of Tastes', in O. Murray and V. Cazzato (eds), *The Symposion: Drinking Greek Style*, Oxford: 3–10.

Murray, P. (1996), *Plato on Poetry*, Cambridge.

Myers, T. (2019), *Homer's Divine Audience: the Iliad's Reception on Mount Olympus*, Oxford.

Myres, J. (1932), 'The Last Book of the *Iliad*: Its Place in the Structure of the Poem', *JHS* 52: 264–96.

Nagler, M. (1974), *Spontaneity and Tradition*, Berkeley.

Nagy, G. (1979), *The Best of the Achaeans: Concepts of the Hero in Archaic Greek Poetry*, Baltimore.

Nagy, G. (1980), 'An Evolutionary Model for the Text Fixation of Homeric Epos', in J. M. Foley (ed.), *Oral Traditional Literature: a Festschrift for Albert Bates Lord*, Columbus, OH: 390–4.

Nagy, G. (1990a), 'The Death of Sarpedon and the Question of Homeric Uniqueness', in *Greek Mythology and Poetics*, Ithaca, NY: 122–42.

Nagy, G. (1990b), *Pindar's Homer*, Baltimore.

Nagy, G. (1994), 'The Name of Apollo: Etymology and Essence', in J. Solomon (ed.), *Apollo: Origins and Influences*, Tucson, AZ: 3–7.

Nagy, G. (1995), 'An Evolutionary Model for the Making of Homeric Poetry: Comparative Perspectives', in Carter and Morris (1995): 163–80.

Nagy, G. (1996a), *Poetry as Performance: Homer and Beyond*, Cambridge.

Nagy, G. (1996b), *Homeric Questions*, Austin, TX.

Nagy, G. (2000), review of West (1999–2000), *BMCR* 2000.09.12.

Nagy, G. (2009), 'An Apobatic Moment for Achilles as Athlete at the Festival of the Panathenaia', Washington, DC (https://chs.harvard.edu/curated-article/gregory-nagy-an-apobatic-moment-for-achilles-as-athlete-at-the-festival-of-the-panathenaia; first published in *Imeros* 5 (2005): 311–17).

Nagy, G. (2012), 'Signs of Hero Cult in Homeric Poetry', in Montanari, Rengakos, and Tsagalis (2012): 27–71.

Nagy, G. (2020), 'From Song to Text', in Pache (2020): 80–95.

Nagy, G. (2021), 'Athletic Contests in Contexts of Epic and Other Related Archaic Texts', in Futrell and Scanlon (2021): 283–205.

Naiden, F. (2013), *Smoke Signals for the Gods: Ancient Greek Sacrifice from the Archaic through Roman Periods*, Oxford.

Naiden, F. (2020), 'Offerings in Homer', in Pache (2020): 365–8.

Nakamura, B. J. (2019), 'Boxing in the Ancient World', in J. Early (ed.), *The Cambridge Companion to Boxing*, Cambridge: 22–33.

Nannini, S. (2003), *Analogia e polarità in similitudine: paragoni iliadici e odissiaci a confronto*, Amsterdam.

Nappi, M. (2002), 'Note sull'uso di Αἴαντε nell' *Iliade*', *RCCM* 44: 211–35.

Nardelli, J.-F. (2001a), 'Éditer l'*Iliade* I. La transmission et ses débats: perspectives critiques', *Gaia* 5: 41–118.

Nardelli, J.-F. (2001b), review of West (1999–2000), *BMCR* 2001.06.21.

Nardelli, J.-F. (2003), 'Citations épiques chez les orateurs attiques: le cas d'Eschine', *Gaia* 7: 355–77.

Neal, T. (2006), *The Wounded Hero: Non-fatal Injury in Homer's Iliad*, Bern.

Nelson, T. J. (2023), *Markers of Allusion in Archaic Greek Poetry*, Cambridge.

Nelson, T. J. (2024), 'Sappho's Rose-Fingered Moon and Traditional Referentiality', *GRBS* 64: 147–61.

Neuser, K. (1982), *ANEMOI: Studien zur Darstellung der Winde und Windgottheiten in der Antike*, Rome.

Nicholson, N. (2014), 'Representations of Sport in Greek Literature', in Christesen and Kyle (2014): 68–80.

Nicholson, N. (2021), 'The Hippic Contests', in Futrell and Scanlon (2021): 242–53.

Nickau, K. (1977), *Untersuchungen zur textkritischen Methode des Zenodotos von Ephesos*, Berlin.

Nicolai, W. (1973), *Kleine und grosse Darstellungseinheiten in der Ilias*, Heidelberg.

Nicolet-Pierre, H. (2006), 'Les talents d'Homère', in P. G. van Alfen (ed.), *Agoranomia: Studies in Money and Exchange Presented to John H. Kroll*, New York: 1–20.

Nielsen, T. H. (2014), 'An Essay on the Extent and Significance of the Greek Athletic Culture in the Classical Period', *Proceedings of the Danish Institute at Athens* 7: 11–35.

Nielsen, T. H. (2018), *Two Studies in the History of Ancient Greek Athletics*, Copenhagen.

Nielsen, T. H. (2024), 'A Brief Essay on Sport and Greek Unity in the Late Archaic and Early Classical Period', in K. Buraselis, C. Müller, and T. H. Nielsen (eds), *Unity and Diversity in Ancient Greece: Reflections on the Occasion of the 2500th Anniversary of the Battle of Plataiai* (*Classica et Medievalia* Supplementum 1), Copenhagen: 67–90.

Nieto Hernández, P. (1995), 'Mensajeros divinos en Homero: Iris y Hermes en la *Iliada* y en la *Odisea*', in J. P. Nieto Ibáñez (ed.), *Estudios de religión y mito en Grecia y Roma*, León: 37–52.

Nikolaev, A. (2013), 'The Aorist Infinitives in -εειν in Early Greek Hexameter Poetry', *JHS* 133: 81–92.

Nothdurft, W. (1978), 'Noch einmal πεῖραρ/πείρατα bei Homer', *Glotta* 56: 25–40.

Nünlist, R. (2009), 'The Motif of the Exiled Killer', in C. Walde and E. Dill (eds), *Antike Mythen: Transformationen und Konstruktionen*, Berlin and New York: 628–44.

Nünlist, R. (2020), 'The Human Condition According to the Similes in Homer's *Iliad*', *SO* 94: 33–58.

Nussbaum, J. (1986), *Head and Horn in Indo-European*, Berlin.

Olisová, V. (1989), 'Chariot Racing in the Ancient World', *Nikephoros* 2: 65–88.

O'Maley, J. (2018), 'Diomedes as Audience and Speaker in the *Iliad*', in J. L. Ready and C. Tsagalis (eds), *Homer in Performance: Rhapsodes, Narrators, Characters*, Austin, TX: 278–98.

Onians, R. S. (1953), *The Origins of European Thought*, 2nd ed., Cambridge.

O'Nolan, K. (1978), 'Doublets in the *Odyssey*', *CQ* 28: 23–37.

Otto, N. (2009), *Enargeia: Untersuchung zur Charakteristik alexandrinischer Dichtung*, Stuttgart.

Pache, C. O. (ed.) (2020), *The Cambridge Guide to Homer*, Cambridge.

Packard, D. W. (1974), 'Sound Patterns in Homer', *TAPhA* 104: 239–60.

Paipetis, S. (ed.) (2008), *Science and Technology in Homeric Epics*, Dordrecht.

Palmer, L. R. (1962), 'The Language of Homer', in S. Wace and F. Stubbings (eds), *A Companion to Homer*, London: 75–178.

Pantelia, M. (1993), 'Spinning and Weaving: Ideas of Domestic Order in Homer', *AJPh* 114: 493–501.

Papakonstantinou, Z. (2002), 'Prizes in Early Archaic Greek Sport', *Nikephoros* 15: 51–67.

Papakonstantinou, Z. (2014), 'Ancient Critics of Greek Sport', in Christesen and Kyle (2014): 320–31.

Papakonstantinou, Z. (2019), *Sport and Identity in Ancient Greece*, London.

Paraskevaides, H. A. (1984), *The Use of Synonyms in Homeric Formulaic Diction*, Amsterdam.

Parker, R. (2011), *On Greek Religion*, Ithaca, NY.

Parks, W. (1990), *Verbal Duelling in Heroic Narrative: the Homeric and Old English Traditions*, Princeton, NJ.

Parry, M. (1971), 'The Traditional Epithet in Homer', in A. Parry (ed.), *The Making of Homeric Verse: the Collected Papers of Milman Parry*, Oxford: 1–190 (tr. of M. Parry (1928), *L'Épithète traditionnelle dans Homère: essai sur un problème de style homérique*, Paris).

Passa, E. (2001), 'L'antichità della grafia ευ per εο, εου nell'epica: a proposito di una recente edizione dell'*Iliade*', *RIFC* 129: 385–417.

Pedaros, G. (1988), 'Homerische Begräbnisbräuche', *Kernos* 1: 195–206.

Perpillou, J.-L. (1982), 'Verbs de sonorité à vocalisme expressif en grec ancien', *REG* 95: 233–74.

Perpillou, J.-L. (1996), *Recherches lexicales en grec ancien: étymologie, analogie, représentations*, Paris.

Perpillou, J.-L. (2004), *Essais de lexicographie en grec ancien*, Louvain and Paris.

Perpillou, J.-L. (2005), 'Hypostases homériques', *RPh* 79: 267–77.

Perry, T. (2014), 'Sport in the Early Iron Age and Homeric Epic', in Christesen and Kyle (2014): 53–67.

Person, R. (1995), 'The "Became Silent to Silence" Formula in Homer', *GRBS* 37: 327–39.

Pestalozzi, H. (1945), *Die Achilleis als Quelle der Ilias*, Erlenbach–Zurich.

Petermandl, W., and Ulf, C. (eds) (2012), *Nikephoros Special Issue: Youth, Sports, Olympic Games*, Hildesheim.

Peters, M. (1998), 'Homerisches und Unhomerisches bei Homer und auf dem Nestorbecher', in J. Jasanoff, H. Melchert, and L. Oliver (eds), *Mír Curad: Studies in Honor of Calvert Watkins*, Innsbruck: 586–602.

Petropoulos, J. (2017), 'Poseidon's Homeric Epithets and Titles', in D. Katsonopoulou (ed.), *Helike V. Ancient Helike and Aigialeia. Poseidon, God of Earthquakes and Waters: Cults and Sanctuaries*, Athens: 99–109.

Petropoulou, A. (1988), 'The Interment of Patroklos (*Iliad* 23.252–57)', *AJPh* 109: 482–95.

Pfeiffer, R. (1949–53), *Callimachus*, 2 vols, Oxford.

Pinsent, J. (1983), 'ἑταῖρος and ἕταρον in the *Iliad*', in C. Froidefond (ed.), *Mélanges Édouard Delebecque*, Aix-en-Provence: 311–18.

Pirenne-Delforge, V. (1994), *L'Aphrodite grecque*, Liège.

Pirenne-Delforge, V. (2018), '"Nyx est, elle aussi, une divinité"', in A. Chaniotis (ed.), *La nuit: imaginaire et réalités nocturnes dans le monde gréco-romain*, Geneva: 131–72.

Pisano, C. (2014), *Hermes, lo scettro, l'ariete: configurazioni mitiche della regalità nella Greca antica*, Naples.

Pisano, C. (2017), 'Iris et Hermès, médiateurs en action', in G. Pironti and C. Bonnet (eds), *Les dieux d'Homère: polythéisme et poésie en Grèce ancienne* (*Kernos* Supplement 31), Liège: 113–34.

Plath, R. (1994), *Der Streitwagen und seine Teile im frühen Griechischen*, Nürnberg.

Platte, R. (2017), *Equine Poetics*, Washington, DC.

Poliakoff, M. B. (1986), *Studies in the Terminology of the Greek Combat Sports*, 2nd ed., Frankfurt am Main.

Poliakoff, M. B. (1987), *Combat Sports in the Ancient World: Competition, Violence, and Culture*, New Haven.

Poliakoff, M. B. (2021), 'Greek Combat Sport and the Borders of Athletics, Violence, and Civilization', in Futrell and Scanlan (2021): 221–31.

Pontani, F. (2024), 'Textual Variants in Homer: an Overview', in G. Most (ed.), *Variants and Variance in Classical Textual Cultures: Errors, Innovations, Proliferation, Reception?*, Berlin: 231–56.

Popham, M., Toulopa, E., and Sackett, L. H. (1982), 'The Hero of Lefkandi', *Antiquity* 56: 169–74.

Porter, A. (2011), '"Stricken to Silence": Authoritative Response, Homeric Irony, and the Peril of a Missed Language Cue', *Oral Tradition* 26: 493–520.

Porter, A. (2019), *Agamemnon: the Pathetic Despot*, Center for Hellenic Studies, Washington, DC.

Porter, J. I. (2011), 'Making and Unmaking: the Achaean Wall and the Limits of Fictionality in Homeric Criticism', *TAPhA* 141: 1–36.

Postlethwaite, N. (1995), 'Agamemnon Best of Spearmen', *Phoenix* 49: 95–103.

Pötscher, W. (1987), *Hera: eine Strukturanalyse im Vergleich mit Athena*, Darmstadt.

Pötscher, W. (1997), 'Die Bedeutung des Wortes γλαυκῶπις', *Philologus* 141: 3–20.

Powell, B. B. (1991), *Homer and the Origin of the Greek Alphabet*, Cambridge.

Powell, B. B. (1993a), 'Did Homer Sing at Lefkandi?', *Electronic Antiquity* 1.2 (https://scholar.lib.vt.edu/ejournals/ElAnt/V1N2/powell.html).

Powell, B. B. (1993b), 'Obloquy: Did Homer Sing at Lefkandi? A Reply to J. R. Lenz', *Electronic Antiquity* 1.3 (https://scholar.lib.vt.edu/ejournals/ElAnt/V1N3/powell.html).

Pratt, L. (2007), 'The Parental Ethos of the *Iliad*', in A. Cohen and J. B. Rutter (eds), *Constructions of Childhood in Ancient Greece and Italy* (*Hesperia* Supplement 41), Athens: 25–40.

Pratt, L. (2009), 'Diomedes: the Fatherless Hero in the *Iliad*', in S. Hübner and D. Ratzen (eds), *Growing Up Fatherless in Antiquity*, Cambridge: 141–61.

Preisshofen, F. (1977), *Untersuchungen zur Darstellung des Greisenalters in der frühgriechischen Dichtung*, Wiesbaden.

Probert, P. (2003), *A New Short Guide to the Accentuation of Ancient Greek*, London.

Probert, P. (2006), *Ancient Greek Accentuation*, Oxford.

Probert, P. (2015), *Early Greek Relative Clauses*, Oxford.

Proietti, G. (2014), 'Annual Games for War Dead and Founders in Classical Times: between Hero-Cult and Civic Honours', *Nikephoros* 27: 199–214.

Pucci, P. (1987), *Odysseus Polutropos: Intertextual Readings in the Odyssey and the Iliad*, Ithaca, NY.

Puhvel, J. (1964), 'The Meaning of Greek Βουκάτιος', *ZVS* 79: 7–10.

Puhvel, J. (1983), 'Homeric Questions and Hittite Answers', *AJPh* 104: 217–27.

Puhvel, J. (1988), 'Hittite Athletics as Prefigurations of Greek Games', in W. Raschke (ed.), *The Archaeology of the Olympics: the Olympics and Other Festivals in Antiquity*, Madison, WI: 26–31.

Puhvel, J. (1991), *Homer and Hittite*, Innsbruck.

Pulleyn, S. (1997), *Prayer in Greek Religion*, Oxford.

Pulleyn, S. (2006), 'Homer's Religion: Philological Perspectives from Indo-European and Semitic', in M. J. Clarke, B. G. F. Currie, and R. O. A. M. Lyne (eds), *Epic Interactions: Perspectives on Homer, Virgil, and the Epic Tradition Presented to Jasper Griffin by Former Pupils*, Oxford: 47–74.

Pulleyn, S. (2019), *Homer: Odyssey 1*, Oxford.

Purves, A. C. (2010), 'Wind and Time in Homeric Epic', *TAPhA* 140: 323–50.

Purves, A. C. (2011), 'Homer and the Art of Overtaking', *AJPh* 132: 523–51.

Purves, A. C. (2019), *Homer and the Poetics of Gesture*, Oxford.

Pye, D. W. (1964), 'Wholly Spondaic Lines in Homer', *G&R* 11: 2–6.

Quattordio Moreschini, A. (1984), *Le formazioni nominali greche in -nth*, Rome.

Radin, A. P. (1988), 'Sunrise, Sunset: ἦμος in Homeric Epic', *AJPh* 109: 293–307.

Rakoczy, T. (1996), *Böser Blick, Macht des Auges und Neid der Götter: eine Untersuchung zur Kraft des Blickes in der griechischen Literatur*, Tübingen.

Rank, L. P. (1951), *Etymologiseering en verwante verschijnselen bij Homerus*, Assen.

Raven, D. S. (1962), *Greek Metre: an Introduction*, London.

Ready, J. (2011), *Character, Narrator and Simile in the Iliad*, Cambridge.

Ready, J. (2019), *Orality, Textuality, and the Homeric Epics*, Oxford.

Ready, J. (2023), *Immersion, Identity, and the Iliad*, Oxford.

Reece, S. (1993), *The Stranger's Welcome: Oral Theory and the Aesthetics of the Homeric Hospitality Scene*, Ann Arbor.

Reece, S. (2005), 'Homer's *Iliad* and *Odyssey*: from Oral Performance to Written Text', in M. Armodio (ed.), *New Directions in Oral Theory: Essays on Ancient and Medieval Literatures*, Tempe, AZ: 43–89.

Reece, S. (2009), *Homer's Winged Words: the Evolution of Early Greek Epic Diction in the Light of Oral Theory*, Leiden.

Reed, N. B. (1990), 'A Chariot Race for Athens' Finest: the "Apobates" Contest Re-examined', *Journal of Sport History* 17: 306–17.

Reese, D. (1995), 'Equid Sacrifices/Burials in Greece and Cyprus: an Addendum', *JPR* 9: 34–42.

Reichel, M. (1994), *Fernbeziehungen in der Ilias*, Tübingen.

Reinhardt, K. (1961), *Die Ilias und ihr Dichter*, Göttingen.

Reitz, C., and Finkmann, S. (eds) (2019), *Structures of Epic Poetry*, Berlin.

Renaud, J.-M., and Wathelet, P. (2008), *Les relations familiales dans l'épopée grecque archaïque*, Lille.

Rengakos, A. (1993), *Der Homertext und die hellenistischen Dichter*, Stuttgart.

Rengakos, A. (2002), 'The Hellenistic Poets as Homeric Critics', in Montanari and Ascheri (2002): 143–57.

Rengakos, A. (2007), 'The Smile of Achilles, or the *Iliad* and Its Mirror-Image', in M. Paizi-Apostolopoulou, A. Rengakos, and C. Tsagalis (eds), Ἄθλα και ἔπαθλα στα ομηρικά ἔπη: από τα πρακτικά του Ι' Συνεδρίου για την Οδύσσεια, 15–19 Σεπτεμβρίου 2004, Ithaki: 101–10.

Rengakos, A. (2015), '*Aithiopis*', in M. Fantuzzi and C. Tsagalis (eds), *The Greek Epic Cycle and Its Ancient Reception*, Cambridge: 306–17.

Richardson, N. J. (1974), *The Homeric Hymn to Demeter*, Oxford.

Richardson, N. J. (2010), *Three Homeric Hymns: to Apollo, Hermes, and Aphrodite*, Cambridge.

Richardson, S. (1990), *The Homeric Narrator*, Nashville, TN.

Richter, W. (1968), *Die Landwirtschaft im homerischen Zeitalter: Archaeologia Homerica II*, Göttingen.

Rieder, H. (2005), 'Wurfgeräte der Altsteinzeit: Steine, Wurfhölzer, Speere', *Nikephoros* 18: 9–20.

Riehl, S. (1999), *Bronze Age Environment and Economy in the Troad: the Archaeobotany of Kumtepe and Troy*, Tübingen.

Riggsby, A. M. (1992), 'Homeric Speech Introductions and the Theory of Homeric Composition', *TAPhA* 122: 99–114.

Rix, M. (2002), 'Wild about Ida', *Cornucopia: the Magazine for Connoisseurs of Turkey* 26: 56–75.

Rodda, M. A. (2021), *A Corpus Study of Formulaic Variation and Linguistic Productivity in Early Greek Epic*, DPhil diss., Oxford.

Roisman, H. (1988), 'Nestor's Advice and Antilochus' Tactics', *Phoenix* 42.2: 114–20.

Roisman, H. (2005), 'Old Men and Chirping Cicadas in the Teichoskopia', in R. J. Rabel (ed.), *Approaches to Homer*, Swansea: 105–18.

Roller, L. E. (1977), *Funeral Games in Greek Literature, Art, and Life*, PhD diss., University of Pennsylvania.

Roller, L. E. (1981a), 'Funeral Games for Historical Persons', *Stadion* 7: 1–18.

Roller, L. E. (1981b), Funeral Games in Greek Art', *AJA* 85: 107–19.

Romano, D. G. (2021), 'Greek Footraces and Field Events', in Futrell and Scanlon (2021): 209–20.

Romm, J. S. (1992), *The Edges of the Earth in Ancient Thought*, Princeton, NJ.

Rose, C. B. (2014), *The Archaeology of Greek and Roman Troy*, Cambridge.

Rose, C. B. and Körpe, R. (2015), 'The *Tumuli* of Troy and the Troad', in O. Henry and H. Kelp (eds), *Tumulus as Sêma: Space, Politics, Culture and Religion in the First Millennium BC*, 2 vols, Berlin: I.373–85, II.168–77 (plates).

Roth, C. L. (1990), *Mixed Aorists in Homer*, New York and London.

Rougier-Blanc, S. (2005), *Les maisons homériques: vocabulaire architectural et sémantique du bâti*, Nancy.

Rousseau, P. (1990), 'Le deuxième Atride: le type épique de Ménélas dans l'*Iliade*', in M. Mactoux and E. Geny (eds), *Mélanges Pierre Lévêque 5. Anthropologie et société*, Paris: 325–54.

Rousseau, P. (1992), 'Fragments d'un commentaire antique du récit de la course des chars dans le XXIIIᵉ chant de l'*Iliade*', *Philologus* 136: 158–80.

Rousseau, P. (2010), 'L'oubli de la borne: *Iliade* XXIII', in C. König and D. Thouard (eds), *La philologie au présent: pour Jean Bollack*, Villeneuve-d'Asc: 27–56.

Ruijgh, C. (1957), *L'élément achéen dans la langue épique*, Assen.

Ruijgh, C. (1967), *Études sur la grammaire et le vocabulaire du grec mycénien*, Amsterdam.

Ruijgh, C. (1971), *Autour de 'te epique': études sur la syntaxe grecque*, Amsterdam.

Ruijgh, C. (1981), 'L'emploi de ἤτοι chez Homère et Hésiode', *Mnemosyne* 34: 272–87.

Ruijgh, C. (1995), 'D'Homère aux origines proto-mycéniennes de la tradition épique: analyse dialectologique du langue homérique, avec un *excursus* sur la création de l'alphabet grec', in Crielaard (1995): 1–96.

Ruijgh, C. (2011), 'Mycenaean and Homeric Language', in Y. Duhoux and A. Morpurgo Davies (eds), *A Companion to Linear B: Mycenaean Greek Texts and Their World*, Louvain-la-Neuve: II.253–98.

Russo, J. (1994), 'Homer's Style: Nonformulaic Features of an Oral Aesthetic', *Oral Tradition* 9.2: 371–89.

Russo, J. (2004), 'Odysseus' Trial of the Bow as Symbolic Performance', in A. Bierl, A. Schmitt, and A. Willi (eds), *Antike Literatur in neuer Deutung*, Munich and Leipzig: 95–102.

Rutherford, I. (2008), 'Achilles and the Sallis Wastais Ritual: Performing Death in Greece and Anatolia', in N. Laneri (ed.), *Peforming Death: Social Analyses of Funerary Traditions in the Ancient Near East and Mediterranean*, Chicago: 223–36.

Rutherford, I. (2020), 'Substitute, Sacrifice, and Sidekick: a Note on the Comparative Method and Homer', in J. Price and R. Zelnick-Abramovitz (eds), *Text and Intertext in Greek Epic and Drama: Essays in Honor of Margalit Finkelberg*, London: 132–48.

Rutherford, R. B. (1992), *Homer, Odyssey Books XIX and XX*, Cambridge.

Rutherford, R. B. (2019), *Homer, Iliad Book XVIII*, Cambridge.

Sacks, R. (1987), *The Traditional Phrase in Homer: Two Studies in Form, Meaning and Interpretation*, Leiden.

Said, S. (2012), 'Animal Similes in *Odyssey* 22', in Montanari, Rengakos, and Tsagalis (2012): 347–68.

Sammons, B. (2014), 'A Tale of Tydeus: Exemplarity and Structure in Two Homeric Insets', in C. Tsagalis (ed.), *Theban Resonances in Homeric Epic* (*Trends in Classics* 6.2), Berlin: 297–318.

Sansom, S. A. (2021), review of Dué 2019, *CPh* 116: 135–9.

Sansom, S. A. (2025), 'Breaking Hermann's Bridge from Homer to Nonnus: towards a Stylometry of Caesurae', *CQ* 75: 1–17.

Sansone, D. (1984), 'On Hendiadys in Greek', *Glotta* 62: 16–25.

Sanz, M. (1999), 'εὐηγενής and εὐηφενής in *Il.* 11.427 and 23.81', *Glotta* 75: 107–13.

Sarischoulis, E. (2008), *Schicksal, Götter und Handlungsfreiheit in den Epen Homers*, Stuttgart.

Sauge, A. (1994), '*Iliade* 23: les jeux, un procès', *Ziva Antika* 44: 5–43.

Saunders, K. B. (2004), 'Frölich's Table of Homeric Wounds', *CQ* 54: 1–17.

Scanlon, T. F. (2004), 'Homer, the Olympics, and the Heroic Ethos', in M. Kaila et al. (eds), *The Olympic Games in Antiquity: Bring Forth Rain and Bear Fruit*, Athens: 61–91 (republished in Scanlon 2015).

Scanlon, T. F. (ed.) (2015), *Greek Poetry and Sport*, Classics@ 13 (https://classics-at.chs.harvard.edu/volume/classics13-greek-poetry-and-sport/).

Scanlon, T. F. (2018), 'Class Tensions in the Games of Homer: Epeius, Euryalus, Odysseus, and Iros', *BICS* 61: 5–20.

Schadewaldt, W. (1975), *Der Aufbau der Ilias: Strukturen und Konzeptionen*, Frankfurt am Main.

Scheid-Tissinier, E. (1994), *Les usages du don chez Homère: vocabulaire et pratiques*, Nancy.

Schein, S. (1997), 'The *Iliad*: Structure and Interpretation', in Morris and Powell (1997): 345–59.

Schein, S. (2002), 'The Horses of Achilles in Book 17 of the *Iliad*', in M. Reichel and A. Rengakos (eds), *EPEA PTEROENTA: Beiträge zur Homerforschung. Festschrift für Wolfgang Kullmann zum 75. Geburtstag*, Stuttgart: 193–206 (also in Schein 2016: 11–26).

Schein, S. (2016), *Homeric Epic and Its Reception*, Oxford.

Scheliha, R. von (1943), *Patroklos: Gedanken über Homers Dichtung und Gestalten*, Basel.

Schironi, F. (2018), *The Best of the Grammarians: Aristarchus of Samothrace on the Iliad*, Ann Arbor.

Schlesier, R. (1992), 'Olympian versus Chthonian Religion', *SCI* 11: 38–51.

Schnapp-Gourbeillon, A. (1981), *Lions, héros, masques: les représentations de l'animal chez Homère*, Paris.

Schnapp-Gourbeillon, A. (1982), 'Les funérailles de Patrocle', in G. Gnoli and J.-P. Vernant (eds), *La mort, les morts dans les sociétés anciennes*, Cambridge and Paris: 77–88.

Schnaufer, A. (1970), *Frühgriechischer Totenglaube: Untersuchungen zum Totenglauben der mykenischen und homerischen Zeit*, Hildesheim.

Scodel, R. (1999), *Credible Impossibilities: Conventions and Strategies of Verisimilitude in Homer and Greek Tragedy*, Stuttgart.

Scodel, R. (2008), *Epic Facework: Self-Presentation and Social Interaction in Homer*, Swansea.

Scodel, R. (2021), 'Homeric Suspense', in I. M. Konstantakos and V. Liotsakis (eds), *Suspense in Ancient Greek Literature*, Berlin: 55–72.

Scott, W. C. (1974), *The Oral Nature of the Homeric Simile*, Leiden.

Scott, W. C. (1997), 'The Etiquette of Games in *Iliad* 23', *GRBS* 38: 213–27.

Scott, W. C. (2009), *The Artistry of the Homeric Simile*, Hanover and London.

Scullion, S. (1994), 'Olympian and Chthonian', *ClAnt* 13: 75–119.

Scully, S. (1984), 'The Language of Achilles: the ΟΧΘΗΣΑΣ Formulas', *TAPhA* 114: 11–27.

Scully, S. (2020), review of Pache (2020), *CR* 71: 20–3.

Seaford, R. (2004), *Money and the Early Greek Mind: Homer, Philosophy, Tragedy*, Cambridge.

Segal, C. (1971), *The Theme of the Mutilation of the Corpse in the Iliad*, Leiden.

Sekita, K. (2022), 'Between Justice, Fertility, and the Underworld: Problems with the Chthonians Revisited', *BICS* 65: 150–61.

Shakeshaft, H. (2019), 'The Terminology for Beauty in the *Iliad* and the *Odyssey*', *CQ* 69: 1–22.

Shapiro, H. A. (1991), 'The Iconography of Mourning in Athenian Art', *AJA* 95: 629–56.

Shapiro, H. A. (1994), *Myth into Art: Poet and Painter in Classical Greece*, London and New York.

Shear, I. M. (2004), *Kingship in the Mycenaean World and Its Reflections in the Oral Tradition*, Philadelphia.

Sherratt, S. (1990), 'Reading the Texts: Archaeology and the Homeric Question', *Antiquity* 64: 807–24.

Sherratt, S. (2004), 'Feasting in Homeric Epic', *Hesperia* 73: 301–37.

Shipp, G. P. (1972), *Studies in the Language of Homer*, 2nd ed., Cambridge.

Shive, D. (1987), *Naming Achilles*, Oxford.

Simondon, M. (1982), *La mémoire et l'oubli dans la pensée grecque jusqu'à la fin du Vᵉ siècle avant J.-C.*, Paris.

Sinos, D. (1980), *Achilles, Patroclus, and the Meaning of Philos*, Innsbruck.

Snodgrass, A. M. (1997), 'Homer and Greek Art', in Morris and Powell (1997): 560–97.

Snodgrass, A. M. (1998), *Homer and the Artists: Text and Picture in Early Greek Art*, Cambridge.

Sommerstein, A. H. (2014a), 'What Is an Oath?', in Sommerstein and Torrance (2014): 1–5.

Sommerstein, A. H. (2014b), 'The Language of Oaths: How Oaths Are Expressed', in Sommerstein and Torrance (2014): 76–85.

Sommerstein, A. H., and Torrance, I. C. (eds) (2014), *Oaths and Swearing in Ancient Greece*, Berlin.

Sourvinou-Inwood, C. (1995), *Reading Greek Death: to the End of the Classical Period*, Oxford.

Spariosu, M. (1991), *The God of Many Names: Play, Poetry and Power in Hellenic Thought from Homer to Aristotle*, Durham, NC and London.

Spatafora, G. (1997), 'Esigenza fisiologica e funzione terapeutica del lamento nei poemi omerici: studi sul significato di κλαίω, γοάω, στένω, οἰμώζω-κωκύω, ὀδύρομαι', *AC* 66: 1–23.

Spatafora, G. (2005), 'Riflessioni sull'arte poetica di Nicandro', *GIF* 57.2: 231–62.

Stähler, K. P. (1967), *Grab und Psyche des Patroklos: ein schwarzfiguriges Vasenbild*, Münster.

Stampolidis, N. C. (1995), 'Homer and the Cremation Burials of Eleuthema', in Crielaard (1995): 289–308.

Stanford, W. B. (1936), *Greek Metaphor: Studies in Theory and Practice*, Oxford.

Stanford, W. B. (1968), *The Ulysses Theme: a Study in the Adaptability of a Traditional Hero*, 2nd ed. rev., Oxford.

Stanford, W. B. (1981), 'Sound, Sense, and Music in Greek Poetry', *G&R* 28: 127–40.

Stanley, K. (1993), *The Shield of Homer: Narrative Structure in the Iliad*, Princeton, NJ.

Stefanelli, R. (2004), 'Greco λιάζομαι: una nota lessicale', *Quaderni del Dipartimento di Linguistica (Università di Firenze)* 14: 179–89.

Steiner, D. (2010), *Homer: Odyssey Books XVII and XVIII*, Cambridge.

Stella, F. (2021), *Νόος e νοεῖν da Omero a Platone*, Besançon.

Stelow, A. R. (2020), *Menelaus in the Archaic Period: Not Quite the Best of the Achaeans*, Oxford.

Stewart, E. (2014), '"There's Nothing Worse Than Athletes": Criticism of Athletics and Professionalism in the Archaic and Classical Periods', *Nikephoros* 27: 273–93.

Stocking, C. (2023), *Homer's Iliad and the Problem of Force*, Oxford.

Stocking, C., and Stephens, S. (2021), *Ancient Greek Athletics: Primary Sources in Translation*, Oxford.

Stoevesandt, M. (2004), *Feinde, Gegner, Opfer: zur Darstellung der Troianer in den Kampfszenen der Ilias*, Basel.

Stoyanov, T. (2015), 'Warfare', in Valeva, Nankov, and Graninger (2015): 426–42.

Straten, F. T. van (1995), *HIERA KALA: Images of Animal Sacrifice in Archaic and Classical Greece*, Leiden.

Sweet, W. E. (1987), *Sport and Recreation in Ancient Greece: a Sourcebook with Translations*, Oxford and New York.

Swift, L. (2018), 'Thinking with Brothers in Sappho and Beyond', *Mouseion* 15: 71–87.

Swift, L. (2019), *Archilochus: the Poems*, Oxford.

Taplin, O. (1992), *Homeric Soundings*, Oxford.

Tasso, A. (2013), *Pylai Aidao: un percorso iconografico e letterario sulla diffusione del tema delle Porte dell'Ade da Oriente a Occidente*, Oxford.

Thalmann, W. (1984), *Conventions of Form and Thought in Early Greek Epic Poetry*, Baltimore.

Thalmann, W. (1988), *The Swineherd and the Bow: Representation of Class in the Odyssey*, Ithaca, NY.

Thesleff, H. (1954), *Studies on Intensification in Early and Classical Greek* (Societas Scientiarum Fennica, Commentationes Humanarum Litterarum 21.1), Helsingfors.

Thiel, H. van (1982), *Iliaden und Ilias*, Basel.

Thiel, H. van (1991), *Homeri Odyssea*, Hildesheim.

Thiel, H. van (1996), *Homeri Ilias*, Hildesheim.

Thomas, O. (2020), *Homeric Hymn to Hermes*, Cambridge.

Thompson, R. (2024), 'The Mycenaean Language', in J. T. Killen (ed.), *The New Documents in Mycenaean Greek, Volume 1: Introductory Essays, Drawings of Selected Tablets*, Cambridge: 232–54.

Thornton, A. (1984), *Homer's Iliad: Its Composition and the Motif of Supplication*, Göttingen.

Tichy, E. (1983), *Onomatopoetische Verbalbildungen des Griechischen*, Vienna.

Trachsel, A. (2007), *La Troade: un paysage et son héritage littéraire. Les commentaires antiques sur la Troade, leur genèse et leur influence*, Basel.

Trédé, M. (1992), *KAIROS: l'à-propos et l'occasion. Le mot et la notion d'Homère à la fin du IVe siècle avant J.-C.*, Paris.

Trümpy, H. (1950), *Kriegerische Fachausdrücke im griechischen Epos: Untersuchungen zum Wortschatze Homers*, Basel.

Tsagalis, C. (2004), *Epic Grief: Personal Laments in Homer's Iliad*, Berlin.

Tsagalis, C. (2017), *Early Greek Epic Fragments I. Antiquarian and Genealogical Epic*, Berlin.

Tsagalis, C. (ed.) (2024), *Herakles in Early Greek Epic*, Leiden.

Tsagarakis, O. (1980), 'Homer and the Cult of the Dead in Helladic Times', *Emerita* 48: 229–40.

Tsagarakis, O. (2001), *Studies in Odyssey 11*, Stuttgart.

Tsitsibakou-Vasalos, E. (2007), *Ancient Poetic Etymology*, Stuttgart.

Tuna-Nörling, Y. (2002), 'Attisch-schawrzfigurige Kermaik aus Alt-Smyrna (Bayrakli): Addenda', *Asia Minor Studien* 44: 1–24.

Turkeltaub, D. (2007), 'Perceiving Iliadic Gods', *HSCP* 103: 51–81.

Turkeltaub, D. (2020), 'Immanence', in Pache (2020): 165–6.

Tzamali, E. (1997), 'Positive Aussage plus negierte Gegenaussage im Griechischen. Teil I: Die ältere griechische Dichtung', *MSS* 57: 129–68.

Ulf, C. (2004), 'Ilias 23: die Bestattung des Patroklos und das Sportfest der "Patroklos-Spiele"', in H. Heftner and K. Tomaschitz (eds), *AD FONTES! Festschrift für Gerhard Dobesch zum fünfundsechzigsten Geburtstag am 15. September 2004: dargebracht von Kollegen, Schülern und Freunden*, Vienna: 85–111.

Unruh, D. (2011), '*Skeptouchoi*: a New Look at the Homeric Scepter', *CW* 104.3: 279–94.

Valavanis, A. (2021), 'Patterns of Politics in Ancient Greek Athletics', in Futrell and Scanlon (2021): 109–23.

Valeva, J., Nankov, E., and Graninger, D. (eds) (2015), *A Companion to Ancient Thrace*, Oxford and Malden, MA.

Valk, M. van der (1949), *The Textual Criticism of the Odyssey*, Leiden.

Valk, M. van der (1952), 'Ajax and Diomede in the *Iliad*', *Mnemosyne* 5: 269–86.

Valk, M. van der (1963–4), *Researches into the Text and Scholia of the Iliad*, 2 vols, Leiden.

Vergados, A. (2012), *The Homeric Hymn to Hermes*, Berlin.

Vermeule, E. (1974), *Götterkult: Archaeologia Homerica III V*, Göttingen.

Vermeule, E. (1979), *Aspects of Death in Early Greek Poetry and Art*, Berkeley.

Visa-Ondarçuhu, V. (1999), *L'image de l'athlète d'Homère à la fin du Vᵉ siècle avant J.-C.*, Paris.

Visa-Ondarçuhu, V. (2015), 'Le héros nu: Jason à l'épreuve ou les souvenirs athlétiques d'Achille et d'Ulysse dans les *Argonautiques*', in Scanlon (2015) (https://archive.chs.harvard.edu/CHS/article/display/6058).

Visser, E. (1997), *Homers Katalog der Schiffe*, Stuttgart and Leipzig.

Vivante, P. (1982), *The Epithets in Homer: a Study in Poetic Value*, Bloomington.

Vlachou, V. (2012), 'Addendum to Vol. VI: 1.e. Death and Burial in the Greek World, IV: Greek Funerary Rituals in Their Archaeological Context', in *Thesaurus Cultus et Rituum Antiquorum VIII*, Los Angeles: 363–84.

Waanders, F. M. J. (1983), *The History of* ΤΕΛΟΣ *and* ΤΕΛΕΩ *in Ancient Greek*, Amsterdam.

Waanders, F. M. J. (1992), 'Mycenaean Evidence for the Indo-European Roots **tel-* and **kʷel-* in Greek', in J.-P. Oliver (ed.), *Mykenaïka: actes du IXᵉ Colloque international sur les texts mycéniens et égéens*, Paris: 591–6.

Wachter, R. (1991), 'The Inscriptions on the François Vase', *MH* 48: 86–113.

Wachter, R. (1998), 'Griechisch χαῖρε: Vorgeschichte eines Grusswortes', *MH* 55: 65–75.

Wackernagel, J. (1916), *Sprachliche Untersuchungen zu Homer*, Göttingen.

Wade-Gery, T. (1952), *The Poet of the Iliad*, Cambridge.

Waele, J. A. K. E. de (1998), 'The Layout of the Lefkandi "Heroon"', *ABSA* 93: 379–84.

Wagner, G. A., Pernicka, E., and Uerpmann, H.-P. (eds) (2003), *Troja and the Troad: Scientific Approaches*, Berlin and Heidelberg.

Wakker, G. (1994), *Conditions and Conditionals: an Investigation in Ancient Greek*, Amsterdam.

Walde, C. (2001), *Die Traumdarstellungen in der griechisch-römischen Dichtung*, Stuttgart.

Walsh, R. T. (2005), *Fighting Words and Feuding Words*, Lanham, MD.

Ward, M. (2019), 'Glory and Nostos: the Ship-Epithet κοῖλος in the *Iliad*', *CQ* 69: 23–34.

Warwick, C. (2019), 'We Two Alone: Conjugal Bonds and Homoerotic Subtext in the Iliad', *Helios* 46: 115–39.

Wathelet, P. (1970), *Les traits éoliens dans la langue de l'épopée grecque*, Rome.

Wathelet, P. (1983), 'Les Phéniciens et la tradition homérique', in E. Gubel, E. Lipinski, and B. Servais-Soyez (eds), *Sauvons Tyr: histoire phénicienne. Studia Phoenicia I–II*. Leuven: 235–43.

Wathelet, P. (1988), *Dictionnaire des Troyens de l'Iliade*, 2 vols, Liège.

Webb, R. (2010), 'Between Poetry and Rhetoric: Libanios' Use of Homeric Subjects in his *Progymnasmata*', *QUCC* 95: 131–52.

Webber, C. (2011), *The Gods of Battle: the Thracians at War 1500 BC–AD 150*, Barnsley.

Webber, J. (2018), *Bronze Age Formulae and Helmets of Invisibility: Meriones and Early Greek Epic*, BA diss., Oxford.

Webber, J. (2023), *Panhellenism and Local Tradition in Early Greek Epos*, DPhil diss., Oxford.

Wees, H. van (1992), *Status Warriors: War, Violence and Society in Homer and History*, Amsterdam.

Wees, H. van (1994), 'The Homeric Way of War: the *Iliad* and the Hoplite Phalanx', *G&R* 41: 1–18 (I), 131–55 (II).

Wees, H. van (1998), 'A Brief History of Tears: Gender Differentiation in Archaic Greece', in L. Foxhall and J. Salmon (eds), *When Men Were Men: Masculinity, Power and Identity in Classical Antiquity*, London: 10–53.

Wehr, O. (2013), *Die Ilias und Argos: ein Beitrag zur homerischen Frage*, Frankfurt am Main.

Weiler, I. (1974), *Der Agon im Mythos*, Darmstadt.

Weiler, I. (gen. ed.), Aigner, T., Mauritsch-Bein, B., and Petermandl, W. (2002), *Quellendokumentation zur Gymnastik und Agonistik im Altertum VII. Laufen: Texte, Übersetzungen, Kommentar*, Vienna.

Weiler, I. (gen. ed.), Doblhofer, G., Mauritsch, P., and Lavrencic, M. (1993), *Quellendokumentation zur Gymnastik und Agonistik im Altertum III. Speerwurf: Texte, Übersetzungen, Kommentar*, Vienna.

Weiler, I. (gen. ed.), Doblhofer, G., and Mauritsch, P. (1995), *Quellendokumentation zur Gymnastik und Agonistik im Altertum IV. Boxen: Texte, Übersetzungen, Kommentar*, Vienna.

Weiler, I. (gen. ed.), Lavrencic, M., Doblhofer, G., and Mauritsch, P. (1991), *Quellendokumentation zur Gymnastik und Agonistik im Altertum I. Diskos: Texte, Übersetzungen, Kommentar*, Vienna.

Weiler, I. (gen. ed.), Doblhofer, G., Petermandl, W., and Schachinger, U. (1998), *Quellendokumentation zur Gymnastik und Agonistik im Altertum VI. Ringen: Texte, Übersetzungen, Kommentar*, Vienna.

Weiss, M. (1998), 'Erotica: on the Prehistory of Greek Desire', *HSCP* 98: 31–61.

Wender, D. (1978), *The Last Scenes of the Odyssey*, Leiden.

Wéry, L.-M. (1967), 'La fonctionnement de la diplomatie à l'époque homérique', *RIDA* 14: 169–205 (= 'Die Arbeitsweise der Diplomatie in homerischer Zeit', tr. by H. Froesch, in E. Olshausen (ed.) (1975), *Antike Diplomatie*, Darmstadt: 13–53).

West, M. L. (1966), *Hesiod: Theogony*, Oxford.

West, M. L. (1978), *Hesiod: Works and Days*, Oxford.

West, M. L. (1982), *Greek Metre*, Oxford.

West, M. L. (1985), *The Hesiodic Catalogue of Women*, Oxford.

West, M. L. (1988), 'The Rise of the Greek Epic', *JHS* 108: 151–72 (= 2011–13: I.35–73).

West, M. L. (1997a), *The East Face of Helicon*, Oxford.

West, M. L. (1997b), 'Homer's Metre', in Morris and Powell (1997): 218–37.

West, M. L. (1998), 'The Textual Criticism and Editing of Homer', in G. W. Most (ed.), *Editing Texts – Texte Edieren*, Göttingen: 94–110.

West, M. L. (1999), 'The Invention of Homer', *CQ* 49: 364–82.

West, M. L. (1998–2000), *Homerus: Ilias*, 2 vols, Stuttgart.

West, M. L. (2001a), *Studies in the Text and Transmission of the Iliad*, Stuttgart.

West, M. L. (2001b), response to Nagy 2000 and Nardelli 2001b, *BMCR* 2001.09.06.

West, M. L. (2005), '*Odyssey* and *Argonautica*', *CQ* 55: 39–64.

West, M. L. (2011), *The Making of the Iliad*, Oxford.

West, M. L. (2011–13), *Hellenica: Selected Papers on Greek Literature and Thought*, Oxford.

West, M. L. (2013), *The Epic Cycle: a Commentary on the Lost Troy Epics*, Oxford.

West, M. L. (2017a), *Homerus: Odyssea*, Berlin and Boston.

West, M. L. (2017b), *The Making of the Odyssey*, Oxford.

West, S. R. (1967), *The Ptolemaic Papyri of Homer*, Cologne.

West, S. R. (1988), in J. B. Hainsworth, A. Heubeck, and S. R. West (1988), *A Commentary on Homer's Odyssey: Introduction and Books I–VIII*, Oxford.

Whallon, W. (1969), *Formula, Character, and Context: Studies in the Homeric, Old English, and Old Testament Poetry*, Cambridge, MA.

Wheeler, E. L. (1982), '"Hoplomachia" and Greek Dances in Arms', *GRBS* 23: 223–44.

Whitley, J. (2013), 'Homer's Entangled Objects: Narrative, Agency and Personhood in and out of Iron Age Texts', *Cambridge Archaeological Journal* 23: 395–416.

Whitman, C. H. (1958), *Homer and the Heroic Tradition*, Cambridge, MA.

Wiesner, J. (1968), *Fahren und Reiten: Archaeologia Homerica I F*, Göttingen.

Wilamowitz-Moellendorff, U. von (1916), *Die Ilias und Homer*, Berlin.

Wilkinson, C. (2013), *The Lyric of Ibycus*, Berlin.

Wilkinson, R. H. (1991), 'The Representation of the Bow in Art of Egypt and the Ancient Near East', *JANES* 20: 83–99.

Willcock, M. M. (1973), 'The Funeral Games of Patroclus', *BICS* 20: 1–11.

Willcock, M. M. (1976), *A Companion to the Iliad*, Chicago.

Willcock, M. M. (1983), 'Antilochos in the Iliad', in C. Froideford (ed.), *Mélanges Édouard Delebecque*, Aix-en-Provence: 479–85.

Willcock, M. M. (1984), *The Iliad of Homer*, 2 vols, London.

Willcock, M. M. (1997), 'Neoanalysis', in Morris and Powell (1997): 174–89.

Willcock, M. M. (2002), 'Menelaos in the *Iliad*', in M. Reichel and A. Rengakos (eds), *EPEA PTEROENTA: Beiträge zur Homerforschung. Festschrift für Wolfgang Kullmann zum 75. Geburtstag*, Stuttgart: 221–30.

Willcock, M. M. (2004), 'Traditional Epithets', in A. Bierl, A. Schmitt, and A. Willi (eds), *Antike Literatur in neuer Deutung: Festschrift für Joachim Latacz anlässlich seines 70. Geburtstages*, Munich: 51–62.

Willi, A. (1999), 'Zur Verwendung und Etymologie von griechisch ἐρι-', *HSF* 112: 86–100.

Willi, A. (2011), 'Language, Homeric', in Finkelberg (2011): II.458–64.

Willi, A. (2018), *The Origins of the Greek Verb*, Oxford.

Willis, A. H. (1941), 'Athletic Contests in the Epic', *TAPhA* 72: 392–417 (reprinted with addendum in T. Scanlon (ed.) (2014), *Oxford Readings in Sport in the Greek and Roman Worlds, Volume I: Early Greece, the Olympics, and Contests*, Oxford: 60–90).

Willmott, J. (2007), *The Moods of Homeric Greek*, Cambridge.

Willms, L. (2010), 'On the IE Etymology of Greek (*w*)*anax*', *Glotta* 86: 232–271.

Wilson, D. F. (2002), *Ransom, Revenge, and Heroic Identity in the Iliad*, Cambridge.

Winter, I. (1995), 'Homer's Phoenicians: History, Ethnography, or Literary Trope? [A Perspective on Early Orientalism]', in Carter and Morris (1995): 247–72.

Wolzogen, C. von (1885), *Schillers Leben: Verfasst aus Erinnerungen der Familie, seinen eigenen Briefen und den Nachrichten seines Freundes Körner*, Stuttgart and Tübingen.

Wyatt, W. F. (1969), *Metrical Lengthening in Homer*, Rome.

Wyatt, W. F. (1994), 'Homeric Loss of /w/ and Vowels in Contact', *Glotta* 72: 119–50.

Yamagata, N. (1989), 'The Apostrophe in Homer as Part of the Oral Technique', *BICS* 36: 91–103.

Yamagata, N. (1994), *Homeric Morality*, Leiden.

Yamagata, N. (1997), 'ἄναξ and βασιλεύς in Homer', *CQ* 67: 1–14.

Yamagata, N. (2012), 'Use of Homeric References in Plato and Xenophon', *CQ* 62: 130–44.

Younger, J. G. (2021), 'Sport and Spectacle in the Greek Bronze Age', in Futrell and Scanlon (2021): 47–61.

Zaborowski, R. (2002), *La crainte et le courage dans l'Iliade et l'Odyssée*, Warsaw.

Zanetto, G. (2017), 'Fighting on the River: the Alpheius and Pylian Epic', in A. Bierl, M. Christopoulos, and A. Papachrysostomou (eds), *Time and Space in Ancient Myth, Religion and Culture*, Berlin: 229–38.

Zanker, A. (2019), *Metaphor in Homer: Time, Speech, and Thought*, Cambridge.

Zanker, G. (1994), *The Heart of Achilles: Characterization and Personal Ethics in the Iliad*, Ann Arbor.

Zanni, D. G. (2008), 'Ambrosia, Nectar and Elaion in the Homeric Poems', in Paipetis (2008): 391–400.

Zarker, J. W. (1965), 'King Eëtion and Thebe as Symbols in the "Iliad"', *CJ* 61: 110–14.

Zimmermann, B. (2009), 'Am Anfang der Irrfahrt durch die Jarhunderte: Odysseus in der *Odyssee*', in Gehrke and Kirschkowski (2009): 11–18.

Zink, N. (1962), *Griechische Ausdrucksweisen für warm und kalt im seelischen Bereich*, diss. Mainz, Heidelberg.

Zunker, A. (1988), *Untersuchungen zur Aiakidensage auf Aigina*, St. Ottilien.

INDEXES

INDEX OF SUBJECTS

Numbers refer to pages

INDEX OF GREEK WORDS

Numbers refer to pages

INDEX OF PASSAGES

Numbers refer to pages

Homer, *Odyssey*